Supply Chain Management

From Vision to Implementation

Supply Chain Management

From Vision to Implementation

Stanley E. Fawcett

Lisa M. Ellram

Jeffrey A. Ogden

PEARSON

Prentice Hall

Upper Saddle River, NJ 07458

Library of Congress Cataloging-in-Publication Data

Fawcett, Stanley E.
  Supply chain management: from vision to implementation / Stanley Fawcett,
  Jeffrey Ogden, Lisa Ellram.
    p.   cm.
  Includes index.
  ISBN 0-13-101504-4
  1. Business logistics.   I. Ogden, Jeffrey A.   II. Ellram, Lisa M.   III. Title.
HD38.5.F385 2007
658.7—dc22

2006049836

AVP/Executive Editor: Mark Pfaltzgraff
Editorial Director: Jeff Shelstad
Assistant Editor: Barbara Witmer
Senior Managing Editor (Production): Cynthia Zonneveld
Production Editor: Melissa Feimer
Permissions Supervisor: Charles Morris
Manufacturing Buyer: Diane Peirano
Manager, Print Production: Christy Mahon
Composition/Full-Service Project Management: BookMasters, Inc.

Credits and acknowledgments borrowed from other sources and reproduced, with
permission, in this textbook appear on appropriate page within text.

Pearson Education LTD.   Pearson Education Australia PTY, Limited
Pearson Education Singapore, Pte. Ltd   Pearson Education North Asia Ltd
Pearson Education, Canada, Ltd   Pearson Educación de Mexico, S.A. de C.V.
Pearson Education–Japan   Pearson Education Malaysia, Pte. Ltd

10 9 8 7 6 5 4 3 2 1
ISBN 0-13-101504-4

DEDICATION

I would like to thank the pioneers in academe and practice who have contributed to our understanding of best practices in supply chain management. Without their active support, our knowledge would be meager. To my wife, Dee, I say thanks for who you are and who you have helped me to become. To my children, Carisa, Tannen, Kjanela, Dallin, Keana, and Taft, I say thank you for your smiles and laughter—they make life a truly fantastic journey.

Stanley E. Fawcett

I would like to thank Drs. Bernard "Bud" LaLonde and Martha C. Cooper for teaching me about supply chain management before most people had heard the term. Most importantly, I would also like to thank my husband, Jeffery S. Siferd, and daughter, Celeste, for their support, understanding, and patience, and for the joy, love, and fun that they bring into my life each and every day.

Lisa M. Ellram

I would like to thank Drs. W. Bruce Handley and Stephen H. Russell for encouraging me to pursue a graduate degree in supply chain management. I would also like to thank all of the professors at Arizona State University for helping me understand supply chain management's importance in today's global economy. I would also like to thank my wife, MaryAnne, and children, Jessica, Rebecca, Jonathan, and Ryan for their patience, love, and support over the past several years.

Jeffrey A. Ogden

Brief Contents

TABLE OF CONTENTS

PART III: COLLABORATING ACROSS THE SUPPLY CHAIN 339

PREFACE

Supply Chain Management: From Vision to Implementation

BACKGROUND AND OVERVIEW

Today's marketplace is more fiercely competitive than ever before. Globalization, technological change, and demanding customers promise to make mediocrity an endangered species. New managerial practices and unique business models emerge and fade constantly as managers strive to help their companies succeed in this less-kind, less-gentle, and less-predictable world. Increasingly, managers must follow the advice of Thomas Edison: "If there is a better way, find it."

For several years, the pundits have said that the very nature of competition is changing. They have claimed that the day is rapidly coming when companies will no longer compete against other companies. They foresaw a world in which supply chains will compete against other supply chains for market supremacy. For example, Wal-Mart and its suppliers will battle Carrefour and its suppliers in consumer markets around the world. Likewise, Toyota and its suppliers will clash with Ford and its suppliers for global competitive advantage. Similar rivalries will emerge in the other industries from electronics to pharmaceuticals, and from apparel to fast food. In other words, companies will choose sides and form cohesive teams that will compete across borders in the quest to increase productivity and capture global market share.

The possibilities in a supply chain world are astounding, but the challenges that lie along the path to supply chain excellence are equally formidable. Indeed, companies have struggled for years to achieve true cross-functional process integration within their own four walls. Perhaps this is one reason why the cohesive supply chain team has never fully emerged. Even so, the integrated supply chain concept is relatively new, and managers across numerous industries are determined to make it work. They are experimenting with all sorts of alignment mechanisms and organizational forms. They are investing in systems, tweaking measures, and looking to technology and people to find the key to more effective interorganizational cooperation. To help future managers achieve success in this arena, this text articulates a framework for designing and implementing a high-impact supply chain.

CONCEPT AND OBJECTIVES

This book is designed to provide a strategic understanding of the supply chain, enabling managers to participate in the vision and implementation of world-class supply chain networks. To help students grasp the supply chain phenomenon, this text:

- Defines supply chain management theoretically and practically.
- Identifies supply chain management's role in enhancing customer fulfillment.
- Emphasizes systems thinking and process management as the foundation of Supply Chain Management (SCM).
- Examines the role of environmental scanning to define the forces driving greater collaboration.
- Discusses the critical issues involved in supply chain design.
- Discusses the vital bridges to supply chain integration and collaboration.

The Supply Chain Road Map is a process model that provides a guiding framework to help students understand the decisions involved in designing a supply chain strategy. The road map is supported by a continuously running "Opening Story" that appears at the beginning of each chapter. These vignettes help students see the challenges managers face as they seek to implement a winning supply chain strategy. End-of-chapter cases highlight critical decisions, practices, and tools required to achieve supply chain success. The best-practices diagnostic was not included in the book. Finally, a series of quantitative supplements help students learn and/or review basic tools that are used in day-to-day decision-making. Overall, the discussion and tools developed in the book provide insight to help future managers as they and their companies endeavor to make headway along the arduous journey to supply chain leadership.

This text helps students appreciate the supply chain discipline by demonstrating that SCM runs counter to many traditional practices. Tightly coupled supply chain relationships do not spontaneously come into existence. An appropriate metaphor is found in the world of athletics. All successful sporting teams are comprised of outstanding athletes; however, championship teams possess something more—they possess "chemistry." Building the corporate chemistry so critical to supply chain success requires a new way of viewing the world, analyzing problems, and working together. We join Eckhard Pfeiffer in his assessment that, "Nothing is harder than casting aside the thinking, strategies, and biases that propelled a business to its current success. Companies need to learn how to unlearn, to slough off yesterday's wisdom." Of course, the key is to know which skills to keep and which ones to discard or outsource. The text will help students gain the knowledge and analytical tools to perform this analysis and to act as change agents within their organizations.

BOOK POSITIONING AND DESIGN

Supply Chain Management: From Design to Implementation takes a strategic, holistic view of supply chain management and is designed for use in either an undergraduate or M.B.A.-level course. The book can be used in programs where the students take only one SCM course or as the text for the introductory class in full-fledged SCM programs involving a series of supply chain-related courses.

The text is comprised of three major sections, each consisting of five concise chapters.

- Section 1 defines SCM and links it to corporate strategy and customer fulfillment. The notions of systems thinking and process integration are introduced and used to help students understand two critical processes—product development and order fulfillment.
- Section 2 discusses the critical elements of supply chain design—environmental scanning, supply chain mapping, strategic costing, core competencies, outsourcing, and network rationalization.
- Section 3 focuses on building and managing more collaborative relationships, highlighting the key integrative mechanisms that lead to "corporate team chemistry."

The chapters can be used selectively to support the professor's teaching objectives, the curriculum design, and the students' background. Furthermore, the quantitative supplements enable professors to tailor the course to take either a strategic or analytical approach to SCM.

The material in each of these sections can be successfully tied together by following the Supply Chain Roadmap found at the beginning of each chapter.

FOR INSTRUCTORS

To help professors bring to life the challenges and opportunities encountered in today's supply chain world, the text uses short case studies and vignettes in each chapter to illustrate and reinforce the application of key concepts. Real-world, global examples from a variety of business sectors are used. Extensive teaching materials support the book to assist those faculty who are less familiar with SCM and provide direction for those who would like to get deeper into the concepts. Teaching materials include the following:

- **Instructor's Resource Manual** (available in print or electronically) contains sample syllabi, teaching tips, project recommendations, answers to end-of-chapter exercises, and case questions.
- **PowerPoint** slides to support each chapter and to supplement, the Instructor Resource Manual.
- **Test Item File** (TestBank available in print or electronically) can be used with Prentice Hall's Test Generator Program.
- **TestGen software** is a computerized package allowing instructors to custom design, save, and generate classroom tests based on the test bank questions provided in the Test Item File. The test program permits instructors to edit, add, or delete questions from test banks; edit existing graphics and create new graphics; analyze test results; and organize a database of tests and student results. This software allows for flexibility and ease of use. It provides many options for organizing and displaying tests, along with a search and sort feature.
- **Instructor's Resource CD-ROM** contains the Resource Manual, PowerPoint slides, and TestBank. The materials available on this CD-ROM are also available on the Instructor's Resource page at www.prenhall.com/fawcett (registration is required before downloading).

- **Supply Chain Management Videos** to reinforce chapter content and supplement lecture

For the students, a Companion Website (available at www.prenhall.com/fawcett) will supplement the text with the following:

- **Online Study Quizzes** for self-practice
- **Virtual Tours** of company websites
- **Links** to relevant Supply Chain Management Web sites

AUTHORS' UNIQUE CAPABILITIES

The authors are active teachers, consultants, case writers, and researchers in the areas of supply management, cost analysis, logistics, global business, and supply chain integration. They have worked extensively with supply chain leaders across a variety of industries and around the world for the past fifteen years and have published extensively (more than 200 articles) on the topics discussed in the book. The book is both research-based and managerially relevant; that is, it reflects leading-edge thought and is filled with examples of what companies are doing to make supply chain collaboration a reality.

ACKNOWLEDGMENTS

We would like to deeply thank and acknowledge Dee Fawcett for her attention to detail, patience, and diligence in editing the manuscript. We are also grateful for the many reviewers whose suggestions have molded this book:

Janet Hartley—Bowling Green State University
Theodore P. Stank—University of Tennessee
Rhonda R. Lummus—Iowa State University
Sime Curkovic—Western Michigan University
Samar K. Mukhopadhyay—University of Wisconsin-Milwaukee
Metin Cakanyildirim—University of Texas at Dallas
Michael E. Smith—Western Carolina University
Charles Petersen—Northern Illinois University
Lee Buddress—Portland State University
Dr. James S. Keebler—University of South Florida
Frank Davis—University of Tennessee
Craig Carter—University of Nevada, Reno
Sridhar Seshadri—New York University
Dale Franklin Kehr—University of Memphis
Dr. Chris I. Enyinda—Alabama A&M University
Melvin R. Mattson—Radford University
Pedro M. Reyes—Baylor University
Drew Stapleton—University of Wisconsin La Crosse
John N. Pearson—Arizona State University
Kaushik Sengupta—Hofstra University
Ike C. Ehie—Kansas State University
Kimball Bullington—Middle Tennessee State University
Richard E. Himmer—Auburn University
R. Glenn Richey—The University of Alabama
Soonhong Min—The University of Oklahoma
Matthew O'Brien—Bradley University
Britt Shirley—The University of Tampa
Ted Farris—University of North Texas
Ghaith Rabadi—Old Dominion University

We would also like to thank the members of the Prentice Hall editorial, marketing, and production teams who have made this book possible: Mark Pfaltzgraff—Executive Editor, Barbara Witmer—Assistant Editor, Melissa Feimer—Production Editor, and Debbie Clare—Executive Marketing Manager. Finally, we must thank our

readers and students to whom we wish the best on their journey through Supply
Chain Management.

Stanley E. Fawcett
Brigham Young University

Lisa M. Ellram
Arizona State University

Jeffrey A. Ogden
Air Force Institute of Technology

About the Authors

Stanley E. Fawcett is the Donald L. Staheli Professor of Global Supply Chain Management in the Marriott School at Brigham Young University. He earned his undergraduate, M.B.A., and M.A. in International Studies from Brigham Young University before obtaining his doctorate at Arizona State University. He began his academic life at Michigan State University before joining the faculty at the Marriott School. He has taught executive programs in SCM in Europe as well as North and South America.

Lisa M. Ellram, earned her C.P.A. (M.N.), C.P.M., C.M.A., Ph.D. in Business Administration (Logistics) with a minor in Industrial Engineering; M.S. in Logistics, The Ohio State University; and M.B.A. and B.S.B. in Accounting (with high distinction), University of Minnesota, Twin Cities. She is Chairperson of the Department of Management and the Richard and Lorie Allen Professor of Business at Colorado State University. Prior to that, she was The John and Barbara Bebbling Professor of Business at Arizona State University's W.P. Carey School of Business. She was named as a "purchasing practitioner to know" by *Supply and Demand Chain Executive,* 2004. She was also named as a Dean's Council of 100 Distinguished Scholar at ASU in 2001.

Jeffrey A. Ogden earned his Ph.D. and M.B.A. in Supply Chain Management from Arizona State University and a B.S. in Accounting from Weber State University. He is currently an Assistant Supply Chain Management Professor at the Air Force institute of Technology.

The Building Blocks of Supply Chain Strategy

PROLOGUE

> *Know, develop, and exploit your strengths.*
>
> —PETER F. DRUCKER

*T*oday's marketplace is more fiercely competitive than ever. Globalization, technological change, and demanding customers promise to make mediocrity an endangered species. To succeed in this exciting but challenging world, managers have begun to pursue **business models** that enable them to follow Peter Drucker's advice. In their quest to know, develop, and exploit their own strengths, managers have reexamined their companies' competencies, placing more emphasis on what they do extremely well. They then work to build strong relationships with supply chain partners who possess essential complementary capabilities.

They do this because the nature of competition is changing. Although companies still compete against other companies, they increasingly leverage the strength of suppliers and customers to gain a competitive edge. Perhaps the day will come when companies will choose sides and form cohesive teams. As teams, they will compete across borders in the quest to increase productivity and capture global market share. Success will depend on how well companies collaborate to manage important processes across company boundaries to better meet customer needs.

This first of the book's three modules introduces supply chain management (SCM) and explains why a strategic approach to managing supply chain relationships is so important. We discuss SCM's underlying goal of customer success and basic philosophy of process integration. We also describe SCM's functional building blocks. This first module's five chapters are as follows:

1. Chapter 1 defines SCM. We show how a supply chain (SC) mind-set affects and supports corporate strategy. A road map for supply chain integration is presented to guide the reader through the book's remaining chapters.
2. Chapter 2 looks at the role of the customer in SCM. We answer the question, "How does SCM affect customer relationship management?" An SC approach to customer fulfillment is described.
3. Chapter 3 defines process management, highlighting the need for systems thinking. We discuss process visibility as well as both trade-off and total cost analysis.
4. Chapter 4 presents the functions of marketing, R&D, and finance from an SC perspective. We show how effective process management can help these functions translate customer needs into winning products through the product development process.
5. Chapter 5 presents the functions of sourcing, operations, and logistics from an SC perspective. Again, we show how effective process management can turn these functions that control the physical flow of products from supply to demand into a winning order fulfillment capability.

Chapter 1

Supply Chain Management and Competitive Strategy

Can supply chain management (SCM) help my company compete?

After reading this chapter, you will be able to:

1. Define supply chain management and identify how supply chain collaboration can improve performance.
2. Discuss the extent to which supply chain strategies are being implemented.
3. Define strategic management and discuss how supply chain management supports the development and execution of a winning competitive strategy.
4. Identify the four process steps involved in designing and implementing a supply chain strategy.

Opening Story: The Dawn of SCM at Olympus Inc.

The serenity of a Caribbean sunrise contrasted sharply with Doug's thoughts as he pondered the challenges of the coming week. Doug and his new bride Charlene were at the end of a weeklong Caribbean honeymoon and would be leaving for the airport in a couple of hours. As director of logistics at Olympus Inc., a leading manufacturer of consumer-packaged goods, Doug's opportunity to sell his vision of supply chain management (SCM) was set for first thing Wednesday morning when he would meet with Joe Andrus, CEO of Olympus, and the company's executive steering council. Doug knew that he had only 2 days to put out any fires that had flared up during his absence and finalize his presentation. Doug was chagrined that the meeting had, at the last minute, been rescheduled for just a couple days after his honeymoon. Yet the realist in Doug acknowledged that sometimes you don't get a second chance to make a difference in a company's performance, culture, and future.

Doug had first become intrigued with the supply chain concept a year earlier, when he and Charlene were copresenters on the topic of alliance management at the national meeting of the Council for Supply Chain Management Professionals. Charlene, a partner at TDG Consulting, had pointed out that, in theory, companies in a well-run supply chain should work together as flawlessly as a well-choreographed Broadway musical. Certain that Olympus's logistics operations could benefit from better "choreography," Doug immediately began researching SCM, looking for evidence of its applicability to Olympus. Charlene pointed him to the results of a supply chain initiative management approach known as **Collaborative Planning, Forecasting, and Replenishment (CPFR)**. Through CPFR implementation, Wegmans, an East-coast grocer, and Nabisco had increased sales of Nabisco's product line by over 50 percent while reducing inventory by one-third. The fact that a rival achieved such outstanding results through supply chain coordination riveted Doug's attention.

Doug began to tout SCM's competitive benefits. At first, nobody listened. A few colleagues suggested he stay focused on the day-to-day challenges of reengineering Olympus's distribution network. But Doug had persisted, seeking to learn as much as he could about SCM so that he could make the business case for pursuing a supply chain strategy. Anecdotes were plentiful, but hard data were hard to find. Doug knew that this would make it difficult to overcome skeptics' objections. Doug himself was not totally sure where to begin, but he was certain that adopting SCM would require significant, even painful, organizational change at Olympus. Doug had therefore assembled a set of SCM success stories from world-class companies. His three favorites—Wal-Mart, Dell, and Honda—came from diverse industries.

- Wal-Mart was Olympus's largest and most demanding customer. Wal-Mart and Kmart were founded in the same year. Yet in 2001, when Kmart filed for bankruptcy, Wal-Mart became the nation's largest grocer with $56 billion in grocery sales. By 2003, Wal-Mart topped the *Fortune* 500 with $248 billion in sales. Wal-Mart's secret of "everyday low prices" on a huge variety of products was made possible by an inventory replenishment system that combines information technology and unique logistics processes.
- Dell was the world's largest and most profitable personal computer manufacturer. Amazingly, Dell had launched a brutal price war at the beginning of the 2000–2001 economic downturn. Leveraging

its direct-to-customer sales channel and relying on contract manufacturers to keep its costs down, Dell generated profits while competitors lost money in their PC operations. Dell's dominance had forced Hewlett-Packard and Compaq to merge in an effort to build a winning PC business.

- Though not the biggest car manufacturer, Honda had established itself as a dominant brand. Honda is year-in-year-out one of the most profitable automakers and is consistently rated as one of the highest-quality car companies. Honda's ingredients for success include engine design and a hugely successful approach to supplier management—suppliers account for approximately 85 percent of Honda's cost.

Doug was a little envious of these companies. He admired Wal-Mart's integrated processes and logistics prowess. At the same time, he wished that Olympus had Dell's marketing and supply efficiencies so that Olympus could profitably win a price war in the midst of a recession. And Doug longed for Honda's proactive supply relationships. If Doug was going to help Olympus establish a reputation as a leading supply chain company, he would have to make the presentation of his life on Wednesday. At a minimum, he needed to

1. Provide a definition of SCM that captures its breadth but is still practical. He needed to tie the diverse aspects of SCM together so that Joe Andrus could get his hands around them.
2. Present a vision of what SCM could do for Olympus. Wal-Mart, Dell, and Honda had harnessed the power of SCM to create powerfully successful business models. Doug hoped he could help the same happen at Olympus.
3. Obtain support for a senior-level task force that could collect the data needed to develop an executable supply chain vision. Doug needed to mobilize Olympus's management team and workforce.

Charlene interrupted Doug's thinking as she entered the room, asking, "Why the serious look? You're not thinking about work already?" Doug could only say, "You know me." Glancing at his watch, Doug suggested, "If we hurry, we can take one last walk along the beach before we head to the airport."

Consider As You Read:

1. What is supply chain management? *Note:* Wal-Mart, Dell, and Honda each take different and unique approaches to SCM. If you were Doug, how would you go about defining SCM?
2. How would you suggest Doug organize his presentation to capture senior management's imagination?
3. Looking ahead, what do you think Doug's biggest challenge is?

What makes Dell and Wal-Mart successful? It's the business model, and supply chain is an enabler. That's why you're seeing this growing importance of supply chains. People realize this is the weapon of the future.

—Robert W. Moffat Jr., IBM

The Theory of Supply Chain Management

For as long as managers can remember, companies have tried to design effective business models. The goal is to meet customer needs better than competitors. Success depends on building processes that can design, make, and deliver the innovative, high-quality, low-cost products and services that customers demand. As managers try to do this, they often find that their companies lack needed resources and skills.[1] They are therefore beginning to look more proactively beyond their companies' walls to consider how the resources of suppliers and customers can be used to create value.[2] These efforts to align goals, share resources, and collaborate across company boundaries are the essence of **supply chain management (SCM)**.[3]

SCM is essentially the economic theory of comparative advantage applied at the company level. Adam Smith argued that (1) the wealth of a nation is the product of its labor and (2) the greatest improvements in the product of labor result from the division of labor. Through specialization and trade, wealth is increased. The result: Consumers worldwide enjoy higher living standards. Similarly, SCM is collaborative specialization. SCM allows a company to do a few things very well for which it has unique skills. Other activities are outsourced to suppliers or customers that possess the needed skills.[4] Relationships are established to assure that each company in the chain performs in a way that improves the success of the entire supply chain. Strategy consultant Kenichi Ohmae has pointed out, "Companies are just beginning to learn what nations have always known: In a complex, uncertain world filled with dangerous opponents, it is best not to go it alone."[5]

The sporting world provides a metaphor that can help us visualize SCM. Winning teams are comprised of great athletes; however, championship teams possess the added ingredient of "chemistry." Many teams with great athletes and huge payrolls never become champions. As frustrating as it is for fans, some very talented teams never get all of the pieces to fit together. As a result, they under-achieve. SCM's goal is to build a corporate "team" consisting of suppliers, finished-goods producers, service providers, and/or retailers. Champion supply chains likewise consist of great companies and develop chemistry—a common understanding of supply chain objectives and individual roles, an ability to work together, and a willingness to adapt in order to create and deliver the very best products and services possible. These teams of companies form an integrated supply chain, which competes and wins against other, less cohesive supply chains in today's global marketplace.[6]

Figure 1.1 shows two simplified supply chains—one service and one manufacturing example. These supply chains are viewed from the perspective

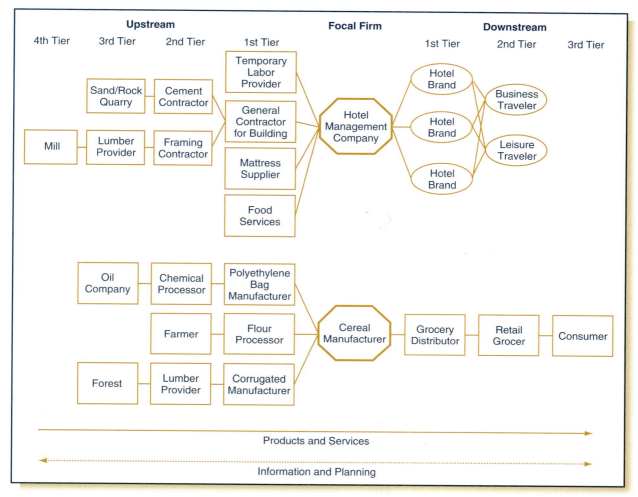

Figure 1.1 Simple Service and Manufacturing Supply Chains

of a "focal firm," the company that is depicting the relationships among its suppliers and customers. Companies are shown in columns, called "tiers," which are numbered in sequence from the focal firm. Purchased goods and services flow from upstream suppliers, through the focal firm, to downstream customers. Information, however, flows in both directions as supply chain members plan and coordinate their efforts.

Take, for example, Marriott International, a company that traces its roots to a small root beer stand opened in Washington D.C. in 1927. Over the years, Marriott specialized in providing lodging for travelers. As Marriott grew into a company that operates over 2,600 hotels and resorts in almost 70 countries, managers realized that there are a lot of distinct kinds of travel needs. Marriott therefore defined its role as understanding the needs of each customer segment and designing hotels to meet those needs at rates customers are willing to pay. Marriott developed a wide range of brands beyond traditional conference hotels and resorts. These brands include Fairfield Inn for the budget-minded traveler, Courtyard for the business traveler, and Residence Inn for the extended-stay traveler. Marriott, however, did not try to integrate backward into the construction or furniture industries. Rather, Marriott relies on specialized suppliers to build and furnish its hotels. These companies in turn rely on suppliers for the materials that are used to construct a hotel or make a mattress. By focusing on what it does best and outsourcing the rest, Marriott has become a leading worldwide hospitality company.

Of course, it is easier to talk about building a cohesive supply chain team than it is to make it happen. For example, the cereal manufacturer shown in the lower panel of Figure 1.1 is a member of the food distribution supply chain. In the early 1990s, as part of the efficient consumer response (ECR) initiative, an industry-wide study was performed to identify opportunities to improve chain competitiveness. A key finding was that 104 days of finished-goods inventory filled the pipeline. Further, nearly 300 days were required to move product from the farm to the consumer.[7] The main reason for the large inventories and inefficient processes was that members of the supply chain viewed themselves as distinct entities and failed to work together to share information and speed the flow of product through the chain. These inefficiencies impose huge cost burdens in an industry that survives on small margins.

Supply Chain Management Defined

Supply chain management is often discussed as managing the flow of information and materials from the "suppliers' supplier to the customers' customer." The reality is that companies do not engage in such extensive supply chain integration.[8] From a practical point of view, managers associate SCM with better information exchange, shared resources, and win–win relationships among the members of the chain. The job of the SC manager is to find opportunities to work with customers and suppliers to reduce costs while improving service. The goal is to use technology and teamwork to build efficient and effective processes that create value for the end customer. The Institute for Supply Management's definition, which is used throughout this book, states that

> Supply chain management is the design and management of seamless, value-added processes across organizational boundaries to meet the real needs of the end customer.

The Internal Value Chain

Before processes can be managed effectively up and down the supply chain, they must be managed well inside the focal firm. Within any company, a variety of functions have responsibility for making decisions that will determine how much value is created. Michael Porter coined the term **value chain** to describe the interconnected nature of these internal functions (see Figure 1.2).[9] For example,

- Executive management defines company strategy and allocates resources to achieve it.
- Research and development (R&D) is responsible for new product design.
- Supply management coordinates the upstream supply base, finding the right suppliers and building the right relationships with them.
- Operations transforms the inputs acquired from suppliers into more highly valued products.

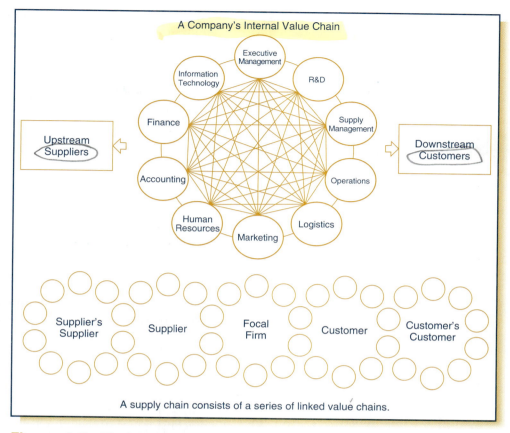

A supply chain consists of a series of linked value chains.

Figure 1.2 The Internal Value Chain

- Logistics moves and stores materials so they are available when and where they are needed.
- Marketing manages the downstream relationships with customers, identifying their needs and communicating to them how the company can meet those needs.
- Human resources designs the systems used to hire, train, and develop the company's employees.
- Accounting maintains business records that provide information needed to control operations.
- Finance acquires and controls the capital required to operate the business.
- Information technology builds and maintains the systems needed to capture and communicate information among decision makers.

Better processes and more competitive products result when managers in the various functions understand customer needs, company strategy, and work well together. However, many company cultures and structures do not promote close working relationships within a company. For example, supply managers in the food distribution supply chain often forward buy large quantities of product on sale without coordinating with logistics managers, who are then left to scramble to find ways of storing the product when it arrives. Supply management costs go down, but the company's inventory, and perhaps total, costs may go up. Such trade-offs are common.

The Bullwhip Effect

A supply chain is made up of a series of linked company-level value chains. Communication up and down the supply chain can help build processes that enable the entire chain to make and deliver winning products and services. However, costs and inefficiencies go up when members of the chain fail to communicate and cooperate. In the food distribution chain discussed earlier, the 104 days of inventory exist because the cereal manufacturer, the distributor, and the retailer all hold just-in-case inventory. Just-in-case inventory, or safety stock, is kept on hand to compensate for poor information sharing and possible transportation delays. Nobody wants to be out of stock when a customer wants to buy cereal.

For example, the grocer forecasts demand for cereal and places an order with the distributor. If the grocer's forecast is wrong, then the order will be too small or too large. To make sure that product is available even if demand is greater than the forecast, the grocer will hold extra inventory in its warehouse. The distributor does the same thing, aggregating all of the orders from different retailers so that it can place one large order with the manufacturer. It too holds safety stock to make up for poor forecasts and possible supply disruptions. The same story is repeated at the manufacturer. In most chains, greater uncertainty exists farther away from the final consumer.

Figure 1.3 illustrates this phenomenon, which is called the **bullwhip effect**. The bullwhip effect says that demand variations are likely to be exaggerated as decisions are made up the chain. Increases in demand begin at the retail level. To fulfill expected future orders, the retailer places a larger order with its distributor. Not wanting to run out of inventory, the distributor places an even larger order with the upstream manufacturer. The manufacturer responds similarly, placing an even larger order with its suppliers. Later, when the retailer's demand diminishes, its upstream suppliers are holding excess inventories, so they reduce their orders. The end result is that small changes in retail-level demand get magnified as they ripple through the supply chain like a bullwhip. It has been estimated that bullwhip-related costs can be as high as 12 to 25 percent for each member of the supply chain. If point-of-sale information were immediately and simultaneously available to all members of the chain, the bullwhip effect could be reduced. Additional steps to combat the bullwhip effect might include retailers working with distributors and manufacturers to develop a collaborative forecast as well as to plan future product promotions. The Wegmans and Nabisco example in the opening story shows that SC costs can be reduced and end-customer satisfaction increased when members of the chain collaborate.

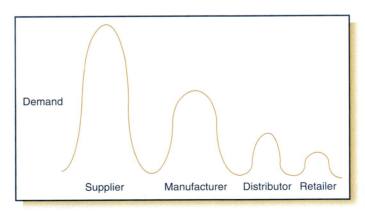

Figure 1.3 The Bullwhip Effect

Companies have always been members of a chain (or more accurately said, network) of organizations; however, most companies still view themselves as separate, distinct entities. They do not effectively work together to reduce inventory levels and costs up and down the chain. Nor do they coordinate decisions to improve customer service. And why should they? Few companies see their stock price increase based on the performance of their suppliers or customers. Reward systems keep managers focused on their own operations and their immediate customers. Managers are too busy trying to cope with the challenges of a tough business world to worry about touchy-feely collaboration. Although the idea of cooperation is intuitively appealing, most managers find it difficult to collaborate meaningfully.[10] This is true within the company and across the chain. Effective collaboration is rare and most often occurs with a company's most important first-tier customers and suppliers. Indeed, research has shown that over 95 percent of collaborative efforts target the first tier.[11]

Figure 1.4 shows various degrees of supply chain integration:

- *Internal process integration.* The goal is to increase collaboration among the company's functional groups.
- *Backward process integration with valued first-tier suppliers.* Leading companies are extending this form of integration to second-tier suppliers (their suppliers' suppliers).
- *Forward process integration with valued first-tier customers.* To date, few companies have targeted integration with their customers' customers.
- *Complete forward and backward integration from the "suppliers' supplier to the customers' customer."* This is the theoretical ideal.

Figure 1.4 Degrees of Supply Chain Integration

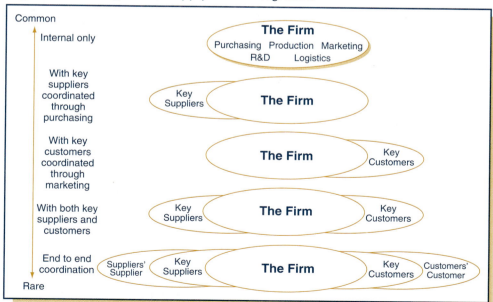

Bridging the cultural and operational gaps that separate the inbound and outbound sides of a company is difficult. Marketers see the world differently from supply managers. Poor information sharing also impedes cooperation. The first order of business for many companies is therefore to make decision outcomes visible and to provide training to help managers understand how the decisions they make influence the rest of the company. For example, both supply and logistics managers need to weigh the pros and cons of forward buying to determine whether or not it makes sense to buy large quantities of a product simply because it is on sale.

Looking beyond internal integration, Jeff Trimmer, director of operations and strategy at DaimlerChrysler, noted, "It's not good enough to optimize the firm—we have to optimize the supply chain. *But no one is king of the supply chain.*"[12] Without a powerful sovereign to make decisions for the entire chain and see that they are carried out, managers maximize the profitability and success of their own departments or companies. The result: Collaboration is limited. The upstream collaboration that occurs typically occurs with a small number of key suppliers, which represent 2 to 20 percent of the direct materials supply base. Collaboration farther upstream is often limited to second-tier purchasing agreements, which are used to leverage purchasing volume. The focal firm generally hands off responsibility for managing beyond the first tier to its direct supplier with only minimal measurement and follow-up. A similar story occurs on the customer side—most collaboration occurs with a few important first-tier customers. As supply chain practice matures and companies learn how to collaborate, we will see more innovative collaboration taking place across the chain. The director of SCM at a leading supply chain company predicts that this day is coming: "We're relatively new at this. As we gain more experience, we will extend our collaborative efforts beyond the first tier."

Revisiting the world of sports, track and field's relay races provide insight into the current status of SC practice. The 4-by-100 meter and 4-by-400 meter relay races involve teams of 4 runners who individually sprint their portions of the race before handing the baton off to the next member of the team. The team whose runner crosses the finish line first—with the baton in hand—wins. Success depends on having fast athletes *and* on making quick, clean handoffs. For most of the race, individual runners focus on what they do best—running fast. As the teammate with the baton approaches the 10-meter handoff zone, the next sprinter begins to run so that the exchange takes place with both teammates running at close to full speed. World-class relay teams practice the handoff tirelessly because they realize that technique is the difference between victory and defeat.

SCM follows the same pattern with each company doing what it does best and then passing the baton to the next company in the chain. Two vital differences exist between the track world and the business world. First, relay teams work out together under the direction of a coach who teaches proper technique, enforces practice, and helps the team catch the vision of the relay while helping individual runners master the details of their individual performance. No SC coach exists in the business world. Individual buyer–supplier relationships may be managed with great care, but nobody has a view of the entire "supply chain" race. Managers focus on a pair of handoffs—one with the customer and one with the supplier. Second, in the track world, each relay involves only three handoffs. Success in the business world depends on executing many handoffs flawlessly. Companies' functional organizations mean that a series of handoffs takes place within the company (a 4-by-100 relay). And even simple supply chains consist of hundreds if not thousands of companies (the 4-by-400 relay). A dropped baton anywhere in this complex 4-by-100-by-400 relay threatens the competitiveness of the entire chain. Establishing a supply chain coach may be the key to long-term supply chain competitiveness.

As the relay metaphor suggests, SCM is not the domain of any function; it is strategic, cutting across the entire organization. Because SCM is strategic, you need to understand the basics of strategic management. The following section discusses how SCM affects and supports strategy development and execution.

INTEGRATING SUPPLY CHAIN THINKING INTO CORPORATE STRATEGY

The Greek verb *stratego* means "to plan the destruction of one's enemies through the effective use of resources."[13] Managers have experience in the competitive arena where rivals seek to take their market share. They know how to wage war against a competitor that can be seen, analyzed, and confronted. Yet this view of strategy often yields poor results because strategy gets defined and measured in terms of the competition. Competitive strategies become reactive—always responding to the actions of key competitors.

Winning strategies should help the company do more than just beat the competition; they should help the company meet the real needs of customers. Sun Tzu observed that the smartest strategy in war is the one that achieves key objectives without having to go to battle.[14] Kenichi Ohmae elaborated on this idea:

> The visible clashing between companies in the marketplace—what mangers frequently think of as strategy—is but a small fragment of the strategic whole. Like an iceberg, most of strategy is submerged, hidden, out of sight. . . . most of it is intentionally invisible—beneath the surface where value gets created, where competition gets avoided.[15]

Michael Dell's creation of the direct-to-customer business model for personal computers allowed Dell to avoid confronting the established PC manufacturers. Recognizing that a market existed for low-cost, standardized computers, Michael Dell had to find a way to get his computers to customers. Dell lacked the clout to arrange for distribution through traditional channels. Besides, Dell almost certainly would have been crushed in a head-to-head confrontation with IBM, Compaq, or Hewlett-Packard. The direct-to-customer model was an ideal approach. It allowed Dell to fly under competitors' radar until Dell had developed a winning business model. By the time other PC makers saw the potential of the direct-to-customer model, Dell had perfected it and established the foundation for years of market dominance.

The Essence and Evolution of Strategic Management

Strategic management is not new. Comparing the duties of a military general and a business manager, Socrates showed Nichomachides that, regardless of setting, the role of strategy is to plan the use of resources to meet objectives.[16] Today's managers still seek to use resources to achieve corporate goals. Competitive threats, demanding customers, and an uncertain business world have increased the need for good strategic decision making.

Contingency Theory

Modern strategic thinking emerged when **contingency theory** conceptualized the relationship between a changing environment, managerial decision making, and performance. Managers need to recognize the implications of a changing environment and use company resources to respond effectively.[17] This contingent response determines how well a company adapts to a dynamic world.[18]

Kmart's early market dominance in the low-price retail segment evaporated as the competitive landscape changed. Its two main rivals, Wal-Mart and Target, changed the rules of the game by pioneering supply chain practices like bar-coding and cross-docking. Kmart's inability to assess and adapt led to bankruptcy.

Building on the foundation of contingency theory, two theories—industrial organization theory and resource-based theory—now guide strategy formulation and the development of a company's business model.

Industrial Organization Theory

Industrial organization (IO) theory claims that market forces should drive decision making. Harvard's Michael Porter noted that a company's power to influence the market is determined by power held by five entities—suppliers, buyers, existing rivals, potential rivals, and providers of substitute products.[19] IO theory's core questions are (1) "Where does market power exist?" and (2) "What are the sources of this power?" By analyzing these five forces, managers can understand their company's operating environment and make decisions to leverage their company's power and thereby its competitiveness in the market.

When Kimberly Clark's CEO Darwin Smith decided to sell off the company's paper mills, most people thought he was crazy. However, he implicitly understood that mill operators lacked market power. As a mediocre paper company, Kimberly Clark had little chance to win in the market. Smith also recognized that Kimberly Clark's primary source of market power came from it's only branded product—Kleenex. Selling the mills provided the money Smith needed to leverage the Kleenex brand and turn Kimberly Clark into a winning consumer products company.[20]

Resource-Based Theory

Resource-based theory emphasizes the management of internal resources to establish a hard-to-imitate advantage.[21] Resource-based strategic management focuses on building organizational skills and processes that enable a company to deliver distinctive products and services. When a company develops unique skills and processes that lead to competitive advantage, it is said to possess a **core competence**.[22]

Honda is the model for resource-based theory. Honda brought together a diverse set of skills found in engineering and production to develop a core competence in engine design and manufacturing. Consumers around the world value Honda's engines for their power, efficiency, and reliability. Honda has used its engine expertise to capture significant share in the automobile, motorcycle, all-terrain vehicle, yard maintenance equipment, and other markets that rely on outstanding engine performance.

The Four Decision Areas of Strategy

The ideas on which contingency, industrial organization, and resource-based theories are built combine to yield a holistic view of strategy that emphasizes four decision areas: environment, resources, objectives, and feedback. Managers must consider these four decision areas to develop strategies that effectively use resources to satisfy customers better than rivals. Each decision area is described in the following sections.

Environment

Managers do not make decisions in a vacuum. Great managers are acutely aware of what is going on in their competitive, economic, legal, and political environments (see Figure 1.5). They also recognize the vital role culture plays in global operations. They know that a company's internal environment, including company culture, functional relationships, and reward systems, influence decision making. The internal and external environments determine which competitive factors should be evaluated to help formulate a winning competitive strategy.

Resources

Business **resources** include all assets, including people, technology, infrastructure, materials, and money. Managers pay close attention to tangible assets like infrastructure and technology. However, the days when "bricks-and-mortar" assets drive success are gone. Competitors can copy infrastructure and buy off-the-shelf technologies. Success now requires investments in knowledge and processes, which are much more difficult to copy. Hard-to-copy capabilities are built on processes that integrate human and technology resources.

Objectives

A business objective is a goal that unifies decision making throughout a company. Typical business objectives focus on earnings, profitability, and stock price. However, Procter & Gamble's CEO, A.G. Laffley, argues that an organization's foremost objective is to create customer value. He claims that in the long run, financial goals can only be met when the company efficiently satisfies customers. Focusing on the right objective is the key to aligning efforts and building winning competencies.

Feedback

Feedback helps managers adapt the organization's strategy to meet the demands of a changing world. In the marketplace, customer expectations change, company capabilities develop and decline, and competitors act and react. Businesses also need information about general factors that can change unpredictably, like exchange rates, government policies, technologies, the weather, and other natural occurrences.

Figure 1.5 Environmental Considerations

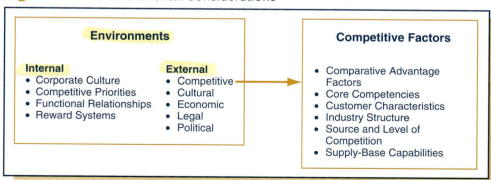

The Influence of SC Thinking on Strategy

Since the dawn of the industrial age, companies have participated as members of one or more supply chains—buying inputs, making products, and selling these products to customers. Until recently, the interdependencies among these diverse companies have been largely ignored—except, of course, when a breakdown occurs in the chain. Even today, many companies develop their strategies independently. They do not consider (1) how the capacities and capabilities of other chain members might be used to create a hard-to-replicate competence or (2) how their strategy affects other members of the chain. SCM changes this traditional, inward-looking approach to strategy formulation and execution.

SC thinking requires that managers look at the world differently—through a new pair of eyes. When they do, they see opportunities to build unique SC-enabled business models. Think: Dell's use of contract manufacturers for enhanced speed and flexibility, Honda's reliance on suppliers for 85 percent of the cost (and quality and innovation) of each car, and Wal-Mart's cross-docking, which requires synchronization among a myriad of product suppliers and transportation service providers. What do these companies' business models have in common? They all leverage the resources and skills of diverse companies in the supply chain to deliver exceptional value to the chain's end customer. The following paragraphs discuss in greater detail how SC thinking influences strategy's big picture view of business model development as well as the four decision areas of strategy.

SC Thinking and Strategic Business Model Design

Strategy's most important role is to define a company's business model. A valid business model must answer two questions: "What is our business?" and "How can we do it better than anyone else?"[23] The first question, "What is our business?" is answered by evaluating two related questions: "Who are our customers?" and "What is the real value that we offer them?" Peter Drucker emphasized that "there is only one valid definition of business purpose: to create a customer. What the customer buys and considers value is never just a product. It is always a utility, that is, what a product or service does for him."[24] A company's identity is defined by its ability to meet the real needs of its customers. For example, Wal-Mart's promise of "Everyday low prices" resonates clearly with a large portion of consumers in every market Wal-Mart has entered.

The second question, "How can we do it better than anyone else?" defines how a company should use its resources to meet customers' needs. Managers must learn how to use basic resources including people, technology, and infrastructure to build unique organizational capabilities. Such capabilities are almost always process-based. Because they are "collective and cross-functional" and encompass "the collective learning in the organization" they are difficult for competitors to imitate.[25] Wal-Mart's supply base, logistics infrastructure, and people enable it to consistently deliver on its everyday-low-price promise, helping it become the world's largest and most profitable retailer.

When managers look through SC lenses, they see these questions differently. Instead of asking, "What is our business?" the SC strategist inquires,

- What is the overall supply chain's value proposition?
- How does our company uniquely help the chain deliver on its value proposition?

Instead of asking, "How can we do it better than anyone else?" the SC strategist explores such issues as,

- What valued capabilities do other members of the chain possess?
- How can we bring these complementary competencies together in a way customers value?
- What types of relationships should we maintain with other members of the supply chain?
- Are any customer-valued competencies missing? If so, who is best positioned to develop them?
- How much of the value-added process should we control?

As managers explore these questions, they realize that an SC vision affects the entire strategy formulation process. They also see that new skills are needed to execute an SC-enabled business model.

SC Thinking and the Four Decision Areas of Strategy

SC managers must also explicitly look at the four decision areas of strategy through their new SC lenses. Table 1.1 describes how SC thinking alters a manager's view of each decision area.

Environment. Starting with environment, SC managers see that today's global competitive environment pits SC teams against each other. For example, Wal-Mart and its suppliers go head to head against the French retailer Carrefour and its suppliers in consumer markets around the world. As the world's two largest retailers, Wal-Mart and Carrefour are engaged in a quest to build the best SC network to ensure access to the right products in sufficient quantities to meet the varying wants and needs of global consumers. Coordinating their global networks relies on sophisticated technology systems. However, to do this effectively, they must learn how to assess the unique needs of consumers in diverse country markets. Because doing

Table 1.1 SCM's Influence on the Four Decision Areas of Strategy

STRATEGY DECISION AREA	COMMON STRATEGIC POSTURE	SUPPLY CHAIN ENABLED PERSPECTIVE
Environment	• React to environmental changes—view them as a threat. • Independent environmental scanning.	• View change as a challenge and an opportunity. • Leverage relationships and technology to anticipate, define, and respond to changes in the competitive environment.
Resources	• Manage company-specific resources. • Buy the best inputs available. • Maintain good supplier relationships.	• Develop unique, boundary-spanning capabilities. • Develop and manage supplier capabilities. • Leverage customer resources when possible. • Build world-class supply chain team.
Objectives	• Deliver customer satisfaction. • Achieve sustainable competitive advantage. • Achieve profitability. • Achieve growth in stock price.	• Help the supply chain satisfy end-customer needs. • Help first-tier customers become more competitive. • Build continuous-improvement-based advantage. • Achieve sustained profitability.
Feedback	• Measure internal activity performance. • Monitor supplier performance. • One-way flow of information from customers to suppliers.	• Measure process and supply chain performance. • Share performance data to drive learning. • Two-way information and idea sharing with both customers and suppliers.

business in Brazil is very different from doing business in China, each must learn how to identify country-specific suppliers and manage in new operating environments where culture, infrastructure, and regulations are dramatically different. The retailer that does the best job of scanning the environment and then building the right SC team will gain an important advantage in the battle for global market share.

Resources. One of the most important jobs of an SC manager is to see how the resources of different SC members can be shared to improve the overall chain's performance. This requires that managers be able to accurately assess the capacities and capabilities of both suppliers and customers. Equally important, SC managers must develop the skills—communication, training, and trust building—to motivate other members of the chain to share their know-how and resources willingly. When this happens, the SC team is able to do things that no single company can. Honda has done more perhaps than any other company to develop its suppliers and then get them to work as a team to build great cars worthy of the Honda name. Honda is so concerned about its suppliers' commitment to the end customer that it invests time and money to help suppliers improve their production processes. Honda's investment in supplier capabilities speaks volumes about its commitment to meeting customer needs. Other companies are catching the vision of managing resources across company boundaries. Procter & Gamble manages much of its in-store inventory at leading retailers, including Kroger and Wal-Mart. Rockwell Collins sends out teams of engineers to help suppliers improve their process capabilities. John Deere invites suppliers to participate in the earliest stages of new product design. A senior manager at Deere commented, "If you visit our design center, 8 out of the first 10 engineers that you meet will be suppliers' engineers." Shared resources can change companies' processes and business models.

Objectives. Strategy defines competitive objectives. When looking through SC lenses, managers see that the only person who really puts money into the chain is the end customer. Therefore, SC strategy emphasizes fulfilling the needs of the end or final customer. Satisfying the immediate customer is still critical; however, each company in the chain must understand who the final consumer is and what it needs to do to fulfill this end customer's expectations. Part of the secret behind Honda's success is that managers work to make sure suppliers know that they are not making just another auto part. Rather, they are building a Honda—a car that drivers love because of its high quality and dependability.[26] This message is communicated constantly to suppliers. As a result, every supplier knows exactly how its parts affect final customer perceptions. Perhaps more important is the satisfaction they feel knowing that they helped make a car that owners love to drive. This satisfaction helps drive their commitment to Honda.

Feedback. Finally, SC managers see that the chain only works if everyone is working from the same playbook. Collaboration requires intensive feedback across the chain. Consistent performance measurement, good information systems, and frequent, honest information sharing are vital components of an SC feedback system. Rockwell Collins has established a Web-based system to share production scheduling information with suppliers on a rolling-horizon basis. Wal-Mart's Retail Link uses the Web to share historic and forecast demand information with its supply partners. Suppliers can monitor the sales of their products at every Wal-Mart where the product is sold on a real-time basis. They can also see exactly how well they are performing to promise in terms of delivery, inventory, sell through, and margin. This information helps them plan their own operations more efficiently. John Deere uses its feedback system to seek supplier input that can improve process efficiency. Any savings obtained through supplier ideas are then shared with the suppliers. Capturing the information needed to coordinate a supply chain's activities and drive learning up and down the chain is much more difficult than monitoring the activities of a single organization. But doing so well can create a powerful competitive advantage—and this is the goal of corporate strategy!

A Look Ahead: A Process Road Map for Strategic SCM

Supply chain management involves more than the implementation of one of many popular initiatives. Practices like collaborative planning, forecasting, and replenishment (CPFR); vendor-managed replenishment (VMR); integrated product development (IPD); customer relationship management (CRM); and supplier development are just building blocks. They must be assembled appropriately to promote meaningful collaboration. Each of these practices will be discussed in future chapters.

A systematic approach to SC analysis can help companies develop an SC-enabled business model and execute a winning SC strategy.[27] Leading SC companies use an iterative 4-step process that emphasizes assessment, planning, execution, and learning. Managers at these companies constantly ask and answer the following four questions that define the road map to SC success (see Figure 1.6). This process model is the unifying theme for this text.

Who Are We?

Every company has its own unique culture and a set of core values that influence decision making. This cultural foundation establishes the beliefs and principles that guide conduct and determine how the organization operates. This identity drives the development of the organization's vision and mission as well as its distinctive competencies. Answering the question "Who are we?" defines why a company exists as well as what it does better than anyone else. The SC executive uses this question to focus the entire organization on meeting downstream customer needs. This unifying focus regarding why the company exists helps promote the systems thinking needed to bridge functions and create winning product development and order fulfillment processes.

How Do We Fit? How Should We Fit?

To design a world-class supply chain, managers need to understand how the chains in which their company participates really operate. Many issues must be evaluated to fully understand the dynamics of the chain. Some of the many questions that must be answered include

- What are the competitive rules?
- Who are our customers—both immediate and farther downstream?
- What are their real needs?
- How can these needs be met efficiently and better than by competing chains?
- What competencies, processes, and technologies are needed to meet these needs and who has them?
- Where are the costs in the chain?
- Who possesses the power in the chain and what is the source of this power?
- Where are the opportunities to optimize the chain's operations and relationships?

Developing an "as-is" SC map can help managers evaluate the strengths, weaknesses, opportunities, and threats of their company's current position. The "as-is"

Figure 1.6 The Supply Chain Road Map

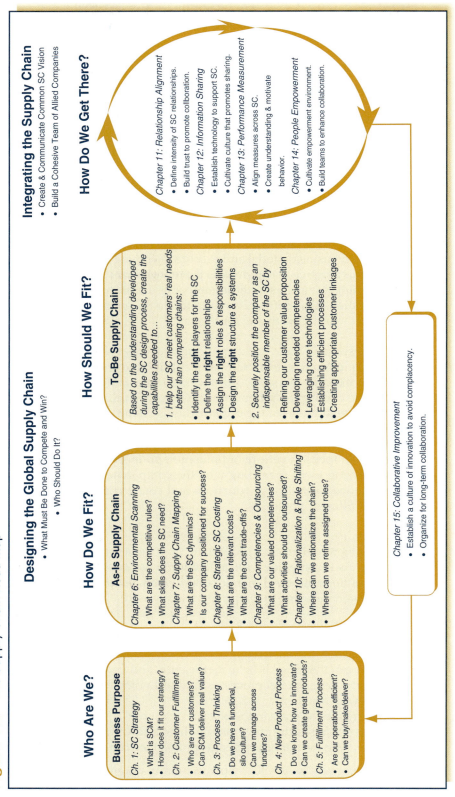

Designing the Global Supply Chain
- What Must Be Done to Compete and Win?
- Who Should Do It?

Who Are We?

Business Purpose

Ch. 1: SC Strategy
- What is SCM?
- How does it fit our strategy?

Ch. 2: Customer Fulfillment
- Who are our customers?
- Can SCM deliver real value?

Ch. 3: Process Thinking
- Do we have a functional, silo culture?
- Can we manage across functions?

Ch. 4: New Product Process
- Do we know how to innovate?
- Can we create great products?

Ch. 5: Fulfillment Process
- Are our operations efficient?
- Can we buy/make/deliver?

How Do We Fit?

As-Is Supply Chain

Chapter 6: Environmental Scanning
- What are the competitive rules?
- What skills does the SC need?

Chapter 7: Supply Chain Mapping
- What are the SC dynamics?
- Is our company positioned for success?

Chapter 8: Strategic SC Costing
- What are the relevant costs?
- What are the cost trade-offs?

Chapter 9: Competencies & Outsourcing
- What are our valued competencies?
- What activities should be outsourced?

Chapter 10: Rationalization & Role Shifting
- Where can we rationalize the chain?
- Where can we refine assigned roles?

How Should We Fit?

To-Be Supply Chain

Based on the understanding developed during the SC design process, create the capabilities needed to...

1. Help our SC meet customers' real needs better than competing chains:
- Identify the **right** players for the SC
- Define the **right** relationships
- Assign the **right** roles & responsibilities
- Design the **right** structure & systems

2. Securely position the company as an indispensable member of the SC by
- Refining our customer value proposition
- Developing needed competencies
- Leveraging core technologies
- Establishing efficient processes
- Creating appropriate customer linkages

Integrating the Supply Chain
- Create & Communicate Common SC Vision
- Build a Cohesive Team of Allied Companies

How Do We Get There?

Chapter 11: Relationship Alignment
- Define intensity of SC relationships.
- Build trust to promote collaboration.

Chapter 12: Information Sharing
- Establish technology to support SC.
- Cultivate culture that promotes sharing.

Chapter 13: Performance Measurement
- Align measures across SC.
- Create understanding & motivate behavior.

Chapter 14: People Empowerment
- Cultivate empowerment environment.
- Build teams to enhance collaboration.

Chapter 15: Collaborative Improvement
- Establish a culture of innovation to avoid complacency.
- Organize for long-term collaboration.

map helps managers see and grasp the nuances that define how the chain works. They then comprehend what must be done for both the company and the chain to compete and win. They also understand better who should be on the SC team.

Once managers understand how the chain works, they are ready to begin their SC redesign. The goal is to use their newfound understanding to create the capabilities to (1) assure that the chain meets customers' real needs better than rival chains and (2) securely position the company as an indispensable member of the chain. A "to-be" SC map guides this process by creating visibility regarding the right players, the right relationships, the right roles and responsibilities, and the right organizational structure and systems. The "to-be" map guides critical decisions involving process design, technology development, outsourcing, alliance development, and supply-base rationalization.

How Do We Get There?

Managers must articulate a compelling migration plan to move the company to its desired position. Creating and communicating a common SC vision is the first step. The second step is identifying the internal and external barriers to greater collaboration. Specific programs or initiatives can then be prioritized. Four decision areas that can be used to promote better collaboration are (1) relationship management, (2) information sharing, (3) performance measurement, and (4) people empowerment. Finally, periodic environmental, technology, and industry scans coupled with best-in-class benchmarking promote continuous learning and improvement.

The supply chain road map emphasizes SC-level planning and scanning. Planning creates understanding and directs resource utilization in a way that mitigates threats and capitalizes on opportunities. Scanning helps managers understand evolving competitive, industry, and market environments. Together, scanning and planning help identify opportunities for improved collaboration. Companies must plan and scan in order to select and build the right capabilities and establish creative and productive SC relationships. The opening stories at the beginning of each chapter chronicle Olympus Inc.'s journey as it starts down the SC road.

CONCLUSION

Thomas Edison provided sound advice to the supply chain manager: "If there is a better way, find it." As IBM's Robert Moffat noted at the beginning of the chapter, SC collaboration can enable better, more competitive business models. Looking at the track record of companies like Dell, Honda, and Wal-Mart, many managers are beginning to see the potential of SCM. As they begin to integrate key business processes from raw materials to the final consumer, the nature of competition will change. Roger Blackwell[28] describes a possible future competitive environment:

> Great firms will fight the war for dominance in the marketplace not against individual competitors in their field but fortified by alliances with wholesalers, manufacturers, and suppliers all along the supply chain. In essence, competitive dominance will be achieved by an entire supply chain, with battles fought supply chain versus supply chain.

Toyota and its suppliers vie against General Motors and its suppliers for global market share. Similar rivalries exist in industries from electronics to pharmaceuticals and from apparel to fast food. A senior executive at Wal-Mart has suggested that the day will come when companies will choose sides and form teams to compete across borders in the quest to increase productivity and capture global market share. The possibilities are amazing, but hard to predict. The challenges are formidable, and very visible. This may explain why the cohesive supply chain team—where objectives are aligned, communication is open, and both resources and risks/rewards are shared—is not yet a reality. Even so, managers across many industries are committed to increase collaboration across the supply chain.

SUMMARY OF KEY POINTS

1. Supply chain management is the theory of comparative advantage applied at the company level. It allows companies to do what they do well. Other activities are outsourced to companies with complementary capabilities.

2. SCM is the design and management of seamless, value-added processes across organizational boundaries to meet the real needs of the end customer.

3. A focal firm's supply chain includes both upstream suppliers and downstream customers. Each company in a chain must manage its own value chain effectively to help the overall chain compete. All supply chains are made up of a series of linked company-level value chains.

4. Supply chain collaboration involves one or more types of process integration: internal integration, backward integration, forward integration, or complete forward and backward integration. Most companies are integrating internally while improving supplier and customer relationships.

5. Strategy's role is to guide managerial decision making to develop a winning business model. Strategic

planning helps managers use resources effectively in a changing marketplace to create value for the customer.

6. Strategic thinking has evolved over time. Three basic theories guide modern strategy formulation and execution: contingency theory, industrial organization theory, and resource-based theory.

7. Four decision-making areas must be considered in strategy formulation and execution: environment, resources, objectives, and feedback.

8. SC thinking can be used to identify and develop unique business models. It also affects each of the four strategy decision-making areas. SCM requires managers to evaluate how the resources of the entire chain can be used to better meet the needs of the end customer.

9. SC leaders engage in an iterative process that emphasizes assessment, planning, execution, and learning. They constantly ask the four questions that define the road map to SC success: "Who are we?" "How do we fit?" "How should we fit?" and "How do we get there?"

REVIEW EXERCISES

1. Define supply chain management. Explain how you would communicate the ideas expressed in your definition in a way that could be operationalized.

2. Imagine you have been assigned the task of developing a slogan to promote SCM at your company. Suggest a slogan that would convey the meaning of SCM in a memorable way.

3. Draw the supply chain for an apparel manufacturer selling cotton slacks.

4. Explain one reason why companies have yet to achieve end-to-end supply chain integration.

5. What is strategy? Identify three strategy theories. What are the characteristics of each?

6. What are the basic decision areas of strategy? Discuss how each decision area is affected by SC thinking.

7. How might SC thinking help a company develop a uniquely competitive business model? Identify and describe one example not discussed in the chapter.

8. What are the questions that an SCM analysis framework must answer to facilitate the formulation and execution of a viable SC strategy? Why are these questions so important?

Case   SCM—Latest Fad or Strategic Imperative?

Don Kagey sat exhausted in his car in the YMCA parking lot. He had just won the city-league 40-and-over racquetball tournament. Don had scarcely had time to savor his victory before workplace worries encroached on his thoughts. It was Friday evening, which meant that Don had only the weekend to decide whether or not to recommend that Med-Tec pursue SCM as a response to increasing customer demands for customized products delivered just in time. Customers were not willing to pay more for the increased service; indeed, they were relentless in their desire to "squeeze" costs out of their supply base. As Don began the drive home, he reviewed his company's situation and the month-long investigation he and his team had been through.

Don Kagey was vice president of purchasing and operations at Med-Tec, a supplier of disposable medical equipment to the hospital industry. At Don's urging, Med-Tec had spent the past 2 years implementing six-sigma quality and lean manufacturing. Med-Tech had also increased its use of global sourcing. The results were impressive: Defects were down to 250 parts per million, productivity was up 5 percent, and order fulfillment times had been reduced from 7 to 4 days. Don's management team was frazzled from the hectic pace they had maintained during the implementations.

Despite these improvements, Med-Tec's best customer, Allegiance Corp., had just approached Don with a request for an entirely new level of delivery performance and customer service. Katie McDonald, senior purchasing manager at Allegiance, had suggested that Med-Tec look at SCM as a possible approach to improving service.

Don wasted little time in investigating SCM. He called a couple of friends whose companies faced the same challenges as Med-Tec. The first conversation was with Mark, a friend who worked for a major supplier in the auto industry. Mark was adamant that SCM was just the latest fad and that it would soon disappear from the headlines. Mark compared SCM to TQM, noting that they both had come to "mean everything and nothing at the same time." Don's second call was to Cheryl, a friend who worked as a logistics manager for a major electronics company. Cheryl's first words were, "Without doubt, SCM is one of our most important areas of emphasis. On a scale of 1 to 10, SCM is an 11. It's clearly the key to our future success or failure." It seamed clear that SCM was not for every company. Don jotted down

a summary note: "SCM can't succeed without top management commitment."

Two days after his meeting with Katie McDonald, Don had met with his management team to communicate to them Allegiance's customer service expectations. The team had spent the next 3 weeks evaluating both SCM and Med-Tec's readiness to implement it successfully. The most important findings were summarized on a white board, as follows:

- At many companies, SC strategies lack specificity.
- Two forces drive SC collaboration: the need to (1) meet customer demands and (2) reduce costs.
- Managers involved in implementing SCM are frustrated by the lack of organizational buy-in.
- SCM can help a company achieve the following benefits:
  - Increased customer responsiveness
  - More consistent on-time delivery
  - Shorter order fulfillment lead times
  - Reduced inventory costs
  - Better asset utilization
  - Lower cost of purchased items
  - Higher product quality
  - Ability to handle unexpected events
  - Faster product innovation
  - Preferred and tailored relationships
- Human nature is a barrier to SCM. People don't like change, and SCM requires change.
- Poor information systems, inconsistent measurement, and conflicting objectives are barriers to SCM.

It was clear that Med-Tec could benefit from a well-designed and executed an SC strategy; however, it was unclear whether Med-Tec had the commitment to make it happen. Don was inclined to move forward and cultivate an SC program. But an editorial in *The Wall Street Journal* titled, "Don't Get Hammered by Management Fads," had caught his attention. Four comments had stuck in Don's mind:

- An estimated 10,000 business books have been published worldwide over the past 3 years, many touting management "tools" promising to make their users incredibly successful by showing them new ways of doing business. Beware.
- Most tools set unrealistic expectations. They overstate benefits and understate costs. Over

time, employees grow fatigued as they are whipsawed from one tool to the next. As one wary store manager recently sighed to me, "If I'm told to jump on one more bandwagon, I'm jumping ship."

- Which tools create the most pain for the least gain? It seems to be those getting the most hype.
- Managers who jump on new-tool bandwagons presuming to boldly go where no one has gone before are doomed to repeat perilous mistakes of the past.

As Don pulled into his driveway, he asked himself, "Is SCM just a fad or is it for real?" Don desperately wanted to avoid embarking on a dead-end journey. Yet his competitive instincts drove him to wonder whether SCM could take Med-Tec to the next level of market success.

CASE QUESTIONS

1. Is supply chain management for real or is it just another fad? Does the answer to this question depend on how a company pursues SCM?
2. What efforts would you make to assure that managers at Med-Tec did not treat SCM as just another flavor-of-the-month management program?
3. Suggest a possible analysis framework Don could use to weigh the facts and determine whether or not SCM is the right thing to do.

ENDNOTES

1. Fine, C. H. (1998). *Clockspeed.* Reading, MA: Perseus Books. Tyndall, G. R., & Kamauff, G. W. (1998). *Global supply chain management.* New York: John Wiley & Sons, Inc.
2. Blackwell, R. D. (1997). *From mind to market: Reinventing the retail supply chain.* New York: Harper Business. Christopher, M., & Ryals, L. (1999). Supply chain strategy: Its impact on shareholder value. *International Journal of Logistics Management, 10*(1), 1–10. Dell, M., & Fredman, C. (1999). *Direct from Dell: Strategies that revolutionized an industry.* New York: Harper Business.
3. Poirier, C. (1999). *Advanced supply chain management.* San Francisco: Berrett-Koehler Publishers, Inc. Ballou, R., Stephen, M., & Mukherjee, A. (2000). New managerial challenges from supply chain opportunities. *Industrial Marketing Management, 29*(1), 7–18.
4. Rich, N., & Hines, P. (1997). Supply-chain management and time-based competition: The role of the supplier association. *International Journal of Physical Distribution and Logistics Management, 27*(3/4), 210–225. Laseter, T. M. (1998). *Balanced sourcing.* San Francisco: Jossey-Bass Publishers. Cox, A. (1999). Power, value and supply chain management. *Supply Chain Management: An International Journal, 4*(4), 167–175. Sheridan, J. H. (1999, September 6). Managing the chain. *Industry Week,* 50–66. Quinn, F. J. (2000). The clockspeed chronicles. *Supply Chain Management Review, 3*(4), 60–64.
5. Ohmae, K. (1989). Managing in a borderless world. *Harvard Business Review, 67*(3), 151–161.
6. Henkoff, R. (1994, November 28). Delivering the goods. *Fortune,* pp. 64–78.
7. Morehouse, J. E., & Bowersox, D. J. (1995). *Supply chain management.* Washington, D. C.: The Food Marketing Institute.
8. Akkermans, H., Bogerd, P., & Vos, B. (1999). Virtuous and vicious cycles on the road towards international supply chain management. *International Journal of Operations & Production Management, 19*(5/6), 565–581. Kilpatrick, J., & Factor, R. (2000). Logistics in Canada survey: Tracking year 2000 supply chain issues and trends. *Materials Management and Distribution, 45*(1), 16–20.
9. Porter, M. (1980). *Competitive strategy.* New York: The Free Press.
10. Mentzer, T. M., Dewitt, W., Keebler, J. S., Min, S., Nix, N. W., Smith, C. D., & Zacharia, Z. G. (2001). Defining supply chain management. *Journal of Business Logistics, 22*(2), 1–25.
11. Fawcett, S. E., & Magnan, G. N. (2002). The rhetoric and reality of supply chain management. *International Journal of Physical Distribution and Logistics Management, 32*(5), 339–361.
12. Nelson, D., Moody, P. E., & Stegner, J. (2000). *Purchasing Machine.* New York: The Free Press.
13. Bracker, J. (1980). The historical development of the strategic management concept. *Academy of Management Review, 5*(2), 219–224.
14. Tzu, S. (2003). *The art of war.* Philadelphia, PA: Running Press Book Publishers.
15. Ohmae, K. (1988). Getting back to Strategy. *Harvard Business Review, 66*(6), 149–156.
16. Bracker, J. (1980). The historical development of the strategic management concept. *Academy of Management Review, 5*(2), 219–224.
17. Hofer, C. (1975, December). Toward a contingency theory of strategy. *Academy of Management Journal,* 784–810.
18. Galbraith, J. (1973). *Designing complex organizations.* Reading: Addison-Wesley.
19. Porter, M. (1980). *Competitive strategy.* New York: The Free Press.

20. Collins, J. (2001). *Good to Great*. New York: Harper-Collins Publishers, Inc.
21. Dierickx, I., Cool, K. (1989). Asset stock accumulation and sustainability of competitive advantage. *Management Science, 35*(12), 1504–1511. Barney, J. (1991). Firm resources and sustained competitive advantage. *Journal of Management, 17,* 99–120.
22. Prahalad, C. K., & Hamel, G. (1990). The core competence of the corporation. *Harvard Business Review, 68*(3), 79–91. Stalk, G., Evans, P., & Schulman, L. E. (1992). Competing on capabilities: The new rules of corporate strategy. *Harvard Business Review, 70*(2), 57–69. Leonard-Barton, D., Bowen, H. C., Clark, K. B., Hollaway, C. A., & Wheelwright, S. C. (1994). How to integrate work and deepen expertise. *Harvard Business Review, 72*(5), 121–130.
23. Drucker, P. F. (1994). The theory of the business. *Harvard Business Review, 72*(5), 95–104.
24. Drucker, P. F. (2001). *The essential Drucker.* New York: Harper Collins Publishers, Inc.
25. Prahalad, C. K., & Hamel, G. (1990). The core competence of the corporation. *Harvard Business Review, 68*(3), 79–91. Stalk, G., Evans, P., & Schulman, L. E. (1992). Competing on capabilities: The new rules of corporate strategy. *Harvard Business Review, 70*(2), 57–69.
26. Nelson, D., Mayo, R., & Moody, P. E. (1998). *Powered by Honda.* New York: John Wiley & Sons, Inc.
27. Tyndall, G. (1998). *Supercharging supply chains.* New York: John Wiley & Sons, Inc. Kuglin, F. A. (1998). *Customer-centered supply chain management.* New York: AMACOM.
28. Blackwell, R. D. (1997). *From mind to market: Reinventing the retail supply chain.* New York: Harper Business.

Supplement A

The Beer Game

The Beer Game was originally developed at the Massachusetts Institute of Technology to simulate the performance of a simple, 6-tier supply chain. To help satisfy end-customer demand for a product, a raw materials supplier ships inputs to a factory, which ships to a distributor, which ships to a wholesaler, which ships to a retailer, which sells to the end consumer as shown in Figure A.1. For this game, players assume the role of one

Figure A.1 Basic Supply Chain

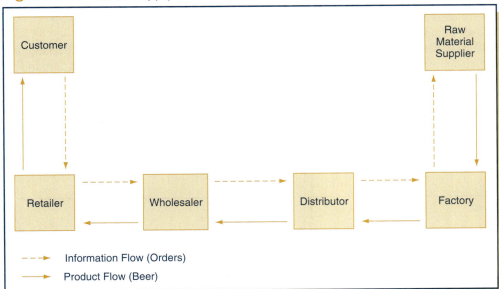

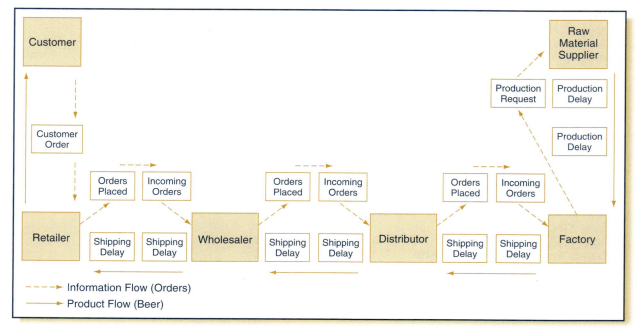

Figure A.2 Shipping and Order Delays

--→ Information Flow (Orders)
— Product Flow (Beer)

of the tiers in the supply chain and make decisions about how much inventory to order from their immediate supplier. To facilitate this ordering and shipping process, inventory is represented by pennies or poker chips and orders are communicated along the supply chain using little slips of paper.

The game is played in a series of periods. Each period corresponds to 1 week. To make the game more realistic, order delays and shipping delays are built in. Each order has a 2-week delay and each shipment has a 2-week delay (see Figure A.2). The exception to these delays occurs between the retailers and their customers. When possible, customer orders are filled when they occur.

As with most supply chains, there are costs associated with having too much inventory (i.e., inventory carrying costs) and costs associated with not having enough inventory (i.e., backlogs, lost sales, lost

customers). In this simulation, the trade-offs occur between inventory and backlogs. To hold a unit of inventory for 1 period (1 week) costs $1.00. Each unit of backlog costs $2.00 per week. Inventory and backlog levels are tracked during the game on a form similar to the one shown in Table A.1.

Inventory levels are determined by simply counting the various pennies and poker chips at the end of each period or week. Backlogs are cumulative and are calculated as follows:

Backlog = previous period backlog
+ current period demand
− amount shipped in current period

The goal of the game is to meet demand at the lowest possible total cost at each of the tiers along the supply chain. The performance of each tier will be

Table A.1 Game Record (By Week)

WEEK	INVENTORY	BACKLOG	ORDER
1			
2			
3			

compared against the performance of the same tier in other supply chains. To play the game, there must be at least one and at most two individuals positioned at each tier of the supply chain with the exception of the customer tier, which requires no players.

Game Steps

Players must complete four basic steps during each week or period of the game. These four steps are

1. Receive inventory and transport orders—During this step of the game, the products that are in the shipping delay boxes are advanced downstream one position on the game board.
2. Look at and fill incoming orders—This step involves looking at the incoming order card for your particular tier and shipping the requested number of units (plus any existing backlog), if possible, into the empty shipping delay box created during step 1. If you don't have enough inventory, ship as much as you can and add any unfilled orders to your backlog.
3. Record inventory or backlog levels—Count up your inventory or calculate your backlog and record it on the provided form.
4. Place an order—During this step, you must decide how many units to order from your immediate supplier. Once you have decided, advance your previous period's order from the order-placed box into the incoming order box of your supplier and place your new order in the order-placed box. Be sure to place these orders face down on the game board so that they cannot be seen by your supplier until the appropriate period.

Rules of the Game

1. If there are two people assigned to your tier of the supply chain, you may communicate with that person while making decisions about how much to order from your supplier. However, the only communication that takes place between the various tiers of the supply chain is through the order cards that are passed face down along the supply chain as discussed earlier.
2. Customer demand is determined in advance and is placed in the customer order box on the game board. Retailers are not allowed to share this information with other tiers along the supply chain.
3. Each of the four steps needs to be completed by each of the tiers for the current period before the next period can be started.
4. The game is stopped after a suitable number of periods have transpired.

Chapter 2

Customer Fulfillment Strategies

How does my company view customers? Can I help it better meet demanding customer expectations?

The Supply Chain Road Map

Who are we?

Business Purpose

Chapter 1: SC Strategy
- What is SCM?
- How does it fit our strategy?

Chapter 2: Customer Fulfillment
- **Who are our customers?**
- **Can SCM deliver real value?**

Chapter 3: Process Thinking
- Do we have a functional, silo culture?
- Can we manage across functions?

Chapter 4: New Product Process
- Do we know how to innovate?
- Can we create great products?

Chapter 5: Fulfillment Process
- Are our operations efficient?
- Can we buy/make/deliver?

After reading this chapter, you will be able to:

1. Discuss how information has empowered customers, raising the competitive bar for today's companies.
2. Explain how customers define value and what a company must do to deliver value. Describe the competitive contributions of cost, quality, flexibility, delivery, and innovation capabilities.
3. Explain the nature of customer service and satisfaction and how they differ from customer success.
4. Explain why the end customer should be the focal point for the entire supply chain.
5. Segment customers based on strategic importance. Describe the relationships, systems, and processes needed to deliver desired levels of service to different customers.
6. Discuss the role of operational excellence in assuring profitable customer relationships.

Opening Story: The Insatiable Customer

It was a beautiful, sunny Tuesday afternoon, yet Doug was perplexed. He and Charlene had returned from the Caribbean to find things running smoothly at their respective workplaces. But things changed quickly. At the last minute, Charlene's boss asked her to make a presentation on collaborative planning at the European Forum on Advanced Logistics. Her flight departed late Monday. As for Doug, the moment he had sat down to put the finishing touches on his supply chain presentation, Diane Merideth, Olympus's North American marketing manager, burst into his office. She was not happy and she let Doug know it, saying, "Doug, we have a problem. I was just on the phone with Sarah Hartley, VP of global sourcing at Goliath, and it seems we missed a delivery window at their Dallas cross-dock facility. I haven't been able to track the shipment down, but I know it left our distribution center on time. Goliath is our largest and most important customer. Sarah didn't hesitate to remind me of this, nor did she hold anything back in expressing displeasure regarding our service levels."

Doug had invited Diane to sit down while they sorted things out. He then called David Amado, a senior transportation manager, to find out what happened. David said he would track the shipment down and promised expedited delivery. He did, however, express surprise at Sarah Hartley's harsh comments regarding Olympus's delivery record, noting, "We've never performed better. Our on-time record and complete orders are at the highest levels we've ever achieved. We're no industry slouch."

Satisfied that David would resolve the immediate crisis, Doug called Tameka Williams, a member of the information systems group, to check on Olympus's overall delivery performance. Tameka pulled up the delivery statistics and confirmed that Olympus had improved its on-time delivery to 98 percent and was hitting the recently established 99 percent complete order goal. She added, "Our recent investments in routing and scheduling software are really beginning to pay off. Efficiencies are way up and so are our service levels."

Diane wasn't fully satisfied with David and Tameka's assessment. She commented, "You may have improved performance on average, but we're not meeting Goliath's expectations. And the penalty clause makes missing delivery windows expensive. These service failures are damaging our operating alliance. Sarah reminded me that we cannot afford not to meet Goliath's requirements. And our other customers are almost as demanding. They are sure to follow Goliath's lead in imposing higher service levels. You should know that come January Goliath is tightening its delivery time windows. They also expect us to take on the responsibility for promotional packaging, store-ready displays, and labeling orders for specific stores. And the continuous improvement clause means that they want us to do it all for 5 percent less next year."

Susan Mass, Olympus's director of global supply, who had stepped into Doug's office to check on Doug's preparation for Wednesday's big presentation, joined the conversation. She pointed out that Olympus was viewed as equally demanding by its own suppliers. She noted, "Just as Goliath soaks up every ounce of service we can provide, we turn around and use our leverage to squeeze costs out of our supply relationships." Although true, this fact did not alter the sense that Olympus was under siege.

Doug acknowledged that Olympus had to raise the service bar even higher. After Diane and Susan left his office, he called David to share some final thoughts. "We've made steady progress in the last couple of years with respect to our customer fulfillment capabilities. Nevertheless, today's service failure has made it clear that we need to reevaluate the nature of our customer relationships. We know that not all customers possess the same clout, yet we still manage to averages. Although we strive for excellence, maybe our one-size-fits-all mentality is outdated. Today's crisis makes that point! The question is, 'what are we going to do about it?' Our best customers demand more, but want to pay less. They want tailored services, but don't seem willing to collaborate in a meaningful way. In many cases, we can't even get them to share information regarding their expected sales or product promotion plans. We need to redefine how we relate to our customers and design the infrastructure to support the new relationships! We need to know what questions to ask and then we need to answer them. That's your next task, David. I'm putting you in charge."

Doug's thoughts regarding Wednesday's presentation had evaporated under the heat of the customer fulfillment challenge raised by Sarah Hartley's call. As he tried to focus on tomorrow's meeting with Joe Andrus, Doug wondered how he might use today's experience to help make the case for SCM. Solving customer fiascos was Charlene's specialty; he wished she weren't in Europe. He could use some advice.

If we aren't customer-driven, our cars won't be, either.

—Donald E. Petersen, Ford

THE INFORMATION-EMPOWERED CUSTOMER

Information is power, especially in the hands of customers. Today's customers are empowered with a broad range of product and pricing information. The Internet reduces the costs of information acquisition, allowing customers to compile product specifications and compare prices. For example, a car buyer can look up JD Power quality and reliability statistics, consider *Consumer Reports* "Best Buy" evaluations, check out *Car and Driver* write-ups, and obtain factory invoice information on Edmunds.com all before visiting a dealership. She enters the showroom as an information-empowered customer who can confidently tell the salesperson exactly which options she prefers and how much she is willing to pay. Some car buyers bypass the dealer and simply buy the car on-line. The technology even exists for the buyer to track the progress of her new car as it proceeds down the production line.

Customer empowerment is occurring across the supply chain. Sourcing professionals can identify potential suppliers, compare their capabilities, and evaluate their pricing strategies. They enter buyer/supplier relationships as informed negotiators. And better database technology combined with data-mining tools helps customers track and benchmark supplier performance. Further, reverse auctions, which place rival suppliers in a real-time competitive-bidding event, provide greater leverage to buying organizations. For the manager who knows how to use them, these tools create leverage within the supply chain. As a result, channel power is shifting down the supply chain toward the end consumer.

Customer empowerment means that companies up and down the supply chain must increase their ability to deliver value. Information availability and shifting power have created customers that use their market leverage to constantly demand higher levels of service at lower costs. These customers have been called "high-service sponges." High-service sponges like Intel, Toyota, and Wal-Mart "soak up" their suppliers' resources to fuel their own quest for market dominance. Although not every customer has Intel's market power, many are adopting the same demanding mentality and high expectations.

Returning to our definition of SCM, the SC manager's goal is to design and manage processes to meet customer needs. To do this, they need to understand how customers view *value* and define *satisfaction*.

CREATING VALUE TO MEET CUSTOMERS' NEEDS

Harvard's Michael Porter noted that to succeed, companies have to develop a distinctive advantage.[1] Distinctive advantage implies that a company differentiate itself in the mind of customers. Beating the competition by capturing the heart of customers is the battle cry for companies like Apple and Nordstrom. If a company were to bring its managers together to brainstorm opportunities to create value, many ideas would be identified. These ideas could likely be classified into one of five basic areas of customer value: *quality, cost, flexibility, delivery,* and *innovation.*

Quality

Managers often define quality as conformance to specifications. However, the real measure of quality is whether or not a product or service lives up to customer expectations. Because quality drives consumer behavior, some analysts have called it the most important factor in achieving long-term success. Besides its influence on the customer, poor quality hurts a company's performance in other areas. For example, at companies that do not manage quality carefully, up to 25 percent of the cost of goods sold can be traced to finding and fixing quality problems. This is one reason why W. Edwards Deming said, "You are not obliged to manage quality. You can also choose to go out of business."[2]

Management can control over 80 percent of quality problems.[3] Best-in-class companies achieve parts per million (PPM) defective quality levels. Motorola launched its 6σ (six sigma) program more than a decade ago to help it make the leap from percent-defective to parts-per-million performance. General Electric's Jeffrey Immelts calls 6σ the common language at GE. He says that everyone from the dock to the CEO's office must speak the language of 6σ. Such commitment to quality has helped a few companies achieve the 6σ goal of only 3.4 defects per million parts produced.

Although this operational view is valuable from a measurement and control perspective, it fails to take customer expectations into full account. SC managers cannot afford to overlook customers. They need to get into the minds of customers to understand how they define quality. Harvard professor David Garvin identified eight factors that comprise quality in the minds of the end user.[4]

- Performance—refers to the primary operating characteristics of the product.
- Features—are the "bells and whistles" or extras that distinguish a product from competitors' offerings.
- Reliability—represents the notion that a product can be counted on not to fail.
- Conformance—measures how well a product matches established specifications.
- Durability—refers to the product's mean time between failures and its overall life expectancy.
- Serviceability—refers to the speed of repair when quality problems arise.

- Aesthetics—deals with perceptions of fit and finish or artistic value.
- Perceived quality—deals with overall perceptions of a product's or brand's quality reputation.

Quality means doing the right things right the first time—every time. Because a finished product's quality can be no better than the quality of the parts that comprise it or the processes used to make and deliver it, SC managers are responsible for a company's quality performance. Because customers demand high quality, outstanding quality must be designed and built into the company's products and processes. This means that quality must really become the common language of both the organization and its supply chains.

Cost

Because customers value low prices, managers face unrelenting pressure to reduce costs. Globalization has increased factor mobility and market access, requiring local companies to match the cost position of global rivals who often possess low-cost labor advantages. Four cost-reduction strategies are widely pursued: (1) productivity enhancement, (2) adoption of advanced process technology, (3) locating facilities in countries with low-cost inputs, and (4) sourcing from the world's most efficient suppliers.[5]

For example, automakers from Europe, Japan, and the United States have automated their production processes, located facilities in low-cost regions, and sourced from efficient global suppliers. At the same time, leading automakers are waging a battle to achieve high levels of assembly productivity. Honda and Toyota require only 18 labor hours to assemble a vehicle compared to over 20 hours for General Motors (the most productive U.S. automaker). Despite its productivity advantage, Toyota proclaims, "We will cut costs like we have never cut costs before."

The cost challenge extends beyond pursuing productivity programs or following competitors around the world to obtain the lowest labor rates. As one manager in the consumer products industry has noted, the real measure of cost performance today is "total landed cost to the customer's trunk." The entire supply chain from raw materials to final consumer must be designed for efficiency. Cost issues drive strategic decisions such as global manufacturing rationalization, outsourcing, and downsizing as firms seek lower labor, materials, and process costs. When cost competitiveness improves, companies can expand market share, increase scale economies, improve profitability, and invest in future capabilities. Cost improvements can drive a powerful cycle of competitiveness.

Flexibility

Flexibility is the ready capability to adapt to new, different, or changing requirements. Chinese philosopher Sun Tzu emphasized flexibility's importance, stating, "Every minute ahead of the enemy is an advantage."[6] A flexible organization operates with short lead times, is responsive to special customer requests, and can adjust rapidly to unexpected events.[7] Flexibility is a cross-functional capability that depends on the adaptability of the firm's people.[8] Flexibility also requires investments in information and automated production and logistics technologies. The following steps are critical to creating a flexibility culture.

- Make cycle time a priority throughout the organization.
- Map processes to make them visible.
- Identify key time-related activities/decisions.
- Benchmark against customer requirements and competitors' capabilities.
- Cross-train workers and organize work in multifunctional teams.
- Design performance measures to value fast-cycle capabilities.
- Develop information systems to track activities and share information.
- Build learning loops into every process throughout the organization.

Amazon.com, The Limited, Toyota, and Wal-Mart have set the standard for flexibility. Amazon.com can trace its success to (1) a "flexible" Web site that self-personalizes to each customer's buying habits and (2) a high level of rapid and complete order fulfillment to customer requests. At The Limited, the goal is to bring the desired product from the mind of the customer to the retail rack within 1,000 hours—about 60 percent faster than the competition.[9] This speed helps The Limited have popular styles and colors available in peak season, when the customer wants them and is willing to pay full price. Toyota's ability to assemble its Camry sedan, Sienna minivan, Highlander SUV, and Lexus RX 330 using the same platform and on the same production line helps it compete in very different but profitable markets. Toyota's promise of a 5-day customized car is an extension of this mixed-model assembly that relies even more on outstanding information systems and supplier support. Wal-Mart combines cross-docking, a satellite communications system, and a private trucking fleet to assure that low-cost products are always on the shelf where the customer expects to find them. These companies demonstrate the importance of combining information, people, and processes to build a flexibility advantage that anticipates and responds to customer needs.

Delivery

Delivery means "doing things fast"—consistently. Fast, reliable delivery requires the reduction of order cycle time and the elimination of variability. By nature, a delivery capability is cross-functional. Anything that increases the time or variability of any portion of the order cycle threatens the firm's ability to deliver on time. An incorrect order entry, a late supplier delivery, a machine breakdown, a transportation delay, or the wrong routing reduces delivery performance and drives costs up. For instance, an electronics manufacturer operating in the Dominican Republic consistently failed to meet production schedules. To deliver on time to customers, the firm had to ship 70 percent of its orders via airfreight at a cost 600 percent higher than ocean shipping.

Sourcing, operations, and logistics play key roles in building a delivery capability. Sourcing manages materials and service suppliers to provide the right materials on time. Operations and logistics often represent 90 percent of the total order cycle time. Efforts to achieve great delivery performance should target all three functional areas. As the following examples show, delivering on short lead times provides a competitive edge.

- Motorola established itself as a world leader in pager manufacturing by reducing production time from 30 days to less than 30 minutes.
- National Semiconductor redesigned its global distribution network to reduce order fulfillment lead times. A 47 percent reduction in delivery time to customers yielded a 34 percent increase in sales.

- Steelcase became a leading furniture manufacturer by promising to deliver and set up 80 percent of its custom line of office furniture anywhere in North America within 12 days from receipt of order.

Innovation

Innovation helps create new markets and changes industry standards. Innovative companies capture market share and enjoy improved profitability.[10] Many companies have reduced concept-to-market cycles by involving suppliers in the conceptualization and development process. **Early supplier involvement (ESI)** is a key element of innovation strategies at industry leaders like Canon, Honda, and 3M. One study showed that early supplier involvement in the product development process accounts for one-third of the reduction in man-hours and 4 to 5 months of the shorter lead times enjoyed by leading innovators in the auto industry. In another study, products introduced 6 months late, but within budget, realized a 33 percent decrease in expected profits over the first 5 years. Products introduced on time, but 50 percent over budget, realized only a 4 percent reduction in profit.[11] The following examples show that product innovations drive market success.

- Canon established itself in the photocopier industry by introducing over 90 new models in 6 years. Xerox eventually stemmed its market share loss by reducing its own product development time and improving quality. However, Canon's persistent innovation enables continued industry dominance.
- Yamaha publicly challenged Honda's position as the world's leading motorcycle maker. Honda responded by introducing or replacing 113 models during the next 18 months. Yamaha managed 37 model changes in the same time. The sophistication of Honda's designs made Yamaha's product line obsolete.[12]
- When Toyota's share of the Japanese market dipped below 40 percent, the CEO pledged to bring exciting new cars to the market. Several vehicles came to market in 18 months (the Ipsum went from concept to market in only 15 months).
- 3M expects 30 percent of all sales to come from products introduced in the last 4 years. 3M invests in research and development even during economic downturns and gives its people time to work on pet innovation projects.[13]

Trade-Offs Versus Synergies

Managers must decide how much emphasis to place on each value area. For years, managers believed that high quality was inherently expensive (see Figure 2.1). Standardization and customization were believed to be at opposite ends of the cost continuum. Likewise, rapid delivery was thought to come at the cost of flexibility. Although trade-offs do exist, modern SC managers seek to build synergies among the dimensions of customer value.

Experience has shown that simplifying the operating environment and creating a fluid organizational culture promotes synergies. For example, 40 percent of all quality problems can be traced back to poor product design and 60 to 80 percent of a product's cost is determined during the design process. Further, the term *hidden plant* was coined to signify that 15 to 40 percent of a firm's capacity is used to find and fix poor-quality work. Leading companies have found that shared information, the elimination of restrictive work rules, and proactive measurement enable cost, quality, flexibility, delivery, and innovation to work together, like the spokes of a wheel, to move the firm forward to a stronger competitive position.

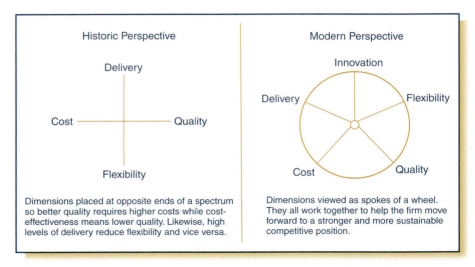

Historic Perspective

Dimensions placed at opposite ends of a spectrum so better quality requires higher costs while cost-effectiveness means lower quality. Likewise, high levels of delivery reduce flexibility and vice versa.

Modern Perspective

Dimensions viewed as spokes of a wheel. They all work together to help the firm move forward to a stronger and more sustainable competitive position.

Figure 2.1   Components of Customer Value: Trade-Offs or Synergies

UNDERSTANDING SATISFACTION TO FULFILL CUSTOMERS' NEEDS

When a customer makes a purchase, she is buying a set of "satisfactions." Satisfaction results as customers use a product. It also emerges from the services used to sell and support the product. Figure 2.2 emphasizes the fact that a customer's expectations

Figure 2.2   Expectations, Satisfaction, and Customer Decision Making

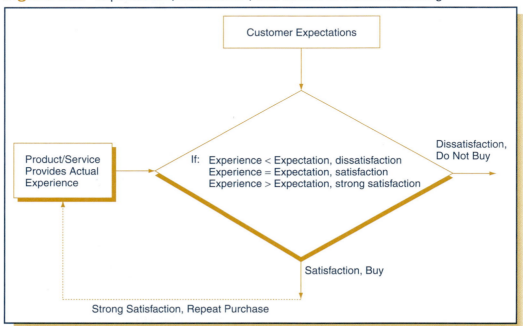

and her actual experience with a product determine her level of satisfaction.[14] She is satisfied when her experience meets a priori expectations. When expectations are exceeded, she views the experience favorably and may become a repeat customer. A negative gap between expectations and experience leads to dissatisfaction. The key to satisfying customers is to understand their needs so that unique products and services can be developed to meet those needs.[15] Creating satisfaction should be the goal of a company's culture and structure.[16]

Nordstrom, the Seattle-based clothier, has made its mark by creating a customer-centric culture that delivers an unparalleled customer service experience. Nordstrom's mission statement is "Offer the customer the best possible service, selection, quality and value." The focus is on the total customer experience. Linda Finn, marketing director, explains Nordstrom's focus this way, "The strategy is to draw customers to the store, then 'delight and surprise them.'" This means empowering employees to get into the customer's mind so they can solve unspoken needs. It also means having the "right merchandise in the right store at the right time—every time."[17] Store design, product selection, and employee training and recognition come together to create the Nordstrom mood. Patrick Kennedy, a department manager, summarized Nordstrom's customer goal: "When you stop worrying about the money, and concentrate on the customer, the money will flow."

Few companies have created a truly customer-centric culture that is supported by appropriate structure and systems. The American Customer Satisfaction Index shows that companies have made little progress in living up to customer expectations (see Figure 2.3). Satisfaction levels have remained stagnant since the mid-1990s. Achieving satisfaction and turning it into loyalty is challenging.[18] Xerox asked customers to rate their satisfaction on a 5-point scale. They found that those who rated 4 (largely satisfied) were 6 times more likely to defect to the competition than those who rated 5 (completely satisfied). Modern customers are demanding and capricious. They view promises to "meet or exceed their expectations" skeptically.

Figure 2.3 Customer Satisfaction Index (1993–2002)

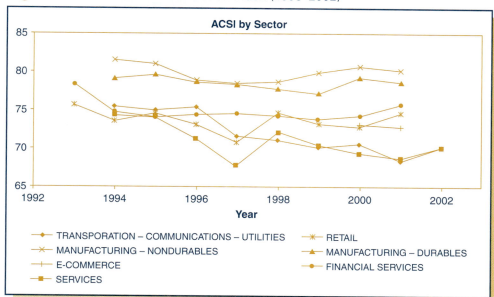

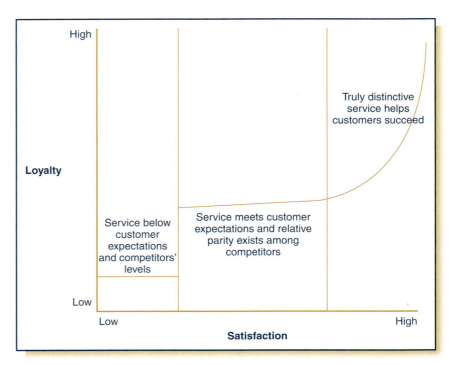

Figure 2.4 Customer Satisfaction and Loyalty

To match promised value to customers' desires, SC managers should revisit such questions as "What are customers really looking for?" and "How do our products uniquely meet these desires?" Only when a company excels at something customers value will it achieve loyalty. Loyalty is important because it leads to profitable repeat business. Figure 2.4 shows the relationship between satisfaction and loyalty. When customers feel a company's service offerings are inferior, they do not come back. Repeat business occurs when the service experience enters the zone where it is comparable to competitors'. However, customers will defect to rivals if it is convenient to do so—managers must not mistake convenience for loyalty. When an intrinsically higher-level experience is provided, customers become truly loyal.

Apple has created such a unique feel and experience with its products that Mac users seldom defect to rivals. When Apple introduced the iPod, its storage capacity combined with a fresh look and an easy-to-use customer interface immediately captured consumers' imagination. The iPod quickly became the best-selling portable digital music player. The iPod mini, though viewed as too pricey by most analysts, sold out within a week of its introduction. The iPod nano stirred similar need-to-have desires among music lovers, helping Apple maintain its 70 percent market share. The challenge for Apple, and other companies, is that most products can be copied by the competition—often in less than 1 year. Apple realizes this and has continued to bring out new and exciting products that have upgraded the customer experience and kept customers loyal. Executives at Apple know that advantages are short-lived if they are not constantly improved.

Loyalty results when a company helps its customers improve their own competitiveness. Managers must learn how to use constrained resources to help preferred customers go beyond satisfaction to enhanced competitive performance.[19] The evolution of customer fulfillment strategies is discussed next.

Customer Service Strategies

Traditional customer service efforts focus on internal service levels and goals. Managers hope that, by doing so, customers' needs will be met. Service measures take the form of percent defective products, percent on-time delivery, and **fill rate** (percent of products ordered that are actually delivered) from distribution centers. Table 2.1 highlights basic limitations of traditional customer service strategies. For example, because many internal measures related to cost, time, and performance are used, managers may feel they are delivering great service even when customers feel otherwise. Without customer feedback, it is easy to emphasize the wrong service activities or focus on the wrong service measures. When this happens, resources are wasted on becoming great at something customers do not value.[20]

For example, a division of one company set quality performance standards at a level lower than the customer's (a sister division) expectations. Shipment after shipment that passed the internal standards was returned as unacceptable. Aligning quality standards with the higher level set by the customer would have required additional investment and training but would have lowered long-term costs and eliminated counterproductive intra-firm rivalry. When managers emphasize efficient operations over appropriate customer understanding, discrepancies like this occur, leading to **service gaps**.

Customer Satisfaction Strategies

Customer satisfaction efforts require direct input from important customers regarding their service expectations. Typical approaches to gathering customer feedback include surveys, focus groups, in-depth personal interviews, and ethnographic studies. At some companies, senior executives spend up to 20 percent of their time with customers to gain a better understanding of their needs. Key account teams and interorganizational collaboration can also provide insight into

Table 2.1 Limitations of Different Customer Fulfillment Strategies

STRATEGY	FOCUS	LIMITATIONS
Customer Service	Meet internally set expectations	• Fail to understand what customers value. • Expend resources in wrong areas. • Measure performance inappropriately. • Fail to deliver more than mediocre service. • Operational emphasis leads to service gaps.
Customer Satisfaction	Meet customer-driven expectations	• Ignore operating realities while overlooking operating innovations. • Constant competitor benchmarking leads to product/service proliferations and inefficiency. • Maintain unprofitable relationship. • Vulnerable to new products and processes. • Focus on historical needs of customer does not help customer meet new market expectations.
Customer Success	Help customers meet their customers' needs	• Limited resources require that "customers of choice" be selected; that is, customer success is inherently a resource-intensive strategy.

customer needs and expectations. An effective customer feedback system answers the following questions:

- How do important customers define quality, on-time delivery, responsiveness, and other key value areas?
- Are our internal measures consistent with customers' measures?
- Does our current performance meet our customers' requirements?
- Would an improvement in our performance really be valued by our customers?

Customer input helps managers (1) align measures to customer expectations, (2) allocate resources and reevaluate priorities, and (3) adopt new policies or practices. The goal is to eliminate service gaps by meeting customer-defined expectations. However, because obtaining accurate customer information is costly in terms of both time and money, many companies fail to collect reliable and valid data from customers. Further, companies that do look outward to their customers face certain risks. An inappropriate emphasis on satisfaction can reduce efficiency and profitability. For example, when a desire to satisfy customers leads managers to make promises that cannot be fulfilled, customers are alienated. Likewise, when service and product offerings proliferate, inefficiencies arise. Finally, satisfaction initiatives that focus too much on what has worked in the past leave the supply chain vulnerable to the dynamics and competition of a global marketplace. Managers need to learn to **benchmark** against customer requirements.

Customer Success Strategies

Customer success strategies use SC knowledge to help customers become more competitive. To do this, managers must understand what their customers' customers really want. By mapping the downstream chain, managers gather intelligence that can be turned into advantage for the customer. Jack Kahl, CEO at Manco, commented on the need for downstream knowledge, saying, "I have to know more about my customers than I know about myself."[21] Another CEO summarized the idea behind success strategies as follows: "We turn our customers into winners. Their success is cash in our bank. Our customer is our most important partner in cooperation—his customer benefits from this as well."[22]

As managers gain knowledge of downstream requirements, they become consultants to their customers. They can then assist them in areas where they lack skills. For example, a supplier to the retail drug store industry shared its knowledge of industry **best practices** to help its small, independent retail customers improve their inventory and merchandising skills. This training lowered the independent retailers' costs while helping them increase sales. As profits improved, they were able to remain competitive in the face of stiff competition from larger chain stores. The helpful supplier became an indispensable member of the SC team.

Another firm, an electrical components manufacturer, brought its customer success philosophy to life through the slogan, "Pride in helping customers compete!" The phrase quickly appeared on walls in reception areas, corporate offices, and manufacturing facilities. More importantly, the company provided the resources and training to make the slogan a reality. The company became a preferred supplier to the largest U.S. appliance manufacturer as well as to two of the world's leading automakers. One corporate official summarized the company's customer success philosophy as follows:

> We feel it is no longer adequate to simply provide our customer good service since that has become the standard in our industry. It isn't even adequate to satisfy them if that means meeting their expectations since their past experience may lead them to expect certain problems to arise with their suppliers. Instead, we feel that the most appropriate thing for us to do is to do our best in making our customers better competitors in their industries. If they are more successful due to our ability to provide them with better products, more timely delivery, lower total costs, or whatever, then they will gain market share and grow. Of course, when they grow, we grow!

Success strategies consist of (1) a clearly communicated goal to help customers succeed, (2) a clear understanding of downstream requirements, (3) investments in customer-valued capabilities, (4) training provided to customers, and (5) resources shared with customers.

The End Customer

The end customer takes center stage in SCM—she is the only one who really puts money into the chain. Therefore, every organization in the chain must know how to satisfy that end customer's needs and wants. Downstream companies typically have the best understanding of customer needs, but they rely on upstream suppliers to produce needed parts and products. Successful companies, therefore, share information that helps the chain focus on the end customer.

For example, retailers cannot thrive if they do not have the hot products that customers desire available on the shelf. Wal-Mart has established a Web tool called *Retail Link* to provide preferred suppliers up-to-date customer demand and inventory status information. By logging onto Retail Link, suppliers can find out how well their products are selling at individual stores or in different geographic regions. They can also download training modules that help them better meet Wal-Mart's expectations. Similarly, Honda shares information and expertise with suppliers to help them produce better parts and components more efficiently. Honda's efficiency experts visit supplier facilities to help them solve problems and improve productivity and quality on the production line. Suppliers are then expected to help their own suppliers do the same. The end result: a supply chain better able to deliver unparalleled value and satisfaction to end customers.

To summarize, the following questions guide a company's efforts to execute a winning customer fulfillment strategy:

- What are the real needs of our immediate customers?
- What are the real needs of our customers' customers?
- What are the real needs of our supply chain's end customers?
- What information must be shared up and down the supply chain to meet these customer needs?
- What capabilities must be developed up and down the supply chain to meet these customer needs?
- How can we help other SC members improve the overall chain's customer fulfillment capabilities?

IMPLEMENTING A CUSTOMER-CENTRIC FULFILLMENT STRATEGY

Companies need to put in place the processes and systems that enable their customer fulfillment strategy to deliver the value and satisfactions customers expect. Managers should consider two facts as they strive to match the right kinds and levels of service to specific customers:

- Not all customers are equal and they do not all deserve the same high level of service.
- Not all customers require the same service.

A Phoenix-based bank discovered these realities as it tried to improve its customer service image. Managers failed to recognize critical differences in customer needs across the metropolitan area. Branch offices located in Tempe, the home of Arizona State University, served a large number of college students who demanded fast service for their frequent, small transactions. College students want their limited financial services delivered efficiently and without hassle. Conveniently located ATMs often offer the perfect service solution. On the other side of the valley, the bank's clientele consisted of older individuals living in one of the many different retirement communities. Retirees' financial needs are more complex, and often more profitable than their college-aged counterparts, but their lifestyles are a little more relaxed. These customers desired accurate, but friendly and personalized, service. Managing branch banks across the valley using a single efficiency-based formula led to frustration and customer dissatisfaction. When managers tailored customer service definitions, employee training, and performance measures for specific branches to fit unique customer needs, service and satisfaction improved.

Matching Fulfillment Strategies to Customer Needs

Identifying specific customer needs and then matching the company's promises and capabilities to those needs is the key to implementing a successful customer fulfillment strategy. The flowchart shown in Figure 2.5 can guide decision makers as they strive to build the right competencies and the right relationships to meet customer needs. Three types of analysis are needed to effectively tailor SC service levels.

Customer Analysis

Customer analysis identifies customer needs, helping managers segment customers. **Customer segmentation**—the identification of unique groups of customers who possess similar needs—helps managers develop the products and establish the systems needed to fulfill the needs of different customer groups.

Marriott Corporation has made a science out of understanding unique customer needs across a variety of segments. Specific brands have been created and designed to meet the needs and budgets of business travelers, luxury vacationers, and budget-conscious travelers. Toyota's new Scion brand is specifically targeted at young, less-affluent drivers who still want to own a well-designed, reliable car. Toyota believes that Scion owners will graduate to either the Toyota or Lexus brand. At both Marriott and Toyota, a careful customer analysis precedes the launching of new brands and new products.

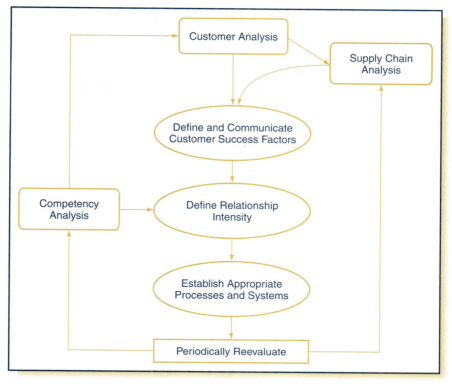

Figure 2.5 A Flowchart for Customer-Centric Supply Chain Management

Supply Chain Analysis

SC analysis identifies the end-customer needs and the capabilities that must exist in the chain to meet those needs. This insight is used to define customer success factors for each segment. **Customer success factors** are the capabilities that first-tier customers need to satisfy their downstream customers.

For instance, in the automobile industry, short concept-to-market times have become a key to success. Toyota's ability to bring new cars to the market in as little as 15 months has helped it become the second largest automaker in the world. Toyota's stated goal is to become the world's largest carmaker by 2010. A supplier that possesses valued technology and that can send an engineer to work on-site at Toyota as a contributing member of Toyota's new product design group can become an invaluable team member. At IBM, the sales force focuses on understanding success factors in particular industries. Salespeople who work in the banking industry take classes at the Wharton School of Business in finance and banking so that they understand the needs and circumstances of their customers. The objective is to help salespeople understand customer success factors better than the customers themselves.[23]

Competency Analysis

A **core competency** is something that your company does so well that it provides the company a competitive advantage.[24] For example, Honda, the company that was used as the model for core competencies, is a leader in engine design. Honda uses its engine-design expertise to compete in a variety of markets from lawn mowers to motorcycles to automobiles. To identify a core competency, two questions should be asked: "What are we known for that makes us uniquely good?" and "What do we do better than anyone else?" True core competencies are almost always cross-functional—a small part of many people's jobs, not a large part of a few.[25] Therefore, these questions should be directed to managers in engineering, production, logistics, marketing, and corporate strategy. Surveying important suppliers and customers provides added insight to confirm the firm's own internal analysis.

Defining Relationship Intensity

The goal in every company is a profitable customer portfolio. As Figure 2.5 illustrates, the right analysis helps managers define the appropriate type of relationship to build with each customer. Relationship intensity should be based on the value of each customer. Classifying customers by sales volume can help define relationship intensity. Figure 2.6 shows "ABC" classification, a tool based on the **Pareto principle**. Also called the *80/20 rule,* the Pareto principle suggests that about 80 percent of sales are generated by about 20 percent of all customers. "A" customers are the most important 5 to 10 percent who generate a disproportionately large percentage of a company's sales. They receive premium, often customized, service. "B" customers account for another 10 to 15 percent of a company's clientele. They also generate significant sales and should receive great service. The remaining 75 to 85 percent are considered "C" customers; they are treated fairly and efficiently, but receive little managerial attention. After classifying customers by sales volume, managers should explicitly

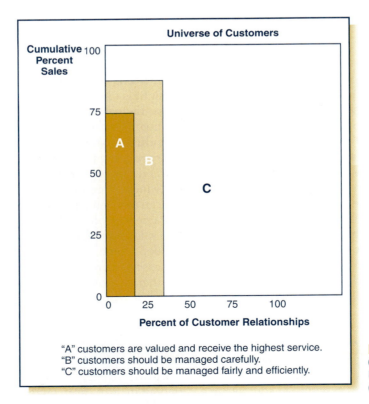

Figure 2.6
Customer Segmentation Using "ABC" Classification

evaluate strategic issues such as relationship profitability, future potential, and linkages to key downstream customers to modify individual customer classifications.

Figure 2.7 shows the competency–success factor alignment matrix, a tool for determining the level of resources to dedicate to specific customer relationships. The vertical axis of the matrix represents customer success factors. The horizontal axis maps the company's competencies. Mapping customers into one of the four quadrants identifies opportunities for market success. The upper-right hand quadrant represents the ideal customers—company competencies are aligned to customer success factors. Close alignment with "A" customers suggests an excellent opportunity to build strong, profitable relationships. Dedicating resources to customers mapped to the other quadrants probably will result in diminished focus and unprofitable customer relationships.

Customer-of-Choice Relationships

Customers of choice are the "A" customers whose needs the company is well positioned to fulfill. They are also profitable relationships (more on this later). Therefore, it makes sense to dedicate the resources needed to build strong relationships with them. Customer-of-choice relationships are characterized as follows.

- Frequent communication occurs between the two firms at many levels, including marketing, engineering, logistics, and senior management.
- Interorganizational teams are formed to solve problems or to work on SC initiatives such as new product development.
- Information systems are linked to enable real-time information exchange on inventory levels, order status, and future demand.
- Fulfillment processes are designed for flexibility to accommodate customers' special requests.
- Policies and procedures support extraordinary efforts to meet unexpected needs or unusual requests.

These relationships are resource intensive and therefore should be very selective. Companies lack the resources to offer tailored product and services to more than a few customers of choice.

Figure 2.7 The Competency–Success Factor Alignment Matrix

	Competencies	
Customer Success Factors (High)	Efforts to pursue activities where no advantage exists result in diminished focus and dissipated capabilities.	**Effective Alignment results in Profitable Customer Takeaway.**
(Low)	Low customer priority and low firm competence suggest that these activities be avoided. Resources expended here are wasted.	Effort and resources dedicated to nonvalued activities result in low customer takeaway.

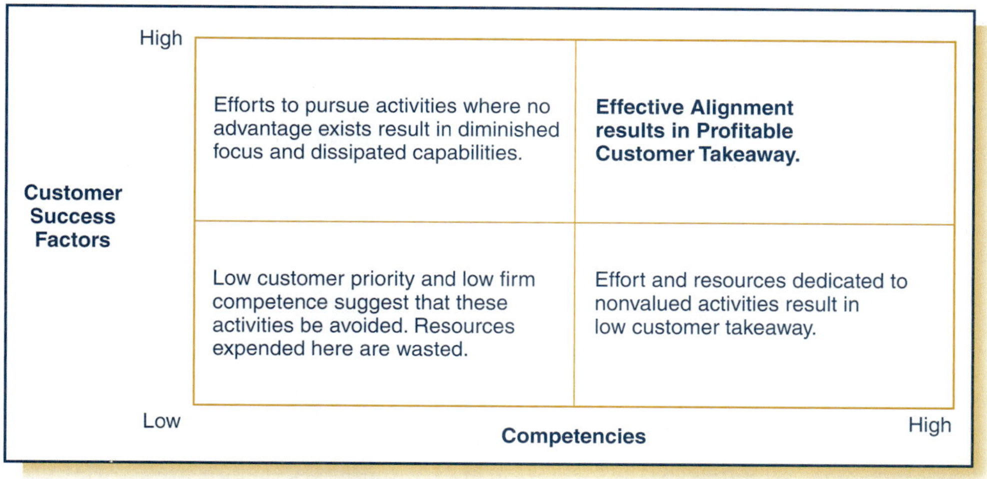

Highly Valued Relationships

Many "A" and most "B" customers are candidates for highly valued relationships. Customer input is actively sought and utilized to meet expressed expectations. These relationships do not merit the resource dedication of close alliances; however, they are important to long-term success. Members of this group often become tomorrow's customers of choice. Formal relationships supported by long-term contracts often make sense. Dedicated customer account teams are used to establish a consistent point of contact and a personal touch. Where possible, information systems are linked to share information and reduce the costs of transactions. Policies and procedures acknowledge the importance of these customers but also take into consideration the costs associated with meeting their needs.

Transaction Relationships

Although "C" customers receive very little personal attention, leading SC companies strive to provide high levels of standardized service excellence. Today's "C" customers may emerge as key industry players in the future. Intel and Microsoft started out as struggling companies operating on "shoestring" budgets. Providing high levels of standard service requires efficient processes and systems. Service recovery, an effort to pacify dissatisfied customers, is used to regain the confidence of customers when a service failure occurs. As data-capturing technologies improve, even "C" customers will be candidates for more tailored satisfaction strategies.

Evaluating the Profitability of Customer Relationships

Satisfying customer expectations profitably is a challenge. SC managers must assure that buyer/supplier relationships yield competitive advantage, and profit, to both firms. Some firms that adopted a "customer-delight-at-any-cost" strategy found that they were losing money trying to keep demanding customers happy.[26]

At one *Fortune* 500 company, the fact that "key" relationships were unprofitable was not discovered until activity-based costing was adopted. **Activity-based costing** ties specific costs directly to the customers that create them. By the time more accurate costing information became available, the company had already begun to eliminate smaller, "less-important" accounts. The cost analysis, however, showed that many of these "C" customers were the company's most profitable relationships.

Table 2.2 exemplifies the importance of understanding the costs associated with specific relationships. Two important lessons can be learned from this example. First, managers need to know how much it costs them to serve specific customers. Losing money to keep customers happy is not a viable long-term strategy. Second, operational excellence is required to profitably provide the value demanded by today's high-service sponges.[27] A cost-efficient provider of exceptional value can almost always negotiate a fair price for its services. Most customers are willing to pay a fair price for the value they receive. However, accurate costing data may be needed to persuade the customer that it is paying a fair price.

Using Customer Relationship Management Systems

Customer relationship management (CRM) software has increased the sophistication of customer segmentation. CRM systems incorporate data-capturing, storage, and analysis capabilities to help companies create customer profiles. A customer profile shows a customer's buying habits and determines the customer's profitability. This information helps managers design appropriate fulfillment strategies for

Table 2.2 Evaluating the Profitability of Customer Relationships

In the following simplified example, AquaFit has $230,000 of costs a week. Traditional accounting allocates the costs to specific areas like salaries and supplies. Process-oriented, activity-based costing allocates the same costs to the value-added activities that generate them.

TRADITIONAL COSTING		PROCESS COSTING	
Salaries	$120,000	Receive material	$86,600
Supplies	30,000	Move material	84,600
Depreciation	20,000	Expedite material	58,800
Overtime	15,000	Total	$230,000
Space	30,000		
Other	15,000		
Total	$230,000		

A single customer, H.S. Sponge, represents 25% of orders and sales. H.S. Sponge pays $63,000 for the product it purchases. Closer analysis shows that H.S. Sponge drives 25% of the receiving, 30% of the movement, and 40% of the expediting costs. How much does it cost to meet H.S. Sponge's service requirements based on both traditional and process costing perspectives? Is the relationship profitable?

Traditional costing allocates costs based on the percent of orders or sales a customer represents. Therefore,

$$.25 \times \$230,000 = \$57,500$$

Process costing allocates costs based on the costs of activities required to meet a customer's needs. Therefore,

$$.25 \times \$86,600$$
$$+.30 \times 84,600$$
$$+.40 \times 58,800 = \$70,550$$

What are AquaFit's options? What would you suggest?

---

each customer. For example, First Union Corp. codes its credit-card customers with green, yellow, or red squares to communicate to service representatives how much service to offer. Customers with green squares are granted fee waivers while red-square customers have no negotiating power.[28]

Preferred customer cards make it easy to collect information. Every time the card is used, details regarding the purchase are automatically captured and stored in a customer database, making it easy to track purchase frequency and buying habits of "preferred" customers. Information regarding whether purchased products were on sale can be monitored and used to calculate customer profitability. Some grocers have stopped using traditional circulars, preferring to target their most profitable customers with mailed invitations to upcoming sales. Others mail customized coupon packages to their best customers. By targeting preferred customers, grocers reduce the incidence of "cherry picking" by customers who only buy sale items with low or negative margins. Profits and satisfaction increase simultaneously.

The Limited has adopted a system that augments a customer profile by allowing sales representatives to make comments regarding customer likes and dislikes as well as past purchases. This feedback is input into the computer after a sale is completed. When a customer makes future purchases, the salesperson can look up this information and personalize the transaction by asking questions like, "How do you like the red sweater you bought last month?" or "Are you enjoying your art classes?"[29] Continental Airlines has adopted a similar system that allows every gate, reservation, and service agent to view the history and value of each customer and to enter into the database details about the preferences of important customers. By focusing on its best customers, Continental increased the number of passengers flying on higher-cost, unrestricted fares by 25 percent.[30]

Internet retailers have a built-in advantage because they can track every "click" a customer makes while browsing the Web site. Amazon.com creates customer profiles and suggests additional titles that might be of interest. Victoria's Secret has used its data to redesign the layout of its Web site to optimize sales. For instance, a lace-up gown was selling well in the site's "top 10" area but poorly in the portion of the site reserved for gowns. By displaying the gown more prominently in the gown section, not only did sales of the lace-up gown increase but overall sales throughout the gown section increased as well.[31] The challenge for Internet retailers is to sort through huge quantities of information to identify the "clicks" that explain buying behavior.

Although CRM systems enable companies to provide their best customers unprecedented service, their use is not without pitfalls. In a cover story titled, "Why Service Stinks," *Business Week* brought attention to the dark side of these systems, noting, "Companies know just how good a customer you are—and unless you're a high roller, they would rather lose you than take the time to fix your problem." The problem is that past buying habits do not always predict future behavior. Situations and lifestyles change in ways that make today's nuisance customer tomorrow's preferred customer. Likewise, a customer's perceptions of previous service encounters can influence lifetime buying decisions. Low levels of activity may reflect a customer's dissatisfaction with current or past service offerings. The bottom line: Managers need to treat each customer contact as an opportunity to make an unprofitable customer profitable or make a profitable customer more profitable.[32]

Recognizing Barriers to Effective Customer Fulfillment

Tom Peters has noted that customer service in America stinks. The question is, "Why?" Three explanations help us understand the persistent gaps between customer expectations and service levels. First, many companies seek to improve service levels, but direct their efforts toward the wrong activities—things customers do not value. The failure to get into the mind of the customer leads to service gaps. When this happens, it takes just as much effort to be mediocre as it does to be excellent.

Second, many companies claim to be service oriented, but fail to deliver on their promises. They are more committed to talking about customer satisfaction than to really improving service levels. For example, many companies have copied part or all of L.L. Bean's customer service policy:

- Customers are not dependent on us; we are dependent on them.
- Customers are not an interruption of our work, but the purpose for it.
- We are not doing our customers a favor by serving them; they are doing us a favor by giving us the opportunity to do so.
- A customer is not someone to argue or match wits with.
  NOBODY ever won an argument with a customer!

They say this, but then do nothing to support the policy. Commenting on this reality, one vice president in the health care industry provided the following definition of customer service, highlighting the gap between the walk and the talk: "Customer service is lip service paid to all customers generally incorporating shallow commitments, hollow promises, and some dandy clichés about how the customer is always right."

Third, access to better information has led some companies to purposely deliver low levels of service to customers who are perceived as "less valuable." They actually use their CRM systems to justify treating low-priority customers poorly.

All three explanations ring true. Companies are more discriminating in whom they serve. They make promises that their capabilities and commitment cannot deliver on, and they misdirect resources. As a result, employees and customers naturally view companies' satisfaction promises skeptically. The good news: Research shows that just a few impediments prevent companies from delivering higher customer satisfaction. Customers have identified the following four issues as the source of dissatisfaction in almost 80 percent of customer service "horror stories."

- Training—employees do not know how their behavior and performance affects customer perceptions.
- Measurement—measures do not reinforce appropriate attitudes and behavior toward customers.
- Empowerment—employees do not have authority to solve problems and respond to customer needs.
- Policies—policies and procedures are inflexible and often run counter to real service and satisfaction.

Once managers make the commitment to raise service levels, tackling these impediments is doable!

CONCLUSION

Meeting customers' needs better than the competition creates loyalty and yields valuable long-term relationships. A rather unique twist on the notion of long-term SC relationships emerged from an SC analyst's visit to Japan. Seeking to understand the intimate nature of a particular relationship, he asked the owner of a Japanese manufacturer how long his company had been doing business with a specific customer. After a long pause, the owner responded that his ancestors had begun doing business with this customer back in 1062. Of course, not all SC relationships will, or should, last 1,000 years. Nevertheless, the point was clear: "What is a profitable relationship worth over the lifetime of the relationship?"

Max and Erma's, an Ohio-based restaurant, took a serious look at this question. Crunching the numbers revealed that its best customers yielded $25,000 profit over a lifetime. Poor service threatened the loss of not just a $20 meal or a $5 tip, but $25,000 profit.[33] Capturing a "lifetime stream of profits" requires that companies build appropriate SC relationships that help them do the right things efficiently. And from an SC perspective that means building collaborative relationships that help the company design great new products that can be made and delivered efficiently, quickly, and with high levels of quality and service. This performance satisfies customers, creating the loyalty that keeps them coming back.

As one executive put it, "The only sure way to grow is to share in the growth of our customers. If we are the preferred supplier and they are their customers' choice, we can jointly identify breakthrough opportunities. Jointly, we can outperform the competition."

SUMMARY OF KEY POINTS

1. With information readily available, customers are more savvy and demanding up and down the chain.
2. Competitiveness depends on a company's ability to deliver the value customers expect. Opportunities to deliver customer value occur in five areas: *quality, cost, flexibility, delivery,* and *innovation.*
3. Customers don't just buy products; they purchase a set of satisfactions that come from buying, using, and servicing a product.
4. Customers are satisfied when their actual experience with a product or service meets expectations. A negative gap between expectations and experience leads to dissatisfaction.
5. Customer service emphasizes performance to operational standards. Customer satisfaction focuses aligning performance to needs expressed by the customer. Customer success uses knowledge of the entire chain to help customers compete more effectively.

6. Customer success is driven by knowledge and capability. It relies on the strength of upstream suppliers while working to enhance the competitiveness of downstream customers.
7. Implementing a customer-centric fulfillment strategy requires the building of the right relationships with customers and then using the company's competencies to augment customer success factors.
8. Customer relationship management systems help companies provide their best customers great service and satisfaction. However, past buying habits do not always predict future behavior. Nor do they provide all of the needed insight into the reasons for the behavior.
9. Customers continue to complain about poor service. Sources of dissatisfaction include a lack of managerial commitment, poor training of service personnel, poor measurement, and inflexible policies.

REVIEW EXERCISES

1. Describe how the information revolution has changed the dynamics of the buyer/supplier relationship. How do you use the Internet to improve your ability to get the best deal for the purchases you make?
2. Discuss the five areas of customer value. Which areas are most important to you? Why? Identify at least one company that differentiates itself in each area of customer value.
3. Explain why customer satisfaction levels have remained stagnant over the past decade despite all of the talk regarding the importance of customers.
4. Explain why customer loyalty is so rare. Why are customers so willing to defect? As an SC manager, describe how you would address this challenge.
5. Describe the distinctive characteristics of customer service, customer satisfaction, and customer success strategies. Explain when each of these customer fulfillment strategies would be appropriate.

6. Looking at Table 2.2, what are AquaFit's options? Explain how you would manage the relationship with H.S. Sponge.
7. Describe the challenges an SC manager is likely to encounter during the implementation of a customer-centric fulfillment strategy. Map the challenges to each of the steps identified in Figure 2.5.
8. Discuss the actions you would take to improve the likely outcomes of customer relationships mapped to each of the three nonaligned quadrants of the alignment matrix shown in Figure 2.7.
9. Explain why "service in America stinks." Discuss the issues behind your explanation. Describe two or three specific actions you would take to address these issues.
10. Describe how you could use the "lifetime-stream-of-profits" concept to increase managerial commitment to customer satisfaction.

Case   SCM²

It was a hot, dry afternoon in Mexico's northern Sonora Desert and Rey was in a sour mood. Rey Uribe, the normally energetic and optimistic president of Sony de Mexico, had just received the news that Sony's Mexican operations were to be shut down in a cost-cutting move. Corporate had decided that to remain competitive, capacity should be shifted to Southeast Asia, where labor costs were a fraction of Mexico's fully burdened hourly labor rates of $3.50. Of course, the news was not totally unexpected. Rey had been aware of the discussion that was taking place back in Japan, but he had hoped that the geographic proximity to the large and lucrative U.S. market would provide sufficient motivation to keep the Mexican operation running. Rey wondered whether there was anything that could be done to reverse the decision. Sony de Mexico had performed so well for so long, and Rey loved the people he worked with. There had to be a way to turn things around—to change the destiny of Sony de Mexico. Could he find it?

The shared 2,000-mile border between the United States and Mexico had driven tremendous growth in the so-called *maquiladora* industry. The opportunity to use comparative advantage to achieve competitive advantage had not gone unnoticed by U.S. and other global companies. The huge U.S. consumer market was just across the border from an abundant source of high-quality, low-cost labor. And managing across the border was much easier than managing across an ocean. As a result, at its peak, approximately 3,000 maquiladora operations turned out everything from leather gloves to consumer electronics; from auto parts to semiconductors. Over 1.5 million people were employed and maquiladora operations were the second leading source of foreign exchange behind oil. However, the maquiladora industry was under siege. The incredibly low-cost labor in China and throughout Southeast Asia was siphoning off foreign direct investment. In the past 12 months alone, more than 300,000 jobs had been lost. Rey and his colleagues had begun calling China the "Black Hole" because it was sucking up vast quantities of foreign manufacturing investment. The question everyone was asking was, "How on earth can anyone hope to win a battle against a black hole?"

While others scoffed at the idea that Sony de Mexico could survive, Rey felt there had to be a way. The proximity to customers in the United States had to provide some advantage that couldn't be undermined by labor costs. Unfortunately, like most maquilas, Sony de Mexico had long relied on its cost advantage and tariff exemptions for its competitive strength. This overreliance on cost had left Sony de Mexico without any differential advantage. As Rey and his top management team had pondered the possibility that Sony Corporate might move to shut down the Mexican operations, they had begun to look for a new advantage—a new justification for their existence.

To assist their quest for survival, Rey and his team had adopted the 6σ mantra of, "Forget what you think you know and let the data prove it to you." Rey felt certain that the only viable solution would be found in the mind of the customer. Therefore, they had sought to listen to the voice of the customer and try to redesign the supply chain to overcome customer frustrations and meet customer needs. With this in mind, the team had developed three core questions: "Who is our customer?" "What is important to them?" and "How are they measuring our performance?" So far they had identified a few salient facts:

- Dealers were frustrated because they were having difficulty anticipating actual customer demand across Sony's product line. The only way to make sure that the right product was in the store ready for sale was to carry large, expensive inventories.
- Despite proximity to the U.S. market, Sony de Mexico's inventory equaled 60 days of sales.
- The average lead time to dealers was approximately 8 weeks.
- Sales forecasts from the dealers were notoriously inaccurate—to the point that managers throughout Sony de Mexico complained about the inefficiencies caused by poor forecast accuracy.

These facts led the team to realize that Sony de Mexico had done little to leverage its geographic presence. The 8-week lead time offered no advantage over Asian production. Would customers truly value shorter lead times and greater responsiveness? Rey was confident they would and that they would also appreciate the opportunity to reduce their inventory costs. Could the supply chain be redesigned to achieve results in these areas? Certainly, Asian operations couldn't match a speed-based advantage that provided better integration with customers. Rey wondered if speed could make money and save Sony de Mexico.

CASE QUESTIONS

1. Is it possible to save Sony de Mexico? Or is Rey refusing to see the writing on the wall?
2. What does Rey need to do to determine whether a time-based advantage is viable?
3. What changes would need to take place within Sony de Mexico?

ENDNOTES

1. Porter, M. (1980). *Competitive strategy.* New York: The Free Press. Porter, M. (1985). *Competitive advantage: Creating and sustaining superior performance.* New York: The Free Press.
2. Deming, W. E. (1986). *Out of crisis.* Cambridge, MA: MIT, Center for Advanced Engineering Study.
3. Juran, J. M., & Gryna, J. F. M. (1980). *Quality planning and analysis.* New York: McGraw-Hill.
4. Garvin, D. A. (1983). Quality on the line. *Harvard Business Review, 61*(4), 65–75.
5. Skinner, W. (1986). The productivity paradox. *Harvard Business Review, 64*(4), 55–59. Gunasekaran, A. (1998). Experiences of a small company in productivity improvements. *Production and Inventory Management Journal, 39*(2), 49–54. Scully, J. I., & Fawcett, S. E. (1994). International procurement strategies: Opportunities and challenges for the small firm. *Production and Inventory Management Journal, 35*(2), 39–46. Ferdows, K. (1997). Making the most of foreign factories. *Harvard Business Review, 75*(2), 73–88.
6. Tzu, S. (1963). *Art of war.* Oxford: Carendon Press.
7. Bower, J. L., & Hout, T. M. (1988). Fast-cycle capability for competitive power. *Harvard Business Review, 66*(6), 110–118. Bowersox, D. J., Calantone, R. J., Clinton, S. R., Closs, D. J., Cooper, M. B., Droge, C. L., Fawcett, S. E., Frankel, R., Frayer, D. J., Morash, E. A., Rinehart, L. M., & Schmitz, J. M. (1995). *World class logistics: The challenge of managing continuous change.* Oak Brook, IL: Council of Logistics Management. Stalk, G. (1988). Time—The next source of competitive advantage. *Harvard Business Review, 66*(4), 41–51.
8. Upton, D. M. (1995). What really makes factories flexible. *Harvard Business Review, 73*(4), 74–84.
9. Blackwell, R. D. (1997). *From mind to market: Reinventing the retail supply chain.* New York: Harper Business.
10. Hayes, R., Wheelwright, S. C., & Clark, K. B. (1988). *Dynamic manufacturing: Creating the learning organization.* New York: The Free Press. Porter, M. (1990). The competitive advantage of nations. *Harvard Business Review, 68*(2), 73–93.
11. Birou, L. M., & Fawcett, S. E. (1994). Supplier involvement in integrated product development strategies: A comparison of U.S. and European practices. *International Journal of Physical Distribution and Logistics Management, 24*(5), 4–14.
12. Ibid. Stalk, #7.
13. Stewart, T. A. (1996, August 19). It's a flat world after all. *Fortune,* pp. 197–199.
14. Oliver, R. L. (1980, November). A cognitive model of the antecedents and consequences of satisfaction decisions. *Journal of Marketing Research, 17,* 460–69. Spreng, R. A., Mackenzie, S. B., & Olshavsky, R. W. (1996, July). A reexamination of the determinants of consumer satisfaction. *Journal of Marketing, 60,* 15–32. Yi, Y. (1990). A critical review of consumer satisfaction. *Review of Marketing.* Chicago: American Marketing Association, 68–123. Zeithaml, V. A., Berry, L. L., & Parasuraman, A. (1993, Winter). The nature and determinants of customer expectations of service. *Journal of the Academy of Marketing Science, 21,* 1–12.
15. Oliver, R. L. (1997). *Satisfaction: A behavioral perspective on the consumer.* New York: The McGraw-Hill Companies, Inc.
16. Anderson, E. W., Fornell, C., & Lehmann, D. R. (1994, January). Customer satisfaction, market share, and profitability: Findings from Sweden. *Journal of Marketing, 58,* 53–66. Fornell, C., Johnson, M. D., Anderson, E. W., Cha, J., & Bryant, B. E. (1996, October). The American customer satisfaction index: Nature, purpose, and findings. *Journal of Marketing, 60,* 7–18.
17. Ibid. #14.
18. Jones, T. O., & Sasser, J. W. E. (1995). Why satisfied customers defect. *Harvard Business Review, 73*(5), 88–99. Stewart, T. (1995, December 11). After all you've done for your customers, why are they still not happy? *Fortune,* pp. 178–118. Fierman, J. (1995, December 11). Americans can't get no satisfaction. *Fortune,* pp. 186–194. Stewart, T. A. (1997, July 21). A satisfied customer isn't enough. *Fortune,* pp. 112–113.

19. Drucker, P. F. (1994). The theory of the business. *Harvard Business Review, 72*(5), 95–104.
20. Stock, J., & Lambert, D. (1992). Becoming a "world class" company with logistics service quality. *International Journal of Logistics Management, 3*(1), 73–80.
21. Ibid. #9.
22. Ginsburg, I., & Miller, N. (1992, May–June). Value-driven management. *Business Horizons,* 23–27.
23. Yarbrough, J. F. (1996, November). The best sales forces. *Sales and Marketing Management,* 46.
24. Ohmae, K. (1988). Getting back to strategy. *Harvard Business Review, 66*(6), 149–156.
25. Stalk, G., Evans, P., & Schulman, L. E. (1992). Competing on capabilities: The new rules of corporate strategy. *Harvard Business Review, 70*(2), 57–69. Ibid. #19.
26. Fawcett, S. E., & Swenson, M. J. (1998). Customer satisfaction from a supply chain perspective: An evolutionary process in enhancing channel relationships. *Journal of Consumer Satisfaction, Dissatisfaction and Complaining Behavior, 11,* 198–204. Ibid. Bowersox, #7.
27. Tyndall, G. (1998). *Supercharging supply chains.* New York: John Wiley & Sons, Inc.
28. Brady, D. (2000, October 23). Why service stinks. *Business Week.*
29. Ibid. #9.
30. Ibid. #27.
31. Totty, M. (2003, October 20). How can e-tailers get to know you better? *The Wall Street Journal,* p. R4.
32. Ibid. #28.
33. Ibid. #9.

Supplement B

Productivity and Quality Management

Introduction

To stay competitive, companies must achieve the minimum standard of performance across the five basic areas of customer value: *quality, cost, flexibility, delivery,* and *innovation.* They must then distinguish themselves by delivering exceptional value in one or more areas. However, the foundation for success in most industries is built on a company's cost and quality performance. That is, the cost of a ticket to play in today's global competitive arena is to be cost and quality competitive. You need to understand the basics of productivity and quality management practices. If you have not studied the basics of productivity and quality management elsewhere, the following tutorials will help you become familiar with these key topics that are so important to creating customer value.

Productivity Management

As mentioned earlier in the chapter, most managers face unrelenting pressure to reduce costs. One way that managers can reduce costs is by improving productivity. Most business processes have inputs, some sort of transformation process, and outputs, as shown in Figure B.1. Most of the costs that managers deal with come from either the inputs to the transformation process or the transformation process itself.

There are two primary types of productivity statistics. The first, labor productivity, measures output per hour of labor. Automobile manufacturers such as GM or Toyota, for example, track the number of labor hours that it takes to produce a vehicle, including hours of labor in metal stamping, engine assembly, and final assembly. In 2004, Toyota used 6.4 fewer labor hours

Figure B.1 Basic Business Process Diagram

per vehicle than GM did to build a vehicle.[1] Because of the costs associated with labor, or other inputs to a process, productivity differences can result in overall cost differences as well. The labor input difference between GM and Toyota translates into about a $400 difference in the cost of the cars. Consequently, reducing inputs while maintaining outputs or increasing outputs with a given set of inputs can have a dramatic impact on an organization's bottom line.

The second type of productivity statistic, multifactor productivity, goes beyond labor and measures output per unit of combined inputs, which consists of labor and capital, and, in some cases, intermediate inputs such as fuel. The U.S. Department of Labor tracks multifactor productivity statistics for many industries. These statistics are available at www.bls.gov/bls/productivity.htm.

Because of the importance of productivity, every manager should know how to calculate and interpret productivity numbers. Productivity is simply a ratio of the outputs achieved divided by the inputs required to achieve those outputs. For example, if a brake manufacturer requires 10 labor hours (inputs) to make 50 brake pads (outputs) then the productivity is expressed as 5 brake pads per labor hour.

Example 1:

$$\text{Productivity} = \frac{\text{Output}}{\text{Input}}$$

$$\text{Productivity} = \frac{50 \text{ brake pads}}{10 \text{ labor hours}}$$

$$\text{Productivity} = 5 \text{ brake pads per labor hour}$$

This information, by itself, is not typically useful to the organization. It is important to put productivity information into a context by comparing it to either historical data or other organizations. Trends or changes in productivity are the most important to organizations. An important measure to changes in productivity is the percent increase or decrease that has occurred. For example, during 2004, GM reduced the number of hours it took to produce a vehicle by 2.2 percent. Without anything to compare this reduction to, it may appear that GM did quite well. When this information is compared to Toyota, however, which reduced the number of hours to produce a vehicle by 5.9 percent

over the same time period, the 2.2 percent doesn't seem quite as impressive.[2]

Calculating increases or decreases in productivity is fairly straightforward. For example, suppose that after receiving some training the brake manufacturer employees were able to produce 60 brake pads for every 10 labor hours. The percent increase in productivity can be calculated by

Example 2:

$$\begin{matrix}\text{Percent} \\ \text{Increase in} \\ \text{Productivity}\end{matrix} = \frac{\text{Change in Productivity}}{\text{Productivity Prior to Change}}(100)$$

$$\text{Percent Increase in Productivity} = \frac{6-5}{5}(100)$$

$$\text{Percent Increase in Productivity} = 20$$

Companies can increase productivity over time by (1) decreasing the number of inputs while holding outputs constant, (2) increasing the number of outputs while holding inputs constant, (3) increasing outputs at a faster rate then increasing inputs, (4) decreasing inputs at a faster rate than decreasing outputs, (5) simultaneously increasing outputs while decreasing inputs, or (6) through some combination of these methods. If the previously mentioned brake manufacturer were to increase production to 60 brake pads while using 5 labor hours, overall productivity would be increased to 12 brake pads per labor hour.

It is important to consider both sides of the input/output ratio when examining productivity changes. Too often managers focus solely on the output side of the productivity ratio (in terms of quantity or quality) while ignoring the input side. For example, suppose the quality levels of the brake pad manufacturing process went from 90 percent to 95 percent. Is this change good or bad? Without more information on the inputs, it is hard to tell. Suppose that this increase in quality levels was due to the hiring of 20 additional employees to perform detailed inspections during the manufacturing process. If this is the case, perhaps the increase in quality has not been necessarily good for the organization. On the other hand, suppose that this increase in quality was due to the elimination of several non-value-adding steps in the process where the brake pads were frequently damaged. This would be viewed as beneficial to the organization.

---

[1]White, Joseph B. (2005, June 3). GM's productivity growth does little for woes. *The Wall Street Journal*, p. B.3.
[2]Hawkins, Lee Jr. (2005, August 22). GM workers hunt for cost reductions; UAW hopes more productivity gains soften auto maker's stance on possible cuts. *The Wall Street Journal*, p. B.2.

There are short-term and long-term ways to improve productivity. When managers are measured solely on productivity improvements, they often take steps to increase short-term productivity, such as running machines without regular maintenance, at the expense of long-term productivity. Wickham Skinner has said, "Experience regularly observes a '40, 40, 20' rule. Roughly 40 percent of any manufacturing-based competitive advantage derives from long-term changes in manufacturing structure. Another 40 percent comes from major changes in equipment and process technology. The final 20 percent—no more—rests on conventional approaches to productivity improvement." Because major changes are often disruptive to the short-term productivity gains that many managers are measured by, those managers are reluctant to make needed changes. For example, redesigning an assembly operation may be time-consuming, costly, and disrupt outputs for a little while, but could result in great overall increases in productivity. Consequently, many managers focus on short-term solutions to productivity gains, which pursue minimal, and often counterproductive, productivity increases rather than focusing their efforts on long-term, rule-changing productivity improvements.

The true role of productivity measurement in organizations is to drive learning and improvement. When the ratio of inputs to outputs changes, managers need to find out why it changed and whether it was because of short-term fixes that are going to cost the company in the long run, or whether it was because real learning or innovation has occurred within the organization. If real learning has occurred, it should be shared throughout the entire organization. This is a job for proactive SC managers.

EXERCISES

1. A lawn mowing service has 3 employees. During an 8-hour day, the lawn mowing service can mow a total of 25 lawns. What is the productivity level of the lawn mowing service in terms of lawns per labor hour?
2. Given the answer from exercise 1, what would the percentage change in productivity be if the lawn mowing service were to hire an additional employee and be able to mow 29 lawns during an 8-hour day?
3. An old machine can produce 20,000 plastic cups using 1,000 watts of electricity. A new, more energy efficient, machine can produce 30,000 plastic cups using the same amount of electricity. What percentage increase in productivity would the new machine provide?
4. An old car uses 40 gallons of gas to go 480 miles. A new hybrid vehicle uses 20 gallons of gas to go 600 miles. Determine the productivity of each vehicle as well as the percentage change in productivity that would occur if a person switched from using the old car to using the new car.
5. A company that manufactures solar panels had sales last year of $2,725,400. Total labor costs for the year were $1,750,000; material costs were $500,000; and capital costs were $300,000. What was the company's productivity based on this information?
6. Larry Jones makes tents for winter camping. Larry and his 5 employees each spend 40 hours per week to make 100 tents. What is their productivity? If Larry and his employees can increase their production to 150 per week, what will their new productivity be? How much of an increase in productivity would this change represent?

WEB EXERCISES

1. Visit the U.S. Department of Labor: Bureau of Labor Statistics at www.bls.gov and examine the most recent data on productivity changes. Write a 1-page summary of your findings.
2. Read Alan Greenspan's remarks at the U.S. Department of Labor and American Enterprise Institute Conference in Washington, D.C., on October 23, 2002, available at www.federalreserve.gov/boarddocs/speeches/2002/20021023/. What did he have to say about productivity? Summarize his remarks into a half-page report.
3. Visit Harbour Consulting's Web site at www.harbourinc.com. Harbour Consulting publishes the annual study of automotive manufacturing performance. Exploring this Web site, what can you infer about the relative productivity of the major auto manufacturers?
4. Use the Internet to come up with at least three ways that you could improve your personal productivity.

Quality Management

Quality is an important aspect of customer satisfaction and may be more important than cost in certain industries. In fact, a recent customer satisfaction survey of U.S. vehicle owners indicates that although focusing on costs and running cost promotions such as "employee pricing" may give automakers gains in the short-term, improving quality is more important in the long run.[3] Indeed, while other automakers were lowering their prices during the summer of 2005, Toyota raised its prices, but because of its high quality levels it still received the highest satisfaction score in the survey.

Though high quality levels can lead to increased profits, the inverse is also true. Quality problems can hurt sales and can lead to other problems as well. For example, pharmaceutical companies run the risk of injuring their customers or even causing death if their quality levels aren't where they should be. In March 2005, the FDA seized two Glaxo drugs on quality-related production concerns.[4] In this case, the drug *Avandamet* was not being uniformly distributed throughout the tablets. Though not life-threatening, it was a cause of concern for the FDA, which pulled thousands of bottles of the drug off the market. Quality is one of the crucial areas of customer value that organizations need to carefully manage.

Quality problems typically result from variations in business processes. Variation is common in most business processes and can be random or systematic in nature. Random variations, as the name implies, are sporadic, difficult to predict, and difficult to manage or control. Systematic variation, on the other hand, is caused by a specific contributing factor—a factor that can often be controlled. To consistently achieve high quality levels, managers must identify and remove the sources of systematic variation. The following quality practices help companies manage processes to achieve high levels of quality performance.

Control Charts

Companies use control charts to help differentiate between process variation due to common or random causes and special causes. When special causes are detected, intervention is often necessary to correct the situation and remove the corresponding variation. When only random causes are observed, it is best to avoid making changes that might introduce special causes.

Most control charts are based on the notion of a normal probability distribution. A centerline of the control chart represents the mean of the process or the target value. Upper control limits (UCL) and lower control limits (LCL) are calculated around this mean or target value to ensure that the statistical probability of a value being either above the upper control limit or below the lower control limit is very small, as shown in Figure B.2.

The general formula for control limits is as follows:

$$\text{Control Limit} = \mu \pm Z\sigma$$

Where: μ = mean or target
Z = the number of standard deviations from the mean
σ = process standard deviation

Control charts can be constructed for product attributes or for product variables. Each of these types of control charts is discussed in greater detail in the following sections.

Attribute Control Charts (p-Charts) P-charts are used when the process characteristic is counted rather than measured. For example, in the semiconductor business, yield is everything. Yield is basically the number of chips manufactured that are good versus those that are defective and need to be tossed out. It's commonly accepted that in producing chips, a certain percentage are going to get thrown out. One of the reasons for Intel's success against its competitors like AMD has been its higher yields. Companies in this industry carefully count and track the number of good and defective chips that are being produced by their processes. These values can then be converted into percentages. Perhaps 75 percent of the chips in a particular batch are good and the other 25 percent are defective.

As with most calculations dealing with normal probability curves, a relatively large number of samples should be taken in order to construct the control chart. One batch of semiconductors would not be very useful in determining the upper and lower control limits for the control chart. Numerous batches of chips should be examined when constructing control charts.

---

[3]Car Owners Value Quality Over Cost, Survey Suggests. *The Wall Street Journal* (2005, August 16), p. D.2.
[4]Munoz, Sara Schaefer, & Whallen, Jeanne. (2005, March 7). FDA seizes two Glaxo drugs on production-quality concerns. *The Wall Street Journal*, p. A.6.

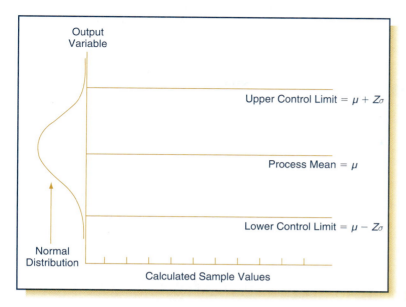

Figure B.2   Control Chart

After observing a number of manufacturing batches, the process mean can be calculated using the following equation:

$$\frac{\text{process}}{\text{mean}} = \bar{p} = \frac{\text{total number of defectives}}{\text{number of samples} \times \text{sample size}}$$

For example, let's assume that after observing the semiconductors in 20 batches, each of which contained 90 chips, you observe that there were a total of 300 defective chips. The process mean would be calculated as follows:

$$\bar{p} = \frac{300}{1,800}$$

$$\bar{p} = 0.1667 \text{ or } 16.67 \text{ percent}$$

The standard deviation of the process is determined by using the following formula:

$$\text{Standard Deviation} = \sigma = \sqrt{\frac{\bar{p}(1 - \bar{p})}{n}}$$

Where: n = sample size

In this example, the standard deviation would be determined as follows:

$$\sigma = \sqrt{\frac{0.1667(1 - 0.1667)}{90}}$$

$$\sigma = 0.03929$$

The control chart is then constructed by taking this information and utilizing the following formulas:

$$\text{Upper Control Limit} = \text{UCL} = \bar{p} + Z\sigma$$

$$\text{Lower Control Limit} = \text{LCL} = \bar{p} - Z\sigma$$

Assuming a z-score of 1.96, for a 95% confidence level, the upper and lower confidence intervals would be calculated as follows:

LCL = 0.1667	UCL = 0.1667
−1.96(0.03929)	+1.96(0.03929)
LCL = 0.0897	UCL = 0.2437

These values for the mean (16.67 percent), upper control limit (24.37 percent), and lower limit (8.97 percent) are used to construct the control chart similar to Figure B.2. If the lower control limit is negative, zero should be used as the lower control limit. After the control chart has been constructed, future observations are made and additional sample data is collected and plotted on the control chart to determine whether the process is in control or not.

Variable Control Charts (x-Bar Charts)   X-bar charts are used when the observation values take on numerical values within a range. For example, suppose that rather than counting the number of bad chips in a batch of semiconductors, we are now concerned with the overall diameter of the batches of semiconductors.

Suppose that 10 samples were taken and that each sample was comprised of 3 batches yielding the following data:

Sample	Batch 1 Diameter (cm)	Batch 2 Diameter (cm)	Batch 3 Diameter (cm)
1	25.25	27.20	25.00
2	24.40	25.80	24.05
3	26.95	23.45	24.80
4	24.15	25.15	26.65
5	24.20	25.90	25.25
6	25.10	25.00	24.40
7	23.00	24.05	26.95
8	27.65	24.80	24.15
9	25.70	26.65	24.20
10	24.30	22.25	27.20

To construct an x-bar control chart for this data, we again need to start with the mean. However, in this case, the mean that we need is not the mean of each individual sample, but is the overall or grand mean. This overall or grand mean is calculated by either taking the mean of each sample and then taking the mean of those sample means or by simply taking the mean of all 30 observations.

Sample	Batch 1 Diameter (cm)	Batch 2 Diameter (cm)	Batch 3 Diameter (cm)	Sample Mean
1	25.25	27.20	25.00	25.82
2	24.40	25.80	24.05	24.75
3	26.95	23.45	24.80	25.07
4	24.15	25.15	26.65	25.32
5	24.20	25.90	25.25	25.12
6	25.10	25.00	24.40	24.83
7	23.00	24.05	26.95	24.67
8	27.65	24.80	24.15	25.53
9	25.70	26.65	24.20	25.52
10	24.30	22.25	27.20	24.58
Overall or Grand Mean				25.12

$$\text{Grand Mean} = \bar{\bar{x}} = 25.12$$

In this simplified case, the standard deviation can be the standard deviation of all 30 of the observations. However, for purposes of constructing an x-bar chart, the standard error is utilized rather than the regular standard deviation. This standard error is calculated by dividing the standard deviation by the square root of the sample size, as shown in the following equation:

$$\text{Standard Error} = \frac{\sigma}{\sqrt{n}}$$

The standard deviation for the observations is 1.329, so the standard error is calculated as follows:

$$\text{Standard Error} = \frac{1.329}{\sqrt{3}}$$

$$\text{Standard Error} = 0.7673$$

The control charts are then constructed using the following formulas:

$$\text{Upper Control Limit} = \text{UCL} = \bar{\bar{x}} + Z(\text{Standard Error})$$

$$\text{Lower Control Limit} = \text{LCL} = \bar{\bar{x}} - Z(\text{Standard Error})$$

In this case, assuming a z-score of 1.96, the upper and lower control limits are calculated as follows:

$$\text{UCL} = 25.12 + 1.96(0.7673) \quad \text{LCL} = 25.12 - 1.96(0.7673)$$

$$\text{UCL} = 26.62 \qquad\qquad \text{LCL} = 23.62$$

Again, as with the p-charts discussed earlier, these values for the grand mean (25.12), upper control limit (26.62), and lower limit (23.62) are used to construct the control chart similar to Figure B.2. If the lower control limit is negative, zero should be used as the lower control limit. After the control chart has been constructed, future observations can be made to collect and plot sample data on the control chart to determine whether the process is in control or not.

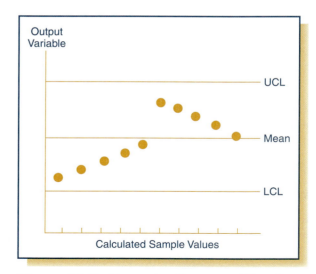

Figure B.3 Upward or Downward Trends

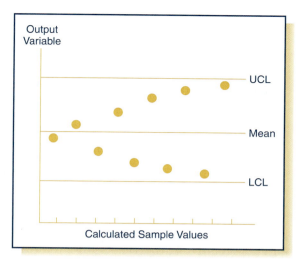

Figure B.4 Widening Gaps

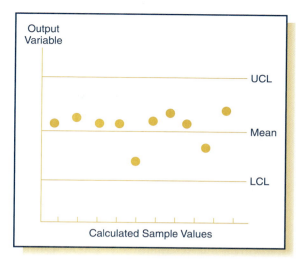

Figure B.5 Many Consecutive Values Above or Below the Mean

Is the Process in Control? Generally, when the plotted sample values are between the upper and lower control limits, the process is said to be in control. With only random variation present, one would expect the values to randomly jump above and below the mean of the control chart. However, even if all of the values are within the control limits, any nonrandom pattern in the observations, such as

(1) upward or downward sloping trends (Figure B.3), (2) widening gaps between the observed values below the mean and above the mean (Figure B.4), or (3) several values in a row either above or below the mean value (Figure B.5) indicate the presence of systematic or controllable variation.

EXERCISES

1. Given the following data, what is the overall standard deviation and the standard error?

Sample Number	Values		
1	59	45	51
2	45	57	41
3	42	43	45
4	57	57	50
5	53	55	40
6	52	48	50
7	50	51	45
8	49	47	56
9	56	50	41
10	60	40	50

2. Given the answers calculated for exercise 1 and a target of 50, calculate the upper and lower control limits using a 3-sigma performance level.
3. A production process consists of assembling 5 components to make a small transistor radio. Every 3 hours a sample of 25 radios is collected and each radio is tested. Historically, 1.3 radios on average have failed the test. Calculate the 2-sigma control limits for the *p*-chart.
4. A candy manufacturer produces bags of assorted Easter candy. Each assorted bag should ideally have 30 percent chocolate bunnies, 30 percent marshmallow treats, and 40 percent chocolate robin eggs. Several samples were taken in an effort to ensure that these percentages were being met.

	Sample 1	Sample 2	Sample 3	Sample 4	Sample 5
Bunnies	70	46	62	60	56
Marshmallows	46	68	64	50	58
Eggs	84	88	78	90	84
Total	200	202	204	200	198

Calculate the mean and standard deviation of the p values for the bunnies.

5. Completed forms from a particular department of an insurance company were sampled on a daily basis as a check against the quality of performance of that department. To establish a tentative norm for the department, one sample of 100 units was collected each day for 15 days, with these results:

Sample	Sample Size	Number of Forms with Errors
1	100	4
2	100	3
3	100	5
4	100	0
5	100	2
6	100	8
7	100	1
8	100	3
9	100	4
10	100	2
11	100	7
12	100	2
13	100	1
14	100	3
15	100	1

Develop a p-chart using a 95 percent confidence level (z-score = 1.96).

6. Plot the data from the following 10 samples on the p-chart that you constructed for exercise 5. Is the process in control? Why or why not?

Sample	Sample Size	Number of Forms with Errors
1	100	5
2	100	6
3	100	4
4	100	7
5	100	3
6	100	4
7	100	5
8	100	6
9	100	7
10	100	8

7. A vitamin company utilizes x-bar charts to ensure that each tablet contains the correct dosage of a particular vitamin. The company's vitamin C tablets should contain a minimum of 6 milligrams of vitamin C. The control charts that were first established for the vitamin C tablets utilize a UCL of 6.56 and an LCL of 5.84 milligrams. Over the past few days, the company has taken 5 random samples of 4 tablets each and have found the following:

Sample	Tablet Weight (Milligrams)			
1	6.5	5.9	6.0	6.5
2	6.2	5.9	6.0	6.2
3	5.6	5.2	4.8	6.3
4	6.3	5.9	6.0	6.0
5	5.9	6.9	6.6	6.3

Is the process still in control?

8. A company manufactures LED flashlights. When the flashlights are performing properly, they utilize 1.25 watts of electricity. A 3-sigma control chart program is used to monitor the performance of the lights. Each sample contains 30 flashlights. Data from the last 10 samples were as follows:

Sample	Sample Mean
1	1.15
2	1.30
3	1.27
4	1.29
5	1.22
6	1.20
7	1.25
8	1.24
9	1.26
10	1.25

The standard deviation for all 300 of these observations was 1.2 watts. Set up an x-bar chart using this information.

9. Bottles of juice are being filled using a high-speed automated machine. The machine is being set up to fill the bottles with 100 ounces of juice.

   To set up the machine and to create a control chart to be used throughout the run, 15 samples were taken with 4 bottles in each sample. The complete list of samples and their measured values are as follows:

Sample Number	Readings			
1	101	99	98	98
2	99	99	100	99
3	99	100	101	108
4	101	102	100	99
5	101	101	100	99
6	99	100	99	105
7	98	99	98	102
8	100	98	99	99
9	100	98	105	100
10	99	100	100	97
11	99	100	99	98
12	101	99	99	101
13	98	99	98	100
14	99	99	98	98
15	101	100	100	99

What are the upper and lower control limits of the x-bar chart that is developed from this data?

10. A furniture manufacturer is producing cushions for their premier line of leather sofas. In order to fit in the sofas, the cushions need to be approximately 24 inches wide. The following 10 cushion samples were taken over a weeklong period. Construct an x-bar chart using this data.

Sample Number	Inches			
1	23.75	24.22	23.85	24.17
2	24.08	24.27	23.51	23.94
3	24.56	24.30	24.10	24.15
4	23.89	23.51	23.57	24.10
5	24.01	23.82	24.00	24.52
6	24.15	23.97	24.08	24.05
7	24.12	23.90	24.15	24.61
8	23.80	23.77	23.95	24.15
9	23.51	24.75	24.51	23.75
10	24.00	25.01	23.05	23.67

WEB EXERCISES

1. Search on-line for the term *statistical process control* and report on three firms that have used statistical process control.
2. Use the Internet to find at least three service processes to which control charts could be applied. Report on the implications of using control charts on these services.

Process Capability

Control charts are used to monitor processes so that variations in those processes can be detected and then reduced. Reducing the variations creates higher levels of product or service quality. Control charts are used to assess the *stability* of a process. However, just because a process is stable or in control doesn't mean that it is *capable* of meeting the required specifications.

Specification (or tolerance) limits are set by design engineers based on the design requirements for a product or service. For example, in order to fit with other engine components, a piston ring may need to be between 2.753 inches and 2.782 inches in diameter. These specification limits, like control limits, are expressed in terms of an upper specification limit (USL) and a lower specification limit (LSL). Figure B.6 illustrates a situation where the process is out of control but within specifications. Figure B.7 shows a scenario where the process is in control but out of specification.

Process capability refers to the ability of a process to meet the targeted specifications. Once processes are in control, as determined by the use of control charts, companies can track overall changes in variation by using a process capability index or C_{pk} index. Until the process is in control, the process capability values may or may not be representative of the true process capability. Process capability indices are ratios that quantify the ability of a process to produce products within the specifications. Process capability indices measure the ratio of the desired process variation to the actual process variation. The formula for the C_{pk} is

$$C_{pk} = \min \{C_{pu}, C_{pl}\}$$

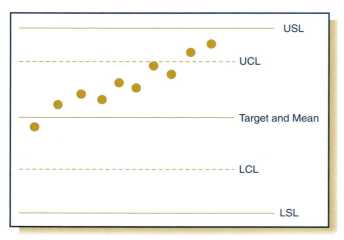

Figure B.6 Out of Control But Within Specifications

where:

$$C_{pu} = \frac{(USL - \mu)}{3\sigma}$$

$$C_{pl} = \frac{(\mu - LSL)}{3\sigma}$$

USL = Upper Specification Limit
LSL = Lower Specification Limit

μ = Process mean
σ = process standard deviation

A C_{pk} of 1.00 indicates that the process is producing product that conforms to the specifications. In this case, because 3σ was utilized in the equation, a C_{pk} of 1.00 indicates that the process will be within the specification limits 99.73 percent of the time, resulting in no more than 3 values outside the specification limits for every thousand products. When C_{pk} has a value less than 1.00, it indicates the process is producing products that do not conform to specifications. A C_{pk} value greater than 1.00 indicates the process is producing products that conform to specifications. A negative C_{pk} value indicates that the process mean is outside one of the specification limits.

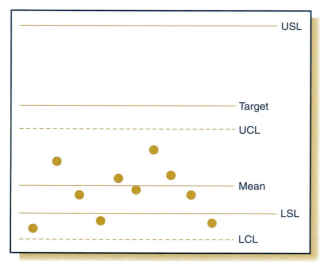

Figure B.7 In Control But Out of Specification

EXERCISES

1. Given a mean of 5, an upper specification limit of 7, a lower specification limit of 4, a target of 5.5, and a standard deviation of 0.26, calculate the C_{pk}. What does this information tell you about the process?

2. Given a mean and target of 20, an upper specification limit of 28, a lower specification limit of 12, and a standard deviation of 5, calculate the C_{pk}. What does this information tell you about the process?

3. Given mean of 4.27, an upper specification limit of 4.59, a lower specification limit of 4.13, a target of 4.36, and a standard deviation of 0.075, calculate the C_{pk}. What does this information tell you about the process?

Problem Solving

The goal of quality management is not simply to identify capability or stability problems, but to correct them or remove them from the process, thereby increasing overall quality and increasing customer service, customer satisfaction, and customer success. Various problem-solving methodologies have been developed to assist in these correction or removal efforts. A simple cause and effect diagram (commonly called a *fishbone* or *Ishikawa diagram*) can be a useful tool in identifying the causes of the capability or stability variations that are discovered. Figure B.8 shows a basic cause and effect diagram.

Brainstorming is utilized to develop the various branches of the fishbone diagram. First the main causes of the problem are identified and then the items that may be influencing those main causes are identified. The problem in Figure B.8 is a flat tire. The main causes of the flat tire may be a puncture or hole, damaged tread, or underinflated tire. Each of these main causes can be linked to other underlying causes such as a lack of knowledge about correct air pressure or a lack of time to perform regular maintenance.

The goal of using cause and effect diagrams is to identify root causes of problems so that they can be addressed and corrected. This tool can be useful in manufacturing and service organizations. For example, a hospital in Pittsburgh, Pennsylvania, used a cause and effect approach to trace problematic infections in some

Figure B.8 Cause and Effect Diagram: Flat Tire

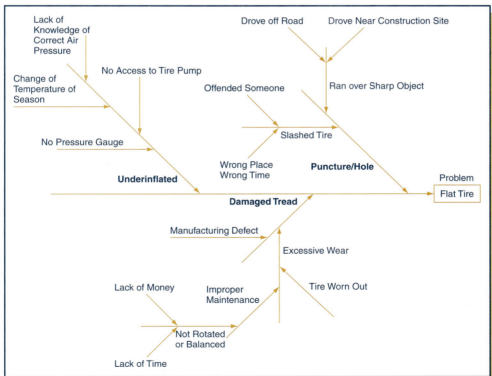

patients to their source, prompting two intensive-care units to change the way they insert intravenous lines.[5] This resulted in a 90 percent drop in the number of infections after just 90 days of using the new procedures and saved the hospital almost $500,000 a year in intensive-care-unit costs. Other hospitals are using similar tactics to reduce patient wait times, to prepare operating rooms faster, and to move patients through a hospital stay or doctor visit with fewer errors.

Cause and effect diagrams are a good way of identifying and organizing the potential causes of a problem, but further investigation and analysis are usually required to determine which of the potential problems are actually causing the problem. Individuals or teams can be assigned to further investigate, assess, and correct (if necessary) the potential causes identified using the cause and effect diagram. Items that should be considered when trying to determine potential problems include people, processes, machines, materials, measurements, resources, management, and the environment in which the process takes place.

Another useful tool in identifying and prioritizing the causes of variation is a Pareto chart. In 1906, Italian economist Vilfredo Pareto created a mathematical formula to describe the unequal distribution of wealth in his country. He observed that 20 percent of the people owned 80 percent of the wealth. This observation has since been labeled the 80/20 Rule. Over the years, many others have observed similar phenomena in their own areas of expertise. One of these individuals, Dr. Joseph Juran, a quality management pioneer, recognized a universal principle he called the "vital few and trivial many." The 80/20 Rule means that in many instances a few (20 percent) are vital and many (80 percent) are trivial.

Applied to quality problems, the 80/20 Rule would state that a small number of causes are leading to a large majority of your problems. The trick is being able to identify which of the causes fall into this category. Pareto charts are used to assist in this process.

For example, suppose that an oak handrail company is concerned that its installation projects are taking longer than the times that they are promising their customers. The owner of the company decides to utilize a Pareto analysis to find out what is causing the delays. By observing her installers in the field for 2 weeks, she collects the following data:

Type of Problem	Frequency
Broken equipment	2
Missing necessary components	18
Sick employees	3
Wrong material delivered to job site	7
Scheduling conflicts	1
House locked/no one home when promised	3

Ranking these problems in order of their frequency and calculating a percentage of the total number of problems caused by each type of problem yielded the following results:

Type of Problem	Frequency	Percentage
Missing necessary components	18	52.9%
Wrong material delivered to job site	7	20.6%
Sick employees	3	8.8%
House locked/no one home when promised	3	8.8%
Broken equipment	2	5.9%
Scheduling conflicts	1	2.9%
Total	34	100%

A Pareto chart (see Figure B.9) was then constructed using this information. From this analysis, it became clear that missing components and the wrong materials were the "vital few" problems that accounted for a combined 73.5 percent of the company's total problems. Based on this information, the owner set out to find a new parts supplier that would correctly deliver all of the components necessary to finish the handrail installations. Time and effort spent on correcting some of the other causes of lengthy installations would not have nearly the overall impact that addressing the missing components and wrong material issues had.

Cause and effect diagrams and Pareto charts are just two of the many tools that managers can utilize to help identify and prioritize the causes of stability or capability problems. Interestingly, as it relates to productivity, the causes of these problems can be from the process itself but are often associated with one of the inputs to the process. Cause and effect diagrams help managers understand the relationship between these inputs and the outputs or results that are achieved.

---

[5]Wysocki, Bernard Jr. (2004, April 9). Industrial strength: To fix health care, hospitals take tips from factory floor; adopting Toyota techniques can cut costs, wait times ferreting out an infection; what Paul O'Neill's been up to. *The Wall Street Journal*, p. A.1

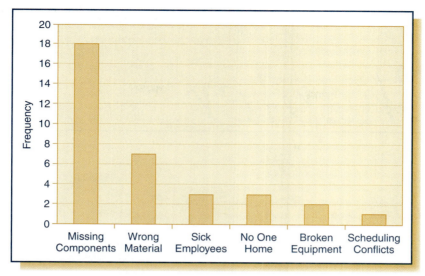

Figure B.9 Pareto Frequency Chart for Handrail Installation Problems

1. Visit www.isixsigma.com and search for statistical process control, process capability, cause and effect diagrams, or Pareto charts. Briefly discuss your findings in a half-page report.
2. Use the Internet to find at least two other tools that might be useful for managers seeking to identify and prioritize the causes of problems within their organizations.
3. Visit the JD Power and Associates Web site at www.jdpower.com. Look at the recent quality statistics for global automakers. What types of quality does J.D. Power evaluate? Which of these is most important? Is quality correlated to profitability?

Chapter 3

Process Thinking: SCM's Foundation

How is my company organized? Can I help it build customer-winning, value-added processes?

The Supply Chain Road Map

Who are we?

Business Purpose

Chapter 1: SC Strategy
- What is SCM?
- How does it fit our strategy?

Chapter 2: Customer Fulfillment
- Who are our customers?
- Can SCM deliver real value?

Chapter 3: Process Thinking
- **Do we have a functional, silo culture?**
- **Can we manage across functions?**

Chapter 4: New Product Process
- Do we know how to innovate?
- Can we create great products?

Chapter 5: Fulfillment Process
- Are our operations efficient?
- Can we buy/make/deliver?

After reading this chapter, you will be able to:

1. Identify and describe the challenges created by functional thinking.

2. Discuss the anatomy of a typical process. Describe the flows that comprise a process.

3. Explain the role of systems thinking in process design and management. Discuss the requirements and impediments to systems analysis.

4. Describe the company as a series of interactive decisions made across functional boundaries and resource types.

5. Explain process reengineering, describing how it can be used to design world-class processes.

Opening Story: Managing SC Change at Olympus

Doug was cautiously excited. Two days had passed since his presentation to Joe Andrus and the clock was ticking. Doug's proposal had been politely received, which was better than Doug had feared might happen. Just minutes before the meeting, Tim Rock, Olympus's chief financial officer, had greeted Doug with the words, "I'm looking forward to hearing your proposal on cost reduction. We need to drive costs down if we're going to keep shareholders happy." Disappointed that Tim had defined SCM so narrowly, Doug felt confident that his definition of SCM would present a broader picture of SCM and its competitive potential. Doug had defined SCM as "the design and management of seamless, value-added processes across organizational boundaries to meet the real needs of the end customer."

Before the meeting, Doug had feared that members of the executive council would feel threatened by the cross-functional nature of Doug's SC definition. To make his collaborative vision a reality, traditional organizational boundaries would have to be altered radically. Doug knew that turf was closely guarded, even among members of the executive council. Thus, Doug welcomed the absence of any real objections to his proposal that a task force be assembled to evaluate the attractiveness of SCM at Olympus.

Even so, Doug was nobody's fool. He knew that no one had gone out on a limb to endorse SCM. He sensed that the success stories had caught Joe Andrus's attention, but Joe was not fully convinced. Other members of the executive council had raised the concern that although SCM had proven successful at other companies, it might not be right for Olympus. Doug felt the pressure of the unspoken challenge to prove that SCM was the right thing to do. Joe Andrus's final comments placed the burden for proof squarely on Doug's shoulders.

Doug, we'll trust you on this one. Your view of SCM is intriguing. Heaven only knows how demanding customers are these days. And our competitors aren't cutting us any slack either. It would be great if SCM could buy us some breathing space, but from where I sit, this looks like an uphill climb. You've got 6 months to gather the data and present a viable plan. Remember, I'm from the "show-me state." You pick the people you want on your task force, and I'll see that you get them. But don't waste their time; we have too much to do to hem and haw on something that won't deliver bottom-line results.

Joe's words, "we'll trust you on this one," still echoed in Doug's mind. Twelve years building his reputation as a get-things-done manager would be put to the test over the next 6 months. Doug could see the mountain that Joe had referred to—could he get Olympus to the top without a higher level of organizational commitment? Doug realized that the weight he would have to shoulder was Olympus's functional—or, better said, dysfunctional—organization. The managers on the executive council were willing to let him expend his energies pushing for SCM as long as he didn't disturb their domains too much. They had seen other "change" initiatives come and go and had avoided meaningful change. Doug felt certain that they expected history to repeat itself once more with SCM.

Doug wished Charlene was back from Europe. She always seemed to take an analytical, yet practical approach to change management. Doug could almost hear her saying, "Make a list of points you have going for you Then make a list of the challenges you face. You'll figure out how to use your leverage points to move the stumbling blocks out of your way." Doug laughed as he envisioned the more difficult members of the executive council as stumbling blocks. Doug quickly jotted down two short lists:

POINTS IN MY FAVOR

- Joe Andrus is on record as supporting SCM. Joe approved a task force to study SCM's feasibility and promised that I could pick the members of the team.
- Customer demands together with intense competition have the executive council running scared. Olympus's stock price is down and market share stagnant. These outside forces might be the lever to move those stumbling blocks.
- Others . . . (I'm blessed with my own in-house consultant.)

CHALLENGES TO BE OVERCOME:

- Senior functional managers are not fully committed to SCM.
- Olympus is organized functionally rather than by key processes. Turf is going to be a serious issue.

- Processes, policies, and procedures will make data collection difficult. Tim Rock is going to want to see the direct profit-and-loss impact of any SC initiative.
- Others . . . (This could be a never-ending list. I need to prioritize and target the pivotal challenges.)

Consider As You Read:

1. What do Joe Andrus's words "we'll trust you on this one" really mean?
2. How can Doug use a challenging competitive environment to motivate change?
3. In what ways might a functional organization make SCM difficult to implement?
4. Who should Doug include on the task force? What characteristics would you want people on your team to possess?
5. How should Doug assess and document SCM's competitive viability?

Our company's basic philosophy is that business is an organic process and system. It's a holistic system. Business is like the human body. If the kidney isn't working, the heart's affected.

—JACK KAHL, MANCO

A NEED FOR PROCESS MANAGEMENT

For years, managers have recognized a need to find better ways to organize work. Jay Forrester, in 1958, foresaw a day when integrative, process decision making would replace compartmentalized thinking.[1]

> Management is on the verge of a major breakthrough in understanding how industrial company success depends on the interactions between the flows of information, materials, money, manpower, and capital equipment. The way these five flow systems interlock to amplify one another and to cause change and fluctuation will form the basis for anticipating the effects of decisions, policies, organizational forms, and investment choices.

Despite Forrester's prediction, the breakthrough to systems or process thinking has not occurred on a widespread basis. David Robinson, president of CSC Index, reiterated the need for process thinking, saying, "It's a shift from competing on what we make to how we make it."[2] The "how" Robinson is talking about is the difference between functional and process management. He is trying to point out that because functional structures limit cooperation and impede creative thinking, companies that rely on functional decision making are destined to lose future competitive battles. By contrast, process management promotes collaboration, enabling companies to satisfy customers at lower costs.

Despite its potential benefits, process integration remains rare. Michael Hammer, the thought leader behind reengineering, estimates that "no more than 10 percent of large enterprises have made a serious and successful effort at it."[2] One reason so few companies have changed the essence of how they do work is that such innovation entails a departure from familiar norms. Process thinking requires major changes in how people relate to one another and work across functions. It affects every aspect of the company from measurement and job design to managerial roles and organizational structure. Executive leadership must therefore embrace process thinking for it to have a real chance to take root and change people's approach to getting work done. Only then can SCM enable a more competitive business model.

Progressive Insurance exemplifies the competitive potential of process integration. Progressive achieved sevenfold growth in just over a decade by inventing new ways of doing work in the auto insurance industry. Progressive reinvented claims processing by introducing what it calls *immediate response claims handling*. Following an accident, a policyholder can reach a Progressive representative by phone 24 hours a day. The representative schedules a time for an adjuster to inspect the vehicle. Working out of a mobile claims van, the adjuster can examine the vehicle, prepare an on-site estimate of the damage, and write a check—all within 9 hours of the initial contact.

Progressive made process redesign a fundamental part of its competitive strategy. It introduced a system that allows customers to compare Progressive's rates with those of three competitors. Progressive even devised a better way to assess a driver's risk, which allows the company to quote the right rate. The key was the realization that an applicant's credit rating is a good proxy for responsible driving behavior. As part of the application process, Progressive's computer systems automatically contact those of a credit agency so that the applicant's credit score can be factored into the price quote. Creating processes that deliver better service at lower prices enabled Progressive to take market share from larger, better-known rivals.[3]

The key for Progressive, and other companies, is to recognize the limiting nature of functional organizations and then to instill process thinking throughout the company. This 2-step approach enables the design and execution of customer-winning value-added processes.

FUNCTIONAL ORGANIZATION AND ITS CONSEQUENCES

Functional organization impedes process thinking. **Functional organization** is the grouping of resources into specific departments, such as research and development, purchasing, production, logistics, and marketing. Each department performs specific tasks to help the company achieve desired goals. Specifically,

- *Research and Development* translates customer needs into tangible products. The goal is to build appealing, easy-to-make products with shorter concept-to-market lead times.
- *Purchasing* acquires the right materials at the right price for use in operations. Purchasing's goal is to select the right suppliers and then build the right relationships with them.

- *Production* transforms inputs into a more highly valued and desirable product or service. The goal: to use capital, energy, knowledge, and labor to build processes that make low-cost, high-quality goods.
- *Logistics* moves and stores goods so they are available for use in operations or for sale to customers. Logistics seeks to leverage critical activities like transportation, warehousing, and order processing to make sure materials and products are where they need to be when they need to be at the lowest cost.
- *Marketing* identifies customer needs and communicates to the customer how the company can meet those needs. Marketing's objective is to perform a liaison role between the company and its customers.

Traditional organization structures drive functional thinking—managers begin to see the world from a narrow, functional perspective, acting as if their function were the company. Functional thinking is built into modern management. Responding to recruiters' requests for specialists, business schools monopolize a business student's course load with function-driven classes.[5] Then, to establish a successful track record, managers become functional specialists early in their careers. Functional thinking is often magnified by physical distance, as different functions are located on different floors or in separate buildings. Over time, managers come to see only their function and its performance. They lose awareness of the rest of the company.

What does this mean? It means that managers view every decision from their own function's perspective, ignoring other viewpoints. Decisions are made to achieve the local, functional optimum regardless of how they affect other areas of the firm. As this happens, managers from different areas of the company fail to recognize the value added in other areas. In extreme cases, managers may even begin to see colleagues elsewhere in the company as competitors rather than collaborators as they fight over scarce resources. The outcome: The company's competitiveness deteriorates. Costs increase and service suffers.

Figure 3.1 shows the typical goals, decisions, and performance measures that might be found in four departments—purchasing, production, logistics, and marketing—of a functionally organized company. By examining the goals and measures of success, we can identify inherent conflicts in decision making among departments. For example, marketing managers, who are evaluated on their ability to increase sales, promise customers exceptional service. Great customer service means delivering the right products when and where the customer requests, even on short notice. Marketers therefore prefer high levels of inventory staged in multiple locations as close as possible to key customers. Marketers also want short fulfillment lead times from logistics so that they can respond to unique customer needs.

By contrast, because logistics managers are often evaluated on a cost basis, their goal is to minimize costs. Logisticians make every effort to reduce inventory levels and to hold inventory in as few centralized locations as possible. They want ample notice from marketing regarding customer demand while seeking rapid replenishment from manufacturing. Such conflicting objectives are common.

Although the roles performed by each department are needed for the company to satisfy customers, the functional organization leads to conflicting interests and counterproductive actions. The lack of overlap across "ideal" worlds creates a tug of war within the company as each function pulls the organization in the direction that it perceives as best. Process thinking—aligning decisions with corporate strategy and coordinating activities across functions—can reduce the inefficiencies of functional organization and unleash great competitive potential. High levels of process thinking do not exist in most companies, largely because managers do not understand the basic nature of a process.

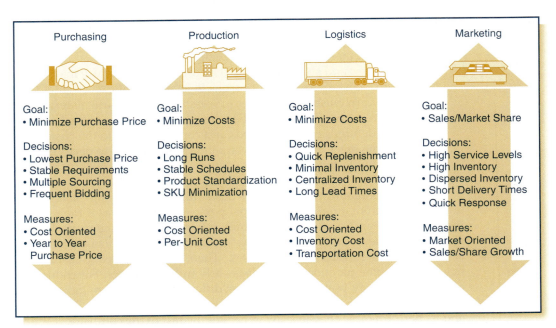

Figure 3.1 The Challenge of Conflicting Functional Objectives

THE ANATOMY OF A PROCESS

Because many managers grow up in a functional world, they have no idea what it means to manage an integrated process. Perhaps the best way to improve our understanding is to take a close look at the anatomy of a process. Every process consists of a set of identifiable flows and value-added activities. Three distinct, but related, flows define each process: an information flow, a physical flow, and a financial flow. Most processes begin with an information flow, which triggers a specific value-added activity. However, the sequence of flows and the type of activities depends on the nature of the process. Figure 3.2 and Figure 3.3 depict two value-added processes—new product development and materials acquisition. Let's dissect these two processes.

Looking first at the new product development process, we see that

1. Product development begins with an idea derived from insight into a customer need or an engineering breakthrough. Once an idea is envisioned, conceptualization and design activities begin.
2. The most important financial flow occurs in project evaluation, approval, and budgeting. If the project is viewed positively, then money is allocated so that specific physical activities can begin.
3. The physical flow begins as a prototype is built, tooling is acquired, production is ramped up, and full-scale manufacturing occurs.
4. Specific decisions are made regarding each activity (conceptualization, evaluation, ramp-up) across several functional areas, including strategy, marketing, operations, research and development, sourcing, and finance. For example, in new product evaluation, a cross-functional team determines whether a product

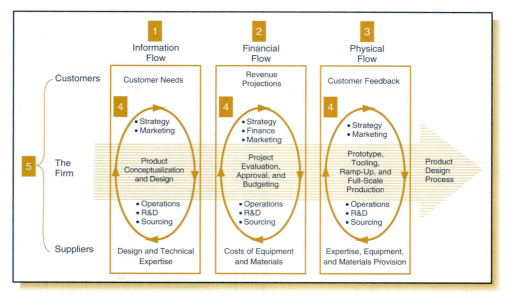

Figure 3.2   Anatomy of a Value-Added Process: New Product Development

can be profitably produced and sold in a competitive market. To do this, the team evaluates revenue projections, materials and equipment cost information, and the firm's own capabilities

5. The company, its customers, and its suppliers all work together to design a great product. Customers provide insight into product viability and potential sales. Suppliers share commodity, design, and technical expertise. They also provide capital equipment and product components.

Figure 3.3   Anatomy of a Value-Added Process: Materials Acquisition

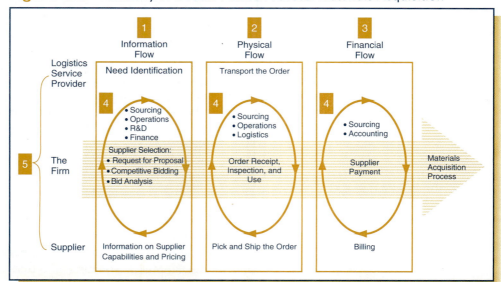

Examining the materials acquisition process, we see that

1. The materials acquisition process begins when a need is identified and communicated. If the item is a new purchase, a request for a proposal (RFP) is sent to potential suppliers. Suppliers respond with appropriate information regarding their capabilities and pricing. After suppliers' responses are analyzed, a supplier is selected.
2. The physical flow consists of several activities including order picking and shipping by the supplier, transportation by a logistics service provider, and order receipt and inspection at the buying firm. The acquired materials are then used to create products and services for delivery to customers.
3. The financial flow concludes the materials acquisition process. Once a product shipment has been received, inspected, and accepted, payment is made. For some organizations, the payment process has been streamlined so that no inspection takes place. As soon as the shipment is matched to an outstanding order, payment occurs via electronic funds transfer.
4. Decisions regarding each activity (supplier selection, product shipment, payment) are made in the areas of operations, R&D, sourcing, logistics, finance, and accounting. At many companies, a commodity team consisting of sourcing, operations, R&D, and finance often manages the supplier selection decision.
5. The buyer, a supplier, and a logistics service provider perform critical roles. Expertise and investment in specialized equipment make all three valued members of the process team.

Many processes such as order fulfillment and customer service must also be managed for a company to succeed. However, the essential elements of process management do not vary much. Every process depends on (1) the timely *flow* of information, (2) the efficient *flow* of physical materials, and (3) effective cash *flow* management. The activities that comprise these three flows and the decisions that affect them are managed across functions as well as up and down the supply chain. This fact is critical: Every value-added process is made up of many activities that take place in different locations and at different times. No single person or company controls all of these activities. Process management by definition depends on collaboration.

Understanding the basic anatomy of a process helps managers collaborate meaningfully. For example, The Limited changed the rules of the very tough fashion retail market by bringing products from the mind of the customer to her body in 1,000 hours.[6] To do this, new product development and order fulfillment processes had to be dissected and then integrated. This, in turn, required intensive cross-functional collaboration supported by good information and logistics systems. Bringing it all together enabled short-cycle design and replenishment. By designing fashionable clothes and getting them on the rack quickly, The Limited delivers to the customer what she wants when she wants it without expensive markdowns and stockouts.

SYSTEMS THINKING AND PROCESS MANAGEMENT

Moving from a functional organization to process management mandates a new way of thinking. It requires the adoption of systems thinking. **Systems thinking** is the holistic process of considering both the immediate local outcomes and the longer-term systems-wide ramifications of decisions. Whereas traditional functional thinking seeks the local optimum—often at the expense of overall system's performance—systems thinking aligns efforts, getting everyone to pull in the same direction. Such united effort creates a stronger, more competitive team.

To cultivate systems thinking and promote organizational transformation, managers need to recognize and understand the following five requirements for managing a company or a supply chain as a system.

A Holistic View

Managers do not see all of the interrelationships, nor do they understand all of the trade-offs that occur within their organizations. Although senior-level managers set the strategic direction of the company, they do not see the details of individual value-added processes. Managers who are intimately involved with the details often lack exposure to what is going on with other value-added activities throughout the company. No one sees the company from a holistic viewpoint.

At one company, a consultant hired to help improve the company's order-processing capability arrived and said, "I'm an order; process me." The consultant led the management team through every step of the process. At the end of the tour, an inch-thick stack of documents and disks sat on the table. Until that moment, nobody within the company understood the process as it actually worked—it was invisible and it was costly. Process visibility is a prerequisite to systems thinking. The need for a holistic view is even greater when the process being managed involves more than one company.

Information Availability and Accuracy

Tremendous amounts of data must be collected, analyzed, and translated into knowledge before well-informed, holistic decisions can be made. Modern information technology now makes it possible to collect and analyze huge amounts of data. Specifically,

- Bar codes and scanning devices make it possible to collect mountains of data. Radio frequency identification (RFID) tags will make it even easier to collect accurate, real-time product and process information.
- Data warehouses and data-mining software make it easy to store and analyze data.
- Enterprise resource planning systems enable better dissemination of data.

Though technology has reduced the limits that a lack of information places on systems thinking, most managers still identify missing or inaccurate information as a barrier to great decision making. They note that greater effort needs to be made to determine exactly what information is needed and then to get it to the right decision maker so that better operational and strategic decisions can be made and executed.

For example, one retailer ran into an information accuracy problem that hurt its customer service. The problem was discovered only after an angry customer wrote a letter to a company vice president. The customer was angry because she had visited the store on three separate occasions trying to buy a specific product. Each time, however, she found the shelf empty. She explained that she was a frequent shopper and that the company would lose significant sales if she were to take her business to a rival. She also told the vice president that he should care enough about customers to make sure that advertised products were in stock. When the vice president investigated, he found that the computer indicated the store had 14 units of the desired item in stock. A physical check revealed that both the shelf and the back room were empty. A physical count of all the items in the store revealed that the inventory status recorded in the computer system was inaccurate for 65 percent of the 10,000 stock-keeping units sold by the retailer. Despite the use of modern technology, poor inventory accuracy information led managers to make decisions that drove costs up and service down.[7] Better data tracking, analysis, and sharing is still needed to help managers make good, holistic decisions.

Cross-Functional and Interorganizational Teamwork

Sub-unit loyalties make holistic decision making difficult. Goals, roles, responsibilities, and training are often functionally oriented. As Figure 3.1 shows, marketing focuses on hitting sales targets; manufacturing is concerned with productivity; and logistics is preoccupied with lowering distribution costs. Working to achieve these goals is desirable, but not at the expense of the rest of the organization. A functional focus can cause managers to view themselves as members of the engineering, marketing, or product development group instead of members of the Barilla, General Motors, or Sony team. Although functional camaraderie is commendable, managers and employees must not lose sight of company and supply chain goals. They must also learn to work together.

The most common approach to building a borderless culture is cross-functional and interorganizational teaming. At Kohl's Department Stores, merchandising teams consisting of marketing, sourcing, logistics, and finance managers make all of the key decisions to get product from source to customer. To promote continuous contact and collaboration, the members of the commodity team work out of the same office space. Co-location promotes spontaneous discussion and collaborative decision making.

At the supply chain level, Rockwell Collins, a manufacturer of aeronautics equipment, sends teams of development engineers to work on-site at a supplier's facility for several months at a time. Rockwell Collins has even established permanent customer advisory boards and supply management councils to bring its managers and those from key SC partners together to discuss new initiatives and resolve thorny issues as they arise.[8]

Measurement

Recognition for a job well done, including bonuses and promotions, is often tied to local, short-run results. As long as personal career success depends on whether "Linda met the sales goal" or "Andreas hit the cost-reduction target," managers will strive to achieve measured expectations. People will not make holistic decisions when they are measured on local, functional outcomes. Measures must consistently support the organization's most important objectives. Aligning measures is one of the biggest challenges companies face.

When managers at Ford Motor Company began to hear stories indicating that supply relationships were deteriorating, they wanted to know why. As they talked to suppliers, it became evident that many suppliers viewed Ford as untrustworthy. Because Ford was convinced that it could not succeed without supplier support, it brought in a consultant to design an instrument to measure the trustworthiness of Ford's culture. Senior managers wanted both internal employees and suppliers to know that Ford was serious about building trust-based relationships. Unfortunately, the measurement was not aligned with the stated goals.

Similarly concerned about maintaining positive supply relationships, Wal-Mart recognized that in their quest to be tough, individual buyers might use Wal-Mart's immense buying power to squeeze suppliers inappropriately. Wal-Mart began to ask every buyer's six most important suppliers to assess the buyer's behavior and professionalism. These assessments were initially viewed as a vital component of each buyer's overall performance evaluations. But concerned about the fairness of formally including outside evaluations in the measurement of buyers, the practice became more of an ad hoc, informal practice. At both Ford and Wal-Mart, initiatives to build trust-based supply relationships failed to change buyer behavior because they were not supported and sustained through systematic measurement. Communication without supportive measurement almost never changes behavior.

Systems Analysis

The previous four requirements promote a culture that values and promotes systems thinking. The fifth requirement is for the company to put in place a systematic approach to systems analysis. Making good holistic decisions requires that a clear goal be set, that system boundaries be defined, information be gathered, and both trade-offs and constraints specifically be considered. Figure 3.4 outlines these process steps.

Establish the Core Goal

Clear, overarching goals must guide system behavior. To get all contributors pulling in the same direction, they need to know what they are trying to accomplish as a "team." Without a well-thought-out and well-communicated goal, individual groups will do their own thing.

Figure 3.4 Process Steps for Systems Analysis

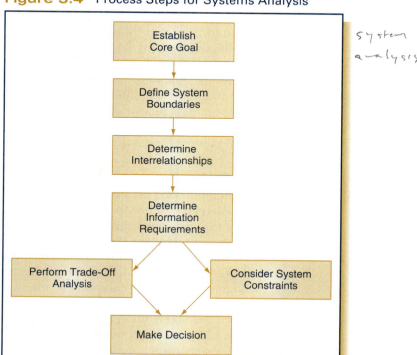

Define System Boundaries

Defining the goal is a prerequisite to identifying the **system boundaries;** that is, who is a member of the team. Systems can be defined at any level. In an ideal world, the entire supply chain should be managed as a system. In practice, systems should be defined at the level that can most effectively accomplish the chosen goal. If the goal is to profitably satisfy customers, the system is generally defined as the company. The company "system" includes the functional areas of accounting, engineering, finance, human resources, logistics, marketing, operations, and purchasing. Each member of the system must perform certain definable tasks in order to meet customers' needs profitably.

Determine Interrelationships

Defining roles of team members and their interrelationships is the next step in describing the system. Different members of a team perform specific roles to achieve success. For example, to satisfy customers efficiently, marketing must determine what customers' real needs are, R&D must design a product to meet these needs, production must make the product, purchasing must acquire the best inputs for use in the production process, logistics must manage the movement and storage of materials, accounting must cost processes and then track costs, and finance must provide capital. The failure to perform any of these roles leads to a product that customers do not want or will not pay for.

The managerial challenge is to determine how a decision made in one area will affect decisions and operations in other areas of the system. The cross-functional implications of individual decisions should be explicitly considered. This is what determining interrelationships is all about. Determining interrelationships in a complex system like a company requires the mapping of critical processes to make specific flows and activities visible. The number of interactions that must be considered makes systems thinking an information-intensive endeavor.

Determine Information Requirements

Information makes systems analysis possible. The key is to identify the needed information, how it can best be captured and analyzed, and how it can be efficiently shared with decision makers. Information about the competitive environment, customers' needs, and internal capabilities defines the goals and boundaries of the system. Information regarding functional strengths and weaknesses and the nature of functional interactions defines interrelationships, highlighting important trade-offs. For information to enable systems-based decision making, it must be accurate, relevant, and timely.

Perform Trade-Off Analysis

Decisions made in one area affect performance in other areas. When marketing promises delivery of a product without verifying inventory and production status, production and/or logistics may have to perform expensive expediting. When purchasing opts for the lowest-priced component without analyzing the supplier's quality and delivery capabilities, purchasing costs may decrease, but production costs may rise. Trade-offs permeate decision making. Although managers recognize many obvious conflicts, many remain unseen. This is because the consequences of many decisions occur in a distant part of the organization or after a time delay. Managers must identify consequences and make all relevant trade-offs visible. Only then can managers determine how to optimize systems-wide results. Process mapping and total cost analysis help mangers identify and evaluate system trade-offs.

Consider System Constraints

Every system has constraints that limit available decision-making options. Some constraints are internal to an organization and include policies and procedures, physical capacities, behaviors, measurement, and insufficient information. Other constraints such as government regulations, customer requirements, and supplier capabilities are imposed externally. Constraint analysis identifies limiting factors, diagnoses their influence on the system, and proposes steps to relieve them. Resources are wasted when managers focus on symptoms rather than the root-cause constraint. After the analysis is done, managers are well-informed and ready to make a decision.

Systems Thinking at Work

The promise of systems thinking is that managers can make better, more competitive decisions when trade-offs are understood. The "total-cost-of-ownership" concept, a simple example of systems thinking at work, shows that buying the lowest-priced component may not deliver the greatest competitive advantage. The real cost of an item can only be assessed by evaluating the costs associated with purchasing, transporting, using, warranting, and disposing of the item. Buying at the lowest price may not be a good deal if the product is delivered late, wears out early, or creates environmental liabilities. For example, many expensive trade-offs occur in global sourcing. Attracted by extremely low wage rates, companies often source products globally only to discover that additional costs outweigh the labor cost savings. Some companies fail to consider the challenge of managing distant suppliers for quality and on-time delivery. Others underestimate the costs of international shipping and insurance. Table 3.1 lists the cost categories encountered in global operations. Of course, some companies successfully outsource globally by identifying qualified suppliers, building winning relationships, and establishing outstanding logistical support. The difference in outcome is determined by a combination of perspective and analysis.

Adopting a systems view can lead to unique solutions to common problems. The process of systems analysis—from goal setting to trade-off and constraint analysis—enlarges the vision of decision makers, providing greater insight into value-added processes. Systems thinking helped Dell, Honda, and Wal-Mart take a different road to meeting customer needs than their rivals. Their hard-to-imitate business models have enabled rapid, profitable growth.

Dell

Dell's direct-to-consumer business model relies on contract manufacturing. Dell does not manufacture many of the computers it sells; rather, customer orders are transmitted

Table 3.1 Costs Incurred in Global Operations

• Unit price	• Cost of money
• Relationship maintenance costs	• Risk of obsolescence
• Language and cultural training costs	• Cost of rejects
• International transportation costs	• Damage in transit
• Inland freight costs (domestic and foreign)	• Inventory holding costs
• Insurance and tariffs	• Technical support
• Brokerage costs	• Employee travel costs
• Letter of credit	• Export taxes

directly via the Web to contract manufacturers that assemble the computers and ship them directly to the consumer. Dell never touches many computers that wear its brand. Dell's outsourcing decision and the distribution system design reflect the process transparency and trade-off analysis that characterize systems thinking. Dell's first-mover advantage in developing its unique business model also suggests that Dell was not constrained by the thinking that had led all other competitors to use traditional sales channels to get their products into the customers' hands.

Honda

Approximately 85 percent of the value of every Honda comes from suppliers. Honda's reputation for quality and reliability rests heavily on its ability to manage supplier capabilities. Honda has therefore invested in developing its suppliers, helping them build skills. The costs of sending process engineers to work on-site at suppliers' facilities are large enough to discourage most competitors from undertaking similar efforts.[9] Justifying this investment required Honda to redraw the boundaries of its system in order to view sending engineers to suppliers' facilities as an integral part of its value-added operations. The return on investment in terms of productivity, superior quality, and joint innovation has made Honda's supplier relations the envy of the automotive industry. Few companies have emulated Honda's supplier development—largely because they have yet to show the same dedication to systems thinking.

Wal-Mart

Wal-Mart operates one of the largest private trucking fleets in the world. Many businesses outsource transportation in order to minimize cost and focus on their main business. Wal-Mart operates a trucking business because transportation is viewed as a part of a larger distribution process that has become one of Wal-Mart's core competencies. By combining a private fleet with a cross-docking warehouse operation, Wal-Mart can purchase product from suppliers in full truckloads, mix and match products from different suppliers at its cross-docking facilities, and use its own trucks to deliver truckload quantities to its retail centers. This distribution model makes frequent deliveries at lower costs possible. Wal-Mart delivers to its stores twice as frequently as most competitors. Systems thinking helps Wal-Mart to promise everyday low prices for products that are consistently on the shelf.

If systems thinking leads to better decisions and uniquely competitive business models, why don't all companies do it? The answer is simple: Although they recognize the counterproductive aspects of a "silo" mentality, most companies lack the discipline to act on the five requirements discussed earlier. The fact that not all decision making is rational further complicates the quest for systems thinking. As individuals we each see the world through unique, personal lenses. We make different decisions even when confronted by the same circumstances. These realities make it even more difficult to build consensus, align efforts, and establish cross-functional and supply chain processes.

A PROCESS VIEW OF THE COMPANY

The competitive world has changed dramatically in recent years. As a result, both the type of work and the way it must be done have changed. Unfortunately, the way companies organize has not changed. They still organize functionally when they should be designed around processes. So, the question arises, "What should a

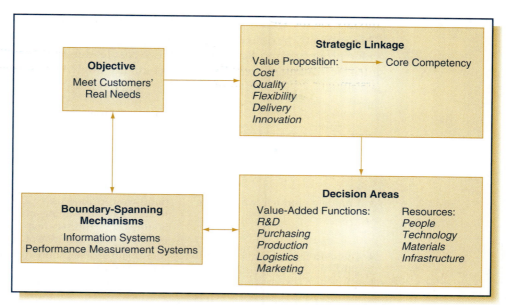

Figure 3.5   The Company As a Value-Added System

process-oriented company look like?" Figure 3.5 depicts a process view of the company that links systems thinking to the elements of strategy introduced in Chapter 1. This process view emphasizes collaborative decision making to meet customer needs. Remember Peter Drucker's advice: "There is only one valid definition of business purpose: to create a customer." Decisions made throughout the organization should all focus on using available resources to create customer value. Systems thinking and the process view highlight four key relationships:

1. A company's customer focus defines its value propositions and drives competency development.
2. Competency development guides functional decision making. Value is created when functional activities are coordinated to build unique core competencies.
3. Competency development directs resource allocation decisions.
4. Information and performance systems help align efforts and create cohesion within the firm.

The Strategic Linkage

Selecting the right value propositions and building the right core competencies are the essence of strategy.[10] Let's quickly review the basics. A **value proposition** is the value a company promises to deliver to customers. **Competencies** are the skills and processes that are developed to create the promised value. A **core competency** is something the company is so good at that it provides the company a competitive advantage. Core competencies are rare and very hard for competitors to copy. Strategy's role is to direct the use of resources so that a company can develop capabilities uniquely able to meet customer needs. Harvard's Michael Porter identified two strategies that are most often employed: cost leadership and differentiation.[11]

Cost Leadership

There can only be one cost leader in any market. Everyone else must offer some other value proposition to succeed. To achieve **cost leadership,** a company must create an intrinsic advantage. For example, a company might seek to develop the following advantages:

Source of Cost Leadership	Company Examples
• Economies of scale	As the world's largest retailer, Wal-Mart's size creates unparalleled buying power and allows it to promise everyday low prices.
• Uniquely productive processes	Southwest Airlines uses a 15-minute "turnaround" to keep its planes flying and generating revenue. Southwest's processes help it achieve the lowest costs per passenger mile of any major airline.
• Low-cost factor inputs	McDonald's global sourcing network provides access to low-cost resources in every region where it operates as well as from around the world.

Differentiation

Differentiation requires a company to develop a product or process attribute that reduces price sensitivity. Differentiation mitigates the constant pressure to compete on price. When a company pursues differentiation, competition shifts to one of the other value propositions: delivery, flexibility, innovation, or quality.[12] Differentiation strategies cultivate brand awareness as the company seeks to promote its unique market position. For example, Toyota is known worldwide for superb quality; Intel is recognized for the speed of its processors; and Coke is accepted as the "Real Thing." The key is to be distinctively better than anyone else. Uniqueness can result from any of the following:

Source of Differentiation	Company Examples
• Advanced product technology	Airbus pioneered the "fly-by-wire" technology that has helped it take share from Boeing and become the world's largest airframe manufacturer.
• Advanced process technology	Schneider National Logistics was the first motor carrier to employ global satellite positioning to track shipments. Don Schneider calls his company a technology company. Advanced processes have helped Schneider become the fastest growing third-party logistics company in the world.
• An extensive distribution network	Coca-Cola may be the most ubiquitous product worldwide. Coke now sells more than 130 beverages and is found in almost every country worldwide.
• Better, more user-friendly products	Apple's iPod was the first portable digital music player to effectively use a miniature hard drive to hold a user's favorite songs. Its sophisticated design and user interface have made the iPod the market leader despite its higher prices.

A low-cost position may not be incompatible with differentiation. Combining low cost and high quality is often needed just to survive. Table 3.2 shows some of the specific choices that might be made as a company formulates a cost leadership or differentiation strategy.

Table 3.2 Using Strategy to Match Value-Added Systems to Customer Needs

DIFFERENTIATION	INNOVATION	DELIVERY/FLEXIBILITY/ QUALITY	COST LEADERSHIP
Goals of Value-Added System	• Short concept-to-market cycle time • Technologically advanced products • Unique service options • Availability despite demand uncertainty	• Rapid, consistent delivery • Availability • High-quality product/service • Responsiveness to customer, i.e., ability to handle small orders and expedited shipments	• Minimum cost—but ensure an "acceptable" service level
Purchasing	Identify and develop suppliers who can assure: • Design expertise • Technological support • Flexibility to changes in specs • Process capabilities	Identify and develop suppliers who can assure: • Rapid, consistent delivery • Certified quality • Full-line availability • Responsiveness	Identify and develop suppliers who can assure: • Productivity/low prices • Learning curve efficiencies • Scale/scope economies • Quantity price discounts
Production	• Work closely with R&D, i.e., concurrent engineering • Support process engineering	• Shop floor control—due-date performance • Shorten cycle times • Cross-train workers • Extensive process control • Reduce inventories	• Reduce inventories • Increase repetitiveness • Increase part commonality • Utilize low-cost labor • Increase worker productivity
Logistics	• Utilize technology including bar codes, satellite tracking, electronic data interchange, and automated picking/packing to offer customized services	• Use private fleet or dedicated contract carrier to assure on-time delivery • Use information technology to increase responsiveness and ability to handle unexpected events • Implement process control and other quality improvement approaches	• Use low-cost transport (rail and/or TOFC) • Use high utilization (truckload) and/or multiple car rates • Use volume contracts • Minimize inventory • Centralize decision making

Resource Management

Every company manages four resources as part of its own value-added system or as part of the larger supply chain. These resources are people, technology, materials, and infrastructure. Capital, a fifth resource, must be managed to finance company operations. Successful companies use efficient and effective resource management to deliver value to customers. For example, resource management allows

- Federal Express to deliver 3 million packages daily in over 200 countries.
- McDonald's to sell $19 billion of Big Macs, Cokes, and fries through 31,200 restaurants in 119 countries.
- Toyota to net $10 billion in income by selling almost 8 million cars and trucks worldwide.

Managerial philosophies and competitive environments govern the way companies manage their resources. The fact is that there is no single right way to manage a company's resources. For example, in 2005, Caterpillar generated over $30 billion in revenues and $2 billion in profits by operating in 180 countries, employing over 76,000 people, purchasing over $8 billion in goods and services, and investing $4 million a day in product and process technologies. Caterpillar builds well-engineered construction equipment, but its ability to use its resources to keep customers' equipment up and running makes it a valued SC partner. Caterpillar promises to deliver spare parts to any location in the world in only 48 hours.

By contrast, Nike's 2005 global sales of more than $13 billion and profits of $1.2 billion were generated with only 24,600 employees (revenues/employee: $528,000 at Nike versus $394,000 at Caterpillar; profits/employee: $48,000 at Nike versus $26,000 at Caterpillar). The difference is that Nike outsources its production. Rather than making the shoes it sells, Nike carefully manages the intellectual assets employed in the design and marketing of athletic apparel. This increases revenues and profits per employee, but not without risks. In the late 1990s, a failure by Nike to oversee its subcontractors led to accusations of human rights abuses and worker exploitation. The abuses were extremely embarrassing and cost Nike considerable goodwill. Nike now takes an active role in managing its contract manufacturers to protect its brand reputation.

Caterpillar and Nike are two very different companies operating in two very different industries with two very different resource-utilization models. Yet, they are both extremely successful. That is because they have both distinguished themselves in their customers' minds by doing what they do better than anyone else. The ability to outperform the competition depends on the way a company transforms its resources into competencies and subsequently into products and services that customers value. Because resource decisions are so important, each resource type is briefly discussed in the following sections.

People

People determine the productivity and quality of the work performed. At leading companies, education and training are the foundation for successful human resource policies. They use performance measurement to instill a sense of fairness within the organizational culture. Empowerment unleashes passion and creativity. Perhaps the most important lesson learned by General Motors in its NUMMI joint venture with Toyota was that getting people and technology to work together as complementary parts of the value-added system is the key to efficiently building high-quality cars. Managers at Toyota know that technology by itself seldom yields a real distinctive advantage. People provide the creativity and passion that drive success.

Technology

Technology includes the equipment and software used to make and deliver goods and services. Effectively employed, technology improves productivity. For example, the advent of mechanized farm equipment dramatically increased agricultural productivity over the past hundred years. In 1900, 40 percent of the U.S. population worked to feed the country. Today, it takes only 2 percent, thanks to productivity increases.[13] Information technology has similarly revolutionized modern business practice, enabling better SC communication and coordination. For example, computer-aided design coupled with collaboration software enables Deere to work with suppliers to reduce the cost of tractor design while yielding better, easier-to-manufacture designs in less time. Bar codes, satellite tracking, warehouse management systems, radio frequency technologies, routing programs, and network modeling simulations have enabled a revolution in logistics management.

Materials

Materials, in the broadest sense, include the goods and services that are bought for use in the value-added process. Materials management begins in product design as engineers set product specifications. Purchasing must then acquire the right inputs from suppliers, leveraging global sourcing, partnering relationships, and vendor-managed inventories to add value. In production, materials decisions facilitate lean production and total quality management to help the company compete on productivity, quality, and responsiveness. Logistics decisions assure on-time delivery of materials. Documentation, inventory, order processing, packaging, transportation, and warehousing decisions all affect the level of service provided to customers.

The Toyota production system, often called *just-in-time* or *lean manufacturing*, demonstrates the value of effective materials management. By redesigning the way materials are purchased, transported, and used in the auto-manufacturing process, Toyota built a reputation as one of the world's best auto companies. Toyota is now the second largest car company in the world and has set the goal of becoming number one by 2010.

Infrastructure

Infrastructure refers to the physical, bricks-and-mortar assets a company uses in the value creation process. Infrastructure decisions determine the deployment and productivity of a company's resources. Vital infrastructure decisions include facility location, process design, capacity planning, and technology selection. These decisions determine the organization's cost structure and service capability.

For example, worried that its distribution network was too unwieldy and expensive, managers at Nabisco asked the simple question, "Do we really need all 11 of our distribution centers (DCs) to meet our customers' service requirements?" A zip-code analysis of customer demand revealed that 5 to 7 well-placed DCs would reduce costs without hurting service levels. Nabisco also discovered that many of its retail customers operated trucking fleets that moved product along the same routes traveled by Nabisco products. Rather than hire expensive less-than-truckload carriers to ship Oreos and other products, Nabisco worked out an arrangement to ship its product on customers' trucks. Nabisco's decision shows that SC strategies often rely on the infrastructure and skills of other SC members.

Coordinating Resource Decisions

Coordinating resource decisions across the company's primary functional areas of R&D, purchasing, production, logistics, and marketing can provide a competitive advantage that is difficult to duplicate. Figure 3.6 shows the 4-by-5 function/resource matrix that represents the organization's critical decision areas. Specific functional and resource initiatives should be mapped to the 20 cells shown in the matrix. Managers can then look for consistency among the initiatives as well as alignment to the company's strategy and value propositions.

Wal-Mart follows this approach, posting a chart on the conference room wall that links every initiative back to a strategic objective. Resources are only dedicated when visible linkages between activities and goals are established. This mapping exercise is critical because delivering on Wal-Mart's everyday-low-prices value proposition depends on careful coordination of complex processes. Wal-Mart's strategy relies heavily on employees who identify new customer needs, a private trucking fleet, satellite communications, carefully located and designed stores, cross-docking at regional distribution centers, and strategic alliances with suppliers. Wal-Mart has woven these resources into a low-cost delivery competency that no one else has been able to match. Take away any of the individual pieces of the competency puzzle and Wal-Mart's competitive advantage would be greatly diminished.

Figure 3.6   The Function/Resource Decision-Making Matrix

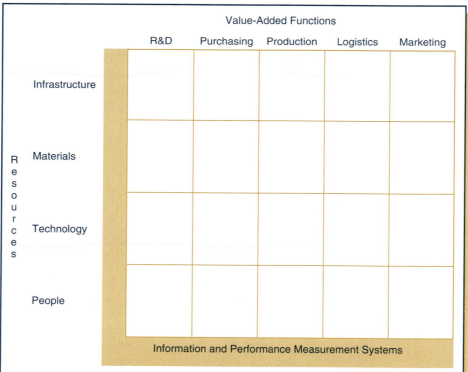

Boundary-Spanning Mechanisms

As noted previously, many potential conflicts exist across resource and functional decision areas. To promote decision-making consistency, information must be shared and behavior must become cooperative. Information and measurement systems can perform this unifying role.

Information Sharing

Information sharing promotes process management by communicating strategic objectives and organizational roles. People need to know how to help the company succeed. Otherwise they will seek the local optimum. Information regarding cross-functional interdependencies facilitates trade-off analysis and helps build better working relationships. Information also plays a role in educating managers and workers regarding the benefits of integrated decision making and process management.

Managers collect and analyze the following types of information to formulate strategy, build competencies, and manage day-to-day operations efficiently.

- Customer-related information defines goals, value propositions, and competencies.
- Information on firm capabilities and processes identifies strengths and weaknesses so that an effective strategy can be developed and implemented.
- Information on competitors' strategies and capabilities is used to anticipate competitive threats as well as competitors' reactions to the company's own strategic moves.
- Information about the external operating environment helps identify potential threats and opportunities such as the opening of a new market or the emergence of a new technology.
- SC operating information is used to make good day-to-day decisions like how many and what types of suppliers are needed to support the firm's production schedule.
- "Success stories" provide the information needed to create momentum for process integration.

Performance Measurement

Measurement must reinforce information sharing to build a process-oriented culture. People pay more attention to what is measured than they do to what is said. Therefore, performance measures must (1) be aligned with strategic objectives and (2) clearly communicate expectations and responsibilities to everybody in the organization. A well-designed measurement system

- Creates understanding regarding strategic objectives and tactical plans
- Promotes behaviors that are consistent with achieving chosen objectives
- Documents actual results, monitoring progress toward goals
- Benchmarks capabilities vis-à-vis competitors' abilities and customers' expectations
- Motivates continuous improvement

Figure 3.7 shows how information about objectives, roles, and measures cascades throughout the organization, facilitating consistency of priorities and action. Feedback and ideas for improvement promote the reengineering needed to build world-class processes.

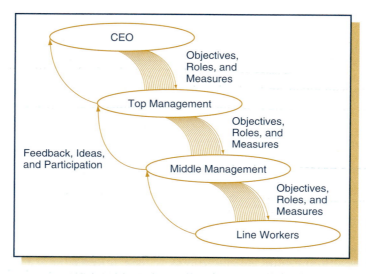

Figure 3.7 The Information-Measurement Integration Waterfall

PROCESS REENGINEERING

Process reengineering describes the radical redesign of business processes made possible by systems thinking and improved information technology.[14] You might ask, "How is reengineering different from traditional restructuring?" Traditional restructuring replaces other resources with technology without changing the basic process design. Reengineering builds processes from scratch. Proponents of reengineering claim that technology makes it possible to improve the way that work is done.

The question that drives reengineering is, "If we were to design a process to accomplish this task today, what would the ideal process look like?" Managers can answer this question by (1) using systems thinking to get beyond traditional organizational constraints, (2) adopting new technologies, and (3) taking advantage of new workers' skills and responsibilities. Imagination and information technology combine to overcome outdated assumptions about how processes do work.

Reengineering begins with an initial process analysis. If this analysis does not identify real opportunities to improve performance, then the selected process is not a good candidate for reengineering. The analytical effort is not wasted if insight gained into how the process works is used to promote incremental improvements. If the selected process is a good candidate for radical process redesign, the following steps should be implemented.

Identify Desired Outcomes

Processes should be designed to fulfill a specific customer need. Process reengineering therefore begins by asking, "Why is this process performed?" If the need no longer exists, the process should be eliminated. At many companies, costly activities are perpetuated because they represent the way the company has always done something. Nabisco's use of 11 DCs instead of 7 exemplifies the opportunity to eliminate activities when they no longer make sense. If the process still delivers value but not as efficiently or effectively as possible, current outcomes are documented and compared to desired outcomes. The process is then redesigned to deliver the desired outcomes.

Make the Process Visible

Many processes perform poorly simply because nobody fully understands them. A process map can be used to make the process visible so that it can be redesigned appropriately. Process mapping identifies individual activities, their specific roles, the people involved, and critical performance dimensions such as time taken by each step. This understanding helps identify opportunities to change the way work is done.

Reorganize the Process

Once a process is understood, opportunities to reorganize work can be identified. In some instances, tasks can be consolidated. In others, individual activities can be eliminated altogether. A simple rule is to design each worker's job to involve performing as many of the tasks required to complete the process as possible.

At Shell Lubricants, cycle time was improved by redesigning the order fulfillment process so that one person handles the entire order instead of seven people performing narrow aspects of the overall process.[15] Because the transformation of work responsibility was radical, it occurred in three steps. Step 1 placed a single manager over all of the departments involved in the process. Step 2 created cross-functional teams involving people from the various departments. The final step, Step 3, involved training each team member to handle the entire order. Though this was the original goal, Shell moved in a deliberate stepwise fashion to make the transition as painless as possible.

Assign Responsibility for Work

The responsibility for the process redesign should be placed where the work is done. No one else has as clear an understanding of how the process actually works. Those individuals who do the work are also likely to have had many ideas for improving the process that have never been acted upon. The reengineering effort thus opens the opportunity for people not only to share their ideas but also be creative in a way that counts.

Figure 3.8 shows a process responsibility chart, which can be used to identify the individuals who should be involved in the process redesign. The responsibility assessment chart initially defines the as-is roles and responsibilities of the people who are involved in the new product design process. This is done by looking at the process map and listing individual process activities in the left-hand column of the chart. Each individual who touches the process is then asked to define his or her specific responsibility for the success of each activity. Responsibility levels range from "process owner" to "no responsibility." For the example shown, Alicia briefly explains why she feels responsible at the identified level. After everyone fills out the responsibility assessment chart, the findings are compiled in the responsibility assignment chart. Alicia's results are shown in column M1. With the findings recorded, everyone is aware of each other's roles and responsibilities. Candid discussion can now take place regarding how roles and responsibilities can be redefined and assigned to improve overall process performance.

Leverage Technology

Emerging technologies make it possible to do work in a new way. However, managers need to explicitly rethink process design to take advantage of new technologies. For example, information technology can expand a process to include related activities formerly performed by specialized departments.

Figure 3.8 Process Responsibility Charting

Responsibility Assessment Matrix:

Name: Alicia DeSoto
Indicate level of responsibility for process or activity success:
O = Process Owner   K = Key Contributor   S = Supportive Role   N = No Role/Responsibility

Process	Responsibility	Rationale
New Product Design		
Process Activities		
Conceptualization	N	Not involved
Team Selection	O	Team leader—new product process manager/expert
Project Evaluation	K	Team leader—represent NPD team
Project Budgeting	K	Team leader—represent NPD team
Product Design	S	Provide general guidance
Materials Specs.	N	Not involved
Process Design	S	Provide general guidance
Tooling Specs.	N	Not involved
Prototype	S	Provide general guidance
Ramp-Up	S	Provide general guidance

Responsibility Assignment Matrix:

Instructions: After each manager has completed the assessment matrix, transfer the entries into the assignment matrix. Where multiple managers have "claimed" ownership of a single process, circle the one you have selected as the single process owner.

O = Process Owner   K = Key Contributor   S = Supportive Role   N = No Role/Responsibility

Process	M1	M2	M3	M4	M5	M6	M7
New Product Design							
Process Activities							
Conceptualization	N	N	N	N	N	N	N
Team Selection	O	N	N	N	K	N	K
Project Evaluation	K	O	S	N	S	N	S
Project Budgeting	K	O	S	N	N	N	N
Product Design	S	S	N	O	O	O	N
Materials Specs.	N	S	K	O	N	N	N
Process Design	S	S	S	S	S	S	S
Tooling Specs.	N	S	K	S	O	S	S
Prototype	S	N	S	K	K	O	K
Ramp-Up	S	N	S	K	S	S	O

At Ford, the materials receiving process was redesigned to eliminate physical inspection of incoming shipments from certified suppliers. When the shipment arrives, a computer database is accessed to verify that the Bill of Lading matches the purchase order. If it does, the shipment is automatically accepted. Information technology can also bridge functional and geographic distance. At 3M, a knowledge system allows managers anywhere in the company to identify individuals working on similar projects or technologies. They can then share expertise and experiences and reduce redundant efforts. Information technology merges the efficiency of centralization with the responsiveness of decentralization.

Reimagine Systematically

Reengineering efforts have produced mixed results. One reason for less-than-hoped-for results is that system boundaries are often defined too narrowly. As a result, companies achieve dramatic improvements in individual processes only to watch overall results decline.[16] Another impediment is that too many efforts emphasize technology without accounting for the challenge inherent in bridging functional boundaries. Michael Hammer makes the following suggestions to help managers reimagine processes successfully:[17]

- First, look for role models outside your industry. When Xerox wanted to improve its order fulfillment process, it copied key elements of L.L. Bean's delivery system.
- Second, identify and defy a constraining assumption. Toyota's just-in-time production system negated the assumption that inventory is an asset; rather, it argues that inventory should be eliminated whenever possible.
- Third, make the special case into the norm.
- Fourth, rethink the following 7 dimensions of work.

Dimensions of Work	Progressive's Immediate Response Claims Handling
• *What results* (value) the work delivers	• Fast, convenient claims processing
• *Who* performs the work	• Call center representative works with a claims adjuster
• *Where* the work is performed	• On-site at the customer's location
• *When* the work is performed	• Within 9 hours of the initial claim
• *Whether* the work should be performed	• Yes—claims processing drives customer satisfaction
• *What information* the work employs	• Accurate repair costs for the vehicle in the specific market
• *How* thoroughly the work is performed	• Repair costs are a major expense; therefore, damage estimates must be complete and accurate

Progressive's immediate response claims-handling process discussed at the beginning of the chapter exemplifies the reimagination process.

CONCLUSION

A few years ago, Mike Wells, vice president of logistics at Hershey, commented, "If you ask me what I stay awake at night thinking about, its cross-functional processes." Making the move from functional organizations to process-driven companies continues to cause insomnia, especially as managers ponder Mike Well's follow-up comment, "The challenge is to become more process focused while maintaining functional expertise." His point—distinctive processes built on functional excellence constitute the foundation for competitive success.

Michael Hammer has claimed that the twenty-first-century corporation will be built on processes not departments.[18] In an effort to streamline customer service, American Express financial advisors reconfigured 180 divisions into 45 "clusters" led by process owners.[19] At GE Medical Systems, process integration created some unique organizational units, including a unit headed by a vice president of global sourcing and order remittance.[20] At these and other companies, the transition from function to process is driven by imagination, experimentation, and systems analysis. As companies become proficient at process management, they will be prepared for more extensive SC integration. After all, SCM is really just process management extended across company boundaries.

SUMMARY OF KEY POINTS

1. Meeting customer expectations requires a shift from a functional organization to a process orientation. Excellent execution requires effective cooperation across functional departments.
2. Functional thinking is an artifact of traditional organizational structures and cultures. Many business practices including hiring and training practices perpetuate a functional mind-set.
3. Every valued process consists of a set of identifiable flows and value-added activities. Three distinct flows define each process: an information flow, a physical flow, and a financial flow.
4. The requirements for systems thinking are (a) a holistic view of the system, (b) access to accurate information, (c) cross-functional teamwork, (d) supportive measurement, and (e) rigorous systems analysis.
5. Systems analysis consists of the following steps: (a) establish a core goal, (b) define the system boundaries, (c) determine interrelationships, (d) define information requirements, (e) perform trade-off analysis, and (f) evaluate system constraints.
6. A process view of the company links systems thinking to strategy so that all of the company's functional and resource decisions are consistently focused on achieving the company's most important objectives.
7. Process reengineering is the radical redesign of business processes. Systems thinking, modern information technology, and imagination make it possible to change the way that work is done.
8. One of the most serious challenges is to achieve process integration's agility and differentiation without losing functional expertise. Both are needed to win a global battle for the customer's loyalty.

REVIEW EXERCISES

1. Explain why companies have struggled to integrate processes despite the fact that managers have been calling for greater cross-functional collaboration for almost 50 years.
2. Diagram a value-added process other than materials acquisition or new product development. Discuss the critical flows. Identify the critical value-added activities and who performs them.

3. Explain the underlying idea behind systems thinking. Identify and describe two instances where systems thinking has led to either superior decision making or to a unique business model.
4. List the steps involved in systems analysis. Which step do you think is the most neglected? Why?
5. Given the ability of systems thinking to enhance competitiveness, explain why companies haven't made systems thinking their standard decision-making approach. What would you do to overcome these issues?
6. Identify a company that uses either a cost leadership or a differentiation strategy. Describe the company's value propositions. Identify its core competencies. Using Figure 3.6, identify one decision for each cell in the function/resource matrix that would support the company's strategy. How do information sharing and performance measurement support the strategy?
7. Looking at Figure 3.8, what potential problems do you see? *Hint:* Identify the process owner for each activity in the new product design process.
8. Define process reengineering. Identify one process that you are aware of that needs to be reengineered. Describe the critical steps that need to be performed to reengineer this process.

Case　Global Semiconductor's Market Share Slide

Tim Thomas, director of logistics at Global Semiconductor, Inc., sighed deeply as he hung up the phone. It was 2:50 P.M. on Wednesday, and Kindra Alexander, vice president of marketing, had called to share the latest sales numbers. They weren't good. Worldwide sales had declined for the fifth straight quarter. Worse yet, Global Semiconductor (GSI) had lost market share to each of its major rivals. Something needed to be done soon to shorten delivery times to customers.

Kindra had grilled Tim about logistics' intended response to marketing's request for faster order fulfillment. She wanted to know when marketing could promise more competitive delivery times. Tim hated to admit it, but logistics didn't have a plan yet. GSI's worldwide manufacturing and distribution networks simply weren't designed to provide the level of customer responsiveness that marketing was requesting. Every option that the logistics task force had looked at had generated heated debate and serious opposition. Tim had been forced to stall, promising Kindra that he would get "something" to her soon. Tim knew he couldn't buy much more time. In fact, Tim hoped that his 3:00 P.M. meeting with the logistics task force would provide some of the answers Kindra was looking for. As Tim headed for the meeting, he reviewed the situation.

Global Semiconductor was a perennial powerhouse in the semiconductor industry. Until 2 years ago, the future had looked bright. GSI had a recognized brand, offered state-of-the-art technology, and maintained excellent customer relationships. Almost overnight, however, the rules had changed. Excess global capacity had led an Asian rival to drop prices by 30 percent and to cut delivery times in half. Other industry players quickly followed, leaving GSI with a serious competitive quandary. Although it could match the lower price, it couldn't meet the standard for delivery—at least not profitably. A market research study revealed that rapid delivery really was the critical buying criterion for GSI's major customers. This finding complicated Tim's life because logistics was given the mandate to cut lead times in half without increasing costs. Tim and his task force quickly discovered that GSI's worldwide network of manufacturing and distribution facilities simply could not perform at the requested service and cost levels. The network was designed to meet regional needs via local warehousing and motor transportation. As Tim entered the conference room, he said, "The time for debate is over. Our credibility is on the line. We need to cut our delivery cycles in half. How are we going to do it? And do it without increasing logistics costs? I'm all ears. Talk to me!"

Luke Stahely, GSI's warehousing manager, was the first to speak up, saying, "We've looked at the simple alternatives. I think its time to evaluate our network configuration. I've crunched a few numbers, and I think we could dramatically reduce lead times by using fewer warehouses that are part of an information-connected network that makes transshipment possible."

Jack Ramsey, GSI's inventory manager, quickly agreed, noting that, "Fewer warehouses means less redundant inventory and a lower risk of stockouts. One of our challenges has been shipping complete orders. Entire orders often sit for days, waiting for manufacturing to get us a shipment of a critical SKU. This dwell time kills our delivery times."

"And we have to expedite a lot of product, which really hits our transportation budget," added Sherri

Dale, GSI's transportation manager. "Of course, any change in number or location of warehouses will have a huge impact on our transportation planning. Luke, have you considered the impact on transportation costs?"

"You're right, Sherri. There would definitely be an impact. I have no idea what it would be, but I'm sure that rationalizing our DCs is the way to go," Luke replied.

"Have you given any thought to getting out of the distribution business altogether?" interjected Tamara Clark, GSI's purchasing manager. "FedEx or UPS might beat our delivery times at a lower overall cost to us. That would be the ultimate DC rationalization!"

"That's a radical idea, Tamara. Do you really think a third party could maintain our customer relationships if we outsource distribution? I question whether a third party would have our best interests at heart," mused Jack.

Randy Johns, GSI's packaging manager, joined the discussion, saying, "Your points are valid, Jack. We've always been suspicious of outsourcing, but we haven't been able to come up with a better option. We really need to forget about protecting our own turf and look at the really tough options."

Sherri wondered out loud, "Are we, each of us, truly ready to live with the consequences of some of these decisions? I know we're under pressure to do something, but the ideas on the table are filled with risk. GSI hasn't always rewarded risk taking."

Tim decided it was time to chime in. Responding first to Sherri's observation, he said, "Sherri, unfortunately, that's true. However, neither our customers nor the competition are leaving us an easy way out. Several ideas merit consideration: outsourcing, DC rationalization, and other possibilities like switching transportation modes or integrating information systems with key customers. We've avoided considering these options because they threaten the way we do business. I need a workable plan to present to Kindra at the end of the month. We need some hard numbers. Luke, how many warehouses should we have and where should they be located? Sherri, Jack, what does this option mean for each of you? Tamara, what about outsourcing? Is it a real option? Time is running out! Let's go to work!"

CASE QUESTIONS

1. What do you think about the task force's conversation? Are there other options that merit attention? What are the pros and cons of each? Which option would you pursue?
2. What types of analysis should be performed? What behavioral issues threaten to derail efforts to radically improve GSI's customer responsiveness?
3. Is this a good opportunity for process reengineering? Why or why not?

ENDNOTES

1. Forrester, J. W. (1958, July–August). Industrial dynamics: A major breakthrough for decision makers. *Harvard Business Review, 38,* 37–66.
2. Jacob, R. (1995, April 3). The Struggle to Create an Organization for the 21st Century. *Fortune,* 90–97.
3. Hammer, M. (2004). Deep change. *Harvard Business Review, 82*(4), 84–93.
4. Ibid. # 3.
5. Kuglin, F. A. (1998). *Customer-centered supply chain management.* New York: AMACOM.
6. Blackwell, R. D. (1997). *From mind to market: Reinventing the retail supply chain.* New York: Harper Business.
7. Dehoratius, N., Raman, A., & Ton, Z. (2001). The Achilles heel of supply chain management. *Harvard Business Review, 79*(5), 25–27.
8. Fawcett, S. E., & Magnan, G. N. (2001). *Achieving world-class supply chain alignment: Benefits, barriers, and bridges.* Phoenix: National Association of Purchasing Management.
9. Nelson, D., Mayo, R., & Moody, P. E. (1998). *Powered by Honda.* New York: John Wiley & Sons, Inc.
10. Stalk, G., Evans, P., & Schulman, L. E. (1992). Competing on capabilities: The new rules of corporate strategy. *Harvard Business Review, 70*(2), 57–69.
11. Porter, M. (1980). *Competitive strategy.* New York: The Free Press.
12. Hayes, R., Wheelwright, S. C., & Clark, K. B. (1988). *Dynamic manufacturing: Creating the learning organization.* New York: The Free Press.
13. Jones, D. (2004, June 14). How productivity is measured. *USA Today.*
14. Hammer, M. (1990). Reengineering work: Don't automate, obliterate. *Harvard Business Review, 68*(4), 104–131.
15. Ibid. # 3.
16. Hall, G., Rosenthal, J., & Wade, J. (1993). How to make reengineering really work. *Harvard Business Review, 71*(5), 119–131.
17. Ibid. # 2.
18. Ibid. # 14.
19. Jacob, R., Rao, R. M., & Musi, V. J. (1995, April 3). The struggle to create an organization. *Fortune,* pp. 90–97.
20. Ibid. # 19.

Supplement C

Decision Making Under Uncertainty

The transformation from a functional organization to a process-driven company is challenging under the best of circumstances. One of the biggest hurdles is the uncertainty introduced by the transformation. As the chapter's closing case ("Global Semiconductor's Market Share Slide") illustrated, managers seldom know exactly how to redesign processes. The consequences and trade-offs of many decisions are likewise unknown. These realities introduce tremendous amounts of uncertainty to the SC decision-making environment. In fact, so many SC decisions involve the unknown that it might be fair to say that SCM is decision making under uncertainty.

SC managers should therefore include in their problem-solving toolbox some tools such as **expected value analysis** and **decisions trees** to help them cope with uncertainty. This class of tools is often called *probabilistic decision making*. If you don't have a strong background in probabilistic decision making, the following tutorial will help you understand the basics of decision making under uncertainty.

The Nature of Uncertainty

People usually don't have perfect information when making decisions. Most people don't have crystal balls that allow them to accurately predict what the future holds. The same holds true for business managers—the lack of perfect information creates uncertainty. Decision making within functional areas is difficult enough because of this uncertainty and the risk it introduces. Systems thinking, at least initially, adds uncertainty because it introduces change. As boundaries are redefined, interrelationships determined, and trade-offs evaluated, new ideas and options emerge. Most of these will change the decision-making environment in ways that may be hard to evaluate. This brings additional uncertainties and risks that need to be considered. As mentioned in the chapter, traditional functional thinking can lead to decisions that optimize individual activities at the expense of overall system performance. Learning how to incorporate cross-functional uncertainties, risks, and trade-offs into the

decision-making process is an important skill for supply chain managers.

One particular risk involves uncertainty about what the future holds. Suppose, for example, that after some careful research, several meetings, and lots of cross-functional interaction and discussion, the team at Global Semiconductors has identified three potential solutions to its dilemma: (1) The company could redesign its logistics network by changing the location and number of its distribution centers at a cost of $500,000; (2) the company could outsource its warehousing and transportation needs to a third-party logistics company (3PL) at a cost of $700,000 for the next 10 years; or (3) the company could start using airplanes rather than trucks to ship its products at a cost of $900,000 for the next 10 years. One of the risks of outsourcing the warehousing and transportation is that the 3PL might not be able to handle the large quantities that would be required. If the outsourcing is unsuccessful, it will cost Global Semiconductors another $200,000 to shift the warehousing and transportation to another 3PL or to bring the warehousing and transportation back within its organization. Another factor that needs to be considered is Global Semiconductor's share of the market. The team has determined that there are three possible outcomes concerning Global Semiconductor's sales: (1) They could increase by 20 percent; (2) they could remain the same; or (3) they could decrease by 20 percent. An increase in sales would mean an extra $ 1.2 million in revenue for the company. A decrease in sales would lead to a $1.0 million decrease in revenue for the company; constant sales would have no effect on revenues.

A decision tree can be useful for organizing this information and assessing the decisions that need to be made. Figure C.1 shows a decision tree for the Global Semiconductor company example. Square nodes in the decision tree represent decision points where the company must choose between existing alternatives. The branches emanating from these nodes represent the various alternatives for that particular decision. Circular nodes represent uncertain events. The branches stemming from these nodes represent the possible outcomes

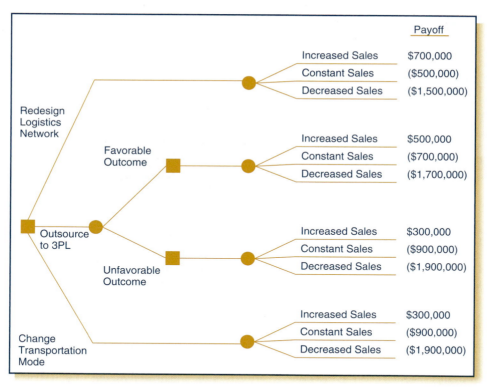

	Payoff
Increased Sales	$700,000
Constant Sales	($500,000)
Decreased Sales	($1,500,000)
Increased Sales	$500,000
Constant Sales	($700,000)
Decreased Sales	($1,700,000)
Increased Sales	$300,000
Constant Sales	($900,000)
Decreased Sales	($1,900,000)
Increased Sales	$300,000
Constant Sales	($900,000)
Decreased Sales	($1,900,000)

Redesign Logistics Network

Favorable Outcome

Outsource to 3PL

Unfavorable Outcome

Change Transportation Mode

Figure C.1 Decision Tree

or states of nature that pertain to the selected alternative. The payoff for redesigning the logistics network if sales increase is calculated by subtracting the additional costs that would be incurred ($500,000) from the additional revenues that would be received ($1.2 million) to arrive at the $700,000 payoff.

The information in Figure C.1 is useful for mapping out the various decisions that can be made; however, it should be interpreted with caution. Obviously, the largest payoff is associated with redesigning the logistics network, if sales increase. However, the company is unsure whether sales are going to increase or not.

A better way to approach the problem would be to assign probabilities to the various events occurring based on information collected from various functional areas. Suppose that if the logistics network is redesigned there is a 25 percent chance that sales will increase, a 50 percent chance that sales will remain constant, and a 25 percent chance that sales will decrease in the future. Suppose that because of the difficulties

often associated with outsourcing important customer service-related processes, there is a 50 percent chance that sales will remain constant, a 15 percent chance that sales will increase, and a 35 percent chance that sales will decline if the outsourcing route is chosen. Suppose also that there is a 50/50 chance that outsourcing the warehousing and transportation will be unsuccessful. Also suppose that if the transportation mode is change that there is a 60 percent chance that sales will increase, a 20 percent chance that sales will remain the same and only a 20 percent chance that sales will decline. This probability information is included in Figure C.2.

With this information in the decision tree, we can now calculate expected values for each of the circular nodes and determine which initial decision has the highest expected payoff. This is done by starting at the right side of the diagram and working toward the left. Calculate the expected values for the circular nodes on the right side of the diagram by multiplying the payoff amounts by the probabilities associated with those payoff amounts and adding those values together.

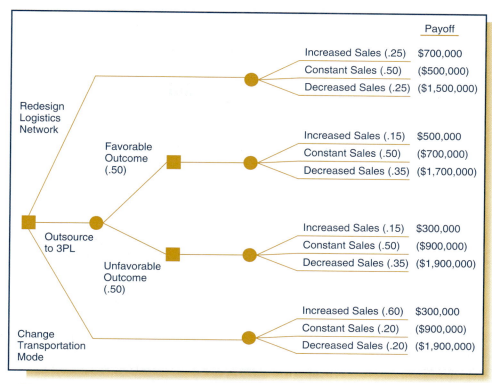

Figure C.2 Decision Tree with Probabilities

For example, the expected value for redesigning the logistics network = .25(700,000) + .50(−$500,000) + .25(−1,500,000) = $−450,000. These expected values can be written next to the circular nodes in the diagram (see Figure C.3).

Next, continue working your way left on the diagram to the next decision node associated with a circular node. After calculating the expected value of the circular nodes, determine which alternative has the highest payoff at that decision node. You can note this on the diagram by crossing out the alternative with the lower expected payoff. Continue to move from right to left using that alternative and its payoff when calculating the expected payoff for the next circular node to the left.

In this case, it appears as though changing the transportation mode has the highest expected value, or in this case the lowest total cost. However, this expected value does not mean that changing the transportation mode will only cost $380,000. The payoff in this case will either be $300,000, $−900,000, or $−1,900,000 depending on what happens to sales.

Expected values are only one way of making decisions using decision trees.

In this case, and in many other business decisions, sensitivity analysis should be performed to see how changes in the values or probabilities used in the decision affect the outcome of the decision. For example, suppose that the cost of redesigning the logistics network is decreased from $500,000 to $300,000. What impact would this have on the initial decision? Or, alternatively, suppose that new technology was developed that could increase the probability of a successful outcome from the outsourcing decision. Or suppose that a new sales forecasting method could more accurately predict the effect of these changes on sales. When the decision result is affected by small changes in the input information, the decision is not very robust. If, on the other hand, major changes in the input information do not change the resulting decision, the decision is referred to as being robust. Sensitivity analysis helps determine the robustness of the decision being made. Managers have more confidence in the resulting decision when their analysis is robust.

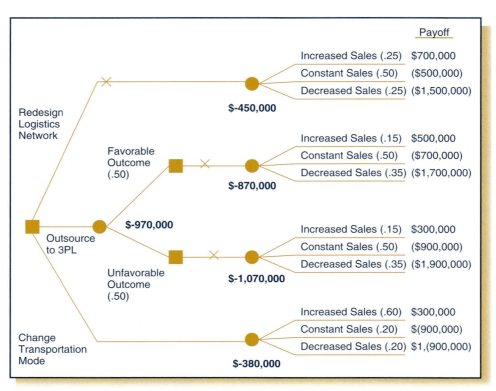

Figure C.3 Decision Tree with Expected Values

EXERCISES

1. Construct a basic decision tree for a situation that has two alternatives (1 and 2) and two possible states of nature (A and B). The payoff and probability information for each of the states of nature are given in the following table:

Alternative	State of Nature	
	A	B
Alternative 1	$67,000 (.25)	$25,000 (.75)
Alternative 2	$40,000 (.80)	$10,000 (.20)

Which alternative would you select, based on the expected values of the alternatives?

2. Bob Jones runs an umbrella store in Portland, Oregon. He places his orders with suppliers about 6 months before the rainy season, which usually begins in October. The more it rains, the more umbrellas he usually sells during the season. The local weather station predicts that there is a 60 percent chance of a lot of rain, a 15 percent chance of moderate rain, and a 25 percent chance of very little rain this season. Bob needs to decide what size of an order to place with his supplier for the upcoming rainy season. The following table shows the payoff amounts of the various alternatives.

Size of Order	Rainfall		
	Little	Moderate	A lot
Small	3	3	3
Medium	3	6	6
Large	3	6	9

Based on this information, which size of order would you recommend that Bob make?

3. A candy factory received an order for 200 peppermint candy canes. The factory produces these candy canes on a specialized machine. The factory sells the candy canes for $1 each. Candy canes that are produced correctly by the machine cost the factory $.80 to make. Candy canes that need to be run through the machine a second time, because of a defect, cost the factory an extra $0.35.

Various adjustments can be made to the machine before the candy canes are produced. The following table outlines the percentage of defective candy canes and the probabilities associated with these defective percentages for three types of adjustments: (1) no adjustment, (2) minor adjustment, and (3) major adjustment.

| | Probabilities | | |
Defective	No Adjustment	Minor Adjustment	Major Adjustment
1 percent	50%	80%	95%
2 percent	30%	10%	5%
3 percent	12%	10%	0%
5 percent	8%	0%	0%

Minor adjustments cost the factory $4.20. Major adjustments cost the factor $10.00. Based on this information, which adjustment policy maximizes the factory's profit on this order?

4. How would your answer to exercise 3 change if the order was for 100 peppermint candy canes? How about for 500 peppermint candy canes? What if the cost of the minor adjustment increased to $6.00? What if the cost of the major adjustment decreased to $8.00? Based on this information, how robust was your original analysis and decision?

5. Construct a decision tree for a decision that you face at work or in your personal life.

WEB EXERCISES

1. Go to www.decisiontoolpak.com or www.palisade.com/html/ptree.asp and download the free trial version decision tree add-in for Excel from these sites. Experiment with these add-ins using the exercises listed earlier.

2. Use the Internet to come up with at least three different decisions where companies can utilize decision tree analysis. Construct basic decision trees for these decisions that show the basic alternatives as well as the various conditions that may be present.

3. Go to www.decisionframeworks.com/Making Decisions.pdf and read this document about decisions in the oil and gas industry.

Chapter 4

The New Product Development Process: Managing the Idea Infrastructure

How does my company view innovation? Can I help it use the new product process to profitably create value?

The Supply Chain Road Map

Who are we?

Business Purpose

Chapter 1: SC Strategy
- What is SCM?
- How does it fit our strategy?

Chapter 2: Customer Fulfillment
- Who are our customers?
- Can SCM deliver real value?

Chapter 3: Process Thinking
- Do we have a functional, silo culture?
- Can we manage across functions?

Chapter 4: New Product Process
- **Do we know how to innovate?**
- **Can we create great products?**

Chapter 5: Fulfillment Process
- Are our operations efficient?
- Can we buy/make/deliver?

After reading this chapter, you will be able to:

1. Describe the new product development process and how it affects company and SC success.
2. List the risks involved in the new product process. Explain how to mitigate these risks.
3. Describe the marketing process and discuss its role in the new product process.
4. Define target costing and explain its role in developing new products and services.
5. Describe the finance process and discuss its role in the new product process.
6. Discuss EVA, profitability, and cash flow as key financial metrics for organizations.

Opening Story: Frozen Despair

Charlene was tired. She had not expected to return from her honeymoon to be sent immediately to Europe and then out again to help a domestic client resolve a crisis. Fortunately, the problem seemed routine and shouldn't require more than a few days on the road. The client company, Frozen Delight, had experienced several new product disappointments: new products that customers didn't embrace or that weren't profitable. With the tight freezer space allotted in groceries, and average grocery store chain profit margins of 1 to 2 percent, Frozen Delight could not continue to disappoint and expect the grocery chains to stock its products. Further, Frozen Delight risked its slotting fees, which are the fixed charges that manufacturers often pay grocery chains for each store that provides shelf space for an additional product. When a new product does not meet sales expectations, the grocer can replace it with a different product, with no refund of the slotting fees.

When Charlene met her client, Mr. Dan Fritz, president and founder of Frozen Delight, on a hot afternoon in Phoenix, he was anything but delighted. He paced the room, agitated. "Charlene, I am infuriated with our marketing department. They promised me that this latest product would be a success. But customers aren't buying it. They don't seem to like, 'moo-moo chocolate mango.' I don't know how they could let me down this way. We paid for consumer focus groups, we paid for test markets . . . it seemed perfect. Here, try some." Mr. Fritz turned to the freezer behind his large desk and got out a pint of the moo-moo mango and a spoon, handing them to Charlene. It was all she could do not to groan. She had just eaten lunch and was not a fan of premium, high-fat ice cream. Oh, well—all part of the job. She would work out a bit longer tomorrow. She opened the lid, and dug in. Ugh! It wasn't the silky-smooth, high-fat taste she expected. There was some graininess to the chocolate; it just wasn't quite right.

Dan's eyes met hers. "See? See what I mean? Your reaction should have been, 'Mmmmm,' or maybe a sigh. Not a look of shock and disappointment. Anyway, the marketing folks blame finance for making the new product group cut the cost and the quality of the ingredients. Marketing wanted a product that the consumers were dying to buy. The finance folks say that there is no point in selling unprofitable products, like our fabulously popular Mesquite Mélange. We lose a few cents on every pint that we sell! They're both right. But we have to find some middle ground and work together so that we can produce products that customers will flock to the freezer case to buy *and* we can make money on. That's where you come in, Charlene. We need help looking at our new product development process."

Charlene smiled. Getting people to work together was her forte. The circumstances reminded her of her husband Doug's situation in trying to get people at his company actively engaged in SCM. "When do I get to talk to all of the players involved?" Charlene asked Dan. "I've got meetings set up starting in just a few minutes with marketing, then finance, and you'll finish with the new product team. And here . . . ," Dan extended his hand toward the ice cream Charlene was holding. "Let me take that stuff away. I just wanted you to experience it."

Charlene needed to gather her thoughts quickly and develop the right questions to make effective use of her interviews with each of these groups. She knew that there would be no clear bad guy in this situation. The issues would be familiar: poor communication, not getting the right people involved at the right time, conflicting goals, and so on.

Consider As You Read:

1. If you were in Charlene's situation, what questions would you ask marketing, finance, and new product development?
2. What do you think the organization structure, reporting relationships, and reward systems at Frozen Delight look like? Are these issues relevant to what is happening here? Why or why not?
3. What are some of the mechanisms within the organization that can be used to help these functions, and others within the company, work more closely toward common goals?

The only entity that puts money into the supply chain is the end customer. Until that customer decides to buy a product for his final usage, the rest of us are all shuffling money back and forth among the various supply-chain members.

—JEFF TRIMMER, DAIMLERCHRYSLER[1]

INTRODUCTION

The development of viable, profitable, customer-pleasing new products and services is a challenge for all companies. It is a challenge that seems to be growing as consumer tastes shift more quickly and information on new styles, technologies, and options become available rapidly and ubiquitously on television and the Internet. Yet it is a challenge that is more and more important to meet. New product development costs are high. A company cannot ride forever on its reputation for past success. It needs to continue to deliver, or its reputation will fall off rapidly.

We are all familiar with companies who had winning products, failed to innovate, and suffered decline. Atari wrote the book on home video games in the early to mid-1980s and was obliterated later by Nintendo's superior technology, which in turn was overshadowed by Sony's PlayStation. Wang was the name in office word processing, but failed to see the real threat of multipurpose personal computers in time to adapt. Motorola owned the cell phone market in the early to mid-1990s, but failed to respond to customer demands for digital technology and has since been far surpassed in market share by Nokia. Nokia was a paper company until it merged with Finnish Rubber Works and Finnish Cable Works in 1967.[2] Today, Nokia is ranked as the world's sixth-most valuable brand, because Nokia has met or surpassed customer expectations.[3] Motorola, on the other hand, was founded in 1930 and has been making mobile radios since the 1930s.[4] However, it fell behind on the technology curve and began disappointing consumers in the mid-1990s. It currently ranks number 74 among the top 100 most valuable global brands.[5]

As important as it is, few companies have mastered the new product development process. Each step of the new product development process is fraught with risk. Experts say that more than 9 out of every 10 new products introduced fail. And new product development is expensive. For example, it costs approximately $30 million to develop a new ASIC (application-specific integrated circuit). In order to justify this expense, a target market size of around a billion dollars is needed.[6]

At the heart of the new product development process is the customer satisfaction cycle, as illustrated in Figure 4.1. The customer satisfaction cycle shows that new product development is truly a cross-functional process, requiring extensive collaboration throughout a company. Specifically, marketing works with potential customers to identify customer needs, R&D conceptualizes and develops a product, and finance verifies that the product is viable; that is, that it will provide an adequate return on invested capital. How a company defines these activities and then organizes to carry them out influences its success as an innovator. Some companies continue to manage innovation functionally. Others have adopted cross-functional teams. SC leaders rely heavily on a teaming approach that includes customers and suppliers early in the process. They often give the new product team responsibility for the entire customer satisfaction cycle.

After presenting risk management issues in new product development, the remainder of this chapter will focus on the four steps of the customer satisfaction cycle.

- *Step 1:* Get into the mind of the customer to identify and articulate current and future needs.
- *Step 2:* Conceptualize and develop the new product to meet customer needs better than existing options.

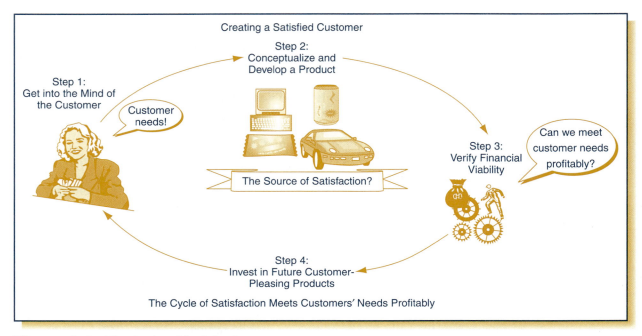

Figure 4.1   The Cycle of Satisfaction

- *Step 3:* Verify the financial viability of the new product. That is, determine how the product can be developed, produced, and delivered profitably.
- *Step 4:* Continue the cycle by continuously investing in future customer-pleasing products and services.

We will show how marketing, R&D, and finance must work together as part of an integrated process to bring profitable product concepts to life and satisfy customer needs.

MITIGATING RISK IN NEW PRODUCT DEVELOPMENT

The challenges of new product development continue to grow. One challenge is time compression. Companies like Intel have seen their product life cycles compress from 4 or 5 years to 4 or 5 months. Good ideas for the next generation of products must be in the pipeline before the current good idea is even launched. This creates extreme pressure to get products out to market now, perhaps at the expense of higher cost or risk. However, with short product life cycles, there is even less time to fix problems once the product is launched. The organization may completely miss the window of opportunity.

A second major challenge is cost. New product or service development is expensive, as is the cost of new product or service failure. Gillette spent $700 million on R&D to create its Mach III razor. This didn't include promotional expenses, factory changes, qualifying suppliers, and other critical activities.[7] Total development and introduction costs exceeded $1 billion. Honeywell's Engine Division estimates that it costs them about $1 million a week to develop a new product. Speeding the development time and lowering the risk of failure are essential to recovering this investment.

Formalized Risk Management

The first critical step in managing and controlling risk is to recognize what risks exist in a situation. For examples, car insurance providers have learned from experience that key risk factors in auto claims include the driver's age, driving record, type of car, and annual mileage driven. Companies likewise need to identify the key risks in their supply chains and reduce those risks before a new product or service is introduced.

Intel has developed an excellent, formalized risk management process for new product development. Because of its short product life cycles and continuous need to introduce new products that meet or exceed market expectations, this is a critical capability at Intel. A commodity manager takes ownership for the risk management process, overseeing risk assessment, completing a risk scorecard, and reporting results. Intel analyzes 8 risk factors:

- Design
- Cost
- Legal issues
- Supply availability
- Manufacturability
- Quality
- Supply base
- Environmental, health, and safety impacts

The risk factors for "supply availability" become part of risk matrix, as shown in Table 4.1, to enable systematic assessment. There is a similarly detailed matrix for each of the other 7 risk factors. Across the top, there is a scale of 5 to 1, where 5 represents the highest risk level (a "showstopper") and 1 represents the minimum risk level possible (or that a supplier is "qualified"). There are also gradations in between. The types of availability risk are listed on the left side of the matrix, with a definition of what qualifies for each level of risk, 1–5, listed in the matrix. For example, for the risk factor *technologically capable,* a level-5 risk occurs when the industry is moving toward a different standard than the technology chosen. This would be a "showstopper" in that the project would not proceed without lowering the risk level, or getting top management approval to continue down this high-risk path.

To add to the objectivity of the risk assessment, a cross-functional team, rather than an individual, gathers data for each risk element and assigns a risk score. Risk reduction plans are developed and documented, and a clear owner is designated for each risk reduction plan. Specific timetables are established for achieving progress. Progress is reported regularly to the product development team, and the overall project risk is reported to top management, with any showstoppers highlighted.[8] A format like that in Table 4.1 is used for scoring, reporting, and tracking risk, with space added for each risk element to indicate current risk level, action plan, owner, and reduction timetable. This is done for all 8 risk factors. Since implementing this system, Intel has virtually eliminated surprises in its new product introductions, recognizing and reducing or eliminating risk before it occurs. Although this risk assessment approach represents a large investment of time, it is one that has a very high payoff.

Going beyond formal risk assessment, companies are experimenting with a variety of approaches to help reduce the technical and SC risks of new product development and introduction. Four of these are briefly discussed here.

Table 4.1 Intel's Scorecard for Availability Risk

RISK FACTOR: AVAILABILITY	SHOWSTOPPER 5	4	3	2	QUALIFIED 1
Incoming Materials	No source identified	Raw material scarcity	Sole sourced, with multiple production operations in close proximity	Sole sourced, with multiple production operations separated by 50 miles	Multiple sources with no supply shortages
Source Process Capability	Unknown, new technology/ supplier	Manufacturing capability only proven on pilot scale	Manufacturing or services capability demonstrated for similar material	Date-demonstrated process is in specification	Source process is stable and capable
Volume Capacity	Availability requirements not supported with existing sources	Suppliers identified; plans to support volumes not in place	Capacity plans developed by supplier and implementation in process	Capacity mostly in place; no known issues	Capacity fully in place
Technologically Capable	Industry moving toward different "standard"	Industry movement toward different "standards" known with no plans to address	Industry movement toward new "standard" understood with plans to address	Industry adopting multiple "standards"	Technology chosen is "standard"
Supplier Lead Time	No quick turn capability exists from supplier	Quick turn capability for new design is greater than lead time	Supplier lead-term reduction plans on track	Quick turn capability for new design lead time or meets goals	Supplier and supplier tooling meets lead-time goals

Early Involvement of Critical Supply Chain Players

The use of new product development (NPD) teams reduces the risk that comes from poor communication. Because costly misunderstandings often occur with upstream suppliers, the NPD team should include key suppliers of inputs and services. Their involvement should begin very early in the process, before irreversible design and distribution decisions have been made. This is referred to as **early supplier involvement, or ESI**. The firm chooses external suppliers, logistics providers, distributors, and others based on their expertise. Aside from improving communication, inviting these SC members to participate on the NPD team provides important competitive benefits. These SC members may have direct customer feedback, or be aware of trends in technology or demand that could prevent costly mistakes and create a competitive advantage.

For example, in the relationship between Phelps Dodge Mining Corporation and Michelin Tire, Michelin provides Phelps Dodge with its latest tire technology for use at

Phelps Dodge mines. In turn, Phelps Dodge gives Michelin access to the tires while in use, so that Michelin can see how they perform under various conditions and provide continuous improvement. Michelin, the tire expert, keeps Phelps Dodge up to date on the latest products and substitutes. Both companies benefit. The cooperation streamlines the development process and enhances future products.

Due, at least in part, to the need for quick, early involvement of competent suppliers in new product and service development and rollout, companies like Honda, Harley-Davidson, Toyota, and General Mills seek long-term relationships with key suppliers. Working together over a sustained time period helps them get to know their suppliers' capabilities and risk factors. Suppliers also improve their understanding of their customers' needs. Mutual trust is built and the NPD process can proceed with lower risk as well as greater confidence.

Core Competencies

Risk is reduced when expertise is identified and applied. By bringing together the expertise that exists throughout the company as well as up and down the supply chain, NPD risk can be mitigated. This also implies that companies stay within their competency zone during the NPD process. As part of the design process, it is important for each company to know what it is good at, what its core competencies are, and where it needs help and should outsource. Even if it is not good at something today, it may need to invest resources in becoming good in those areas where customers perceive important value. A company should never outsource its core competency or activities that support it. Making the wrong decision on what to do internally versus what to outsource can make or break a company.

Think of the classic example of IBM's outsourcing its software to Microsoft. In the early to mid-1990s, when Microsoft was surpassing IBM on profits from the PC market, IBM attempted to introduce its own operating system, OS2. It failed, at least in part, because businesses were already entrenched in the Microsoft Windows platform. A few years later, IBM was actually losing money in the PC market. In 2005, IBM sold its PC manufacturing business to Lenovo, a Chinese firm. It continues to purchase many of the IBM-branded PCs and laptops from Lenovo.[9] Core competencies and outsourcing are discussed in more depth in Chapter 8.

"Design for" Considerations

Explicitly focusing on downstream requirements can take risk out of the development and introduction process. Many "design for" issues should be considered when a company is designing its products and services. These include issues such as design for manufacturability, design for purchasing, design for logistics, design for environment, design for disassembly, and so on. Each of these design-for initiatives entails just what it sounds like: considering the impact of the design on how easy it will be to (1) manufacture the product, (2) support the product using the existing supply base, (3) distribute the product through the chain, (4) protect the environment, and (5) take the product apart for recycling and reuse of parts. Design for reuse is another initiative, in which the organization tries to use existing parts and specifications wherever possible. Why would it do that? To reduce the risk, cost, and time associated with developing and qualifying a new part or supplier. Design for reuse represents the realization by many organizations that all change does not represent true innovation or improvement. Rather, change can become a "habit" that does not add value, but adds unnecessary complexity and risk.

Modular Versus Integral Product Design

Modular products are ones that can be manufactured in "pieces and parts" by a variety of sources and then assembled. Modularity is facilitated by standardization and invites the opportunity for part substitution and outsourcing. This works well if a company is planning on relying on outside suppliers and standard technology for much of its product, reducing the risk of dependence on sole sources or proprietary technology. Cars are becoming more and more modular, as we can opt for limited features, and buy our sound system, spoiler, and other amenities in the aftermarket. When we have our car repaired, we can often opt for original equipment manufacturer (OEM) parts, or "generic" substitutes. Although modular products may reduce the risk of supplier dependence and create more options for the consumer, there is greater opportunity for niche competitors to enter the market to excel in a certain module.

For example, the original IBM PC became a modular product, with companies such as Intel, Microsoft, and Seagate selling "parts" and allowing customers to upgrade their PCs without buying new ones. Apple, on the other hand, designed an integral product in its Macintosh computers. If a customer wants to modify her Mac, she must buy the parts from Apple. There are fewer options and less competition. Both modular and integral approaches have their risks and rewards. Though the IBM or "Wintel" platform has captured the lion's share of the PC market, IBM has not profited. Apple has an integrated niche strategy, focusing more on publishing, graphic design, and the creative market. Yet Apple has really controlled the direction and future of its product. The downside: Apple has a very small, but loyal following, commanding less than 5 percent of the market share for PCs.

MARKETING AND THE CRITICALITY OF THE CUSTOMER

The first step in the cycle of satisfaction is to get into the mind of the customer to identify customer needs and desires. This is marketing's specialty. Marketing brings the voice, the mind, and the heart of the customer into the company where the customer's desires are translated into viable, profitable products and services. How do companies continue to win customers year after year? How do newcomers steal customers from other companies? The answers lie in effective marketing, which focuses on understanding customers' current needs while seeking to identify and articulate their future wants. As taught in any basic marketing class, the marketing mix is made up of four Ps: product, price, place, and promotion. These four Ps must complement each other to delight the customer, purchase after purchase, year after year.

- *Place* deals with having the product where it is needed and when it is needed, and relies heavily on logistics.
- *Promotion* deals with effective advertising and sales techniques to increase the visibility and perceived desirability of the product.
- The notion of *product* has expanded beyond the physical good to encompass intangibles and services that satisfy customer needs.[10] Thus, when we use the term *product*, we refer to both goods and services unless we specify either goods or services.
- *Price* focuses on determining how much value a customer places on satisfying a need.

Some people have added a fifth *P*, **product positioning**. Marketers may position a product through promotion and product design to serve the specific needs of a market segment. The focus in this chapter is on product development, pricing, and positioning. That is, we focus on creating a product that addresses unmet needs and pricing it so the customer sees the product as a good value. This is really what the NPD process is all about—creating customer value.

Marketing is an increasingly complex task. The marketing process begins with understanding the organization's goals, strategies, image, and competitive position. This entails a classic **SWOT** analysis of a company's strengths, weaknesses, opportunities, and threats, which is discussed in detail in Chapter 6. A company's internal strengths and weaknesses can include its cash flow position, research and development team, speed and agility in getting ideas to market, and customer relationships. Marketing is increasingly staying in close touch with its customers through dedicated customer account teams and customer relationship management (CRM) software, such as that offered by firms like SalesForce.com, SalesLogix, and Siebel (now part of Oracle).[11] CRM software allows a company to capture all data related to customers in a single location, in order to provide better service and analytics. CRM software also allows the company to put a single face forward to the customer, improving consistency in dealing with customers.

Externally, marketing must identify the company's and the chain's current and emerging competitors, understand their strengths and weaknesses, and predict their next moves. To find new opportunities, the marketing group may conduct research, including customer surveys, interviews, and focus groups. Marketing may gather data by monitoring Internet and in-store purchasing patterns, or by observing product usage patterns with in-home video cameras. Marketers also scan the market for new technologies and discuss opportunities with their own NPD teams. Most viable ideas for new products don't come as a flash of insight, but rather from hard work and research.[12]

Customer-Driven Marketing and the Importance of the Product

Essentially, what is required of marketing is to get into the mind of the customer and create customer-driven solutions meant to meet the customer's wants and needs. This is in sharp contrast to the approach of many early e-tailers, who created technology-driven solutions, most of which clearly did not meet customer needs. As a result, these e-tailers failed. Good marketing, advertising, and a sharp Web site cannot sell a product with little apparent value.

But satisfying customer needs is not the job of the marketing department alone. It is the task of the entire supply chain, sometimes called a **demand chain** by customer-focused marketers. The product that a customer buys is not just the physical product. The augmented product includes the service associated with the product, the product's ease of use and performance, the after-sale support, the purchasing experience, and even the way that the salesperson treats the customer. Failure in any aspect of the tangible or intangible product experience can leave a bad taste in the customer's mouth and cause an organization to lose future sales. Thus, it is the job of all members of the supply chain to understand, serve, and satisfy the end customer.

Harley-Davidson and Its Supply Chain

In order for a supply chain to be effective in meeting the needs of the customer, everyone in the supply chain must have the end customer in mind. Rather than only meeting the needs of its direct customer, each player must focus simultaneously on meeting the needs of every downstream customer. This changes and broadens the mind-set of each member of the chain, and provides a common goal. Customer focus requires that organizations look not only at their own operations, but also at the external supply chain. One company that embodies this approach is Harley-Davidson. Back from near-bankruptcy in the 1980s, Harley changed its tune and began to listen to, and respond to, its customer's needs and concerns for quality, value, and image.

Recognized today as the 46th most valuable brand in the world,[13] Harley instills the idea of serving customers at all levels of its internal and external supply chain. Harley believes that it is not simply selling a product—it is selling a dream! Owning a Harley is an experience. It gives the owner access to a whole network of other Harley owners, special events, parties, concerts, and Web sites. Harley-Davidson has successfully captured the heart and loyalty of its customers. Because of its 1980s experiences, Harley knows that it cannot be complacent; it must continue to evolve and serve the needs of customers.

To that end, its product offerings continue to evolve. Harley acquired a majority interest in Buell Motorcycle, which produces lower-end Harleys as "starter" bikes. Yet these bikes are very high quality and in line with the Harley image. It is very careful about licensing its name for products, licensing only high-quality items and distributing them selectively. To help its associates better understand its needs, Harley gives all employees the opportunity to attend motorcycle rallies to talk to customers and get a feel for customer wants and needs.

In the upstream supply chain, it establishes long-term relationships with suppliers, and instills in them the need for quality, reliability, and image consistent with the desires of its end customers. This includes holding key supplier conferences where attendees have the opportunity to ride Harleys. This gives suppliers a chance to "catch the vision" and understand that they are making a Harley, not simply providing a part.

In the downstream supply chain, Harley selects its dealers carefully and has extensive educational facilities for its dealer network, to train them to communicate better with customers, to instruct customers on product usage, and to merchandise and lay out its stores. Although virtually all other motorcycle manufacturers outsource heavily to foreign suppliers, Harley has held fast to its "made in the U.S.A." image as part of the value perceived by its customers. Thus, Harley is a master at designing its supply chain and positioning its product to meet the needs of its customer base.

Product Positioning

As the Harley-Davidson example illustrates, understanding your customers and positioning the total package to meet their needs is critical to customer loyalty. Bank One is a company that has been an innovator in understanding its customers' changing wants and needs, and in positioning innovative new services ahead of the curve so that it increases its customer base, and creates a loyal following.

Bank One (now part of JPMorgan Chase) has grown a thousand-fold since the 1960s, to capture over $100 billion in assets today. How has it done this? By constantly innovating and anticipating the customer's changing needs. It helped popularize and make consumer credit cards widely available in the 1960s, creating a new area of financial freedom for consumers. It partnered with a manufacturer to create the first ATM machine, introduced in Columbus, Ohio, in 1970, giving people ready access to their money, instead of being confined to proverbial banker's hours. This positioned Bank One as sensitive to customers' needs for flexible and convenient services, as did its other innovations, such as the drive-through banking windows and overdraft protection. It transformed itself from a bank to a consumer financial center, partnering with industry leaders when it did not have the technology or where-withal to implement its ideas alone.[14] Bank One's clever service positioning, customer focus, and leveraging its supply chain partners has won it loyal customers and a leadership position in a very dynamic and competitive industry. It also made it an attractive acquisition target for JPMorgan Chase.

Pricing to Meet Consumer Demand

In terms of pricing, marketing has a tendency to focus on meeting customer price points. What is the customer willing to pay for this product or service? At what price will the customer see our offering as an attractive value? This becomes the company's "target price" for the product or service. Marketing may also have goals for achieving a certain level of pretax profit margin. In order to meet the profit margin goal and sell at the target price, marketing subtracts the target profit margin from the target price to come up with the target cost. This target cost is all-inclusive: It must encompass the cost of materials, labor, logistics, product development, packaging, equipment, utilities, and sales and marketing itself. Cost management and product development beyond the concept stage are not marketing's areas of expertise. It must team with new product development and finance to support its pricing goals.

NEW PRODUCT DEVELOPMENT

The second step in the cycle of satisfaction is to take the product from idea to market. New product and service development is both a process and a function at most organizations. Those in new product development may have a variety of names in different companies and industries: designers, research and development engineers, new product scientists, and so on. The **new product development (NPD)** process begins when an organization identifies an unmet customer need and determines that the potential demand justifies further investigation. The organization can then take a sequential approach or a concurrent approach to NPD. **Sequential NPD** is a traditional approach based on strict functional boundaries. As illustrated in Figure 4.2, each functional area does its part and then passes work along to the next function, which does the same.

Sequential NPD is time-consuming and inefficient, because the firm must complete the entire process before it evaluates the idea and the input contributed by each department. For example, the production group may specify an expensive, hard-to-attain material for a component of a new product. If it talked to potential suppliers about what it was trying to accomplish, the suppliers might be able to provide a very attractive substitute material. However, if suppliers are only given a specification, they will provide a price quotation based on that. Thus, without early supplier involvement, an important opportunity for innovation and improvement is lost. The product may be abandoned, or the process may return to an earlier stage for improvement. Either way, significant resources are wasted, and the company may miss an important market window of opportunity.

Concurrent NPD is the approach advocated by most SC leaders. Concurrent NPD uses a cross-functional team to develop a new product with a targeted unit cost. Team composition varies greatly, depending on company resources and the complexity of

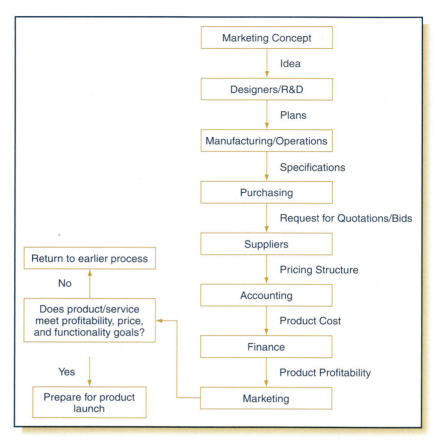

Marketing Concept
↓ Idea
Designers/R&D
↓ Plans
Manufacturing/Operations
↓ Specifications
Purchasing
↓ Request for Quotations/Bids
Suppliers
↓ Pricing Structure
Accounting
↓ Product Cost
Finance
↓ Product Profitability
Marketing

Return to earlier process
↑ No
Does product/service meet profitability, price, and functionality goals?
↓ Yes
Prepare for product launch

Figure 4.2 Sequential New Product/Service Development

the project. However, the typical team will include managers from marketing, R&D, engineering, production, and purchasing. As previously noted, many companies have invited external members of the chain to participate as valued members of the NPD team. These external members include customers, suppliers, and service providers.

NPD teams often rely on an integrative approach known as "target costing" to guide discussion and decision making. As shown in Figure 4.3, the first step in target costing and concurrent NPD is to identify the product features and their relative importance to the customer. This is usually a joint effort of the marketing and NPD groups. Meeting the customer's needs is critical. There may be some give and take here based upon what is technically feasible, and how long a time frame the marketing group is willing to allow from the initial idea to product rollout. Purchasing and suppliers should also be involved at this stage in order to help generate alternatives and perhaps begin working on some of the cost management activities identified in Figure 4.3. The next sections highlight key aspects of the concurrent approach to NPD, using the framework of target costing.

Target Price, Profit, and Cost in NPD

To determine a target cost for a new product, the firm has to consider a target price and a desired profit margin. The first challenge of the NPD process is determining the **target price**, what the customer is willing to pay for the product. Marketing often

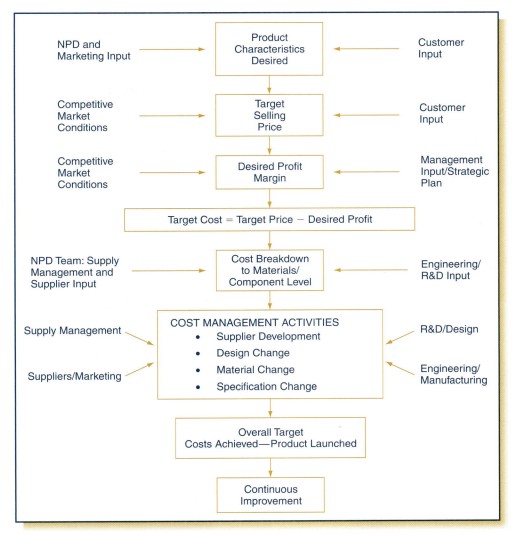

Figure 4.3 Target Costing/Pricing

wants to charge a low price to stimulate sales. Finance generally wants a high price to cover costs and generate profit. NPD may prefer a higher price that avoids the struggle of cutting costs without reducing value.

Pricing is truly a strategic decision. If the price is too high, consumers may not buy the product and the investment will be lost. If the price is too low, the company may not be able to cover its costs and make a reasonable profit, forcing it to forgo future product development altogether. The major inputs that affect the target pricing decision are shown in Figure 4.4.

Next, the target profit margin for the product is determined by looking at the market, as well as what the firm needs to make shareholders and debtors happy, and to reinvest in the company. Deducting the target profit from the target price yields the target cost. This represents the most the organization can spend to make the product or deliver the service profitably.

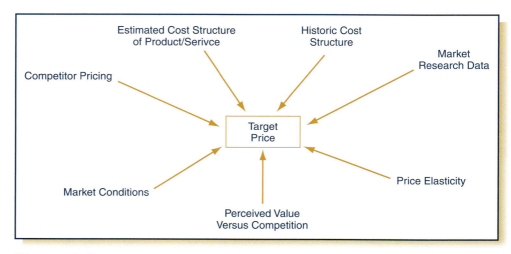

Figure 4.4   Determinants of Target Price

The organization is also very concerned that the cost is market competitive. The approach to ensuring cost competitiveness for new products taken by one large electronics firm is shown in Figure 4.5. It develops targets for all key costs: materials costs, labor, building costs, salaries, marketing and promotion expenses, and so on. Through its competitive cost benchmarking process, it explores market

Figure 4.5   Competitive Target Costing at a Large Electronics Firm

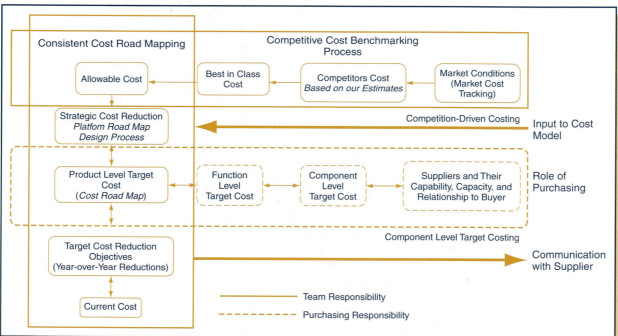

Source: Ellram, 1999.[15]

conditions and competitor pricing so that it can develop a **best-in-class** cost for its product. This helps ensure that customers perceive the product as being a superior value in the marketplace. Based on this, managers develop strategic cost-reduction plans while determining its allowable product-level costs. Product-level costs are broken down to target costs based on the function the item is to perform. Component-level costs are then developed and communicated to suppliers. Each of these steps involves a close interaction between finance, marketing, and NPD. During this stage, the finance group will also likely run profitability, cash flow, economic value-added (EVA), and other analyses on the product or service to see how it meets the firm's other financial targets and measures. If the product does not look good at this point, development may be halted or the product modified before proceeding. Once a product is introduced, the bottom-left corner of Figure 4.5 also shows that year-over-year cost reduction is embedded as part of the target costing process, and goals are continually communicated to the supplier.

Target Cost Breakdown and the NPD Team

The next step involves breaking the overall target cost into its component parts. This effort is frequently led by finance people who have an excellent understanding of cost accounting. It is often based on historical cost breakdowns for similar products. A team of representatives from relevant functions is formed to participate in the NPD process. This would generally include someone from operations who understands how the manufacturing or service delivery process would be performed; someone from purchasing to work with the suppliers and get their input; NPD, to work with suppliers and internal engineering and operations functions to concurrently engineer the product or service; marketing, to keep the customer perspective in focus; and finance, to help manage the costs. Packaging engineers, logistics associates, and others involved in the production and delivery of the product or service may also be involved to the extent that their area has a significant impact on the product or service cost or functionality. A key difference between this approach and the traditional, sequential approach to NPD is that the key NPD activities are taking place simultaneously or concurrently, with various groups sharing ideas and progress on a regular basis, making trade-offs, and modifying their approach accordingly. This saves significant time, effort, and resources, and should result in a product or service that better meets the customers' price and feature demands.

Each team member is given an understanding of the time frame, the volume expectations, the overall target cost as well as the cost target for their piece, and the key elements of customer value. The team members often have subteams within their own functions and report back to the main team for updates on a regular basis, often weekly. It is not unusual for key suppliers and key customers to actively participate in the subteams. Getting suppliers involved early through an ESI program is critical to the success of complex development efforts. ESI mitigates supply risk while providing a forum for incorporating suppliers' innovative ideas and technology into the design stage. This approach is far more productive than reactively "fixing things" later. This is all part of the concurrent engineering process. Remember, suppliers are the experts in their field, unless your company is working with the wrong suppliers. Suppliers may be in a position to recommend new solutions and options that allow NPD to make cost savings or functionality—adding changes to a product.

Cost Management Activities During NPD

All members of the team may participate in some of the cost management activities shown in Figure 4.3. This is often the most intense aspect of the NPD process. Time invested in cost management activities during the design phase is time well spent, as illustrated in Figure 4.6, which shows the percentage influence that design has on a product's costs over its life cycle.

Figure 4.6 shows us that although the organization might spend only 5 percent of the total, cumulative product cost on design, the design influences 70 percent of the total cost. Thus, it behooves companies to "get it right the first time." Yet traditionally, most of the efforts toward managing cost come after the product or service has been introduced, when the company feels it has breathing room to "fix" things that it did not have time to fix during the design stage. Considering the cost and quality implications in the design stage is a better approach.

For example, when John Deere designs a tractor, the design includes what materials will be used, tolerances, weight, the lumens of the head and tail lamps, and so on. With these as given, most of the cost to purchase components and manufacture the product has been set. Thus, although materials will make up approximately 50 percent of the total amount spent on this product over its life cycle, the design stage determines the nature and specifications of those materials. Once a product's specifications have been agreed to, we are limited in how much we can influence total product costs through materials, or direct labor, or overhead, because most of the decisions that affect each of these costs are made during the design stage. While the team is working on cost management activities, it must keep in mind that the new product it is creating must meet the customer's needs.

One challenge inherent in the NPD process is balancing the potentially conflicting goals of the various functions. The key is to set goals that cut across functional areas. All team members must be held accountable for meeting customer needs, product rollout schedules, and price and profitability targets.

In the early 1990s, Honda of America Manufacturing was not meeting the target costs it set for cars. The purchasing and financial associates would identify cost problems during the design and development stages, but the designers simply did not get around to changing the designs. This is because the designers were focusing on

Figure 4.6 Percent of Influence of Each Element on Total Cost to Produce a Good

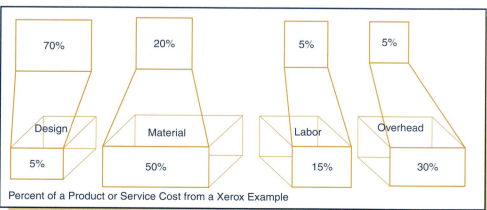

Source: Ellram and Choi, 2000.[16]

Table 4.2 Key Areas of Strategy Tracking and Reporting New Product Review Meetings

PRODUCT REVIEW MEETINGS
• Target: Has a target cost been determined that acknowledges both the margin requirements and the competitiveness of the products?
• Team: Are cross-functional cost advisory teams chartered to identify relevant issues and competitors and to drive cost of goods to meet or beat the targets?
• Activity coordination: Are all the subteams meeting the timetables and merging results as necessary?
• Value and features: Are we retaining the key features identified as critical to the customers as we refine the design and cost?
• Progress: How are we progressing in our plan to get to best-in-class and target COGS?
• Manufacturing road map: Is there a manufacturing road map for the product?
• Suppliers: Have our key suppliers been identified?
• Risks: Have key risks in cost, supply, timing, pricing, and so on been identified and a plan developed for mitigating these risks?
• Launch: For new products, will the product/offer be at best-in-class COGS when launched?
• Communication: Have we communicated key news to top management, so that we continue to have their support to proceed, and don't have any surprises?

doing what they were measured on and rewarded to do: creating the next new model. They were not held accountable for meeting product cost targets. Seeing this problem, Honda changed the designer's reward and measurement systems to include a heavy weight for meeting product cost targets. Honda has consistently met or beaten its cost targets, while adding features, every year since then.

The importance of goal congruence and good communication among all members of the NPD team cannot be underestimated. Table 4.2 shows some of the key discussion points included during update meetings. Notice that a broad range of issues are considered—everything from activity coordination to key product values and features to risk mitigation.

New Product Launch

Cost management efforts continue until the team meets or beats the cost targets. Once the new product or service has been launched, the NPD team generally disbands and turns the product or service over to operations, which is then responsible for continuous improvement and ongoing cost management. The NPD process and target costing process are complementary processes, as illustrated by the way that a large aerospace firm maps NPD activities with target costing activities in Figure 4.7. For example, when NPD is in the concept stage, the focus of target costing activities is on historic costs, in order to provide early cost estimates. On the other hand, at detailed design, the cost estimates are refined based on detailed specifications, and should be much more accurate.

When a product or service is launched, finance and marketing continue to be heavily involved in its management, understanding its success and making modifications as necessary. The NPD group will likely no longer be involved. The success of the new product development process will ultimately be judged by the sales of the new product, product profitability, and a high level of ability to meet market demand.

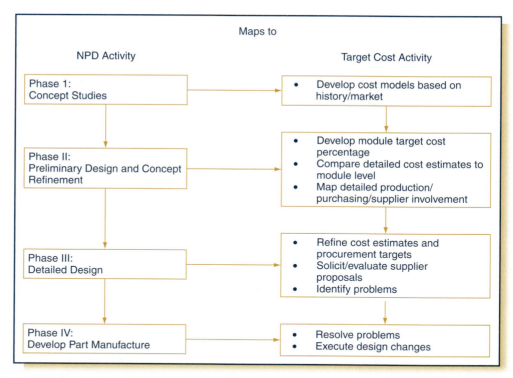

Figure 4.7 Major New Product Development Activities and Relation to Target Costing

Source: Ellram, 1999.[17]

THE ROLE OF FINANCE IN NEW PRODUCT DEVELOPMENT

The third step in the cycle of satisfaction is to verify the financial viability of new products. As suggested earlier, this step is performed concurrently with step 2: product conceptualization and development. Finance and accounting are the firm's scorekeepers, and they communicate performance results throughout the organization and to the outside world. In terms of financial results, we live in a very reactive time. The world financial markets respond very quickly to earnings surprises of any kind. As a result, companies try to manage earnings. They delay expenses if earnings are below previous announcements, or spend money earlier if it looks like earnings will exceed expectations, in order to hedge their bets for future quarters. Finance is a tool for monitoring and managing business activities.

The Boundary-Spanning Role of Finance at Intel

Given the constant pressure on publicly held companies to make money, it is no wonder that finance usually reports directly to the president and/or CEO, and plays a prominent role in corporate decision making. For example, at Intel, although people in the finance department are assigned to support local business units and functional areas throughout the corporation, these managers only have dotted-line reporting

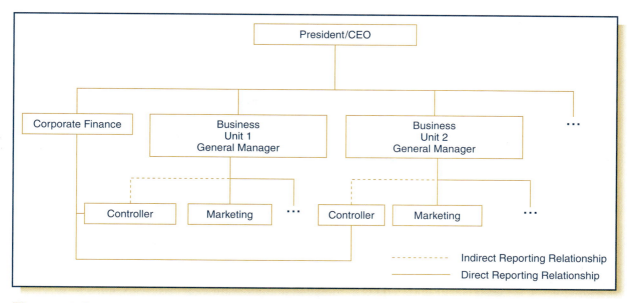

Figure 4.8 Finance Reporting Relationships

relationships to their local clients. The finance personnel have a solid line, direct-reporting relationship to corporate finance. This structure helps retain the objectivity of each local finance group, creating greater loyalty to the overall corporate good than to any particular business or function. If a business unit's finance group thinks that a business decision is flawed, business unit management can expect to hear about it directly. If the business continues on a questionable path, corporate finance may give the matter further review and attention. This willingness to question and challenge the business is generally not the purview of business unit finance, but is made possible by the relatively independent reporting structure, as shown in Figure 4.8.

The finance department at Intel sees itself as a facilitator of cost management by providing the right tools and support. It also sees itself as a facilitator across businesses and functions that provide checks and balances to management decisions to assure sound and ethical practices.

Measures of Profit

Finance is concerned with several measures of a firm's financial performance. At the most basic level, it is concerned that the company make a reasonable profit—enough money to be an attractive investment to shareholders and enjoy steady growth in stock prices. **Profit** is a measure of how much a company makes after paying all its expenses. There are two relevant types of profit. **Operating profit** represents how much money a company makes from the ongoing business of selling its goods and services. This is before tax, and before money that the company makes or loses from other activities, such as investment and financing gains and losses. Finance is concerned with this number for both new and existing products.

A hypothetical profit-and-loss statement for Taystee, a food manufacturer, is shown in Table 4.3. This shows the key elements of a profit-and-loss statement (also known as an *income statement*). Table 4.4 shows the cost breakdown for a new gourmet cookie that Taystee plans to sell to grocers for $2.00 a box. It costs Taystee

Table 4.3 Profit-and-Loss Statement for Taystee

Cost Category	(000's)
Sales	$20,000
Cost of goods	(12,500)
Gross profit	7,500
G&A	(2,500)
Operating profit	5,000
Nonoperating cost (interest expense)	(1,250)
Profit before tax	3,750
Taxes	(1,250)
Profit after tax	$ 2,500

$.75 for ingredients, $.25 for packaging, and 25 for fixed and variable manufacturing costs, including depreciation, labor, and all plant expenses. This sums to $1.25, and is referred to as "cost of goods." In addition, it has to pay $.25 for its share of the allocation of corporate overhead, known as general and administrative expenses (G&A), including business unit and headquarters finance, advertising, marketing, new product development, human resources, and other expenses. This leaves Taystee with an operating profit of ($2.00 − $1.50) = $.50 for each box it sells, right? Well, from a strictly internal perspective, if we sell every box we make at full price, that might make sense. But looking at this from a broader supply chain perspective, and the way that we interact with our customers and our suppliers, many other things can happen that we need to take into account.

The target selling price may not turn out to be the actual average selling price. For example, that $2.00 per box selling price may be eroded. Marketing might run special promotions and offer discounts to grocers and other customers for buying large quantities, for trying the product, or for including the product in its advertisements. Some boxes of cookies may be damaged or returned by retailers in an unsalable condition. We may have to write those off. We may also have to pay storage charges for excess product and transportation charges for returns. And we may decide to issue coupons for the product, which we will have to pay for from our promotional budget. All of these factors will ultimately affect the profitability of this product, and must be taken into account. Our expectations for these additional

Table 4.4 Cost Breakdown for New Cookie

Cookie Costs per Box	
Ingredients	$ .75
Packaging	.25
Manufacturing costs	.25
Subtotal costs of goods	$1.25
Corporate overhead/G&A	.25
Total cookie cost	$1.50

cost or revenue shortfalls may be factored into our planned profit as "allowances" or deductions.

Our production costs may also vary due to internal factors, such as manufacturing efficiencies that differ from plan, or the need to run overtime or extra shifts at higher hourly labor rates. Our costs may also differ from plan due to external cost factors. For instance, the volume of purchases from our suppliers may vary because our sales volume is higher, lower, or more variable than planned. If our volume is lower than planned, a supplier may raise the price of inputs due to lower efficiency levels. If our volume is higher than planned, a supplier may either ask for higher or lower prices, depending upon how it affects their operating costs. If demand is very erratic, a supplier is likely to ask for price increases as their inability to plan and schedule raises their internal costs and those of their suppliers.

The bottom line: Estimating the profitability of products is actually more complex than it first appears. To make up for all of the risks involved, the finance group may suggest a higher price, say $2.25 or $2.50 per box to offset all the allowances. Marketing might protest, saying that it has researched consumer price points, and a price above $2.00 is not acceptable. Finance might then suggest that costs be cut. Depending on the areas of cost-cutting, product quality or customer service might be affected, threatening sales, and raising objections from marketing. It is no wonder that functional groups often disagree.

But finance is not only concerned with operating profits. **Profit before tax** represents the sum of operating profits plus or minus gains and losses from other activities. Thus, in the previous example, where the cookies were contributing $.50 per box to operating profit, finance must also be concerned with other nonoperating income and expenses. Does the company have investment losses or large interest costs that it must repay? They will show up after operating profit, and must be covered if the company is to make a profit for its shareholders.

Thus, a company must consider both operating profit and profit before tax. If a company is making money from its day-to-day business, but has made bad investment or financing decisions, its cash flow and ability to invest may be impaired. On the other hand, a company with good long-term investments may look profitable before taxes, but actually be losing money on operations.

For example, in the fourth quarter of 2001, Amazon.com appeared to actually make money for the first time. Closer analysis revealed that it made $16 million in foreign currency gains, largely because the euro fell versus the dollar. This gave Amazon a net of $5 million, offsetting its loss from operations.[18] Only a close look at the company's financial statements would reveal this fact.

Cash Flow

The concept of **cash flow** is one that has received increased attention in recent years. It is the timing of cash payments and receipts that can make a difference to a company's liquidity, not just the amount of these flows. Cash flow analysis can apply to a product, a business unit, or to an organization. The cash-to-cash conversion cycle for a typical firm is shown in Figure 4.9. As shown in Figure 4.9, cash enters a business from three sources. Creditors make loans, investors provide new capital, and operations generate cash that the company may reinvest. The company uses this cash in the various stages of its operations. It may acquire property, plant, and equipment; buy raw materials; produce the goods; and market and sell them. Cash flows into the company when receivables are collected, the company borrows money, or sells shares of stock. Cash flows out to pay for the goods and services

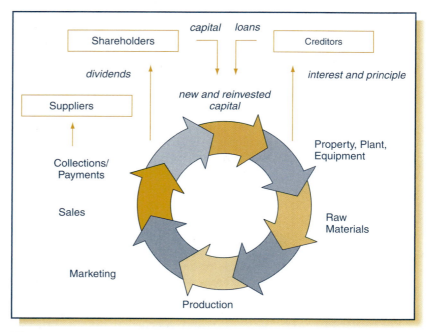

Figure 4.9   Cash Flow Cycle

used in operations. Cash also flows out to repay investors with dividends and creditors with interest and principal payments.

Let's walk through this for the cookies example we introduced earlier. First, we all know that in order for a company to remain in business in the long run, it must provide an attractive return to its shareholders and be able to repay its creditors on a timely basis. Any money invested to make new cookies, perhaps $1,000,000 on a piece of equipment, must come from either loans or from earnings that we retain and reinvest, rather than paying them to our shareholders. In return for this money, the creditors expect interest payments and a return of their principle. The shareholders expect dividend payments and/or stock appreciation on their money that the company is using.

To simplify this example, let's assume that we took out a loan for the entire amount. It is payable in 5 years, with annual interest payments of $70,000. The company must also purchase raw materials. Assuming we plan to make and sell 1,000,000 boxes a year, and that materials include the $.75 for ingredients and the $.25 for packaging, our materials costs are $1,000,000/year in the product we have sold. We also have $.25/unit for production costs, including the depreciation on the new equipment, for a total of $250,000 a year, and $.25 for corporate overhead costs (G&A), or $250,000/year. The marketing group also plans on spending an additional $250,000 on promotions and slotting fees to get retailers to try the product. We pay all of these expenses this year. We have already incurred some expenses for purchases to make additional cookies for the coming year, but have not yet paid our suppliers for those, so they do not affect our cash flow. We don't have much other expense or inventory buildup, because we have a responsive production system that operates pretty close to a just-in-time basis. We do sell 1,000,000 boxes of cookies, but we have a 1 percent damage/return rate, and we have only received payment from 90 percent of our customers by year end.

Table 4.5 Income Statement for Cookies

Sales	$1,980,000
Cost of sales	1,250,000
Gross profit	730,000
G&A	250,000
Additional promotional expenses	250,000
Operating profit	230,000
Other expenses	70,000
Profit before tax	$ 160,000

As shown in Table 4.5, our revenue is (1,000,000 × 99% × $2.00) = $1,980,000. But we have only collected $1,782,000 of this amount ($1,980,000 × 90%). Thus, our cash flow is $1,782,000 − $1,820,000 = −$38,000, even though we made a pretax profit of $160,000 and an operating profit of $230,000 (adding back the $70,000 interest expense). The cash inflow and outflows are shown in Table 4.6. If this were our only product, we would not have cash to be able to make the full interest payment on our loan, and could be in danger of having the loan called or declaring bankruptcy. In this simple situation, the company's timing of cash inflows and outflows did not match. In reality, Taystee probably would have been having problems paying its bills all year. This could create ill will with suppliers, who might delay shipments or even cut Taystee off completely. We also need to be setting aside cash to pay our $1,000,000 equipment loan in 5 years. We made the simplifying assumption that our product did not take long to produce, and that we did not hold much inventory. A long production time or high inventory levels would tie up even more cash, putting us in a very tough position with creditors, suppliers, and employees. Managing cash flow as well as profit is critical for the long-term viability of a company.

Economic Value-Added

There is yet another measure that has become popular in finance to measure the true value that a product or an organization returns to its shareholders: **economic value-added (EVA)**. The simple explanation of economic value-added is that it considers

Table 4.6 Statement of Cash Flows

Sources of Funds:	
Payments received from customers	$1,782,000
Uses of Funds:	
Interest	$ 70,000
Raw materials	1,000,000
Production	250,000
Corporate overhead costs	250,000
Promotional expense	250,000
Total uses of funds	$1,820,000
Net cash flow	($ 38,000)

how much money the company makes from operations after taxes, less the cost of the capital that the company had tied up to make that money. It is essentially a measure of the surplus value generated by an investment. If the value is negative, the investment did not pay for itself. If it is zero, the investment basically broke even, considering what else could have been done with the capital employed. A positive EVA demonstrates that a company is really adding value.

The simplified formula is

$$EVA = Operating\ Profit - Taxes - (Total\ Capital\ Employed \\ \times Company's\ Cost\ of\ Capital)$$

In reality, the calculation is very detailed and complex, and takes into account the timing of significant cash flows. It can easily require 100 or more adjustments.[19] This complexity is the obvious reason why not all companies use EVA analysis. Stern Stewart & Company, who trademarked the term *EVA*, has hundreds of clients, and caters to large and mid-market companies.

Let's take a look at a grossly simplified calculation of EVA for our cookie project. The operating profit for our first year was $230,000. At a corporate tax rate of 35 percent, our after-tax operating profit is $149,500. We know we have an investment of $1,000,000 of capital tied up in the equipment. However, we also have capital tied up in inventory and accounts receivable, and we have to take part of the allocation for the factory. Thus, our total capital employed is $1,600,000. Our cost of capital is 11 percent. This is a blended rate based on the rate at which we can borrow and the rate the stock market demands for a small-cap company like ours, thus, our EVA = $149,500 - (11% \times $1,600,000) = -$26,500. We actually diminished the value of the company this year by introducing our new cookie.

To be fair in this evaluation, we would want to look at the EVA of this project over its expected life, taking into account the time value of money and adjusting the cash flows accordingly. EVA gives a longer-term perspective on whether a project is generating or destroying the firm's value over the project life cycle. This may not be obvious by looking at operating earnings. EVA goes beyond traditional net present value analysis of new investments by considering capital tied up in accounts receivable, inventory, and related assets. It provides a more comprehensive picture. Considering either EVA or cash flow as metrics for the cookie project, it does not look very promising. Such findings severely limit Taystee's ability to proceed to the fourth step in the cycle of satisfaction—invest in future customer-pleasing products. Because innovation is the source of renewal—the lifeblood of a company—Taystee needs to take costs out of its new product or do something to increase its attractiveness in the marketplace.

CONCLUSION

This chapter opened with the concept of mitigating risk in new product and service development. Recognizing potential risk, and involving internal and external players early in the NPD process, is critical to effective risk mitigation. Understanding the high risk involved in NPD makes the importance of establishing an intimate working relationship between marketing, finance, and new product development personnel more apparent. This chapter illustrates just how important it is to bridge the gaps between these functions. They must all share a common goal, perform their specific roles efficiently, and work together collaboratively to support the success of the organization. Marketing, new product development, and finance are each functional areas as well as processes. The processes of each are very much dependent upon the processes of the others to successfully support the customer satisfaction cycle.

Marketing plays the critical roles of identifying unfulfilled customer needs and working within the organization to create products and services to meet those needs. Although the ultimate goal of the firm is often stated as profitability, the firm must first have customers and desirable products to sell those customers. This is a fundamental first step on the road to profitability. Due to decreasing product life cycles, a firm's ability to rapidly and successfully introduce profitable new products and services is more important than ever. This chapter provided an overview of the target costing process as an approach to provide common goals and a framework to facilitate successful new product introduction. A firm must concurrently involve the NPD function and other functional areas to improve time to market while meeting customer goals. The traditional, sequential approach to NPD is often too slow and inefficient.

Finance plays a key role in facilitating the target costing process. Finance is also the "voice" of the company in communicating performance to investors, potential investors, and creditors. Thus, finance is concerned with multiple measures of the firm's financial performance, including cash flow, economic value-added, and various profitability measures.

SUMMARY OF KEY POINTS

1. Business success is short-lived for companies that do not respond to the needs of the customer. The customer is the driver of SCM. Everyone in the chain should focus on the same end customer, and meeting that customer's needs.

2. Risk management is a critical dimension of new product and service development. Risk management includes (1) early supplier involvement to reduce supply risks, (2) ensuring that the company is not outsourcing core competencies, and (3) design considerations such as whether products should be modular or integral.

3. The interface between marketing and SCM lies in developing the right product at a fair price and then positioning it properly in the marketplace.

4. Target costing provides a step-by-step approach to involve cross-functional teams to ensure that a product can be priced to appeal to the customer while still making a reasonable profit.

5. New product development exists as both a function and a process in many organizations. An effective NPD team includes many functions, common goals, and a focus on both meeting customer needs and cost targets.

6. Finance and accounting are the firm's scorekeepers. They communicate performance results throughout the organization and to the outside world. Finance is responsible for assessing the organization's investments, including its products.

7. Financial measures that are commonly applied to new and existing products include profitability, cash flow, and economic value-added.

REVIEW EXERCISES

1. Identify and discuss three reasons to keep the end customer in mind while designing new products

2. Describe Harley-Davidson's approach to defining customer needs.

3. Discuss the causes of conflict between the marketing and finance functions. Identify a couple of ideas for resolving these conflicts.

4. Define the concepts of a target price and a target cost. Discuss how target pricing relates to the target cost.

5. Explain how new product development is both a function and a process. Provide an illustration of your ideas.
6. Discuss the importance of cash flow. Explain how it is possible for a firm to make a profit and still not be able to pay its bills.
7. Using the simplified concept of EVA presented in this chapter, explain how a profitable company could have a negative EVA.
8. Identify several of the risks in new product and service development. Present a plan to reduce or eliminate these risks.

Case *Reorganizing for New Product Development and Ongoing Customer Management*

Bill Johnson shook his head and sighed. His director, Lydia Jones, had just sent him an e-mail telling him that his engineering staff and marketing were at each others' throats over the new personal digital organizer that the company, *Time Flies*, was developing.

> Bill:
>
> The fighting among your staff and marketing has got to stop; this is getting embarrassing. At the directors' meeting today, Steve (the marketing director) claimed that your staff is both behind schedule and over cost. He also said that he got wind at a trade show that a competitor is developing a product very close to ours, and that they may beat us to market at the pace things are moving. Apparently he feels that your staff spends more time explaining why things can't work than they do finding solutions. Worse, the solutions they do suggest are obscure, expensive, and based on untested technology. We're starting to look like villains and developing a real image problem throughout the rest of the company. I am going to be meeting with the business unit president in a few days. I'd like you to brief me about your perception of the situation and what you recommend to improve the working relationships and the output. I've set up a time on your calendar on Thursday at 1:00 P.M.
>
> Thanks,
> Lydia

This gave Bill 2 days to come up with some answers. He remembered reading the story about Chrysler in the early 1990s, and how it had cut new product development times and costs tremendously while achieving higher levels of customer satisfaction by co-locating all the team members and making them jointly responsible for all key elements of new product success. He remembered reading a similar story about IBM: how it had lost its way in the PC business because it rewarded its design engineers based on how many design awards they won rather than how well their products were received by customers. It had gotten to the point where IBM's development cycle was several times longer than its product life cycle.

Bill could see elements of all of this at *Time Flies*. Various functions did not speak to each other. They had different goals. Finance translated the total product viability into EVA measures, but no one seemed to be held accountable for achieving them, or at least it wasn't clear how. Marketing wanted a new product packed with features, low cost, reliable, and ready to hit a mass market today. The engineers wanted to design quality products using innovative technologies, where they felt they could make their mark. Bill sighed. The next couple of days were going to be long ones. Yet Bill knew this problem had been going on for some time. Decreasing product life cycles were making the problem more serious and more visible. Bill knew that some organizational changes were needed and hoped he could be part of the solution.

CASE QUESTIONS

1. If you were Bill, where would you begin? What steps should he follow to be sure that he has not missed any of the key points?
2. What are the specific changes that need to occur at *Time Flies* to get the new product development process in general, and this product in particular, back on track?
3. Could the target costing process be helpful here? Explain why or why not, providing specific reasons.

ENDNOTES

1. Vinas, T. (2001, October) Supply chain strategist. *Industry Week,* www.industryweek.com/CurrentArticles/asp/articles.asp?ArticleID=1133.
2. History in brief. www.nokia.com/link?cid=EDITORIAL_3913.
3. Anonymous. (2002, August 5). The top 100 brands. *BusinessWeek,* pp. 95–99.
4. 1930s Motorola history highlights. www.motorola.com/content/0,1037,117–282,00.html.
5. Ibid. #3.
6. Ogawa, J. (2004 November 23). Living in the product development "valley of death." *FPGA Journal,* www.fpgajournal.com/articles/ 20041123_altera.htm.
7. McMath, R. (1999, March) New product failures: The high cost of forgetfulness. *Exec,* www.unisys.com/execmag/1999–03/journal/viewpoints2.htm.
8. Zsdisin, G. & Ellram L. M. (1999, June). Supply risk assessment analysis. *Practix,* 9–12.
9. IBM corporation Web site. www.ibm.com/ibm/us/en/pcannouncement, accessed January 2, 2006.
10. Vargo, S. L., & Lusch, R. F. (2004). Evolving to a new dominant logic for marketing. *Journal of Marketing,* 68(1), 1–17.
11. See ecrmmadtery.com at www.crmmastery.com/software-eval-selection-assistance.cfm or software.com at www.2020software.com/software/display.asp?tMethodID=5&tMethod=category&ic_campID=26&ic_pkw=crm%20software for a comparison of features of various CRM software packages. The www.siebel.com Web site also provides an excellent description of the benefits of CRM.
12. Drucker, P. F. (2002). The discipline of innovation. *Harvard Business Review, 80* (8), 95.
13. Ibid. #3.
14. Blackwell, R. D. (1997). *From mind to market.* New York: Harper Business.
15. Ellram, L. M. (1999). The role of supply management in target costing. Tempe, AZ: CAPS Research.
16. Ellram, L. M., & Choi, T. (2000). Percent of product or service cost from a xerox example. *The Supply Management Process.* Tempe, AZ: National Association of Purchasing Management, 127.
17. Ibid. #15.
18. (2002). Amazon announces fourth quarter profit. www.amazon.com.
19. Stern Stewart & Company. www.eva.com.

Supplement D

Evaluating the Return on a New Product Project

After reading the chapter, you should clearly understand that SC managers need to learn to speak the language of finance. The chapter discussed core finance concepts like cash flow as well as advanced financial thinking as represented by EVA. In both cases, the tools were used to evaluate the attractiveness of a new product introduction. The chapter also mentioned a tool that every SC manager should have in her toolbox—net present value (NPV) analysis. Most companies that do not use EVA rely heavily on this NPV analysis. Many companies that have adopted EVA still use NPV concepts. If you are not confident in your NPV analysis skills, take a close look at the following tutorial.

The Time Value of Money

One of the key concepts in the language of finance is the time-value-of-money concept. The basic premise of this concept is that $1 today is not the same as $1 in the future. This is an important concept to consider when assessing the financial feasibility of new products and prioritizing those new products for introduction to the marketplace. The chapter pointed out the boundary-spanning role of finance within Intel. Intel utilizes the time-value-of-money approach to discount expected future cash flows from projects under development to their net present value in order to make better decisions concerning these projects. Intel estimates these future cash flows by utilizing forecasted revenues and costs, taking into account the expected life cycles of the products and the underlying technology, relevant market sizes, and industry trends.[1] Intel also uses net present value analysis when making decisions about process changes or technology changes within its organization. For example, in 2002, Intel performed a net present value analysis to assess the financial viability of installing wireless local area networks (WLAN) within their buildings. Intel's information technology (IT) function estimated a net present value return on investment of $4.6 million for the large-scale implementation, $940,000 for a medium-scale deployment, and $280,000 for the small-scale installation.[2] This information was used to justify the implementation of WLANs throughout Intel's organization. Intel's IT function has learned that it is far more productive to team with Intel's finance function from the start in order to make a business case for changes to technology or processes than it is to go it alone and only meet when presenting the case to cost-conscious senior managers.

How are these important time-value-of-money calculations performed? Suppose that an organization is considering investing $100,000 in a new product that will provide an annual return of $40,000 for the next 3 years. Because the return of $120,000 (3 × $40,000) is greater than the initial $100,000 investment, one might conclude that the firm should accept this project. However, it is important to remember that the $100,000 is paid out today and that the $40,000 returns will be received over a period of 3 years. Some simple calculations are used to determine whether or not the organization should accept this project.

Two basic formulas are commonly used to calculate the time value of money. The first is used to calculate the *future value* of a sum of money and the second is used to calculate the *present value* of a sum of money.

Future Value

The general formula for calculating the future value of a sum of money is as follows:

$$\text{Future Value} = C_0 \times (1 + r)^T$$

Where:

C_0 = Cash to be invested at time 0
r = the interest rate for each period
T = the number of periods over which the cash is invested

This formula assumes that the initial investment occurs at the beginning of time period 0 and that interest payments are made at the end of each period.

For example, let's assume that an organization invests $500 for 5 years at an interest rate of 15 percent. Where does this interest rate come from? Companies such as Intel typically derive these interest rates or discount rates from a weighted average cost of capital analysis, adjusted to reflect the relative risks inherent in each entity's development process, including the probability of achieving technological success and market acceptance. Given a 15 percent interest rate, what is the future value of the original $500? Plugging the values into the formula listed earlier yields the following results:

$$\text{Future Value} = 500 \times (1 + .15)^5$$
$$\text{Future Value} = 500 \times 2.0114$$
$$\text{Future Value} = \$1,005.68$$

Thus, $500 invested today at 15 percent interest for 5 years has a future value of $1,005.68.

Present Value

The general formula for calculating the present value of a sum of money is as follows:

$$\text{Present Value} = \frac{C_i}{(1+r)^i}$$

Where:

C_i = Cash at time period i
r = the interest rate for each period
i = the number of time periods

For example, suppose that as part of a multiyear sales contract, an organization will receive $500 two years from now. At an interest rate of 10 percent, what is the present value of that future payment? The solution is obtained as follows:

$$\text{Present Value} = \frac{500}{(1+.1)^2}$$
$$\text{Present Value} = \frac{500}{1.21}$$
$$\text{Present Value} = \frac{\$413.22}{\$413.22}$$

Thus, the present value analysis tells us that a payment of $500 received 2 years from now has a present

[1]Intel Corporation 1999 Annual Report.
[2]Cio White Paper. Intel IT Uses Test Results, ROI to Gain Business Support for WLAN Deployment, accessed at http://www.cio.com February 15, 2006.

value of $413.22. In other words, at an interest rate of 10 percent, the organization would be indifferent as to whether it received $413.22 today or $500 in 2 years.

New Product Evaluation Using NPV Analysis

The net present value (NPV) of an investment represents the value of future cash flows minus the present value of the cost of the investment. Net present values less than zero represent projects that will cost the organization money overall. Net present values greater than zero will provide an overall return to the organization. The net present values of different projects can be compared against each other. Higher net present values represent projects with higher returns to the organization. However, sensitivity analysis should be conducted before choosing between various projects to determine the effect of changes to the assumptions used in the NPV calculations.

$$\text{NPV} = - \text{Initial Cost} + \text{Present Value of Future Cash Inflows} - \text{Present Value of Future Cash Outflows}$$

Using the various formulas that have been presented in this section, let's return to the initial example problem listed earlier and determine whether the organization should invest the $100,000 in the new product. Assuming an interest rate of 10 percent, the net present value of the project is calculated as follows:

Year	Initial Cost	Future Cash	Calculations	Present Value
0	−$100,000.00			−$100,000.00
1		$40,000.00	(40,000/1.1)	$36,363.64
2		$40,000.00	(40,000/1.21)	$33,057.85
3		$40,000.00	(40,000/1.331)	$30,052.59
			NPV	−$525.92

A NPV of −$525.92 suggests that the organization will not recover its initial $100,000 investment if they choose to invest in this particular new product. Therefore, managers should only invest in this project if there are other, nonmonetary benefits to the organization that have not been captured by this analysis.

EXERCISES

1. What is the net present value of a $25,000 payment 3 years from now assuming a cost of capital of 12 percent?

2. What is the value of $12,000 5 years from now assuming an interest rate of 20 percent?

3. What is the net present value of an investment that costs $50,000 and has a salvage value of $25,000? The annual profit from the investment is $15,000 each year for 5 years. The cost of capital at this risk level is 15 percent.

4. Using a cost of capital of 12 percent, calculate the net present value of the following project:

Year	Cash Expenses or Costs	Cash Incomes or Revenues
0	$75,250	
1		$125,000
2		$100,000
3	$1,275	$75,000
4		$50,000

5. A wind turbine company is thinking of developing a new turbine, the XP9. The company estimates that creating the XP9 will require an initial investment of $125,000 today, $250,000 of engineering related costs at the end of the first year, and $49,000 of marketing costs at the end of the second year in order to be successful. However, the company estimates that sales will be increased in years 3 through 10 by $75,000 each year. The company's current cost of capital is 15 percent.
   a. What is the net present value of the XP9?
   b. What is the net present value if sales are only increased by $50,000 in years 3 through 10?
   c. Using the $75,000 estimate of the increase in sales, how does the net present value calculated in part a change if the cost of capital is increased to 18 percent?

6. The initial cost of an investment in a new product is $85,000 and the cost of capital is 10 percent. The estimated return is $18,000 per year for 9 years. What is the net present value of the investment?

7. An investment will produce $2,900 3 years from now. What is the present value of the investment if the interest rate is 10 percent?

8. Roger Johnson has been asked to evaluate two different product development projects. After some investigation, he determines that they have the following costs:

	Project A	Project B
Original cost	$257,500	$285,200
Labor cost per year	$23,700	$21,900
Other costs per year	$1,275	$1,585
Increased revenues per year	$75,000	$80,000

Each project has a 5-year life span and requires a 12 percent return.

a. What is the net present value of Project A?
b. What is the net present value of Project B?
c. Which project should Roger recommend?

The Order Fulfillment Process: Managing the Physical Flow Infrastructure

How does my company deliver to promise? Can I help it harness order fulfillment to deliver customer value?

The Supply Chain Road Map

Who are we?

Business Purpose

Chapter 1: SC Strategy
- What is SCM?
- How does it fit our strategy?

Chapter 2: Customer Fulfillment
- Who are our customers?
- Can SCM deliver real value?

Chapter 3: Process Thinking
- Do we have a functional, silo culture?
- Can we manage across functions?

Chapter 4: New Product Process
- Do we know how to innovate?
- Can we create great products?

Chapter 5: Fulfillment Process
- **Are our operations efficient?**
- **Can we buy/make/deliver?**

1. Describe how purchasing, production, and logistics decisions work together to create customer value.

2. Identify and describe the steps in the purchasing process.

3. Identify and discuss design and control decisions in production operations management. Describe the underlying principles and practices of lean manufacturing. Describe the characteristics of service operations.

4. Identify the key decision-making elements of the logistics process. Discuss order fulfillment, transportation, and distribution strategies.

5. Describe how physical flow decisions affect the cost and service positions of the company as well as the design of the overall supply chain.

Opening Story: Coco Loco's Sweet Dilemma

When Lisa Green's Coco Loco Confectionary was in trouble, she turned to Charlene, her best friend from college. Once again, Charlene found herself driving a rental car to a town she hadn't heard of until a week earlier. When she picked up the phone last Friday evening and heard Lisa's voice, she had no idea it would lead to a hastily planned visit to Alpine, Utah. Lisa's frustration was palpable as she explained that her shop, Coco Loco, had become hugely popular, creating delectable chocolates sold throughout the Rocky Mountain West. Orders were increasing at better than 20 percent per year, yet the company had begun losing money—at an alarming pace.

Lisa had explained the situation: "We created irresistible candies and made a name for ourselves. We even managed to eke out a profit since we first opened the doors. Now, our inventory is increasing, but we still can't get product out the door in time to meet customer orders. Just before I called you, I tried to find out where the order for Heber City's Swiss Days celebration was. Nobody could find it. Robert, our purchasing manager, informed me that we hadn't even started production. It turns out that we were out of a critical ingredient—hazelnuts. You can't make cherry hazelnut truffles without hazelnuts. It's an all too familiar story these days. We can't deliver on time without the right ingredients and once you miss Swiss Days, the customer is lost forever. If we don't get things figured out, our image will be gone. Almost half our orders are late! I'm afraid the phone is going to ring and it will be Steve Townsend, wanting to know when his truffles will be delivered. I don't know what to tell him. Please, Charlene, this is your thing; is there any way I can talk you into coming to my rescue?"

When Charlene arrived at Coco Loco, Lisa explained that the immediate crisis had been solved. "We got the truffles out the door yesterday. I drove them to Heber City myself. I think the personal touch combined with a bonus tray of maple hazelnut drops will salvage the relationship. But I can't hand deliver every late order, especially orders coming from across the country and around the world."

"You're right, Lisa," Charlene agreed. "That would be a lot of frequent flier miles and some very expensive truffles. You mentioned that customer complaints are increasing, costs are rising, and some internal friction is developing. Tell me more about the in-house disputes."

Lisa's smile melted. "We have been such a tight company—largely because we've worked together and succeeded. However, the late orders and lost profitability are creating real tension. Marketing is proud of increased sales, but we can't always deliver on their promises. Terry, our marketing manager, insists that marketing has to accept orders for when the customer wants them. We sell over 100 standard products, mixing and matching according to customer demand. We also made over 200 custom products last year. You know—the one-time order of macadamia coconut caramel crunch. Jack, our production manager, is frustrated with the extreme variability. He constantly points out that we have limited capacity and he just can't switch from a dark to a white chocolate without incurring costs and delays."

Charlene smiled.

Lisa continued, "I'm glad you find my situation amusing. Robert, our purchasing manager, was so upset earlier in the week that he walked out of a planning meeting. Terry accused him of dropping the ball on the hazelnuts, placing a valued account in jeopardy. Jack echoed Terry's criticism, and then attacked Terry for causing the problem by accepting an express order without checking to see if we had available production capacity. Of course, Terry angrily justified her decision. Things turned ugly in a hurry. Where do you think we should start? I can walk you through the facility and arrange for interviews with anyone you want to talk with."

"Well Lisa," Charlene replied, "I'd love to see your operation; it sounds to me like everyone ought to take a closer look at the entire fulfillment process. Before the day is over, I want to sit down with Terry, Jack, Robert, and you and see if we can't make the whole process visible."

Consider As You Read:

1. Why is Charlene interested in making the entire order fulfillment process visible? What do you think the root cause of Coco Loco's problems is?
2. What questions would you ask Terry, Jack, and Robert? Are the organization structure, reporting relationships, and reward systems at Coco Loco relevant to the current crisis? Why or why not?
3. What mechanisms might help the order fulfillment process better meet customer requests? Specifically, what policies, procedures, processes, and measures are needed?

> *Operations is either a competitive weapon or a corporate millstone. It is seldom neutral.*
>
> —WICKHAM SKINNER

> *In logistics, if you go an hour without a screw-up, you've had a great day.*
>
> —GUS PAGONIS

FUNCTIONAL COMPONENTS OF THE PHYSICAL FLOW

If you have ever gone to the store and found the product you were looking for out of stock, you have personally experienced a breakdown in the order fulfillment process. You probably don't care where the breakdown occurred; all you know is that the product isn't available, and you've been inconvenienced. Three functions, purchasing, production, and logistics, are responsible for order fulfillment, which is the process that actually makes and delivers a product or service. **Purchasing** acquires the inputs used to support production and day-to-day business activities. **Production** converts sourced inputs into a product or service that customers value. **Logistics** transports and stores goods, assuring that inbound materials are available for operations and that outbound finished products are available when and where the customer wants to buy them. Making good, collaborative purchasing, production, and logistics decisions can spell the difference between delighted and disgruntled customers.

The role played by purchasing, production, and logistics depends on a number of factors including industry type and the company's chosen competitive strategy. For example, retailers like Carrefour, Kohl's, and Lands' End do not make the products they sell; rather, their business models rely on acquiring the right products at the right time from global suppliers and then getting them to the customer as efficiently as possible. They must therefore manage their sourcing and logistics practices meticulously. Carrefour and Kohl's operate extensive, dispersed distribution systems designed to move product rapidly and make it available for purchase by consumers in the communities where they live. Because Carrefour operates in international markets and sells a wider variety of products than Kohl's—including grocery, clothing, and consumer hard goods—its sourcing and logistical requirements are more complex and dynamic. At the other end of the spectrum, Lands' End, a catalog retailer with a relatively limited product line, buys from fewer suppliers and employs a centralized distribution system, which allows it to efficiently ship product directly to the customer's front door. Although retailers do not manufacture a product, they must still manage in-store operations to provide outstanding service at the lowest possible costs. Carrefour claims that the majority of its opportunities to improve efficiency and service are found in the "last 100 meters" of the supply chain; that is, within its own retail stores.

Manufacturers like Bosch Seimens, Rockwell Collins, and Toyota must also manage sourcing and logistics for competitive success; however, their ability to satisfy customers depends on their own production capacity and capabilities. For instance, Bosch Seimens's sells innovative, quality household appliances in markets from Europe to South America to China at affordable prices. Bosch Seimens's success has come from an intense effort to rationalize manufacturing to leverage both design efficiencies and manufacturing scale economies. At Rockwell Collins, a totally different approach is required because the vast majority of the sophisticated avionics and communications equipment it sells are produced in very small batch sizes. A team approach that emphasizes shared learning is the key to Rockwell Collin's success. Finally, Toyota's unique just-in-time production system helped it gain a reputation in the 1980s as one of the world's best manufacturing companies and revolutionized the way managers thought about manufacturing. Twenty years later, Toyota's relentless efforts to improve its operations continue to make it a formidable competitor and the benchmark for manufacturing efficiency.

When purchasing, production, and logistics work in concert, directed by the company's overall strategy, they help the company deliver great products and services to customers. These functions are the building blocks of a successful SC strategy. The Supply-Chain Council's (www.supply-chain.org) Supply-Chain Operations Reference (SCOR) model shown in Figure 5.1 highlights this fact. The SCOR® model helps create a common vision for managing and coordinating five primary SC processes.

- *Plan:* Processes that balance demand and supply to develop a course of action to meet sourcing, production, and delivery needs. This process aligns the supply chain plan with the financial plan.
- *Source:* Processes that purchase goods and services to meet planned or actual demand. Emphasis is on selecting suppliers, establishing policies, scheduling deliveries, and assessing performance.
- *Make:* Processes that transform product to a finished product to meet demand. Emphasis is on scheduling production, measuring performance, managing inventory, and configuring the network.
- *Deliver:* Processes that provide finished goods and services to customers. Emphasis is on order management, warehouse management, and transportation management.
- *Return:* Processes associated with the return of products for any reason, and includes post delivery customer support. Emphasis is on reverse logistics and long-term customer support.

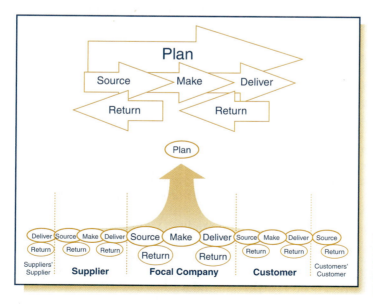

Figure 5.1 The Supply-Chain Council's Supply-Chain Operations Reference Model (SCOR)

The SCOR model points out that every company performs a "chain" of plan, source, make, deliver, and return processes. Decisions made at one point in the chain affect other points in the chain. For example, when Aisin's brake parts facility burned to the ground, its most important customer, Toyota, quickly ran out of parts and had to shut down its own assembly lines. Toyota's decision to source a critical component from a single supplier left it vulnerable to the unforeseen disaster. Interestingly, the brake part affected by the fire was only one of a handful of parts that Toyota had decided to sole source. In another example, a failure to meet production due dates at one of Westinghouse's manufacturing facilities located in the Dominican Republic forced managers to expedite shipping to meet promised customer delivery dates. The use of expensive airfreight instead of ocean shipping offset much of the production costs savings obtained by locating in the Dominican Republic.

The SCOR model enhances collaboration by developing a common SC language and a set of standards to guide SC integration. As managers gain an understanding of the role of each process as well as a vision of how the processes relate to one another, they can make decisions that bridge the gaps within and between organizations. Best practices in each process area can be more easily identified and shared with the members of the Supply-Chain Council to help create the insight needed to build world-class processes. Because success depends on the effective coordination of purchasing, production, and logistics activities, these functional areas are discussed in the pages that follow.

ACQUIRING THE GOODS: THE NATURE OF PURCHASING MANAGEMENT

Marketplace changes have driven purchasing to evolve from a simple clerical function to a competitive weapon. Purchasing's arrival as a strategic function was hastened by four vital developments during the 1980s and 1990s. First, purchased inputs became a primary operating cost. Second, the just-in-time manufacturing revolution placed much greater emphasis on cooperative, long-term buyer–supplier relationships. Third, new information technologies made it possible to store and track the large amounts of information needed to strategically manage buyer–supplier relationships. Fourth, better trained and more competent managers began to enter the supply arena. Purchasing, also called *sourcing* or *supply management*, could now take on a proactive role in helping companies meet new competitive threats.

Manufacturers spend about 55 cents of each sales dollar on purchased goods and services. This equates to about 60 to 80 percent of operating expenses.[1] As shown in Table 5.1, purchased inputs—materials and capital equipment—represent the single largest cost category for many industries. By comparison, direct manufacturing labor costs have decreased to 5 to 15 percent of total operating costs (as little as 2 percent in some high-tech sectors). Service industries depend less on purchased materials than manufacturers. However, they still purchase some materials, office supplies, and maintenance, repair, and operating (MRO) items as well as clerical help, computer programming, overnight mail, and other services. The cost of these purchased inputs is often substantial. For example, the value of purchased inputs represents 30 percent of AT&T's sales. Sourcing decisions play a central role in determining the cost competitiveness of most organizations.

Table 5.1 Purchased Inputs as a Percent of Sales

NAICS CODE	INDUSTRY	COST OF MATERIALS (1,000s)	CAPITAL EXPENDITURES (1,000s)	MATERIALS AND CAPITAL EXPENDITURES (1,000s)	INDUSTRY SHIPMENTS (1,000s)	MATERIAL SALES RATIO	PURCHASE SALES RATIO
314992	Tire cord and tire fabric	790,743	70,152	860,895	1,207,840	0.65	0.71
322226	Surface-coated paperboard	800,159	14,137	814,296	1,155,716	0.69	0.70
336212	Truck trailer mfg.	3,764,716	88,895	3,853,611	5,500,475	0.68	0.70
321211	Hardwood veneer and plywood	1,755,698	71,682	1,827,380	2,856,487	0.61	0.64
334111	Electronic computer mfg.	40,239,744	1,053,379	41,293,123	65,923,736	0.61	0.63
321991	Manufactured home	6,105,063	137,052	6,242,115	10,167,746	0.60	0.61
322232	Envelope mfg.	1,882,776	145,487	2,028,263	3,582,016	0.53	0.57
311991	Perishable prepared food	1,357,722	124,723	1,482,445	2,740,447	0.50	0.54
335911	Storage battery mfg.	2,238,893	171,434	2,410,327	4,422,702	0.51	0.54
335221	Household cooking appliance	1,754,600	120,678	1,875,278	3,540,221	0.50	0.53
313221	Narrow fabric mills	606,166	72,537	678,703	1,390,642	0.44	0.49
333313	Office machinery mfg.	1,180,516	97,724	1,278,240	2,667,886	0.44	0.48
339920	Sporting and athletic goods	4,679,110	345,602	5,024,712	10,458,222	0.45	0.48
332313	Plate work mfg.	1,190,533	78,103	1,268,636	2,707,463	0.44	0.47
331511	Iron foundries	5,174,792	512,167	5,686,959	12,266,373	0.42	0.46
334419	Electronic component mfg.	4,385,786	424,939	4,810,725	10,375,635	0.42	0.46
316992	Handbags and purses	158,768	8,336	167,104	372,430	0.43	0.45
325920	Explosives mfg.	542,828	34,009	576,837	1,318,404	0.41	0.44
336611	Ship building and repairing	4,286,697	241,691	4,528,388	10,441,434	0.41	0.43
327113	Porcelain electrical supply	355,681	68,329	424,010	1,167,201	0.30	0.36
334417	Electronic connector mfg.	1,818,892	237,872	2,056,764	5,666,430	0.32	0.36

Source: U.S. Bureau of the Census. 1997 Economic Census, Washington, DC: U.S. Government Printing Office.

Today's focus on core competencies has led many companies to outsource value-added activities such as light assembly, inventory management, and distribution services. Supply management professionals control a large and important set of resources that reside in the supply base. As a result, suppliers are often managed as an extension of the company, and sourcing professionals take on the role of acquiring not just inputs but also supplier capacity and capabilities. The impact of sourcing on company competitiveness is thus magnified. For example, quality expert Philip Crosby claimed that up to 50 percent of a company's quality problems can be traced to defective purchased materials. Effective sourcing decisions can also reduce order fulfillment lead times. And early supplier involvement in the new product development process can speed product development.

Sourcing professionals must possess highly developed skills and substantial managerial judgment to build and manage a world-class supply base. How well supply managers select the right suppliers, build the right relationships, and help key suppliers develop their own capabilities influences a buying firm's competitiveness. A supply manager's ability to scan the environment and take on new roles helps the company achieve greater competitive success.

The Purchasing Process

Figure 5.2 illustrates the general **sourcing** process, which consists of four phases. The process begins when a need is identified and communicated. A supplier is then selected. An order is placed and the transaction is managed. Finally, performance is measured and an appropriate relationship is developed. The specific steps in the actual process vary depending on what an organization is buying. Services are managed differently from raw materials, and MRO items are managed differently from sophisticated technological components. Each company therefore performs the following steps of the purchasing process at varying degrees of sophistication and formality.

Figure 5.2 The Sourcing Process

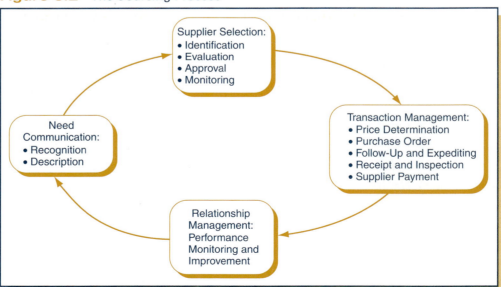

Recognition and Description of Need

The sourcing process begins when someone within the organization identifies a need to acquire some input. Many standard purchases are communicated automatically through a computerized system that monitors inventory levels and reorder points. Otherwise, recognizing that a need exists is the responsibility of the user. The well-managed company uses a purchasing policy or procedure handbook to guide interactions between internal users and sourcing. For new, unique, or one-time purchases, a clear and precise set of guidelines must be in place to assure clear communication.

A **purchase requisition** is used to clearly describe and communicate needs to sourcing. The purchase requisition contains the following information: the item description, requisitioning department, authorizing signature, purchase quantity, delivery date, and location. The information should be stated clearly to assure that the purchasing process goes smoothly. For example, the delivery date should be specific to a day and time and not "ASAP." A user should not exaggerate the urgency of an order. Getting an item 2 weeks before you need it might require a higher price than having the item delivered "on-time." Realistic and accurate information is needed to establish good working relationships. A clear description of the item is particularly critical. The less experience purchasing has with an item, the more clear and specific the description must be.

Supplier Selection

Supplier selection is arguably the most important step in the purchasing process. An effective sourcing manager requires suppliers to provide the highest-quality product at the lowest total cost supported with the best service. To achieve these goals, supply managers must identify candidate suppliers, assess them, and invite the most promising suppliers to participate on the SC team.

The process used to identify good suppliers depends on the importance of the item being purchased. For instance, sourcing might give little attention to suppliers of MRO items in order to focus its resources on analyzing suppliers of major components such as engines or flat panel displays. The higher the dollar value or the greater the impact of the purchased item on the end product's performance, the more resource-intensive the supplier selection process.

The supplier selection process is characterized by four stages: identification, evaluation, approval, and monitoring.

1. *Identification* involves making a list of all potential suppliers. A purchaser might look to the company's purchasing database or directories such as the *Thomas Register of American Manufacturers* (www.thomaspublishing.com) to identify potential suppliers. The *Thomas Register* lists over 150,000 companies.
2. *Evaluation* involves the identification of supplier selection criteria and the gathering of performance information that can be used to assess and compare possible suppliers. Frequently used criteria include quality, price, delivery dependability, capacity (current and future), service responsiveness, technical expertise, managerial ability (attitude, skills, and talent), and financial stability.
3. *Approval* identifies the suppliers that are eligible to receive an order if their price and other terms are competitive at the time the order is being placed. The number of suppliers on the approved list depends on the nature of the item being purchased. For commodity-type items, multiple suppliers are generally used; for unique items, a sole-sourcing arrangement may be preferable.

4. *Monitoring* assures high levels of performance. Scorecards are often used to provide an overall supplier rating. John Deere uses this rating to categorize suppliers into one of four groups: partner, key approved supplier, approved supplier, or conditional supplier. All suppliers are expected to use the scorecard information to drive continuous improvement.

Determination of Price

Price is only one factor in the supplier selection decision, but it is the factor used most frequently to evaluate the sourcing group's performance. The "best" price is actively pursued using one of three approaches: buying at list price, competitive bidding, and negotiation. Buying at list price is used for lower-volume or lower-valued items that do not merit the managerial time and effort needed to obtain a lower-than-list price. Competitive bidding relies on market forces to get suppliers to offer a low price. Competitive bidding is an efficient means of obtaining a fair price when the dollar value of the purchase is high enough to justify the work needed to run a successful bid. Real-time, on-line bidding, sometimes called *reverse auctions*, has achieved 10 to 30 percent price reductions. Suppliers, however, resent what they perceive to be a cutthroat behavior. Finally, negotiation is used when the dollar value of the purchase is large, high uncertainty exists, or a long-term relationship is desired. Negotiation generally goes beyond price determination to develop an overall agreement that is mutually beneficial to both negotiating parties.

Preparation of Purchase Orders

After sourcing selects a supplier and determines the contract details, it prepares a **purchase order (PO).** A PO is a document that specifies the terms and conditions of the purchase agreement and initiates supplier action. Every PO should be filled out correctly. Specifying the wrong part number or delivery details can negate the benefits of careful supplier selection and astute negotiating. Efforts to streamline the purchasing process have focused on reducing the paperwork and costs associated with POs.

For example, a **blanket order** specifies the overall terms of agreement for a given time period—often 1 or 2 years—and covers the entire quantity to be purchased even though smaller quantities will be delivered periodically during the agreement. Once the blanket order is on file, the buying organization issues a materials release to trigger a new shipment. This is often done via computer as part of an e-procurement program. The longer-term sourcing arrangement promises the supplier future business, often qualifying the buyer for a quantity discount.

Web catalogs and corporate procurement cards are also used to streamline the purchasing process. Intel developed a Web catalog for use in all standard buys. Supplier selection and contract issues are managed up-front by the sourcing team. The sourcing team also works closely with the Web designers to create an easy-to-use Web interface. The end user simply pulls up the on-line catalog, identifies the appropriate product, and places an order with the click of the mouse. Beyond reducing the use of expensive POs, the Web catalog allows sourcing to negotiate volume discounts with preferred suppliers.

National Semiconductor adopted procurement cards to reduce the costs of small, nonstandard buys. Instead of issuing a PO for each small-dollar purchase, end users are issued a "p-card," which works just like a standard credit card. All of the small-budget purchases are paid for by the procurement card issuer, which then bills National Semiconductor on a monthly basis. National Semiconductor claims that p-cards have reduced the costs of purchases from $30 per order to a few cents each.

Follow-Up and Expediting

Regular follow-up helps assure that suppliers comply with the purchasing agreement. A diligent supply manager can identify problems with quality or delivery as they arise. When problems occur, a supply manager might (1) increase the frequency of follow-up efforts, (2) send personnel to work with the supplier, (3) use higher-cost emergency transportation, (4) arrange for delivery from an alternative supplier, or (5) alter the buying organization's production schedule. Supply managers should take into account the problem type, the order's importance, and the nature of the buyer/supplier relationship before deciding on a specific action.

Expediting refers to efforts to speed up the delivery of an order. A well-managed organization expedites only a _small_ percentage of total shipments. If sourcing performs well, only suppliers capable of delivering as promised are selected, and if production adequately plans its materials requirements, requests for early shipments should be rare.

To avoid delivery problems, many companies build **penalty clauses** into the purchasing agreement. One company charges $5,000 for the first late delivery, $50,000 for the second late delivery, and removes the supplier from the approved list for a year after the third late delivery. Another company has written its penalty clause so that suppliers have an incentive to let it know when problems arise so the two organizations can work together to eliminate the source of the problem. When a supplier fails to notify the company of delivery problems, the monetary penalty is severe.

Receipt and Inspection

When an order arrives at the buying company, it must pass through a receiving process, which matches the invoice to the contents via a physical count and quality inspection. The goal is to make sure that the sourced inputs are fit for use. Receipt and inspection are managed by a separate organizational unit to assure objectivity. Purchasing gets involved when an incoming shipment fails to pass inspection. Two primary reasons for failure are that the count is off—either too much or not enough was shipped—or that the quality is inferior. When an order does not meet specifications, sourcing must work with the supplier to correct the problem.

Supplier certification simplifies the receiving process. Certification programs focus on improving the supplier's ability to produce high-quality products so that inspections can be eliminated. Making sure the supplier has the procedures and skills to deliver the right quantities on time is also a consideration in the certification process. Once the supplier achieves certification, incoming inspection is eliminated and incoming orders are moved directly to storage or the production area where they will be used. These certified suppliers are often referred to as *dock-to-stock suppliers*. Inspections are only performed if problems occur in the future. Better quality and reduced cycle times are two important benefits of supplier certification.

Invoice Clearance and Supplier Payment

Suppliers deserve to be paid on time; moreover, timely payment helps build good relations with capable suppliers. Efficient procedures for invoice clearance makes good financial sense because payment terms often include discounts for prompt payment. That is, many suppliers offer a 2 percent discount if payment is made within 10 days with full payment due in 30 days (2/10, net 30). This discount equates to an annual return of 36 percent. Actual payment is done by accounts payable, but purchasing should design a system that clears and submits the invoice as quickly as possible.

Many companies' e-procurement programs have entirely automated this process. At Ford, supplier certification became the catalyst for redesigning the accounts payable process. The goal was to create "invoiceless processing." When an order arrives from a certified supplier, a computer database is checked to make sure that a corresponding order is expected. If a record of the order is found on the database, the order is accepted without inspection and accounts payable issues payment directly from the PO.

Performance Monitoring

Supplier performance should be tracked carefully and the sourcing database updated to provide supply managers with good information for future decision making. Performance monitoring provides the insight needed to identify candidates for more collaborative, long-term relationships. Four types of information should be tracked: (1) current status of all POs, (2) performance on selected evaluation criteria for all suppliers, (3) information on each part type or commodity, and (4) information regarding all contracts and relationships. If a current contract commits the company to a total annual volume, managers need to know how much has been ordered to date. If a contract stipulates that the supplier will reduce the item price by 3 percent a year over the life of the relationship, sourcing needs to know if the supplier is living up to its obligation. Care should be given to design and maintain a database capable of providing accurate, relevant, and timely information.

Purchasing Skills for a Supply Chain World

When the steps in the sourcing process are performed well, a company gains access to the best inputs available worldwide. Supply management is the gateway to supplier capabilities all the way back to raw materials. Sourcing professionals need to build the following skills, which are discussed in detail elsewhere in the book.

Knowledge Management

Commodity expertise, an understanding of suppliers' capacities and capabilities, and a clear idea of upstream processes are needed to manage sourcing for competitive advantage. Few companies have pursued the management of suppliers beyond the first tier. Most efforts to extend the company's influence upstream have focused on second-tier purchasing contracts, which are simply efforts to consolidate purchase requirements at the second tier to obtain volume discounts. Proactive SC sourcing will require the mapping of the physical and technological flows associated with critical components. Supply managers will then be able to selectively work with upstream suppliers to resolve problems, coordinate efforts, and build capabilities. In addition, because many excellent suppliers are located in countries around the world, supply managers need to increase their global awareness and skill set.

Relationship Management

SC management means building the right relationships with all suppliers. Today's supply managers need to build alliance relationships with a few critical suppliers. Knowing when and how to build collaborative relationships is critical. At the same time, supply managers must maintain fair relationships with all suppliers, so they can encourage good service and develop additional resources. Efficient transaction mechanisms must be used to manage the numerous small or infrequent purchases. Establishing a supplier support infrastructure that assures efficiency, treats all suppliers fairly, and promotes collaboration is the modern supply management challenge.

Process Management

SC sourcing requires process expertise. Sourcing professionals must (1) constantly improve the sourcing process described earlier; (2) manage collaborative processes such as supplier certification, new product development, and cycle-time reduction; and (3) help suppliers improve their own processes. The supply manager's role in supplier development is to identify potential supplier participants, persuade them to participate, and then work with process engineers in the supplier education effort. Honda and Rockwell Collins have made supplier development a cornerstone of their sourcing strategy. John Deere is a leader in supplier education, actively helping suppliers improve their own production processes and purchasing practices so that they can more proactively manage upstream suppliers.

Technology Management

Web catalogs, Web scorecards, real-time information exchange, electronic funds transfer, and on-line bidding events are just a few of the areas where technology helps streamline purchasing management. Sourcing managers need to be technology savvy to effectively employ new technologies to reengineer the sourcing process. E-procurement promises many efficiency gains. Likewise, sourcing managers need to increase their familiarity with information technologies employed in other areas of the organization so they can provide insight into technology-related acquisition decisions. Because enterprise resource planning (ERP) systems, CRM software, and other applications are expensive and difficult to implement, the decision regarding which system to acquire is often made at senior management levels. Sourcing managers can, however, provide insight to help avoid expensive and embarrassing mistakes. The same is true regarding information management outsourcing decisions.

PRODUCING THE GOODS: THE NATURE OF PRODUCTION MANAGEMENT

Production management, also known as **operations** *or manufacturing management*, creates value for customers by transforming capital, technology, labor, and materials into more highly valued products and services. Whether we are watching television, driving to work, participating in recreational activities, or consuming a Big Mac and Coke, we use products and services that did not exist before an operations process was performed. Managed well, production and operations management drives productivity growth, is the wellspring of innovation, and generates higher living standards.[2]

Outstanding operations practices have been employed throughout history. For example, Venetian shipbuilders in the early fifteenth century employed labor specialization and a large-scale assembly line to equip their fighting galleys. By towing the galleys through a water channel between warehouses, the galleys could be completely outfitted at a pace of one ship every 36 minutes.[3] These same Venetians offer an early example of parts standardization via their practice of making rudders on warships interchangeable.[4] By being able to quickly change battle-damaged rudders, the Venetians achieved a key combative advantage.

Over the years, several factors have influenced the role of production management.

- The industrial revolution substituted machine power for human power, increasing productivity.
- Personal wealth and leisure time created a consumer society, which demanded better operations to produce the variety of products consumers wanted to buy.
- Frederick Taylor applied the scientific method of observation, improvement, training, and monitoring to standardize operations practices.[5]
- Quantitative analysis transformed operations from an art to a science. Computers made it possible for complex algorithms to be applied routinely in situations where judgment and guessing previously prevailed.[6]

Dramatic improvements in manufacturing management following World War II led John Kenneth Galbraith to claim, "We have solved the production problem."[7] However, global competition has reminded managers that operational excellence is a prerequisite to success. In the face of global competition, every company must design and implement outstanding operations processes to make the innovative, high-quality, low-cost goods and services global customers demand. The alternative: Extinction!

The Production Process

There is no such thing as a standard production process. The artisan-based, glass-blowing process used by Orrefours to produce fine leaded crystal looks completely different from the massive, highly-automated assembly lines employed by General Motors to build automobiles. Likewise, the semifixed assembly process utilized by Embraer to manufacture regional jets appears to have little in common with the flashy, entertaining process employed by Benihana's restaurants to captivate diners during the production of their delicious dinner.

Despite differences in physical layout and the specific activities performed, operations processes must manage the same core set of decisions to yield world-class results. These core decisions can be classified into two groups: design decisions and control decisions (see Figure 5.3).

Figure 5.3   World-Class Operations Management

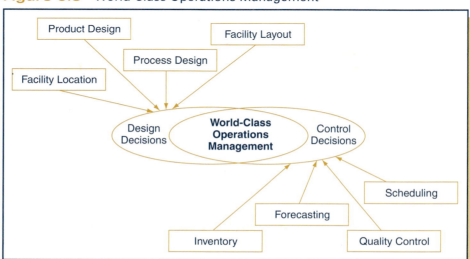

Design Decisions

Design decisions focus on infrastructure, product, and process. These decisions tend to be resource-intensive and have a long-term impact on corporate competitiveness.

Facility location decisions affect access to factor inputs and customer markets. When deciding where to locate a factory, manufacturers focus primarily on labor costs or resource proximity. Service companies pay more attention to where customers are located. Issues that should be considered in almost every location decision include the cost of land, construction, and energy; tax rates; transportation rates and availability; labor availability and productivity; materials cost; the location of customers and competitors; and lifestyle considerations.

Facility layout decisions determine the positioning of equipment, the flow of materials, and the number of times each item must be handled. The ideal layout minimizes movement and handling, creating a simple and smooth flow of materials through the facility. Over time, once-efficient layouts become circuitous as the products being produced and the processes used to produce them change. Because disrupting production to improve a facility's layout is expensive, managers need to learn when to modify or redesign an existing layout.

Product design decisions represent the company's ability to profitably capture future market share.[8] Product development begins with the generation of good ideas and culminates with a successful product launch. Fewer than 1 in 10 promising ideas ever becomes a marketplace success. Rapid product introduction helped Hewlett-Packard dominate the ink-jet printer market. Likewise, Nokia captured 40 percent of the cell phone market by rapidly bringing fashionable products to market. By contrast, Motorola's inability to design and introduce in a timely fashion the cell phones consumers wanted to buy led to an erosion of its market-dominant position. Most design efforts focus on reducing concept-to-market time by emphasizing the concurrent or simultaneous design of a product and the process used to make it.

Process design involves technology selection and work design. Technology choice is based on production volumes, financial resources, labor cost, the interchangeability of capital and labor, and the technology used by competitors. Regarding work design, specific jobs should be designed and grouped together in a way that promotes efficiency and quality. The objective of work design is to increase worker motivation and process efficiency. Poorly designed jobs—comprised of tedious, narrowly defined tasks—alienate workers, reduce productivity, and stifle learning. To counteract this situation, managers may emphasize job enlargement, job enrichment, and employee involvement programs.

Control Decisions

Control decisions take place on a day-to-day basis and define how materials move through the production process. Compatible design and control decisions can create a lean operating environment, which is needed to achieve world-class performance.

Forecasting provides an estimate of what products need to be produced and when they need to be produced. Forecasts are used to plan production, determine capacity needs, refine workforce plans, and determine inventory levels. Forecasting techniques range from simple moving averages to advanced econometric models. Most techniques use historical data, looking specifically at the sales trends. By nature, forecasts are almost always wrong. This fact drives the quest for more accurate information and for greater operating flexibility.

Inventory control determines how much and when to make specific products. The question of "how much to produce" can be answered by calculating an economic order quantity, which balances the cost of setting up production with the cost of storing goods. Larger production runs yield lower unit costs, but raise inventory costs. Low inventories can mean missed sales and customer frustration. The question of "when to produce" can be answered by calculating a reorder point, which compares the amount of inventory currently available to the rate of demand.

Scheduling occurs at two levels. First, aggregate planning determines what needs to be produced and provides a rough idea of the timing for the desired production. Inputs for aggregate planning include a measure of production capacity, a demand forecast, and cost data for different resources. Second, the work to be done at each workstation at any point in time must be defined. In a low-volume setting where multiple jobs might be waiting to be processed at a workstation, scheduling decisions assign priorities to each job. These priorities determine the sequence in which the jobs will be processed. For high-volume assembly operations, scheduling is defined via assembly-line layout. In one-of-a-kind projects such as the construction of an apartment complex, scheduling is done using project planning tools (these tools are also used for ERP implementations and other major initiatives that require careful resource management).

Quality control focuses on designing, building, and inspecting quality into both the process and the product. After all, no amount of inspection can make a bad product into a good one.[9] The goal is to make it right the first time, every time. A number of statistical tools are used to guide product design, monitor process quality, and evaluate the quality of finished products. Quality control is equally important in the delivery of services; however, because service quality is often viewed from the perspective of customer satisfaction, it is more difficult to quantify. Nonetheless, statistical techniques can and should be applied.

Toyota's Quest for Lean Production

For most of the twentieth century, mass production on assembly lines was considered to be the best way to produce high-volume products. By the late 1970s, Toyota, under tremendous competitive pressure, introduced just-in-time (JIT) manufacturing to the world. Toyota had patterned its production process, as closely as possible, to that found in the process industries. In JIT production, inventory is reduced to minimal levels and material flows are synchronized so that as one item moves out of a workstation, another is ready to move in. Materials flow through the facility like water through a pipe.

By altering the nature of the manufacturing environment, Toyota changed the cost/volume relationship, dropping the learning curve for JIT beneath that of the standard volume-dependent curve. A learning curve expresses the cost relationship between the number of items produced and the cost per item. Every time the cumulative production volume doubles, the cost of the nth item produced decreases by a certain percentage. If a company is on a 90 percent learning curve and production of the 100th unit cost $10, then the production of the 200th part will cost $9.

On a volume-dependent curve, the key to low-cost production is to build large factories to increase volume. Toyota discovered that on a JIT learning curve most of the economies are achieved when production reached 200,000 cars per year. While other carmakers were willing to settle for a 5 to 15 percent learning rate, Toyota achieved better than a 30 percent learning rate.[10] The difference was that Toyota designed and controlled its processes in a way that identified and eliminated waste. The Toyota approach required workers to actively participate in designing and managing the production system. Through JIT, Toyota improved productivity, raised the quality bar, and compressed cycle times. Over the years, the basic principles of

Table 5.2 Basic 5S Principles

THE 5 Ss	BASIC PRINCIPLE
Sort	Eliminate clutter. Remove all supplies, materials, tools, and paperwork not required in the operation. Keep only that which is needed to perform the process.
Set in Order	Organize the work area to make it easy to find what is needed. Everything has a place and everything is in its place.
Shine	Clean the work area. Make it shine. This includes aisles, walls, and meeting storage places.
Standardize	Create and use policies, procedures, and practices to assure that the first three of the 5S activities are performed regularly.
Sustain	Create a 5S culture by putting in place mechanisms that support, enhance, and extend 5S practices. Involving, measuring, and recognizing people are critical.

JIT have evolved into the current lean production philosophy. The best way to understand the "logic of lean" is to look at the adaptations to the operating environment that are required for success.

Waste Elimination

The goal of lean operations is to identify and eliminate waste wherever it is found. Toyota's 5S program, a comprehensive methodology for cleaning, organizing, and sustaining a productive work environment, exemplifies waste elimination (see Table 5.2). Simply stated, the 5S program for workspace management requires that "everything have a place and that everything be in its proper place." When tools—from jigs to staplers—are where they belong, wasted motion and effort are eliminated.

Often, the greatest opportunity for eliminating waste is inventory reduction. Inventory covers up the problems in the process that if removed, would improve quality, increase productivity, and shorten lead times. Lean companies reduce inventories in a systematic way that brings problems to light so they can be eliminated.

Workforce Participation

The JIT practice of "Jidoka"—or line stop—allows workers to stop the production line when a quality problem occurs. The Japanese symbols for Jidoka literally translate into "man-and-machine system." This level of worker participation requires serious investments in the problem-solving skills of individual workers. Worker participation in every facet of the value-added process becomes the social norm as (1) every member of the workforce is trained, (2) every individual takes responsibility for action, and (3) workers are effectively integrated into all aspects of the process.

Managerial Responsibility

When workers take responsibility for their own work and actively participate in problem solving, managers take on the role of teacher, team facilitator, and motivator. A spirit of cooperation replaces an adversarial attitude, allowing workers and managers to jointly work toward continual improvement. Not every manager is suited to fulfilling this coaching role. Skeptical managers who hesitate to give up authority and empower workers thwart lean initiatives.

Process Development

Because line workers are best positioned to improve processes, they must receive adequate statistical training and be empowered to make decisions. They can then solve problems and improve processes. The classic example of process improvement was Toyota's modification of a heavy press used to stamp hoods and fenders. Toyota reduced changeover time from 4 hours to 12 minutes—this type of improvement greatly improves production efficiency and flexibility. Toyota has recently built time buffers, which serve as active learning centers, into the assembly process. A time buffer is extra, or slack, time built into a process to allow process engineers to experiment with new tools or techniques to perform the work. The time buffer prevents major disruptions to the production process. The goal is to continue to improve already efficient processes by testing new assembly methods. These buffers are real-time learning and experimentation zones.

Network Orientation

Toyota believes that lean principles should be practiced upstream among its most important suppliers. The goal is for the supplier to become an extension of Toyota's processes. Long-term contracts, consolidated purchases, and co-located facilities make process integration possible. Greater value can be created when stability is increased and resources shared. Toyota's dependence on its key suppliers is evidenced by its willingness to increase its ownership stake in select suppliers to prevent General Motors and other competitors from gaining access to them.

Synchronization

A "pull" or "kanban" system is driven by customer demand, and it requires control and discipline to assure that materials arrive just in time to be used in production, to produce subassemblies just in time to be used in the final assembly process, and to deliver finished goods just in time to be used by the customer. The word "kanban" means little card. In its simple form, a kanban system transfers little cards to trigger production. When a "little card" is transferred to a workstation, production begins. The "kanban" system is thus a visual system that triggers production only when parts are needed "downstream." Because complexity makes synchronization difficult, lean organizations carefully manage the active number of inventory items or stock keeping units (SKUs), simplify product design, streamline production flows, work with fewer suppliers, outsource complete modules, and pursue the development of excellent information systems. Simplification is an important key to synchronization.

Continual, Incremental Improvement over the Long Term

Lean operations depend on incremental productivity gains and consistent innovation. Masaaki Imai, the Japanese continuous improvement guru, calls this quest for constant improvement *kaizen*. Companies that master the *kaizen* philosophy cultivate two attributes—a high level of workforce training and an organizational attitude that everyone is responsible for the organization's success. These attributes enable the lean company to adopt major breakthroughs when and if they occur.

Toyota learned early that success requires a long-term perspective. The modifications to Toyota's hood and fender press took 5 years to design and implement. The need for a long-term perspective is exemplified by the following story. At the end of a plant tour, an American manager asked his Japanese counterpart, "Why are you sharing all of this with us? Don't you realize that we are going to go home and copy

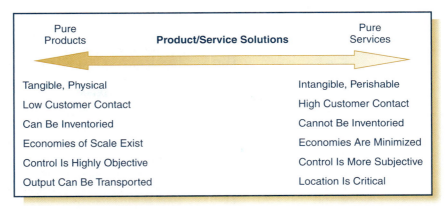

Figure 5.4 Continuum of Manufacturing and Service Operations

the things you are showing us?" This question prompted an unexpected response: "It has taken us years and years to develop and implement this system. We do not believe that you have the patience and determination to make it work."

Operations Management in the Services Setting

SC managers need to understand the distinctive characteristics of service operations for several reasons (see Figure 5.4). First, many SC processes are actually services. Purchasing, logistics, and new product development are examples of internal service operations. Second, services now dominate economic activity and service companies like banks rely on excellent SC practice. Finally, customers want to buy solutions, not just products.

This reality led IBM to transform itself from a computer manufacturer to an information solutions company. IBM offers consulting, hardware, and complete managerial support to companies interested in outsourcing their information needs. IBM even sells competitors' hardware as part of its information solutions. In the auto industry, General Motors discovered that setting up a finance division not only facilitated the purchase of its cars but also made it possible to use very low financing rates as a competitive weapon. General Electric likewise found that financing is an important aspect of selling turbines and other capital equipment. GE Capital is often the most profitable division at GE.

Critical differences between production and service operations are highlighted in the following sections.

Tangibility

Production outputs are tangible—they can be touched and closely examined. By contrast, service outputs are intangible—they cannot be touched, but must be experienced. When you buy a ticket to fly to Cancun for vacation, you cannot evaluate your satisfaction with the flight until you are consuming it. By then, it is too late to return the ticket for a refund. Because goods are physical, they can be stored and transported; services cannot. The physical nature of goods also allows for objective measures of quality, especially in terms of conformance to specifications. Intangibility affects many operations decisions, including facility location, facility layout, inventory, scheduling, and quality management.

Customer Contact

Customers of manufactured products have little contact with the production process. In services, customers are often involved in the delivery process.[11] For example, customers often bag their own groceries, and at Fuddruckers, the eclectic hamburger chain, customers assemble their own design-to-order hamburger from a set of fresh ingredients available in the dining area.

Perhaps the automated teller machine (ATM) in banking best exemplifies customer involvement. Using an ATM, a customer can perform routine transactions including deposits and withdrawals any time of the day or night without teller assistance. The customer becomes the service operator, enhancing productivity and satisfaction. On-line banking extends customer involvement in financial services, allowing the customer to perform a variety of transactions from the comfort of home 24 hours a day.

Ability to Inventory

Because physical goods can be stored, manufacturers can produce now to meet future demand. Services, by contrast, are generally produced and consumed simultaneously, making capacity and demand management critical. Companies can build for peak demand and live with excess capacity in off-peak hours, or they can build for average demand and lose sales during peak times. Matching capacity to demand is a challenge.

For example, once an airplane takes off, an empty seat cannot be sold. The capacity is lost forever. American Airlines pioneered yield management to put a body in seats that would otherwise go unfilled. Yield management attempts to maximize revenue by offering reduced-fare seats on each flight in a way that minimizes lost opportunities to sell full-fare seats. Using its automated reservation system SABRE (semiautomated business research environment), American uses historical demand information, forecasts of future demand, and seat availability to allocate discounted fares on each flight. If a flight is relatively empty, more seats are discounted at a higher rate. As seats become scarce, fares rise. Variable pricing increases the likelihood of filling as many seats as possible at the highest fare possible. American estimated that yield management increased its revenues by $1.4 billion in the period from 1989 to 1992, a number 50 percent higher than its net profit of $892 million for this same period.[12] Marriott Hotels and other service companies now use yield management to help them match supply to demand.

Economies of Scale

Labor productivity tends to be higher in production operations than in service operations. Because physical goods can be produced for future consumption and shipped to customers worldwide, manufacturers can build huge facilities that leverage scale economies. These large-scale operations are often highly automated and capital intensive. Services typically rely on smaller operations located close to customers. Service operations tend to be labor intensive. Thus, production operations tend to produce greater revenues and profits per labor hour than service operations.

For example, in 2005, Wal-Mart generated revenues of $285 billion and employed almost 1.7 million people. Wal-Mart's revenue per employee was about $167,778. By contrast, General Electric generated revenues of $134 billion with 305,000 employees. Its revenues per employee were over $482,147. The contrast is even greater when the focus is on profitability per employee. Wal-Mart earned $6,039 per employee compared to General Electric's $53,267 per employee. Table 5.3 shows similar comparisons for typical *Fortune* 50 manufacturing and service companies.

Table 5.3 Labor Productivity in Manufacturing and Service Companies (2003–2004)

MANUFACTURERS	EMPLOYEES	REVENUES	REVENUES/ EMPLOYEE	PROFITS	PROFITS/ EMPLOYEE
Exxon Mobil	85,900	$263,989,000,000	$3,073,213	$25,330,000,000	$294,878
General Motors	324,000	$193,517,000,000	$597,275	$2,805,000,000	$8,657
General Electric	307,000	$148,019,000,000	$482,147	$16,353,000,000	$53,257
Altria Group	156,000	$63,963,000,000	$410,019	$9,416,000,000	$60,359
Pfizer	115,000	$51,298,000,000	$446,070	$8,085,000,000	$70,304
Procter & Gamble	110,000	$56,741,000,000	$515,827	$7,257,000,000	$65,973
Dell	55,200	$49,205,000,000	$891,395	$3,043,000,000	$55,127
Dow Chemical	43,203	$46,307,000,000	$1,071,847	$4,515,000,000	$104,507
Microsoft	61,000	$39,788,000,000	$652,262	$12,254,000,000	$200,885
Boeing	159,000	$52,457,000,000	$329,918	$1,872,000,000	$11,774
Manufacturer Average			$846,997*		$92,573**

SERVICE COMPANIES	EMPLOYEES	REVENUES	REVENUES/ EMPLOYEE	PROFITS	PROFITS/ EMPLOYEE
Wal-Mart	1,700,000	$285,222,000,000	$167,778	$10,267,000,000	$6,039
Verizon Com.	210,000	$71,283,000,000	$339,443	$7,831,000,000	$37,290
Home Depot	325,000	$73,094,000,000	$224,905	$5,001,000,000	$15,388
State Farm Insurance	79,200	$58,800,000,000	$742,424	$5,300,000,000	$66,919
Federal Express	250,000	$29,363,000,000	$117,452	$1,449,000,000	$5,796
Target	292,000	$46,839,000,000	$160,408	$3,198,000,000	$10,952
Time Warner	84,900	$42,089,000,000	$495,748	$3,363,000,000	$39,611
Morgan Stanley	53,284	$39,549,000,000	$742,230	$4,485,000,000	$84,172
UPS	384,000	$42,581,000,000	$110,888	$3,870,000,000	$10,078
Walgreen	163,000	$42,201,000,000	$258,902	$1,559,000,000	$9,564
Service Average			$336,018*		$28,581**

*Average revenue per employee
**Average profit per employee

Objectivity of Control

Productivity and quality can be objectively measured in manufacturing. Intangibility and customer involvement complicate the control of a service operation. For example, the dimensions and characteristics of a product can be, and are, measured to determine if it is fit for use. By contrast, the customer experience in the service setting is seldom measured directly. Customer comment cards and suggestion boxes are often used in the service setting; however, the accuracy, frequency, and quality of the feedback provided are limited. Beyond that, customer behavior is often beyond the control of the service provider. We've all had to wait in the checkout line of a grocery store for the person in front of us to find a lost debit card.

Transportability

Because physical goods can be transported, manufacturers can locate production anywhere as long as their landed cost—the sum of production and transportation costs—is competitive. Services are generally consumed where they are produced. They are very difficult to transport—unless of course the output can be digitized. For example, on-line banking can be done from the customer's own home. The outsourcing of services such as call centers and software programming has become an important economic and political phenomenon. More exotic examples exist. An MRI can be performed in Boston, shipped via cyberspace to Bangalore where it is interpreted by an Indian radiologist, with the results being sent back the next day. India has become a popular destination for these service jobs because of its large, highly educated, English-speaking workforce. Forecasts suggest that over 3 million service jobs will be outsourced by 2015. However, for the vast majority of services that cannot be easily digitized, customers must come to the service. Peapod, the pioneer in grocery home delivery, continues to struggle to achieve consistent profitability.

Operations Skills for a Supply Chain World

Achieving great operational performance within the walls of the organization via the application of lean principles is the goal of most operations. However, in a world where rival supply chains compete, companies must strive for operational excellence throughout their chains by (1) careful outsourcing management, (2) supplier integrated manufacturing, and (3) the dissemination of best practices. Today's managers need the skills to do this; otherwise, they risk obsolescence. After all, the supply chain is only as strong as the weakest link.

Outsourcing

Outsourcing allows a company to invest in a few specific skills while relying on outsource partners to perform other vital activities. Managed appropriately, this specialization can improve both service and efficiency. Dell's business model relies on ultra-efficient contract manufacturers and exemplifies the opportunity to use outsourcing to enhance overall SC efficiency. Dell's challenge is to add enough value to retain its role as the SC captain.

Supplier Integrated Manufacturing

Defining what needs to be done and who should do it is a critical part of supply chain design. Increasingly, companies are learning to share resources in new and unique ways to improve their value-added capabilities. Volkswagen's truck assembly facility in Resende, Brazil, is an interesting experiment in the shifting of value-added roles and responsibilities. Volkswagen built the assembly facility and invited seven key suppliers to establish assembly lines within the facility. Suppliers provide their own capital equipment and assembly personnel, and they do not get paid until the finished vehicle passes final inspection.

Best Practices Dissemination

Companies need to learn how to share best practices across organizational and geographic boundaries. Payless ShoeSource uses an annual audit to share best practices with its suppliers. When an outstanding practice is identified at one supplier, it is incorporated into the audit so that the practice can be shared with other suppliers. The goal must be to create the learning supply chain.

DELIVERING THE GOODS: THE NATURE OF LOGISTICS MANAGEMENT

Logistics is the art and science of moving things from one point to another and storing them along the way. Logistics bridges the physical and temporal gaps in a global supply chain. Indeed, efficient logistics makes a global economy possible, lowering the costs of living for the people of the world. Today, a supermarket in London might sell fish from Maine and Vietnam and fruits from California and Chile. A North American apparel retailer might sell products sourced from over 50 countries in over 4,000 retail outlets located on 3 continents. People can also vacation in once-remote locations or visit family across continents. The performance of modern logistics systems affects almost every aspect of our lives, and they work so well that we take them for granted.

The Council of Supply Chain Management Professionals (CSCMP), the leading professional association of logistics and supply chain managers and educators, has defined logistics as follows:

> Logistics management is that part of SCM that plans, implements, and controls the efficient, effective forward and reverse flow and storage of goods, services, and related information between the point of origin and the point of consumption in order to meet customers' requirements.

Logistical excellence has become a cornerstone of the competitive strategy of such well-known companies as Benetton, Hershey's, The Limited, and Whirlpool. Outbound logistics costs account for between 7 and 10 percent of each sales dollar. Though logistics costs are sizable, the real potential of logistics lies in its ability to help differentiate the company from the competition, increasing customer loyalty, sales, and profits. Donald Bowersox, a logistics thought leader, pointed out that today's customers want (1) to receive exactly what they ordered: no more, no less, no substitutions, no defects, no breakage, no spoilage; (2) delivery of their perfectly filled orders at the agreed-upon time; and (3) to pay as little as possible. This is today's logistical mandate.

The Logistical Process

The logistics process often is discussed in terms of inbound and outbound flows. **Materials management** is concerned with the inbound movement and storage of raw materials, purchased components, and subassemblies entering and flowing through the conversion process. The central objective of materials management is to ensure that production has the necessary inputs at the right time and place. *Physical distribution* focuses on the outbound transportation and storage of finished products from point of manufacture to where customers wish to acquire them. The goal of physical distribution is to meet or exceed customer service expectations at the lowest possible costs.

A company's overall logistics capability is defined by the way it organizes and manages people, facilities, equipment, and operating policies. Table 5.4 shows the basic roles and responsibilities of core logistical activities. These activities must be planned in concert with other internal and external processes. For instance, logistics must coordinate forecasting and inventory control decisions with production management. Packaging decisions must involve marketing input and downstream customer concerns.

Order Fulfillment

Logistics creates value by delivering orders when and where they are needed. The order cycle is the sequence of activities that begins when a need is recognized and ends when the product is delivered and available for use. Figure 5.5 shows the key activities that comprise a typical order cycle. By definition, the order cycle begins and ends with the buying company. The buyer must recognize a need and place an order. The supplier must then process the order. Order processing involves (1) order entry, (2) production or picking of the order, and (3) preparation and packaging for

Table 5.4 Basic Logistics Activities

ACTIVITY	BASIC ROLES AND RESPONSIBILITIES
Customer Service	Customer service focuses on understanding what customers want and measuring logistics performance against these customer requirements.
Demand Forecasting	Forecasts—estimates of demand—must be developed to help plan other logistics activities, allocate resources, and provide high levels of service at low costs.
Documentation	Accurate documentation helps assure that the product gets to the customer on time. Documentation is particularly vital in international shipments.
Information Management	Data on carriers, customers, and inventories must be turned into useful decision-making information. Information replaces inventory in today's logistics systems.
Inventory Management	Product must be available to meet production requirements and customer demand. However, inventory is expensive. Inventory control must support high levels of customer service with as little inventory as possible.
Material Handling	Because handling materials costs money and can lead to damage, factories and warehouses are designed to minimize the total amount of required handling.
Order Processing	Order processing initiates work. Many orders are transmitted electronically, improving the speed and accuracy of the fulfillment process.
Packaging	Packaging protects the product throughout the distribution process. Packaging also conveys information about the product and presents an attractive appearance.
Parts and Service Support	Needed spare and replacement parts must be available to support sales. Caterpillar promises delivery of needed replacement parts anywhere in the world within 48 hours. This type of after-sales support increases customer loyalty.
Site Selection/Location	Location can provide access to inputs like low-cost labor and materials. It can also affect customer service levels, providing access to important consumer markets.
Return Goods Handling	Defective products and inaccurate orders must be returned efficiently. "Reverse logistics" is very important to achieving high levels of customer satisfaction.
Salvage and Recycling	Handling excess materials is often overlooked. However, this is an important logistics activity, especially when hazardous materials or recyclable items must be managed.
Transportation Management	Transportation is the most visible logistics activity. Six modal options exist: rail, truck, air, water, pipeline, and cyberspace.
Warehouse/ DC Management	Storing products until they are ready for use is the role of warehousing. A variety of products are also consolidated into a single customer shipment.

shipment. The order is then shipped from the supplier to the buyer. Once the order arrives at the buyer's receiving dock, it must be inspected and accepted before it is moved to the point of use.

An important issue is to reduce order cycle times. Managers realize that much of the fulfillment lead time is nonproductive time. A measure known as the **dwell time ratio** evaluates the number of days inventory sits idle compared to the number of days the inventory is moving. In many instances 90 percent of the total order cycle is nonproductive. To reduce the cycle time, one or more of the activities that make up the order cycle must be managed more efficiently. Figure 5.6 shows the five primary activities that must be managed to improve order fulfillment.

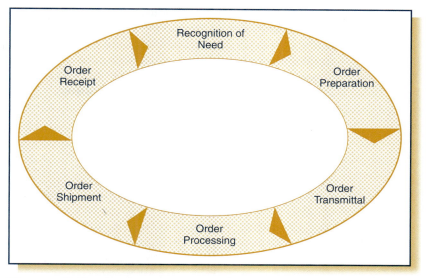

Figure 5.5 The Order Cycle

- Placing facilities in the right location and leveraging appropriate process technologies can help a company reduce the combined production and delivery time.
- Carrying the right quantity and mix of inventory allows the company to rapidly fill complete orders.
- Streamlining order processing eliminates unnecessary steps. Assuring that orders are entered accurately helps eliminate delays and fill orders as specified.
- Developing good relationships with reliable transportation companies reduces transit times and increases on-time delivery performance.
- Adopting appropriate technologies and implementing innovative materials handling processes like cross-docking can increase the speed at which materials flow through warehouses.

Fast-cycle order fulfillment depends more on how well a company coordinates all of the activities that comprise the order cycle than on how well its performs any single activity. For example, in an effort to improve customer service through better fulfillment, National Semiconductor closed six warehouses in different areas of the world.

Figure 5.6 Activities That Facilitate Order Fulfillment

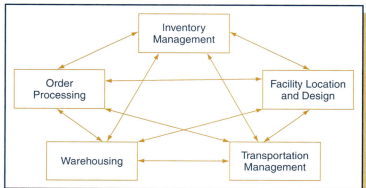

The inventory in the warehouses was consolidated into a single 125,000-square-foot distribution center in Singapore. This move reduced the total amount of inventory that needed to be held while increasing the probability that National Semiconductor could deliver complete orders. However, the only way to provide acceptable delivery times to worldwide customers from a single distribution center was to switch transport modes to airfreight. By combining airfreight with consolidated inventory in a single distribution center (DC), National Semiconductor reduced delivery time 47 percent while lowering total distribution costs by 2.5 percent. More importantly, sales increased by 34 percent.[13]

Another question associated with any order is, "Who is going to manage and pay for the transportation?" The two primary options are to buy product collect or prepaid. Sam's Club analyzes all of its purchases to determine which buying terms are most advantageous. When a company buys collect, it takes ownership of the product at the supplier's dock and arranges for necessary transportation. In the prepaid option, the supplier arranges and pays for the transportation, passing the costs on to the buyer. A transportation allowance is often offered to the retailer. Sam's Club knows that the allowance often does not cover the added freight charge, and that suppliers often push the prepaid option because it gives them an opportunity to make a little money in the freight management process. This hidden supplier margin motivates Sam's Club to decouple purchase price and transportation cost. Because Sam's Club makes the effort to do the analysis, it can choose the low-cost option for each order.

Transportation Management

Transportation cost, availability, and reliability play a vital role in logistics system design. They influence the number and location of facilities needed to serve worldwide customers.[14] Transportation also influences inventory management, product and packaging design, and customer service strategies.[15] Effective transportation strategies can greatly enhance competitiveness. Therefore, decisions such as modal choice, carrier selection, transportation routing, and logistical outsourcing should be considered carefully. Because modal choice determines the service characteristics and costs of the transportation system, it is the driver of transportation system design.[16]

Logistical managers can select from six general modes of transportation: rail, motor carrier, pipeline, airplane, ship, or cyberspace. For most companies, choosing a transportation mode depends on the type of product being shipped, the origin and destination points, the infrastructure available, customer requirements, and the cost/service characteristics of the available modes. An evaluation of the characteristics highlighted in Table 5.5 reveals that each mode possesses advantages and disadvantages depending on the situation. The goal is to select the lowest-cost mode capable of achieving the desired service level.

The modal selection decision is complex, requiring careful costing and trade-off analysis. For instance, managers at Sam's Club, in their bid to compete with Costco, initiated a modal cost analysis. Their goal was to leverage Sam's Club's logistical expertise to overcome Costco's merchandising advantage. They found that even within the motor carrier mode, options and costs varied greatly. Truckload (TL) shipments yielded the lowest costs. "Milk-run" style multiple stop truckload shipments cost 25 percent more. Less-than-truckload (LTL) shipments, which involve product from multiple shippers being consolidated into a full truckload quantity, cost 250 percent more than the base TL cost. Parcel service costs were 700 percent higher, and airfreight over 1,000 percent higher than TL costs. The cost differences were greater than many managers expected. This new understanding led managers to analyze the entire logistical network to identify opportunities to ship more freight via TL carrier.

Table 5.5   Evaluation of the Major Modes of Transportation

	LAND		
	RAIL	MOTOR CARRIERS	PIPELINE
Cost	High fixed, low variable cost structure Inexpensive, especially for bulk goods	High variable (90%), low fixed (10%) More expensive than rail	High fixed, low variable Very inexpensive
Speed	Relatively slow, average car speed 20 MPH (unless utilizing double stack unit trains, effectively doubling speed)	Medium speed where sufficient roads exist, about twice as fast as rail (50 MPH)	Nature of product makes speed a nonissue
Quantities	Large quantities; full carload increments most cost-effective	Limited capacity of about 80,000 lbs; larger capacity combination vehicles are geographically limited	Large quantities of limited products
Geographical Coverage	Widespread on some continents; limited by tracks, landmass	Widespread on some continents; limited by roads, landmass	Widespread on some continents; limited by unidirectional movement and the availability of landmass to support pipelines
Environmental Concerns	High impact of new tracks, low air pollution	High pollution, especially in developing countries, high impact of new roads	Pipeline leakage, high impact on wildlife, scenic value
Distances	Medium to long	Short to medium	Medium most common
Required Infrastructure	Tracks, rolling stock	Roads, vehiclesRouting limited by road location	Pipeline between two points required
Product Variety	Large variety of products; ideally suited for bulk goods	Large variety of products	Primarily petroleum products; only practical for liquid, liquid-carried, or gas products
Reliability	Low loss, damage, less timely (delays at sidings, terminals)	Limited loss, damage, more timely than rail	Very low loss or damage, usually timely
Flexibility	Routing limited to track location, little door-to-door delivery (side spur required)	Routing limited to road locations, but still good for JIT, extensive access in countries with well-developed highway systems, door-to-door delivery possible with appropriate roads	Routing limited to pipelines
	WATER	AIR	CYBERSPACE
	SHIP	AIRPLANE	INTERNET
Cost	High variable, low fixed Very inexpensive, about $.008/ton mile (1/4 cost of railroad) Less fuel needed	High variable, low fixed Very expensive (2 to 3 times as high as motor carriers, 12 to 15 times as high as rail); lower packing costs than ship	Low variable, low fixed Extremely inexpensive, where infrastructure is in place

(continued)

Table 5.5 Continued

	WATER	AIR	CYBERSPACE
	SHIP	AIRPLANE	INTERNET
Speed	Inland waterway: Slow, about 4 to 5 MPH Ocean: faster, fewer stops (10–12 days Pacific crossing)	Fast speed within and between continents; measured in hours or days	Extremely fast
Quantities	Large. Container ships carry up to 40 equivalent unit containers	Relatively small	Limited by number of source transmission lines available, or satellite access
Geographical Coverage	Global, but limited to natural and constructed waterways	Widespread on some continents; limited by air terminal availability	Widespread on some continents; limited by transmission capability availability
Environmental Concerns	Spillage from accidents, leakage, high impact on fisheries	Noise pollution near major population centers	None except where new transmission line construction occurs, then less than other modes
Distances	Long to very long	Medium to very long	Very short to very long
Required Infrastructure	Ports, ships Routing limited by waterway, ocean availability	Airports, navigational aids, airplanes Routing limited by airport location	Telephone lines, satellite, cellular transmission capability Routing limited by transmission path
Product Variety	Low variety of heavy, bulk, or low-value-by-weight items, often commodities	Large variety of small, high-value-by-weight, often perishable items	Limited to digital information; software, music, video, documents, information
Reliability	Loss, damage tends to be relatively high, especially for bulk shipments	Low loss or damage, very timely	No loss, except through piracy, great variations in timely delivery
Flexibility	Port to port	Air terminal to air terminal	Computer to computer

Distribution Management

Warehousing performs the vital storage function, decoupling manufacturing from consumption and making product available when it is needed. Two common warehousing options exist: (1) to store product in a finished goods warehouse located at a manufacturing facility and (2) to store the product in a **distribution center (DC),** which acts as an intermediate storage location between the manufacturing facility and the customer. Distribution centers are used when many different items from diverse production sites are to be stored in a single location. Many value-added activities beyond holding inventory are performed in warehouses and DCs:

- Shipping and receiving goods and materials
- Materials handling and order processing
- Consolidating and distributing shipments

- Transportation management, such as routing, tracing, and monitoring movements
- Product packaging and labeling (form postponement)
- Re-packaging and mixing of products
- Preparation of in-store displays (ready store delivery pallets)
- Light manufacturing or assembly
- Scrap and disposal

Because holding inventory costs money, product flow is critical in distribution operations. The cost of capital tied up in inventories can be large. Other costs incurred when products sit in storage include product obsolescence, damage, and loss. Therefore, most companies try to keep product in storage for the shortest time possible. Efficient warehousing operations that receive product, place it in inventory, pick it to fill orders, and move it quickly out the door help keep distribution costs down. Wal-Mart's flow-through or cross-dock operations exemplify efficient movement of product through a DC, as shown in Figure 5.7.

Wal-Mart designed its distribution centers to gather and redistribute goods from multiple suppliers to multiple retail supercenters. Each regional DC covers an area 27 acres in size and supports approximately 120 supercenters. Full truckloads of product arrive at one loading dock, where the product is unloaded, broken down and mixed with other products that have recently arrived from other suppliers, and then dispatched to individual retail stores in full truckloads. Most product never sits in inventory, but flows from one dock to another. The goal is for product to be dropped, unloaded, mixed, packed, and shipped within 48 hours. Cross-docking consolidates and stages inventory so that customer service levels can be raised while production and transportation scale economies are obtained. Cost and performance trade-offs must be evaluated to determine how warehousing can best improve distribution operations.

Designing an effective distribution network requires that managers make decisions regarding the number, location, ownership, and automation of warehouse operations. Few companies operate ideally designed distribution networks. The problem arises from the fact that networks tend to grow over time. As demand grows, new warehouses are added. Further, demand patterns change, as do customer networks.

Figure 5.7 A Cross-Docking Operation

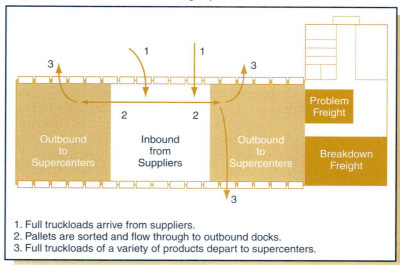

1. Full truckloads arrive from suppliers.
2. Pallets are sorted and flow through to outbound docks.
3. Full truckloads of a variety of products depart to supercenters.

Over time, what was once a well-designed network can become costly and inefficient. Managers should therefore reevaluate their logistical operations periodically. Taking a "start-from-scratch" mind-set can provide insight into the types of change that may be needed. Nabisco returned to the basics as it reevaluated its distribution network.

Nabisco initiated a network redesign with the following goal: "To reduce the cost of total product and information flow from the point of origin to the point of consumption, and to accelerate the response time to meet changing customer demand." Nabisco's as-is map of its distribution network revealed that it managed over 2,000 SKUs sourced from 106 production and co-packing facilities. These products were delivered to 10,500 different customer DCs and stores via 30 major transportation carriers. To support this network, Nabisco had decided to outsource DC operations so it could focus on its core activities and leave the warehousing to the specialists. They employed 12 regional third-party DCs located in Portland, Oregon; Modesto, California; Buena Park, California; Denver, Colorado; Kansas City, Kansas; Grand Prairie, Texas; Chicago, Illinois; Columbus, Ohio; Mechanicsburg, Pennsylvania; Franklin, New Jersey; Morrow, Georgia; and Jacksonville, Florida.

After comparing distribution costs with the service levels provided, Nabisco decided that it needed to reduce the number of DCs. A zip-code based analysis of customer demand suggested that six DCs could provide adequate national coverage. (Most zip-code analyses suggest that national coverage can be obtained with five DCs located in Los Angeles, California; Dallas, Texas; Chicago, Illinois; Mechanicsburg, Pennsylvania; and Atlanta, Georgia.) Nabisco planned to phase out three or four DCs, but these plans were put on hold when Nabisco was acquired by Kraft Foods. The details of a world-class distribution system depend on the whole picture, and Nabisco's picture had just changed.

Logistics Skills for a Supply Chain World

Making logistics more efficient and effective can be daunting and complex, but the potential payoff is large. Managers generally tackle less complex reforms as they strive to improve company performance. One manager described this situation: "We've done most of what we need to do to be competitive. We've changed the way we develop products, manufacture, market, and advertise. The one piece of the puzzle we haven't addressed is logistics. It's the next source of competitive advantage. The possibilities are just astounding."[17] To use logistics as the thread that ties a supply chain's value-added activities together, managers need to build the skills needed to do the following.

Logistics Outsourcing

The complexity of logistics operations has led many companies to outsource their logistics operations. Third-party logistics (3PL) is a multibillion-dollar industry and continues to grow. Many companies simply lack the resources to provide world-class logistics support for their own operations. Others prefer to avoid the tangled mess that global logistics represents. UPS manages National Semiconductor's global distribution center. UPS also stores and delivers repair parts for Dell's server business. Schneider National Logistics manages General Motors' parts operations. Managers must now ask and answer two related questions: "When is logistical outsourcing the most competitive option?" and "Among the third-parties, who can do the best job?"

Shared Logistics Services

Shipping small quantities offers greater customer responsiveness, but it is extremely costly. Companies therefore do everything they can to move product in full truckload quantities. To maximize transport efficiencies, more companies are experimenting with shared logistics services. For example, ServiceCraft, a California-based **third party logistics company (3PL)**, consolidates product from several different packaged goods companies for full truckload delivery to retail stores. ServiceCraft's coordinating role allows smaller, but more frequent shipments to be made economically. Nabisco has even shipped product via its customers' transportation fleet. Shared logistics offers tremendous opportunities to reduce inefficiencies like empty backhauls and partially filled trucks. However, what action do you take to remedy late or damaged shipments when your best customer is moving your freight?

Network Rationalization

As the Nabisco example demonstrates, managing the many logistics decisions required to support commercial operations is a complicated challenge. Managers often acknowledge that simplifying the logistics system will yield "a pot of gold," but they quickly note that they are not eager to tackle what they describe as tangled webs of complexity.[18] Most companies are just now beginning to seriously consider rationalizing their logistics network. This will require a better understanding of customer needs, supplier capabilities, and service provider options. It will also require much more sophisticated information technology to track all of the DC location options, carrier selection decisions, and routing alternatives. Finally, logistics managers will need to master the art of relationship management to make a rationalized network run effectively.

CONCLUSION

Turning great ideas into customer value requires the coordinated management of purchasing, production, and logistics. Because no company has the capital and expertise to do it all, diverse SC members must learn to work together to design and manage key physical flows across the supply chain's infrastructure. Managers must become skilled at building efficient networks of facilities, equipment, and processes that combine specialized capabilities found up and down the chain. Dell has done a great job of not only reaching customers to create demand but also of integrating the production skills of Solectron and other contract manufacturers into Dell's build-to-order, direct sales delivery system. Frito-Lay has created tremendous appetite for its snack foods, and it meets that demand through an extensive network of distribution centers and local drivers who keep retailers' racks stocked with Frito-Lay products.

Companies have become both strategically and operationally interconnected. As consumers and managers, we recognize that purchasing, production, and logistics decisions define the physical flow; yet we often forget how they affect strategy formulation. We also forget that a problem anywhere in the physical flow can bring the entire chain to a screeching halt—remember, the fire at Aisin's brake plant shut mighty Toyota down in a matter of hours. Moreover, remember that customers really don't care where the problem occurs up and down the chain; they only know that service failures represent broken promises.

Understanding the nature and role of purchasing, production, and logistics and how they work together to fulfill orders enables managers to assess the value of unique competencies and delegate specific roles and responsibilities throughout the supply chain. If managers want their companies to be valued SC team members, they need to know how to acquire, transform, and deliver goods and services efficiently and effectively.

SUMMARY OF KEY POINTS

1. Making and delivering a valued product or service is the responsibility of purchasing, production, and logistics. These functions are the building blocks of an SC strategy.

2. Purchasing acquires the inputs used to produce a finished good or service. The purchasing process begins with the recognition of a need and concludes when acceptable products are available for use.

3. Supply management professionals are the gatekeepers to upstream capacities and capabilities. They control a huge portion of the value added in most supply chains.

4. Production converts sourced inputs into a product or service that customers value. No standard production process exists. Critical decision areas include inventory control, scheduling, quality control, and productivity management.

5. Operational excellence is a prerequisite to success, making the application of lean principles and the sharing of best practices across organizational boundaries critical.

6. Logistics' main role is to manage storage and transportation to achieve outstanding levels of order fulfillment.

7. To use logistics as the thread that ties a supply chain's value-added activities together, managers need to know how to use the logistical capabilities and infrastructure of the entire supply chain to reduce costs and improve service. Using 3PLs and sharing logistics services can improve logistical efficiency.

8. Managers need to understand purchasing, production, and logistics processes to effectively select the right competencies and assign other activities to the right SC members.

REVIEW EXERCISES

1. Explain how the management of purchasing, production, and logistics processes affects customer satisfaction.

2. Think of a couple of occasions when you were dissatisfied with a product you purchased. Where did the breakdown in the management of the physical flow occur that caused your dissatisfaction?

3. What is the Supply Chain Council? Describe the characteristics of the SCOR model. Identify the strengths and weaknesses in the SCOR approach.

4. Describe the purchasing process. What are the key steps in the process? How might greater SC integration affect each step? How can technology be used to streamline the process?

5. Discuss the critical production management decision areas. How has lean management affected each

of these decision areas? Identify the three greatest impediments to lean operations.

6. Describe the difference between the operational characteristics of products and services. Which lean principles are applicable to service operations? Which are not? Why?

7. Discuss the movement and storage roles of logistics management. Why did Gus Pagonis claim, "In logistics, if you go an hour without a screw-up, you've had a great day"?

8. Identify five ways companies can work more closely to achieve efficient management of the purchasing, production, and logistics activities that are so critical to managing the supply chain's physical flow.

Case   *The Club War*

The battle lines were drawn in the membership warehouse sector and the competitive intensity was ratcheting up. As Jim Brau looked out the airplane window through the clouds, he pondered the charge to improve efficiency and cut costs through logistical redesign. His

flight would be landing in a few minutes and he would be back in the office within the hour. Jim had just completed a tour of three Midwestern stores and was eager to get back to work. Jim and his reengineering team had been given the mandate to "provide a competitive advantage to Sam's Club by having merchandize flow through the Sam's Club supply chain at the *lowest possible cost*."

EXISTING INEFFICIENCIES

To date, the team had analyzed the "as-is" supply chain and identified 10 sources of inefficiency. Jim knew that the challenge was to determine how to exploit the inbound network to transform the following inefficiencies into opportunities for competitive advantage.

1. Too much freight was moving in non-truckload quantities. Freight cost analysis revealed that TL was by far the low-cost option. Multistop TL cost 25 percent; LTL, 250 percent; parcel, 700 percent; and airfreight, 1040 percent more.
2. Delivery options from suppliers were not always analyzed adequately. Cross-docking leveraged TL economies; yet the team wondered whether other options might be more cost-effective at times.
3. Despite all of Sam's Club's efforts, empty backhauls were still prevalent. Wal-Mart also suffered from empty backhaul inefficiencies.
4. Freight imported from Asia landed almost exclusively on the West Coast and was then shipped by truck to DCs and individual stores. Everyone wondered if this was the most efficient option.
5. Sam's Club shipped millions of pounds of freight LTL. There was no way to create milk runs or buy certain products in larger quantities; still, the team wondered if some other alternative might be found.
6. Industry practice was to buy product with shipping prepaid. Although suppliers often offered a shipping allowance, the question was whether or not this was really the best way to manage inbound freight.
7. Scores of carriers and thousands of routes were used to move product from suppliers to DCs and then on to stores. Was Sam's Club using the most efficient options, especially with respect to shipping points?
8. The loss and damage bill seemed excessive and materials handling costs were high. Transportation costs for some low-density products like garden ponds really took a toll on profit margins.
9. It appeared that the impact of purchasing decisions on transportation efficiencies was often ignored, leading to poor capacity utilization and excessive damage.
10. The team knew that a trailer's capacity is determined by weight and volume; yet this fact had not been taken into consideration in defining trailer loading policies and procedures.

INDUSTRY BACKGROUND

The members-only shopping craze began in 1976 when the first Price Club opened in a converted airplane hanger in San Diego, California. By 2002, almost 1,000 club stores were in operation worldwide, most in the United States. Two companies dominated the market—Costco and Sam's Club. Costco operated 390 stores and generated sales of about $35 billion in 2001. Sam's Club claimed over 46 million members, operated over 500 warehouse stores, and generated sales of $30 billion. Both promoted a similar value proposition and operated using comparable efficiency-driven business models.

Costco	Sam's Club
Costco is dedicated to bringing our members the best possible prices on quality brand-name merchandise.	SAM'S CLUB offers exceptional value on brand-name merchandise at "members only" prices.
Our operating philosophy has been simple. Keep costs down and pass the savings on to our members. Our large membership base and tremendous buying power, combined with our never-ending quest for efficiency, result in the best possible prices for our members.	SAM'S CLUB operates by selling merchandise at very low profit margins, passing savings along to members in the form of low, warehouse prices. SAM'S CLUB consistently works to meet member expectations by operating in a cost-effective manner, offering big deals on general merchandise and other services.

The typical warehouse store is over 100,000 square feet and maintains a spartan look and feel. To keep costs down and prices low, each club is patterned after a working warehouse. This no-frills format features cement floors and steel racks from floor to ceiling packed with merchandise, which is often displayed on shipping pallets. The product line consists of over 4,000 items, including apparel, appliances, automotive, books, consumer packaged goods, electronics, fresh and frozen foods, home furnishings, and office supplies. Many items are available year round; however, other items are found strictly on a seasonal basis. Other products are on hand through a unique special buy and are obtainable on a one-time-only basis. Because customers never know whether these products will be available at a future time, a treasure-hunt mentality results, driving impulse buying. Of course, to make this format work and fulfill the value promise made to members requires operational excellence not only in store operations but also in sourcing and logistics.

CASE QUESTIONS

1. For each source of inefficiency, what are Jim's options? What policies and procedures could help eliminate the inefficiencies?
2. Identify the appropriate analyses for each option: What information is needed? What issues should be considered?

ENDNOTES

1. Tully, S. (1995, February 20). Purchasing's new muscle. *Fortune*, pp. 75–83. Monczka, R., Trent, R., & Handfield, R. (2002). *Purchasing and supply chain management*. Cincinnati: South-Western College Publishing.
2. Skinner, W. (1969). Manufacturing—missing link in corporate strategy. *Harvard Business Review, 47*(3), 136–145. Drucker (1991). The new productivity challenge. *Harvard Business Review, 69*(5), 69–79.
3. Ruch, W. A., Fearon, H. E., & Wieters, C. D. (1992). *Fundamentals of production/operations management*. St. Paul: West Publishing Company.
4. Chase, R. B., & Garvin, D. A. (1989). The service factory. *Harvard Business Review, 67*(4), 61–69.
5. Schroeder, R. (1993). *Operations management*. Boston: McGraw-Hill/Irwin.
6. Ibid. #1.
7. Galbraith, J. K. (1998). *The affluent society*. New York: Houghton Mifflin.
8. Wheelwright, S., & Clark, K. (1992). Creating project plans to focus product development. *Harvard Business Review, 70*(3), 70–82.
9. Ibid. #1.
10. Schonberger, R. J. (1986). *World class manufacturing*. New York: The Free Press.
11. Ibid. #2.
12. Davis, P. (1994). Airline ties profitability to yield management. *SIAM News, 27*(5).
13. Henkoff, R. (1994, November 28). Delivering the goods. *Fortune*, pp. 64–78.
14. Aikens, C. H. (1985). Facility location models of distribution planning. *European Journal of Operations Research*, 263–279. Brandeau, M. L., & Chiu, S. S. (1989, June). An overview of representative problems in location research. *Management Science*, 645–678. Fawcett, S. E., & Magnan, G. N. (2002). The rhetoric and reality of supply chain. *International Journal of Physical Distribution and Logistics Management, 32*(5), 339–361.
15. Bowersox, D. J., Closs, D. J., and Copper, M. B. (2002). *Supply chain logistics management*. New York: McGraw Hill.
16. Lambert, D., & Cooper, M. (2000). Issues in supply chain management. *Industrial Marketing Management, 29*(1), 65–83. Wood, D. F., & Johnson, J. C. (1996). *Contemporary transportation*. Upper Saddle River, NJ: Prentice Hall.
17. Henkoff, R. (1994, November 28). Delivering the goods. *Fortune*, pp. 64–78.
18. Fawcett, S. E., & Magnan, G. N. (2001). *Achieving world-class supply chain alignment: Benefits, barriers, and bridges*. Phoenix, AZ: National Association of Purchasing Management.

Supplement E

Forecasting and Inventory Management

Efficiently managing the order fulfillment process from raw materials to the customer's dock, door, or trunk requires that managers throughout the supply network must anticipate what customers at each tier of the chain will want to buy and when they will want to buy it. Even in simple supply chains, companies buy materials from a variety of suppliers, make a number of distinct and often diverse products, and sell to a host of different customers. This complexity makes it almost impossible to have perfect information regarding product demand.

What does this mean? It means that managers must make many "guesses" about the timing and quantity of their purchasing, production, and logistics activities. Unfortunately, bad guesses cost the company and the chain time and money. Remember the beer distribution game from Chapter 1. Even in that super simple supply chain—each team purchased from only one supplier, produced only one product, and sold to only one customer—a lack of perfect information led to increased costs and poor customer service.

To help overcome the challenges related to matching supply to demand and managing the physical flow of materials through the chain, managers have developed sophisticated decision tools in the areas of forecasting and inventory managing. As an SC manager, you will want to have a sound understanding of these tools. The following tutorials will help you put these fundamental tools in you decision-making toolbox.

Forecasting

As mentioned in the chapter, airlines use forecasting to help improve their yield and thereby improve their profitability. As part of this forecasting process, the airlines need to predict what the demand for a certain route will be so that they can know how many planes and flights to assign to that route. If the airlines overestimate demand, they may allocate too many planes or flights to a particular route and have a lot of empty seats. If they underestimate demand, they may have full flights but may be missing out on the potential revenues that could be generated with greater capacity.

A certain percentage of people who purchase tickets for air travel do not actually show up for the flight. To compensate for this, airlines typically overbook each flight based on their forecast of how many "no-shows" there will be on each flight. If they overestimate the number of no-shows, they may have empty seats, which reduce their yield. If they underestimate the number of no-shows, they may have more passengers show up than they can fit on a plane. When this occurs, the airlines have to delay passengers in order to have them take the next flight. If the next flight isn't leaving soon after the original flight, the airlines may also be required to pay for meals and lodging for passengers while they wait.

Accurately forecasting airline travel not only affects the airlines but also their suppliers. Boeing, for example, plans its production partially based on what the consumer

demand for air travel is. When this demand, and consequently airline profits, falls short of expectations, airlines consider canceling existing contracts for airplanes or have difficulty paying for planes that are delivered. Boeing delivered only half as many of its model 767 airplanes in 2003 than it did in 2002 partially because of sagging demand for air travel.[1]

In addition to forecasting the demand for air travel, airlines are also concerned with forecasting items on the cost side of the revenue equation. Airlines try to forecast the price of fuel for their planes. Historically, some airlines have been able to forecast these prices better than others. Southwest airlines paid 95 cents per gallon during the third quarter of 2005 because its forecasts suggested that it hedge against future price increases by locking in rates. Over the same period, Alaska Airlines paid $1.56, JetBlue paid $1.70, Continental Airlines paid $1.88, and American Airlines paid $1.89 per gallon.[2]

These examples demonstrate the importance of being able to accurately forecast items such as customer demand and the prices of inputs to the service or manufacturing processes. Companies utilize this information when making decisions about their purchasing, production, and logistics processes. Companies can use either qualitative (i.e., surveys, test markets, panel of experts) or quantitative methods to generate these forecasts. Several different types of quantitative forecasting are discussed in the following sections. They include simple moving average, weighted moving average, exponential smoothing, and regression forecasting.

Simple Moving Average

The simple moving average uses the average of data from a few recent time periods to forecast the next period's demand. The number of previous periods used in the calculations influences the forecast that is generated. Suppose that the actual customer demand for the past 7 weeks was as follows:

Week	Demand
1	350
2	397
3	375
4	342
5	381
6	366
7	348

[1]Wallace, James. (2003, March 12). Boeing keeps fingers crossed for American Airlines. *Seattle Post*, p. C.1.
[2]Koenig, David. (2005, October 21). Airlines that hedged against fuel costs reap benefits. *The Washington Post*, p. D.02.

The 3-week moving-average forecast for week 8 would be calculated by averaging the demand from the previous 3 weeks as follows:

$$\text{Forecast}_{(periods=3)} = \frac{348 + 366 + 381}{3} = 365$$

Similarly, 5-week and 7-week moving-average forecasts would be calculated by averaging the demand from the previous 5 or 7 weeks as follows:

$$\text{Forecast}_{(periods=5)} = \frac{348 + 366 + 381 + 342 + 375}{5} = 362.4$$

$$\text{Forecast}_{(periods=7)}$$

$$= \frac{348 + 366 + 381 + 342 + 375 + 397 + 350}{7} = 365.6$$

The number of periods used in moving-average forecasts represents a trade-off between stability and responsiveness. The greater the number of periods used, the less the forecasts are affected by rapid or dramatic changes in the historical data. In other words, the more periods used, the more stable the forecast. However, because these forecasts use a greater number of periods, they may fail to react swiftly enough to the changes that are occurring (i.e., they are less responsive). Managers should experiment with different numbers of periods when using simple moving averages in order to find the number of periods that most closely follows the actual data and provides the right balance between stability and responsiveness.

EXERCISES

1. Using the data from the previous example, calculate the moving-average forecast for week 8 using a 4-week moving average.
2. Using the data from the previous example, calculate the moving-average forecast for week 8 using a 6-week moving average.
3. Using the 3-week moving-average forecast from the previous example, calculate the 3-week moving-average forecast for week 8.
4. Suppose that a company's stock prices for the past 5 days were as follows. Calculate a 3-day and 5-day moving-average forecast for the stock price on day 6.

Day	Stock Price
1	$15.94
2	$16.01
3	$16.27
4	$16.08
5	$16.15

5. A local grocery store recorded sales over the past 6 months as follows:

Month	Sales
January	$27,500
February	$28,300
March	$26,700
April	$29,200
May	$31,400
June	$30,500

a. Forecast sales for July using a 2-month moving average.
b. Forecast sales for July using a 3-month moving average.
c. Forecast sales for July using a 4-month moving average.
d. Forecast sales for July using a 5-month moving average.

6. T-shirt sales for the past 8 months at a hotel gift shop were as follows:

Month	T-Shirts Sold
May	523
June	819
July	757
August	692
September	543
October	558
November	423
December	398

a. Forecast the number of t-shirt sales for January using a 2-month moving average.
b. Forecast the number of t-shirt sales for January using a 3-month moving average.
c. Forecast the number of t-shirt sales for January using a 5-month moving average.
d. Forecast the number of t-shirt sales for January using a 6-month moving average.

Weighted Moving Average

One of the disadvantages of the simple moving average is that every previous period carries the same weight in the calculated forecast. Because newer data may be more representative of the future than older data, managers often use a weighted moving average approach to forecasting. For example, managers could use a 4-week weighted moving average by assigning a weight of 0.1 to the fourth oldest data, 0.2 to the third oldest data, 0.3 to the second oldest data, and 0.4 to the most recent data. Any combination of weights that summed to 1.00 or any number of periods could be included in the weighted moving average.

Suppose we return to the demand information listed earlier, only this time let's calculate a 4-week weighted moving average forecast for week 8 using the weights listed in the previous paragraph. This 4-week weighted moving average would be calculated as follows:

Week	Demand
1	350
2	397
3	375
4	342
5	381
6	366
7	348

$$\text{Forecast} = 0.1(342) + 0.2(381) + 0.3(366) + 0.4(348)$$
$$= 359.4$$

EXERCISES

1. Calculate a 5-period weighted moving average forecast for period 6 using the following data and corresponding weights:

Period	Price	Weight
1	$125.47	0.1
2	$165.26	0.1
3	$105.14	0.2
4	$129.91	0.2
5	$141.33	0.4

2. Using the data from exercise 1, calculate a 3-period weighted moving average forecast for period 6 using the following weights: most recent = 0.6, second most recent = 0.2, third most recent = 0.2.

3. Monthly sales for hammers at a local hardware store were as follows:

Month	Sales
January	27
February	28
March	29
April	31
May	35
June	32

   a. Forecast July sales using a 6-month weighted average using .1, .1, .1, .2, .2, and .3, with the heaviest weights applied to the most recent months.

   b. Forecast July sales using a 4-month weighted average using .2, .2, .3, and .3, with the heaviest weights applied to the most recent months.

   c. Forecast July sales using a 3-month weighted average using .2, .3, and .5, with the heaviest weights applied to the most recent months.

4. A local pest-control company is considering the purchase of a new truck. The decision will rest partly on the anticipated mileage to be driven next year. The miles driven during the past 5 years are as follows:

Year	Mileage
1	35,000
2	27,000
3	32,000
4	33,000
5	29,000

   a. Use a weighted 3-year average with weights of .2, .2, and .6, with the heaviest weights applied to the most recent years, to forecast next year's mileage.

   b. Use a weighted 5-year average with weights of .05, .05, .2, .2, and .5, with the heaviest weights applied to the most recent years, to forecast next year's mileage.

Exponential Smoothing

As noted earlier, managers want to find the right balance between forecast stability and forecast responsiveness. Exponential smoothing is a forecasting technique that helps managers meet these two objectives. Exponential smoothing forecasts are more stable because the forecasts take into account errors made in previous forecasts. In exponential smoothing, the forecast for the next period is equal to the forecast for the previous period plus an adjustment for the error made in predicting the previous period's forecast. Therefore, the formula for exponential smoothing is as follows:

$$Forecast_{t+1} = \alpha Actual_t + (1 - \alpha)Forecast_t$$

The smoothing constant α in the previous equation can assume any value between zero and one. The greater the α, the more responsive the forecast is to changes in the data.

As an example, let's calculate the exponential smoothing forecast for period 12 using the following data. In this case, the forecasts for periods 7 though 11 were calculated using an exponential smoothing constant of 0.328.

Period	Actual Demand	Forecasted Demand
7	48	52.69
8	45	51.15
9	47	49.13
10	45	48.43
11	40	47.31

The forecast for period 12 is calculated as follows:

$$Forecast_{12} = \alpha Actual_{11} + (1 - \alpha)Forecast_{11}$$
$$Forecast_{12} = 0.328(40) + (1 - 0.328)47.31 = 44.91$$

Now, let's look at a similar set of forecast data that was calculated using an exponential smoothing constant of 0.793.

Period	Actual Demand	Forecasted Demand
7	48	52.69
8	45	48.97
9	47	45.82
10	45	46.76
11	40	45.36

As you can see, the exponential smoothing constant of 0.793 more closely follows the general downward trend in the historical data than the exponential smoothing constant of 0.328. In this case, the forecast for period 12 is calculated as follows:

$$Forecast_{12} = 0.793(40) + (1 - 0.793)45.36 = 41.11$$

EXERCISES

1. Calculate the forecasts for periods 21 through 26 using the data in the following table and an exponential smoothing constant of 0.645.

Period	Actual Price	Forecasted Price
21	$1.97	$2.00
22	$2.15	
23	$2.05	
24	$2.09	
25	$2.12	

2. Calculate the forecasts for years 2 through 6 using the data in the following table and $\alpha = .5$.

Year	Actual Sales	Forecasted Sales
1	$25,000	$27,000
2	$32,000	
3	$48,000	
4	$57,000	
5	$62,000	

3. The following table provides information on the raw material requirements for a manufacturing firm.

Week	Actual Raw Material Requirements	Forecasted Raw Material Requirements
42	480	500
43	525	
44	395	
45	750	
46	628	
47	299	
48	805	
49	586	

a. Forecast the raw material requirements for weeks 43 through 50 using an $\alpha = .3$.
b. Forecast the raw material requirements for weeks 43 through 50 using an $\alpha = .5$.
c. Forecast the raw material requirements for weeks 43 through 50 using an $\alpha = .7$.

1. Search the Internet for at least three companies that provide forecasting help to businesses. What services are offered by these companies?
2. Search the Internet for at least three jobs that involve forecasting. Write a brief summary of each of these types of jobs.

Regression

Linear regression is often used as a forecasting technique. Ordinary least squares regression can be used to determine the straight line, which minimizes the sum of squared differences between the actual values and the forecasted values. The equation for this line is

$$\hat{Y} = b_0 + b_1 x$$

where:

$\hat{Y}$ = Forecast for time period x

b_0 = the intercept of the line = $\dfrac{\sum y}{n} - b_1 \dfrac{\sum x}{n}$

b_1 = the slope of the line = $\dfrac{n \sum xy - \sum x \sum y}{n \sum x^2 - \left(\sum x \right)^2}$

x = the time period variable

where:

n = the number of observations
x = independent variable values
y = dependent variable values

The following example illustrates the use of this forecasting technique. The demand data for small engine repair shop is contained in the following table. Use linear regression to compute the forecast for week 15.

Week (x)	Number of Repairs (y)
1	59
2	73
3	41
4	62
5	48
6	57
7	69
8	70
9	46
10	50

The solution would be calculated as follows:

Week (x)	Number of Repairs (y)	x^2	xy
1	59	1	59
2	73	4	146
3	41	9	123
4	62	16	248
5	48	25	240
6	57	36	342
7	69	49	483
8	70	64	560
9	46	81	414
10	50	100	500
$\sum x = 55$	$\sum y = 575$	$\sum x^2 = 385$	$\sum xy = 3115$

b_1 = the slope of the line
$$= \frac{10(3115) - 55(575)}{10(385) - 55^2} = -0.5758$$

b_0 = the intercept of the line
$$= \frac{575}{10} - (-0.5758)\frac{55}{10} = 60.67$$

$$\hat{Y} = 60.67 + (-0.5758)x$$

To forecast week 15, we enter 15 into the regression equation as follows:

$$\hat{Y} = 60.67 + (-0.5758)15 = 52.03$$

1. Enter the data from the preceding example into Excel and use the slope and intercept functions to calculate the slope and intercept portions of the previous equation.

2. Use the slope and intercept functions in Excel to forecast the raw material price for week 20 using linear regression.

Week	Raw Material Price (per pound)
1	$3.85
2	$3.72
3	$3.88
4	$3.80
5	$3.95
6	$3.82
7	$3.78
8	$3.75
9	$3.81
10	$3.87
11	$3.86
12	$3.84
13	$3.88
14	$3.91
15	$3.92

3. Use linear regression to develop a forecast for week 50 for the following data:

Week	Raw Material Requirements
42	480
43	525
44	395
45	750
46	628
47	299
48	805
49	586

4. Using linear regression, develop a forecast for month 9 for the following data:

Month	Warehouse Space Requirements (square feet)
1	15,525
2	16,750
3	17,250
4	18,000
5	18,257
6	18,785
7	19,280
8	19,575

Measuring Forecast Error

The sad truth about forecasts is that they are almost always wrong. It is very difficult to predict the future with precision. There are many events or scenarios that can change actual results. As the forecast horizon lengthens, confidence in the accuracy of the forecast diminishes because the historical patterns on which the forecast is based may not continue into the future.

Two basic ways of measuring forecasting error are the mean squared error (MSE) and the mean absolute deviation (MAD). These two methods are discussed in greater detail in the following sections.

Mean Squared Error   The mean squared error (MSE) is the average of all the squared errors. To calculate the MSE, square the differences between each actual value and the forecasted value, add these squared values together, and then divide by the total number of observations. The following data, used in the exponential smoothing section of this supplement, can be used to illustrate this calculation.

Period	Actual Demand	Forecasted Demand	Error	Squared Error
7	48	52.69	−4.69	22.00
8	45	51.15	−6.15	37.82
9	47	49.13	−2.13	4.54
10	45	48.43	−3.43	11.76
11	40	47.31	−7.31	53.44

Total = 129.56

$$MSE = \frac{129.56}{5} = 25.91$$

The MSE of 25.91 resulted from forecasts obtained using an exponential smoothing constant of 0.328 in the previous exponential smoothing section. For comparison sake, let's calculate the MSE of the forecasts obtained using an exponential smoothing constant of 0.793.

Period	Actual Demand	Forecasted Demand	Error	Squared Error
7	48	52.69	−4.69	22.00
8	45	48.97	−3.97	15.76
9	47	45.82	1.18	1.39
10	45	46.76	−1.76	3.10
11	40	45.36	−5.36	28.73

Total = 70.98

$$MSE = \frac{70.98}{5} = 14.20$$

As you can see, the MSE for the forecasts obtained by using a larger exponential smoothing constant was smaller in this instance, indicating that the forecasts more closely matched the actual data.

Mean Absolute Deviation The mean absolute deviation (MAD) is calculated by removing the negative and positive signs from the differences between the actual values and the forecasted values (i.e., taking the absolute values) and then dividing the sum of those values by the number of observations. The MAD is easier to interpret than the MSE because the MAD represents the average error for the prior number of forecasts, whereas the MSE can be thought of as being the variance of the forecast error. The MAD for the previously listed data can be calculated as follows:

Period	Actual Demand	Forecasted Demand	Error	Absolute Value
7	48	52.69	−4.69	4.69
8	45	48.97	−3.97	3.97
9	47	45.82	1.18	1.18
10	45	46.76	−1.76	1.76
11	40	45.36	−5.36	5.36

Total = 16.96

$$MAD = \frac{16.96}{5} = 3.39$$

EXERCISES

1. Calculate the MSE and MAD for the following actual and forecasted data.

Year	Actual Demand	Forecasted Demand
1	4,800	5,000
2	5,200	5,100
3	5,000	4,900
4	5,500	4,700
5	4,500	4,800
6	6,000	4,200
7	4,200	5,000
8	4,000	3,500
9	4,700	4,200
10	3,300	4,900

2. Calculate the MSE and MAD for the following actual and forecasted prices.

Year	Actual Price	Forecasted Price
1	$385	$387
2	$392	$395
3	$388	$390
4	$378	$373
5	$375	$372
6	$372	$369
7	$365	$365
8	$367	$365

3. Calculate the MSE and MAD for the following actual and forecasted prices.

Month	Actual Sales	Forecasted Sales
1	$22,700	$26,275
2	$28,300	$24,841
3	$32,250	$30,900
4	$31,147	$31,150
5	$26,275	$34,428
6	$28,780	$24,784
7	$25,910	$26,667
8	$30,633	$29,615

Inventory Management

As the chapter discussed, products flow throughout the various stages and processes of the supply chain in the form of inventory. These inventories can be raw materials, work-in-process, or finished goods inventories. In some form or another, most organizations carry inventory. In fact, the money that is tied up in inventory and the costs associated with ordering, moving, and storing inventory represents huge costs for most organizations.

If organizations have too much inventory, they have extra capital tied up and incur extra costs in moving and storing the excess inventory. They also run the risk of having the inventory become damaged, spoiled, or obsolete. Wal-Mart, for example, carefully considers how many seasonal items, such as show shovels and heaters, to order, knowing that if it orders too many, it may be forced to sell off the excess at steep discounts.[3]

If, on the other hand, organizations run out of inventory, they can disappoint customers, lose sales, lose market

---

[3]Hudson, Kris. (2005, November 30). Moving the market—tracking the numbers/outside audit: Wal-Mart's discounts exact a price; As retailer lures shoppers, some fret risky reductions might harm profitability. *The Wall Street Journal*, p. C.3.

share, and may potentially go out of business. Although some have claimed that shortages are part of the strategies for products such as the Apple iPod and Microsoft's Xbox 360, most companies prefer not to run out of inventory.[4] Inventory levels not only affect costs, but they also affect customer service levels. Consequently, most organizations are concerned about having the right amount of inventory.

Inventory management involves two basic questions:

1. How much inventory should the organization order?
2. When should orders for inventory be placed?

Several inventory models or approaches have been developed to help managers answer these two questions. Two basic models are fixed order quantity and fixed order interval approaches. Fixed order quantity approaches order the same quantity every time an order is placed. Fixed order interval approaches, on the other hand, order on a regular basis, but the size of the order may vary from one order to the next.

An example of a fixed order interval approach might be a lumberyard that places an order for plywood every Monday morning with its supplier. Before placing the order, the lumberyard counts how much inventory it has on hand and then orders enough inventory to bring the total amount up to a predetermined level. If sales have been good for a given week, the order might be large. Small orders may result from slow sales the previous week.

Fixed order interval approaches are fairly simple and do not require complex calculations. Fixed order quantity approaches, conversely, can require calculations ranging from very basic to very complex and intricate. We will spend the next few pages discussing some basic versions of these fixed order quantity models in greater detail.

To set the stage for some of these models, let's first discuss a basic inventory cycle using what is commonly referred to as a "sawtooth" diagram. Figure E.1 shows a basic sawtooth diagram that represents several inventory cycles. In this scenario, inventory levels start at 100 units and constantly decrease to zero, at which point another shipment of 100 units arrives. The reorder point indicates that once the inventory levels reach about 20 units another order is placed. The time between the placing of the order and the arrival of the shipment is called the *lead time* or *order cycle time*. The order quantity, labeled "Q" in the diagram, is 100. The average inventory level in this scenario is 50 or 1/2Q.

Economic Order Quantity Approach

Before discussing the economic order quantity (EOQ) approach in greater detail, it is important to discuss some of the assumptions of this model, many of which are illustrated by Figure E.1. The first assumption of the EOQ model is a constant and known demand rate. The second assumption is that all of the consumer demand is satisfied (i.e., there aren't any shortages). The third assumption is that the lead time or order cycle time is constant and known. The fourth assumption is that the price paid for the units of inventory is constant.

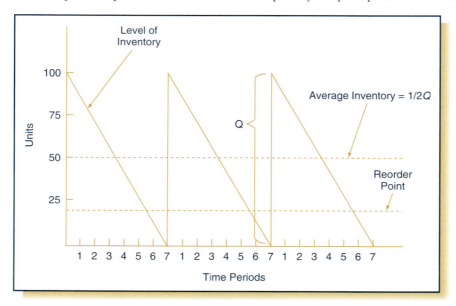

Figure E.1 Inventory Levels—Fixed Order Quantity Approach

---

[4]Wingfield, Nick, & Guth, Robert A. (2005, December 2). Why shortages of hot gifts endure as a Christmas ritual. *The Wall Street Journal*, p. B.1.

The economic order quantity (EOQ) approach examines the trade-off between two costs: ordering or setup costs and carrying costs. Ordering or setup costs occur whenever an order is placed or a batch is started. Ordering costs include the cost of placing the purchase order, tracking the shipment, receiving the shipment, inspecting the shipment, matching the receiving document to the purchase order and invoice, and paying the invoice. Setup costs can include labor or materials used to change the settings of machines or the labor and materials involved to clean machines between batches. For example, a creamery incurs costs to switch from making chocolate ice cream to producing vanilla ice cream. Each of the involved machines needs to be taken apart, cleaned, and then reassembled.

Figure E.2 shows the relationship between ordering or setup costs and the size of the order. The smaller the order size, the more frequent the ordering or setup costs are incurred. For example, suppose an organization requires 1,000 units on an annual basis and that each purchase order it places costs $50. If it orders 100 units with each order, then it will place 10 orders per year at an annual cost of $500 (the number of orders per year can be calculated by dividing the annual demand by the order size). If, on the other hand, it orders 500 units with each order, then it will place only 2 orders per year at an annual cost of $100. Thus, annual ordering costs are expressed as:

$$\text{Annual Order Costs} = \frac{A}{Q}S$$

Where:

A = Annual Demand
Q = Order Quantity
S = Cost Per Order or Setup

Carrying costs are the costs incurred to store or "carry" inventory. These costs include warehousing, overhead, capital, insurance, labor, and tax costs. Carrying costs are usually expressed as either a percentage of the price of an item in inventory or as a dollar amount. For example, suppose an item costing $100 has a carrying cost of 25 percent. The carrying cost would be $25 for each unit per year. At most companies, carrying costs are between 20 and 30 percent of the value of the product. Because the average inventory level, as shown in Figure E.1, is one-half of the order quantity, annual carrying costs can be expressed as:

$$\text{Annual Carrying Costs} = \frac{1}{2}QCP \text{ or } \frac{1}{2}QW$$

Where:

Q = Order Quantity
C = Cost per Unit of Inventory
P = Carrying Costs as a Percentage
W = CP or the Annual Cost to Carry One Unit in Dollars

Figure E.2 shows that carrying costs increase in direct proportion to the size of the order. This makes sense because as the size of the order increases, the size of the average inventory also increases.

The combination of order or setup costs and carrying costs yields the annual total cost curve shown in Figure E.2. The formula for the annual total cost is

$$\text{Total Costs} = \frac{1}{2}QCP + \frac{A}{Q}S$$

The economic order quantity (EOQ) is the minimum point on the total cost curve, which corresponds to the

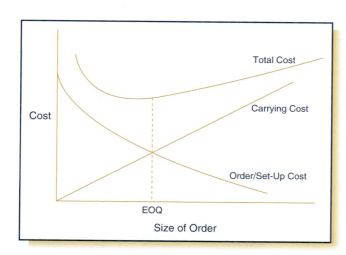

Figure E.2 Inventory Costs

point at which ordering costs are equal to carrying costs. The formula for determining the EOQ is

$$EOQ = \sqrt{\frac{2AS}{CP}} \text{ or } \sqrt{\frac{2AS}{W}}$$

For example, suppose that in order to find the economic order quantity for measuring cups, the manager of Hogan Kitchenwares gathered the following data. He expects to sell 44,000 measuring cups this year. Hogan purchases the measuring cups for $0.75 each from its supplier, Shatter Industries. Every order that is placed costs Hogan $8.00 to process. The manager at Hogan estimates his company's inventory carrying cost to be 12 percent. Hogan Kitchenwares is open for business 365 days per year.

Given this information, the economic order quantity can be calculated as follows:

$$EOQ = \sqrt{\frac{2(44,000)(8.00)}{0.75(0.12)}} = 2,796.82 \text{ units}$$

To verify that this is the correct answer, let's calculate the annual ordering costs and the annual carrying costs to see if they are indeed the same. These values are calculated as follows:

$$\text{Annual Order Costs} = \frac{44,000}{2796.82} 8.00 = \$125.86$$

$$\text{Annual Carrying Costs} = \frac{1}{2}(2796.82)(0.75)(0.12) = \$125.86$$

Hogan Kitchenwares' total costs are minimized by using an order quantity of 2,796.82 measuring cups. The total annual costs ($251.72) of this order size are calculated by adding the annual order costs to the annual carrying costs (125.86 + 125.86). Thus, the EOQ calculations help answer the first inventory management question of how much inventory to order. Note that you can't actually order fractional units and the decision to round up slightly increases annual carrying costs, while rounding down slightly increases annual ordering costs.

Reorder Point

The second inventory question of when to order inventory can be answered by calculating the reorder point. Suppose that in the previous example the lead time between when an order is placed with Shatter Industries and when it is received is 8 days. By dividing the annual demand by the number of days that Hogan Kitchenwares is open for business, we can calculate the daily demand as follows:

$$\text{Daily Demand} = \frac{\text{Annual Demand}}{\text{Number of Days Open for Business}}$$
$$= \frac{44,000}{365} = 120.55 \text{ units}$$

The reorder point is calculated by multiplying the daily demand by the length of the lead time as follows:

$$\text{Reorder Point} = \text{Daily Demand} \times \text{Order Lead Time}$$
$$= 120.55 \times 8 = 964.40 \text{ units}$$

Thus, when the inventory level reaches 964 or 965 units, an order for measuring cups should be placed with Shatter Industries. This reorder point ensures that Hogan will not run out of measuring cups prior to receiving the next order. However, this calculation assumes that the demand rate is known and constant.

If the demand is not known or constant, then additional inventory, called "safety stock," needs to be held to ensure that the demand doesn't exceed supply. Figure E.3 illustrates the addition of safety stock to a sawtooth diagram where demand is not constant. Without the addition of safety stock inventory, the organization would run out of inventory in periods when demand for products was high. Various calculations can be performed to calculate what level of safety stock should be held in order to avoid inventory shortages.

Purchase Price Discounts

One assumption of the EOQ model that can be easily relaxed is the assumption of a constant price. Many suppliers offer discounts when buyers purchase large quantities of products. These discounts may be offered due to transportation cost differences, production economies of scale, or simply as incentives to have buyers purchase more products. To illustrate, let's assume that Shatter Industries sells its measuring cups for $0.73 each if buyers are willing to order batches of 5,000 or more units. Should Hogan Kitchenwares order 5,000 measuring cups at a time to take advantages of these savings? If it does, its carrying costs will increase because it will hold more average inventory. However, its ordering costs will decrease because it will be ordering fewer times per year. In order to calculate the total annual difference between the two alternatives, we need to add another term to the total annual cost equation listed earlier. The new equation would be

$$\text{Total Costs} = \frac{1}{2}QCP + \frac{A}{Q}S + AC$$

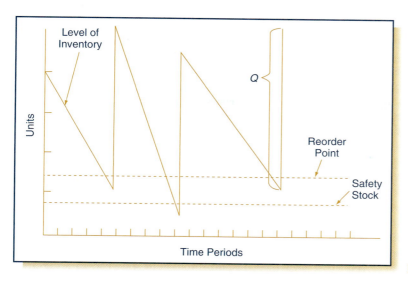

Figure E.3 Safety Stock

Where:

A = Annual Demand

C = Cost per Unit of Inventory

The steps for determining whether or not Hogan Kitchenwares should take advantage of this quantity discount are as follows:

1. Calculate the EOQ. If the EOQ is greater than the quantity required to take advantage of the discount, then go ahead and do so. If not, then move on to step 2.
2. Calculate the total annual costs of both options and select the option with the lowest annual total costs.

In this case, because the EOQ of 2,796.82 units is less than the 5,000 units required to take advantage of the quantity discount, we need to compare the total annual costs of the two alternatives. We calculated the total annual costs of the EOQ option with the exception of the new AC term, which represents the actual price paid for the product. Combining this value with values for carrying costs and ordering costs yields the following annual cost for EOQ:

$$\text{Total Costs}_{EOQ} = \frac{1}{2} 2796.82(0.75)(0.12) + \frac{44000}{2796.82} 8.00$$
$$+ 44000(0.75)$$

$$\text{Total Costs}_{EOQ} = 125.86 + 125.86 + 33000$$

$$\text{Total Costs}_{EOQ} = \$33,251.72$$

Similarly, the total annual costs of the 5,000 unit order size is calculated by changing the quantity size and the price paid for each item in the total cost equation as follows:

$$\text{Total Costs}_{5,000} = \frac{1}{2} 5000(0.73)(0.12) + \frac{44000}{5000} 8.00$$
$$+ 44000(0.73)$$

$$\text{Total Costs}_{5,000} = 219 + 70.4 + 32120$$

$$\text{Total Costs}_{5,000} = \$32,409.40$$

In this scenario, notice how the carrying costs increased from \$125.86 to \$219.00, the ordering costs decreased from \$125.86 to \$70.40, and the price paid for the measuring cups decreased from \$33,000 to \$32,120. Overall, by ordering in quantities of 5,000, Hogan Kitchenwares would save \$842.32 on an annual basis. Consequently, it should take advantage of the quantity discounts offered by its supplier, Shatter Industries.

Implications of EOQ

Some have criticized the EOQ model as being very unrealistic for most companies because of the assumptions that it makes. Additional models have been developed that extend the basic EOQ formula by relaxing many of those assumptions. Many of these models relax the assumptions of known and constant demand and lead times. However, even in its basic form, the EOQ model is fairly robust and can provide insight into how to better manage inventory levels and many organizations.

One interesting observation that some have made is the impact of technology on the EOQ model. Many have noted that technologies such as the Internet have the potential to reduce transaction costs (such as the costs to place a purchase order) to basically zero by electronically automating them. In a situation where ordering costs and even setup costs are reduced to zero, the economic order quantity becomes 1. This corresponds to the ideal order size advocated by a just-in-time (JIT) or lean approach to inventory management. By focusing on reducing ordering and setup costs, companies will be able to reduce their total annual inventory costs by ordering more frequently, which means carrying less inventory and having fewer costs associated with carrying that inventory.

EXERCISES

1. Given a constant daily demand of 40 units and a lead time of 4 days, what should the reorder point be?
2. If a company has an annual demand of 50,000 units and orders 400 units per order, how many orders are placed during a year?
3. If each of the orders in exercise 2 costs the company $200, what are the company's annual ordering costs?
4. Suppose it costs an organization $53 to hold 1 unit of inventory for 1 year. If the organization's order size is 3,000 units, what is its total annual carrying cost?
5. Suppose a company's carrying costs are 25 percent. If it costs $15 to buy 1 unit of inventory from a supplier and the average inventory level is 250 units, what is the company's total annual carrying cost?

Use the following information to answer exercises 6 through 10.

Charlene Baker, owner/CEO of Quicktime Cooking, manages all of the sourcing and sales for her company from her home office. Charlene's most popular product, the "Quick Chef Cooker," sells at an average pace of 12,500 cookers per month. Each cooker costs Charlene $100. The annual carrying cost for each cooker is 10 percent. Each order that Charlene places for the "Quick Chef Cooker" costs $300, covering clerical and delivery expenses. The order lead time is 6 days and Quicktime Cooking is open for business 365 days per year.

6. What is the economic order quantity?
7. What is the annual order cost?
8. What is the annual carrying cost?
9. At what inventory level should Charlene place an order?

10. Charlene has the option of buying in quantities of 4,000 at a price of $95 per unit. Should she take advantage of this option? Why or why not?

Use the following information to answer exercises 11 through 15.

Mr. John Rhoads, owner of a bicycle shop in Tempe, Arizona, sells 12,000 model XT4 helmets every year. Although he mainly sells these helmets to college students, the demand for these helmets is constant throughout the year. In an effort to find out what the optimum order size is for these helmets, Mr. Rhoads has gathered the following data. Each helmet costs Mr. Rhoads $12.00. He sells these helmets to college students for $22.00. Regular customers pay $24.00 for the same helmets. Each helmet weighs 2 pounds. It costs Mr. Rhoads $50.00 to process each purchase order that he submits for helmets. Mr. Rhoads' carrying costs are 10 percent. Mr. Rhoads' bicycle shop is open for business 300 days per year.

11. Find Mr. Rhoads's EOQ for the helmets.
12. Using the EOQ, what is the annual cost for ordering the helmets?
13. Using the EOQ, what is the annual cost for storing the helmets?
14. Given the EOQ calculated in exercise 11, determine the number of orders Mr. Rhoads would place each year for helmets and the time interval between orders.
15. Mr. Rhoads's supplier has agreed to give him a 10 percent discount on orders of 1,000 or more helmets. Should he take advantage of this discount? Why or why not?

WEB EXERCISES

1. Many companies today are outsourcing the management of their inventories to suppliers in vendor managed inventory (VMI) programs. Use the Internet to learn more about VMI programs and why companies are utilizing them. Come up with a list of advantages and disadvantages of such programs.
2. Use the Internet to learn more about safety stock and the various models that are used to calculate safety stock levels.

3. Contact managers at three different companies of your choice via e-mail and ask them how much it costs them, on average, to hold 1 unit of inventory for 1 year, either as a percentage or as a dollar value.
4. Go to the Web site of a large business consulting firm and see what type of inventory management assistance they provide.

Part I Epilogue

The Building Blocks of Supply Chain Strategy

> *As the economy changes, as competition becomes more global, it's no longer company versus company but supply chain versus supply chain.*
>
> —HAROLD SIRKIN,
> BOSTON CONSULTING GROUP

Supply chain management is the design and management of seamless, value-added processes across organizational boundaries to meet the real needs of the end customer. As Part 1 shows, the development and integration of people and technological resources are critical to successful SC integration. Supply-chain leaders . . .

- Are relentlessly customer-centric
- Recognize interfirm collaboration as critical
- View open communication as a must
- Are obsessed with performance measurement
- Are driven to improve asset efficiency
- Focus on processes rather than functions
- Factor people into every decision
- Invest in technology as an enabler

SCM is intuitively appealing and represents what most people consider common sense. That is, companies can win by working closely together. Unfortunately, the devil is in the details. Boundless details and complexity make SCM very hard to do and very few companies have

The Supply Chain Road Map

Designing the Global Supply Chain
- What must be Done to Compete and Win?
- Who Should Do It?

Integrating the Supply Chain
- Create & Communicate Common SC Vision
- Build a Cohesive Team of Allied Companies

How Do We Get There?

Chapter 11: Relationship Alignment
- **Define intensity of SC relationships.**
- **Build trust to promote collaboration.**

Chapter 12: Information Sharing
- **Establish technology to support SC.**
- **Cultivate culture that promotes sharing.**

Chapter 13: Performance Measurement
- **Align measures across SC.**
- **Create understanding & motivate behavior.**

Chapter 14: People Empowerment
- **Cultivate empowerment environment.**
- **Build teams to enhance collaboration.**

How Should We Fit?

To-Be Supply Chain

Based on the understanding developed during the SC design process, create the capabilities needed to…

1. Help our SC meet customers' real needs better than competing chains:
   - Identify the **right** players for the SC
   - Define the **right** relationships
   - Assign the **right** roles & responsibilities
   - Design the **right** structure & systems

2. Securely position the company as an indispensable member of the SC by
   - Refining our customer value proposition
   - Developing needed competencies
   - Leveraging core technologies
   - Establishing efficient processes
   - Creating appropriate customer linkages

How Do We Fit?

As-Is Supply Chain

Chapter 6: Environmental Scanning
- What are the competitive rules?
- What skills does the SC need?

Chapter 7: Supply-Chain Mapping
- What are the SC dynamics?
- Is our company positioned for success?

Chapter 8: Strategic SC Costing
- What are the relevant costs?
- What are the costs tradeoffs?

Chapter 9: Competencies & Outsourcing
- What are our valued competencies?
- What activities should be outsourced?

Chapter 10: Rationalization and Role Shifting
- Where can we rationalize the chain?
- Where can we refine assigned roles?

Who are we?

Business Purpose

Ch 1: SC Strategy
- What is SCM?
- How does it fit our strategy?

Ch 2: Customer Fulfillment
- Who are our customers?
- Can SCM deliver real value?

Ch 3: Process Thinking
- Do we have a silo culture?
- Can we learn to collaborate?

Ch 4: New Product Process
- Do we know how to innovate?
- Can we create great products?

Ch 5: Fulfillment Process
- Are our operations efficient?
- Can we buy/make/deliver?

Chapter 15: Collaborative Improvement
- **Establish a culture of innovation to avoid complacency.**
- **Organize for long-term collaboration.**

mastered its intricacies. The SC roadmap shown on previous page can help you manage the intricacies by helping you understand the nature of SCM. It will also guide your efforts to analyze, design, and integrate a supply chain.

Part I has focused on the building blocks of SCM—strategy, customers, and processes. Only when managers understand their company's strategy, how the company meets customer needs, and how people think about and manage core processes do they understand the company, why it exists, and how SCM can begin to help the company succeed. The analysis and thinking presented in Part I can help you understand the intricacy of SCM. Let's quickly summarize.

The details begin with customers and their ever-rising service expectations. No company has the resources to be everything to every customer. Therefore, managers must define the appropriate type of relationship to build with individual customers. They must then build the processes to create and deliver the value customers demand.

Designing and building great processes is difficult for at least two reasons. First, companies have been organized and people trained along functional lines for as long as we can remember. Most managers therefore do not know what a great process should look like. Second, great process design requires a level of detailed systems analysis that is seldom performed. Even so, well-designed processes make it possible for a supply chain to work as a team, leveraging complementary capabilities to create unique customer value. Understanding the anatomy of a process and cultivating systems thinking can help managers mitigate conflicting objectives and build great processes.

Process excellence is needed in two areas: (1) creating products that meet customers' needs and (2) managing the physical flow of materials from source to consumption. Great products are developed when marketing gets into the minds of customers to identify vital needs, new product teams translate these needs into desirable products, and finance supports the entire process to assure profitability. Of course, satisfying customers and making money require the production and delivery of outstanding products. Best practices in the areas of purchasing, production, and logistics make it possible to profitably satisfy customers' real needs.

The devil is indeed in the details; however, managers that get the details of customer satisfaction, process design, and product development and delivery right will win tomorrow's competitive battles.

Part

Designing the Global Supply Chain

PROLOGUE

When the sun goes up, the world has changed.

—LAURI KIVINEN, NOKIA

*C*harles Fine,[1] MIT Professor and author of *Clockspeed*, called SC design the company's "ultimate core capability." Why? Simply stated, a supply chain's design enables, or limits, the company's competitive ability. SC design answers two questions:

- What must be done to create customer value more efficiently than competing supply chains?
- Who in our supply chain is best positioned to perform specific value-added activities?

Answering these questions helps SC leaders coordinate the complementary activities of various channel members to deliver unparalleled value to the end customer. SC design is similar to but more complex than assembling a group of outstanding athletes to form a championship team. Although becoming champions is the goal of most sports franchises, few ever "win it all." Success requires more than great players; it depends on getting everyone to accept specific roles and responsibilities. Great supply chains win profitable market share because they are comprised of excellent companies that perform specific, valued roles excellently.

[1]Fine, C. H. (1998). *Clockspeed*. Reading, MA: Perseus Books.

The Supply Chain Road Map

Designing the Global Supply Chain
- What Must Be Done to Compete and Win?
  - Who Should Do It?

Who Are We?

Business Purpose

Ch. 1: SC Strategy
- What is SCM?
- How does it fit our strategy?

Ch. 2: Customer Fulfillment
- Who are our customers?
- Can SCM deliver real value?

Ch. 3: Process Thinking
- Do we have a functional, silo culture?
- Can we manage across functions?

Ch. 4: New Product Process
- Do we know how to innovate?
- Can we create great products?

Ch. 5: Fulfillment Process
- Are our operations efficient?
- Can we buy/make/deliver?

How Do We Fit?

As-Is Supply Chain

Chapter 6: Environmental Scanning
- What are the competitive rules?
- What skills does the SC need?

Chapter 7: Supply Chain Mapping
- What are the SC dynamics?
- Is our company positioned for success?

Chapter 8: Strategic SC Costing
- What are the relevant costs?
- What are the cost trade-offs?

Chapter 9: Competencies & Outsourcing
- What are our valued competencies?
- What activities should be outsourced?

Chapter 10: Rationalization & Role Shifting
- Where can we rationalize the chain?
- Where can we refine assigned roles?

How Should We Fit?

To-Be Supply Chain

Based on the understanding developed during the SC design process, create the capabilities needed to...

1. Help our SC meet customers' real needs better than competing chains:
- Identify the **right** players for the SC
- Define the **right** relationships
- Assign the **right** roles & responsibilities
- Design the **right** structure & systems

2. Securely position the company as an indispensable member of the SC by
- Refining our customer value proposition
- Developing needed competencies
- Leveraging core technologies
- Establishing efficient processes
- Creating appropriate customer linkages

Chapter 15: Collaborative Improvement
- Establish a culture of innovation to avoid complacency.
- Organize for long-term collaboration.

Integrating the Supply Chain
- Create & Communicate Common SC Vision
- Build a Cohesive Team of Allied Companies

How Do We Get There?

Chapter 11: Relationship Alignment
- Define intensity of SC relationships.
- Build trust to promote collaboration.

Chapter 12: Information Sharing
- Establish technology to support SC.
- Cultivate culture that promotes sharing.

Chapter 13: Performance Measurement
- Align measures across SC.
- Create understanding & motivate behavior.

Chapter 14: People Empowerment
- Cultivate empowerment environment.
- Build teams to enhance collaboration.

This second of the book's three modules discusses five critical steps in the SC design process and explains why each is so important. We focus on designing a supply chain that leverages global resources to meet the needs of worldwide customers. This module's five chapters are as follows:

- Chapter 6 shows how SCM emerged as a response to an evolving global marketplace. Environmental scanning is introduced and the rules of global strategy are discussed. Global network design is introduced.
- Chapter 7 details SC mapping. Mapping helps answer the two questions posed earlier. Mapping reveals the company's "as-is" position and helps define desired "to-be" roles and responsibilities.
- Chapter 8 shows how strategic cost management provides insight needed to define and evaluate the roles each SC member performs, enabling managers to access trade-offs and make better design decisions.
- Chapter 9 discusses core competencies and the outsourcing decision. A great SC design allows a company to do what it does better than anyone else. Other firms provide needed complementary skills.
- Chapter 10 discusses SC rationalization. As part of the ongoing design process, managers must optimize and re-optimize the network. This effort helps them strategically manage complexity, focusing on processes and relationships that really add value.

Chapter 6

Scanning and Global Supply Chain Design

Do we understand today's competitive rules? Can I use scanning to design a competitive global SC network?

The Supply Chain Road Map

Designing the Global Supply Chain
- What Must Be Done to Compete and Win?
  - Who Should Do It?

How Do We Fit?	**How Should We Fit?**
As-Is Supply Chain	**To-Be Supply Chain**

As-Is Supply Chain

Chapter 6: Environmental Scanning
- **What are the competitive rules?**
- **What skills does the SC need?**

Chapter 7: Supply Chain Mapping
- What are the SC dynamics?
- Is our company positioned for success?

Chapter 8: Strategic SC Costing
- What are the relevant costs?
- What are the cost trade-offs?

Chapter 9: Competencies & Outsourcing
- What are our valued competencies?
- What activities should be outsourced?

Chapter 10: Rationalization & Role Shifting
- Where can we rationalize the chain?
- Where can we refine assigned roles?

To-Be Supply Chain

Based on the understanding developed during the SC design process, create the capabilities needed to…

1. Help our SC meet customers' real needs better than competing chains:
- Identify the **right** players for the SC
- Define the **right** relationships
- Assign the **right** roles & responsibilities
- Design the **right** structure & systems

2. Securely position the company as an indispensable member of the SC by
- Refining our customer value proposition
- Developing needed competencies
- Leveraging core technologies
- Establishing efficient processes
- Creating appropriate customer linkages

After reading this chapter, you will be able to:

1. Discuss the emergence of SCM as a strategic response to a changing competitive environment.
2. Explain the transition from ownership (vertical) to relationship (virtual) integration strategies.
3. Discuss how managers can use scanning and planning processes to define the rules of competition.
4. Describe the forces driving change in today's market and their effect on decision making.
5. Identify the issues driving globalization. Explain how globalization has changed the rules of competition.
6. Discuss the critical issues involved in designing a global supply chain network.

Opening Story: The Task Force's Dilemma

Doug's SC task force had been up and running for almost 4 months. The task force consisted of 6 managers, all selected because of their reputations for creativity, hard work, and passion. Doug had selected individuals who were highly credible within their own functions. Each manager brought not only functional expertise but also a vibrant personality and unique skills to the team effort. Doug reflected on why he appreciated each task force member:

- Joel Sutherland, senior financial analyst, believed decisions should be financially justified and was great quantitatively. Although respected by Tim Rock, Joel was more of a visionary than the CFO.
- Susan Maas, director of global supply, was relentless in her pursuit of purchasing excellence. She was not satisfied with the status quo and believed in building a world-class supply base.
- Tameka Williams, information systems specialist, brought energy and curiosity to the team. She questioned everything and felt that technology possessed the ability to transform Olympus.
- Diane Merideth, North American marketing manager, never lost sight of customer needs. Diane was always ready to take action. She was a team player—as long as her opinions were valued.
- Vijay Gilles, director of operations, was intimately familiar with the details of production. He knew the importance of constraints, but didn't discount possibilities. Vijay was the model of meticulousness.
- David Amado, senior transportation manager, was a master of details. He knew transportation and technology. Despite delving into details, David managed to keep the big picture in focus.

If Doug could get this group of respected managers excited about SCM, their enthusiasm would be contagious. These initially resistant managers were becoming a team and Doug was tempted to call the new working style "chemistry." Susan had captured Doug's feelings when she said, "If we can

---

learn from one another, we will be better managers and a better team. We can then make SCM work for Olympus." The team had come a long way, but Doug wondered if they were moving fast enough. The team had been busy evaluating the viability of SCM and assessing Olympus's readiness. The goal of today's task force meeting had been to decide what it all meant. The task force had come to a consensus on two major points:

1. Using a model Susan discovered in a report by the Center for Advanced Purchasing Studies, the team had identified the following "Benefits, Barriers, and Bridges" for Olympus pursuing an SCM initiative:

Benefits	Barriers	Bridges
• 30% less inventory • 40% faster delivery to customers • 10% sales growth • 10% profit growth • 20% shorter product development cycles	• Lack of SC commitment • Poor forecast accuracy • Turf conflicts • Lack of trust • Poor communication	• Task force enthusiasm • A learning environment • Great SC relationships • Great measurement • Great information systems capabilities

2. Olympus was only marginally ready to implement SCM. As Joel pointed out, SCM truly was "a different breed of cat" and would require drastic change in the way decisions were made at Olympus.

Given the potential benefits the task force had identified, Doug was confident he could make the case for SCM. *But, should he?* Olympus's marginal readiness made him uneasy. The need for real change and the lack of organizational commitment were serious barriers. The task force had identified key bridges to success, some of which were already in place. Others still needed to be built. Could the task force really make SCM a competitive force at Olympus? Where should the task force focus its efforts now? As Doug left his office for the evening, he thought, "Two months to go! Joe Andrus, you can trust me on this one."

EARLY THE NEXT MORNING IN CHARLENE'S GARDEN

"Doug, don't you just love the beautiful flowers?"

"Yes, Charlene, they are beautiful, but they're a ton of work. I never thought I'd find myself crawling around on my hands and knees planting bulbs. With fall in the air, it seems like an odd time of the year to be planting. What's this supposed to look like next spring?"

Charlene's response surprised Doug. "I'm sure you'll get questions like that when you present your SC plan in a few weeks. Everyone always wants to know what the harvest will be before the planting. Next spring these bulbs will be beautiful crocuses, daffodils, and irises. They will be stunning." Charlene paused and then added, "Doug, I've spent a little time thinking about where your task force might want to go next. You need to take a closer look at the competitive environment. You and the members of the task force feel a sense of urgency. Your research has convinced you that the world is changing and that Olympus needs to change, too. Your job is to convince Joe Andrus of the type and magnitude of change that is needed. To do this, you need to do more than document SCM's opportunities. You need to help him see the threats Olympus is likely to face if you do not move forward with an SC initiative. You've talked about industry consolidation as a real threat. You need to make that threat tangible, using real numbers to show Olympus's vulnerability. You need to define tomorrow's competitive rules. And because Olympus is deeply rooted in its past successes, you need to create a "significant emotional event" to catch people's attention and help them be willing to look beyond their comfort zones. Then, and only then, will you be ready to look for a surefire pilot project to document how SCM can help Olympus meet the threats successfully. If you can do that, you'll be on your way to changing Olympus's culture of complacency."

Consider As You Read:

1. Does Doug have all the right people on the task force? What changes would you make?
2. What do you think of Charlene's idea? Can an environmental scan create a sense of urgency across Olympus? What other benefits might an environmental scan provide?
3. What role does each of the following play in helping overcome a culture of complacency? A SWOT analysis? A significant emotional event? A successful pilot project?

If the rate of change inside an organization is less than the rate of change outside, the end is in sight.

—JOHN F. WELCH, GENERAL ELECTRIC

WHY SUPPLY CHAIN MANAGEMENT NOW?

What topics are being discussed in planning sessions throughout the corporate world? The odds are that SCM is high on the agenda. How has SCM found its place among the hot strategic issues of the day? The answer is simple—SCM enables winning business models. Today, a company's business model must help it (1) meet the needs of demanding customers worldwide, (2) build unique competencies to fend off fierce rivals, (3) span the globe to acquire the best resources, and (4) do all of these efficiently. Using global resources to meet worldwide customers' needs better than anyone else is a daunting task. Nevertheless, this is today's competitive mandate. Andrew Grove, former CEO of Intel, described the challenge as follows:

> The new environment dictates two rules: First, everything happens faster; second, anything that can be done will be done, if not by you, then by someone else, somewhere. Let there be no misunderstanding: These changes lead to a less kind, less gentle, and less predictable workplace.[1]

The performance bar has been raised and is likely to be ratcheted up even higher in coming years. The quest for survival in a competitive world has led managers to step tentatively out of their comfort zones. As they have reevaluated business fundamentals, they have witnessed the demise of traditional rules regarding customer service, channel relationships, and resource utilization. The go-it-alone business model—where a company controls all the key value-added processes—lacks the agility and speed demanded by the marketplace. To deliver unsurpassed customer value, companies must develop unique competencies, relying increasingly on capable SC partners. It is within this setting that SCM has emerged as a strategic weapon.

THE JOURNEY FROM OWNERSHIP TO RELATIONSHIP INTEGRATION

In the early twentieth century, Henry Ford decided that vertical integration represented the ideal business model. To increase scale, reduce costs, and control the entire value-added process, Ford acquired the critical pieces of the automobile supply chain from extracting natural resources to delivering the finished car to the consumer. Unfortunately for Ford, General Motors' less integrated but more flexible strategy delivered attractive cars at an affordable price. Enough customers opted for GM's cars to help it win the competitive battle and become the world's largest automaker. Ford's experiment with integration failed to deliver the cost advantage, the control, and the innovation needed to win the automotive war.

The Decline of Ownership Integration

Few companies attempted to achieve Ford's goal of end-to-end vertical integration. Even so, vertical integration strategies remained popular for most of the twentieth century. Harvard's Robert Hayes and Steven Wheelwright identified two objectives that led to the decision to vertically integrate: (1) the desire to reduce costs and (2) the desire to increase control.[2] Cost reductions are supposed to emerge as overhead is reduced, designs are better coordinated, and communication is enhanced. Improved control comes from assuring supply sources, enhancing cooperation, and exerting direct influence over product quality and delivery. The theory: Ownership should increase influence.

Experience, however, told a different story. The theoretical benefits of vertical integration almost never emerged. Ironically, decreased competitiveness was attributed to the vertical integration strategies undertaken to improve performance. Managers could never master the diverse value-added activities up and down the vertically integrated company. Retailing, distribution, manufacturing, and design are all distinct activities that require specialized knowledge. Trying to do it all was an overwhelming challenge. Diluted managerial focus, increased bureaucracy, and inertia increased costs and decreased control.

The Rise of Relationship Integration

In the 1980s, economic globalization and the arrival of hugely successful Japanese companies such as Nippon Steel, Sony, and Toyota pressured U.S. and European manufacturers to cut costs. The Japanese *kieretsu*, or buyer/supplier network, provided Japanese companies a competitive edge. Toyota and Honda relied on suppliers for approximately 80 percent of a car's value. Sole sourcing arrangements with certified suppliers were often used. American carmakers, by contrast, maintained control of the production process, relying on suppliers for about 30 percent of the assembled car. Suppliers were pitted against each other to drive down prices on purchased inputs.

The Japanese business model yielded superior quality matched by a $2,000 per vehicle cost advantage, enabling Toyota and Honda to capture market share.[3] This competitive disparity led U.S. and European managers to rethink the desirability of arms-length, adversarial buyer–supplier relationships. Relationship integration via collaborative buyer–supplier alliances was born.

At the same time, a shift in the balance of channel power from manufacturers to retailers also began to promote integration via relationships. Once again, globalization played a key role, increasing the number of competitors in markets around the world. As customers gained access to a wide array of competitive offerings, power began to shift toward the customer. "Category killers" like Wal-Mart, Home Depot, and Toys"R"Us established dominance in their respective industries. Their size created the leverage needed to further shift channel power away from product producers. Manufacturers were forced to devote more resources to building closer customer relationships. For example, Procter & Gamble's status as a Wal-Mart supplier was put to the test by Wal-Mart's demands for shorter delivery lead times and increased fill rates. P&G's desire to be a preferred supplier to the world's largest retailer provided the motivation to build new capabilities. Today, P&G has leveraged its logistical skills and its ability to manage customers' in-store inventories to help it become a preferred supplier to many of the world's largest grocery retailers.

Henry Ford's early twentieth-century vision of a completely integrated company is now viewed as impractical and unwieldy. Collaborative relationships up and downstream deliver cost savings and provide the flexibility needed to adapt to rapid marketplace changes. Relationship integration has redefined the roles of SC participants, underscoring a new reality—that only by working as "partners in profit" can companies thrive in today's competitive environment.

What can we learn from the preceding description of evolution toward relationship integration? For one thing, the competitive environment is constantly changing. New rules are emerging to govern competition. New skills are needed to win an ever-changing competitive game. Smart SC managers proactively keep their eyes open so they can identify the new rules and learn the new skills before their rivals do.

A Changing Supply Chain World

Charles Fine, a professor at Massachusetts Institute of Technology, noted that in a modern world sustainable competitive advantage is dead.[4] He claims

> All advantage is temporary. No capability is unassailable, no lead is uncatchable, no kingdom is unbreachable. Indeed, the faster the clockspeed, the shorter the reign. Sustainable advantage is a slow-clockspeed concept; temporary advantage is a fast-clockspeed concept. And, clockspeeds are increasing almost everywhere.

The threat of faster clockspeeds is real, making renewable advantage the goal. Competitive success depends on how well a company, and its supply chain, adapts to new market demands. Making good decisions in a complex, uncertain, and rapidly changing marketplace requires that managers devote more time and effort to learn about the world in which their companies do business. Managers must learn to scan, understand, and act. Only then can they identify the forces driving change, anticipate how these forces will change the competitive rules, and structure SC resources to win the new competitive game.

Environmental Scanning

Environmental scanning is the acquisition and use of information about events, trends, and relationships in an organization's internal and external environments.[5] By looking at both internal and external forces, managers can place their company's initiatives and strategies in the context of the broader, competitive marketplace. They thus identify their firm's strengths and weaknesses and know where the company stands vis-à-vis competitors' capabilities and customers' expectations.

Scanning can be passive or active. Almost every manager observes changes in the marketplace as they occur, responding in an informal and ad hoc manner. For example, a manager might hear about a new technology at a professional luncheon or observe a delighted customer's response to a competitor's product. At most companies, these observations do not initiate rigorous analysis. Nor do they lead to improved planning. Some companies, however, incorporate such observations into a proactive search for information that can help them gain unique insight into a changing world. Scanning becomes a primary mode of organizational learning. These companies make it part of everyone's job to help the company anticipate and adapt to an ever-changing environment.

Proactive scanners use insight gained to avoid surprises, identify opportunities and threats, and improve both tactical and strategic decision making. Their scanning systems pursue the following objectives.

1. Detect important cultural, economic, legal, political, social, and technological events and trends.
2. Help managers accurately and objectively understand the company's strengths and weaknesses.
3. Identify and define potential opportunities and threats implied by identified events and trends.
4. Provide a common and correct perception for tactical and strategic planning.
5. Promote an adaptable, forward-looking mind-set among managers and employees.

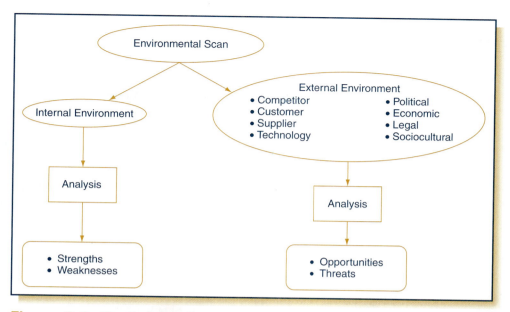

Figure 6.1 The Scanning Process

To do all of this, scanning initiatives must systematically gather and analyze information. Motorola, one of the early strategic scanners, established an extensive methodology to collect information regarding technology developments worldwide. Technical developments in Japan were viewed as particularly important. Motorola invested heavily to learn the language, obtain technical literature, and build long-term relationships with researchers and research organizations. These scanning efforts helped Motorola stay on the cutting edge of technology for many years. Figure 6.1 shows that information should be gathered for both internal and external environments. With respect to the external environment, managers should seek to understand behavior and trends occurring in the following areas: customers, competitors, suppliers, and technology. They should also track economic, legal, sociocultural, and political conditions and trends. A variety of methods are used to collect information. Informal approaches include talking to personal contacts, participating in professional associations, monitoring the media, reviewing public opinion polls, and analyzing anecdotes. More formal gathering techniques include detailed literature searches, key-informant surveys, focus groups, in-depth interviews, facility visits, and "futuring," or visualization exercises. Effective scanning assembles information using many if not all of these practices.

Regardless of how the data are gathered, a careful analysis is needed to identify common themes and trends. Simple graphic techniques can bring key insight to light. Cluster analysis, frequency charts, trend diagrams, and timelines are commonly used tools. Sophisticated data-mining software is also used at some companies. A critical step in the analysis is to organize the findings in a way that communicates a compelling story. For this reason, SWOT (strengths, weaknesses, opportunities, and threats) analysis often accompanies scanning efforts. A SWOT matrix such as the one shown in Figure 6.2 helps make findings easier to interpret. Figure 6.2 identifies a few typical strengths, weaknesses, opportunities, and threats. It also lists some commonly asked questions that are used to identify these core ideas. Questions asked in one of the SWOT areas often provide insight elsewhere. Managers often find performing a mock

Positive Factors:	Negative Factors:

	Positive Factors:	**Negative Factors:**
Internal Factors:	**Strengths** • Excellent customer relationships • Production costs are lowest in the industry • Great information technology systems • Talented people **Questions to ask:** • What do we do better than anyone else? • What are our major sources of revenue and profit? • What is our market share in each segment? • How have market share and profitability changed? • What do our customers see as our strengths? • What do our suppliers see as our strengths? • What resources do we have unique access to? • Do we have the right people? Are they motivated? • Are we adaptable? • How have we responded to competition in the past?	**Weaknesses** • Poor product quality • Inferior delivery speed • Lack of global infrastructure • Slow decision making because of bureaucracy **Questions to ask:** • In what areas do we receive customer complaints? • In what areas has performance declined recently? • What does our financial position look like? • What are our least profitable product lines? • Who are our least profitable customers? • Do we have the right infrastructure in place? • Are our capabilities aligned with customer needs? • Do we manage technology well? • Are we aware of changes in our environment? • Do we bring new products to market effectively?
External Factors:	**Opportunities** • Growing market in Asia • Key customers looking for longer-term relationships • Major competitor bet on wrong technology • Technology linkages are becoming more important **Questions to ask:** • What new technologies are coming to market? • Are any new lifestyle trends emerging? • Are demographics changing in key markets? • How are government policies changing? • Are there opportunities to extend brands? • Are there any inexpensive acquisition opportunities? • What do global markets look like? • Can we innovate or markets new channels? • Can the company move up or down the supply chain? • Are there opportunities to modify SC relationships?	**Threats** • Overly dependent on a few customers • Excess production capacity coming on line • Tough rivals emerging in China • Shifting consumer tastes and lifestyles **Questions to ask:** • Have margins been under pressure? If so, why? • What initiatives have competitors launched? • Is changing technology threatening our position? • Do we have adequate cash to withstand a surprise? • Are our sources of supply stable? • Are there new competitors vying for market share? • Are government or trade regulations changing? • Are socio cultural trends affecting our market? • Are customer preferences changing? • What legal changes are taking place?

Figure 6.2   Strength, Weaknesses, Opportunities, Threats (SWOT) Analysis

SWOT analysis for key competitors a useful part of the scanning process. Effective scanning and planning can improve organizational learning and performance.

Finally, managers should avoid the pitfalls often found in scanning efforts. For example, many efforts fail to involve the people who can act on the insights discovered. Other efforts fail to incorporate diverse sources of information or fail to use multiple methods of gathering information. Others fail to look at the information from diverse viewpoints. Still others do not consider both internal and external issues and perspectives. It is likewise easy to overlook interactions among many of the environmental trends. Indeed, much scanning analysis is too superficial or too narrowly focused. Managers need to push one another to think more creatively and rigorously as they try to interpret the data. Only then can unique insight be gained and realistic expectations promoted.

Jim Collins avoided these pitfalls as he used scanning techniques to research and design his best-selling book, *Good to Great*. Specifically, his research team performed a detailed literature search going back nearly 50 years for every company highlighted in the book. After compiling a file for each company, each article was read and systematically coded so that underlying themes could be identified. With this groundwork in place, interviews were conducted with appropriate executives. The research team held many open-forum discussions to identify and define good-to-great practices. During these forums, members of the research team prodded and poked at one another, challenging each other's thinking, prompting each participant to take a fresh look at the world. Rigorous scanning combined with creative and challenging thought helped create one of the most read and influential business books of the last 20 years.

Forces Shaping Today's Supply Chain Environment

A careful environmental scan helps managers identify the forces that are likely to affect their company and industry. Although many factors are industry-specific, 10 forces are shaping the environment in which today's SC managers make decisions.[6] Because these issues will define the rules of the new competitive game, they are briefly discussed here. Table 6.1 summarizes these core issues, highlighting the competitive imperatives associated with each issue.

Table 6.1   Forces Changing the Decision-Making Environment

ISSUE	COMPETITIVE IMPERATIVES
Competitive Pressure	• Must reduce costs relentlessly • Must seek innovation and non-imitable products/processes • Must create switching costs via relationships
Corporate Social Responsibility	• Must understand how customers define "good" or ethical business practice • Must understand global social norms and track working conditions in SC • Must develop, implement, and communicate company codes of conduct
Customer Expectations	• Must get into the minds of downstream customers • Must realize that the best way to adapt to the future is to create it • Must build learning organization that thrives on continuous improvement
Role Shifting	• Must establish valued core competency to avoid disintermediation • Must make supply chain visible • Must actively and formally evaluate role-shifting opportunities
Financial Pressure	• Must recognize that stock markets are not always right • Must establish viable long-term strategy and stick to it • Must create incentives that will not lead to short-term decision making
Global Capacity	• Must reduce costs relentlessly • Must seek innovation and non-imitable products/processes
Globalization	• Must establish global reach—physically and via alliances • Must establish seamless outstanding performance • Must compete in rivals' home country/region
Mergers and Acquisitions	• Must realize that mergers and acquisitions are hard to do successfully • Must formally evaluate soft issues—culture, processes, policies, people
Technological Innovation	• Must monitor technological developments closely • Must establish technology policy to guide adoption
Time Compression	• Must enhance internal and interorganizational cooperation • Must measure time explicitly

Competitive Pressure

Fierce, unrelenting competition is the common denominator in today's economy. Companies from countries around the world vie to become legitimate players on the global stage. For example, Korea's Samsung is no longer content to be a low-cost producer of imitative products; rather, it desires to be recognized as a cutting-edge brand equivalent to Sony.[7] China has entered the World Trade Organization and is intent on leveraging its huge 1.3 billion-person consumer market and its low wages (often less than $100 per month) to become an economic superpower. As long as aggressive and hungry competitors loom on the horizon, competitive intensity will increase.

Corporate Social Responsibility

Corporate social responsibility (CSR) is emerging as a critical issue. Companies must now be aware of what is often called the *triple bottom line*: economic, environmental, and social performance. The existence of nongovernmental organizations (NGOs) that survey and publicize corporate misdeeds has raised the bar for socially responsible conduct. Nike learned the hard way that what happens upstream at suppliers' operations can impact a company's reputation and fortunes. Nike's problem was that its contract manufacturers in Southeast Asia had been accused of running sweatshops that exploited workers. The bad press tarnished Nike's image. Companies that operate global SC networks took note and are now far more proactive. Most participate in one of several organizations like the Fair Labor Association or Social Accountability International, which are designed to help companies assure that their SC partners observe international working standards. Companies like the Gap and Home Depot have established and published codes of conduct to govern their SC operations. They use their proactive social and environmental programs as marketing tools. In tomorrow's business world, running your own business ethically will not suffice. You will need to promote high environmental standards and good working practices throughout your supply chains.

Customer Expectations

Customer expectations have risen over the past decade. Customers throughout the supply chain expect near perfect quality, immediate responsiveness, universal availability, and continuous innovation. And they expect all this at the same or lower costs. Meeting customer expectations while mitigating performance trade-offs is a huge challenge for SC managers.

Role Shifting

Defining who should contribute and what role each company should play in a world where roles are shifting among SC participants is a key theme for coming years. The growth of contract manufacturing has made it highly attractive for companies like Apple, Hewlett-Packard, and Nike to outsource much of their manufacturing, making them essentially design and marketing organizations. Nortel sold its own manufacturing operations to Flextronics, a leading contract manufacturer, to reduce its production costs. Flextronics now operates these facilities, producing product for Nortel and other electronics companies.[8] The Internet has made it possible for other companies to eliminate intermediaries and sell directly to the end consumer. The bottom line: Managers need new skills to manage relationships in a world where organizational boundaries are blurring and roles and responsibilities are ever shifting. They must learn to share the risks and rewards of collaboration. And they must build relationships for the long haul, even as they consider the circumstances that might call for the relationship to end.[9] Few companies have mastered the art and science of role shifting.

Financial Pressure

William Steele, an analyst for Bank of America, emphasized the need for outstanding financial performance, saying, "What you really want is consistent double-digit EPS growth." Modest failures to meet analysts' expectations can batter a stock's price. To remind employees that shareholder value should be in continual focus, many companies have placed a stock ticker in their lobbies. Unfortunately, meeting quarterly profit expectations can lead to poor, and sometimes unethical, decisions. Important long-term investments in R&D or SC relationships are often overlooked because they may not yield immediate gains in profitability.

Global Capacity

Geoffrey Colvin, senior editor at *Fortune Magazine*, noted, "There are too many chip plants, too many steel mills, too many fishing boats, too many cargo ships; there are too many tires, trucks, airline seats, and cars, too much plastic, too much capital for making loans and writing insurance. . . . Creating capacity is easier than ever." The desire to get into the competitive game has driven companies to add capacity at breakneck speed. Capacity in the auto industry is about 80 million cars per year compared to worldwide demand of 55 million vehicles. Excess capacity is equal to 150 percent of the annual demand in either the United States or Europe. Until demand catches up to supply, managers face a serious dilemma—making money in a world where too many products are chasing too few customers.

Globalization

Technology has made the world smaller, bringing not only far away events but also distantly produced products into the homes of consumers worldwide. SC managers must design global manufacturing and distribution networks to make and deliver these products. They must also learn to identify and build relationships with the best suppliers from around the world. Challenges in the form of communication, culture, distance, and documentation make the SC manager's job both interesting and challenging. Global knowledge and flexible mind-sets are needed to succeed in a global market. Because globalization is such an important topic, it is discussed in detail later in the chapter.

Mergers and Acquisitions

Industry consolidation and the pursuit of scale have led to an unprecedented number of mergers and acquisitions. The goal is often to thwart the competitive attack of dominant rivals. Daimler acquired Chrysler to broaden its product portfolio, create geographic diversification, and compete more effectively with Toyota and its luxury Lexus nameplate. Hewlett-Packard bought Compaq to defend against a rapidly advancing Dell. Despite the fact that a majority of acquisitions fail to achieve strategic goals, companies continue to pursue them to obtain skills and scale that they could not obtain on their own.

Technological Innovation

Technology has helped to shrink the world, compress time, raise customer expectations, and enable SC integration. Unfortunately, rapid technological change creates a fundamental challenge—how can managers harness technology to enable value creation without investing in inappropriate "silver-bullet" technologies? No company wants to fight tomorrow's competitive battles with yesterday's outdated and obsolete technologies. Yet chasing technological innovation for the sake of having the latest technology can dilute focus and consume scarce resources without delivering real value.

Time Compression

Companies have competed on the basis of speed since the just-in-time revolution. Today, the pressure to take time out of key processes is greater than ever. Many practices including concurrent engineering and supplier integrated manufacturing are being implemented to eliminate waste wherever it is found. Wasted time and effort are the primary targets of continuous improvement efforts. SC managers must build knowledge, skills, and relationships to eliminate waste and compress fulfillment and new product cycle times.

To summarize, managers cannot opt out of the competitive environment in which their companies operate. They must deal with the forces that are converging to change the competitive landscape. Because globalization is profoundly affecting SC design, the following section discusses it in detail.

THE GLOBALIZATION OF MARKETS

The world has steadily marched toward a globally integrated economy. Companies rely on suppliers from diverse geographic regions for critical resources and sell to customers in various countries around the globe. Our standard of living depends on the specialization and scale afforded by global operations. Looking in our closets, we see evidence of global economic interdependence. Our clothing is made in countries ranging from England to China and from Italy to Brazil. Globally branded products produced in countries from around the world fill our homes. We have become accustomed to the benefits of the low-cost labor and technological innovation found in distant lands. However, globalization has brought with it some serious challenges that include pollution, workers' rights violations, and job displacement. Even so, most worldwide consumers and workers perceive that they are better off after 50 years of economic integration than any previous generation.

Forces Driving Globalization

Technology has overcome much of the distance created by geography and culture. Television was the first technology to propel globalization. As early as 1983, Theodore Levitt[10] argued that television had "made isolated places and impoverished peoples eager for modernity's allurements. Almost everyone everywhere wants all the things they have heard about, seen, or experienced via the new technologies." According to Levitt, technology had changed consumer attitudes, irrevocably homogenizing wants and needs. Levitt underestimated the power of culture; nevertheless, he correctly forecast that worldwide consumers would expect the latest innovations coupled with superior quality and low cost. It has even been said that the Eastern Bloc's thirst for Coca-Cola and Levi's brought down the Berlin Wall. Today, the pace of economic globalization depends on three primary forces: advances in information and communication technology, the availability of reliable transportation, and the reduction of protectionist trade policies. SC managers must understand these forces as they design and manage a global SC team.

Information Availability

The cost of information exchange has always limited economic integration. Today, telephones, satellites, and e-mail make communication relatively inexpensive. Citizens in the most remote village in Bangladesh now have access to the world through a satellite digital phone.[11] The Internet is bringing the latest news and fashions into homes and businesses worldwide. Better communication also enables managers to coordinate geographically dispersed operations and track competitors' actions. Similarly, consumers can better comparison shop. The time from first action to competitive response is shrinking. Just as television changed wants; digital communication is changing capabilities.

Logistics Capabilities

Physical distance has always increased costs and limited market size. Today's logistics systems provide consistent, reliable, and timely service at known, affordable prices. The selective use of airfreight and better service from third-party intermediaries reduce the uncertainty and variability in scheduling and costs that have long plagued international transportation. Technology has also enhanced logistical coordination. Advanced shipping notices, global geographic tracking systems, and electronic customs clearance make it possible for managers to accurately schedule the movement of goods to and from diverse locations worldwide. Better logistics have lowered the barriers to a global economy.

Free Trade

Since World War II, the General Agreement on Tariffs and Trade (GATT) has reduced tariffs and other barriers to the free flow of goods. From 1947 to the end of the twentieth century, worldwide tariffs decreased from over 40 percent to an average of less than 5 percent. GATT's successor organization, the World Trade Organization (WTO), continues to work to reduce tariffs and eliminate protectionist practices. Regardless, countries still seek to protect domestic industries from global competition via tariffs and other barriers, including domestic-content regulations, ownership restrictions, quotas, and subsidies. Protectionism remains a structural impediment to a fully integrated global economy.

Globalization's Implications

To make good day-to-day decisions, managers need to understand the competitive implications of globalization. SC managers should factor three trends into their strategic planning: (1) Competition is intensifying, (2) global markets are increasingly important, and (3) domestic and global business are different.

Intensified Competition

The term "rust belt" was coined in the 1980s to describe America's decaying industrial heartland. Hundreds of thousands of workers lost their jobs because their companies could not compete against fiercely competitive Japanese companies like Nippon Steel, Sony, and Toyota. The real story of the 1980s was that global competition had arrived. Today, serious global rivals compete in almost every industry from airframes and automobiles to chemicals and computers to semiconductors and services. Competition comes from several sources. Competitors like Nokia and Unilever possess the capital and technology needed to challenge rivals in markets around the world. Further, companies like Korea's Samsung are no longer content to be low-cost producers of imitative products; rather, they want to be recognized as cutting-edge brands. At the same time, unknown firms like China's Haier, a manufacturer of electronic appliances, use low-cost labor to achieve competitive advantage. Andrew Grove,[12] former CEO of Intel, has noted that intense competition is the one constant in a global economy:

> Business knows no national boundaries. Capital and work—your work!— can go anywhere on earth. The consequence of all this is painfully simple: If the world operates as one big market, every employee will compete with every person in the world who is capable of doing the same job. There are a lot of them, and many of them are very hungry.

Global Markets

Did you know that 95 percent of the world's population lives outside the United States? And almost 80 percent of the world's gross domestic product (GDP) is produced beyond America's borders. And did you know that India's middle class is now larger than America's? What does this mean? We live in a global market that managers can no longer ignore.

Another fact: Consumer behavior has changed. Educational background and disposable income often eclipse culture and ethnicity as factors that motivate consumption decisions. This fact has created market segments that cross geographic and cultural boundaries. This is particularly true among the almost 1 billion consumers who live in industrialized nations with per capita GDP approaching $20,000 or more (see Table 6.2). The spending capacity of this affluent market is huge. Companies must learn how to build global brands while establishing a local presence in diverse markets to achieve success. Procter & Gamble reorganized its global operations away from geographic regions to product lines specifically to build and leverage global brands. New products are developed so that they can be simultaneously introduced to critical markets around the world.

The approximately 5 billion consumers who live in emerging markets have shown that they are more demanding consumers, no longer willing to buy outdated models. Their per capita GDP is increasing to the point that they have disposable income to spend. Another characteristic of this market is that it is overwhelmingly young—in many countries, 50 percent or more of the population is under 20 years old. Companies that take advantage of first-mover advantages to capture the hearts and minds of these young consumers can look forward to a substantial stream of revenues as their earning power matures. Figure 6.3 shows that global consumer markets account for a growing percent of many firms' sales and profits. U.S. companies are exporting goods and services for global consumption at record levels. Further, the foreign affiliates of U.S. companies have dramatically increased their sales to worldwide markets in recent years. What does this mean? Global markets are a source of great profit opportunity. The Bureau of Economic Analysis reported that U.S. companies earned $315 billion of profits overseas in 2004, up 78 percent over the past decade—a pace that far outstrips domestic profit growth. This trend is likely to continue as economic growth and consumer spending outside the U.S. market continues to expand. In fact, General

Table 6.2 Demographic and Economic Statistics for Representative Countries Around the World

Industrialized Economies	Population (x1,000)	GDP ($Billion)	GDP/Capita	Exports ($Billion)
Australia	19,358	445.8	23,200	69.0
Austria	8,110	188.5	23,200	94.6
Belgium	10,251	229.6	22,300	197.4
Canada	31,209	875.0	27,700	273.8
Denmark	5,340	161.4	30,100	70.2
Finland	5,181	120.9	23,200	51.9
France	58,892	1,302.8	21,400	370.9
Germany	82,205	1,846.1	22,400	629.5
Hong Kong	7,211	181.0	25,400	204.0
Ireland	3,787	102.9	26,900	90.4
Italy	57,189	1,088.7	18,800	304.3
Japan	126,772	3,150.0	24,900	450.0
Luxembourg	439	19.6	44,100	29.2
Netherlands	15,926	379.8	23,700	248.4
New Zealand	3,864	67.6	17,700	14.6
Singapore	4,300	109.8	26,500	137.0
Sweden	8,872	209.8	23,600	108.1
United Kingdom	59,766	1,424.1	23,700	401.8
United States	275,000	10,943.0	27,154	1,103.0
Total	**783,672**	**22,846.4**	**29,153**	**4,848.1**

Emerging Economies	Population (x1,000)	GDP ($Billion)	GDP/Capita	Exports ($Billion)
Argentina	37,385	476.0	12,900	26.5
Brazil	174,469	1,130.0	6,500	55.1
Chile	15,328	153.1	10,100	18.0
China	1,273,111	4,500.0	3,600	232.0
Czech Republic	10,264	132.4	12,900	28.3
Hungary	10,106	113.9	11,200	25.2
India	1,029,991	2,200.0	2,200	43.1
Indonesia	228,438	654.0	2,900	64.7
Korea	47,904	764.6	16,100	172.6
Malaysia	22,229	223.7	10,300	97.9
Mexico	97,000	611.0	6,300	180.0
Peru	27,484	123.0	4,550	7.0
Philippines	82,842	310.0	3,800	38.0
Poland	38,634	327.5	8,500	28.4
Russia	145,470	1,120.0	7,700	105.1
Slovakia	5,415	55.3	10,200	12.0
Taiwan	22,370	386.0	17,400	148.4
Thailand	61,798	413.0	6,700	68.2
Uruguay	3,360	31.0	9,300	2.6
Venezuela	23,917	146.2	6,200	32.8
Total	**3,357,515**	**13,870.7**	**4,131**	**1,385.9**

Source: The world factbook.[13]

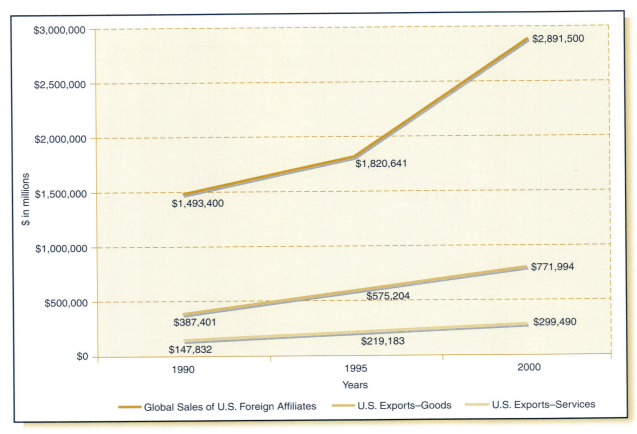

Figure 6.3   The Importance of Global Markets

Electric estimates that 60 percent of its revenue growth over the next decade will come from emerging markets.[14]

Global supply markets are also more important. Low wage rates have made countries like Mexico a great place to assemble labor-intensive products. In 2001, Mexico's maquiladoras exported goods valued at $76.8 billion. However, even lower wage rates in China have made Mexican wage rates of $3.50 an hour seem high. China is the number one destination for foreign capital, attracting over $50 billion in foreign direct investment per year in recent years. Contract manufacturers located in China produce products for Dell and Nike. Capital equipment is also sourced globally. General Motors used a target costing campaign to obtain the lowest price for critical die tooling for its stamping operations. GM sourced its dies from a new Korean supplier as well as an established German supplier.[15] Access to global resources allows companies to remain competitive.

Domestic and Global Business Are Different

SC designers often overlook the differences between domestic and global operations. Even outstanding companies like Wal-Mart have struggled to adapt their operations and product lines to the needs of consumers outside their home country. When Wal-Mart opened its first supercenter in Sao Paulo, Brazil, among the items it had for sale were leaf blowers and American footballs. People who live in a concrete metropolis of 20 million inhabitants have little need for leaf blowers. And although

Brazilians love their "football," they have little desire to play the American version. Over time, Wal-Mart improved its product mix to match Brazilian tastes, but the learning process was costly. Managing the details of global operations is a challenge. SC managers must consider four issues.

1. *Politics.* Managers must evaluate the political stability of potentially attractive markets. Instability can lead to a variety of problems from stagnant economic growth to violent civil disobedience. The riots in Argentina that erupted following the 2001 currency devaluation were indicative of popular frustration with a corrupt government. Similarly, the surprise victory in 2004 of India's Congress party in parliamentary elections led to a dramatic stock market decline as investors feared the newly elected government would reverse economic reforms that had helped create thousands of high-paying service jobs. Managers need to assess political undercurrents that might jeopardize a global business strategy.

2. *Legalities.* In France, English advertising is banned. In Singapore, the sale of chewing gum is regulated. Small details to be sure, but such details increase the costs of doing business globally. Other issues like bribery, product liability standards, labor laws, domestic content regulations, and advertising laws complicate decision making. Competent legal counsel is vital to global supply chain management.

3. *Finance.* The most important financial issue in international business is managing exchange rates. When the euro was first introduced in 1999, it was worth $1.17. By 2002, the euro had hit a low of $.82, making European exports to the United States more attractive to U.S. consumers. However, fortunes change and by 2006, the euro had increased in value to $1.26, reducing the cost competitiveness of European manufacturers. Individual transactions are subject to exchange rate fluctuations. For instance, a contract to source mechanical parts from a German supplier denominated in euros cost a U.S. buyer 57 percent more in dollars in 2004 than 2 years earlier. A hedging strategy can reduce a firm's exposure to exchange rate risk. Taxation is another financial issue that merits attention and expert assistance.

4. *Culture.* Culture affects the way people view almost every aspect of life including time, personal space, worker/manager relations, and individual accountability.[16] In many countries, building close personal relationships precedes the establishment of business relationships. The Chinese word "guanchie" means relationship and points to the need to invest in relationships; otherwise, bureaucratic hurdles can stop business in its tracks. The cultural challenge is one of awareness and flexibility. Observant managers who do their homework and are willing to adapt can succeed in global settings.

Globalization's Rules

As globalization progresses, the rules of competition are changing. Managers make good decisions when they understand clearly the rules of the global competitive game. Of course, the rules governing competitive success vary depending on company size and industry structure. However, most companies—regardless of size, location, or resource status—participate as members of global supply chains. Very few products are made with 100 percent domestic content. Moreover, every lucrative market attracts competition from global rivals. Thus, every SC manager should adopt a global perspective. SC managers should seek to understand the following 6 imperatives that are shaping the competitive landscape and driving SC strategy across most industries.

Establish a Triadic Presence

Companies need to operate in three major world markets—the United States, the European Union, and Asia. This triad represents the wealthiest and most populous economies in the world. Product introduction must be simultaneous across the three markets to preempt competition, gain first-mover advantages, and generate the cash flows to support new product development and global expansion. For instance, Gillette spent over $1 billion to develop and launch the Mach 3 razor. These huge costs required Gillette to get the Mach 3 onto as many stores shelves throughout the triad as quickly as possible. After all, Schick and American Safety Razor introduced competing 3-bladed razors within a year. In most product areas, aggressive competitors can now copy most new products and introduce their own versions into the market in less than a year, creating almost immediate margin pressure. A **triadic presence** also helps hedge against economic slowdowns. Except in the most dire circumstances, one of the three major markets is likely to be growing at any given time.

Utilize Beachheads

Companies need to use operations in the industrialized countries as the bridge into emerging markets. For example, a company's German operations make an excellent platform from which to enter Central and Eastern Europe. Close proximity yields better (1) market knowledge, (2) cultural understanding, (3) control, and (4) logistical support. A similar platform-and-bridge approach works well for expansion within each region. For example, Black & Decker and Kimberly-Clark established production beachheads in Mexico and Brazil as the launching point for their South American market entry strategies.

Achieve Seamless Performance Across Markets

Companies must consistently perform at very high levels across global markets. Seamless performance is the catchphrase. Seamless means that the company delivers the same high-quality product with the same excellent service everywhere it does business. The point is simple. If a customer has a positive experience with your product in Europe, it expects the same positive experience in Asia, the United States, or wherever you do business. Equally important, because companies are working to reduce the number of suppliers they buy from, customers look for suppliers who can support their operations around the world. Thus, you had better do business everywhere your customers do business. Otherwise, they will find another supplier to fill the void. The competing supplier becomes a potential rival in every market where it does business. Steelcase, a leading office equipment manufacturer, has established a global logistics capability so that it can provide great service to customers wherever they want to buy and use Steelcase furniture. Duane Bucklin, senior vice president for global logistics, noted, "We never said we wanted to be a global logistics company, but multinational companies have pulled us out of North America." Customers who do business worldwide expect their suppliers to "be there" to support their operations.

Extend Reach Through Alliances

Companies need to use alliances to create global reach. When Wal-Mart first entered Mexico, it did so through an alliance with Cifra SA. After gaining much needed experience in the Mexican market, Wal-Mart bought out its former ally. When General Motors realized that it could no longer build a customer-friendly small car, it turned to Toyota to gain valuable manufacturing expertise. Companies pool resources because going global is costly. Alliance partners can provide market knowledge, technological expertise, operating know-how, and/or financial resources.

Compete in Competitor's Home Market

Companies must compete in competitors' home markets. Competition prevents cross-profit subsidization. For years, GM and Ford complained about the cost advantage of Japanese rivals. Yet not until the 1990s did a U.S. carmaker market a competitive vehicle in Japan. The lack of competition allowed Japanese automakers to use profits from the Japanese market to subsidize efforts to capture U.S. market share. Wal-Mart entered Germany and England to encircle Carrefour. The goal was to sidetrack Carrefour's global expansion by forcing it to protect its home market. Other reasons to compete in the competitors' backyard are to gain access to technology, advanced supplier capabilities, and competitive intelligence.

Coordinate Global Activities

Companies need to coordinate global operations to create synergies.[17] Procter & Gamble reorganized along product lines instead of geography to increase coordination of product-related efforts taking place independently in different geographic regions. For instance, for years P&G operated independent research operations in Europe, Japan, and the United States. More than once, the three research groups worked on the same type of new product projects without knowing it. They failed to share ideas and technological breakthroughs that would have helped P&G bring better products to market faster and at lower costs. Since the realignment, P&G has found that better coordination increases cross-pollination of ideas while reducing redundancy. Productivity has improved, new products go from concept to market faster, and higher levels of tailored customer service have been achieved. Global category management and centralized purchasing leverages scale economies, making P&G more competitive in its global battle for market share with arch rival Unilever.

Designing a Global Network

How have companies responded to the new rules of a global marketplace? They have built operating networks that span the globe. These networks enable a company to sell its products to customers around the world while providing the firm access to worldwide resources. They consist of production facilities, distribution centers, and retail outlets. However, the physical infrastructure does not need to be owned by a single company. The SC goal is to access worldwide markets through a virtual network—one that uses the facilities and capabilities of far-flung suppliers, distributors, retailers, and other intermediaries such as freight forwarders and transportation providers. Working together, these companies combine their diverse skills to design, build, and deliver great products to customers around the world. Because virtual networks are used, even small companies can participate in the global marketplace. The prerequisite to join in the global arena is to possess "skills" that make your company an attractive member of the SC team.

Global networks evolve over time, with one piece of the network puzzle being added at a time. A new manufacturing plant is needed to increase production capacity. A new DC is required to serve customers. A supplier alliance is entered into. Or a new country market is selected for entry and development. Even when each decision appears to make sense when it is made, over time, the global network can easily become unwieldy. A systematic approach to network design can help keep the network manageable. Four critical decision areas—compatibility, configuration, coordination, and control—should be evaluated to make sure that each network design decision yields a more competitive global network.

Compatibility

Compatibility refers to the need to align network-design decisions with the company's overall strategy. Many companies fail to explicitly consider strategic compatibility. Some companies "island hop," moving operations from one country to another to obtain ever-lower wage rates. Others decide to begin operations in a new country simply because the competition is "doing it." Such decisions may or may not make strategic sense.

For example, chasing low-cost labor rates can wreak havoc on a company's quality performance, making it impossible for the company to compete as a producer of premium products. Several years ago, Mercedes and BMW decided they needed to reduce costs to compete with Japanese luxury brands. The obvious place to build cars outside Germany was the United States. Because of its lower costs and close proximity to the U.S. market, Mexico was also considered. Ultimately, both carmakers decided that "Built in Mexico" was not an appropriate label for high-priced "German" luxury cars. Every network decision should be carefully analyzed to make sure that it supports the company's value-added strategy.

Configuration

Configuration refers to the decision of where to locate value-added activities. In the Mercedes example, the decision was made to build cars in the United States. As Mercedes considered possible production sites, it sought an abundant, hard-working, and flexible workforce. A key goal was to avoid labor unions. Mercedes also wanted to have access to existing, high-quality suppliers. Among the other issues considered in the location decision were the quality of the transportation infrastructure, the cost of real estate, utility rates, and tax incentives. After comparing several options using these criteria, Mercedes decided to build its new assembly plant in Alabama.

The configuration challenge is to identify and consider all of the issues that will affect network performance. Too many companies focus on one or two issues such as labor costs or tax rates as they decide where to locate value-added activities. They are then surprised when labor turmoil stops work, the electricity fails each afternoon, local suppliers fail to deliver on time, or the transportation infrastructure breaks down. Good configuration decisions require careful research and detailed analysis.

Coordination

Coordination refers to the challenge of integrating geographically dispersed activities. Basic activities like sharing information or transporting goods among worldwide facilities are almost always more difficult than in domestic operations. Physical distance, cultural diversity, and bureaucracy create confusion, raise costs, and diminish performance.

Procter & Gamble's R&D efforts illustrate the challenge. When Wahib Zaki became vice president of R&D, he found that U.S. researchers were working on improved builders (ingredients that break down dirt) while the Japanese subsidiary was formulating a new surfactant (the ingredient that removes grease). Neither group had incorporated breakthroughs achieved by P&G's European subsidiary, nor were they sharing their research with each other. Zaki recognized an opportunity to coordinate efforts to develop and launch a truly powerful liquid laundry detergent. He formed a team to analyze market needs, combine dispersed technical knowledge, and develop product specifications. The result was a "world" laundry detergent sold as Liquid Tide in the United States, Liquid Cheer in Japan, and Liquid Ariel in Europe.[18]

Control

Control refers to the day-to-day decisions involved in managing operations. Global networks only improve competitiveness when the many decisions made on-site at production facilities, distribution centers, and supplier operations improve productivity, quality, and other performance characteristics. However, differences in language, reward systems, workforce relations, and infrastructure can make control decisions more difficult in global operations.

One company did a nice job of evaluating the compatibility, configuration, and coordination issues involved in setting up a maquiladora co-production operation in Mexico. However, the plant manager was not willing to adapt to the Mexican culture. His communication style and measurement practices alienated the workforce. Poor morale led to inferior quality and high costs. The manager was eventually replaced by one of his Mexican assistants. Productivity and quality quickly improved to world-class levels. Poor on-site control can undermine otherwise good network design decisions. Similarly, great control decisions help global networks create and deliver outstanding value.

CONCLUSION

Today's business world is rapidly changing. Customers are more demanding, competitors more aggressive, and circumstances more complex and uncertain. Success requires that managers understand the implications of Charles Darwin's observation that "only the adaptable survive." Companies that master the art and science of environmental scanning can anticipate changes before they occur. They are positioned to interpret and adjust to the rules that emerge as the environment evolves.

Globalization is just one trend that has ushered in new competitive rules and changed the very nature of competition. By adopting strategies that rely more on relationships than ownership, SC managers are developing flexible global SC networks. These networks provide access to the best resources available worldwide, enabling companies to design, make, and deliver great products to global consumers.

SUMMARY OF KEY POINTS

1. SCM has emerged as a strategic response to changes in today's competitive environment.

2. Ownership and relationship integration strategies determine the percent of value added to a product within the company. In a fast-paced marketplace, relationship integration offers greater flexibility and has become a preferred strategy.

3. Environmental scanning is the acquisition and use of information about events, trends, and relationships in an organization's internal and external environments. It is a valuable tool in the SC manager's toolkit.

4. Some of the forces influencing today's decision-making environment include intensifying competition, rising customer expectations, the shifting of value-added roles among SC members, relentless financial pressure, excess global capacity, economic globalization, an increase in merger and acquisition activity, constant technological innovation, time compression, and a greater emphasis on corporate social responsibility.

5. Globalization has created both opportunities and threats. Because the forces driving globalization are likely to persist, managers need to take advantage of

globalization's opportunities while mitigating its threats.

6. Globalization has changed the rules of competition. SC managers need to understand globalization's six basic rules: establish a triadic presence, utilize beachheads, strive for seamless performance, extend reach through alliances, compete in the competitor's home market, and coordinate global activities.

7. One response to globalization's rules is to build a global SC network. Effective global SC network design requires careful management of four issues: compatibility, configuration, coordination, and control.

REVIEW EXERCISES

1. Why is SCM a strategic initiative and a valued contributor to company success?

2. Define ownership (vertical) and relationship (virtual) integration and compare their advantages and disadvantages.

3. Define environmental scanning. Imagine you have just been given the responsibility to design your company's scanning program. What would an effective scanning program look like? What pitfalls would you want to be sure to avoid? Be specific.

4. Identify 10 forces that are changing today's competitive landscape. Based on your observations, what are the three most important forces affecting each of the following industries: automotive, biotechnology, computer, grocery retail, and pharmaceutical? Are these forces transitory or permanent?

5. What are the three most important forces affecting the industry in which you would like to work? How are these forces changing the rules of competition in this industry?

6. Discuss the three primary forces driving globalization. What do you think will happen to each of these forces over the next decade? How will these changes affect globalization?

7. Identify the six rules of globalization. How does each affect decision making and competitiveness in the industry in which you would like to work?

8. From the business press, identify a company making a global SC network design decision. What are the primary issues the company is evaluating? How do they compare to the issues discussed in the chapter?

Case   *The Scanning and Planning Internship*

Debbie Clare was thrilled. She had landed the ideal internship with Dynamic World (DWC), a *Fortune* 1000 consumer electronics retailer. Tom Tucker, director of order fulfillment at DWC, had just invited Debbie to lead a 5-intern task force. The task force would perform an environmental scan to be used as input in DWC's 1-, 5-, and 10-year strategic SC road maps. As a first-year SC major in Michigan State's MBA program, Debbie's excitement was matched only by an intense feeling of trepidation. Tom had assured her that the team consisted of outstanding students from Arizona State, Ohio State, Tennessee, MIT, and Wharton. Yet, introspectively, Debbie wondered whether she had the skills to deliver the expected results. This was the real world; the results of her work would make a difference—this wasn't just another classroom assignment.

Debbie perceived DWC to be an early adopter of leading-edge SC practices. DWC trusted its employees to share ideas and drive change. DWC was the company Debbie wanted to work for after she finished her MBA. She knew that the internship was a 3-month job interview. From her previous interviews with Tom, Debbie knew that the past 5 years had been fraught with challenges in the retail sector, but that DWC had navigated them better than anyone else. As a result, DWC had added almost 150 stores per year over the past 3 years, had increased same-store sales by 8 percent, and had developed a national reputation for having a broad assortment of brand-name products consistently available at the low prices consumers expected.

During their phone conversation, Tom had shared with Debbie his concern that more than a little luck had helped DWC achieve its market-leading status. Tom assured her that he didn't want future success to depend on good fortune. Tom concluded the call saying, "The best way to predict the future is to create it. We want to make our own luck by being prepared when opportunity knocks, and we believe that great environmental scanning can help us be ready. We look forward to having you help us build a scanning and planning culture." Given the magnitude of the task, Debbie decided that she had better start her own planning. She only had 6 weeks before the first day on the job. Debbie recorded several concerns Tom had shared as he had described Debbie's responsibilities.

- Tom was certain that the economy could not sustain the growth of the past 10 years. There was already too much retail floor space—companies had added stores believing that "if you build it, consumers will come." Debt made it doubtful that consumers could keep coming and spending. Too many stores were chasing too few consumer dollars.
- Tom was worried about the globalization of retail competition. Retailing had been sheltered from the global threat, but Tom felt that the global retailer loomed on the horizon. What could DWC do to protect its home market while striving to penetrate lucrative markets worldwide?
- Tom noted that the threats and opportunities of an evolving Internet were not yet defined. Could DWC leverage distance shopping to create greater customer loyalty? Would manufacturers learn how to use the Web to market directly to end consumers— eliminating the need for retailers like DWC?

"Of course," Tom pointed out, "other factors will change the way we do business. We aren't sure what they are or how they will affect us. But, that's why we are bringing you in." Surprised that such a vital task would be given to interns, Debbie had asked Tom to discuss the rationale for establishing an intern-driven task force and what he thought the "deliverable" should look like. Tom's response was simple: "We need a fresh perspective. As a successful company, we look at the world through the same lenses that helped us achieve success. Although there is nothing wrong with the way we look at the world, we don't want to miss anything. Besides, interns are a lot less expensive than consultants and they bring with them passion and cutting-edge thinking. And we'll have a parallel in-house team performing a similar analysis." A successful project would deliver at least two takeaways:

- Trends would be identified and driving forces documented.
- Priorities would be recommended for 1-, 5-, and 10-year time horizons.

Tom had reiterated the importance of clear, concise, and compelling communication. Every member of the steering committee was busy and wouldn't be inclined to wade through a weighty report. Given the power of corporate inertia, the team needed to come up with an attention-grabbing approach to drive home key findings. Debbie couldn't help but feel overwhelmed, but she was pleased that Tom and DWC trusted her to lead such an important project. She wanted to make sure that she delivered.

QUESTIONS

1. Where should Debbie begin? What can she do between now and the first day on the job?
2. How could Debbie use SWOT analysis to create a compelling case for their environmental scan?
3. Suggest a presentation format to help Debbie's team deliver a thought-provoking presentation.

ENDNOTES

1. Grove, A. S. (1995, September 18). A high-tech CEO updates his views on managing and careers. *Fortune*, p. 229.
2. Hayes, R., & Wheelwright, S. (1984). *Restoring our competitive edge: Competing through manufacturing.* New York: John Wiley and Sons.
3. Haas, E. A. (1987). Breakthrough manufacturing. *Harvard Business Review, 65*(2), 75–81.
4. Fine, C. H. (1998). *Clockspeed.* Reading, MA: Perseus Books.
5. Choo, C. W. (2001). Environmental scanning as information seeking and organizational learning. *Information Research, 7*(1). Coreia, Z., & Wilson, T. D. (2001). Factors influencing environmental scanning in the organizational context information research. *Information Research, 7*(1).
6. Fawcett, S., & Magnan, G. (2005, August 1). Beware the forces that affect your supply chain. *Supply Chain Strategy, 9.*
7. (2002, August 5). The best global brands. *BusinessWeek.*
8. (2004, June 29). Nortel reaches deal to outsource manufacturing to Flextronics. *The Wall Street Journal,* Online News Roundup.
9. Bowersox, D. J. (1990). The strategic benefits of logistics alliances. *Harvard Business Review, 68*(4), 1–7.
10. Levitt, T. (1983). The globalization of markets. *Harvard Business Review, 61*(3), 92–102.
11. Jordan, M. (1999, June 25). It takes a cell phone. *The Wall Street Journal,* pp. B1, B4.
12. Ibid.
13. Central Intelligence Agency. (2002). OECD in figures, statistics on the member countries. *The world factbook.*

14. Hilsenrath, J. E. (2005, April 4). U.S. multinationals reap overseas bounty. *The Wall Street Journal*, p. A2.
15. Simison, R. (1999, April 2). General Motors drives some hard bargains with Asian suppliers. *The Wall Street Journal*, pp. A1, A6.
16. Hall, E. T. (1981). *Beyond culture*. New York: Anchor Books/Doubleday.
17. McGrath, M., & Hoole, R. (1992). Manufacturing's new economies of scale. *Harvard Business Review, 70*(3), 94–102.
18. Bartlett, C., & Ghoshal, S. (2003). *What is a global manager? Harvard Business Review, 81*(8), 124–132.

Supplement F

Facility Location

Designing a global SC network requires constant screening and rigorous analysis. The 4Cs framework—compatibility, configuration, coordination, and control— relies on a variety of analysis techniques, none of which is more important than facility location modeling. Good SC performance depends on the location of various facilities such as factories, warehouses, distribution centers, and retail stores. For example, when Edwards Lifesciences Corp., a manufacturer of products used to treat cardiovascular disease, operated its Memphis, Tennessee, DC, only 50 percent of its products could be shipped to its customers within 2 days. After shifting to a location in Columbus, Ohio, Edwards Lifesciences Corp. now ships 80 percent of its products within 2 days.[1] This location change provided the dual benefits of improved customer service and reduced transportation costs.

Similarly, in early September 2005, Bombardier Aerospace officially opened a high-volume 238,000-square-foot aircraft parts distribution center in Chicago and a comparable one in Frankfurt, Germany, to form the nucleus of its redesigned logistics network. The new facilities will reportedly offer Bombardier business jet operators and regional airlines greater speed, accuracy, and quality of service on more than 120,000 unique parts.[2]

As an SC manager, you will want to make sure that facility location analysis techniques are in your toolkit. One tool that will help you appropriately locate facilities is called the *center-of-gravity approach*. It helps determine the point that minimizes the distance traveled or the costs involved in shipping to and from the various locations along the supply chain.

Basic Center-of-Gravity Approach

In its most basic form, the **center-of-gravity approach** helps managers locate the geographic center of a group of locations. For example, suppose that a retail company is trying to decide where to locate a new DC to serve five retail stores. The various locations (or coordinates) of these five retail stores are shown in Figure F.1. These

Figure F.1   Retail Locations

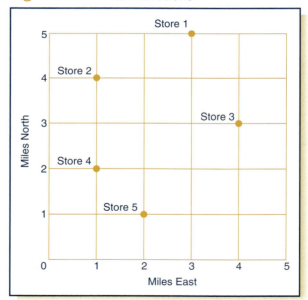

[1]Maher, Kris. (2005, July 5). Global goods jugglers; Outsourced warehouses boom as factories move offshore, people expect quick shipping. *The Wall Street Journal*, p. A.1.
[2]Anonymous. (2005, October). Bombardier inaugurates new worldwide distribution center in Chicago. *Materials Handling Management, 60*(10), 6.

coordinates can be determined by establishing a zero point and then using latitude and longitude data or by simply drawing a uniform grid pattern onto an existing map of the various locations.

The central location of "center of gravity" can be determined by calculating the average North–South coordinates and the average East–West coordinates. In this example, the average North–South coordinate is calculated as follows:

$$\frac{\text{Distance North}_{\text{Store 1}} + \text{Distance North}_{\text{Store 2}} +}{\text{Distance North}_{\text{Store 3}} + \text{Distance North}_{\text{Store 4}} +}$$
$$\frac{\text{Distance North}_{\text{Store 5}}}{\text{Total Number of Stores}}$$

$$\frac{5 + 4 + 3 + 2 + 1}{5} = 3$$

Similarly, the average East–West coordinate is calculated as follows:

$$\frac{\text{Distance East}_{\text{Store 1}} + \text{Distance East}_{\text{Store 2}} +}{\text{Distance East}_{\text{Store 3}} + \text{Distance East}_{\text{Store 4}} +}$$
$$\frac{\text{Distance East}_{\text{Store 5}}}{\text{Total Number of Stores}}$$

$$\frac{3 + 1 + 4 + 1 + 2}{5} = 2.2$$

Thus, in this situation, the central location would be at 3 units North and 2.2 units East, as shown in Figure F.2.

Figure F.2 Central Location

This basic approach minimizes the distance traveled from the DC to the five retail stores, but will only minimize the transportation costs if each location is shipped equal amounts at equal frequencies and the transportation rates are the same for each location. The next sections discuss the calculations that can be made to determine the lowest cost location when these two assumptions are violated.

Unequal Shipment Sizes or Differing Shipment Frequency

In order to minimize transportation costs, facilities should be located closer to locations that require more frequent shipments than to locations that require less frequent shipments. To illustrate, assume that Store 5 in the example requires twice as many shipments as the other stores. If this is the case, then it makes sense to locate the DC closer to Store 5.

To further illustrate this concept, visualize Figure F.2 lying on a flat surface. Now visualize strings leading horizontally from the central location mark to each of the store locations and then vertically through the flat surface. Now envision various weights attached to the ends of the strings. When all of the weights are equal, the center of gravity remains in the same location. However, when the weight of a certain store is increased (in terms of its shipment size or frequency requirements), the additional weight pulls the central location toward that location. However, because of the weight of the other stores, the location is not drawn completely to the "heavier" location.

To illustrate the calculations involved in determining the new center of gravity by using the weight or volume that is shipped to a particular location, let's assume that the five stores introduced earlier receive the annual weights listed in Table F.1.

Rather than being a simple average of the coordinates, as in the basic example described earlier, the new

Table F.1 Transportation Weight Data

LOCATION	EAST–WEST COORDINATE	NORTH–SOUTH COORDINATE	ANNUAL TONS
Store 1	3	5	200
Store 2	1	4	600
Store 3	4	3	400
Store 4	1	2	100
Store 5	2	1	300

center of gravity is simply a weighted average. The coordinates are "weighted" by the weight that is shipped to each location. Thus, in this case, the weighted average coordinates can be calculated as follows:

$$C_{EastWest} = \frac{\sum EastWest(weight)}{\sum (weight)}$$

$$C_{EastWest} = \frac{3(200) + 1(600) + 4(400) + 1(100) + 2(300)}{200 + 600 + 400 + 100 + 300}$$

$$C_{EastWest} = \frac{600 + 600 + 1600 + 100 + 600}{1600}$$

$$= \frac{3500}{1600} = 2.1875$$

$$C_{NorthSouth} = \frac{\sum NorthSouth(weight)}{\sum (weight)}$$

$$C_{NorthSouth} = \frac{5(200) + 4(600) + 3(400) + 2(100) + 1(300)}{200 + 600 + 400 + 100 + 300}$$

$$C_{NorthSouth} = \frac{1000 + 2400 + 1200 + 200 + 300}{1600}$$

$$= \frac{5100}{1600} = 3.1875$$

Thus, the new center-of-gravity coordinates are (2.1875, 3.1875). This location helps minimize the ton-miles that are utilized to distribute goods from the distribution center to the five store locations.

Transportation Rate Differences

In order to find the lowest-cost location, transportation rates should be considered if they differ between the store locations. Differences in transportation rates affect the location of the DC just as different shipment sizes or different shipment frequencies. In order to minimize the total distribution costs, the DC should be located closer to locations that have higher transportation costs. Let's refer to the previous example and add some data on transportation rates to illustrate this point. Suppose that the transportation rates per ton-mile for each of the locations correspond with the data in Table F.2.

Table F.2 Transportation Rate Data

LOCATION	EAST–WEST COORDINATE	NORTH–SOUTH COORDINATE	ANNUAL TONS	RATE $/ TON-MILE
Store 1	3	5	200	$1.55
Store 2	1	4	600	$1.27
Store 3	4	3	400	$1.42
Store 4	1	2	100	$1.75
Store 5	2	1	300	$1.48

In this situation, the various store locations are weighted not only by the tons, but also by the transportation rate. The center-of-gravity location of this scenario can be calculated as follows:

$$C_{EastWest} = \frac{\sum EastWest(weight)(rate)}{\sum (weight)(rate)}$$

$$C_{EastWest} = \frac{\begin{array}{c}3(200)(1.55) + 1(600)(1.27) + \\ 4(400)(1.42) + 1(100)(1.75) + \\ 2(300)(1.48)\end{array}}{\begin{array}{c}200(1.55) + 600(1.27) + 400(1.42) + \\ 100(1.75) + 300(1.48)\end{array}}$$

$$C_{EastWest} = \frac{930 + 762 + 2272 + 175 + 888}{310 + 762 + 568 + 175 + 444}$$

$$= \frac{5027}{2259} = 2.23$$

$$C_{NorthSouth} = \frac{\sum NorthSouth(weight)(rate)}{\sum (weight)(rate)}$$

$$C_{NorthSouth} = \frac{\begin{array}{c}5(200)(1.55) + 4(600)(1.27) + \\ 3(400)(1.42) + 2(100)(1.75) + \\ 1(300)(1.48)\end{array}}{\begin{array}{c}200(1.55) + 600(1.27) + 400(1.42) + \\ 100(1.75) + 300(1.48)\end{array}}$$

$$C_{NorthSouth} = \frac{1550 + 3048 + 1704 + 350 + 444}{310 + 762 + 568 + 175 + 444}$$

$$= \frac{7096}{2259} = 3.14$$

Therefore, the new center of gravity is located at (2.23, 3.14). This location minimizes the transportation costs associated with shipping goods from the distribution center to the various store locations. These calculations also take the annual weight of the shipments being sent to the various locations into consideration.

Other Items to Consider

The center-of-gravity approach provides a starting point to look at in deciding where to locate a facility. However, the exact coordinates of the center of gravity may not correspond to a good site to build or lease a facility. The coordinates may be located in a remote wilderness location or in the middle of a swamp or desert. In addition to the mathematical results of the center-of-gravity approach, several other items should be considered when locating a facility. These items are listed in Table F.3.

Table F.3 Other Items and Issues to Consider When Locating a Facility

Proximity to major highways and airports	State and local tax rates
Proximity to labor force	Proximity to competition
Education level of labor force	Proximity to similar industries
Degree of unionization	Topography
Cost of land	Environmental issues
Construction costs	Availability of shippers or carriers
Weather	Management preferences
Quality of life	Population characteristics
Employment rates	Security

EXERCISES

1. Using the basic center-of-gravity approach, find the center of the following locations.

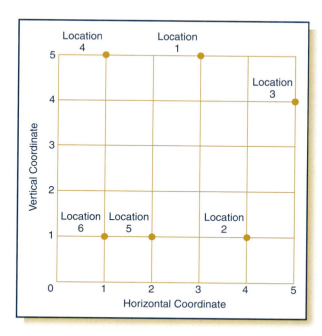

Location	East–West Coordinate	North–South Coordinate	Annual Tons
Store 1	3	5	300
Store 2	1	4	300
Store 3	4	3	300
Store 4	1	2	300
Store 5	2	1	300

3. Using the equations in the Transportation Rate Differences section of the supplement, find the center-of-gravity location for the following data.

Location	East–West Coordinate	North–South Coordinate	Annual Tons	Rate $/ Ton-Mile
Store 1	3	5	200	$1.63
Store 2	1	4	200	$1.63
Store 3	4	3	200	$1.63
Store 4	1	2	200	$1.63
Store 5	2	1	200	$1.63

4. John is the manager of a local warehouse that stores apples, oranges, bananas, pears, peaches, and plums. The storage areas for these different fruits are located throughout the warehouse, as shown in the following diagram. When the warehouse was constructed, the builders forgot to install an office for John. Because John plans to walk between his office and the various storage locations numerous times per day as shown in the following table, he

2. Using the equations in the Unequal Shipment Size section of the supplement, find the center-of-gravity location for the following data.

would like his office in a location that minimizes the distance that he has to travel. Given this information, where do you suggest he locate his office?

Storage Location	Number of Daily Trips
Apples	5
Oranges	8
Bananas	10
Pears	3
Peaches	1
Plums	3

5. An electronics company has retail outlets in seven cities across the United States. Rather than servicing these outlets directly from its factory in Philadelphia, the company has decided to establish a distribution center in a more central location. Using the data in the following table, determine the best location for the company's distribution center.

Location	Latitude	Longitude	Annual Tons	Rate $/Ton-Mile
Phoenix, Arizona	33 degrees N	112 degrees W	1020	$1.96
Los Angeles, California	34 degrees N	118 degrees W	1400	$1.63
Houston, Texas	29 degrees N	95 degrees W	1080	$1.12
Detroit, Michigan	42 degrees N	83 degrees W	800	$1.55
Seattle, Washington	47 degrees N	122 degrees W	400	$1.72
Columbus, Ohio	40 degrees N	82 degrees W	650	$1.45
New York, New York	40 degrees N	73 degrees W	1500	$1.25

WEB EXERCISES

1. Use the Internet to locate the approximate latitude and longitude of the following cities and then find the center-of-gravity location.

   Dallas, Texas
   Atlanta, Georgia
   Boston, Massachusetts
   Orlando, Florida
   Salt Lake City, Utah
   Denver, Colorado

2. Use the Internet to research global positioning satellite (GPS) systems and write a brief report about their possible use in facility location analyses.

3. Use the Internet to compare and contrast two different specific facility locations in different states in terms of at least five of the items listed in Table F.3.

Chapter 7

Supply Chain Mapping

How does our SC work? Can I use mapping to assess and improve my company's position in the chain?

The Supply Chain Road Map

Designing the Global Supply Chain
- What Must Be Done to Compete and Win?
- Who Should Do It?

How Do We Fit?	**How Should We Fit?**
As-Is Supply Chain	**To-Be Supply Chain**

As-Is Supply Chain

Chapter 6: Environmental Scanning
- What are the competitive rules?
- What skills does the SC need?

Chapter 7: Supply Chain Mapping
- **What are the SC dynamics?**
- **Is our company positioned for success?**

Chapter 8: Strategic SC Costing
- What are the relevant costs?
- What are the cost trade-offs?

Chapter 9: Competencies & Outsourcing
- What are our valued competencies?
- What activities should be outsourced?

Chapter 10: Rationalization & Role Shifting
- Where can we rationalize the chain?
- Where can we refine assigned roles?

To-Be Supply Chain

Based on the understanding developed during the SC design process, create the capabilities needed to…

1. Help our SC meet customers' real needs better than competing chains:
- Identify the **right** players for the SC
- Define the **right** relationships
- Assign the **right** roles & responsibilities
- Design the **right** structure & systems

2. Securely position the company as an indispensable member of the SC by
- Refining our customer value proposition
- Developing needed competencies
- Leveraging core technologies
- Establishing efficient processes
- Creating appropriate customer linkages

After reading this chapter, you will be able to:

1. Discuss the concept of SC design and its importance.
2. Explain process mapping and describe mapping's role in SC design.
3. Describe several popular approaches for SC design.
4. Map out a supply chain. Describe key insights a manager can gain from an SC map.

Opening Story: Olympus's Quest for Supply Chain Visibility

Doug and the SC team had been thrilled when Joe Andrus and the executive committee had given them the green light for a broad SC program. Their 6 months of hard work documenting the potential benefits, barriers, and bridges to SCM had paid off. However, the reality of the work that lay ahead sank in when Joe Andrus stepped into Doug's office during the team's brief celebratory discussion and said, "We really like what you've done so far. Your presentation today made supply chain management look attractive. If you can deliver on those benefits, our ability to cut costs and serve customers will go up dramatically. So will our profits and our stock price. Just make sure you get it right. Supply chain management is too important and too resource-intensive to fail. Good luck." With the weight of Olympus resting on their shoulders, the team's enthusiasm turned to sober reflection. Now what?

THREE WEEKS LATER . . .

Although Doug was gaining a degree of acceptance for SCM across many functional groups, many areas in Olympus's internal supply chain needed improvement. Inventory levels were high, and despite steady improvements in service levels, complaints from key customers were as loud as ever. However, the reasons for these problems were not readily apparent. Doug needed to gain an understanding of supply chain operations across business units, functions, and in relation to external SC players. Doug knew the clock was ticking, and Doug still needed to make the case for specific change. He knew that operating performance wasn't what it needed to be, but how could he identify why, and what could be done? Doug didn't want to sound like he was accusing the other functional areas of negligence or telling them how to do their jobs. A knock at his office door interrupted his thought.

Startled, Doug responded, "Come in." Bob Moyers, a quality assurance director, pushed the cracked door open and entered, pile of paper in hand. "Hey, Doug. I hope I am not disturbing you. I know that you are up against a lot of pressure right now trying to figure out how to move ahead on our SC initiatives. Well, I don't know much about that specifically, but I do know that one of the reasons that our inventory is high is because we have some quality problems with the suppliers. The folks in the factory have been asking for bigger order releases than they really need because we have so many quality holds. It seems to me we have some real problems with the way our processes link up internally, as well as how they link up with suppliers."

Doug nodded, recognizing the connection with SC design. Bob continued, "Like I said, I don't know much about SCM, but I know a lot about how to identify problems from my role as QA director. One of the things that we rely on when we are trying to identify and solve problems is process mapping."

Doug nodded, "Yes, I'm familiar with the concept." Bob said, "Great! When we find a quality problem, we observe the process where the problem occurred, talk to people involved, and then we draw a picture of what we see going on—a process map. We run this map by the people involved. Sometimes they make corrections; other times, they point out something going on, like a missing or unnecessary step. The map helps us identify problems and solutions. Sometimes, a simple fix is possible, but sometimes the map becomes the starting point for the redesign of the entire process. We draw the process as it should be in an ideal world, and then work to make the needed changes. We create buy-in by getting everyone involved—we really believe that people support what they help create. Anyway, I thought mapping might help you get started with your SC program. I'll leave you some materials from a training class I give if you are interested."

Doug nodded, thinking about just how he could use this approach. "Thanks, Bob. This might be the tool I'm looking for. I appreciate your help. Maybe we can call on you for some training too, if needed?"

"I'd be happy to help. Anything that helps the supply chain perform better will make my job easier, and will fatten up everyone's bonus check." Bob left, smiling. Doug looked over the familiar explanations of process mapping, wondering how to begin.

Consider As You Read:

1. Does "drawing a picture" of Olympus's core process seem like a good way to identify improvement opportunities? Why or why not?
2. Does extending the idea of process mapping to the supply chain make sense? In what ways would you expect SC mapping to differ from process mapping?
3. Where would you begin in drawing the SC map? Who should be involved?
4. SC mapping answers the questions, "How do we fit?" and "How should we fit?" Why begin with a map of your current process before drawing a map of how you would like things to be?

> *Supply chain design is just too important to leave to chance.*
> *Just as genetic engineering has begun to shortcut the process*
> *of species evolution, proactive chain design will shortcut and*
> *forever make obsolete the slow, incremental processes of*
> *industrial evolution.*
>
> —CHARLES FINE[1]

INTRODUCTION

How does a company determine what its supply chain should look like? Given the ideal supply chain, how does an organization determine how to move from where it is today to where it would like to be? This chapter will help you answer these questions by introducing process and value stream mapping, supply chain design, and supply chain mapping. Process mapping is a tool to chart how individual processes are currently being conducted and to help lay out new, improved processes. Value stream mapping is a type of process mapping that visually depicts the product's or service's "current" and "ideal" flow of information and materials throughout the supply chain. It specifically focuses on reducing waste throughout the system, in line with lean production concepts.[2] SC design creates a vision for where the company would like its supply chain to be. SC mapping provides a picture of the dynamics that govern how an organization's supply chain works today and can be used to provide a road map for the future.

Recall our definition of SCM:

> Supply chain management is the design of seamless value-added processes across organization boundaries to meet the real needs of the end customer.

As you might guess, great supply chains must be consciously designed to effectively meet the needs of customers and other stakeholders. SC design is not a small or a simple task. It involves aligning customer needs with both internal and supply base capabilities. It involves determining who is the best party in the SC network to perform the required tasks. It involves coordinating physical, financial, and information systems to improve responsiveness and efficiency. All of these activities must be performed to create value for the customer and profitability for all SC players.

THE IMPORTANCE OF SUPPLY CHAIN DESIGN

What if an organization does not design its supply chain, but simply allows the chain to evolve based on a series of processes and choices that are made independently over the years? We can expect the following:

- Poor coordination of effort
- Incompatible information systems
- Long cycle times

- Communication problems
- Customer service issues
- Excessive waste and environmental degradation
- Relatively high inventory for the level of customer service achieved
- Lower than optimal profit

So why do all of these problems occur? Because no one planned SC processes to achieve system-wide goals. Because the supply chain lacks transparency, decisions have been made independently to optimize local results without considering the effects on the rest of the chain. For example, a choice of low-cost packaging may fail to protect the product, drive up shipping costs, and drive away customers. Yet predicting those results might be politically and operationally complex. Such complexity is certainly one reason why SC design is still an uncommon practice. The designer must first make the chain visible. Managers must be able to see how processes are conducted, how processes affect other processes, who is doing what, where it is being done, and why it is being done. Visibility is critical to effective SC design and management.

Some believe that an organization's key to success is its ability to design and manage the supply chain in a nimble way, assembling and reassembling the "right" chain of capabilities as the operating environment changes.[3] Let's look at an example of an organization that has successfully designed its supply networks.

Nokia

Nokia is the world leader in mobile phone sales. Although the company was founded in 1865, it was only in the 1960s that it entered the telecommunications business. In the early 1990s, Nokia divested its noncore operations so that it could focus on digital telecommunications technology. One of Nokia's core philosophies is to take a cradle-to-grave approach in designing not just a product but also its supply chain. Thus, Nokia realizes that its suppliers play a huge role in Nokia's and the overall chain's performance, environmental impact, and ability to meet its customers' needs.

Because Nokia outsources a great deal of its manufacturing and assembly, it establishes close working relationships with its suppliers, focusing on excellent communication and coordination. This reduces SC inventory and the associate risk of obsolescence. As part of Nokia's approach to improved SC design and life cycle management, David White, environmental and safety manager, notes that Nokia ". . . works with suppliers to help them develop their own environmental management systems if necessary. This avoids the need for costly, specialized processes later on in the supply chain. By working with suppliers to minimize the amounts of hazardous constituents in a component through design, we save money for everyone. The environment benefits, we benefit, and suppliers benefit."[4]

Nokia's approach to SC design and management is not limited to its supply base. Internally, it focuses on energy consumption, waste reduction, and improved sorting of waste. This reduces SC costs. Another measure that reduces SC costs, improves efficiency, and benefits the customer is Nokia's logistics network design. It locates its facilities centrally to minimize transportation and to respond rapidly to its customers. By taking a big picture approach to SC design, Nokia has continued to profitably grow its global market share, despite increasing competition and difficult economic times.

PROCESS MAPPING

A *process* is defined as an activity that transforms or changes inputs into a new output. For example, a haircut is a process: You enter with one style, undergo the process, and exit with a new and improved look. A process map is a graphic representation of a system that contains a sequence of steps that are performed to produce some desired output. The primary goal behind process mapping is to make complex systems visible. Once the system is depicted and understood, the maps become the focal point for identifying the unnecessary process "complexity" that arises and leads to inefficiencies.

The important point here is that process mapping can break down a system into subsystems where the boundaries of a subsystem under analysis depend on the problem being studied. Therefore, it also becomes important to decide the extent of the supply chain for which the mapping will be conducted. A supply chain is made up of a series of manufacturing or service processes, including procurement, new product development, transformation of raw materials, delivery, and customer service.

Figure 7.1 shows a simplified SC process map. The process mapping symbols identify input and output, processes, delays, decisions, and flow. The input-process-output sequences highlighted in Figure 7.1 are typical of manufacturing processes. In this supply chain, we see that materials are transformed by two manufacturing processes. The chain also involves three warehousing delays and five transportation processes before the final output is delivered to the customer.

By creating a high-level process map, we can better understand the interdependencies and flows within supply chains. We can then look more closely at particular processes to explore whether opportunities exist to improve or eliminate those processes.

Figure 7.1 A Simplified Manufacturing Supply Chain Process

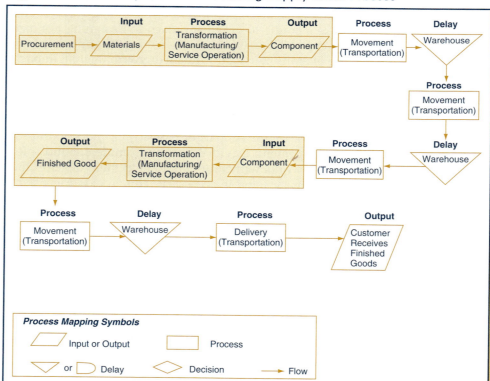

People map processes for many reasons. They hope to gain insight into current activities; drive candid discussions regarding current processes; identify areas for improvement or radical changes, as was mentioned in Chapter 3 in conjunction with reengineering; train new employees; and provide a framework for how things should operate.

When developing a process map, the suggested approach is to

- Determine why you want to draw a process map—this will affect the level of detail and the boundaries of the map.
- Determine who has the required information or experience.
- Determine the level of detail required for the map to support the goals.
- Establish the process boundaries by identifying the processes of interest.
- Analyze the process through observation and interviews, and record the steps.
- Draw the map.
- Have the people who are involved in the mapping process as well as others (including those who actually perform the process) review the map for clarity and completeness.[5]

Figure 7.2 provides a detailed process map for baking a cake. Note that the process times have been added to this process map. To take into account variability

Figure 7.2 A Manufacturing Process Map with Timing—Baking a Cake

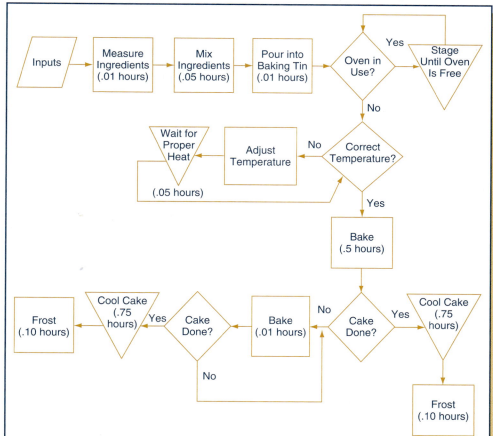

of process times, many maps also show a range of times that the process may take (standard deviations may also be included). Processes that are extremely variable are more difficult to manage. Including times helps identify bottlenecks in the process. In addition, the name of the function and/or individual responsible for each step can be added to improve the clarity and depth of understanding of the process. Again, depending on the rational for mapping the process, inventory levels, quality defects, and other issues may be depicted. The cake-baking process map is simply an expansion of one rectangle representing one manufacturing process in the simplified SC process map shown in Figure 7.1.

PROCESS ANALYSIS

Analysis for the purpose of process improvement is one of the main goals of mapping. Let's explore how to conduct process analysis.

1. Begin process analysis by examining the time, cost, resources, and people involved in each step.
   - Identify the steps that consume the most time or resources.
   - Identify processes that take too long or vary greatly in time.
   - Identify points of delay.
   - Estimate the value added by each step and judge the value against the cost.
   - Consider the reasons for problems and how to improve specific activities or processes.
2. Reexamine each decision symbol.
   - Determine whether the decision is necessary; does it add value?
   - Consider combining decisions or moving them to another point in the process to create more value.
3. Check each rework loop. A rework loop involves iterative processes, like repeatedly checking a cake until it is done baking. Here, consider how rework can be reduced, eliminated, or combined with another step.
4. Finally, look at each process step again. Sometimes a process is done out of habit without verifying its value.
   - Verify that the step adds more value than its cost.
   - Judge if the step is redundant.
   - Consider how steps could be recombined for greater efficiency.

Process mapping can also be very beneficial in identifying non-value-added activities. Looking at the process map in Figure 7.2 for the cake-baking process, there is one activity that clearly does not add value. That is the constant checking as to whether the oven is free and the temperature is set after we have mixed the cake. That should be the first step of the process. The process has been modified to reflect this as shown in Figure 7.3. We know in advance that the oven is the right temperature and that it is available before we begin mixing the cake batter.

A major computer company that was looking for a way to reduce its costs provides a real-life example of the benefit of process mapping as a tool for identifying waste. When managers mapped out some of the process steps in the assembly process, they noticed that the company was spending about $1.00 per unit to put very high-quality brand tags *inside* the computers! This process step and its associated cost were easily eliminated without affecting the customer value proposition.

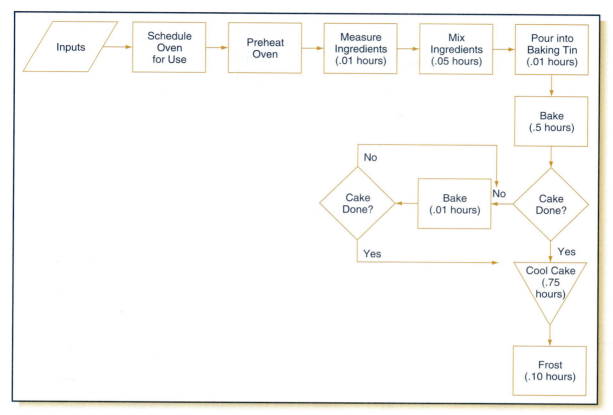

Figure 7.3   Improved Cake-Baking Process

Value Stream Mapping

Value stream mapping is a specific application of process mapping, based on lean manufacturing principles (see Chapter 5). As you may recall, lean manufacturing principles focus on eliminating the nonvalue or wasteful activities from processes. Value stream mapping generally includes much more information than a typical process map, such as times for each process, details on process performance characteristics, and information flows as well as physical flows. When applied, value stream mapping shows the current state of a process as well as the desired future ideal state. The goal is to better understand the current process, and to improve it so that it works more like the ideal process. The processes analyzed in value stream mapping tend to be broad processes, such as mapping the flow of product and information from manufacturer to customer. This is in contrast to traditional process mapping, which may vary in focus from very narrow processes to mapping the entire supply chain.

United Technologies has become an avid believer in the worth of value stream mapping. It not only value stream maps every major process in its own manufacturing operations but it is also working to teach suppliers value stream mapping techniques. United Technologies holds what are called "value stream mapping events." Managers from several suppliers come to a central location where they are taught the basics of value stream mapping. They tour United Technologies facilities and see how value stream mapping is used in daily practice. They may even participate in a process improvement activity. Supplier managers are then expected to return to their companies and begin to map key value streams. Supplier maps are then overlaid on United Technologies' maps to provide a continuous view of key processes across companies' boundaries. Of course, as suppliers reap the benefits of mapping, they are expected to help their suppliers build similar skills. The goal is to build interconnected value stream maps all the way up and down the chain.

As mentioned earlier, a supply chain is made up of a series of processes. Mapping the processes creates visibility of the activities and processes being performed as well as who is performing them. This is important in redesigning and improving existing supply chains. It is just as important when an organization is creating a new product or service and has the opportunity to create a supply chain from ground zero. What should the supply chain look like? What processes must it include? Who is the right party to execute the processes? By laying out the ideal processes, the organization can greatly reduce the waste, redundancy, and inefficiency within its supply chain. By questioning each process and interface in the supply chain an organization can come as close as possible to the ideal supply chain.

SUPPLY CHAIN DESIGN

Designing a supply chain is a relatively new concept. Historically, supply chains evolved, responding to changes in the business environments. As noted earlier, supply chain design involves planning and developing your supply chains to support the value proposition and goals of the organization. It is a proactive approach to serving the customer rather than chasing after changing needs. To clarify design specifics, managers should follow these steps:

1. Begin the process by identifying the chain's end customer.
2. Determine the supply chain's value proposition.
   - Identify the key players at each supply chain level and the value they add.
   - Determine where your company is in the supply chain and the value it adds to the supply chain.
3. Analyze who possesses the power in the supply chain: manufacturer, distributor, retailer, or other party.
   - Determine who has the best linkages with the end customer.
   - Establish the key technologies that drive supply chain success.
   - Assess the core competencies that drive supply chain success.
4. Isolate the major processes required to support the supply chain's value proposition.
   - Determine where there is a significant amount of time and variability in the supply chain.
5. Establish what the ideal supply chain would look like.
   - Ascertain the as-is value-added roles of the various supply chain members.
   - Analyze how much control over supply chain activity we want or need.
   - Clarify the should-be value-added roles of the various SC members.

These high-level questions help managers identify key processes in the supply chain. Once these processes are identified, managers can begin to define ideal processes.

Table 7.1 A Comparison of Traditional and Supply Chain Process Focus

PROCESS	TRADITIONAL	SUPPLY CHAIN
Inventory management approach	Only company-owned	Whole chains, high turns
Cost management approach	Price focus	Total cost
Coordination of sharing and monitoring in chain	Limited	Long horizon for planning
Amount of coordination of multiple levels in the chain	Limited	Extensive
Planning in supply chain	None	Integrated with information technology
Supplier management	Arms-length and/or adversarial	Close relationships with key suppliers
Leadership in supply chain	None	Leadership roles defined among players
Sharing of risks and rewards	None	Defined with key players
Speed of operations, information/inventory flows	Slow, limited	Rapid, extensive
Information technology	Not an issue; internal focus in supply chain	Extensive improvements and linkages
Team process	None with customers or suppliers	Joint teams with key customers and suppliers

They can also determine which processes should be performed internally and which should be outsourced. Outsourcing is discussed in Chapter 9. Table 7.1 contrasts some of the process differences between an SC focus and a traditional approach to management. These perspectives should be considered when designing the supply chain. For example, in a traditional approach there is generally a very limited place for sharing information with others in the supply chain, no process for joint planning exists in the supply chain, no sharing of SC risks and rewards occurs, and no joint teams are in place.

Designing a supply chain implies starting with a new product or service. This "blank slate" approach creates a tremendous opportunity to assess the ideal supply chain. In reality, most supply chain design is supply chain redesign. For example, Hewlett-Packard (H-P) has established an internal group called *SPaM (strategic planning and modeling)* to work with H-P businesses on supply chain design. Most of SPaM's work is directed at improving current SC configuration and execution. The SPaM group at H-P has been involved in many SC redesign initiatives, including efforts to

- *Address obsolescence issues.* This resulted in the use of postponement and standardization so that product differentiation could be delayed to a time when actual demand was known.
- *Assess the global supply chain for printer manufacturing.* This resulted in plant closures and relocations with an increased reliance on contract manufacturers.
- *Determine where H-P should source its parts.* The decision was made to move away from some "low-price" suppliers that actually created higher total costs in the form of long lead times, transportation costs and delays, increased inventory levels, and higher obsolescence costs. Not only did H-P reduce costs by reevaluating its sourcing configuration, but it's ability to respond to changing customer demand also improved.

Design for Supply Chain Initiatives

The 1990s ushered in an era of "design for . . ." initiatives, often referred to as *DFX*. These **designs for initiatives** were directed at the fact that designers of new products, services, and processes often failed to consider certain key elements of product/service performance that were very costly, and often very difficult to change once the product or service had been designed. The overriding principle of DFX is to create an atmosphere where designers work with other key players internally or in the supply chain to ensure that the critical issues are considered and integrated into design. DFX initiatives remind us to

- Design for manufacturability.
- Design for distribution.
- Design for disassembly.
- Design for environment.
- Design for supply.
- Design for the customer.

The list goes on. None of these initiatives alone is sufficient to ensure that the organization designs products, services, and processes that meet customer needs efficiently and effectively. The organization must look at the bigger picture of design for supply chain: How do the issues faced by each function and level in the supply chain affect others? For example, we can design a product that is relatively easy to manufacture, but might be very difficult to disassemble and repair or recycle. Customers may shy away from it because repair costs are high. Thus, it is important to keep the perspective of the supply chain as a whole in mind, not simply the internal perspective or the functional perspective.

Approaches to Supply Chain Design

The following section presents several approaches for designing supply chains. None of the approaches provides a complete "cookbook" methodology for designing supply chains, because each situation is unique. However, each approach provides a different perspective on what should be emphasized in designing supply chains. These approaches could be used together, to provide a big picture of some of the concerns and influences in SC design. SC design is enhanced by supply mapping, an important tool for understanding and improving your current and desired state in terms of SC design and management.

All of the approaches to SC design have some common elements. After we have identified the customers and the value proposition, there are three decisions involved in SC design. Conscious decisions are required to determine (1) the membership of the supply network (who will participate in manufacturing or services), (2) the structure of their relationships (who will supply what to whom), and (3) locus of control (who will actively manage the network).

The membership of the supply networks entails two primary types of decisions. The design engineers first make the creative decisions to design the product that meets the customer's needs. The parts and subassemblies required to produce this product are listed in the **bill of materials (BOM)**. Then, the sourcing managers take this BOM and engage in the **make-or-buy** decision, which requires the identification of the parts and subassemblies that need to be produced or procured from outside sources and the selection of the suppliers for these items. In cases where the design engineers have leveraged the expertise of an existing supplier in the design process, the decision of who will produce the part has already been made. It is now up to purchasing and supply to negotiate the terms and conditions of the agreement. Alternatively, the general terms and conditions may already exist between the buying and supplying companies, and only the specific details need to be worked out.

Management of the supply network entails supplier selection, evaluation, and oversight. This encompasses managing for cost, quality, and delivery of parts from suppliers. In the last two decades, we have seen many large final assemblers (e.g., Ford, General Electric, Hewlett-Packard, IBM, Lucent) delegating these responsibilities to the large top-tier suppliers who perform the manufacturing and create subassemblies. However, many of these large assemblers are very selective in delegating these activities to their suppliers. For instance, the large assembler may still select second- and third-tier suppliers, and engage them in product development. This is known as *buyer-directed sourcing*. For instance, if there is a part or module common across several product lines (e.g., fasteners or door subassemblies), the buyer may require its first-tier suppliers to use these common parts or modules from a particular supplier. In spite of this, they may delegate the responsibility for day-to-day management and supplier evaluation to their first-tier suppliers, but retain the control for cost in-house, leveraging volume with a sub-tier supplier across several products and first-tier suppliers. Whether and how much buyer-directed sourcing is done determines to a large extent the structure of the relationships in the supply network.

Various approaches have been suggested for most effectively designing supply chains to meet the organization's needs. This section briefly reviews the SCOR model, and introduces models based on product "clockspeed," product characteristics, and product life cycle.

SCOR Model

Chapter 5 introduced the Supply-Chain Council's SCOR (supply chain operations reference) model (see Figure 7.4). The SCOR model is very process-focused. It proposes that the supply chain is made up of a series of linked, plan-source-make-deliver-and-return processes. These processes can be mapped, measured, and better understood in order for the organization to improve. It suggests a 4-step approach to SC design that supports the plan-make-source-deliver-return process:

- Analyze the basis for competition: What do you need to do well in order to succeed? How can you measure and monitor your progress in these key areas?

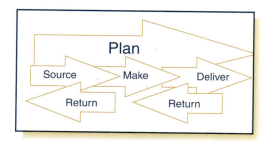

Figure 7.4 The Supply-Chain Council's Supply-Chain Operations Reference Model (SCOR)

- Configure the supply chain as it is and as you would like it to be. Include geographic locations and flows.
- Align performance levels, practices, and systems across information and work flows.
- Implement SC processes and systems, including people, processes, technology, and organization.[6]

Although this is presented as a series of steps, each step involves a significant amount of work, dedicated cross-functional team effort, and top management support. It requires a commitment of internal resources and a vision of what should be. This approach relies heavily on mapping current and ideal processes.

Supply Chain Design and Evolution: The Double Helix[7]

Another way to look at SC design is to understand that supply chains are constantly evolving and changing as the environment in which they compete changes. Some supply chains evolve very rapidly, like those of high-technology industries. Others change very slowly, like the mining industry. Regardless of the rate of change, the design of the supply chain is very important. Companies should look at trends that are occurring in the supply chains of industries that evolve faster than their own in order to anticipate and prepare for changes in their own supply chains. They should then look at their own supply chain in terms of their organizational structure, leading technologies, and their own capabilities. Because supply chains are constantly changing, it is the ability to design and redesign supply chains proactively that creates a real opportunity for competitive advantage.[8]

Within industries, power is constantly shifting and companies are evolving from relatively vertically integrated, self-sufficient organizations to firms that heavily outsource and are very dependent upon suppliers. This happens as suppliers develop better ideas and competencies, and vertically integrated firms decide to focus their own operations on areas where they feel they excel. As vertically integrated firms grow, their organizations often become rigid, impeding innovation. Niche competitors may gain advantage in certain areas because they are more agile. In addition, as products become more complex, niche competitors may also be at an advantage in focusing resources to develop highly profitable proprietary systems utilizing new technology. As will be discussed in the Chapter 9 on outsourcing this is how both Intel and Microsoft were able to grow and gain significant advantage over IBM in the PC market. IBM's response in "dis-integrating" its PC operations and focusing on full-service IT solutions demonstrates that the helix is dynamic. Those who can accurately predict the shifts of the helix stand to profit greatly. Likewise, in order for organizations to be proactive in designing their supply chains, they need to understand how their industry is evolving. This evolutionary concept and the pressures present at various stages are shown in Figure 7.5 and illustrated in the following example.

Organizations need to be aware of where they are in the evolution of their supply chains for a particular industry, and plan accordingly. For example, the modern automotive industry began with Henry Ford as a highly vertically integrated system. Ford Motor Company owned everything from rubber plantations to metal foundries on to final assembly and sales. As time passed, niche competitors developed who specialized in making components like tires, radios, or microprocessors. These agile, smaller specialists could provide equal or better parts at

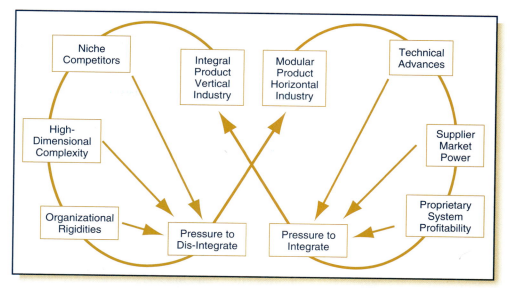

Figure 7.5 The Dynamics of Product Architecture and Industry Structure: The Double Helix

Source: Fine and Whitney; Muffatto and Pawar[9]

lower cost. Their size and specialization allowed them to focus more effectively on technology, and change more rapidly.

This created pressure to "dis-integrate" and create modular products that outside suppliers could create, as was seen in General Motors' spin-off of Delphi, its captive parts supplier. Today, the automotive industry is moving into modular products in a horizontal industry. Based on Fine and Whitney's model, shown in Figure 7.5, suppliers may begin to develop critical, proprietary technology, gaining market power. Thus, auto manufacturers need to be aware of their potential growing dependence on suppliers, and may even have to shift some production back in-house, vertically integrating. They need to take care not to become too dependent on suppliers for knowledge and capability, which are difficult to imitate and replace. They also need to monitor how quickly their industry is changing by paying attention to the most rapidly changing technologies, to allow them to respond positively, rather than take a reactionary approach.[10]

Finally, as a company designs and redesigns its supply chains, it must take full advantage of the DFX approach presented earlier in this chapter. Specifically, a company must design its products and services, processes, and supply chains simultaneously.[11] The interdependencies among these must be recognized and leveraged to create a competitive, responsive supply chain. This approach relies heavily on mapping processes and the supply chain. But an organization can never rest. Managers must be looking ahead at the next supply chain changes as it prepares for the changes beyond, because "supply chain design and development ought to be thought of as a meta-core competency—the competency of passing judgment on and choosing all other competencies and the strategies for competency development."[12]

Nature of the Product or Service

Another approach to SC design suggested by Marshall Fisher[13] is to design the supply chain based upon whether the product or service that you are selling is innovative or functional in nature. Innovative products may be fashion or fad items that have a very short life cycle. Examples are the latest video game and high fashion clothing items. They have relatively high profit margins and very unpredictable, short-lived demand, so the firm must be very flexible in meeting customer needs. On the other hand, the risk of obsolescence is also very high, so inventory levels should be kept to a minimum. The optimum buffers are speed and flexible capacity and distribution. Demand may shift rapidly, and carrying high inventory levels to respond to estimated peak demand can result in costly write-offs when demand shifts. Thus, the ideal supply chain for innovative products is best described as responsive.

Functional products are those items that fulfill a basic need, such as staple foods like sliced bread and basic cars like the Honda Civic. Demand is relatively predictable, the products have a longer life cycle, and there are plenty of substitutes in the market. The ideal supply chain for functional products is an efficient one. The supply chain should minimize handling and transport costs, and provide predictable supply at the lowest possible cost.

Fisher's approach allows an organization to better match the SC design with the type of product or service offering in order to achieve the best fit between customer demands and the firm's profitability. It provides a basic framework that can complement the SCOR or double helix models (presented earlier) or the product life-cycle model (presented next).

Supply Chain Design and the Product Life Cycle

Product life cycle (PLC) is a marketing concept that has been around for many years, but is still a valid one. This concept states that products and services evolve through a life cycle, and that the specific management concerns vary with each stage of the life cycle. In the high-tech arena, where the PLC might be months rather than years long, the organization has to focus on rapidly adapting its supply chain focus and capabilities to support the appropriate stage in the PLC. Figure 7.6 shows how Intel, a company that faces very short product life cycles

Figure 7.6 Product Life-Cycle Concept

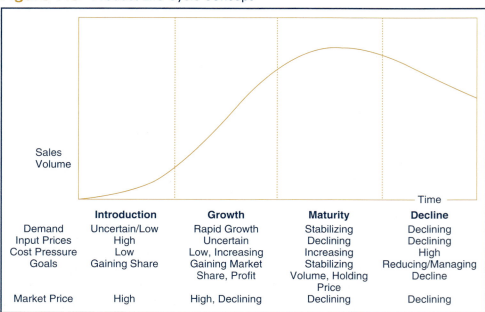

	Introduction	**Growth**	**Maturity**	**Decline**
Demand	Uncertain/Low	Rapid Growth	Stabilizing	Declining
Input Prices	High	Uncertain	Declining	Declining
Cost Pressure	Low	Low, Increasing	Increasing	High
Goals	Gaining Share	Gaining Market Share, Profit	Stabilizing Volume, Holding Price	Reducing/Managing Decline
Market Price	High	High, Declining	Declining	Declining

and very high volumes, applies the PLC concept to its products. This varies slightly from the standard PLC model you might see in a marketing text because Intel's product life cycles are extremely short. The elements listed in Figure 7.6 illustrate how Intel's focus changes over the PLC. Such an approach to designing and managing supply chains might be more important to companies that offer products and services that would be classified as innovative based on the needed characteristics.

In the introduction phase, the company focuses on gaining product acceptance, or market share. In the growth phase, sales volume increases. Although demand is uncertain, sales prices are high and cost pressure is low. As the product volume grows, competitors enter the market and sales prices begin to decline. Input prices are declining due to economies of scale and cost pressures on suppliers. Once the product matures, the cost pressure is very high, as prices continue to decline due to excess industry capacity and potentially shifting tastes. During decline, the item is being phased out, and the volume is dropping.

To support its short life cycles and demands to get its products to market quickly, and respond rapidly as the product moves through various PLC stages, Intel relies heavily on DFX initiatives. These include design for manufacturability and design for reuse, which incorporates existing parts, processes, and suppliers wherever it makes sense to do so; and design for material/purchasing. All of these DFX initiatives make Intel more agile.[14]

SUPPLY CHAIN MAPPING APPROACHES

There are numerous reasons for SC mapping. For example, an organization may decide to map its supply chain when the chain is not performing up to expectations, when it needs to reduce costs or time in the supply chain, or when it wants to gain a better understanding of its supply chain. The rationale for the mapping will affect the level of detail of the SC map. In general, it is good to begin with a high-level supply chain map so that the organization can identify the major linkages and bottleneck areas. Unlike the process maps shown earlier, SC maps should consider linkages with customers and key suppliers.

It would be nearly impossible for a complex organization to ever map its entire supply chain in detail. This would likely entail thousands, if not tens of thousands, of linkages. An organization should determine where it believes the greatest opportunity lies before it begins the detailed mapping process. If outsourcing entails simple parts or materials, the SC map will simply be a chain of dyads or simple triads. One of the goals of process mapping may be to identify the unnecessary process "complexity" that leads to inefficiency. In much the same way, the SC map can be a useful tool for identifying the unnecessary complexity in the supply network so that the SC manager can make a conscious decision whether and how to remove it.

For example, process complexity can be defined as the unexpected steps that must take place to compensate for errors that occur. There are a series of steps in the system that the engineer has designed and the customers are willing to pay for; however, due to unforeseen events and errors, extra steps are required for corrective purposes or to compensate for them. Complexity includes steps that do not add value to the process or output, but simply add cost and/or time to the supply chain.

For instance, in a supply chain, a buying company may have chosen a particular supplier for its special technical capability, but in reality this supplier may lack this capability and, unknown to the buying company, subcontracts to another more technically advanced supplier. To the extent this addition of another supplier in the supply chain has lengthened the delivery lead time, it might be said that additional complexity has been added.

The same basic approach may be used for SC mapping as is used for process mapping. Figure 7.2 showed an example of an SC map using the conventions and symbols of process mapping shown earlier in this chapter, where each major process is identified and laid out. Much information can be added to this map: company names, inventory levels and values, and even a contact person for a specific process. There are so many ways that companies and researchers map supply chains that some have even called for standard practices in SC mapping.[15]

One particularly useful type of SC map is known as the "pipeline map." This type of SC map is noted as a way to "identify the current competitive state of the supply chain."[16] An example of the pipeline map for men's underwear is shown in Figure 7.7.

A step-by-step approach for mapping the SC pipeline for a particular item is provided here. This approach focuses on understanding and improving SC performance.

1. Identify the item that you wish to map.
2. Identify all of the processes that occur on the physical pipeline for that product, including supplier processes. For example, in the case of the men's underwear example, there is the spinning of yarn to make fabric, the knitting of the fabric,

Figure 7.7 Men's Underwear Example

Source: Scott and Westbrook[16]

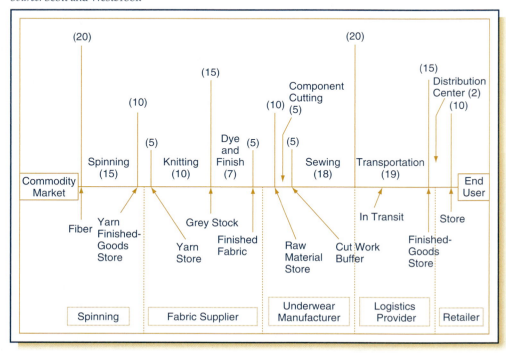

the dyeing and finishing of the fabric, the cutting of the fabric, and the sewing of the underwear. In addition, there is transportation and storage of goods in a distribution center and at the retail level before they are sold to the end customer.

3. Determine who performs each process in the chain. For simple processes, you may know who the players are. For more complex processes, you may have to ask your suppliers, or your suppliers' suppliers.

4. Talk to each of the entities that performs a process for you and determine how long the process takes them, and how much inventory they have at the beginning of the process (raw materials or components) and at the end of the process. Also find out how much they have in transit on average, and the transit time. In this example, the location differences of the spinning, fabric, and manufacturing firms are negligible, so this is not an issue. There is, however, a 19-day transit time from the underwear manufacturer to the distribution center and another 2 days from the distribution center to the retailer.

5. You are now ready to draw the SC pipeline map from raw material to end user. The pipeline map is simply a series of horizontal and vertical lines.

   a. Begin by drawing a horizontal line from the commodity market to the end user.

   b. Sum the times for all of the processes. Note that there is no transportation included other than shipping of finished goods from the underwear manufacturer to the distributor. This is because the spinning, fabrication, and manufacturing all take place in close proximity with negligible transit times. If the transit times were a day or more, they would need to be included in the SC pipeline map. In this case, spinning is 15 days; knitting, 10; dyeing and finishing, 7; cutting, 5; sewing, 18; transportation, 19; and distribution, 2 days. The sum is 76 days. The length of the horizontal line you have just drawn is equivalent to these 76 days. This is the average time spent in the processes between the stockholding points, and is known as the *pipeline length*.[17]

   c. Starting with the earliest process, write the name of the processes in order, above the horizontal line. After the name of the process, indicate the length of time that the process takes. In this case, spinning takes 15 days. Allow space equivalent to 15/76 days to represent the length of the process; then, write in the next process, etc., until you have divided the line for all of the processes, accounting for the full 76 days.

   d. Now draw vertical lines at the beginning and end of each process to indicate the average amount of inventory that each party has on hand in terms of raw materials (at the beginning of the process) and goods that it has transformed (at the end of the process). These represent the average inventory that any party in the supply chain is holding at any point in time. If the product is not physically transformed by the process, as in transportation, distribution, and retail, then only one inventory level is shown. If you add all of these figures on the vertical lines together, the total is the entire inventory in the pipeline that is waiting in some form of processing or finished goods. In this case, that totals 20 + 10 + 5 + 15 + 5 + 10 + 5 + 20 + 15 + 10 = 115 days. This represents the amount of "non-value-added" days of inventory, in all forms, in the supply chain. This is simply buffer inventory, because nothing is actually happening to this inventory during this time. The organization may want to evaluate how much of this inventory is really needed.

    e. As an enhancement, you could also use flow modeling to ". . . identif(y) both the time and cost associated with a process.[18] This involves 76 days of in-process inventory and 115 days held in buffer stock. You may want to focus on the processes with the highest value and the longest delays.

6. Analyze the supply chain for opportunities.

    a. Look at the pipeline length, which we calculated in step 5b as 76 days. Does this seem long? Consider that in order for you to "work off" the entire inventory in the supply chain in case of a decline in demand, it would take 76 days for the fiber in beginning inventory now to work its way to the end of the supply chain. Examine the pipeline map created in step 5c to understand whether any of the processes look particularly long for the activity being conducted. You may need to contact some of the suppliers, or even make site visits.

    b. Map relevant SC processes, as shown in the example in Figure 7.2. Look for unnecessary processes and delays as a starting point. Where are parts being moved multiple times and/or long distances? How does this affect SC costs and lead times? Identify potential improvement opportunities.

    c. Look at the level of buffer inventory identified in step 5d. This is 115 days. This represents assets that SC members have tied up. This increases the cost of doing business, and lowers the agility of the chain. It increases your risk: If a dramatic change occurs in the environment, various members of the chain will have to absorb write-offs of inventory, or may attempt to pass them along to others in the chain. Analyze where you believe the inventories are too high, and may be lowered. Again, you may be best served by talking to or visiting your SC members and focusing on areas with the highest value and longest delays, as suggested by flow modeling.

7. Prioritize your ideas from step 6. Work with the team, suppliers, customers, and other affected parties to implement, manage, and monitor the changes. Don't limit yourself to the first-tier suppliers or customers, as the suppliers' suppliers and customers' customers may also provide excellent ideas or opportunities for SC improvement.[19]

8. Analyze the new supply chain, revisiting step 6 until you are satisfied with the improvement results or they are no longer cost-beneficial.

9. Repeat the procedure with other supply chains where you believe there is opportunity for improvement.

This practical approach to SC pipeline mapping creates an excellent basis for understanding the organization's "as-is" supply chain situation, and a starting point for mapping the "should be" supply chain. With the help of detailed process maps to illustrate key areas of improvement opportunity in the supply chain, SC pipeline mapping can yield excellent results, supporting reengineering efforts and smaller improvement efforts. Mapping creates an improved basis for communicating within the organization as well as with external SC members.

CONCLUSION

The idea that a supply chain can and should be designed is a relatively new concept. Yet designing supply chains can be important to the success of the organizations involved in the supply chain. Whenever an organization does not systematically design its supply chains, and even when it does, it may find that the supply chains are not as effective as the organization would like them to be. Thus, the organization should map the supply chain in order to better understand the processes involved, and where inefficiencies may be occurring. Once potentially inefficient processes have been identified, those processes should be mapped in order to identify improvement opportunities. SC mapping, supplemented by process mapping or value stream mapping, can be an effective means to identify inefficiencies and potential solutions. These tools can also be an effective way to communicate internally, and with SC members. Although we have shown a standard method for process and SC pipeline mapping, these methods are extremely adaptable. Organizations should adapt the information that they include in supply chain and process maps to best suit their needs.

SUMMARY OF KEY POINTS

1. Supply chain design is a relatively new concept that advocates organizations to plan their supply chains rather than allowing them to "happen."
2. A supply chain is made up of a series of processes that involve an input, a transformation, and an output.
3. Process mapping can help managers understand how a process operates and how to improve it.
4. Value stream mapping is an application of process mapping, developed to apply lean principles to process improvement.
5. A DFX initiative is a product development mandate to improve a specified supply chain factor, X, through careful design. For example, products may be "designed for" optimizing manufacturing, supply, and/or usability.
6. There are numerous popular approaches for designing supply chains. These include the SCOR model, proposed by the Supply-Chain Council; the double-helix model based on SC evolution; a model based on the nature of the product or service; and one based upon the product life cycle concept. Each of these approaches can provide valuable insight to help design a supply chain. It is also useful to combine these different approaches to gain a broader perspective of SC design issues.
7. Organizations need to adapt the SC design process to fit their situations.
8. SC mapping uses process mapping techniques to help understand and improve supply chains.
9. SC pipeline mapping includes useful information about the organizations involved, the key SC processes, how long the processes take, how much inventory is being held, and where it is being held in the chain. Flow mapping focuses on process time and costs.
10. Organizations need to control the complexity of their SC maps to focus on their goals.

REVIEW EXERCISES

1. Discuss the importance of SC design to an organization's success.
2. Describe taking a class at a university as a process. Be sure to include the inputs, the transformation, and the output(s).
3. Explain why managers map processes. Identify at least five questions that a manager would answer through the use of a process map.
4. List the key steps in process mapping. Describe the role each step plays in the mapping process.
5. Define DFX. Describe how it relates to SC design.
6. Describe the SC design and evolution approach presented by Charles Fine.
7. Is there one right approach to supply chain design? Justify your answer.
8. Discuss at least three reasons why an organization would engage in SC mapping.
9. Describe the key steps in SC pipeline mapping, with an emphasis on how to analyze the supply chain for improvement opportunities.

Case   *Mapping the Mac*

As part of her internship project at Global Foods, Lillian Smith was charged with understanding and mapping the supply chain for Global Foods' premium macaroni and cheese. This is the macaroni and cheese that comes with the premixed cheese sauce in a can, rather than the powdered mix in a pouch. The selling point is that the sauce in a can tastes closer to homemade. It is priced at 3 to 4 times more than the macaroni and cheese with powdered cheese mix.

The cost of this product was too high, according to management. Because it was already priced at such a premium, marketing believed that there was no way that Global Foods could raise the price of the product to consumers. However the cost increases it was experiencing were squeezing the margins.

Lillian had been given a bill of materials (BOM) for the mix and needed to trace it back to the individual suppliers, their subsuppliers, and any sub-subsuppliers. The BOM that Lillian was given appears in Table 7.2. The ingredients in each finished box of macaroni and cheese weigh approximately 1 pound (lb). There are 24 boxes in a case, and each case contains about .24 hundredweight (cwt) of ingredients, not counting the packaging. The shrinkage or loss costs are built into the unit cost in the far column. Note that the unit costs are per case of 24 boxes. The packaging is also converted to a cost per case of macaroni and cheese. Corrugated shippers and cartons are priced per hundred and need to be converted to a case cost. Loss in manufacturing must also be incorporated. The glue is priced per cwt.

Lillian approached one of the product engineers to give her some insight into reading the BOM. The project engineer provided the following definitions:

- Remember that the unit of measure is 1 case of 24 boxes.
- CWT means hundredweight, which is the same as 100 pounds. It is a common measure in food manufacturing and ingredient buying in the United States.

Answer the following questions to help Lillian get started on her SC-mapping project.

CASE QUESTIONS

1. Evaluate the applicability of each of the four approaches to supply chain design (SCOR, supply chain evolution, nature of the product or service, or life cycle) to Lillian's analysis of the macaroni and cheese supply chain.
2. Where should Lillian begin with mapping this supply chain, and why?
3. Lillian contacted the supplier of the cheese sauce to get the bill of materials for the cheese sauce, as shown in Table 7.3. Note that there is also information to

---

Table 7.2 Bill of Materials for Premium Macaroni and Cheese Mix

24 Box Case
Product Code: 6001
Date of Last Update: 12/20/2004
Approved by: Bill Jenkins, Materials Scientist

INGREDIENTS	SUPPLIER	CODE	% WEIGHT	LOSS	CWT/CASE	COST/CWT	COST/CASE
Durum Wheat Pasta	Noodles-R-Us	11234	75%	2.00%	0.18240	$24.00	$4.47
Cheese Sauce Mix	Stan's Sauces	98549	25%	0.05%	0.06012	$300.00	$18.05
Ingredient Cost			100%		0.24252		$22.52

PACKAGING	SUPPLIER	CODE		LOSS	UNITS/CASE	COST/100	COST/UNIT
Package	Brown Boxes	3567		0.50%	24	$11.50	$2.77
Corrugated Shipper	Acme Boxes	3678		0.02%	1	$50.05	$0.50
Glue (cwt)	Sticky Wicket	3925		2.00%	0.00167	$78.00	$0.13
Packaging Cost							$3.40
Total Material Cost							$25.92

Table 7.3   Bill of Materials for Stan's Sauce Premium Cheese Sauce Mix

100 Unit Box Case
Product Code: 98549 for Global Foods
Date of Last Update: 11/20/2004
Lillian: As you requested, we buy the following items as "raw" materials.

Whey
Partially hydrogenated soy oil
Salt
Paprika
Milk fat
Lactic acid
The rest are already processed when we purchase them.
You will need to check with our suppliers to find out their processes.

MATERIAL NAME	SUPPLIER	PERCENTAGE WEIGHT
Cheddar Cheese	Statler Dairy	60.00%
Water	Local	25.49%
Whey	Statler Dairy	8.00%
Partially Hydrogenated Soy Oil	Greasy Tony	5.00%
Salt	Costco	0.25%
Paprika	Costco	0.01%
Milk Fat	Statler Dairy	0.75%
Lactic Acid	Statler Dairy	0.50%
Total		100.00%

PACKAGING ITEM	SUPPLIER	UNITS
Can	Aluminum Inc.	100 each
Corrugated Shipper	Acme Boxes	1 each
Glue	Costco	.00067/cwt
Total Material Cost		$25.92

particular questions that Lillian had asked this supplier at the top of the BOM. Draw as much of the SC map for the cheese sauce as you can. Note that the supplier chose not to share cost and yield loss data.

4. Identify any areas for improvement in the cheese sauce supply chain.
5. What further information would you request to assist you in analyzing the cheese sauce supply chain?

ENDNOTES

1. Fine, C. (1998). *Clockspeed.* Reading, MA: Perseus Books.
2. iSixSigma.com. (2006, January 10). www.isixsigma.com/dictionary/Value_Stream_Mapping-413.htm. Mid-America Manufacturing Technology Center. (2006, January 10). www.mamtc.com/lean/building_vsm.asp.
3. Ibid.
4. Anonymous. (2002). Supplier network management. www.nokia.com/cda2?id=1148. Anonymous, (2002). Succeeding with suppliers. www.nokia.com/cda2?id=1808.
5. Anonymous. (2000–2002). Basic tools for process improvement module 6: Flowchart. iSixSigma LLC. www.isixsigma.com/offsite.asp?A=Fr&Url=http://quality.disa.mil/pdf/flowchrt.pdf.
6. www.supply-chain.org/slides/SCOR5.0Overview Booklet.pdf. Anonymous. *Supply chain operations reference overview of model 5.0.* Pittsburgh, PA: Supply Chain Council, Inc.
7. This section draws heavily on Charles Fine's work in (1998). *Clockspeed.* Reading, MA: Perseus Books, in Fine, C., & Whitney, D. (1999). Is the make/buy decision process a core competence? and in

Muffatto, M., & Pawar, K. (eds.). *Logistics in the information age.* Padova, Italy: Servizi Grafici Editoriali, 1999. pp. 31–63.

8. Ibid. 1.

9. Fine, C., & Whitney, D. (1999). Is the make/buy decision process a core competence? Muffatto, M., & Pawar, K. (eds.). *Logistics in the information age.* Padova, Italy: Servizi Grafici Editoriali, 31–63.

10. Ibid. 1.

11. Ibid.

12. Ibid.

13. Fisher, M. (1997, March–April). What is the right supply chain for your product? *Harvard Business Review*, 105–116.

14. Ellram, L. M. (1999). *The role of supply management in target costing.* Tempe, AZ: CAPS Research.

15. Gardner. J., & Cooper, M. C. (2003). Strategic supply chain mapping approaches. *Journal of Business Logistics, 24*(2), 37–50.

16. Scott, C., & Westbrook, R. (1991). New strategic tools for supply chain management. *International Journal of Physical Distribution and Logistics Management, 21*(1), 23–33.

17. Ibid.

18. Farris, M. T. (1996). Utilizing inventory flow models with suppliers. *Journal of Business Logistics, 17*(1), 36.

19. Wittmann, C. M., Farris, M. T., & Strutton, D. (2006). The extended supply chain: Value creation, networks, and implications for supply chain theory and practice. Working paper, Department of Marketing and Logistics, University of North Texas, College of Business Administration.

Supplement G

Project Management

In addition to managing processes, SC managers are often called upon to supervise or facilitate the completion of various projects within their organizations or supply chains. These projects range from supplier development projects to distribution network redesign projects to new product development projects. In many respects process and project management are companion practices. Every project involves managing a process. And most process mapping initiatives could be managed as a project using project management tools. Further, the two practices share an important similarity—their complexity requires that managers make them visible in order to manage them efficiently and effectively.

Microsoft, arguably one of the successful project management companies, breaks down every project into dozens or hundreds of milestones to ensure that the project timetables are kept.[1] Companies without skilled project managers, on the other hand, can incur unnecessary costs and lose valuable revenues. For example,

construction company Multiplex Group said continuing problems at its Wembley Stadium redevelopment project in the United Kingdom have forced it to slash its forecast for fiscal 2006 net profit by nearly 80 percent, a reduction of nearly $150 million.[2]

Successfully completing a project of any size requires a good understanding of the interdependencies among the various required activities as well as an awareness of the time and resources necessary to complete these activities. The skills to complete projects on time and on budget are highly valued and should be part of every SC managers toolkit. Fortunately, project management tools have been developed to assist supply chain managers in these endeavors. Three of the best-known project management tools are the **critical path method (CPM)**, **Gantt charts**, and the **program evaluation review technique (PERT)**. These tools help managers plan, organize, and control projects. The basics of these tools are discussed here.

---

[1]Battles, Brett E., & Mark, David. (1996, December 9). Manager's journal: Companies that just don't get it. *Wall Street Journal*, p 1.
[2](2005, December 20). Multiplex group: Forecast slashed on problems with Wembley Stadium project. *Wall Street Journal*, p. 1.

Critical Path Method (CPM)

Employees of DuPont and Remington Rand developed the critical path method (CPM) in the late 1950s. CPM helps project managers schedule and monitor the various activities associated with a project in a way that helps complete the project on time. One of the key concepts of both CPM and PERT is that projects can be broken down into various activities that each require a certain amount of time to complete and that must be accomplished in a specific order. Therefore, the first steps in utilizing CPM are (1) to list the activities required to complete the project, (2) to construct a precedence diagram showing the sequential order that these activities must be completed in, and (3) to estimate the time needed to perform each activity.

Suppose that the activities, times, and precedence relationships for a given project are as follows:

Activity	Time (Days)	Preceding Activities
A	5	none
B	2	none
C	4	A
D	4	A
E	3	B
F	7	B
G	3	D, E
H	2	F
I	4	C, G, H

To construct a precedence diagram based on this information, we will use nodes to represent the various activities and arrows to represent the precedence relationship between and among the various activities as shown in Figure G.1.

To include more information in this diagram, which is useful for the CPM calculations, we will break

Figure G.1 Project Precedence Diagram

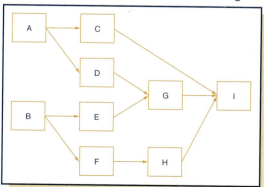

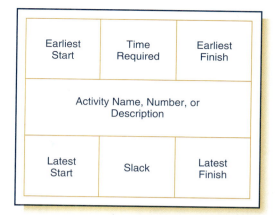

Earliest Start	Time Required	Earliest Finish
Activity Name, Number, or Description		
Latest Start	Slack	Latest Finish

Figure G.2 One Method of Organizing CPM Information

each node into sections that will be utilized as shown in Figure G.2.

The following sections detail the calculations of these values. Figure G.3 utilizes this format and includes the time required for each activity in the diagram.

Once these first 3 steps have been accomplished, the next step in the CPM is to calculate the earliest start and earliest finish times. For these calculations, we assume that the project begins at time zero, so the earliest start times for the activities with no preceding activities is also zero. The earliest finish time for each activity is simply the earliest start time plus the time required for that particular activity. The earliest finish time of a given activity then becomes the earliest start time of subsequent activities.

Earliest finish time = earliest start time + time required for activity

Because a given activity cannot commence until all of its preceding activities have been completed, we use the largest earliest finish time among an activity's immediate predecessors as the earliest start time for that particular activity. Activity G, for example, is preceded by activities D and E. The earliest that activity E can be completed is day 5. However, activity G cannot begin in day 5 because it needs to wait until activity D is completed, which is not until day 7. The calculation of earliest start and earliest finish times is referred to as a *forward pass through the events*, because the calculations are made in the order that the activities are performed. Figure G.4 shows the earliest start and earliest finish times that were calculated for the example project.

The earliest finish time of the last activity is the earliest finish time of the entire project. In this example, the earliest that this project could be finished is in 16 days.

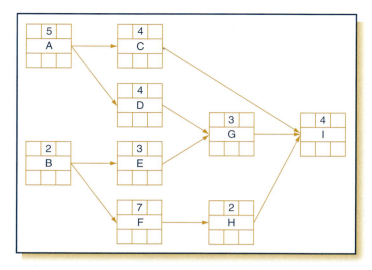

Figure G.3 Expanded Precedence Diagram

The next step in the CPM process is to calculate the latest start and latest finish times. This is accomplished by starting at the end of the project and working backwards through the various activities, a process referred to as a *backward pass*. The latest start time is calculated by subtracting the time required for a given activity from its latest finish time value. When an activity is followed by two or more activities, the smallest latest start value of these subsequent activities is utilized as the latest finish time in the activity preceding these subsequent activities. Figure G.5 shows the latest start and finish values that were calculated for this example.

Latest start time = latest finish time − time required
for activity

The next step in the CPM process is to calculate the amount of slack in each activity. Slack is the amount of time that an activity or a group of activities can slip without causing a delay in the completion of the project. Slack is the difference, if any, between the earliest start time and the latest start time or between the earliest finish time and the latest finish time. The critical path consists of the set of activities that, if delayed in any way, would cause a delay in the completion of the entire project. Critical activities are distinguished by the absence of slack. Figure G.6 shows the slack times of each of the activities and highlights the critical path of this project.

The information about earliest start, earliest finish, latest start, latest finish, and slack can be used to keep a project on schedule. The activities along the critical path

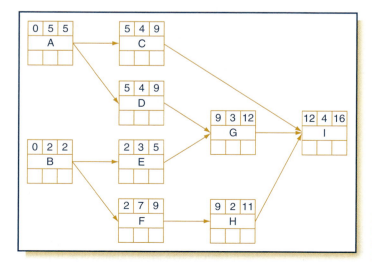

Figure G.4 Results from a Forward Pass Calculation of Earliest Start and Finish Times

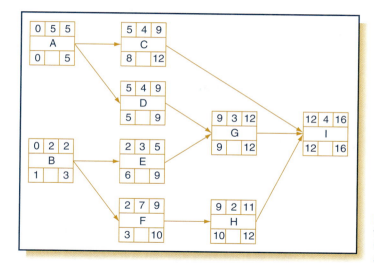

Figure G.5 Results from a Backward Pass Calculation of Latest Start and Finish Times

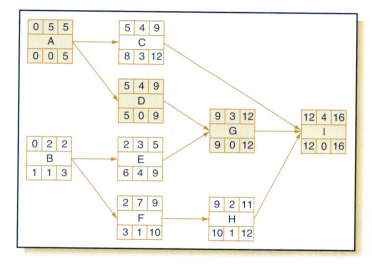

Figure G.6 Slack Calculations and Identification of Critical Path

must be closely monitored if the project is to be completed on time. Occasionally, slack in other activities can be diverted or shifted to activities along this critical path to help ensure that these activities do not slow down the progression of the project. The slack calculated in CPM refers to time, but other slack such as people, financial resources, or equipment may also exist. These other resources can also be applied to the critical path to help ensure a timely completion of the project. It is important to remember that applying additional resources to noncritical path activities will not help compress the overall project timeline.

Companies can also weigh the advantages and disadvantages of adding additional resources to activities along the critical path in order to reduce the time that these activities take. For example, activity times can often be shortened by scheduling overtime, hiring more employees, or adding

an extra shift. A comparison can be made between the normal time and cost required to complete an activity and the costs and times associated with "crashing" or compressing the time normally associated with the activity. For example, Table G.1 lists the normal cost and time as well as the crash cost and time of three activities of a particular project.

Assume that these activities are all performed sequentially, which means that they are all part of the critical path. Shortening any of these activities will shorten the entire project. The normal time to complete this project would be 9 weeks. Suppose that management would like to reduce the amount of time that this project takes by 2 weeks. Which of the activities should be changed and how much more would this crashed project cost the company?

To answer this question, we must first convert the data into values that can be compared across the three

Table G.1 Normal Versus Crash Time and Cost

| | NORMAL | | CRASH | |
ACTIVITY	TIME (WEEKS)	COST	TIME (WEEKS)	COST
A	4	$2,000	2	$4,000
B	3	$1,500	2	$1,750
C	2	$5,000	1	$5,500

activities. To do this, we can calculate a cost per week savings that can be generated by crashing each of the activities. For activity A, we assume that the cost savings are linear and directly proportional to the amount of time that is saved. Thus, if the activity can be shortened from 4 weeks to 2 weeks for an additional cost of $2,000, each week saved has a cost of $1,000 per week. These calculations are shown in Table G.2.

Because it costs more to shorten some activities than other activities along the critical path, it makes sense to select the activities with the lowest cost/time values. In this case, we can save 1 week by crashing activity B at an additional cost to the project of $250. However, this does not reduce the total time required by the project to the 7 weeks called for by management. We must, therefore, select another activity to shorten. Activity C has the next lowest cost/time value. Reducing the time that activity C takes costs the project an additional $500. In total, by shortening both activities B and C by 1 week the project can be completed in the necessary 7 weeks for a total additional cost of $750.

The steps taken when utilizing the critical path method (CPM) are summarized in Table G.3.

Gantt Charts

A Gantt chart is a graphical portrayal of a project's activities over time. Many different variations of Gantt charts can be constructed depending on what exactly the project manager is trying to accomplish. Figure G.7 shows a basic Gantt chart for the CPM example completed earlier. This particular Gantt chart shows the earliest start and finish times as well as the slack for each of the activities. Many project managers use this information to monitor the progress of the various activities. Often this involves placing a vertical line through the chart to show the current time period. This helps project managers know which activities are behind schedule, which activities are in process, which activities have been completed, and which activities are about to begin. These charts are periodically updated and distributed to project stakeholders and participants.

Another way to utilize Gantt charts is to use the horizontal bars to represent the time between the earliest start time and the latest finish time for each activity and then to shade in the bars as the activities are completed, similar to the bar that is filled in when you download files from the Internet or copy large files on your computer. For example, if the activity is 50 percent completed then the bar is filled in halfway.

One of the disadvantages of using Gantt charts is that they do not show the precedence relationships between the various project activities. Therefore, they should be used with CPM to help overcome this disadvantage.

Table G.2 Cost/Week Calculations

| | NORMAL | | CRASH | | |
ACTIVITY	TIME (WEEKS)	COST	TIME (WEEKS)	COST	COST/WEEK
A	4	$2,000	2	$4,000	$2,000/2 = $1,000
B	3	$1,500	2	$1,750	$250/1 = $250
C	2	$5,000	1	$5,500	$500/1 = $500

Table G.3 Critical Path Method Steps

STEP NUMBER	STEP NAME
1	List required activities.
2	Construct precedence diagram.
3	Estimate time necessary for each activity.
4	Calculate earliest start and finish times.
5	Calculate latest start and finish times.
6	Calculate slack of each activity.
7	Identify critical path.
8	Use critical path information to better manage project.
9	If necessary, calculate the cost and benefits of crashing the critical path.

Program Evaluation Review Technique (PERT)

The program evaluation review technique (PERT) was initially developed by the U.S. Navy and Booz Allen Hamilton for use on the Polaris missile project. This complex project involved thousands of activities that needed to be completed in a time-efficient manner.

The major difference between CPM and PERT involves how the time element of the activities is determined. CPM utilizes one specific time estimate of how long each activity will take. CPM assumes that these values are known with certainty or that they can be estimated with a high degree of accuracy. In reality, however, the length of each activity ranges between a set of values rather than being a constant value. There

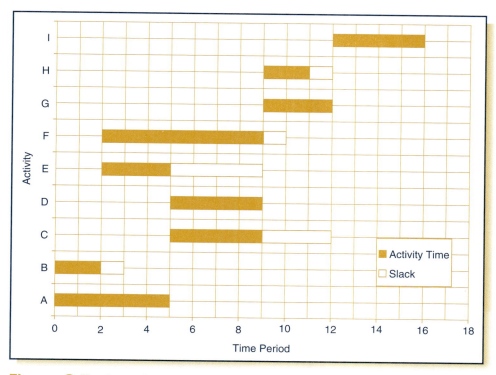

Figure G.7 Gantt Chart for the CPM Example Problem

is a lot of uncertainty pertaining to how long activities will take, especially on new projects. Therefore, PERT utilizes a technique that combines three time estimates into a single value that is used for each activity. The three estimates are

A—Best case (optimistic)	How long would the activity reasonably take if everything worked flawlessly and there were no complications or extenuating circumstances?
B—Worst case (pessimistic)	How long would the activity take if everything that could reasonably go wrong went wrong?
C—Most likely	How long would this activity take place under normal operating conditions?

PERT takes a weighted average of these three estimates and uses that average when calculating the earliest start and finish times as well as the latest start and finish times. The calculation of an expected time value is completed as follows:

$$\text{Time Estimate (mean)} = \frac{A + 4C + B}{6}$$

This weighted average assigns four times more weight to the most likely time estimate. This formula is based on a beta probability distribution.

The variance of each activity's time is calculated as

$$\text{Variance} = \sigma^2 = \frac{(B - A)^2}{36}$$

Calculating the mean and variance of each activity allows the project manager to make probabilistic statements about how long the project will take to complete. This is the main difference between CPM and PERT. The processes of determining the critical path are the same in both methods with the exception that CPM uses a single time estimate for each activity and PERT uses the time estimate that was calculated from the other three estimates.

EXERCISES/PROBLEMS

1. A project has the following activities, times, and precedence relationships:

Activity	Time (Weeks)	Preceding Activities
A	3	none
B	5	A
C	3	A
D	4	B
E	8	C
F	2	D, E

a. Draw a precedence diagram for the project.
b. Calculate the earliest start and finish times for each of the activities.

2. Determine the earliest start, earliest finish, latest start, latest finish, and slack times for each of the activities in the project shown in Figure G.8.

3. A project has the following activities, times, and precedence relationships:

Activity	Time (Weeks)	Preceding Activities
A	3	none
B	5	none
C	3	none
D	4	A, B
E	8	A, B
F	2	D, E

a. Draw a precedence diagram for the project.
b. Calculate the earliest start and finish times for each of the activities.

4. A project has the following activities, times, and precedence relationships:

Activity	Time (Weeks)	Preceding Activities
A	15	none
B	5	none
C	21	A
D	9	C
E	12	C
F	7	D, E, B

a. Draw a precedence diagram for the project.
b. Compute the earliest start times, earliest finish times, latest start times, latest finish times, and slack times. Write these values in the precedence diagram.
c. Determine the critical path.
d. How long is this project estimated to take?

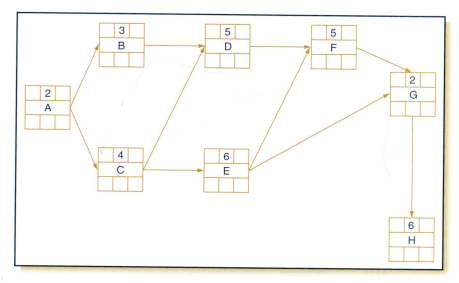

Figure G.8

5. A project has the following activities, times, and precedence relationships:

Activity	Time (Days)	Preceding Activities
A	15	none
B	5	A
C	21	A
D	9	A
E	12	B, D

a. Draw a precedence diagram for the project.
b. Compute the earliest start times, earliest finish times, latest start times, latest finish times, and slack times. Write these values in the precedence diagram.
c. Determine the critical path.
d. How long is this project estimated to take?
e. Construct a basic Gantt chart for this process.

6. Suppose that the following additional information is available for the project in question 5. How much would it cost to shorten the project by 5 days? Which activities would you shorten and by how much?

| | Normal | | Crash | |
Activity	Time (Days)	Cost	Time (Days)	Cost
A	15	$450	10	$850
B	5	$300	2	$350
C	21	$950	18	$1,500
D	9	$600	8	$1,600
E	12	$1,200	6	$2,400

7. A project has the following activities, times, and precedence relationships:

Activity	Time (Months)	Preceding Activities
A	2	none
B	8	none
C	3	none
D	6	B
E	5	C
F	4	B, A
G	1	D, E
H	2	C
I	2	F, G
J	7	D, C, A
K	3	J, I
L	6	B, H, I
M	1	D
N	5	K, L

a. Draw a precedence diagram for the project.
b. Compute the earliest start times, earliest finish times, latest start times, latest finish times, and slack times. Write these values in the precedence diagram.
c. Determine the critical path.
d. How long is this project estimated to take?
e. If the project needs to be shortened, should managers focus their attention on activity G? Why or why not?
f. Construct a basic Gantt chart for this project.

8. Compute the mean and variance for each of the following activities:

Activity	Optimistic	Pessimistic	Most Likely
A	5	10	7
B	3	21	15
C	18	32	25
D	9	11	10
E	8	8	8
F	1	10	6
G	45	95	60
H	12	15	13
I	7	11	9
J	22	80	60

9. A project has the following activities, precedence relationships, and time estimates:

Activity	Predecessor	Optimistic	Pessimistic	Most Likely
A	none	8	10	10
B	A	20	25	22
C	A	14	21	17
D	B	5	9	8
E	C	3	42	15
F	D, E	21	87	45

a. Compute the mean and variance for each of the activities.
b. Draw a precedence diagram.
c. Identify the critical path.
d. If the project needs to be shortened, should managers focus their attention on activity C? Why or why not?
e. Construct a basic Gantt chart for this project.

WEB EXERCISES

1. Visit www.pmi.org and write a 1-page paper summarizing additional information that you learned about the project management tools discussed in this chapter.
2. Visit www.project.net and write a 1-page paper discussing how this application may be useful to project management.
3. Visit www.microsoft.com and learn more about Microsoft's project management software. Write a 1-page paper discussing how this application may be superior to the calculations/methods discussed in this supplement.
4. Use the Internet to find two companies utilizing project management tools. Compare and contrast the companies' use of these tools in a 1-page paper.

Chapter 8

Strategic Supply Chain Cost Management

Do we understand our SC costs? Can I use strategic costing to assess SC design decisions and trade-offs?

The Supply Chain Road Map

Designing the Global Supply Chain
- What Must Be Done to Compete and Win?
- Who Should Do It?

How Do We Fit?

As-Is Supply Chain

Chapter 6: Environmental Scanning
- What are the competitive rules?
- What skills does the SC need?

Chapter 7: Supply Chain Mapping
- What are the SC dynamics?
- Is our company positioned for success?

Chapter 8: Strategic SC Costing
- **What are the relevant costs?**
- **What are the cost trade-offs?**

Chapter 9: Competencies & Outsourcing
- What are our valued competencies?
- What activities should be outsourced?

Chapter 10: Rationalization & Role Shifting
- Where can we rationalize the chain?
- Where can we refine assigned roles?

How Should We Fit?

To-Be Supply Chain

Based on the understanding developed during the SC design process, create the capabilities needed to …

1. Help our SC meet customers' real needs better than competing chains:
- Identify the **right** players for the SC
- Define the **right** relationships
- Assign the **right** roles & responsibilities
- Design the **right** structure & systems

2. Securely position the company as an indispensable member of the SC by
- Refining our customer value proposition
- Developing needed competencies
- Leveraging core technologies
- Establishing efficient processes
- Creating appropriate customer linkages

After reading this chapter, you will be able to:

1. Explain why strategic cost management is important to company and SC success.

2. Apply the three elements of strategic cost management to an analysis within your organization.

3. Explain the relationship between process mapping and strategic cost management.

4. Describe the various types of price and cost analysis strategies applied today.

5. Select the right type of cost analysis tool to best support a particular SC design situation.

6. Develop and explain a total cost of ownership analysis.

Opening Story: Breaking the Cost Management Silo

Doug strode down the hall toward the conference room, eager to begin the next meeting of the SC task force. Today the team would discuss ways that SCM could save the organization money, while not sacrificing performance. But cost management always made people nervous about jobs and relationships with partners. Doug had planned his agenda carefully after discussing with Charlene the pitfalls of most approaches to cost management. Charlene had pointed out the trap of cost cutting in isolation, without regard to the bigger picture or long-term implications. To do it right, Charlene explained, he needed to take a strategic perspective.

Doug opened the meeting. "Good afternoon, team. We have a topic to work with today that can win us a lot of points with top management if we do it right. That is strategic cost management." He heard the expected groans. "I know this is not your favorite topic, but it is critical. This is one of the biggest ways that SCM affects the bottom line."

Diane Meredith, marketing manager for North America, cleared her throat. "What about sales? I mean, cost cutting is great, but we always seem to go too far, and affect quality or service. We'll squeeze our suppliers so much that they start to miss deliveries, or make compromises, and then we miss our deliveries, or have to expedite and increase our cost."

Susan Mass, Olympus's director of global supply agreed: "I can't go through another round of forcing across-the-board price reductions on our supply base. It just doesn't make good business sense when we have invested our time developing relationships. In most cases, we can find a better way to make a bigger bottom-line difference than a 3 percent price decrease. Why not share resources, pool inventory, and work together on development?"

Doug nodded. "Other concerns before we get started?" Doug felt confident.

Dave Amado, the senior transportation manager, interjected, "Vijay and I have been through this too many times. Kathy optimizes her production to lower her unit costs, and then my costs go sky high when I have to store the inventory and move it between distribution centers. Nothing personal, Vijay."

Vijay nodded. "It's true. We need to look at this differently than we have in the past if we want to be effective."

Doug saw his opening. "Great. I am glad we are all in agreement. We need to take a different approach. You remember a few moments ago, I used the term, 'strategic cost management.' Well, that means we take a big-picture perspective. We've done the mapping, so we understand our *value proposition*—that is, why our customers buy from us. We keep the value proposition at the forefront of our minds, so we don't weaken it while we try to cut costs. Anything we do that is not completely transparent to the customer must be evaluated in terms of how it might affect sales."

"Good," Diane chimed in. "We haven't always done that. Remember when we changed the consumer packaging to save money for the Olegra product line! The customers hated it! They said the new packaging didn't close properly after use, and it cost us tons of money to appease them with coupons and giveaways before we changed back to the original material. That was my first assignment as a brand manager!" She rolled her eyes.

"Diane is right," Doug explained. "Most people act like all costs are bad—but whenever we look at a cost driver like the Olegra packaging, we need to ask, 'What value does the cost add?' If we don't know or determine that it doesn't add enough, then maybe we can reduce costs. For Olegra, however, the original packaging did add value. The change we made was painfully apparent to the customer. By ignoring this, we hurt ourselves. We clearly should have taken a closer, or at least a different, look at that one before we implemented it."

"Costs are definitely important, Doug," said senior financial analyst Joel Sutherland. "We've just mapped our supply chain. Let's identify the cost drivers."

Doug nodded again. "Right, and that is where SC analysis and cost management fits in. To start strategic cost management, you map the supply chain, like we've been doing for the past few weeks. From there, you identify the key cost drivers, keeping in mind your value proposition. Then you engage key suppliers and customers before making the cost-cutting moves that could affect your value proposition. Better costing makes the trade-offs transparent. It helps us make better strategic decisions. We can do a better job of evaluating not only what needs to be done, but also who can do it at the right cost!"

"Sounds great, Doug," Susan replied. Then she asked quizzically, "It all seems very logical. What has taken us so long to think about strategic cost management instead of the here-we-go-again-across-the-board cost cuts?"

Consider As You Read:

1. Why do companies engage in across-the-board demands for cost cutting rather than using a strategic cost management approach?
2. What is a good way to identify a promising initial project for strategic cost management?
3. How do problems with current management accounting systems complicate the strategic cost management process?
4. How can a company reduce costs without compromising quality or service?
5. Who needs to participate in strategic cost management?
6. What tools can help a firm understand the broad cost implications of its decisions?

> *The objective of cost management is to instill in everyone in the firm a disciplined approach to cost reduction . . . it must spread across the entire supplier network.*
>
> —ROBIN COOPER AND REGINE SLAGMULDER[1]

> *A cynic is someone who knows the cost of everything and the value of nothing.*
>
> —OSCAR WILDE[2]

THE PROFIT LEVERAGE EFFECT OF SUPPLY CHAIN COST REDUCTION

If your boss is like most, she wants to save money. Major research studies by the Center for Advanced Purchasing Studies (CAPS), Michigan State University, and the AT Kearney Global CEO study show that chief executive officers are consistently concerned about cost management. More importantly, CEOs look to SCM for cost management initiatives. Measurable cost savings that don't hurt sales produce a tremendous improvement on the bottom line. This is often referred to as "the profit leverage effect."

To illustrate profit leverage, Table 8.1 compares the effect of a $1 million cost reduction to a $1 million increase in sales for a manufacturing firm, where cost of sales is initially 60 percent of the revenue. The cost reduction could be as a result of improved logistics operations, lower material costs, improved manufacturing methods, or some combination. As this example indicates, the profit impact of cost reduction is, of course, much larger than the impact of increased sales, because the reduction in cost goes directly to the bottom line. The increase in sales, on the other hand, comes with the additional costs of providing the goods or services that were

Table 8.1 Profit Leverage of Cost Reduction Versus Sales Increase

	BASE CASE	% SALES	COSTS DOWN	% SALES	SALES UP	% SALES
(1000s) Sales	$20,000	100.0%	$20,000	100.0%	$21,000	100.0%
Cost of Sales	12,000	60.0%	11,000	55.0%	12,600	60.0%
Gross Margin	8,000	40.0%	9,000	45.0%	8,400	40.0%
***Operating Expense**	2,000	10.0%	2,000	10.0%	2,000	9.5%
Net Profit Before Tax	$6,000	30.0%	$7,000	35.0%	$6,400	30.5%

*Assume no change in operating expenses is required to generate additional sales or cost reduction.

sold. Thus, a small reduction in cost yields the same rise in profit as a much larger increase in sales. The lower the average profit margin, the greater the effect. For example, in the grocery industry, where profit margins are around 2 percent, changes in cost can have a tremendous impact on profitability.

STRATEGIC COST MANAGEMENT PRINCIPLES

Cost reduction should never be done in isolation. One must always consider the effect on other functions, the supply chain, and the firm's value proposition to its customers. For purposes of this discussion, we will define **strategic cost management** as using cost management techniques to reduce the organization's costs and improve profit while supporting its value proposition. There are three key elements of strategic cost management: supply chain analysis, value proposition analysis, and cost driver analysis.[3]

Supply Chain Analysis

Supply chain analysis is the examination of the management of the flow of information, inventory, processes, and cash from the earliest supplier to the ultimate consumer, including the final disposal process. The firm may examine in detail a particular supplier, customer, product, or service while considering the many inter-relationships and interactions among members of the supply chain. Understanding the supply chain begins with SC mapping (the topic of Chapter 7).

SC analysis has received increased attention for a number of reasons. For example, many researchers and business analysts believe that organizations are now competing supply chain to supply chain rather than firm to firm.

Clearly, decisions related to the design of the supply chain have major implications on the organization's cost structure, value proposition, and ability to compete. Two organizations can appear to have very similar supply chains in terms of their supply base and distribution methods, but still have very different results. This is because of the nature of the relationships that the organization has with its suppliers and the ways roles and responsibilities are shared. For example, one organization may work collaboratively with suppliers, sharing much more information and jointly developing products and promotions. In this case, the results of the physically similar supply chains would be very different.

Value Proposition Analysis

Value proposition analysis considers how your organization competes and is an essential element of corporate strategy. What is it that attracts customers to you to do business rather than to another potential supplier? What advantage do you have to offer your customers above the competition? In order to effectively act upon this, you must understand and speak strategy. This is the only way that you can effectively communicate with top management *and* make the right decisions to achieve organizational success. Some generic value propositions you might recognize include:

Cost leader, or being the low-cost provider
Innovator
Niche service provider[4]

These approaches to competition are still valid today. However, there are many new approaches as well. The most popular among these include:

First to market provider: This was a very popular strategy in the late 1990s and continues to be an important approach to doing business today.
Service/solution provider: This has become one of the key ways for organizations to compete in this decade. Being a full-service solution provider requires a high level of understanding of customer needs and flexibility in willingness to meet those customer needs.
Technology leader: This is a focused innovation approach, whereby the organization competes by providing the latest and greatest technology to its customers.

The service solution provider value proposition is popular among many organizations today. IBM follows this approach in the information technology arena by selling computer hardware, providing staff to run the hardware and support the software at your location, providing help-desk support, and so on. Full-service solution providers often cater to the growing market for outsourcing professional services. On the other hand, Hewlett-Packard has chosen to compete primarily as an innovator and hardware provider, rather than providing on-site support to replace an organization's information technology department. Apple Computer has been very successful by acting as a niche solution provider of personal computer hardware and software to a market that focuses on graphic designers and other non-Windows clients. More recently, Apple has been extremely successful in executing a first-to-market provider value proposition for its iPod.

Organizations may use a combination of the value propositions. In addition, the value propositions used may change over time and vary by product and business unit. MooreWallace used to focus its value on cost leadership and simply provide printed material to order. Today, as a service solution provider, it offers complete forms design, consolidation, standardization, management, and distribution in an electronic environment to meet its customers' needs. Thus, it is important for you to be aware of the current value proposition for the products/services that you support. This is critical to making the best decisions in your job. For example, if you are a buyer, and are not aware of the strategy of your organization in selling its new line of widgets, you will have no way of gauging how to weight supplier selection criteria such as quality, price, and supplier technical innovation. Without this knowledge and understanding of your organization's strategy, you could make the wrong decision and actually undermine the long-term success of the product. Table 8.2 shows the value propositions for Intel and Amazon.com.

Table 8.2 Example Value Propositions

INTEL[5]

Intel is putting the people and resources in place to sharpen our focus on the development of platforms that meet the demands of our customers and provide innovative and exciting new technologies for the marketplace.

—Paul Otellini, Intel CEO

AMAZON.COM

- To use the Internet to transform e-commerce shopping into the fastest, easiest, and most enjoyable shopping experience possible

Note that the value propositions for both Intel and Amazon.com have also changed over time. Both rely heavily on technology. Intel creates and sells the latest technology. Amazon creates and utilizes the latest technology to better serve its customers. Table 8.3 provides a list of questions to answer before you undertake a cost-reduction efforts for your organization. This could prevent you from saving money at the expense of value. Anytime you make a change that is not completely transparent to the customer, the firm's value proposition could be at risk.

The rationale behind these questions is to improve decision making by ensuring that you do not inadvertently negatively affect the firm's value proposition as you work to cut cost. You begin by assessing where you get information about the firm's value propositions, and then ask additional questions to help ensure that your knowledge of the value proposition is current. Finally, you consider how your decision might impact the value proposition in the eyes of the customers.

Cost Driver Analysis

Cost driver analysis relates to what processes, activities, and decisions actually create costs in your supply chain. The cost drivers vary over time and among different products and services. Some of the generic cost drivers include:

1. *Level of outsourcing within a company.* A company that outsources may experience higher costs when asking for additional services than it would if it had internal operations. However, the overall costs may be lower when demand is erratic.

Table 8.3 Questions to Consider Before Undertaking Cost-Reduction Efforts

How do you become aware of what the value proposition is in your organization at any point in time, for any particular product or service?

What is the value proposition for your organization (product, service)?

Does the value proposition vary among business units and products or services?—If so, are you certain you have identified the right value proposition?

Does the value proposition vary over time?
—If so, are you certain you have identified the current or future value proposition?

Will your current or proposed activities be transparent to the customer?
—If not, in what way will they be visible?
—Are these areas that the customer values?
—Will the impact be positive, negative or neutral?

2. *Use of nonstandard materials, components, and parts.* In general, nonstandard items are more costly because there aren't as great economies of scale. However, a nonstandard part may provide better performance, or lower operating costs.
3. *Scale of operations.* For example, a very large manufacturing operation must have high volumes in order to be profitable. A smaller manufacturing operation may actually be unprofitable at high-volume levels due to overtime costs, inefficiency in operations, and machine breakdowns and maintenance issues.
4. *High level of finished goods product mix.* The more options the organization offers its customers, the more inventory it may have to carry, and the more flexible it must be in its production operations.

Cost drivers can also be related to an organization's internal and external processes. One of the key issues to remember when considering cost drivers is that cost drivers are not inherently good or bad. They must be analyzed relative to their value. For example, DS Waters of America focuses on drinking water, sold in bottles at retail (Sparkletts and Hinckley Springs are two of its brands), and delivered directly to consumers and businesses. On the other hand, Coca-Cola focuses on bottled water (e.g., Dasani), soft drinks, and juices. A high level of product mix clearly adds complexity and cost compared to offering a single product. However, Coca-Cola's product mix is part of its value proposition: to benefit and refresh everyone it touches.[6] Thus, one must always look at cost drivers relative to the value that they add.

So what do you think is a key cost driver for Amazon.com? Does that cost driver also add value? One key cost driver for Amazon.com is *inventory*. When Amazon.com first began its operations, it did not own any warehouses. This allowed it to keep inventory cost low. However, it did not allow Amazon.com to be as flexible and timely in its delivery of product to its customers. As this was a key part of what distinguished Amazon.com from the competition, it decided to move into a bricks-and-mortar environment and own both warehouses and inventory. Thus, having better control of inventory is certainly an important part of Amazon.com's value proposition. However, we might ask the question again, is this the only way? Is this the best way? Amazon.com must believe it is, because it has invested heavily in technology and systems to make its distribution operations among the most efficient in the world.[7]

Example of Strategic Cost Management: Southwest Airlines

Southwest Airlines is a company you have to admire, whether or not you enjoy its "no-frills" service. Southwest started business in 1971, became profitable in its third year of business, and has remained profitable every year since then.[8] Southwest Airlines' mission " . . . is dedication to the highest quality of Customer Service delivered with a sense of warmth, friendliness, individual pride, and Company Spirit."[9] Its value proposition centers on low-cost, reliable, and friendly service.

To meet its value proposition and achieve profitability goals while competing against the major airlines, Southwest Airlines needed a great supply chain design that focused on eliminating non-value-adding cost drivers while providing the promised service. In short, it needed a strategic cost management perspective. Some key elements of its successful design include:[10]

- Utilize secondary airports wherever possible in major cities, for lower cost as well as reduced traffic and congestion to improve on-time reliability.
- Standardize on one type of equipment (Boeing 737) to improve the efficiency of pilots and crew, maintenance, flight turnaround, and equipment substitution, when necessary.

- Implement performance-enhancing upgrades to the equipment to lower fuel costs, maintenance costs, noise level, and to improve range, contributing to lower cost and improved customer satisfaction.
- Do not use preassigned seating, different classes of service, or meal service in order to lower cost and speed turnaround of airplanes.
- Implement careful hiring procedures and cross-training of associates so that employees support the mission of friendliness and customer service, and are flexible to meet the needs of whatever job is required, within reason.
- Promote customer self-ticketing, early adoption of ticketless travel, and no use of travel agencies to reduce costs and promote efficiency.

Southwest still touts itself as "the *only* short-haul, low-fare, high-frequency, point-to-point carrier in America."[11] Taken together, Southwest Airlines' value proposition (low-cost, friendly, and reliable service) is supported by both its supply chain design (hub locations, single type of equipment) and its attention to minimizing nonvalue cost drivers (maximizing equipment and employee efficiency and effectiveness) make it an excellent example of strategic cost management implementation. Of course, Southwest Airlines has an excellent strategy and outstanding execution. Part of that execution embraces strategic cost management concepts, and a broad sense of employee responsibility.

RESPONSIBILITY FOR STRATEGIC COST MANAGEMENT

Who should be responsible for strategic cost management within the organization? Historically, accounting and finance people have had responsibility for reporting, and in some cases managing, costs. As we look at the interrelationship of cost in the supply chain and take into consideration how our own processes have an effect on the processes of our customers and our suppliers, it is clear that we need a perspective broader than just accounting, or just finance, or marketing alone, or just engineering. SC managers by themselves do not have all the answers. The bottom line is that everyone in the organization should be responsible for strategic SC cost management in some way, having specific goals incorporated into their performance appraisal.

Industry Examples

At Intel, controllers and cost managers develop models for supply management people to use in working with their suppliers, understanding their suppliers' cost structures, and developing opportunities for improvement. Thus, at Intel, supply management's role in strategic cost management is selecting the right cost management processes and executing them with suppliers. Although accounting and finance have responsibility for developing tools to support supply management, it is the supply managers who have the ultimate responsibility for delivering cost savings to the organization.

In other organizations, such as SBC, a major telecommunications company serving portions of the southern United States and California, an internal consulting group focuses on cost analysis within the supply management organization. This group takes on large or complex projects that individual commodity managers do not have the time or skills to deal with effectively. The group includes people with finance, purchasing, logistics, operations, sales, and engineering backgrounds. It looks at insourcing/outsourcing decisions, SC design decisions, alternative sourcing, opportunities for leverage, and other cost savings opportunities. Although supply management is explicitly responsible for cost management in this organization, management acknowledges that some projects might be too large for an individual commodity manager to undertake without the support of experts.

Supply management cannot be effectively responsible for cost management by itself. Honda of America tells the story of how, in the early 1990s, supply management was held solely accountable for the target costs of new products. When engineers designed a product that did not meet the organization's desired target costs, purchasing returned to the engineers and asked them to make a modification. The engineers would promise to do so. However, the engineers had other, higher priority projects for which they were held accountable. Rarely did the engineers go back and modify the design to better meet target costs. Why not? It was because achieving target costs was not included on their long list of responsibilities.

It did not take the management at Honda of America long to determine that there was a problem with accountability. It made design engineers and supply management jointly responsible for achieving target costs for new products. Since that change in measurement, Honda has been able to meet its target costs and value proposition for new automobiles.

DETERMINING THE TOOLS TO SUPPORT STRATEGIC COST MANAGEMENT

As shown in Chapter 7, a process map helps analysts identify the cost and value drivers in the supply chain, and should be the starting point for strategic cost management. Once processes have been mapped, keeping the value proposition in mind, the organization can determine which tools to use to better understand the costs. Some of these tools include:

> *Cost analysis:* Including "should-cost" analysis or zero-based pricing, as well as analysis of service provider cost elements.
> *Price analysis:* Understanding the prices available in the competitive marketplace.
> *Total cost of ownership:* Analyzing the true cost of acquisition, use, maintenance, and disposal of a good, service, capital equipment, or process.
> *Target costing:* Determining what the market will bear and working backwards to see how much you can afford to produce the product or service for, and still make a profit.

These approaches are often modified or used in combination. Supply managers have to assess their situations to decide which tools to use.

Classification of Supply Chain Decisions

Before you decide to move ahead with an SC decision, it's important to understand as much as you can about the process or decisions that you are dealing with. Once you have a good understanding based on process mapping, you can use a matrix similar to that shown in Figure 8.1 to determine the correct cost analysis approach to

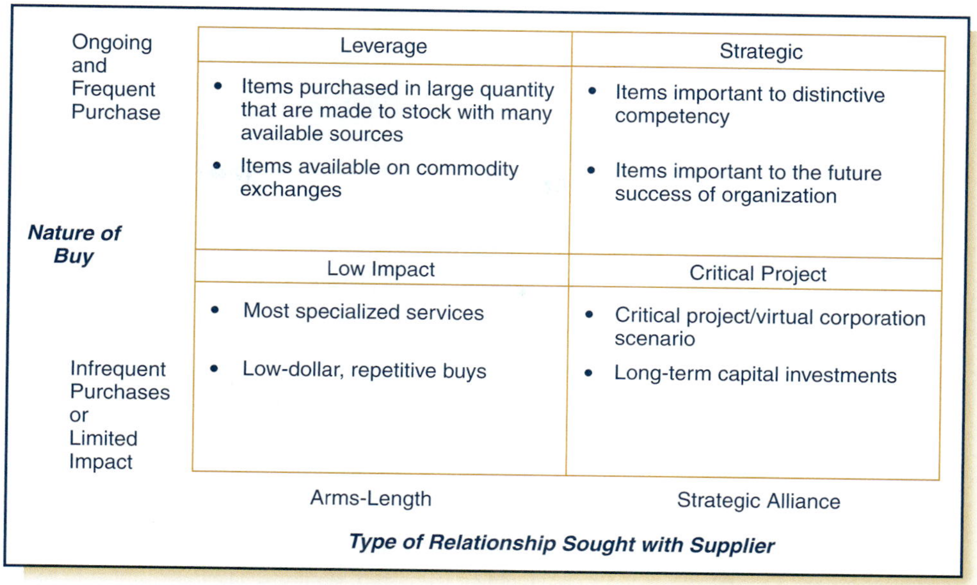

	Leverage	Strategic
Ongoing and Frequent Purchase	• Items purchased in large quantity that are made to stock with many available sources • Items available on commodity exchanges	• Items important to distinctive competency • Items important to the future success of organization
	Low Impact	**Critical Project**
Infrequent Purchases or Limited Impact	• Most specialized services • Low-dollar, repetitive buys	• Critical project/virtual corporation scenario • Long-term capital investments

Nature of Buy

Arms-Length   Strategic Alliance

Type of Relationship Sought with Supplier

Figure 8.1   Classifying Suppliers/Purchases

use for your analysis. This matrix focuses on upstream SC decisions and provides a starting point to determine how to view a particular purchase, supplier, or SC decision from a cost perspective. Downstream decisions follow a similar pattern.

The supplier can be an internal process provider as well as an outsourced provider or a supplier of materials. This matrix approach to classifying purchases is a decision-support tool. This matrix helps classify any of the types of purchases or outsourcing situations a buyer may encounter. It also helps frame the types of relationships the firm would like to have with its internal and external suppliers.

In Figure 8.1 the vertical axis shows the nature of the buy (from "limited impact either/or infrequent purchase" to "ongoing impact and frequent purchase"), and the horizontal axis shows the relationship sought with the supplier (from "arms-length" to "strategic alliance"). This 4-quadrant matrix is a valuable tool in helping buyers determine what kind of cost/price analysis technique to use for a particular situation.

Classification of Cost: Nature of the Buy

The vertical axis, the nature of the buy, asks the question, "Is this a one-time buy?" As we move up to the top, the criteria changes to, "Is this a frequent buy that has ongoing impact?" The questions in Table 8.4 help you make the determination of exactly where along this continuum to place your situation. The more and stronger the "yes," the more the buy moves up to the top of the vertical axis.

Relationship with the Supplier

The second part of the classification is to consider the type of relationship desired with the supplier. Table 8.5 shows some questions about the nature of the supplier relation desired. The relationships can vary widely. Do you want to have more of an open-market sort of relationship—not developing an ongoing relationship with the supplier? Or, do you want this to be a very close working relationship with the supplier, or something in between?

Table 8.4   Nature of the Buy

1. Is the cost of the item or service important, perhaps due to high volume?
2. Is the technology used by the supplier critical to the product's image, performance, or quality?
3. Does the supplier have a critical brand name or image that you can use to generate sales?
4. Is the technology used by the supplier critical to future products, line extensions, or the next generations of products?
5. Is the item critical to getting leverage with supplier for other buys?
6. Could the item create environmental or safety concerns?
7. Are there limited good sources available?
8. Is the item purchase ongoing?
9. What other issues complicate the buying situation for your organization at this time?

Table 8.5   Relationship Sought with the Supplier

1. How long would we like to continue to do business with this supplier?
2. If we desire an ongoing relationship, would we like this supplier to be aware of our intentions?
3. Would we like to share information related to the buy with the supplier?
4. Would we like the supplier to become involved in our product or service development?
5. Would we like the supplier to locate one or more of its employees at our facility?
6. What other issues affect the nature of the desired relationship with this supplier at this time?

Classification of Decisions: Analyzing the Quadrants

Once you have determined which quadrant of the matrix your purchase fits in, you can turn to the second matrix to help you determine the best types of cost analysis tools to apply in your situation.

Low Impact

In Figure 8.2, the bottom-left quadrant lists price analysis techniques appropriate for "low-impact" purchases. Be sure to compare prices for items with the same quality and features and with the same level of service.

There is usually not a huge sum of money involved in these buys, or the item is just so generic that even though there is a fair amount of money involved, it's more of a commodity, and you're more or less a price taker on the open market. What sorts of items might fit this description? Things like office supplies or stationery—perhaps the statement envelopes that you get printed to send bills to your customers. Price comparison is easy here because you can provide suppliers with clear specifications/requirements.

Leverage

The upper-left quadrant in Figure 8.2 represents larger purchases from suppliers who have a routine relationship with the firm. This is the area of leverage buys. Because you are buying products that are available from many sources in relatively large quantity, a little effort in careful purchasing makes a big difference in cost. You may begin pooling your purchases with other business units in your company to gain even more leverage. Unless the item is truly a generic item with many suppliers,

Nature of Buy	Arms-Length	Strategic Alliance
Ongoing Purchases and Impact	Leverage Cost Analysis Focus • Estimate cost relationships • Value analysis • Analysis of supplier cost breakdowns • Cost estimate/"should cost" • Industry analysis • Total cost modeling	Strategic Continuous Improvement Focus • Open books • Target cost analysis • Competitive assessment/ teardowns • TCO analysis • Total cost modeling of the supply chain
Infrequent Purchase or Limited Impact	Low Impact Price Analysis Focus • Landed price/apples-to-apples • Competitive bids • Comparison pricelist/catalogs • Comparison to established market • Comparison to history • Price indices • Comparison to similar purchases	Critical Projects Life-Cycle Cost Focus • TCO analysis/life-cycle costing • TCO analysis of supply chain

Type of Relationship Sought with Supplier

Figure 8.2 Classifying Supplier/Purchases—Consider the Right Tools

you want to understand some of the underlying cost issues of the supplier so that you can favorably influence the supplier's underlying cost structure. A central question here is "Am I getting a fair price based on the cost to the producer?"

The types of buys that come to mind here include desktop hardware for a service firm—its PCs. You can easily determine the major cost drivers that go into a PC. If your organization spends a significant sum of money on PCs, you might want to investigate the costs of the individual components that make up the PC to make sure that you get a fair price.

Strategic Items

The two classifications on the right side of the matrix are oriented toward more important supplier relationships. The strategic classification has a continuous improvement focus and is associated with large buys from important suppliers that have an ongoing impact on the product and services firm sells. The term "strategic" means that you are dealing with issues that are going to make a difference in your company's competitive success and generally relate to items you buy that are used to create the product or service that your firm sells. Purchases in this category often require more time-consuming cost management approaches, such as total cost of ownership (TCO), open books, or two-way cost information sharing with key suppliers and target cost analysis. The focus here is on continuous improvement.

For a company like LG Electronics, which is on the cutting edge of technology for LCD and flat panel televisions, its strategic items are likely to be those providing the latest technological performance breakthroughs—the latest computer chips and display technologies.

Critical Projects

A major difference between critical projects and strategic items is the frequency of the purchase. Strategic items tend to be purchased repetitively; for critical projects, the purchase is infrequent, but has ongoing impact. For example, custom software is a critical project. It is a "one-time" decision, but has larger cost and performance implications. In addition to obtaining the software, the costs involved include installing the software and training your employees. Thus, looking at the total cost of ownership of the software over its life cycle is the right cost analysis approach. Similarly, you want to understand how much it's really going to cost to operate that copier over the life of a copier. The price is just the beginning, because the price of the copier bears little relation to the total cost of using it. How many copies can you get out of it before it needs maintenance? What is the cost of the toner cartridge? How frequently does it need maintenance? What sort of speed does it have? Those are questions that will reveal that ongoing costs will have a bigger impact on your decision than just the initial price.

When TCO analysis is used for a project where costs are incurred over a period of time, the process is also known as a life-cycle cost analysis. TCO will be further discussed later. In addition, whenever you are analyzing projects that have cost or revenue implications that extend beyond a year, you want to consider the time value of money, and perform a net present value (NPV) analysis (see Supplement D on NPV calculations). You need to understand the timing of cash flows and adjust them properly to fairly evaluate projects where cash inflows and outflows extend over time. Production equipment is yet another example of a large capital expenditure that has ongoing impact. You need to understand the true total cost of ownership.

Commodity Classification

As in previous chapters, we used the term "commodity" to mean a group of like items that the organization purchases. Examples of **commodities** include paper, molded plastic parts, and travel services. When applying this matrix, it is important to remember that both axes are a continuum, which means that things can be classified roughly into one category or another. You need to use your judgment, and consider your skills, priority, and the support available should you need it. For example, "paper" is an item that is not straightforward in terms of its classification. It could fit into cost analysis as easily as it could into price analysis, depending on the industry and the type of paper. If your organization buys large quantities of commodity paper, it may be best managed using price analysis. If you purchase a large volume of unique paper, it may be suitable for cost analysis. In either case, if you buy a great deal of paper, it just might be important to understand what's going on in the pulp market. That information can be a gauge to help you determine what you should be paying for paper.

This classification tool should help you make your purchasing analysis from a position of understanding. Simply asking the questions should be helpful in providing insight. Be certain to keep in mind that different business units within your organization may actually classify things differently. Thus, you need to keep the perspective of the relevant internal customer in mind when making classifications. Table 8.6 provides some examples of various buys and their classification. Remember, different industry situations and assumptions may indicate a different answer than the approach recommended in the table. There is an issue that can significantly complicate the ability to get the data you need for strategic cost management: the organization's accounting system. We'll consider that issue next.

Table 8.6 Commodity Classification

ITEM	CLASSIFICATION	RATIONALE
Company fleet	Leverage	Large volume, many suppliers, not critical to our product
Copiers	Critical project	One-time buy with long-term cost implications, many suppliers available
Desktop computers	Leverage	Large volume, relatively undifferentiated, very competitive market
Facilities management	Leverage	Large volume, many suppliers, not critical to our product
Furniture	Leverage	Large volume, many suppliers, not critical to our product
Office supplies	Low impact	Relatively unimportant, easy to switch, many suppliers
Latest high-speed microprocessors	Strategic	Large spend, affects product performance, few suppliers available, may be critical to our leading edge image
Outsourced copy center	Leverage	Large volume, many competitive suppliers
Production equipment	Critical project	One-time buy with ongoing impact
Telemarketing center	Leverage	Large volume, many comparable companies
Technical support call center	Leverage/strategic	Large volume, limited qualified suppliers, may be critical to our firm's image and customer service

ACTIVITY-BASED COST MANAGEMENT[12]

Many people who have not worked in accounting, or closely with accounting and finance, take the cost numbers in internal analysis and external reporting at face value. We are concerned here with managerial accounting systems—those systems that are used by an organization to support internal decision making. This includes, for example, budget data, data generated by cost accounting, and product or service costing systems and internal transfer pricing. Even when you know the data aren't very accurate, it is often the only data you have upon which to make decisions, and it is the data that others in the organization use, so you are bound to use it. **Activity-based cost management (ABCM)** is one possible solution to the many problems associated with traditional accounting systems.

Problems with Traditional Managerial Accounting Systems

Managerial accounting is the organization's approach for distributing costs internally. Ideally, the costs are allocated based on actual expenses incurred, known as *direct costing*. However, many organizational costs are incurred for multiple benefits. For example, a piece of production equipment may be used to manufacture many different products. The human resource (HR) department may support many functions and business units. In general, these costs become part of "overhead." Rather than being directly charged for using the production equipment or the services of human resources, all the overhead costs are lumped together in one "pool," and business units pay a proportion of these and other overhead costs based on some benchmark factor or activity level, such as production volume. Ideally, the firm chooses the benchmark because it tends to vary directly with overhead usage. For instance, a firm might find that the overhead costs of its products and departments are most closely related to revenue, or with direct labor costs, or with manufacturing floor space. The firm then sets its overhead charge as a simple proportion:

Firm's overhead pool / Firm's benchmark activity = Percentage overhead allocation per business unit's level of the benchmark activity

For example, Advanced Consumer Products, Inc. (ACP) finds that its overhead is $10 million, and its direct labor is $5 million company-wide. This gives it an overhead allocation of $10 million/$5 million, or 200 percent. It requires each product line to share overhead at that rate. The nanofilter group spends $2 million in direct labor, so it is charged $4 million in overhead.

Problems arise, of course, when overhead allocations do not reflect reality. For example, although direct labor is one activity that is related to some overhead costs, there are significant costs in the overhead pool that are unrelated to direct labor. For example, the costs of running, maintaining, and replacing equipment is a huge part of the overhead pool for a manufacturing facility, but relate more closely to production volume than direct labor hours. A business unit's use of the actual overhead services may stay constant, even if it can reduce direct labor costs. If direct labor is the benchmark activity for allocating overhead charges, the product may receive an undeserved reduction in overhead charges.

For example, ACP's marketing manager for nanofilters was desperately trying to save money and increase the profitability of his product line. He reviewed the numbers and found that nanofilters had already cut costs to the bone on materials and packaging. His only significant opportunities for savings were labor and overhead, which accounted for the bulk of the expenses. His current product cost structure is shown in Table 8.7, under the heading "Dollars/Unit Before New Line." ACP charged each business unit 200 percent of direct labor as overhead. The marketing manager worked with the engineering group to review alternatives. They identified new production equipment that would use only one-half the amount of direct labor. Thus, the new direct labor would be $0.50 per case rather than $1.00 per case. Better still, the new plant overhead would be 200 percent of the new direct labor, for a cost of $0.50 × 200% = $1.00. The total savings would be $1.50, right? This calculation is shown in Table 8.7, under the heading "Dollars/Unit with Proposed New Line."

Table 8.7 Traditional Cost Allocation in the Current System

Cost Category	Dollars/Unit Before New Line	Dollars/Unit with Proposed New Line
Raw materials	0.95	0.95
Packaging	0.75	0.75
Direct labor	1.00	.50
Total direct costs	**2.70**	**2.20**
Plant overhead (200% of direct labor)	2.00	1.00
Total manufacturing cost (cost of goods)	**4.70**	**3.20**
Selling, general, and administrative expense	0.25	.25
Total product cost	**$4.95**	**$3.45**

In this example, the true cost of changing equipment was distorted. The accounting system allocates overhead to all products in the plant at a rate of 200 percent of direct labor. But what about the depreciation expense related to the new equipment? What about the additional indirect labor incurred to support materials handling? Under traditional cost accounting systems, all the indirect and overhead costs of the plant are put into one pool, and allocated on the basis of direct labor. In effect, other product lines are subsidizing the additional indirect costs associated with adding the new equipment. However, unless you use an activity-based costing system, this cost shift is not apparent. Activity-based accounting provides a more accurate alternative to traditional cost accounting.

The ABCM Solution

ABCM is a managerial accounting approach that attempts to match the indirect costs with the activities and products or services that actually generate those costs, the same way traditional accounting systems handle direct costs. However, ABC attempts to treat indirect/overhead costs more like direct costs. ABCM looks at the activities that actually create the indirect costs, or identifies the cost drivers and allocates costs according to those drivers. So how would ABCM handle the product-costing problem in Table 8.7? The direct costs, as shown in Table 8.7, will not change. Table 8.8 illustrates that the plant overhead costs instead of being the same flat rate per each production line, will be subdivided and allocated based on the activities associated with a line that actually drives the cost. To put it another way, the plant overhead costs associated with line A, for example, would be charged to line A rather than allocated to other lines. Notice that using ABCM, the "Dollars/Unit Before New Line" in Table 8.8 (total cost of $4.40/unit) are actually lower than the allocation in the traditional method ($4.95/unit), with no changes in operations. This is because the nanofilter group's products are manufactured on a fully depreciated, stable line that is being

Table 8.8 Cost Allocation with ABCM

Cost Category	Dollars/Unit Before New Line	Dollars/Unit with Proposed New Line
Raw materials	0.95	0.95
Packaging	0.75	0.75
Direct labor	1.00	0.50
Total direct costs	**2.70**	**2.20**
Depreciation on equipment	0.00	0.60
Line supervision	0.10	0.15
Materials handling	0.20	0.25
Maintenance of line	0.15	0.15
General plant utilities and maintenance (based on floor space)	1.00	1.00
Total plant overhead	**1.45**	**2.15**
Total manufacturing cost (cost of goods)	**4.15**	**4.35**
Selling, general, and administrative expense	0.25	0.25
Total product cost	**$4.40**	**$4.60**

charged with allocated overhead, such as equipment depreciation, from other lines. Under ABCM, other lines will absorb more overhead costs. Although this change would please the marketer of this product, those who are charged a higher, albeit more accurate, indirect amount on their products could be upset.

Looking at Table 8.8, we see that the cost of the product with the proposed new line will actually increase, because using ABCM, the nanofilter products will have to absorb the overhead from the new line—such as depreciation on equipment and higher supervision costs.

Making Better Decisions

So how would the product cost look with the new equipment under the new ABCM system? As illustrated in Table 8.8 under the heading "Dollars/Unit with Proposed New Line," the direct labor cost would decrease due to improved automation, and the depreciation would increase, reflecting depreciation on the new equipment. In addition, line supervision and materials handling would also increase, due to the higher degree of automation and the reduction of line workers. The net effect is an increase in total cost from $4.40 per unit to $4.60 per unit. Purchasing new equipment that increases unit costs is not a wise investment. Yet such decisions are frequently made without regard to the "real" or activity-based costs; such decisions focus instead on misleading accounting data.

Whereas in the previous example the traditional accounting system underburdened products manufactured on the proposed new production line, the opposite may also happen. For example, a firm may develop a product line that uses a fully depreciated piece of equipment, and put it in a manufacturing facility that has a very high overhead rate because it has new, expensive, highly automated equipment for other products. If overhead is allocated based on direct labor, the new product will absorb a very high level of depreciation in overhead that is unjustified. As a result, the firm passes up a profitable opportunity because its traditional accounting system overburdened the venture with costs it would never generate. ABCM better matches costs to the activities that drive those costs. Thus, more accurate cost data is developed, better decisions are made, and the whole system gives a more equitable, accurate representation of reality. If the organization wanted to work on reducing some of the nonvalue cost drivers, it would have an accurate picture of where to begin. However, it's not this simple in all cases.

Problems with ABCM Implementation

Implementing an ABCM system represents a pervasive change in an organization's accounting, reward, and measurement systems. It requires a significant change that many organizations may not be willing to undertake. For example, internal and external users of human resources (HR) may not pay for the purchasing department's services in any visible way. The HR department's expense may be buried in an overhead allocation. Once ABCM is in place, internal and external users will pay for the HR department's services based on their level of use of those services. Although this may be a more equitable approach, it represents a major change. Some groups will pay less for HR's administrative cost; some will pay more. Those who pay more may spend a great deal of unproductive time fighting the new allocation.

Building on the product-costing example, for every product that's being charged extra, some are being charged less. Thus, some benefit from ABCM while others do not. Products that the organization thought were profitable may turn out to be significantly less profitable. The organization may have to rethink its pricing strategies, its marketing and manufacturing strategies, and even who its best purchasers are. Thus, implementing ABCM should not be a casual decision. Total cost of ownership analysis is related to ABCM, in that both try to better match the costs with what actually drives the cost.

TOTAL COST OF OWNERSHIP

Total cost of ownership is defined here as a philosophy for understanding all relevant SC-related costs of doing business with a particular supplier for a particular good/service, or the cost of a process, or particular SC design. In its broadest sense, total cost of ownership looks at the "big" picture, considering many costs beyond price. TCO does not actually require precise calculation of all costs, but instead looks at major cost issues and costs that may be relevant to the decision at hand. In many industries, organizations have done all that they can to lower the price. In order to make significant improvements in their cost management and SC cost structure, they need to look at the costs of doing business . . . their own processes and supply chains. That is where the future lies in terms of competitive opportunity. This is one reason that TCO is a philosophy receiving increased visibility and concern among organizations.

Figure 8.3 shows the five steps to implementing a TCO approach in the organization. From a strategic cost management approach, TCO may be misunderstood, in

Figure 8.3 A 5-Step Approach to Implementing TCO Analysis

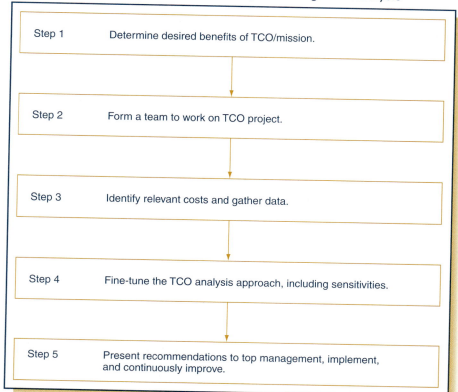

Step 1	Determine desired benefits of TCO/mission.
Step 2	Form a team to work on TCO project.
Step 3	Identify relevant costs and gather data.
Step 4	Fine-tune the TCO analysis approach, including sensitivities.
Step 5	Present recommendations to top management, implement, and continuously improve.

that TCO must also consider revenue implications. In situations where organizations make a change that is not revenue neutral, it is not enough to simply capture the costs of change; the revenue impact must also be captured. The first step in TCO analysis is deciding why the organization wants to conduct a TCO analysis.

Step 1: Determine Desired Benefits of TCO

The first step in a TCO analysis is deciding what benefits you are seeking in conducting the analysis. You probably already have a particular project in mind. There may be multiple reasons to conduct a TCO analysis. A list of some potential reasons is shown in Table 8.9. The benefits that you think you can achieve using TCO analysis must be *very* strong, because TCO analysis requires a big commitment of time and effort on your part, as well as on the part of many others in your organization. At every step of the way in a TCO project, you want to think about cost/benefit. Is it likely that the benefits of the analysis will outweigh the costs? If you answer no, TCO analysis is not recommended. If you can answer yes, then you need to identify whether the project you have chosen has the characteristics that are important in a successful TCO project.

The following list shows some of the characteristics that make a purchase, outsourcing analysis, or process analysis well suited for TCO analysis:

- The firm spends a relatively large amount of money on that item.
- The firm purchases the item with some degree of regularity, in order to provide some historical data, but more importantly, to allow opportunities to gather current cost information.
- Purchasing believes the item has significant transaction costs associated with it that are not currently recognized.
- Purchasing believes that one or more of the currently unrecognized transaction costs is individually significant.
- Purchasing has the opportunity to have an impact on transactions costs, via negotiation, changing suppliers, or improving internal operations.
- Those purchasing/using the item will cooperate in data gathering to learn more about the item's cost structure.

Table 8.9 Possible Reasons to Perform TCO Analysis

- Performance measurement
- Framework for cost analysis
- Benchmarking performance
- More informed decision making
- Communication of cost issues internally and with suppliers
- Encourages cross-functional interaction
- Support external teams with suppliers
- Better insight/understanding of cost drivers
- Build a business case
- Support an outsourcing analysis
- Support continuous improvement
- Helps identify cost savings opportunities
- Prioritize/focus your time on high-potential opportunities

Purchases with these characteristics are ideal for early TCO projects. In order to have others in the organization embrace and accept the potential benefits of a TCO philosophy and analysis, it is critical to have a successful first project. This will help "sell" the concept of TCO throughout the organization. Big savings are also easier to understand and gain visibility for this type of project. In general, you want to make sure that you select a project where you have options—several suppliers in a buying or outsourcing situation. This encourages supplier cooperation. For example, if you work for a large organization that is considering whether to install reverse osmosis cold-water fountains versus getting chilled water coolers with bottled water delivered weekly, the TCO of the alternatives is very different. The water fountains have a relatively high installation cost and a periodic maintenance cost, but no ongoing weekly expenses. The chilled watercoolers have a relatively low initial cost, or may be provided "free" if you commit to water delivery contract. However, there is a weekly variable cost based on water consumed. This is an ideal TCO analysis, because you have options with clearly different cost issues.

On the other hand, assume that you purchase a unique, patented ingredient that you use in small quantities in a critical product. The ingredient is important to you, and the TCO is very high because the supplier has long and unreliable lead times. A TCO analysis may illustrate that the TCO is very high because of high inventory levels at some times and shortages and high airfreight costs to ship the ingredient quickly. The problem is that you are a small customer to this supplier, so it gives you low priority. Also, you have no alternative source for this patented ingredient, and it would be very costly, time-consuming, and perhaps not even possible to change the formula for the product to eliminate the ingredient. This project would not be a good place to begin your TCO analysis. It is unlikely that you would do anything except prove that the supplier has your company between a rock and a hard place. Likewise, a highly politically charged situation is not a good first TCO project.

Capital purchases are virtually always good candidates for TCO analysis, because after what appears to be a relatively large initial outlay, there continues to be costs associated with usage year after year, and day after day. Leading organizations such as Johnson & Johnson do TCO analysis on major purchases such as acquiring a fleet of vehicles. Intel uses TCO analysis on all of its capital equipment, especially the equipment used in production. Other companies, such as Phillips, Heineken, Texas Instruments, Lucent, Bank of America, and Nortel, have used it to select suppliers of parts, components, and services when there are important differences in supplier performance in areas such as quality, service, lead times, and inventory levels.

Throughout this discussion of TCO, we will use the example of purchasing all new printers for our facilities. We are trying to decide between laser printers and deskjet printers. If we purchase laser printers, we will purchase 1 for each 6 people, plus each executive assistant having her own. This will amount to 400 laser printers. If we purchase deskjet printers, each person will have her own, and the executive assistants will still have a laser printer. This will amount to 2,100 deskjet and 50 laser printers.

Step 2: Form a Team to Work on TCO Analysis

Team formation will vary depending on the project under consideration. Sometimes, a team is formed during step 1 when a project is identified. The specific team membership may change as the TCO project is firmed up in step 1. At a minimum, the team should

Table 8.10 Potential TCO Team for Analyzing New Equipment Laser Printing

Name	Expectations/Expertise	How Involvement Supports Team	How Involvement Supports Job
Sarah—Accounting	As accountant, she understands depreciation, cost allocation, and present value	Support financial analysis; help obtain data	Aware of acquisition; be able to properly account for it
Jake—Purchasing	Expert on buying capital, knows suppliers	Work with supplier(s); obtain costs; familiar with past performance problems	Input into process helps selection and ongoing supplier management
Riana—IT	Technical expert	Know maintenance and reliability issues; downtime.	Will be responsible for simple repairs and maintenance; work with repair persons
Conrad—User	Head of executive assistants' network—represents their views	Provide voice of key internal customers	Has input into decision
Nicole—User (Accounts payable manager)	Her department relies heavily on printers	Provide voice of key internal customers	Has input into decision

include purchasing, users, and any functional/technical experts. Finance/accounting should be part of the team to add credibility to the calculations. TCO analysis is most effective in a team setting. Because TCO analysis is time-consuming and complex, it is important to gain the commitment and cooperation of others in advance. Before proceeding, it is also important to consider:

- What is in it for others?
- Why should they cooperate?
- How will it improve their job environment and company performance?
- Do we need top management sponsorship? Who and why?

Gaining participation of others in TCO analysis may require a persuasive sales job. A "TCO Team Members" form should be filled out to determine who should be on the TCO analysis team for the project in question. Table 8.10 shows a completed copy of this form as filled out for the laser printing equipment team. In some cases, the organization might want to include SC members, such as key customers, suppliers, or logistics providers if they have a significant impact on the TCO, or if the outcome of the analysis may have a significant impact on them.

Step 3: Identify Relevant Costs and Gather Data

At this step, the real work begins. It is important at this stage to keep the scope of the TCO analysis reasonable—to make sure benefits exceed cost. To really understand the costs associated with the various printing options, it is necessary to draw a process flow diagram for each option. These are shown in Figure 8.4.

The team uses the process flowcharts to help them with their brainstorming of cost drivers. Brainstorming is an excellent approach for coming up with a laundry list of possible cost elements that will later be narrowed down, based on importance. In brainstorming, the team simply takes turns, one at a time, naming a key cost driver. There is no evaluation, explanation, or selling of ideas. A recorder captures all

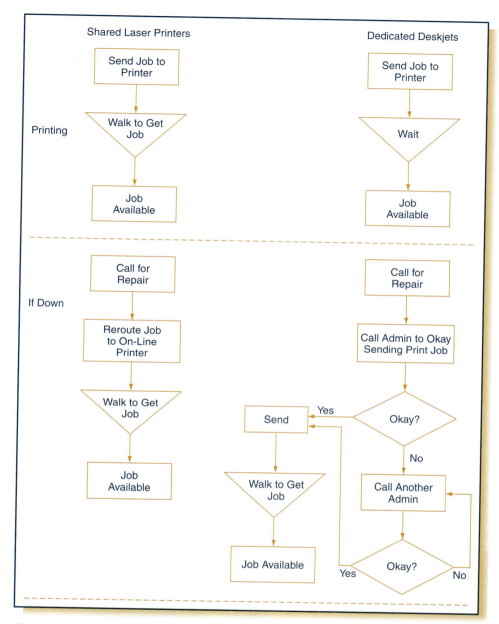

Figure 8.4 Process Flowcharts for Printer Acquisition

of the ideas. When the team exhausts its ideas, it eliminates duplicate ideas, and then determines which costs are really relevant to the decision. Relevant costs are those that are significant and will vary among different decision alternatives. For example, when buying equipment, the disposal value of one option might be considerably higher than another. In the case of the printer alternatives, the company might actually incur a disposal cost in retiring the printers at the end of their lives! However, if the total disposal costs will remain unchanged regardless of the alternative pursued, these costs are not relevant to the decision because they will not affect the decision outcome.

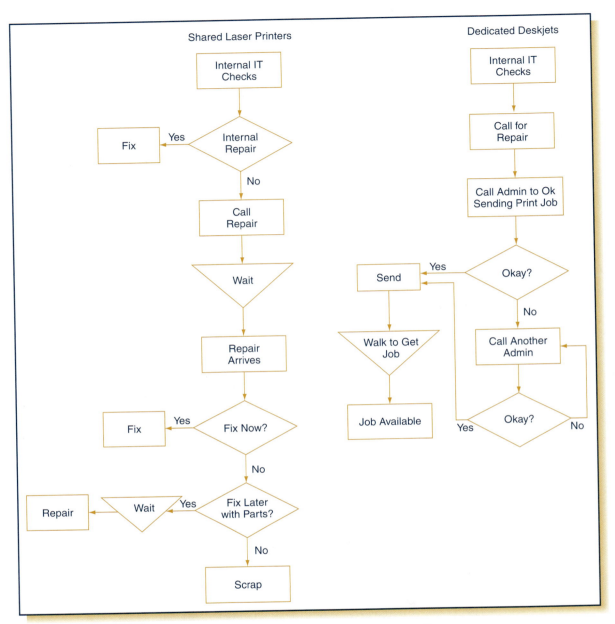

Figure 8.4 Process Flowcharts for Printer Acquisition (continued)

The cost activities identified for the printer purchase are listed in Table 8.11. The team classified the key cost drivers that would need to be investigated for this decision. Note that the noncost items will not be a part of the cost analysis. These issues will be discussed as "soft costs" or other issues. Wait time is not a true or hard cost because the person waiting would be paid regardless of their activity. It would be a hard cost if it caused so much delay that the person was required to work paid overtime as a direct result of a printer problem. In TCO, only costs that are incremental and have a direct impact on the bottom line are included in the calculation. The team is now ready to gather cost data.

Table 8.11 Key Cost Drivers

Critical cost driver?	
Noncost*	• Waiting time for print
Noncost	• Lost time walking to get print
Yes	• Price of equipment
Yes	• Price of ink cartridges/toner
Yes	• Life of ink cartridges/toner
Yes	• Disposal value or cost of equipment
Noncost	• Lost time looking for a printer when primary printer is down
Yes	• Cost per repair
Yes	• Frequency of repair
Noncost	• Time from initial call to repair

*The items indicated as noncost issues have only soft costs and will not be included in the TCO cost calculations. These items can be included as qualitative issues in the final TCO report.

Gathering the cost data can require significant manual effort. Most of the data needed are not readily available in the accounting system. The data sources and cost calculation method are shown in Table 8.12. Most TCO analyses are conducted on spreadsheets, because spreadsheets allow flexibility to change as assumptions change and have sufficient power to handle all but the most sophisticated TCO analysis. To make the comparison of alternatives meaningful, the costs will be translated to a cost per printed page side. Usage estimates were developed by IT and the departments based on past printer paper and ink cartridge usage. Costs must be gathered for each alternative and usage pattern. In this case, we need to know the costs and usage of both the shared laser printer only option and the laser and deskjet printer combination. The analysis indicates

Table 8.12 Gathering Cost Data

COSTS	DATA SOURCE
Price of equipment	Supplier
Price of ink cartridges	Supplier
Life of ink cartridges	Supplier, IT data, external ratings
Disposal value/cost	Supplier, IT data
Cost per repair	Supplier, history
Frequency of repairs	Supplier history
	SAMPLE CALCULATION—TCO
	PRESENT VALUE*

TCO = (price of equipment) + (price of ink cartridge × lifetime cartridge usage) + (cost per repair × lifetime expected repairs) ± end of life disposal cost (value)

$$\text{TCO/page} = \frac{\text{Total TCO}}{\text{Expected lifetime pages}}$$

*The concept of present value is explained in Chapter 4.

that the option of purchasing all laser printers has a present value (cost) of $1,131K over 4 years, while the mixed model of laser and desk jet printers costs $1,704K over the same time frame (see Appendix A, pp. 496–499).

Step 4: Fine-Tune the TCO Analysis, Including Sensitivity Analysis

Many of the costs within the TCO model may be estimates. The team may have a "range" of cost estimates it thinks are reasonable for certain cost elements. In that case, the team should do a "sensitivity analysis," which involves reanalyzing the total model with different cost estimates to see how sensitive the model is to changes in those costs. Which of the relevant costs in the printer decision do you think are the most subject to change? Which of these, if they actually change, would have an impact on the decision? As shown in Appendix A, the cost of the toner versus print cartridges is the largest factor favoring the all-laser option. What might affect that cost?

For example, the toner drum is said to print 5,000 page sides. What if it only prints 4,000? If the number of pages goes down, both options become more expensive on a cost per page. The all-laser printers option cost becomes $1,290K over 4 years, while the mixed model of laser and deskjet printers costs $1,784K over the same time frame. Clearly, the actual output would have to vary significantly to change this decision. Thus, the page yield from a toner drum is not a sensitive option. If deskjet cartridges go down in price from their current $35.00 to under $10.00, the laser only option is unchanged at a cost of $1,131, while the mixed option cost drops to $1,038. It becomes more attractive because the cost per page drops significantly. Do we think this is a possibility? Would the lower priced ink cartridges yield the same number of printed sides? These are all issues to consider.

If the decision recommendation changes as the estimates change, the team should investigate those cost elements more carefully—trying to improve its level of confidence in its estimates. Again, this is a cost/benefit issue. How much time should we invest in getting very precise in certain cost elements that won't have any impact on the outcome of our analysis anyway? If the decision is unaffected as the estimate changes, it is probably not worth the time to refine the estimate for that variable. An analysis that does not change much as assumptions change is said to be "robust," meaning it produces valid results under a broad range of assumptions. When the team is comfortable, it is ready to use the data in decision making, and/or presenting the results to top management. You need to be ready to answer all potential "what-if" questions from top management.

Step 5: Present Recommendations to Top Management

Once team members are comfortable with the data, and have addressed areas of uncertainty through sensitivity analysis and additional data gathering, they are ready to prepare their presentation to management. This presentation should include the quantitative results of the TCO analysis, as well as other "soft" factors that are more difficult to quantify. For example, as we noted in Table 8.11, there are several noncost factors to consider in the selection, such as time spent walking to the printer and waiting time for print jobs. In addition, the user representatives have told us that people really like to have their own printer. However, the quality of the laser print is higher. These issues should be summarized for consideration by the decision makers. A good format to use for a report or presentation to top management includes:

- An executive summary that includes a brief background, a summary of alternatives, key issues, TCO results, key sensitivities, and recommendation
- Summary of TCO analysis results
- Sensitivities
- Noncost issues
- Recommendation
- Appendices, with detailed calculations and assumptions

Once a TCO project is approved, it is important to monitor the implementation and actual results, to learn about how to improve future processes. In addition, project documentation should be retained, preferably in an electronic intranet location, so that future TCO teams can benefit from the lessons of related projects.

Additional Examples of TCO Analysis

As noted earlier, TCO applies to the purchase of materials, parts, and services as well as to capital acquisitions. Cockerill Sambre, a large multinational Belgian steel manufacturer, uses TCO for determining the lowest total cost of materials and components, rather than focusing only on price, as it had prior to TCO implementation.[13] Cockerill Sambre was able to reduce its TCO for ball bearings by 11.5 percent by switching from using two suppliers to using four suppliers, while considering the following elements:

- Price
- Service level
- Ordering costs, invoicing costs, and payment cost (manual elements versus electronic varies among suppliers)
- Purchasing costs, inventory costs, payment terms

Similarly, TCO applies to services. A large electric utility was using contract labor for much of its security services, focusing on the price per hour to obtain qualified personnel. However, it noticed that it was experiencing a higher than desirable turnover, which was costly in terms of hiring new employees, who required careful screening and background checks. Doing a TCO analysis revealed that the cost of qualifying new employees was prohibitive, including background checks, drug screening, and training. This utility discovered that it could actually lower its TCO by paying a slightly higher hourly wage, thereby improving contract employee retention. This made the workforce more efficient and effective, and reduced overtime paid to more qualified employees when the utility was short staffed, or when new hires were being trained.

TCO analysis is widely applicable to many process analyses, outsourcing decisions, and purchase situations. Care should be taken to consider the extra time and effort that may be required to do a TCO analysis versus the potential benefit of the analysis. In addition, TCO analysis can be used jointly with key suppliers and customers to work together to reduce the costs of doing business. Extending TCO analysis into the supply chain can yield even greater benefits in terms of cost savings and value enhancement.[14]

CONCLUSION

There is much more to cost management than simply reducing prices or costs. In order to be effective to the organization in the long run, every cost management initiative should be based on an understanding of why the company wants to better manage costs in a given area, and what the value proposition related to that area is, so that value is not unwittingly sacrificed. Strategic cost management takes a holistic approach to understanding the supply chain, the cost drivers, and the value proposition. It spans the borders of the organization to embrace costs and opportunities in the entire chain. To be effective, it must also span across functions within the organization, leveraging the expertise of finance, supply management, engineering, marketing, and other functions and users relevant to the analysis at hand. In order to be effective, everyone in the organization needs to have some responsibility and accountability for cost management.

There are many tools available to help analyze and manage costs. It is important that organizations choose the right approach for the decision at hand. The cost management matrix helps organizations determine the right cost management approach for a given situation. In this chapter, we delved deeper into total cost of ownership (TCO) analysis. This is a time- and resource-intensive approach to holistically understanding and managing the costs of a purchase, process, or outsourcing decision. Due to the costs and resources involved in conducting a thorough TCO analysis, it is generally reserved for key decisions. It is becoming a more accepted and common approach today, as organizations rely increasingly on outside SC members to add value and provide services.

SUMMARY OF KEY POINTS

1. Strategic cost management is about much more than simply managing or reducing costs. It also embraces understanding what drives the organization's value, and how the supply chain affects both value and cost.

2. Costs and cost drivers are not inherently bad; they must always be analyzed in relation to the value that they add to the organization.

3. In order to be effective on an organization- and supply-chain-wide level, everyone in the organization must have some responsibility for cost management.

4. Process mapping is a valuable starting point for understanding cost issues and opportunities.

5. There are many tools available to assist in understanding and managing costs. The tools used should be appropriate for the situation, based on the nature of the purchase and the type of supplier relationship desired.

6. Companies that use traditional accounting systems may aggregate and assign cost data inaccurately, so cost managers should consider an activity-based approach to identify true costs and make better decisions.

7. Activity-based cost management helps improve the integrity of the organization's managerial accounting data by better matching expenses to the activities that cause those expenses.

8. Total cost of ownership analysis (TCO) is a team-based analysis approach for better understanding the true costs of a sourcing or outsourcing decision, or a process.

9. TCO analysis can provide improved understanding of the true costs of decisions and help the organization to make better decisions.

10. Conducting a sensitivity analysis in conjunction with TCO analysis allows the TCO team to reanalyze the total model with different assumptions and cost estimates to see how sensitive the model is to changes in those costs.

11. TCO analysis can be applied to a variety of situations, from purchases of material, components, services, and capital to process analysis to SC design. It can help companies assess who should do what to make the chain most cost competitive.

1. Describe the three key elements of strategic cost management and how they are related to each other.
2. Why is it important for key decision makers throughout the organization to understand the value proposition for the situation they are working with?
3. When can a high level for a cost driver be desirable? Give an example of a situation (real or hypothetical) when a higher cost decision is better for an organization than a lower cost decision.
4. Who should be responsible for strategic cost management in an organization, and why?
5. What are the problems with most managerial accounting systems today? How does ABCM address these problems?
6. Describe TCO analysis, and where it is applicable.
7. Why is it important to have a team involved in conducting TCO?
8. When conducting TCO analysis, what is sensitivity analysis? Why is it important? When should it be conducted?

Case   *The Costly Packaging Decision*

Selena Diaz felt she had a real opportunity on her hands. She was in her second job rotation of her SCM training program at Noette, a global consumer products manufacturer. Her manager, Wu Li, had explained their packaging problem to her: "We have very long lead times on the plastic packaging for our Noette Platinum skin care line. Because we change the labeling, the style, the sizes, and color offerings of products quite frequently, packaging lead time significantly affects time to market for new products. We don't have a long product life cycle. Further, when we drop a product, any packaging in inventory becomes obsolete. This is costing us about $500,000 a year. In addition, we sometimes have to ship the finished product by air due to the production delays caused by waiting for the packaging material. This costs us another $400,000 a year.

"From a marketing standpoint, it is critical that we adapt our production schedule very quickly, as soon as product demand is realized. But it is often difficult to determine the demand for new products. If we do not have the products available to sell the consumers in the marketplace, we could lose the sale forever. This could cost us millions. We just don't know how much. Ideally, our response time for packaging should be very rapid. This would minimize the risk of lost sales and airfreight charges, as well as the risk of write-offs due to obsolescence. Don't even think about standardizing the packaging or using some cheap labeling technique. This packaging is a critical part of the product's image. Marketing would never stand for it. Take a look at the supply chain and come back to me with ideas for improvement."

Selena had talked with manufacturing, the suppliers, and marketing, and sketched the supply chain in Figure 8.5.

Selena learned that Noette's Platinum skin care products are packaged in specialized high-quality tubes. The label is first printed on "web stock," which is then laminated onto the tube so the words will never rub off. Noette sees its packaging as adding value in quality, image, and even safety because the tubes carry the usage instructions. The tube supplier was chosen to provide a unique, high-quality packaging that fit the image of this upscale cosmetic supplier.

Currently, the need for the tube order is identified when the MRP (materials requirements planning) system is run. This takes approximately 1 day. Next, about half a day is used in placing a purchase order (PO) with the tube supplier, and another half-day in the supplier's scheduling process. Now the queuing process begins. The tube supplier places the PO to schedule printing of the web stock with the label supplier. There is about a 14-day wait until the web stock label is printed.

Printing then takes one day and the label supplier ships the web stock to the supplier of laminated tubes in New Jersey. At this point, the order enters a queue at the tube supplier's manufacturing facility, where it waits for 23 days. After this time, the tube supplier makes the tube and applies the web stock, laminating it to the tube. This takes about 2 days. The tubes are then shipped by truck and boat to Noette's manufacturing facility in Puerto Rico, which takes another 7 days. The current process takes 49 days, from the time the packaging need is identified to the time the tubes arrive in Puerto Rico.

Laminate Tubes

Located in New Jersey, shipped to Puerto Rico

Run MRP
(1 day)

Place PO
(.5 day)

Supplier Schedules
(Queuing Time, Acknowledgment)
(.5 day)

Supplier Schedules Printing of
Web Stock with Label Supplier
(14 day wait)

Print
(1 day)

Web Stock Ships
to Supplier
(1 hour)

Wait for Process
(23 days)

Tube Supplier Converts
(2 days)

Tube Ships to Puerto Rico
(7 days)

**Total Cycle
Time
49 Days**

Figure 8.5 Process Flowchart—49 Days

There, the tubes are filled in a cosmetic manufacturing process, packaged into individual boxes, put into a case, and then shipped out for consumption around the world. However, the continental United States is the largest market for these products.

Selena contacted the tube supplier to get a better understanding of the waiting time. The manufacturer explained, "It's waiting time, just like when you want to go on a ride at Disneyland. Other people got there first."

Selena asked, "Shouldn't we go into the queue when our initial order arrives, rather than when the web stock arrives? After all, you place the web stock order, so you know it is coming."

"No can do. We don't schedule anything until we have all the materials. We are pretty much at capacity, and can't afford any delays or last minute rescheduling when something doesn't show up," the manufacturer explained.

Selena offered an alternative: "Well at Disneyland, you can pay extra to reserve a place in line, or move up in line. They let you schedule in advance now, if you are willing to pay. Would you consider that?"

The manufacturer sighed. "I see where you are coming from. We just don't do business that way. We have to turn customers away due to high demand because of our world-class technology. I'm sorry I can't help you out here."

Selena understood it was not going to be as simple as working with the current suppliers to fix the apparently easy issues in the processes. She was going to have to come up with a creative idea. Yet it had to be an idea that honored marketing's high-end image for the product.

CASE QUESTIONS

1. From a strategic cost management perspective, what are the cost and value drivers in this supply chain?
2. Which costs and associated processes do not add value commensurate with cost, and which should be considered for improvement?
3. Develop some ideas for improving the supply chain of this product, and redraw the process map based on those ideas. How long is the lead time now?
4. Is this project a good opportunity for total cost of ownership analysis? Explain why or why not, including what sort of costs you would try to capture if you do a TCO analysis?
5. Which assumptions and costs related to this process do you think you should perform a sensitivity analysis on, and why?

ENDNOTES

1. Cooper, Robin, & Slagmulder, R. (1999). *Supply chain design for the lean enterprise.* Portland, OR: Productivity, Inc.
2. Ibid.
3. Shrank, J., and V. Govindarajan, (1993). *Strategic cost management.* New York: AMACOM.
4. Porter, M. (1980). *Competitive strategy.* Boston: Harvard Business School.
5. Intel. (2006, February 2). Intel's platform vision. www.intel.com/platforms/vision.htm.
6. www2.coca-cola.com/ourcompany/ourpromise.html.
7. Vogelstein, F. (2003, May 26). Mighty Amazon. *Fortune,* pp. 61–74.
8. Southwest Airlines. (2006, February 3). We weren't just born yesterday. www.southwest.com/about_swa/airborne.html.
9. Southwest Airlines. (1988). The mission of Southwest Airlines. www.southwest.com/about_swa/mission.html, accessed February 3, 2006.
10. Points from this list were taken from the following sources: Freiberg, K., & Freiberg, J. (1997). *Nuts! Southwest Airlines' crazy recipe for business and personal success.* New York: Broadway Books. Ibid. #8. Porter, M. (1996, November–December). What is strategy? *Harvard Business Review,* 61–78.
11. Ibid. #8
12. Ellram, L. (1999, March). The ABCs of fair costing. *Purchasing Today,* pp. 39–41.
13. This example is taken from Degraeve, Z., & Roodhooft, F. (1999). Effectively selecting suppliers using the total cost of ownership. *Journal of Supply Chain Management, 35*(1), 5–10.
14. Ellram, Lisa M. (2006). TCO—adding value to the supply chain. Proceedings of the 4th Worldwide Research Symposium on Purchasing and Supply Chain Management, 15th Annual IPSERA Conference, 17th Annual North American Research & Teaching Symposium, held April 4–6 2006, San Diego, CA.

Chapter 9

Core Competencies and Outsourcing

Who should do what? Can I help my company leverage our competencies with those of SC partners?

The Supply Chain Road Map

Designing the Global Supply Chain
- What Must be Done to Compete and Win?
- Who Should Do It?

How Do We Fit?	How Should We Fit?
As-Is Supply Chain	**To-Be Supply Chain**

How Do We Fit?

As-Is Supply Chain

Chapter 6: Environmental Scanning
- What are the competitive rules?
- What skills does the SC need?

Chapter 7: Supply Chain Mapping
- What are the SC dynamics?
- Is our company positioned for success?

Chapter 8: Strategic SC Costing
- What are the relevant costs?
- What are the cost trade-offs?

Chapter 9: Competencies & Outsourcing
- **What are our valued competencies?**
- **What activities should be outsourced?**

Chapter 10: Rationalization & Role Shifting
- Where can we rationalize the chain?
- Where can we refine assigned roles?

How Should We Fit?

To-Be Supply Chain

Based on the understanding developed during the SC design process, create the capabilities needed to…

1. Help our SC meet customers' real needs better than competing chains:
- Identify the **right** players for the SC
- Define the **right** relationships
- Assign the **right** roles & responsibilities
- Design the **right** structure & systems

2. Securely position the company as an indispensable member of the SC by
- Refining our customer value proposition
- Developing needed competencies
- Leveraging core technologies
- Establishing efficient processes
- Creating appropriate customer linkages

After reading this chapter, you will be able to:

1. Describe the notion of core competency. Identify an organization's competencies and determine whether they pass the threefold test of a core competency.
2. Define outsourcing and discuss reasons why companies outsource.
3. Describe the three phases to developing and executing an outsourcing strategy.
4. Identify and assess some of the potential risks associated with outsourcing.
5. Conduct a make-or-buy analysis to support an outsourcing decision.

Opening Story: Fear of Outsourcing at Olympus

Doug smiled as he looked over the new list of concerns from the executive council for the latest SC task force meeting. Certainly, no one could say that Doug had a dull, routine job. At the top of the list was the whole issue of outsourcing.

In a recent meeting with Joe Andrus, CEO of Olympus, Doug learned that Olympus's chief financial officer, Tim Rock, had attended a CFO conference where some of his colleagues reported cost reductions as great as 30 to 50 percent due to outsourcing. One impetus behind Olympus's interest in SCM was certainly its cost-reduction potential. The council had asked Doug and his task force to address these questions:

1. Where does outsourcing fit into your plans for improving the company's supply chain?
2. What potential areas of outsourcing opportunity do you see for Olympus?
3. What business processes are the best candidates for outsourcing?
4. Where can we get the biggest bang for our buck in outsourcing?

When Doug brought this up at the SC task force meeting, the reaction had been swift and negative. Tameka Williams, information systems specialist, pointed out, "The first thing most companies want to do is to outsource their information systems. They do this blindly, without ever considering the real consequences on the users. In general, it ends up costing the company a lot more, and they get worse performance than they would have if they had just upgraded their internal systems."

"The thing that gets me about this whole outsourcing thing is the drive to go overseas with our production. People never seem to look at the total cost, the inventory implications, the quality issues, and the loss of internal expertise. Frankly, I knew this was coming, but it still concerns me," agreed Kathy Gilles, director of operations.

David Amado, senior transportation manager, nodded in concurrence. "Don't forget that my group is the one that will have to figure out how to get all the goods back and forth; that is, unless we are outsourced, too. I think about the dock strike on the West Coast of the United States before Christmas 2002. What a disaster that was! That sort of thing can wipe out all of the cost savings of using low-cost global suppliers, as well as create a great deal of gray hair!"

The conversation continued for a few more moments, with each task force member airing concerns, constraints, and downright fear at the possibility of outsourcing. Doug decided it was time to step in and bring some perspective to the discussion. Doug was a firm believer in the importance of "clearing the clutter" so that an objective discussion could be held, but he knew that negativity could become contagious. Doug said, "Well, I think it is good to get this out in the open. We need to identify the possible risks associated with outsourcing various activities. We've been developing the tools to help us weigh realistically the pros and cons of this type of decision. So, I'm confident we'll make the right choices for Olympus. Besides, let's keep in mind that no one has said we will outsource anything. The executive steering committee has given us the charge to look at outsourcing as one possibility as we focus on improving the design and the management of our supply chains. This is a real opportunity for us to shape the outsourcing discussion at Olympus. Hold onto that thought. I'd like to take the next hour to do a little nominal group brainstorming. Let's address each of the steering committee's four questions in groups of three. Then we'll report our ideas. Before we get started, let's take a 10-minute break to clear our thoughts. We need to take a serious, objective look at if and how outsourcing can make us more competitive now and in the future. See you in 10 minutes."

Consider As You Read:

1. Do you think that the task force members concerns are warranted? Why or why not?
2. How do you suggest that Doug keep the task force members focused on the topic of outsourcing as a legitimate SC decision, rather than their fears related to their own functional areas?
3. Is this a strategic issue, tactical issue, or both? Explain your answer, and how the task force should address this.
4. What activities and analyses should the task force undertake to address the executive committee's questions?

> *The outsourcing person has to be able to learn from the supplier at a prodigious rate, and learn from people in the business, to stay at the frontier of the field.*
>
> —James Brian Quinn[1]

Do you know what you are good at, and what you are not? When you work as a member of a team, do you immediately volunteer for one particular aspect of the assignment, such as gathering the research articles, writing the first draft, doing the final edit? If you are really, really good at that particular activity, you might view it as your core competency: the set of activities, skills or advantages you have that distinguishes you from others and makes you a valuable member of the team.

For years, companies have struggled with a key organizational design decision: Should they specialize and build an area or two of expertise or should they try to do and control everything through vertical? We have already discussed this issue in broad, historical terms. Remember the example of Ford Motor Company at the beginning of Chapter 6. Over time, fierce competition proved that Ford was not the "best" at all of the activities that it undertook internally. Suppliers entered the marketplace to provide automakers with automotive parts: tires, engines, wiper assemblies, transmissions, and so on. These specialized suppliers were frequently able to provide better and more affordable technology than the large automotive companies because they specialized. They identified their special areas of expertise and stuck to those. As a result, Ford and other automotive manufacturers throughout the world gradually evolved to a less vertically integrated model.

The fact is that the pendulum is swinging toward specialization. Today's emphasis on specialization focuses on the term "core competence" coined by C. K. Prahalad and Gary Hamel in their seminal article, "The Core Competence of the Corporation." Prahalad and Hamel argued that to win in a global marketplace a company must be uniquely good at something, something no one else could do quite so well. Companies that did not develop such a core competency would always find themselves in a battle to preserve their market share and their margins. Interestingly, their role model for core competence was Honda—an automaker. They showed how Honda had leveraged engine design and manufacture to become not just a great automaker but also a valued member of its supply chain. The key for Honda was to identify and focus on a few specific activities that became a hard-to-copy core competency. Other activities—about 85 percent of the value of each Honda automobile—have been outsourced to other supply chain members who are very good at what they do. By bringing complementary competencies together, Honda created a winning SC strategy.

The chapter begins with a discussion of core competencies. We then examine the relative merits and fit of outsourcing versus vertical integration, the benefits and risks of outsourcing, and the outsourcing decision-making and implementation process.

WHAT IS A CORE COMPETENCE?

Once an organization understands its customer needs and success factors, it needs to develop and align its core competencies to meet these needs. Specifically, the company must determine what its role in the supply chain is going to be and decide how to structure and use its resources to add unique value. Because resources are scarce, it is absolutely vital to determine how to most efficiently and effectively use them. Noncritical activities may be outsourced to companies that can better perform them. Establishing the correct mix of internal and outsourced activities is a fundamental part of supply chain design.

In their article, "The Core Competence of the Corporation," C. K. Prahalad and Gary Hamel describe core competencies as ". . . the collective learning in the organization, especially how to coordinate diverse production skills and integrate multiple streams of technologies."[2] Core competencies are based on combinations of attributes or skill sets that give an organization a unique advantage over its competitors.[3] This frequently involves delivering value to the customer by creating synergies among business units and supply chain partners.

How did Honda become the model for core competencies? It developed an exceptional skill and reputation for the blend of quality, reliability, and efficiency of its engines. As you might expect, to do this, Honda established an intensive engine R&D operation. But this is just part of the diverse skills and multiple streams of technology mentioned earlier. Honda also supports an IndyCar racing program. Why racing? Can you think of a better setting to drive the competitive juices to identify and develop new engine ideas or a better place to test them out? In 2005, Honda won the "Manufacturers Championship"—Honda cars and drivers had won more races than anyone else. Of course, Honda supports other racing programs, especially in motorcycles, to power an environment of innovation. What is the next piece to Honda's core competency puzzle? Honda has established outstanding manufacturing practices that enable it to turn new ideas developed for the track into efficient, high-quality engines to power Accords and Civics. But Honda's competency does not lie only in its engine design and manufacture. It is also found in the way that various elements and activities within Honda fit together and support each other. The complementary fit does not happen by chance, but takes careful planning and orchestration. This coordination begins with Honda's egalitarian corporate culture, which emphasizes quality and innovation, as well as the teamwork that the company embodies as part of the "Honda Way." The open, internal communications, long-term suppliers, and employees and teamwork orientation all fit together to create an atmosphere where employees understand the company's objectives, and work in harmony to support them. By leveraging this skill set across its business units and product lines (automotive, boating, motorcycles, and yard care), Honda truly recognizes its engine development and manufacturing as a core competency. Honda customers also recognize its core competency, as seen in its growing and profitable global market share.

Most companies that are truly leaders in their industry build their core competencies around a handful of essential skills. They don't just identify the necessary pieces to the core competency puzzle but they spend tremendous amounts of time figuring out how to assemble them into collective learning and unique capabilities. To determine whether a certain combination of skills is indeed a core competency, organizations should ask the questions shown in Table 9.1.

If an organization can answer yes to these questions, it has probably successfully identified a core competency.[4] Unfortunately, while many companies talk about their so-called core competencies, the fact is that few have established a true core competency that can meet this test.

The concept of core competencies is certainly applicable to the service sector as well. For example, service quality can create a core competency that provides sustainable competitive advantage. Based on service quality attributes such as consistency, responsiveness, and empathy, service companies build their reputation for

Table 9.1 Key Questions to Consider in Identifying a Core Competency

1. Does the identified skill set contribute significantly to what customers perceive as our organization's value-added?
2. Is the skill set difficult for others to replicate or imitate?
3. Are we particularly good at the skill set, or willing to invest the resources to become excellent?
4. Is the skill set broad enough that it allows us the opportunity to enter many diverse markets or businesses (think of Honda and its engines)?

dealing with customers. An outstanding example of this is Southwest Airlines. Some may feel that Southwest Airlines has "poor service" because it does not offer in-flight meals, preassigned seating, and other frills. However, as discussed in Chapter 8, Southwest Airlines has made a strategic choice to create a value proposition that focuses on other service measures, such as responsiveness to customers, on-time arrival, low fares, and consistency of the service experience. This combination of skills and execution creates a core competency in service as demonstrated by the answers to the questions for identifying core competencies.

1. *Does the identified skill set contribute significantly to what customers perceive as our organization's value-added?* Yes. Southwest's service attributes have created a very loyal customer base.
2. *Is the skill set difficult for others to replicate or imitate?* Yes. Other airlines, such as Continental, Delta, and United, have tried to copy Southwest's model and failed.
3. *Are we particularly good at the skill set, or willing to invest the resources to become excellent?* Yes. Southwest's superior performance in its areas of core competency has made it a consistent leader in the airline industry and business in general.
4. *Is the skill set broad enough that it allows us the opportunity to enter many diverse markets or businesses?* Yes. Southwest has successfully used this model to expand into many markets across the United States. It has traditionally focused on short-haul routes, and in the early 2000s started moving to longer routes. Time will tell if it will be as successful with transcontinental, and perhaps international, routes as it has been with shorter routes.

Southwest Airlines is consistently ranked as one of the most admired companies, among the top 10 on the U.S. list of most admired companies for the past 8 years.[5] Why? Again, it does not boil down to any one, simple thing. Rather, it is based on a host of factors in Southwest Airlines' culture and operations. It includes factors such as Southwest Airlines' competency in training and its cross-training policies, its decision to utilize a single type of airplane, concentration on short routes, and use of underutilized airports wherever possible.

To summarize, core competencies are not based on one simple factor, but on how a whole host of decisions and internal competencies work together to provide products and services customers value. Because neither Honda's nor Southwest's core competencies rest on any single issue, they have proven impossible for others to copy to date. This concept of core competency is also referred to as "strategic fit," which emphasizes the need for alignment among activities within an organization.[6]

Once a company defines its core competency, it can design a supply chain to support its competitive strategy, value proposition, and competency development. This almost always involves outsourcing. That is, the company focuses on what it does very

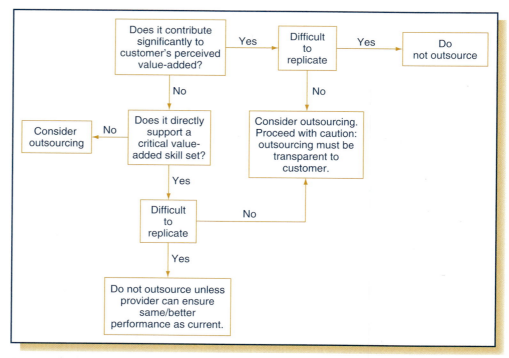

Figure 9.1 Questions to Consider in Outsourcing Activities

well—its core competencies—and relies on SC partners for other aspects of value creation. Because core competencies are composed of many intertwined activities, it may be difficult for an organization to truly identify all the activities that create its core competency. If it does not recognize all the elements of its success, it may mistakenly outsource an activity that should be kept in-house. This could be a very serious threat to the organization's competitiveness. To help the organization mitigate such risks, it should ask itself a modified version of the questions listed earlier, as shown in Figure 9.1. The company is asked to consider how an activity is directly and indirectly related to its core competencies before outsourcing. As a rule, valuable core competencies should not be outsourced, nor should their vital complementary capabilities.

With this perspective on core competencies in mind, we will now take a deeper look at the outsourcing process: the process of bringing together a winning set of competencies at the SC level. We will focus on some of the factors that are influencing the growth in outsourcing today.

THE OUTSOURCING CHALLENGE

Outsourcing is growing in importance and incidence every day. **Outsourcing** is the process of moving an aspect of production, service, or business function from within an organization to an outside supplier. Firms may outsource activities that they feel are not core competencies, that they are not good at, or that they do not otherwise wish to perform inside the organization. When the government or a public agency chooses to outsource, it is called **privatization**.

It is believed that outsourcing is about a $1 trillion global market. Historically, it has been common for companies to outsource services, including logistics, parts, materials, and components. This has been occurring since the dawn of business. Why vertically integrate when there is a supplier who makes the item or provides the service just as well, or better, at a good price?

Outsourcing trends include expansion into contract manufacturing (CM), use of third-party logistics (3PL) providers, offshoring, and outsourcing of business processes. **Contract manufacturing** involves a third party that makes an end product or major components under another company's brand. **Third-party logistics** involve using a supplier to provide some combination of logistics activities such as transportation, warehousing, procurement, manufacturing, inventory management, and customer service.[7] Estimates indicate that about 80 percent of U.S. firms engage 3PLs in some capacity. The dollar spend and percentage of firms using 3PLs has been rising steadily over the past 2 decades.[8] **Offshoring** is another name for outsourcing to a different country. In some cases, it may involve setting up a business office overseas and hiring local employees to do the work. This is not truly outsourcing, because the company employees still perform the work—just different employees at a different location. Offshoring is particularly popular in the information technology (IT) arena.[9] **Business process outsourcing (BPO)** includes everything from logistics to human resource management, payroll processing, purchasing, marketing, sales, accounting, administration, and information technology. BPO is increasingly being performed offshore.[10] Outsourcing is a critical decision. To compete effectively, an organization strives to reap the benefits of outsourcing while retaining its core competencies and without losing control of its products or business.

Outsourcing is really a matter of degree: How much should a company do itself, versus how much should it have its suppliers perform? Companies may decide to have a supplier perform a task (outsource) and later decide to bring the task back inside the company (insource) because they believe that they can perform the task better, more economically, or perhaps because the activity is more strategic in nature and they want to develop their own competency more fully. The decision to insource or outsource is also referred to as the **make-or-buy** decision.

Benefits of Outsourcing

Outsourcing can be a value-enhancing activity. By outsourcing manufacturing, services, and processes that are not strategic in nature, the organization can focus its attention on the issues that are most important to the customers and the activities the organization needs to perform best. Pick up any business magazine today, and you will see articles and advertisements about outsourcing. It seems that everyone is outsourcing everything. The advertisements emphasize cost savings, performance improvement, and the ability to have a third party focus on noncore issues while you focus on the critical ones. The top reasons that companies outsource is found in a recent survey are shown in Figure 9.2.

Not surprisingly, the bottom line in outsourcing comes back to the bottom line. According to this study, more than three-quarters of those surveyed indicate that their primary motivation to outsource is related to cost savings: reducing operating costs, creating a variable cost structure, and conserving capital. The remaining primary motivation comes from the company's desire to focus on its core business—its perceived core competencies. Although globalization is not listed as a specific reason for outsourcing, increasing levels of competition from companies throughout the world are demanding that companies reexamine their processes. Many activities performed

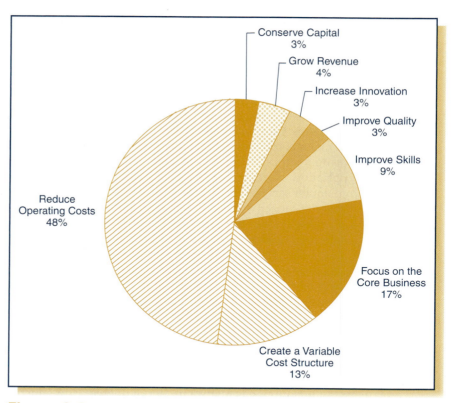

Figure 9.2 Top Reasons That Companies Outsource

Source: The 2005 Outsourcing World Summit® produced by the International Association of Outsourcing Professionals (IAOP).[11]

in affluent countries, such as Germany, France, Japan, and the United States, can be performed for pennies on the dollar in developing countries such as China, India, and Mexico.[12] Indeed, such savings is the primary motivator for offshoring.[13]

As competitors take advantage of low labor costs in other parts of the world, firms in the same industry often follow suit in order to remain cost competitive. For example, the cost of a fully-burdened automotive worker for Ford Motor Company in the United States is around $65 per hour, versus around $2 per hour in China.[14] The pressure to find lower cost global sources often spreads throughout the supply chain. For example, Honeywell, a global provider and manufacturer of aerospace equipment and services, recently urged its Arizona-based suppliers to relocate to Mexico to take advantage of lower labor costs. Honeywell explained this request as its response to competitive pressures in the aerospace industry.[15]

Some companies outsource to conserve capital: They let the suppliers invest in the development and production of new products, plant, and equipment. For example, when Chrysler began to outsource a great deal of its component design and production in the 1980s under the leadership of Lee Iacocca, it was a matter of survival. Conservation of capital and cutting costs were critical, because Chrysler was in bankruptcy.

Other companies outsource so they can benefit from outside expertise and focus on their core competencies. For instance, when Microsoft decided to outsource the manufacturing of its XBox video-game system in the 1990s, XBox was a new product. Microsoft lacked experience as a manufacturer. One of its primary motivations

Table 9.2 Potential Risks Associated with Outsourcing

STRATEGIC RISKS	TACTICAL RISKS
Firm loses knowledge and/or technology to perform activity internally	Firm experiences:
Supplier develops unique, hard-to-replicate expertise	Short-term supply shortages
Supplied activities add unique value recognized by customer	Hidden transaction or management costs
Customer identifies more with the supplier than the original firm	Loss of schedule control
Firm loses sight of market trends	Short-term price fluctuations
Supplier shares knowledge with firm's competitors	

was to utilize the expertise of contract manufacturers. Microsoft had enough insight into its own core competencies to know that more experienced companies could probably manufacturer things better. It wanted to stick to what it knew: software.

Constraints and Risks of Outsourcing

If you outsource a strategic activity, you might lose your position in the market. If you outsource to the wrong organization, your costs and service level might suffer. Organizations must be aware of strategic and tactical risks of outsourcing, as shown in Table 9.2. Strategic risk is a long-term, perhaps irreversible, risk that may occur as a company loses the knowledge it once had related to its core activities. Tactical risks are short-term risks that occur when an organization relies on a supplier for capacity, but not necessarily knowledge. Tactical risks are less costly in the long run.

We look again to the automotive industry, where many firms outsourced myriad processes during the 1980s and 1990s. Today, automakers are outsourcing entire sub-assemblies and subsystems to suppliers. For instance, rather than buying individual parts, such as wiper blades, many automakers outsource the complete wiper assembly, inclusive of the wiper motor. This strategy is not without risk. As the suppliers develop the technology for manufacturing parts, components, and subassemblies, the buyers lose the ability to make and design internally, becoming increasingly dependent on the suppliers. This increased dependency reduces the buyer's relative bargaining power and sets up a situation where the balance of power, and value-added, can shift to the supplier if the buyer is not careful. This approach to outsourcing creates increased interdependence in the supply chain. Concern for this eventuality is demonstrated in a memo sent to 350,000 staff members by Ford Motor Company's chief operating officer. He said, "If we are not our suppliers' customer of choice, they will dedicate their best people, invest their best resources and offer the newest technology and innovation to our competitors—putting Ford at a disadvantage."[16] In its sustainability report, Ford specifically mentions, "Suppliers are an integral part of our business, and our success is interdependent with theirs."[17]

Some managers believe that the strategic risk of making a bad outsourcing decision is so high that it can make or break a company. For example, Charles Fine,[18] author of *Clockspeed*, believes that designing supply chains in terms of knowing what to outsource and what not to outsource is the ultimate core competency. He argues that industries and organizations cycle in and out of vertical integration. Firms move out of vertical integration as suppliers become better at critical activities than they are. However, even as they increase their dependence on suppliers, companies must do so strategically, retaining internally those activities that the customers really value. The ability to make these decisions wisely is critical. Organizations that outsource the activities the customers see as valuable find themselves losing power as they outsource. They may never be able to get that power back. An example of this is IBM in the PC business. It outsourced PC software to an unknown Microsoft, and the microprocessor to a tiny company named Intel. The rest is history. Despite its strong efforts at a comeback, IBM had lost power in the PC hardware industry. To its credit, IBM has successfully reinvented itself as a service provider.

Another potential negative outcome is for a company to help create its future competition. Intel encountered this challenge. Early in its history, Intel outsourced manufacturing to Advanced Micro Devices (AMD) because it could not keep up with demand. AMD then began producing its own chips, becoming a competitor to Intel. Although Intel has been able to maintain the upper hand in the marketplace, it now has another threat that it may not have had, had it not worked closely with AMD in its early growth years. Thus, a strategic assessment of the industry should be performed before entertaining any outsourcing decision.

Establish the Outsourcing Team and Goals

Whether you are considering manufacturing, services, or business processes, the outsourcing process should include three major phases, as shown in Figure 9.3:

1. Establish the mission; generate and screen ideas.
2. Conduct an outsourcing analysis.
3. Establish and manage the outsourcing relationship.

Establish Outsourcing Mission; Generate and Screen Ideas

To begin, an organization needs to state what benefits it hopes to achieve by outsourcing, nominate processes to outsource, screen those ideas, and analyze the best ones. These activities must include representatives from key stakeholder groups who will be affected by the decision, as well as strategists high enough in the business organization to be in tune with competitive issues and planned future strategic direction. Thus, higher-level managers should be involved in the screening of ideas. Without top management's involvement, a business unit might outsource a process that the company really needed to develop as a new strategic technology, or that is part of a core competency. Table 9.3 shows key elements of the outsourcing decision-making process and who should be involved.

The first step in the screening phase of outsourcing is to determine why the company wants to outsource. What are the benefits that it seeks? As shown in Figure 9.2, the benefits vary widely. Top management may establish a leadership team to solicit ideas for outsourcing based on the goals of outsourcing. Ideas can be generated from

Figure 9.3 Outsourcing Process Phases

Table 9.3   Major Outsourcing Phases and Key Participants

PHASES	KEY PARTICIPANTS
Establish mission; generate and screen ideas	Top management, business unit, and functional leaders
Conduct an outsourcing feasibility study	Multidisciplinary team of key stakeholders in the current process
Establish and manage the relationship with the supplier	Purchasing or relationship manager

a variety of sources. A leading manufacturer of imaging products, referred to here as "Image," engaged in extensive outsourcing throughout the 1990s and into the 2000s. The specific goals that Image pursued included (1) cost reduction and (2) a reduction in noncore activities. All managers above a certain level in the organization were asked to identify outsourcing opportunities and provide a rationale for each. A multidisciplinary team of high-level managers screened out unattractive options based on Image's goals, Image's core competency or strategic success factors, potential risks, and strategic impact, as explained in more detail later. In the early stages, the team also considered the internal political ramifications of outsourcing, avoiding making unpopular decisions until it had a few success stories to share.

The next step in this first stage of outsourcing is to compare the ideas for outsourcing to the organization's key success factors or core competencies. By outsourcing activities that are critical to the organization's success, or that directly contribute to critical activities, it may experience diminished performance, thereby reducing its competitive position. For any item being considered for outsourcing, the organization should answer the four questions shown in Table 9.1 to help identify whether the item is a core competency or critical to the organization's core competencies.

If the organization answers "yes" to questions 1 and 2, outsourcing is ill-advised. Questions 3 and 4 are only important if the item is perceived as a potential core competency: a difficult-to-imitate, value-added activity. Table 9.4 shows several of the ideas that were suggested for outsourcing at Image, and the rationale regarding whether or not they were core activities. Failure to properly screen could mean that you retain activities you should outsource, or worse, outsource activities you should retain. For example, food service operations did not initially pass through the screening process to

Table 9.4   Image Potential Outsourcing Projects

PROJECT	DECISION/RATIONALE
Laundry	Outsource—internal support function
Forms Management	Outsource—internal support function
IT	Outsource—important area, but Image did not excel in that area and could not invest to achieve excellence
Supply Management	Do not outsource—critical to internal analysis, maintaining key supplier relationships, and cost competitiveness
Food Service	Outsource—although Image had an excellent cafeteria, it did not provide any value-added to its customers, nor would it be difficult to replicate

be considered as an outsourcing opportunity at Image until it had outsourced many other noncore activities. This is because there were some people in the organization who convinced top management that core competencies were anything that the organization was really good at, and its cafeteria had won awards! In addition, one of management's early goals in outsourcing was to outsource noncontroversial areas. The cafeteria outsourcing was very emotional for some employees. However, the cafeteria did not pass the litmus test of the first question: Does the activity or skill set contribute significantly to what customers' perceive as the organization's value-added? Once it passed through the screening process as a viable outsourcing candidate, it was analyzed according to the process presented in the next phase.

Conduct an Outsourcing Analysis

In this second phase, a team is formed to analyze promising ideas that made it through the screening process and select those to outsource. The team needs to encompass various perspectives, including those involved in the day-to-day activities. It also needs operational-level people from key functions, such as logistics, supply, finance, and others who will be affected to provide data and perform the nitty-gritty analysis. This team should report its findings to the higher-level team that initiated the outsourcing analysis, and have executive sponsorship from the higher-level team. Along with the charter to conduct the analysis, the top management team should share with the operating team why it believes that this is a viable outsourcing project, as well as its expectations in terms of the potential outcome. For example, how strongly do they want to outsource an activity, like food service? Do they want a minimum of 10 percent savings to justify the change? Do they expect service to be improved or maintained, or perhaps even diminished? In addition, if there are any potential risks that have been identified by the management team, they should pass that information on to the analysis team. An organization should not proceed to this phase of conducting the outsourcing analysis until it has completed the previous phase. It must understand its motivations for outsourcing and screen out ideas that do not seem viable. In this phase, the team:

- Develops a better understanding of the organization's needs
- Gathers detailed information on cost, performance, and risks in the marketplace
- Performs a total cost of ownership analysis

The analysis stage of the outsourcing decision begins after the strategic assessment presented in the previous section has determined that this purchase is a potential candidate for outsourcing. The level of detail and information gathered is much more specific in this phase.

Identify Potential Suppliers. The organization must perform a more thorough assessment of the supply market capabilities at this point, considering:

- Are there supply sources available?
- Do the potential supply sources meet capacity, quality, and other organizational needs?
- Are the suppliers interested?
- What risks are present in outsourcing?

If the buying organization answers no to any of these key questions, it must consider whether it wants to develop a supplier to meet its needs, or retain the activity in-house. Supplier development, working with a supplier to help improve its performance, can be a very costly and time-consuming process. Reverse marketing, a type of supplier development, is presented next.

Consider Reverse Marketing.[19] When a firm wants to outsource but can find no qualified supplier, it may engage in **reverse marketing**, the process of recruiting a supplier to provide an item or service. This is different from a routine request for quotation or proposal. In general, the buyer is asking the supplier to do something it is currently not able to do, whether the ability is lacking due to capacity, capability, capital, or other reasons. To increase the probability of success, the candidate suppliers should be in a line of business directly related to the needs of the buyer.

For example, Image decided to outsource the inventory management and ordering of its relatively low-value maintenance, repair, and operating supplies such as janitorial suppliers, nuts and bolts, lubricants, and other miscellaneous low-value plant supplies. The organization had about 600 suppliers for around 10,000 parts. However, because of the diversity of parts it purchased, it looked like it might still end up with 50 to 100 suppliers, far too many to manage effectively, or with which to gain any leverage. This was simply not acceptable. Thus, Image decided to approach suppliers that currently carried many items that Image needed and try to persuade them to expand their offerings specifically to meet Image's needs. Image believed that this would be more effective than approaching a supplier in an unrelated area with this business proposition.

Image then prepared a business case based on its strengths and the potential benefits to the supplier. As part of the reverse marketing plan, Image had to develop an idea for how it would support the supplier in terms of sales volume and technical and financial support. Negotiation ensued. As part of the negotiation, Image realized that no one supplier/distributor would be willing to carry the 10,000 diverse items it needed. Thus, it segregated its needs by like items and came up with six product families, including corrugated containers; bearings, nuts, and bolts; safety and hygiene supplies; electronics, connectors, and cables; and two miscellaneous categories. Once agreements were reached with the suppliers, contracts were put into place. Initially, a reverse marketing arrangement is likely to be a "committed" relationship, with a great deal of effort and attention to making it work. There is much interaction and communication as the supplier develops the required capability with the help of the buying firm. This relationship should be reviewed periodically to determine whether it should be maintained as a committed relationship or changed to a less resource-intensive relationship type. Relationship types are presented in greater depth in the third phase of the outsourcing process, establish and maintain relationships.

Restate the Need and Expected Benefits. Restating the need and desired benefits involves considering the volume and the timing of the requirements as well as weighing whether a complete outsourcing/insourcing solution is needed. This reinforces the screening of potential outsourcing possibilities that occurs in phase 1. This aspect of the make-or-buy analysis involves further analyzing what aspects of the buy are strategic, and where the organization has expertise versus the supply market.

For example, when a major telecommunications service provider was considering outsourcing construction management, it considered simply hiring a general contractor to manage the entire process. It also segmented the buy into three parts: construction management, professional services, and zone general contractor. The firm found that by separating the key activities, it allowed each of the service providers to focus on what it was good at, and the telecommunications company could focus on what it was good at: managing the contracts. It achieved better performance and lower total cost of ownership by separating the construction management into three activities rather than outsourcing it as a whole. Thus, the company retained more of the management than originally anticipated.

Identify and Mitigate Potential Risks.   Most organizations are good at recognizing the potential tactical risks of outsourcing in terms of supply interruption (refer to Table 9.2): What if we become dependent on the supplier, and there is a shortage, a disaster, or a failure in the relationship? Although these are all very important immediate issues, these are operational issues that generally will pass or can be resolved given time. An even bigger issue from a strategic perspective examines: What if we lose our internal capability to perform this activity, and the supplier "holds us hostage," demanding high prices? By increasing power, the supplier might be able to capture a larger share of the overall chain's margins. Although these issues are touched on in the initial screening phase of the overall analysis, risk must be reevaluated here, as the scope and the nature of the outsourcing arrangement may have changed considerably from initial idea inception. Companies need to grasp what it is that they are outsourcing. Are they simply outsourcing capacity, in which case they could move their capacity needs elsewhere if this relationship does not work out? Let's return to our Image example. Was Image just outsourcing capacity when it outsourced laundry, forms, and the cafeteria? Or was Image outsourcing knowledge and capability, in which case it could become increasingly dependent on the supplier? This is the question Image asked as it considered outsourcing its IT, and why Image chose not to outsource supply management.

Thus, at this stage, it is also a good idea for the organization to develop contingency plans for dealing with the risks it has identified. In the case of Image's outsourcing of low value parts, it identified risks in terms of potential capacity and shortages, loss of competitive pricing information by dealing with only one supplier, and hidden transaction and management costs. To help mitigate these risks, Image incorporated the measures shown in Table 9.5 into its planning and contracts.

The next step is to use all of the data the outsourcing team has gathered to develop a good cost analysis, and understand the potential cost impact of the risks identified.

Conduct a Total Cost of Ownership Analysis.   Performing a total cost of ownership (TCO) analysis is an important approach for gaining insight into the true impact of an outsourcing decision on the organization's cost. Once you have determined that there

Table 9.5   Risks and Mitigation Plans in Outsourcing MRO

RISK ISSUE	SAFEGUARD
Capacity or shortages	Identified alternative sources for key parts, keeping in mind that all distributors use the same manufacturers, so shortage is difficult to avoid in an industry-wide shortage
Loss of competitive pricing information	Right to audit manufacturers' bills built into contract Right to test market and go out to receive competitive bids for comparable services Most-favored-customer clause in contract to ensure that Image's price meets or beats the price offered to other customers receiving the same service
Hidden transaction or management fees	Cap fees in contract Right to audit distributor's cost allocations built into contract Contractual clause requiring distributor's bills itemized into major cost categories for management fees, rather than one lump sum

are reasonably good suppliers who are willing to work with you and you have really scoped out your needs, TCO can help you understand the true cost implications.

The basic approach is to determine the total of all costs to the organization if it makes the item or if it purchases the item, and then compare the two. The incremental costs, or costs that change from one decision to another, for that individual firm must be analyzed and compared. Such an assessment must include an analysis of all major cost elements. It should also include sensitivity analysis to account for potential risk. This process was discussed in detail in Chapter 8.

Analysis of all cost elements includes the direct costs of materials, labor, energy, overhead, transportation, inventory, quality, obsolescence, and capital costs. It is easy to overlook some key costs, so a cross-functional team that really understands the current and proposed processes should perform this analysis. In outsourcing, organizations often overlook the fact that they may have to retain employees to manage outsourced relationships. For example, a large chemical manufacturer that outsourced all of its logistical capabilities was very disappointed to find that it needed to retain a large management team to manage the third-party providers and coordinate the information flow and reporting of results. Another common mistake is to recognize savings in wages, when only parts of jobs will be eliminated, so no real reduction in wages will occur. Thus, a TCO analysis considers all direct costs and hidden costs to the extent that these costs are incrementally related to the decision. Costs that will not change are not considered relevant to the decision.

Sensitivity analysis should also be performed in conjunction with TCO analysis. This "what-if" analysis takes into account that many of the costs used in analyzing the outsourcing decision are estimates. After all, projecting anything that has not yet happened involves uncertainty. For example, as with the chemical company mentioned earlier, the organization might make an assumption that it will need to retain 3 of 30 employees to manage the outsourced process. What if that estimate is wrong? What if 6 internal employees are needed? A sensitivity analysis should be performed for all assumptions in which there is some degree of uncertainty. Costs for all strategic decisions including outsourcing should be calculated for the best, worst, and expected scenarios. Assumptions are considered very sensitive if a small change in estimate would change the decision from make to buy or visa versa. In those cases, special care must be taken to get the best available information possible. It is worth investing time and effort into gaining more certainty for those items.

Based on the TCO analysis, including the results of the sensitivity analysis, the team should now be prepared to make a presentation to top management. Based on the cost, the supply base, and the organization's needs, does outsourcing look like the best decision? If so, the organization is ready to consider specific suppliers, the type of relationship it desires, and the breadth of service it seeks. These issues will be presented under "Establish and Manage the Outsourcing Relationship" on page 294.

Example of TCO Analysis for Outsourcing. Organizations such as Image often consider whether they should manage their own parts inventory and ordering for small-dollar, high-variety parts and components. As mentioned in the discussion of reverse marketing, Image had about 600 suppliers for around 10,000 small-dollar items in maintenance, repair, and operating supplies; nuts; bolts; and corrugated packaging. Inventories and obsolescence were high, the paperwork was vast, and shortages were common.

Based on these inefficiencies discovered during the TCO analysis, the organization knew it needed to change its processes. It looked into **integrated supply**.

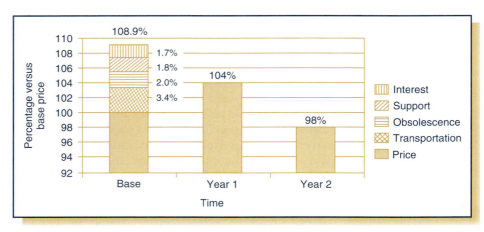

Figure 9.4 TCO Saving Analysis

Integrated supply involves having one or a handful of distributors handle all of the items, rather than ordering from a huge number of manufacturers or small distributors. These "multiline distributors" carry many lines of items; handle all of the inventory management, order placement, and stocking; and provide one monthly bill. In an integrated supply system, some jobs within the firm could actually be eliminated.

Because the array of items that Image was purchasing was so broad, and many of its current distributors had exclusive distribution territories, the multiline distributors had to buy from other distributors, thereby increasing the markup. Thus, some of the prices paid would actually go up. Rather than making a simple price-to-price comparison, Image did a total cost of ownership analysis. The new price that it would pay would be a landed price, including freight. In addition, Image determined that its inventories and obsolescence would go down, because the integrated suppliers would do a better job of managing the inventory. As Figure 9.4 shows, savings in transportation, obsolescence, support, and interest more than compensated for the rise in purchased goods in the first year.

An unexpected benefit of outsourcing was that Image had chosen integrated distributors as suppliers that were truly experts in the items that they sell. As these experts spent time at the manufacturing site and saw how inventory was actually used, they came up with many suggestions for standardizing, substituting, and generally lowering costs. The second bar of the bar chart in Figure 9.4 shows that by the second year, costs had come down another 4 percent, so that the total cost of the outsourced alternative was now about the same as the original price of doing it internally, but with tremendous savings in overhead.

The Case of Business Process Outsourcing. Business processes and functions are increasingly being outsourced today. This includes activities such as purchasing and supply management, logistics, information technology, finance, customer service, payroll, and accounts payable. In general, companies outsource business processes for much the same reasons that they outsource manufacturing: to reduce costs and improve performance. It may be the case that a company does not buy very much from the outside and could leverage its purchasing better by using a third-party professional that combines the volume of multiple organizations. Thus, it decides to outsource purchasing.

A business process outsourcing program should follow the same rigorous analysis approach as manufacturing outsourcing. It is possible that some business processes are strategic to the organization's success and are truly valued competencies. An example of this includes Amazon.com's information technology and Web site management abilities. Other companies, such as Target and Toys"R"Us, have outsourced their Web design and management to Amazon.com because of its expertise. Thus, like anything else being considered for outsourcing, business processes should be reviewed from a strategic standpoint.

Image chose to outsource its entire IT department. In doing so, it went through steps that parallel those used for outsourcing goods. During the idea generation portion of phase 1 of the outsourcing process, the chief information officer (CIO) for Image recommended outsourcing. She noted that information technology was changing rapidly, it was not a core competence for Image, and Image would not be able to afford to keep up with the latest and best trends on its own.

In Image's IT outsourcing situation, it was decided at a strategic level that the firm wanted to outsource IT in order to remain competitive, not necessarily to save money. The first phase of the outsourcing process, *establishing the mission; generate and screen ideas,* was essentially performed by top management on the recommendation of the CIO. Nonetheless, the core issue in phase 2, *conduct the outsourcing analysis,* was a thorough TCO analysis. The TCO analysis was conducted to help identify potential hidden costs and to better understand processes so that process improvements could be built into the new system. The TCO analysis/outsourcing team consisted of the CIO, other technical IT representatives, end users, supply management, and finance. In addition, the IT service provider had an ad hoc team member to provide information and answer questions to support the team's analysis.

The team developed an assessment of key risks and how Image intended to mitigate them, as shown in Table 9.6. There was particularly strong concern about good

Table 9.6 Risks and Mitigation Plans in Outsourcing IT

RISK ISSUE	SAFEGUARD
Poor service to internal customers	Establish internal user survey that links service provider's pay to performance
Poor communication or management of service provider	Dedicated relationship managers at Image Advisory board to meet with relationship manager, service provider, key users to provide feedback, discuss technology needs and trends
Difficulty in controlling costs	Hire a third party to audit service provider, compare rates with other like companies
Loss of internal expertise	Loss in support-level expertise could not be avoided; however, relationship manager, CIO, and others would retain enough strategic knowledge to replace the service provider effectively if needed
Short contract duration/high turnover would be expensive for supplier and frustrating for internal users	Established a 5-year contract with annual reviews and contract extension clauses
Transitioning own employees out of IT and training new employees by service provider	Virtually all current Image IT employees were offered and accepted jobs with service provider to remain at Image

service levels to internal users. To mitigate this risk, Image built in pay-for-performance standards and metrics, where part of the IT provider's pay was based on internal user satisfaction.

Next, Image brainstormed the key cost drivers in the outsourcing arrangement versus the current in-house arrangement. These included (1) ongoing and periodic costs of hardware, (2) software, (3) internal management, (4) professional labor, (5) training, and (6) one-time layoff costs. The team determined that the hardware and software costs would be virtually the same whether Image insourced or outsourced, so those costs were not relevant to the decision and were not included in the decision. In addition, because most of Image's current employees were retained, training and layoff costs were minimal. However, Image determined it would need to retain much of its current IT management to deal with contract and relationship issues. Thus, management savings was minimal. The net result was that there would be moderate savings over the 5-year contract, due to the outsourced IT provider's efficiencies. More importantly, Image anticipated that its IT service and capabilities would be significantly improved versus what Image could provide for itself. Management decided to go ahead with the outsourcing arrangement. IT outsourcing was so successful that the initial contract was extended from 5 years to 10 years.

Establish and Manage the Outsourcing Relationship

In this third stage of the outsourcing process, we will explore the types of supplier relationships and how to manage them. Outsourcing arrangements exist on a continuum from minimal service to full-service or turnkey operations, as shown in Figure 9.5. Outsourcing critical and complex processes requires a closer relationship with suppliers than traditional contract management. This section presents definitions for each type of outsourcing arrangement, where it best fits, and the key issues to consider in determining which type of arrangement is best suited for the situation. These are related to the type of relationship desired and needed with the supplier.

The left side of the continuum represents the suppliers that are easier to replace and add less unique value. As we move to the right, the supplier adds more value, provides more unique value, and is more closely integrated with the organization's operations. There are two types of limited-scope providers identified on the continuum: arm's-length relationship and niche provider. In both cases, the buying firm does not want to influence the supplier's activities to any great extent. It expects them to perform a task to standards, meeting well-defined needs and specifications. Keep in mind that these relationships do evolve over time. A hybrid supplier may evolve into a solutions integrator based on its performance, capabilities, and your trust in its abilities. Table 9.7 offers a scale for defining the breadth of a supplier relationship. This can be useful in determining the right type of supplier relationship for a particular outsourcing situation.

Figure 9.5 The Outsourcing Relationship Continuum

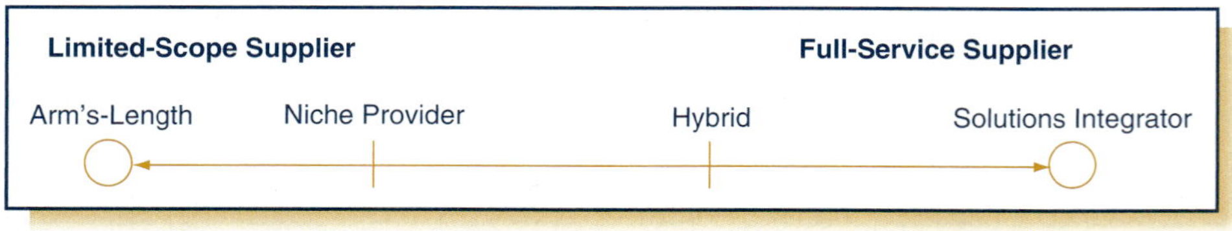

Table 9.7   What Kind of Supplier Do You Need?

Is the value in this process created through specialized expertise or through technology and repeatable routines?	1.............3...........5 Low...........Med........High			
How tightly interconnected are the activities within the process?	1.............3...........5 Low...........Med........High			
To what extent do you want to change this entire process?	1.............3...........5 Low...........Med........High			
To what extent does your own firm have the management bandwidth to manage multiple providers?	1.............3...........5 Low...........Med........High			
To what extent do you need a provider with market power to get the benefits you are seeking?	1.............3...........5 Low...........Med........High			
Total	1–8		9–17	18–25
	Arm's-length	Niche provider	Hybrid	Solutions integrator

Adapted from Linder and Cantrell.[20]

- *Arm's-length relationship.* An arm's-length relationship is best suited for "routine" purchases of goods or services. There is no long-term commitment or special value-added by this supplier. It fits well for nonrecurring purchases of items that aren't critical, or when the market is very competitive, switching costs are low, and the suppliers are not differentiated. Specific examples of this include the provider of unskilled labor for general assembly operations and a print shop. General examples include clearly specified parts and components, and minor, ongoing operating processes.
- *Niche provider.* Niche providers are generally specialized, providing a very specific, limited good or service. Although they do not provide a strategic activity, they may be more difficult to replace than arm's-length suppliers due to their specialized nature. Specific examples of this might be the provider of skilled engineers to monitor and certify water quality, or the provider of a specialized stamping or plating process that you do not need routinely. In general, these are specialized, nonrecurring purchases.
- *Hybrid: Intermediate-level service provider.* Hybrid suppliers provide an intermediate level of service. They are those suppliers that provide items of moderate importance that are somewhat integrated into the organization's operations. They may have responsibility for a whole subsystem or process rather than one clearly defined piece, as do limited-scope providers. They offer standard, "turnkey" solutions and may even run some of the company's internal processes with their own people. As such, the boundaries between the provider and the firm may begin to blur, because it is not always clear where the supplier's scope of responsibility ends.

  Ongoing communication is critical, as any changes made by either party may significantly affect the other. There is definitely a higher degree of ongoing reliance on this type of provider; they are more difficult and expensive to replace than limited-scope providers because they are more integral to the company. Yet they are not impossible to replace, because the nature of what they supply is not unique or strategic. Suppliers in this category provide goods and services on an ongoing basis that are integral to the firm's processes or add value to its products, like subassemblies, meeting and travel planning, and logistical services.

- *Solutions integrator: Full-service solution provider.* Solutions integrators provide strategic items and processes that are entrenched in the firm's own processes. Rather than providing out-of-the-box, turnkey solutions, they offer custom solutions and are often associated with business process outsourcing (BPO) of critical functions. These providers have a very high level of responsibility and accountability. They often suggest processes and process improvements and have a significant presence in the organization, working side-by-side with the organization's employees.

    The open-ended nature of responsibilities makes these relationships harder to evaluate and manage. Some examples include contract manufacturers; BPO of the entire IT process, equipment, and software; and key outsourced processes that interface directly with the customer such as sales and fulfillment. There are definite similarities between hybrid and solutions integrators. The key distinguishing factors are that the items involved are more critical or strategic in nature for the solutions integrators, and the solutions involved are likely to be more custom.

Proactive outsourcers define expectations clearly so that they can choose the right form of outsourcing arrangement. Equally important, the company must clearly communicate those expectations to its outsourcing partner and then closely monitor its performance over time.

Management of Outsourcing Relationships. Can you imagine accepting a job where you had no job description, no clearly defined objectives and goals, and were given no feedback on your performance until the annual review process? Most people would not accept such a job, because the ambiguity would be overwhelming. Yet some organizations treat their suppliers just that way. Based on the outsourcing arrangement identified earlier, we must establish clear expectations, ongoing measurement, and feedback in dealing with third-party providers. The nature and frequency of the oversight varies with the value and complexity of the outsourced process. As in the case of the outsource arrangements, we will look at outsource oversight on a continuum, from routine to committed.

- *Routine* relationships are named for traditional contract management. The contract terms are clear and the deliverables are simple to use and measure. Naturally, effective buyers monitor routine relationships, but they do so in a standard way. Routine relationships are best suited to arm's-length and niche arrangements. In these cases, the suppliers are relatively easy to replace, and the contract or purchase order covers all of the essential issues.
- *Cooperative* relationships are suited to hybrid outsourcing arrangements. The contract defines the relationship, but the suppliers also cooperate on an ongoing basis to redefine expectations and goals based on changing business needs. The relationship is more flexible and evolutionary.
- *Committed* relationships are common between buyers and solutions integrators. The two parties have committed a great deal of resources and efforts to the relationship, and their management style should reflect this.

Depending on the strategic importance of the outsourced item, the relationship should be cooperative or committed. Each of the management and oversight styles will be presented more fully in the following sections. The fit between the type of outsourcing arrangement and type of relationship is summarized in Table 9.8.

Table 9.8 Fit Between Outsourcing Arrangement and Relationship Type

	ROUTINE RELATIONSHIP	COOPERATIVE	COMMITTED
Arm's-length	X		
Niche provider	X		
Hybrid		X	
Solutions integrator		X	X

Supplier relationships are also discussed in additional depth in Chapter 11, "Relationship Management," and Chapter 15, "Collaborative Innovation."

Determine a Proper Level of Oversight. Table 9.9 shows the key factors to consider in determining the type of management and oversight best suited for a particular outsourced relationship. Answer the questions in Table 9.9 for the integrated supply/MRO relationship presented in the TCO example earlier in this chapter, and add up the score.

What did you get for the score? Something between 9 and 17? The authors scored this as 17, at the high end of cooperative relationships. Again, this involves some judgment, so it is a good idea to get a team involved to incorporate different experiences and perspectives.

Table 9.10, a modification of Table 9.9, summarizes the key characteristics of each of the types of supplier oversight and management.

In general, committed relationships will be relatively rare. They are more time-consuming and challenging to manage, so you want to make sure that you have properly classified your relationships. Keep in mind: Improperly overrating relationships can waste valuable company resources and time with suppliers that won't benefit the company proportionately. Improperly underrating relationships means that you could be missing out on opportunities.

Table 9.9 How Should the Supplier Be Managed?

How much management oversight will this process require?	1.........3............5 Low......Med.........High		
What is the strategic importance of this process/item now and in the future?	1.........3............5 Low......Med.........High		
If this is a complex process/item, do we need to be concerned with the level of complexity?	1.........3............5 Low......Med.........High		
How much change do you anticipate in this process/item over the life of the contract?	1.........3............5 Low......Med.........High		
How interdependent is this process with other processes in the firm?	1.........3............5 Low......Med.........High		
How important is it for you to keep this supplier motivated in ways beyond simply providing business?	1.........3............5 Low......Med.........High		
Total	1–8 Routine	9–17 Cooperative	18–30 Committed

Adapted from Linder and Cantrell.[21]

Table 9.10 Characteristics of Types of Oversight/Management

ISSUE	ROUTINE	COOPERATIVE	COMMITTED
Level of management oversight after relationship is established	Low	Low to medium	High
Strategic importance of item/process outsourced	Low	Medium	High
Need to interface with supplier closely to understand processes	Low	Medium to high	High
Anticipated change/improvement over life cycle of relationship	Low	Medium to high	High
Interdependence of our process with supplier	Low	Medium	Medium to high
Our need to be a "preferred customer" to this supplier	Low	Low to medium	High
Level of ambiguity and change in expectations	Low	Low to medium	Medium to high

Ongoing and Post-Audit Evaluation. In all three types of management and oversight approaches, there should be ongoing supplier evaluation and feedback. This is critical if the supplier is to meet expectations and focus on continuous improvement.

- In *routine* relationships, feedback often amounts to simply complaining to the supplier when it performs poorly. Most organizations do not have the time and resources to devote to providing ongoing feedback to suppliers who do not provide them with significant volume or value-added. If the supplier does provide significant volume, the buyer is likely to have a standard "report card" of **key performance indicators (KPIs)**. Buyers generally send report cards to ongoing contractual suppliers monthly or quarterly, or more often if there is a problem with performance. The report compares actual to expected performance on key KPIs, such as ontime performance, quality, and completeness of order/activity.

- In *cooperative* relationships, the supplier would also likely receive a report card on a regular basis. However, it might include one or more unique items, such as "breadth of product line" for a distributor. It could be semicustomized to capture the value the supplier adds. A hypothetical example of such a report card for the outsourced IT relationship presented earlier is shown in Table 9.11.

- In *committed* relationships, a more customized report card is given to establish performance on key issues and initiatives that the outsource provider and customer are working on together. In addition, much of the performance feedback would be verbal, as this is a close day-to-day interaction.

A post-audit goes beyond the ongoing feedback, and is often done prior to contract renewal or renegotiation. It considers all of the elements in the formal report card, but also looks at more strategic issues, such as, "How does this provider fit with our future plans?" and "Should we grow this relationship into other areas?" It also examines any issues with the outsourcing arrangement that were not identified as part of the outsourcing analysis, so that future outsourcing decision processes can be improved.

A post-audit will be a team activity, designed to provide the greatest depth of understanding in terms of how the supplier has been performing from many angles, and where the relationship should go in the future. The major results should be communicated to the provider, giving it the opportunity to respond and improve.

Table 9.11   Report Card for Outsourced IT Service Provider for First Quarter 20XX

PERFORMANCE INDICATOR	RATING	GOAL	COMMENTS
Completes key tasks on time	90%	98%	Was late on transitioning to new inventory system
Meets service levels to internal customers	95% same-day response	92% same-day response	Excellent; keep up the good work!
Follows up on missed service levels within a week	99%	95%	Thanks for your good work!
Client perception survey—Quality	88% meets/exceeds quality expectations	90% meets/exceeds quality expectations	Need to perform a root cause analysis and identify weak area(s) to target improvement
Client perception survey— Technology leadership	95% meets/exceeds technology leadership expectations	90% meets/exceeds technology leadership expectations	Good work!
Operates within budgeted costs unless prior approval given	100%	100%	Good work!

As the third step of our 3-phase outsourcing process, this last phase provides essential closure. It is the oversight and ongoing management of outsourced relationships that provides the critical feedback both internally and to suppliers to "close the loop" on the whole outsourcing process. The information gained by monitoring providers and giving them feedback is important to creating clear expectations and continuous improvement. The information gathered is also useful in contract renegotiations.

Skill Level Required for Buyers

"Traditional" buyers are accustomed to managing contractual relationships that are clearly defined, with clear expectations and performance measures. This is an excellent fit in the case of routine or contractual relationships. However, this approach may not work as well in dealing with cooperative and committed outsource providers, where the expectations and management may be more fluid, depending on the organization's need. Thus, today's supply professionals will likely need different skill sets to manage outsource providers than to manage more traditional relationships.

Outsourcing deals with procedures and processes that are less clearly defined than traditional buying. Those who are managing outsource providers may need additional training in order to be successful. Managing complex relationships may involve facilitating change and evaluating potential improvements, rather than focusing on monitoring day-to-day performance. The new skill set required includes:

Improving two-way communication with suppliers
Looking for continuous improvement opportunities
Developing metrics for soft performance issues, such as responsiveness and innovation, rather than simply looking at on-time deliveries or other hard measures

Motivating the supplier to want to support the organization

Listening to the supplier's concerns and being considered a "preferred customer"

Bringing Activities or Processes In-house

Bringing outsourced activities back in-house is not an unusual process. The firm may decide that it has gone too far in outsourcing, that it can perform better internally, or that it wants to gain a competence in a given area. When that occurs, a process similar to the process for outsourcing would be undertaken, often referred to as **insourcing** or vertical reintegration. Although it seems that most companies today are focusing on outsourcing (buying goods and services from suppliers) rather than vertically integrating (making or providing their own goods and services), historically, firms and industries tend to shift back and forth between vertical integration and dis-integration.[22] This has happened in the industrial construction industry in the United Kingdom, and to some extent globally. Industrial construction began as a very vertically integrated activity, and then became dis-integrated over time as many specialized firms provided expertise in outsourced services. As complexity grew, construction firms had difficulty in effectively coordinating the many different activities of various outsourced parties, especially between design and construction. This created a new opportunity for a full-service-oriented construction business, drawing on a fresh combination of core competencies, providing "one-stop" shopping and total solutions.[23] This is illustrated in Figure 9.5, as organizations may move from a niche provider to a total solutions integrator. Thus, the outsourcing decision is not permanent or irreversible, although it may be expensive to change. As the dynamics of the marketplace, competition, and even what is considered to be a valuable core competency change, the structure of the firm must be adapted.

CONCLUSION

Core competencies are an elusive and changing concept. Core competencies are often defined as a set of skills or attributes that distinguish the organization from its competitors in a way that is valuable to its customers. Core competencies include and are shaped by the organization's culture, as we saw in the cases of both Honda and Southwest Airlines. As companies choose to focus more and more on their core competencies or distinctive areas of value-added, they have a tendency to outsource more manufacturing, services, and business processes.

Analyzing outsourcing versus retaining an activity internally is often referred to as the "make-or-buy" decision. Today, the desire to achieve lower costs is one of the primary drivers of outsourcing. Other factors, such as the desire to focus on core activities, do come into play. A company analyzing potential activities for outsourcing must take care not to outsource areas of core competence. It must also focus on selecting the right suppliers, developing the right types of supplier relationships, and monitoring and correcting supplier performance. These activities may be very time-consuming and costly, reducing the potential benefits of outsourcing. Outsourcing decisions should be made with care because they can be difficult and expensive to reverse. Effective involvement in outsourcing analysis and management may require an additional skill set for buyers. It tends to require buyers to focus more on longer-term, more cooperative supplier relationships, and ongoing supplier management, as the supplier now plays a more significant role in the supply chain.

SUMMARY OF KEY POINTS

1. The concept of core competency requires the organization to develop a deep understanding of how its activities work together to add value in the supply chain. Activities that are integral to the organization's core competencies should not be outsourced.

2. Outsourcing has emerged as an important component of supply chain design. By having others in the supply chain perform activities that the firm is not as good at, the company can save money, improve operations, and focus on where it adds value in the supply chain.

3. Potential outsourcing decisions must always be analyzed from a strategic perspective, not only from the perspective of whether the organization will reduce its costs. Outsourcing can be a long-term, difficult-to-reverse decision.

4. Cross-functional teams should manage the outsourcing process. A high-level management oversight team focuses on strategic issues; an operational-level team focuses on cost and executional issues.

5. Whether you are outsourcing manufacturing, services, or business processes, there are three distinct phases to the outsourcing process:
   - Establish the mission; generate and screen ideas
   - Form a team and conduct an outsourcing analysis
   - Establish and manage the relationship

6. There are many potential risks associated with outsourcing that need to be identified and investigated both in the feasibility phase of outsourcing and during the make-or-buy analysis phase. To help identify the risks, organizations should conduct a total cost of ownership analysis on the outsourcing project, including a thorough sensitivity analysis.

7. Determining the right type of outsourcing arrangement and management oversight is critical to the success of the outsource relationship. Ongoing evaluation and feedback are important to keep the relationship on track, and stay in tune with the organization's changing needs.

8. Buyers involved in outsourcing need to develop a different skill set, directed more at managing the supplier and maintaining the relationship rather than contractual compliance. In some cases, reverse marketing the benefits of doing business to the supplier may be necessary.

9. Companies may decide to insource previously outsourced activities based on the dynamics of the market and their competitive strategy. The insource–outsource decision is a dynamic one, with many companies constantly changing and revisiting what they should do internally versus what they should outsource.

REVIEW EXERCISES

1. Define core competency. Describe the three tests of a core competency.

2. Using the example of Southwest Airlines, or another company you are very familiar with, describe in detail the elements that make up that organization's core competency.

3. Explain why outsourcing has become an important element of competitive strategy.

4. Explain what a sensitivity analysis is, and why an organization should conduct one when considering outsourcing.

5. Describe two operational and two strategic risks that might be associated with outsourcing.

6. Describe the four different types of outsourcing arrangements, and the distinguishing features of each.

7. Describe the three different ways of managing outsourced relationships.

8. Discuss the difference between a post-audit of an outsourced relationship and an ongoing evaluation.

9. Define reverse marketing. Discuss how it fits in with the outsourcing decision.

10. When might a firm decide to insource or vertically reintegrate? Identify an example and discuss the reasons behind the decision.

Case   *Outsourcing for the First Time*

Cindy Anderson has just been hired as an MBA graduate from The Ohio State University. Her new employer, Red Mountain Lab, is an independent testing service that serves the pharmaceutical companies and the FDA. Red Mountain's business is to test pharmaceuticals for purity, following strict Food and Drug Administration (FDA) guidelines. Red Mountain is at the beginning of a process to analyze all of its activities and better understand its value proposition. It is counting on Cindy to use the tools she gained in her MBA program to help them structure their analysis, ask the right questions, gather data, and make changes. Based on the outcome of this analysis, it may decide to undergo a massive reorganization that includes outsourcing many of its activities.

Right now, Red Mountain Labs does most of its work internally. Its pharmaceutical company customers have numerous independent labs they can send their products to for testing. The FDA regulates Red Mountain's labs. Thus, the results of Red Mountain's tests go to both the pharmaceutical company and the FDA. The accuracy of its tests is critical to the lives of patients who are given prescriptions. Yet there is a great deal of pressure to turn the tests around on a timely basis so that the drug lots can be released and go to market. Red Mountain labs has a solid customer base and has built its reputation upon:

- Fast turnaround of tests
- Accurate test results
- Specialty in testing all types of antibiotics
- Excellent computer interfaces with customers, allowing rapid access to data
- Good working relationships with the FDA

Red Mountain is not known for being a low-cost service; indeed, its prices are higher than many of its competitors. However, there is currently a great deal of pressure on the FDA by the pharmaceutical companies to certify more labs for independent testing. The pharmaceutical companies argue that this would bring testing prices down through greater competition. More importantly,

they argue that this would also speed the release of drug lots to the market. Faster testing would significantly reduce inventory levels and associated carrying cost of inventory, so the pharmaceutical companies could lower their prices to the industry.

CASE QUESTIONS

1. If you were Cindy, where would you begin? Outline the key steps and questions to be asked in this process.
2. Who (functions, levels) should Cindy enlist on the cross-functional team to investigate the possible reorganization and outsourcing?
3. What is Red Mountain's core competency?
4. Consider the following four potential outsourcing candidates. For each one, indicate
   - The potential risks to be considered
   - What type or types of outsourcing arrangements would be the best fit
   - What type of management oversight is best suited for each of the following situations:

   Option A: Outsourcing all standard lab supplies to a full-service supplier rather than using 20+ suppliers as is done today.

   Option B: Outsourcing the development and ongoing updates/maintenance of a software system to track the results of all tests for government analysis, and provide a data base for statistical analysis.

   Option C: Outsourcing some unique tests that customers request on average of 3 times a year in total.

   Option D: Outsourcing the payroll processing and management, including time cards; tracking vacation, sick days and holidays; issuing regular paychecks, bonuses, and all employee reimbursement.

ENDNOTES

1. Quinn, J. B. (2004). Managing outsourcing and intellect. Outsourcing Institute. www.outsourcing.com/content.asp?page=01b/articles/intelligence/quinn_interview.html&nonav=true.

2. Prahalad, C. K., & Hamel, G. (1990, May–June). The core competence of the corporation. *Harvard Business Review,* 79–90.

3. Richie, G. (2005). *Dynamic capabilities impacting logistics service competency and performance.* Unpublished doctoral dissertation, The University of Oklahoma.

4. Ibid. #2.

5. Useem, Jerry. (2005). America's most admired companies—2005. *Fortune,* money.cnn.com/magazines/fortune/fortune_archive/2005/03/07/8253419/index.htm, accessed February 6, 2006.

6. Porter, M. (1996, November–December). What is strategy? *Harvard Business Review,* 61–78.

7. Close, D. (2004, November). What's a 3PL? How does my firm decide if we need one? *Logistics Quarterly, 10*(4). www.lq.ca/issues/nov2004/articles/article01.html, accessed February 7, 2006.

8. Ashenbaum, B., Maltz, A., & Rabinovich, E. (2005). Studies of trends in third-party logistics usage: What can we conclude? *Transportation Journal, 45*(3). www.allbusiness.com/periodicals/article/519784–1.html, accessed February 6, 2006.

9. Parry, E. (2004). Gartner: Offshore outsourcing horse has "left the barn." searchcio.techtarget.com/qna/0,289202,sid19_gci913695,00.html. Baker, S., & Kripalani, M. (2004, March1). Software: Will outsourcing hurt America's supremacy? *BusinessWeek,* pp. 84–94.

10. Ibid. #9, Perry. McKinsey Global Institute. (2003). *Offshoring: Is it a win–win game?* San Francisco: MGI.

11. Corbett, M. (2005, March 21). "Trends to Watch 2005," © Michael F. Corbett & Associates, Ltd., All rights reserved, *Fortune,* S12.

12. Ibid. #9, Baker.

13. Ibid. #9, Perry.

14. Elliot, D., & Szczesny, J. (2006, January 30). My goal is to fight Toyota. . . . *Fortune,* 47.

15. Mattern, H. (2002, June 2). Honeywell seeks to cut costs. *The Arizona Republic,* D1.

16. Makintosh J. (2002, September 3), Ford warns staff over suppliers. FT.com site.

17. Ford Motor Company. 2004/2005 Sustainability Report. www.ford.com/en/company/about/sustainability/report/relSuppliers.htm, accessed February 7, 2006.

18. Fine, C. (1998). *Clockspeed.* Reading, MA: Perseus Books.

19. Leenders, M. R., & Blenkhorn, D. L. (1988). *Reverse marketing: The new buyer–supplier relationship.* New York: The Free Press. The concept of reverse marketing was coined in this book.

20. Linder, J. C., & Cantrell, S. (2002). BPO big bang: Turning theory into practice. San Francisco: Accenture and Montgomery Research.

21. Ibid.

22. Ibid. #18.

23. Cacciatori, H., & Jacobides, M. G. (2005). The dynamic limits of specialization: Vertical integration reconsidered. *Organization Studies, 26*(12), 1851–1883.

Chapter

10

Supply Chain Rationalization and Role Shifting

What is an optimal SC? Can I help my company manage complexity to elevate our SC's performance?

The Supply Chain Road Map

Designing the Global Supply Chain
- What Must Be Done to Compete and Win?
  - Who Should Do It?

How Do We Fit?

As-Is Supply Chain

Chapter 6: Environmental Scanning
- What are the competitive rules?
- What skills does the SC need?

Chapter 7: Supply Chain Mapping
- What are the SC dynamics?
- Is our company positioned for success?

Chapter 8: Strategic SC Costing
- What are the relevant costs?
- What are the cost trade-offs?

Chapter 9: Competencies & Outsourcing
- What are our valued competencies?
- What activities should be outsourced?

Chapter 10: Rationalization & Role Shifting
- **Where can we rationalize the chain?**
- **Where can we refine assigned roles?**

How Should We Fit?

To-Be Supply Chain

Based on the understanding developed during the SC design process, create the capabilities needed to…

1. Help our SC meet customers' real needs better than competing chains:
- Identify the **right** players for the SC
- Define the **right** relationships
- Assign the **right** roles & responsibilities
- Design the **right** structure & systems

2. Securely position the company as an indispensable member of the SC by
- Refining our customer value proposition
- Developing needed competencies
- Leveraging core technologies
- Establishing efficient processes
- Creating appropriate customer linkages

After reading this chapter, you will be able to:

1. Articulate the challenge of complexity in SC design. Explain the relevance of Jim Collins's quote, "'Stop doing' lists are more important than 'to do' lists."
2. Identify and discuss the sources of SC complexity.
3. Define SC rationalization, identify the key areas of the supply chain that must be rationalized, and discuss supply-base optimization as an example of the rationalization process.
4. Define role shifting, discussing its benefits and threats. Explain how role shifting improves the competitiveness of an individual company and the entire supply chain.

Opening Story: Olympus's Complexity Challenge

Doug had left the office early on a beautiful Friday afternoon. It was Charlene's birthday, and he wanted to surprise her. After all, the task force had been making great progress and Charlene's encouragement had been invaluable. An environmental scan had been performed. Maps depicting Olympus's primary supply chains were almost complete. Also well underway was the costing of key activities and relationships. Insight created by these efforts invigorated the task force. Opportunities to leverage Olympus's competencies to enhance productivity and service were being defined. This progress led Doug to feel that the task force could quickly establish clear, actionable priorities regarding Olympus's future SC strategy. But, dissension during the task force's meeting earlier in the morning had dampened Doug's optimism. The weekend didn't look quite so tranquil anymore and Doug no longer felt like celebrating.

Doug's quandary emerged shortly after the task force meeting began. Commending the team for its excellent work, Doug had introduced the agenda, saying, "Now that our position in the supply chain is coming into focus, its time to design our ideal "to-be" chain. I've written 4 questions on the board—they should look familiar. After all, we've been working to answer them for the past 6 months! Each is important, but the first two lead to the third and most important question. We need to identify our economic engine and define our unique SC role. Then we can address the 'how to' questions."

1. What needs to be done?
2. Who needs to do it?
3. What will be Olympus's distinctive role?
4. How do we get there?

Diane was the first to speak, saying, "We have great brands! Our snacks portfolio makes customers salivate! The competition can't match our brand recognition. But, we can't consistently get the right product on our customers' shelves. And they can't sell product they don't have. We are also too reliant on past reputation. We haven't brought a 'hit' new product to market in over a year. As a result, customers like Goliath are threatening to allocate us less shelf space. You all know that Goliath is broadening its private-label offerings. It's just a matter of time before Goliath introduces private-label products that compete with ours. To secure our position as a preferred supplier in our customers' chains, we need to address these issues."

"You're right Diane," Vijay replied. "We are too reliant on line extensions. We spend a ton of money on me-too products and new package sizes instead of truly new products. Recent introductions haven't created much customer buzz, but they have created a real burden for operations. Multiply the number of SKUs we make by the variety of promotions you run, and our production forecasts are destined to be off. Factor in changeover and run times and it's next to impossible to match production to actual demand."

"You make an excellent point, Vijay," interjected Susan. "SKU proliferation has created a nightmare for us in sourcing. Every product has a unique, often complex formulation, requiring both greater commodity expertise and a larger supply base. Decisions made in marketing make our job more difficult. We often wonder what we gain by offering all these line extensions. It seems that we just cannibalize our own sales. A friend at P&G told me that they've reached the point that their product offerings are confusing customers. They performed a study that involved giving customers a sample product and asking them to find it in the store. Only about half of the customers could. Too many SKUs not only create complexity and cost but they also confuse customers."

"Let me piggyback on that thought," added David. "We just met with McKinsey. They analyzed our global operating network and concluded that we can't compete without it. However, they suggested that we are wasting close to $100 million every year because of the complexity involved in doing business worldwide. We have created a tangled and expensive web of redundant and sometimes conflicting logistical operations."

Frustrated by her colleagues' comments, Diane reacted, "Your points are valid. Becoming a great company is a complex and complicated business. And that's what we are striving for in marketing. Keeping all of our customers happy isn't easy. Each has specific wants and needs. That's why we have so many SKUs and why we need so many product formulations. And each staging point is essential to our rapid customer response program. Complexity is just a fact of life. You're going to have to deal with it."

Having quietly followed the debate, Joel mused, "Let me see if I understand. Our SC leverage comes from our brand reputation, which is built on a former ability to create exciting products. Diane, I hear you saying that it's the end customer that pulls us into the supply chain. However, the rest of you seem to be saying that we just aren't that good at bringing tantalizing products to market anymore. It also seems that some of our customers find it a hassle to work with us—they don't see us as a reliable partner. Too many SKUs, complex product formulations, an unwieldy supply base, a tangled operating network, and other sources of complexity hinder our service and increase our costs. More importantly, the confusion created by the complexity may be hiding our economic engine and diluting our most important competencies."

Doug had chosen that moment to refocus the discussion, saying, "Thanks Joel, that is an excellent summary. We've all been frustrated from time to time by the complexities of our business, and we've lived with them until now. Complexity is more than a nuisance; it appears to be a real enemy we can no longer afford to live with. We need to clear the clutter to define and renew our source of market advantage. The clutter appears to be everywhere. So, where do you suggest we start?"

At Charlene's Office

"Happy birthday," Doug said as he stepped into Charlene's office. "I've come to take you away from this rat race. How does a weekend of seclusion at our favorite hideaway sound?" Hesitating, Doug added, "A new challenge surfaced this morning. As we drive to the lodge, could you share some of the things your best customers do to mitigate the adverse effects of SC complexity? I'd appreciate your insight."

"Well," Charlene paused for a moment, " . . . I suppose, but only on the drive. After all, it is my birthday."

Consider As You Read:

1. Is all complexity bad? Why or why not? What are the costs of complexity up and down the chain?
2. What are the sources of complexity? Why do so many managers make the decision to "just live with it"?
3. What best practices might Charlene share with Doug regarding how to deal with the challenge of complexity?

"Stop doing" lists are more important than "to do" lists.

—JIM COLLINS[1]

THE CHALLENGE OF COMPLEXITY

When Chrysler decided to make SCM a key strategic initiative in the 1990s, one of the early tasks was to create a simple map showing the number of participants at each level of the chain back to third-tier suppliers. Although only a rough estimate, the map revealed that Chrysler managed 1,500 first-tier direct materials suppliers and depended on the performance of 50,000 second-tier and 250,000 third-tier suppliers (see Figure 10.1). Managers at Chrysler quickly realized that with its vast and complex supply base, managing the value creation process from "suppliers' supplier to customers' customer" was an almost impossible task.

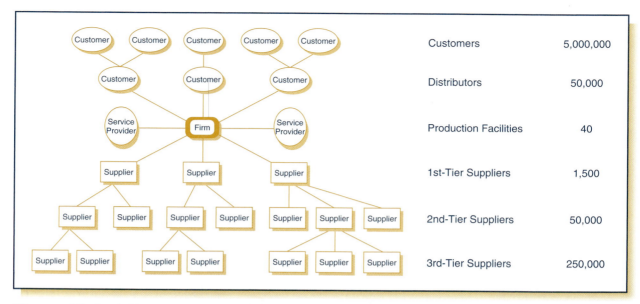

Customers	5,000,000
Distributors	50,000
Production Facilities	40
1st-Tier Suppliers	1,500
2nd-Tier Suppliers	50,000
3rd-Tier Suppliers	250,000

Figure 10.1 A Simple Depiction of Chrysler's Complex Supply Chain

To reduce the complexity and costs associated with its supply base, Chrysler began a 2-stage rationalization program. That is, Chrysler undertook the analysis necessary to make sense of its existing supply operations so that it could eliminate unnecessary or wasteful activities. In a sense, managers at Chrysler took a close look at how and why things were done so that they could create their "stop doing" lists. The motivating force for this supply-base rationalization: Once "stop doing" lists are created and followed, more time would be available to do really well those things that were on the "to do" lists.

The first step was to identify and eliminate redundant suppliers. This required a careful analysis of what was being sourced from every supplier. The creation of a supply management database is critical to this analysis. For example, like other companies who have done this, Chrysler found that it was sourcing a variety of parts that were technically distinct, but that performed the same basic purpose. Often these parts were sourced from different suppliers. Because the performance specifications for the different parts were only minimally different, Chrysler could standardize the parts, select the one or two best suppliers, and aggregate its buy to get a lower cost. This analysis resulted in both fewer SKUs and fewer but higher-performing suppliers.

The second step was to classify remaining suppliers on the basis of importance. As the rationalization process progressed, Chrysler developed the understanding and freed up the resources needed to build more collaborative relationships with its most important suppliers. Suppliers were integrated into Chrysler's new product development process, helping Chrysler reduce its concept-to-market time to a competitive 24 months. Chrysler's reputation for having the best supplier relations among the big three U.S. automakers made it an attractive partner for the Daimler Corporation.

One of the most interesting stories that emerged during Chrysler's transformation involved kitty litter.[2] With more time to focus on key SC relationships, managers at Chrysler began to look closely at who did what to support Chrysler's most important product lines. Starting with the Jeep Grand Cherokee, one of Chrysler's most popular and profitable vehicles, managers examined the production of Jeep's V-8 engines. A small but critical component—a roller-lifter valve—became the focus of analysis. Eaton Corporation, a global automotive supplier, precision-machined these valves from raw metal castings acquired from a small second-tier supplier located near Eaton's facility. The casting process required the use of clay with a unique chemical composition. However, the clay producer had consistently lost money on the sale of casting clay. Without informing the other members of the supply chain, the owner of the third-tier clay supplier had decided to exit the unprofitable casting clay business to refocus his company on making kitty litter. Imagine the consequences. Chrysler was fortunate to discover this pending strategic reallocation of resources at a third-tier supplier before the decision shut down one of Chrysler's most vital production lines. Unfortunately, many potentially detrimental decisions go undiscovered, hidden by SC complexity.

The fact is that complexity creates confusion, increases costs, and can lead to counterproductive decisions and diminished competitiveness. However, not all complexity is bad—some complexity may be absolutely necessary. Would you shop at a grocery store that carried only 20 items? The grocer would have a relatively simple supply chain to manage, but its value proposition would almost certainly fail to meet your needs. Sometimes, one additional SKU or another supplier or a distinctive distribution channel is needed to provide the value that customers demand. As you can see, added complexity is often a necessity. The key is to assure that the added costs associated with the complexity don't outweigh the value created.

Thus, this chapter is placed at the end of our discussion of SC design principles and practices. Until the competitive rules are identified, SC dynamics understood, costs defined, and competencies determined, SC managers do not have the knowledge needed to tell needed complexity from counterproductive complexity. Moreover, until the essential first steps of SC design are well underway, managers are not likely to have the time or the focus needed to tame the challenges of SC complexity. However, with those tools in hand, you are ready to tackle the chaos of complexity, making sense of it, and managing it as part of the ongoing SC design process.

SOURCES OF COMPLEXITY

Where is complexity found? In SCM, complexity is everywhere. Think about it. The number of parts used to assemble a car makes automobile production a very complex process. Similarly, making sure that each of thousands of products sourced from hundreds of suppliers is on the shelf when customers want to buy them is a real problem for retail managers. Globalization has magnified the complexity challenge. The best supplier may be found halfway around the world, and customer needs are often as diverse as the countries in which they live.

Managing such complexity stretches thin the resources of even large, well-run companies. Consider IBM. In 2003, IBM operated 16 manufacturing plants in 10 countries, bought 2 billion parts from 33,000 suppliers, and sold 78,000 products available in 3 million possible variations. IBM's North American operations processed 1.7 million customer orders and maintained 6.5 million records, updating 350,000 every day.[3] Hidden among this complexity are both costs and opportunities. At IBM, the decision was made to take a closer look to see where costs could be removed and competitive opportunities exploited. Early efforts yielded tens of millions in cost savings and a leaner, more responsive IBM. IBM could better compete as a solutions provider on the

Table 10.1 The Pros and Cons of Centralized and Decentralized
Organizational Structures

CENTRALIZED STRUCTURE		DECENTRALIZED STRUCTURE	
PROS	CONS	PROS	CONS
Increases leverage	Increased bureaucracy	Knowledge of local needs	Reduces leverage
Reduces duplication	Reduced flexibility	Better local relationships	Leads to duplication
Facilitates standardization	Can lose touch with reality	Greater responsiveness	Is relatively inefficient
Enables specialization			
Greater control			

global competitive stage. As managers at IBM discovered, the key to managing
complexity is for SC managers to understand the sources and nature of complexity.
The following seven sources of complexity create the greatest headaches for today's
SC manager.

Organizational Structure

A company's organizational structure influences complexity. The real issue is
decision-making authority—is it centralized or decentralized? Centralization
leverages scale to reduce costs. Decentralization relies on local knowledge to build
relationships and promote rapid response. Table 10.1 compares the pros and cons
of both structures. The trend has been toward centralization. However, many
companies, especially multinationals and those that have grown through acquisitions, retain decentralized, often redundant, operations. Companies like General
Motors and Unilever have struggled for years to overcome the costly duplication
that arises from a decentralized structure.

At General Motors, decentralization dates back to the 1920s when the automaker
was formed by joining independent car companies including Britain's Vauxhall
Motors, Germany's Adam Opel, and Australia's Holden together into a single global
giant.[4] Although Alfred P. Sloan described the organizational structure as "decentralized operation and responsibilities, with centralized control," autonomous decision
making became the rule. Over time global fiefdoms emerged, creating redundant
operations and limiting the sharing of ideas and components across product lines.
GM's vice chairman Robert Lutz commented on the diseconomies of GM's structure,
saying, "GM's global product plan used to be four regional plans stapled together."
In Europe, each division ran its own engineering department, designing parts that
were not interchangeable across brands and making it hard to build multiple models
on the same production line. Independent sourcing operations limited GM's ability
to use its scale to reduce the cost of purchased parts. To reduce these complexity
costs, GM is reorganizing, taking power away from its regional groups. GM has
established a global design council in Detroit to drive parts standardization, making
it easier to use common parts on distinctive vehicles. GM is also centralizing sourcing operations, hoping to aggregate common buys and drive down unit costs.

Unilever has experienced similar frustration with its decentralized structure. By
the late 1990s, Unilever was buying 30 types of vanilla for its European ice cream,
and its Rexona deodorant had 48 unique formulations and was sold in 30 different

packages.[5] Each country manager insisted on complete autonomy, handling advertising and branding locally. Commenting on the challenge of getting the different units to work together, Simon Clift, marketing head for Unilever's personal-care division, said, "It was like herding cats. There were no strategic priorities at all." To reduce the duplication and establish strategic direction, in 1999, Unilever began a program called "Path to Growth." Over the next 5 years, Unilever eliminated hundreds of businesses, 1,200 brands, 145 factories, and 55,000 jobs. Though extensive, these changes failed to eliminate costly redundancies—a review in 2004 revealed that Unilever still had three times the number of marketing managers as needed. Unilever therefore launched a new program called "One Unilever" with the goal to create truly global brands and consolidate R&D and sourcing activities.

The quest to reduce unnecessary complexity by finding the right balance between local autonomy and central control is difficult and dynamic. Fierce global competition dictates a need for efficiency. But, distinct local needs must be acknowledged and met. To get the best of both worlds, companies are experimenting with a combination of four practices:

- Team-based structures like GM's global design council are increasingly used. These centralized steering committees can look for standardization opportunities, redundant or wasteful activities, and aggregation or best practice dissemination prospects. They act as review boards and clearinghouses for ideas and product/project plans.
- Policies are adopted to promote a center-led, decentralized organization. Both GM and Unilever now require that dispersed operations share data with a center decision team. After performing rationalization analysis, the center team assigns responsibilities for managing specific activities. Leverage opportunities are managed centrally; activities specific to dispersed operations are managed locally.
- Measurement systems must promote cooperation and support local autonomy and accountability. GM and Unilever struggle to get local managers to cede some of their perceived autonomy. Measures must balance accountability for collaboration with accountability for their local unit's performance. Measures must be clear and help managers feel that they still can make a valued contribution.
- Modern communication and database technologies are used to enable rationalization analysis. Today's information systems enable a more flexible blending of centralization and decentralization, making it possible for managers to proactively reduce the costs of structural complexity.

Value-Added Processes

By their nature, processes like new product development, production, and order fulfillment are complex. They involve a number of people from different functions working together. They consist of a large number of distinct activities. They employ a variety of capital equipment, and they typically design, make, or deliver a wide range of products. The number of "handoffs" involved makes it easy to drop the baton, driving satisfaction down and costs up. Recognizing this challenge, companies now expend vast resources to streamline their value-added processes. Even so, process complexity is a persistent problem. Examples abound:

- Unilever spent years redesigning its product development process only to find that its Knorr's soup innovation center in Germany was working on 900 new products—far too many projects to manage effectively.[6] The redesign had failed to establish policies and practices to standardize the new product approval process.

- An engineering process that promotes complex designs has impacted the quality of European cars. The BMW 7 Series has over 120 electric motors—38 just to adjust the seats. Everything from ambient humidity to the angle at which the wipers rest on the windshield is controlled by dozens of microprocessors.[7] The reliance on so many motors and microprocessors makes the 7 Series susceptible to defects.

Even Toyota, one of the world's leanest companies, has suffered recent quality problems as a result of process complexity. Toyota's ambitious goal to become the world's largest automaker by 2010 has forced it to expand worldwide operations at a pace that has strained its human and technological resources. According to J.D. Power's initial quality survey, Toyota's Camry dropped from America's highest-quality vehicle in 2000 to number 8 in 2004. To remedy the problem, Toyota launched a global campaign to simplify its famed production system.[8] The goal was to get back to the basics. How did Toyota approach the problem?

- Standardized work processes were reemphasized.
- A new emphasis on error proofing was initiated to reduce the number of decisions made by an hourly worker to two or fewer per car.
- A logistical parts-matching process was implemented to deliver the exact parts a worker needs for the car being assembled. The parts arrive at the workstation simultaneously with the car.

Under the new system, the worker actually makes zero decisions in picking parts. Such simplification makes it easy to assemble defect free up to 7 models on a single production line.

The Operating Network

Designing a company's operating network, which may include manufacturing facilities, distribution centers, and retail outlets, is a complex task. When discussing this task, industrial engineers often talk about network optimality. When they do so, they are really talking about using sophisticated mathematical models to design the SC network to minimize or maximize the targeted performance object—typically costs or service levels. Although achieving true optimality in a dynamic global marketplace is a great ideal, it is generally not an attainable long-term goal. Several factors reduce a company's ability to achieve true optimality.

- First, operating networks evolve over time, often rapidly. New facilities are added to an existing network as needs emerge. At Texas Instruments (TI), a global network analysis revealed that "network creep" had created a situation that required multiple touches and extensive backtracking among TI's geographically dispersed facilities to get product to customers. Network creep was costing TI tens of millions of dollars annually in non-value-added costs.
- Second, acquisitions complicate network design. Remember our earlier discussion of Nabisco. Facing stiff competition from Keebler, Nabisco evaluated its operating network. The analysis revealed that Nabisco operated too many DCs, driving its costs up. But, even as Nabisco began the tough process of deciding which facilities to shutter, it was acquired by Kraft. The problem suddenly changed to focus on how to integrate the two companies' networks.

- Third, macroeconomic changes also influence network design. For instance, the addition of 10 countries to the European Union in 2004 changed consumption patterns as well as production and distribution requirements for companies operating in Europe. Shifts in political stability can likewise change operating realities overnight.

These factors combine to create a world where few companies operate an ideal or optimal network.

Nonetheless, careful, and often complex, analysis can help a company achieve the goal of network design: maximum service at minimal cost. Experience shows that managers should begin by asking the following critical questions:

- How many facilities do we really need to achieve desired service levels?
- Where should they be located?
- What activities will be performed in each?
- How will the value-added activities be coordinated and controlled?

To answer these questions, many performance trade-offs must be considered. For example, adding an additional warehouse requires both an up-front facility investment as well as a commitment to day-to-day operating costs. These costs may or may not be justified by decreased transportation costs and/or increased revenues stimulated by better customer service. In real-world networks, these decisions become complicated in a hurry, requiring rigorous research and analysis to accurately weigh their costs and benefits.

For example, Caterpillar faced a serious analytical challenge when it introduced a new line of compact construction equipment a few years ago.[9] To meet its long-term revenue targets, Cat needed a new source of growth. Cat designed a new line of earth-moving equipment to meet the needs of homebuilders and landscapers—a demanding clientele that expects equipment to be available on very short notice. In fact, Cat estimated that 9 of 10 potential customers would buy the competitor's product if Cat's product were not available on the same day the customer wanted it. To make market entry more difficult, Ingersoll-Rand's Bobcat line of equipment was well entrenched in the marketplace with a 50 percent share. Moreover, the new product line would carry small profit margins for both Cat and its dealers. Thus, the dealers would be unwilling to carry large inventories without subsidies from Cat. The small margins also meant that distribution costs had to be minimized. Unprofitable revenue growth was unacceptable! Now for the challenge of managing complexity:

- The new line consisted of 15 models of 3 machines—a rubber-tracked excavator, a scaled-down front-wheel loader, and a skid-steer loader. The first two were to be made in England; the third, in North Carolina.
- Cat designed 102 different interchangeable attachments or work tools including different types of buckets, augers, brooms, pallet forks, and trenchers. Each of the attachments was designed to fit on the rival Bobcat, increasing sales opportunities, but decreasing Cat's ability to accurately forecast demand.
- The work tools are sourced from Cat's manufacturing plants and third parties in the United States, England, Finland, Hungary, and Mexico.
- The dealer network consisted of 207 dealers operating in 90 countries.

How did Cat determine the inventory levels and routing requirements for its new product line? It turned to a group of industrial engineers who used a mathematical network modeling approach called *infinitesimal perturbation analysis.* Cat supplied the basic facts such as factory lead times, transportation costs, the number of tools per truck, sales forecasts, and possible contingencies. When the analysis was done, Cat had target inventory levels and routing plans for all of its work tools. The tools would be routed from their place of manufacture through two DCs located in Illinois and Belgium. These DCs would reroute the tools based on demand levels to a designated group of Cat's Parts Distribution Centers, which would deliver them to dealers. Cat's Robert Briggs noted that the solution was not one that Cat would have come up with, but that it "gave us the highest response, lowest cost, and lowest inventory." Sophisticated optimization modeling can be a valuable tool in SC network design.

The Company's SKUs

Managing the number and type of individual items, known as SKUs, that a company must handle to meet customer needs creates headaches for SC managers. The challenge starts with the company's value proposition. Henry Ford limited SKU complexity by selling only black Model Ts. GM, however, won the market battle by opting for more complexity—it offered customers a variety of models in different colors. The same competitive battle was played out again 50 years later. This time, though, Honda and Toyota chose to minimize SKU complexity by offering a limited number of models available in only three exterior colors and interior fabrics. All other options (stereos, transmissions, etc.) were also limited. Minimizing SKUs helped Honda and Toyota achieve both productivity and quality advantages that helped them take share from GM and Ford.

A similar story can be told in the retail sector. Retailers must also choose between breadth complexity and depth complexity. With well over 100,000 SKUs, Wal-Mart sells everything from groceries to electronics to car batteries. It has vast breadth. However, in any given category, the customer can choose from only a small set of options—limited depth. Tiffany, by contrast, is a specialty jewelry retailer with a very limited variety of SKUs. Tiffany has minimal breadth. But if you are interested in the type of diamond jewelry, watches, or gifts that Tiffany sells, you will find a large variety in each category. Tiffany makes its money on product depth. Each business model imposes certain competitive requirements. A breadth retailer like Wal-Mart relies on inventory turns and efficient operations to make its profit in a low-margin business. A depth retailer like Tiffany depends on high service levels and distinctive products to earn high profit margins in a low inventory turn environment. Both must choose and manage their SKUs well to make money. Interestingly, both Wal-Mart and Tiffany achieve comparable returns on net assets. This is because they both know their customers and they both execute their SKU strategies well. Successful retailers must get three issues right: product category, category depth, and service levels. They can then achieve a viable return via a combination of inventory turns and profit margin.

It is very difficult to be both a breadth and depth retailer. Imagine how large a store would have to be to offer the combined breadth and depth found at Home Depot, PetSmart, Toys"R"Us, and Kroger. Such a store would not just intimidate consumers, but it would also violate most cities' building codes. Of course, such constraints do not exist in cyberspace. Recognizing this, Jeff Bezos chose the name of his company, Amazon.com, to symbolize breadth and depth. But, Amazon.com has discovered that even in cyberspace it is difficult to manage both breadth and depth complexity profitably.

Experience suggests that companies struggle most with breadth complexity. In the retail sector, for example, research has shown that despite continuous replenishment programs, modern information systems, and efficient logistics, retailers seldom achieve in-stock performance levels above 90 percent.[10] This is true for category killers, discounters, grocers, and catalogue retailers. The reality is that customers expect each item to be on the shelf 24/7/365. For this to happen, the retail manager must order the right product from the right supplier at the right time and in the right quantity. At the supplier's DC, the order must be picked, packed, and shipped (this assumes each item is in stock). Once at the retailer's DC, product is sorted and loaded on a semi destined for a specific retail store. Upon arrival, the truck must be unloaded and product must be placed on the shelf before existing inventories sell out. This process must be done for 25 to 150 thousand SKUs, depending on the retail format. Any mishap or delay anywhere along the way means that the product will be out of stock when a customer wants to buy it.

So, how are companies managing SKU complexity? Unfortunately, many aren't. The trend at all but the most disciplined companies is toward SKU proliferation, which can both (1) increase production and logistics costs dramatically and (2) confuse customers, as the P&G story from the opening case showed. We can, however, draw on the success of the disciplined few to identify the following approaches:

- Companies are more proactively managing the breadth versus depth decision. After P&G determined that the sheer number of SKU options it provided customers was costly and confusing, it began to seriously analyze the cost-to-value contribution of the various products in each of its product categories.
- Companies are taking a closer look at the total cost equation for their product portfolios. A few have begun using ABC costing to evaluate individual SKU profitability. Unprofitable SKUs are then eliminated.
- Companies are instituting policies specifically designed to put a halt to SKU proliferation. At one company, the SKU policy was simple—for every new product marketing wanted to bring to market, it had to identify one that would be eliminated from the product portfolio. Most companies that have similar policies allow for exceptions, but only with the approval of a senior management team that looks at the overall cost/revenue implications.
- Companies are implementing **postponement strategies**. Simply stated, companies postpone final manufacturing, assembly, packaging, labeling, or other value-added activities until a final customer order is received. Consider the case of managing the assortment of men's twill slacks sold by Lands' End. Table 10.2 shows that for twill slacks, over 57,000 distinct SKUs could exist. The huge number of SKUs results from the possible combinations of color, fabric type, size, and style. To make the number of SKUs more manageable, Lands' End orders unhemmed slacks, cutting them to length at its DC in Dodgeville, Wisconsin, once a firm order is received. By hemming and cuffing pants to order, Lands' End can reduce the total number of options for twill slacks to fewer than 3,000.
- Companies are making better use of supplier, manufacturing, and customer databases as well as the **data-mining** tools that help managers make sense of them. Let's return to the Lands' End example. Lands' End collects and analyzes vast amounts of customer behavior data. Looking at the sales profile enables Lands' End to offer certain sizes like big/tall in selected colors and waist sizes, further reducing the number of SKUs its SC partners must make and ship.

What do the SKU management approaches listed here have in common? They all rely on a careful analysis of the costs and benefits associated with adding or deleting individual SKUs to help managers establish policies to reduce the adverse effects of SKU proliferation.

Table 10.2 The Impact of Product Options on Total SKUs: Twill Slacks Example

PRODUCT CHARACTERISTIC	NUMBER OF OPTIONS
Color: Charcoal, field khaki, khaki, cognac, brown, olive, steel, navy, and black	9
Fabric: Blended 60% cotton/40% polyester or 100% cotton	2
Front: Pleated or plain	2
Rise: Long, regular, short, big/regular, and big/tall	5
Waist Size: 30, 31, 32, 33, 34, 35, 36, 37, 38, 40, 42, 44, 46, 48, 50, 52 inches	16
Length: 27–38 inches	10
Bottom: Cuffed or plain	2
Total SKUs	$9 \times 2 \times 2 \times 5 \times 16 \times 10 \times 2$ $= 57{,}600$
Simplified SKUs via Postponement	$9 \times 2 \times 2 \times 5 \times 16 \times 1 \times 1$ $= 2{,}880$
Simplified SKUs via Data Mining	1,300

The Supply Base

The sourcing manager's mandate is to develop reliable sources of supply that can deliver high-quality, low-cost materials and services on time every time. Reliable suppliers must be selected for every item purchased. To ensure against supply disruptions and to create leverage to drive costs down, most companies have sourced the same item from multiple suppliers. As a result, the typical company sources from hundreds, if not thousands, of suppliers. Success requires that each transaction be managed efficiently. The right relationship must also be established with each supplier. Indeed, many SC initiatives rely on the collaboration that comes only from long-term, partnership-style relationships. Building these close, collaborative relationships is almost impossible when scarce resources are consumed managing a large and unwieldy supply base.

The desire to more strategically manage the supply base has led companies to launch a supplier reduction initiative. One of the early success stories comes from Xerox. Losing market share to rival Canon, Xerox realized it needed to change the nature of its supply relationships. Xerox consolidated purchase requirements on a global basis, inviting its best suppliers to participate in partnership relationships. Redundant suppliers were eliminated. Xerox slashed its global supply base from about 5,000 suppliers to just over 400. Aggregating purchases led to not just lower unit prices but simplified purchasing also reduced overhead rates from 9 percent of total materials cost to about 3 percent.[11]

Supply-base rationalization has been popular since the 1980s. Because companies have more experience with managing supply-base complexity than with the other complexity areas discussed here, we use supply-base rationalization as the model for a detailed discussion of SC rationalization strategies in the next section.

The Customer Base

The customer base at many companies is even more numerous and complex than the supply base. Moreover, managing customer relations can be very tricky. Not only do customer expectations differ but customers also know who puts the money into the supply chain. And they do not hesitate to threaten to take their money elsewhere—often to lower-cost "global" suppliers. They use this leverage to demand constantly higher levels of customized performance, but they are seldom willing to pay more for the increased service. Keeping customers happy is a tough proposition.

The asymmetrical power relationship between suppliers and customers in SC relationships makes the discussion of customer base rationalization a sensitive topic. That is, customers don't like to be evaluated the same way that they evaluate their suppliers. Historically, they haven't been. After all, customers typically possess the channel power, not the suppliers. Moreover, most companies are under constant pressure to profitably grow sales and increase market share. This fact makes it hard to talk about walking away from some customers' business. This is particularly true at companies where the sales force works on commission. Experience also shows many companies forget about the profit dimension of downstream relationships as they pursue the easier-to-measure quest for sales growth. Nonetheless, more companies are assessing the quality of customer relationships and how they fit with the companies' long-term competitive strategy. How are they doing this? Several practices have become common:

- ABC classification is being applied to customers with the same rigor they use the tool to evaluate suppliers. The goal is to classify customers based on sales volume and profitability. As was discussed in Chapter 2, companies use ABC classification to establish tailored service programs to meet critical customers' needs.
- Customer relationship management (CRM) software is also being used to segment customers. One midwest grocer used CRM software to identify its best customers. Consumption habits were analyzed and customer profiles developed. The grocer then mailed tailored coupons directly to key customers, offering them discounts on the products they typically bought. The grocer also stopped putting out a weekly advertising circular. The result: Sales and profits soared as the key customers increased their purchases. Cherry-picking behavior by unprofitable customers also decreased. CRM software can help manage customer complexity; however, CRM software cannot predict the future and it does not provide insight into why some customers are not very profitable—they may be the company's dissatisfied customers.
- More sophisticated costing techniques are being used to evaluate both customers and specific customer-related initiatives. Foremost among these costing techniques is ABC costing. Many companies have implemented ABC costing programs and discovered that their so-called best customers were actually unprofitable. Some customers are so demanding that the cost to meet their demands exceeds the revenue they generate. Total costing techniques can likewise be used to evaluate specific programs.

The Logistics System

SC managers often describe their logistics system as a "tangled web."[12] The number of options among transportation modes, carriers, and routes is huge. The geographic dispersion of suppliers, production facilities, warehouses, and customers magnifies the complexity. Add in variations in product demand, customer-specified delivery time windows, expensive backtracking, and empty backhauls and you can see that optimizing the logistics system becomes a combinatorial nightmare. You might ask, "Why is optimizing the logistics system so important?" The answer is simple: Poor logistics hampers service and destroys profitability. A missed time window diminishes trust and can lead to a charge back. Likewise, shipping in less than truckload quantities is expensive. Sam's Club determined that LTL shipments cost 250 percent more than full truckloads. Emergency expediting via airfreight costs a whopping 1,040 percent more than TL shipments. To mitigate the costs of logistical complexity, companies have adopted the following practices:

- *Advanced technology.* Numerous software providers including SAP, I2, and Manuguistics offer logistical planning packages to assist in carrier selection, route planning, and vehicle loading. These software programs rely on sophisticated mathematical optimization models to identify optimal logistical solutions. Similarly, many companies are adopting satellite technology and radio frequency tagging to track equipment and product as it moves from origin to destination. This technology enables the logistics manager to know where a container is in route or where a truck has been dropped at the DC.

- *Outsourcing.* Companies like GM and Sony have turned to third-party logistics experts because they no longer want to expend scarce resources trying to manage key parts of their complex logistics systems. Schneider National Logistics took on the challenge of redesigning and managing GM's spare parts distribution system. UPS has built a network of DCs around the world to provide complete distribution services for customers. UPS repairs faulty Sony laptops. When a laptop fails, UPS picks it up and flies it to Louisville, where the problem is diagnosed and the laptop is either fixed or replaced. The now-functioning laptop is returned the next day.[13]

- *Insourcing.* Insourcing is really a specialized form of outsourcing. It refers to the practice of bringing in a third-party service provider to work on-site at a company's manufacturing or distribution facility. Carrier's air conditioner assembly operation in Monterrey, Mexico, exemplifies 3PL insourcing. As you walk from the assembly lines to the adjoining warehouse, you notice that the employees' uniforms are slightly different. That is because they work for DHL. Their job is to manage incoming and outgoing shipments. In effect, they manage large portions of Carrier's warehouse as well as much of Carrier's transportation requirements. DHL, FedEx, and UPS are insourcing leaders.

- *Innovative practices.* The use of milk runs, consolidation centers, and an SC partner's fleet can improve logistical efficiency. Ford designs milk-run routes to make multiple stops at suppliers to pick up parts until a full truckload quantity is achieved. Sam's Club established consolidation centers so that LTL shipments can be consolidated regionally into TL quantities for long-haul movements. Nabisco uses available space on its customers' trucks to deliver product to other customers.

Throughout the previous pages, the primary sources of SC complexity have been identified, the nature of each kind of complexity has been discussed, and leading companies' approaches to dealing with the complexity have been highlighted. Proactive SC managers put in place formal SC rationalization programs to make sure that the their company strategically manages complexity on an ongoing basis.

SC Rationalization: The Case of Supply-Base Optimization

One approach to managing complexity is to rationalize the supply chain. **Supply chain rationalization** is the process of systematically evaluating the company's operating network, suppliers, customers, and product offerings to find and eliminate inefficiencies and redundancies. Rationalization efforts increase SC visibility, helping managers understand the consequences of changes in SC structure. Such changes may involve the number and location of facilities, transportation strategies, inventory deployment, external relationships, and product mix. While most rationalization initiatives focus on simplifying the supply chain, the real goal is to more efficiently allocate scarce resources to a company's most profitable and strategically important SC activities and relationships.

According to a Cap Gemini study, most companies have not seriously begun to rationalize their supply chains.[14] Many companies are just beginning the process of identifying their key suppliers, customers, or products. The study reported that 44 percent of companies have rationalized their supply base, 38 percent have performed a customer profitability analysis, and 28 percent have streamlined product offerings. One reason relatively few companies have undertaken SC rationalization is that rationalization is best done after the supply chain is mapped, customer needs defined, core competencies identified, and costing systems put in place. The understanding created by these efforts makes it possible to (1) differentiate between strategic and redundant activities and (2) accurately assess trade-offs among different SC configurations. Rationalization should be considered as part of the broader strategic SC design process.

To exemplify the rationalization process, the following discussion looks at how companies are optimizing the supply base.

How Many Suppliers Do You Need?

The objective of supply-base optimization is to determine how many and which suppliers a company should buy from.[15] The optimization process should also help managers determine what type of relationship to establish with each supplier. Figure 10.2 depicts the choice—a decision that runs from using many suppliers for a given part to buying from a single source. In today's decision-making environment, the use of many suppliers implies arm's-length, perhaps adversarial, relationships. The choice of the single-sourcing model suggests a close, collaborative relationship. An optimal supply strategy would likely employ a range of relationships running from one end of the continuum to the other—each designed for the commodity strategy being pursued. The rationale for operating at the continuum's two end points is discussed next.

The Case for Multiple Suppliers

For many years, the standard modus operandi was to use multiple suppliers for most purchased inputs. The goal was to pit suppliers against one another. Managers believed that the resulting competition would drive prices down and ensure better service. This logic drives the current popularity of on-line bidding scenarios, which are also known as *reverse auctions*. On-line bidding events identify potential qualified suppliers from around the world and encourage them to bid for a contract in real time. Because the suppliers can see one another's bids and a time limit is in place, intense competition drives prices lower. Savings of 10 to 30 percent have been

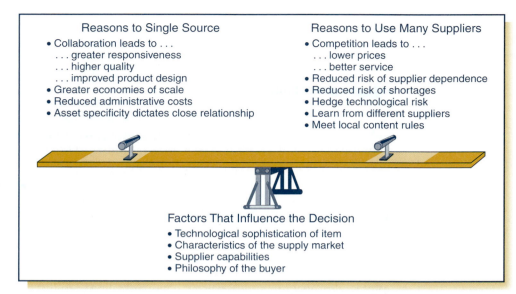

Figure 10.2 The Choice Between Single-Source and Many Suppliers

achieved through competitive on-line bidding events. The power of competition in supply relationships is real.

Companies use multiple suppliers for several other reasons. Few managers are willing to incur the risk inherent in relying on a single supplier, especially for important items. They want to avoid being dependent on any single supplier. A fire at an Aisin production plant highlighted the risks of dependence. The fire at Aisin, a sole-source supplier of brake parts for Toyota, destroyed all of the equipment needed to produce a critical component. Using a JIT system, Toyota maintained only 4 hours of inventory of the part. Production on all of Toyota's production lines quickly came to a halt, costing Toyota thousands of dollars per minute.[16]

The use of multiple suppliers also reduces the risk and potential costs of a supply shortage. The risk of supply disruption is best mitigated via the use of geographically dispersed suppliers. For example, a drought, earthquake, or other natural disaster can greatly reduce the availability of a product. A few years ago, a series of major earthquakes shook Taiwan, disrupting semiconductor production. The resulting shortage of semiconductors quickly crimped the production of laptops and other high-tech consumer products among those companies that sourced their chips strictly from Taiwan.

Using multiple suppliers can also help a company hedge technological risk. That is, when a technology is rapidly evolving or when two technologies are vying for market dominance, it is often wise to source from multiple suppliers. For example, Hewlett-Packard co-funded with Intel the development of the 64-bit Itanium chip. Even so, H-P made the decision to buy AMD's Opteron chip, which could handle both 32- and 64-bit applications.[17] Likewise, some companies adopt a multiple-sourcing strategy as part of their scanning efforts—they want to learn from different suppliers. Finally, multiple suppliers are often used to support global operations, especially when domestic content regulations are in place.

The Case for Single Sourcing

The most important reason for single sourcing is to attain the benefits of collaboration. By eliminating redundant suppliers, purchasing managers have more time and resources to focus on developing closer, long-term relationships with preferred suppliers. Working more closely with suppliers—sharing information and resources with them—allows suppliers to better plan the use of their own resources. Better scheduling reduces supplier costs and improves their ability to respond to customer requests. The certainty of future sales that comes with a long-term contract also promotes supplier investments in process capabilities. Finally, joint problem-solving and supplier development initiatives improve supplier quality and reduce inspection costs. The motive for helping suppliers improve their own capabilities is not altruism. Rather, as Honda's Dave Nelson often said, "There are plenty of benefits on both sides."

Other reasons for sourcing from a single supplier include (1) the opportunity to aggregate purchases, (2) the opportunity to reduce administrative and transaction costs, and (3) the costs of specific assets. First, as the number of suppliers for a part is reduced, the quantity sourced from remaining suppliers goes up. Scale economies can be captured. Second, as previously noted in the Xerox example, working with fewer suppliers reduces administrative costs. Long-term contracts also enable the use of blanket orders, which minimizes transaction costs. Third, many types of production require capital investments in specific tooling such as dies, jigs, and molds. Because these assets are unique or specific to the buying company, the buyer often provides them. Sourcing from fewer suppliers means less investment in these assets.

It is important to note that very few companies actually single source large percentages of their needs. Even Honda, an advocate of close, collaborative supplier relationships, tends to dual source components. For example, it might source the right headlamps from one supplier and left headlamps from another. If something happens at one of the suppliers, a good working relationship and sound production capabilities are already in place at the other. This approach enables Honda to get most of the benefits of sole sourcing without incurring the risks of dependence.

Factors That Influence the Decision

Several factors influence the decision of whether to source from many or few suppliers. Most of these factors focus on the context of the buying situation. To guide the decision, you might ask, "How technologically complex is the item being purchased?" Unique or sophisticated products like car engines are usually sourced from a small number of suppliers. Commodities like wheat or paper clips can easily be sourced from multiple suppliers. Another relevant question is, "How many qualified suppliers are there?" AMD and Intel are the only major suppliers of computer microprocessors. By contrast, many injection-molding suppliers are available. Specific supplier capabilities may also influence the decision. For example, some injection molders have reputations for being superior innovators or for producing the finest quality. If such skills are needed, the number of supply options can be greatly reduced. Finally, the philosophy of the buying company plays a huge role in determining how many suppliers a company needs. Honda has always believed that building quality relationships with a smaller number of suppliers is a sound long-term investment.[18] GM and Ford have only recently begun to seriously shift their thinking toward more collaborative supply relationships.

The Supply-Base Optimization Process

Supply-base optimization is part of an overall sourcing strategy. Remember, the goal is to (1) determine how many suppliers a company needs, (2) identify the right suppliers, and (3) establish the right relationship with them. Achieving this goal requires that detailed analysis be performed at the commodity level. As noted earlier, the pacesetters in supply-base management, companies like Honda and Toyota, typically single

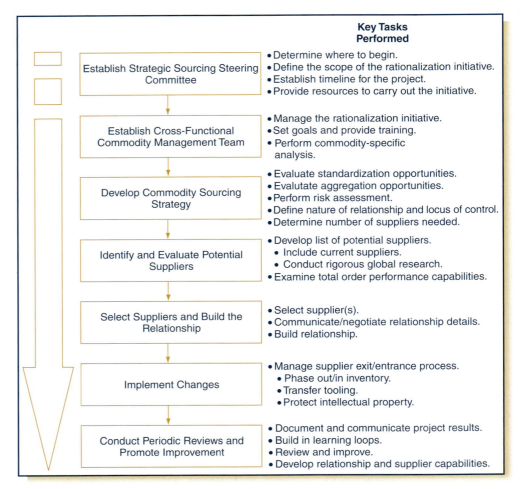

Figure 10.3 The Supply-Base Optimization Process

source at the part-number level but dual source at the commodity level. This hybrid approach drives competition in the supply base and establishes a relationship with a backup supplier should some unexpected event like a fire or strike occur. At the same time, this practice increases the volumes placed with individual suppliers, providing motivation for more collaborative relationships. To determine the right number of suppliers for each commodity, a systematic supply-base optimization process should be used. Figure 10.3 traces the basic steps in such a process.

Establish Strategic Sourcing Steering Committee

The role of the steering committee is to evaluate all strategic sourcing initiatives, deciding which ones to pursue in support of the overall corporate strategy. If the steering committee decides to pursue an optimization initiative, four critical decisions need to be made:

1. Where should the effort begin?
2. How extensive should the effort be?
3. How long should the initiative last?
4. What resources are needed to ensure success?

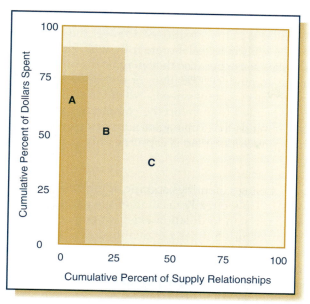

Figure 10.4 "ABC" Supplier Classification using the Pareto Principle

Segmenting the spend can provide the insight needed to make these decisions.

Segmentation provides a profile of purchasing behavior. It helps identify key commodities and vital supplier relationships. Most companies use the Pareto principle to create an "ABC" classification of commodities or suppliers. Such a classification is based on dollars spent (see Figure 10.4). As a rule, 10 to 20 percent of the commodities (suppliers) represent 80 percent of the total spend. These commodities deserve the greatest managerial attention. Other segmentation approaches based on risk or position in the product life cycle should also be used. For example, one semiconductor company performed a traditional ABC classification. The low-volume "C" parts were grouped and bid out as a long-term, blanket contract. A subsequent analysis based on life cycle revealed that many of these "C" items represented emerging technologies. That is, they were in the growth stage of the life cycle. Over time, the volumes would grow dramatically as the technologies became more widely used. The original classification missed this vital implication.[19] Once the appropriate segmentation is performed, managers will have a good feel for where the money is spent, how many suppliers it buys from, and what strategic issues need to be considered. This insight will help them identify where the greatest optimization benefit lies and how to proceed to obtain the benefits.

Establish Commodity Management Team

The creation of a sourcing strategy is an organizational capability. If the company is not already using cross-functional commodity teams to manage its spend, it should establish them to guide the supply-base optimization process. The team's role is to set goals and provide the training needed to perform the specific commodity analysis. The team can then develop and implement a competitive commodity sourcing strategy.

Commodity teams should include members from sourcing, manufacturing, engineering, finance, and perhaps marketing. Obtaining input and buy-in from these stakeholders is vital early in the optimization process, especially if a change in suppliers is anticipated as the outcome. The greater the desired collaboration with potential suppliers, the more important broad-based participation is. For example, engineering may have established specifications to favor a specific supplier.

Involving engineering in the analysis may help key decision makers realize that another supplier is better positioned to meet the company's needs. Only then will engineering be willing to collaborate fully with the new supplier. Besides, involving engineers makes sense because they may be the only managers who understand key issues such as tooling, certification, or emerging technology that influences a supplier's fit with the company's needs. All of the skills represented by the diverse team members are needed to develop the commodity sourcing strategy. Equally important, the fact remains that "managers support what they help create." The value of a commodity optimization plan is captured only as it is implemented.

Develop Commodity Sourcing Strategy

The sourcing strategy identifies specific optimization opportunities. A good starting point is to ask, "Do we really need all of the parts we are currently buying?" Many opportunities for standardization exist. At one company, the implementation of a common manufacturing database identified almost 2 dozen interchangeable fasteners that had been designed to perform a single function. At General Motors, a decision was made to reduce the types of radios used in its cars from 270 to only 50.[20] At John Deere, display boards were put up to show all of the different versions of similar components like tractor headlamps. Managers quickly realized that redundant parts were creating unnecessary supplier management costs. Standardizing parts offers the opportunity to shrink the supply base.

Another relevant question is, "Are there any aggregation opportunities?" Decentralized operations, whether by geography or business unit, often make independent sourcing decisions. As a result, the same commodity may be purchased from multiple suppliers. Not only are volumes and negotiating leverage decreased but opportunities to collaborate in a meaningful way may also be marginalized as each buying group "reinvents the wheel." By creating a spend profile and matching it to company needs, opportunities to aggregate volumes with global or regional suppliers may be found. Another type of aggregation opportunity involves the move from buying individual parts to the purchase of complete modules. General Motors now buys entire mirror and window trim modules from Donnelly. Donnelly then manages all of the suppliers required to build complete mirror modules. This approach, which is often called **tiering**, can dramatically reduce the number of supply relationships a company must manage. Tiering enabled Volkswagen to reduce the number of direct suppliers at its Resende, Brazil, truck operation to only seven. Of course, these remaining relationships merit much more careful and creative management.

Managers should also ask, "What are the risks involved with changing the supply base?" One company identified five types of risk and created a risk profile that portrayed these risks in terms of likelihood and impact. Such information helps determine how many suppliers are needed to safely meet a company's sourcing requirements. It can also be used in the supplier selection decision.

As these, and other questions, are answered, a clearer picture of the number of suppliers needed for a specific commodity comes into view. The team also knows what type of buyer/supplier relationship should be established. Finally, managers develop a strong sense of whether a centralized or decentralized decision-making structure should be used. The team is now ready to identify, evaluate, and select the suppliers that will help the company achieve its competitive goals.

Identify and Evaluate Potential Suppliers

As companies pursue a supplier optimization program, they often focus exclusively on their existing supply base. This is a mistake. Certainly, the list of potential suppliers should include current suppliers that are performing to expectations. However, the optimization effort gives the commodity team a chance to scan the global marketplace for previously unidentified, but outstanding, suppliers. Rigorous global research provides a secondary benefit—the opportunity to benchmark world-class performance in a supply industry. A commodity team from General Motors scoured the world to identify potential die suppliers. At the end of its search, the team sourced dies from two suppliers. One was a German manufacturer that GM had worked with for years; the other was a previously unknown Korean supplier. Managers were surprised to find that a high-quality auto supply base had come into existence in Korea. A final place to look for potential supply capabilities is in-house. Many companies possess internally the skills needed to make parts that they are currently buying. Make–buy analysis should be considered as part of the supplier identification and evaluation process.

To compile a valid list of potential suppliers, the commodity team must examine the performance capabilities of the suppliers. Too often, the focus is on purchase price. The better approach is to evaluate suppliers on the basis of total order performance criteria including cost, quality, delivery, responsiveness, and innovation. Trade-offs almost always exist, especially when comparing suppliers from different geographic regions. A low-price supplier in a developing country may actually be the high-cost option when global transportation costs are added in. Quality and delivery considerations may point to an entirely different option.

Select Suppliers and Build the Relationships

Once the list of potential suppliers is compiled, detailed performance data is gathered. Many companies use an iterative selection process (see Figure 10.5). Early efforts focus on low-cost methods such as sending out requests for a proposal (RFPs). As the list is narrowed down, more expensive but comprehensive data gathering occurs via in-depth interviews, supplier audits, and plant visits. A formal comparison of capabilities using a weighted-factor model can make trade-offs transparent and help managers take the list down to the desired number of suppliers. The decision is communicated and the details of the final arrangement negotiated. Negotiation only occurs when the value of the contract is substantial or the nature of the relationship justifies the cost of

Figure 10.5 The Supplier Selection Process

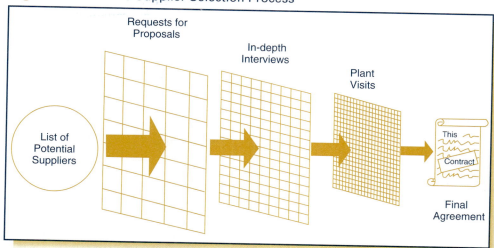

Requests for Proposals

In-depth Interviews

Plant Visits

List of Potential Suppliers

This Contract

Final Agreement

negotiation. The stage is now set to build the appropriate relationship, which is the focus of Chapter 11.

Implement Changes

Rigorous optimization almost always leads to a change in the composition of the supply base. Frequently this involves the phasing out of long-used suppliers. End users within the organization often resist such changes, preferring to buy from the familiar "tried-and-true" sources. Assuring compliance—that is, that buys are made only from preferred suppliers—becomes a real challenge. This is particularly true when a new, unproven supplier is added to the preferred-supplier list. Developing trust by assuring quality, demonstrating on-time delivery, and integrating information systems is critical as the new supply relationship is ramped up. In addition, transferring tooling, phasing out or building up inventory, and protecting intellectual property rights all make the transition from the old to the new supply base the most difficult step in the optimization process. These issues must be managed carefully during the pilot phase of the optimization effort. Otherwise credibility will be damaged and opportunities to take the optimization effort company-wide will be lost.

Conduct Periodic Reviews and Promote Improvement

The final step in the supply-base optimization process is to document and communicate the results. Success stories are powerful motivators for change. The documentation process also helps identify key learning points that can be used in future efforts. Remember, continued success depends on building learning loops into every strategic process. Finally, managers need to remember the environment is dynamic. New technologies emerge, new suppliers become available, and a company's needs change. Today's optimal supply base will have to evolve to achieve world-class performance tomorrow. Periodic reviews, benchmarking, and continuous improvement through supplier development are needed to achieve outstanding relationships and best-in-class performance.

To summarize, supply-base optimization is a strategic sourcing initiative. The objective is to develop and manage a world-class supply base. Sometimes managers lose track of this objective. Under pressure from top management or caught up in management fads, they translate rationalization as reduction. This approach can lead to perverse behavior. For example, one company set a goal to reduce the number of suppliers. Success was measured in terms of how many suppliers were used before and after the reduction initiative. The company proceeded to consolidate all of its purchases of a class of commodities with a single distributor. The distributor continued to source from the original set of 15 suppliers, but charged a 30 percent premium for its services. According to the goal and the measures in place, the effort was a success. However, despite some reductions in transaction costs, the company ended up paying more for the same parts it was buying before the reduction initiative was launched.[21] Following a well-defined process can prevent such outcomes.

SHIFTING ROLES AMONG SC MEMBERS

Historically, individual members of the supply chain fulfilled well-defined roles. Manufacturers made things and retailers sold them. Today, the roles are far less certain. In their quest for profitability, manufacturers may sell directly to the end customer, bypassing traditional retailers. Retailers often design their own "house" lines to compete directly with their suppliers' branded offerings. Managed well, this shifting of roles can help a company increase its power within the chain. As roles shift, however, other SC members may lose power and perhaps their very reason for participating in the chain. If other SC members can better perform the role of a specific company, that company can be shifted out, or **dis-intermediated,** from the chain. The only way to avoid jeopardizing its participation in the chain is for a company to add unique value. Role shifting makes SC design very dynamic, creating opportunities and threats for each member of the chain. The good news: Now that you've performed all of the preceding SC design analysis and begun the rationalization process, you have the insight and the time to look for hard-to-see role-shifting opportunities.

Shifting roles to the SC member best positioned to perform them—a process also called **functional shiftability**—can also improve the efficiency of the entire chain to enhance end customer value. A familiar example of role shifting took place in the retail food chain back in the early 1900s. Clarence Saunders noticed that grocery stores were terribly inefficient and inconvenient. At the time, shoppers presented their orders to clerks who gathered the items, which were often stored in bulk. Shoppers then waited for their orders to be filled. Saunders's idea was to shift the responsibility for picking items to the customer. The self-service grocery store was born. Saunders's first Piggly Wiggly store opened in 1916 complete with many innovations that we take for granted—pre-packaged, pre-priced branded products, open shelves, shopping baskets, and checkout lines. Though many predicted failure, the convenience and efficiency of Piggly Wiggly made it the model for the modern retail store.

As a part of the ongoing SC design process, role shifting is enabled by SC simplification. Eliminating unnecessary complexity frees up time and resources so that proactive SC managers can look for opportunities to shift value-added activities among SC members. To improve SC competitiveness via role shifting, managers must answer two critical questions: "What must be done to create customer value more efficiently than competing supply chains?" and "Who in our supply chain is best positioned to perform specific value-added activities?" Detailed analysis is needed to identify and justify role-shifting opportunities. When analysis is supported by strong, trust-based relationships among chain members, truly innovative role shifts can occur.

Role-shifting opportunities can be found throughout the chain. Ikea, the Swedish retailer, has become the third most influential brand in the world by selling low-cost, fashionable furniture that customers assemble themselves.[22] Ikea gains a competitive edge by getting its customers to perform the assembly role. This role shift allows Ikea to order flat-pack furniture from its suppliers, minimizing transportation and inventory costs. The flat-pack furniture also stores easily at Ikea retail outlets, helping Ikea achieve high in-stock levels without taking up a lot of space. Customers can visit the store and walk out with the furniture they like. They don't have to wait for a delivery truck to bring it to them a day or two later. A final, often unseen benefit of flat-pack furniture is that more space is available on the showroom floor for displays. Ikea uses this space to create model designs that pique customers' interest. Shopping becomes an experience. All of these benefits are made possible because a role-shifting decision was made and implemented well.

At the other end of the supply chain, a semiconductor manufacturer examined the activities required to make a key part. One activity, lead forming, caught the commodity team's attention. A supplier performed this activity. Closer examination revealed that lead forming could be done in-house at a much lower cost. Interestingly, the supplier viewed lead forming as a hassle and did it only at the customer's insistence.[23]

A third, quite distinct, example involves the financing of SC operations. Many companies seek to minimize their cash-to-cash conversion cycles by delaying payment to suppliers. This practice can place a real burden on smaller suppliers that often have higher costs of capital. Schneider National Logistics looks at capital costs and finances joint SC activities for which it has the lower cost of capital. This approach reduces chain-wide costs.

Several other role-shifting practices, which were once perceived as radical ideas, are now considered best practices in SCM. These practices are discussed next.

Second-Tier Sourcing Contracts

Sourcing is a fundamental value-added activity that must be performed in every supply chain. In the past, companies managed their own purchases, selecting suppliers, negotiating contracts, and arranging for delivery. This approach makes sense for most items at most companies. Yet, for some commodities, different members of the chain source the same exact item independently. Aggregation opportunities are often missed. Also, because each company manages its own buys, redundant activities are performed and chain-wide transaction costs rise. Recognizing this, United Technologies examined its own spend and compared it to first-tier suppliers' buying requirements. A number of common items were found. In most instances, United Technologies' annual spend for each common item was larger than that of any of its suppliers. Coordinating with its first-tier suppliers, United Technologies assumed the responsibility for negotiating blanket contracts for the aggregated volumes. Not only did United Technologies lower its unit costs for these items but first-tier suppliers also achieved cost reductions, some of which were passed on to United Technologies. The shared benefits from using second-tier sourcing contracts promoted more cooperative relationships.

Supplier Certification

Whose job is it to assure quality? Although quality should be built into products, for years most companies performed an incoming inspection to verify supplier quality. They simply could not trust suppliers to deliver high-quality parts every shipment. But, inspecting incoming shipments add costs. To eliminate this redundant effort, many companies have implemented supplier certification programs. Supplier certification is the formal process of working with selected suppliers to evaluate and improve supplier quality (see Figure 10.6). Suppliers pass through an intensive quality audit program designed by the buyer to verify that the supplier's quality systems are capable of producing at the required high-quality levels. The actual product also goes through a rigorous quality evaluation before the supplier receives "dock-to-stock" status. "Dock to stock" simply means that incoming inspection is no longer performed and incoming shipments go straight from the dock to either inventory or the production floor. When a quality deficiency is discovered, it is often resolved through a joint buyer–supplier effort. The net result of supplier certification is that it shifts the responsibility for assuring quality back to the source—the supplier.

Managed well, supplier certification is a win–win example of role shifting. The supplier gains access to knowledge and resources that it would not otherwise have. These resources are used to improve the supplier's internal quality processes. Certified suppliers receive preferred supplier status and become eligible for larger volumes and future contracts. Many suppliers use their certified status as a marketing tool—their lobbies are decorated with certification awards from well-known customers.

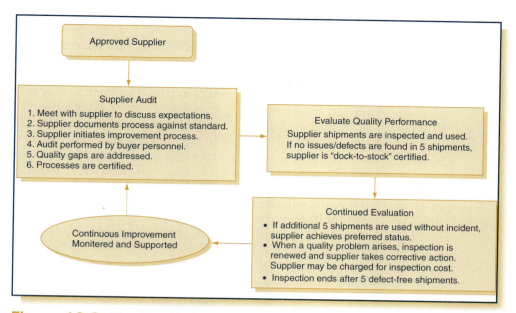

Figure 10.6 The Supplier Certification Process

From the buyer perspective, the return on investment begins with higher-quality purchased parts and extends to the confidence to rely on fewer suppliers as well as the cost and time savings that come from simplified receiving. Supplier certification often sets the stage for more intensive buyer/supplier interaction in areas such as early supplier involvement in new product design, joint cycle-time reduction programs, and productivity enhancement programs.

Vendor-Managed Replenishment

Placing replenishment orders to keep the production line running or the store's shelves stocked has traditionally been the buying company's responsibility. The process works something like this: When an order arrives, individual items are added to inventory; inventory levels are carefully monitored; when they fall below the established reorder point, an order is placed; the supplier fills the order and the process starts over. Back in the 1970s, Frito-Lay changed the basic model, taking over inventory management responsibility at individual retail stores. Frito-Lay's approach, which has evolved as new technologies have become available, is simple. Every time a bag of Doritos is sold, the bar code is scanned. This point-of-sale information is transmitted to Frito-Lay. Overnight, the local distribution center uses this information to create and pick orders, which are loaded on local delivery trucks. Early in the morning, drivers arrive at the DC, check their routes, verify their orders, and begin a day of delivering product. At each store, the driver checks and stocks the customer's shelves, rotates the inventory, and makes sure that Frito-Lay products are displayed with maximum appeal and visibility. The customer authorizes the transaction via a Frito-Lay handheld computer. The primary benefits to Frito-Lay are better merchandising and having the right product on the shelf when customers want to buy snack food. The retailer benefits from lower labor and inventory costs. Variations of this vendor-managed replenishment model have been adopted in other retail and manufacturing settings.

Supplier-Integrated Manufacturing

Turning responsibility for manufacturing and assembly over to the supplier represents the most aggressive effort yet to shift roles in order to reduce costs and shorten cycle times. Volkswagen's truck assembly facility in Resende, Brazil, set the standard for supplier-integrated manufacturing. The operation relies almost exclusively on suppliers for the assembly of the entire vehicle. Volkswagen built the manufacturing facility and invited seven suppliers to establish assembly lines within the facility. Each supplier is responsible for managing an entire module. Maxion builds the truck's chassis. Cummins makes the powertrain. Meritor assembles the suspension. Delga stamps the cab panels in Sao Paulo and welds them together at the Resende facility. VDO assembles the instrument panel and other interior components. Remon handles the wheels and tires. And Carese paints the finished product. Each supplier provides its own specialized equipment, manages its own inventory, and hires and trains its own workers. In fact, suppliers employ approximately 80 percent of the operations workers. Because they all wear the same basic uniform, the only way to tell who is paying the check is to look for a small company insignia located on the worker's shirt pocket. Suppliers are paid when the finished truck rolls off the line and passes a detailed quality inspection.

As companies continue to experiment with role shifting, traditional lines of responsibility are blurring.

CONCLUSION

Complexity is a fact of life for the modern SC manager. A 2004 AT Kearny study found that over 90 percent of companies experienced an increase in complexity in the previous 5 years. Almost 80 percent expected the amount of complexity to increase in the next 5 years. Managers pointed to their companies' growth strategies and product proliferation as the main drivers of complexity. They also identified the need to eliminate non-value-added activities that occur in-house as well as up and down the chain. Most importantly, managers noted that the ability to manage complexity is critical to improved financial performance.

To win tomorrow's competitive battles, managers need to develop the skills to identify and eliminate unnecessary complexity—wherever it is found. They need to understand the basics of SC rationalization. And they need to be able to weigh the trade-offs that are inherent in any rationalization effort. Only then will they be able to strategically allocate resources to the right activities and relationships. They will also be better prepared to evaluate unique role-shifting opportunities that can enhance the company's strategic position and the entire supply chain's competitiveness.

SUMMARY OF KEY POINTS

1. Unnecessary complexity creates confusion and increases costs. SC managers must learn to identify and reduce unnecessary complexity in several areas: organizational structure, value-added processes, the operating network, the company's SKUs, the supply base, the customer base, and the logistics system.

2. Complexity creep occurs because supply chains evolve over time. An optimal network today may not be optimal tomorrow. Few companies have the policies and procedures in place to evaluate the complexity effects of individual decisions in each of the seven areas where complexity is found.

3. Rationalization is the process of evaluating the company's operating network, suppliers, customers, and product offerings to find and eliminate inefficiencies and redundancies. The goal is to efficiently allocate scarce resources to a company's most profitable and important activities and relationships.

4. Because rationalization is best done after the supply chain is mapped, customer needs defined, core competencies identified, and costing systems put in place, many companies are just beginning serious rationalization efforts.

5. Rationalization is most advanced in the area of supply-base optimization, which determines how many suppliers a company needs and which suppliers to buy from. Similar issues exist in the other areas targeted for rationalization. Thus, supply-base optimization exemplifies the rationalization process.

6. A systematic supply-base optimization process consists of 7 steps: establish a strategic sourcing committee, build cross-functional commodity teams, develop a commodity sourcing strategy, identify potential suppliers, select suppliers, implement changes, and conduct periodic reviews.

7. Shifting roles to the SC member best positioned to perform them—a process also called *functional shiftability*—can improve the efficiency of the entire chain to enhance end customer value.

8. Effective role shifting requires that managers (a) define what must be done to create customer value and (b) identify who in the chain is best positioned to perform specific activities. Detailed analysis is needed to justify role-shifting opportunities. Trust among chain members enables risk taking in role shifting.

9. SC simplification enables role shifting by freeing up time and resources so that managers can look for opportunities to shift value-added activities among SC members. Both simplification and role shifting should be considered as part of the broader strategic SC design process.

REVIEW EXERCISES

1. What are the sources of complexity in your own life? Take a few minutes to map out your past week. Where did you spend your time? How much time did you waste dealing with complexity? Describe at least one thing you could do to reduce the costs of complexity in your own life.

2. From your own work experience, identify and discuss an example of the confusion, costs, or counterproductive decisions that resulted from each of the 7 sources of complexity. Alternatively, find and discuss examples from the current business press.

3. Define SC rationalization. Describe how a proactive rationalization program can improve the SC design process and lead to a more competitive supply chain.

4. Define supply-base optimization. Explain how supply-base optimization is different from supply-base reduction.

5. Identify the basic steps in the supply-base optimization process. Select one of the other 6 sources of complexity and draw a rationalization flowchart for this source of complexity. Describe the basic steps in the generic rationalization process.

6. What is role shifting? From the trade press, identify and describe an example of role shifting that resulted in higher levels of company and/or supply chain performance.

7. Explain why most companies have not taken full advantage of SC rationalization and/or role shifting to achieve higher levels of efficiency and customer value.

Case   *Designing a Hybrid Global Sourcing Strategy?*

Donna Rock, director of purchasing at Triton Labs, stared intently out her office window. It was a crisp Friday afternoon in the middle of February, and Donna knew that she had to make some tough decisions before Monday morning's presentation to Triton's board of directors. The Global Sourcing Task Force, which Donna led, had completed an arduous 6-month review of Triton's global sourcing requirements and practices.

At the review's outset, it was clear that Triton's decentralized sourcing structure was not lean enough to help Triton compete against larger rivals in a consolidating industry. Yet centralizing sourcing represented a radical transition that would be difficult to implement over the objections of Triton's worldwide purchasing managers. Donna's challenge was to present a hybrid plan that would yield both efficiency and autonomy.

THE MANDATE FOR CHANGE

A challenging transition in the pharmaceutical industry prompted the strategic review. Two issues were driving dramatic change: First, the end of patent protection for many top-selling drugs meant that margins would come under severe pressure. Second, the search for new, blockbuster drugs was becoming more and more expensive. To cope with this dual challenge, key industry players were merging to increase market power and R&D budgets. Two new giants had been created with the mergers between Glaxo Wellcome and SmithKline Beecham and between Pfizer and Warner Lambert. This consolidation was ratcheting up the pressure felt by Triton. Greater sourcing efficiency would be needed to survive in a behemoth-dominated world.

The Global Sourcing Task Force was created in July of 2003 with a clear mandate—reengineer Triton's purchasing structure so that it would more efficiently support Triton's competitive strategy. Everyone involved with the task force knew that the key word was "efficiency." They also knew that Triton's decentralized structure would need a drastic and painful overhaul to achieve the desired results.

For many years, Triton Labs, headquartered in Rochester, New York, operated production, marketing, and R&D facilities around the world. Autonomous purchasing groups were located in 7 locations in Asia, Europe, Latin America, and the United States. Coordinating Triton's worldwide purchasing requirements would not be easy. Donna's 23 years of purchasing experience combined with her personal credibility and influence throughout Triton's sourcing organization made her an ideal candidate to lead the task force.

TASK FORCE FINDINGS

The Global Sourcing Task Force first sought to understand why Triton had used a decentralized purchasing structure for so many years. They discovered that Triton had relied on a decentralized purchasing organization because both internal and external customers had always demanded high levels of responsiveness from purchasing. The critical performance characteristics had

been (1) short fulfillment lead times, (2) knowledge of local needs and marketplace, (3) flexibility to meet the individual division's needs, and (4) good relationships with the local supply base.

Donna's team discovered that purchasers throughout Triton's decentralized organization took pride in their rapid-response capability and the technical expertise they had developed to meet the needs of the local operations. While Triton's purchasing managers were familiar with the cost arguments behind centralization, they were highly skeptical that greater centralization could really meet Triton's purchasing needs, especially across global operating divisions. As a result, they were firmly committed to retaining a decentralized structure.

The task force then sought to quantify the benefits of centralization. They identified opportunities both to reduce administrative duplication and to leverage Triton's global spend. A comparison of the various divisions' purchase requirements revealed that 60 percent of all purchased items were common to two or more locations. In close to 20 percent of the cases, all seven purchasing groups bought the same or an equivalent item.

The task force's benchmarking efforts also identified several companies that had recently shifted from decentralized to centralized purchasing with dramatic cost savings. A consulting study commissioned by Triton revealed that a centralized organization would reduce Triton's purchasing costs by 7 to 10 percent. The study identified 5 primary areas where centralization would result in costs savings:

- Increased buying volume and leverage
- Reduced administrative duplication
- Standardization of products
- Greater supplier cooperation and coordination
- Enhanced control over purchase commitments

Based on its analysis, the task force concluded that the decentralized organization had become a threat to Triton's long-term competitiveness. The benefits of centralized purchasing appeared to be substantial. However, as the task force began to develop an implementation plan, it quickly discovered that it would be difficult to move to a fully centralized purchasing organization. Not only did Triton's purchasing professionals complain vigorously but various internal customers also voiced serious concerns, arguing that the lost flexibility would more than offset the cost savings.

The Global Sourcing Task Force found itself in a delicate situation—cost savings had to be obtained, but centralization was not a viable option. As the task force reexamined key findings, it decided that as a global company, Triton needed to achieve the cost benefits of centralization while maintaining the flexibility of decentralization. The task force began to focus on creating a hybrid sourcing organization.

THE HYBRID ORGANIZATION

Donna and the entire task force concurred that a hybrid organization had to possess several key characteristics. That is, it had to

- Facilitate component/commodity standardization
- Consolidate common requirements
- Enable the use of the best suppliers worldwide
- Allow divisions to control unique purchases
- Allow divisions to schedule receipt of common items
- Take transportation and other costs into account
- Reduce redundancy across global operations
- Retain the passion of local purchasing managers

Clearly, two keys to success would be (1) the ability and willingness of each division to share information and (2) their willingness to relinquish control while accepting modified responsibilities. From Donna's perspective, the information technology issues could be addressed without too much difficulty. Although Triton would need to upgrade its information capabilities, intranet and extranet technologies appeared capable of meeting the technical demands of a hybrid organization. Data-warehousing and data-mining tools promised to facilitate the assignment of purchasing responsibilities. Donna was more concerned with the willingness of Triton's purchasing managers to make a hybrid model work. Turning control of common purchases and key relationships over to a corporate purchasing group represented a significant change in mind-set and behavior.

As Donna left for home, 3 questions were on her mind.

- What would an ideal hybrid sourcing policy look like?
- What would ideal sourcing procedures look like?
- What would hybrid performance measures look like?

CASE QUESTIONS

1. How would you answer Donna's questions? What type of analysis is needed to answer these questions?
2. Are there any alternatives to the approach Donna's task force has taken? Describe at least one and identify its comparative strengths and weaknesses.
3. What steps need to be taken to prevent "culture shock" as a new sourcing model is implemented? How can Donna make sure that managers in the local operations continue to be passionate about their ability to help Triton compete?

ENDNOTES

1. Collins, J. (2001). *Good to great.* New York: HarperCollins Publishers, Inc.
2. Fine, C. H. (1998). *Clockspeed.* Reading, MA: Perseus Books.
3. Lyons, D. (2003, October 13). Back on the chain gang. *Forbes,* 114–123.
4. Hawkins, L. (2004, October 6). Reversing 80 years of history, GM is reining in global fiefs. *The Wall Street Journal,* A1.
5. Ball, D. (2005, January 3). Despite revamp, unwieldy Unilever falls behind rivals. *The Wall Street Journal,* A1.
6. Ibid.
7. Boudette, N. E. (2004, November 9). A bad report card for European cars. *The Wall Street Journal,* D1.
8. Shirouzu, N., & Moffett, S. (2004, August 4). As Toyota closes in on GM, quality concerns also grow. *The Wall Street Journal,* A1.
9. Spiekman, P. (2000). New victories in the supply-chain revolution. *Fortune,* T208C–T208HH.

10. Taylor, J. C., & Fawcett, S. E. (2001). Retail in-stock performance on promotional items: An assessment of logistical effectiveness. *Journal of Business Logistics, 22*(1), 78–89. Taylor, J. C., Fawcett, S. E., & Jackson, G. C. (2004). Catalogue retailer in-stock performance: An assessment of customer service levels. *Journal of Business Logistics, 25*(2), 119–138.
11. McGrath, M., & Hoole, R. (1992). Manufacturing's new economies of scale. *Harvard Business Review 70*(3), 94–102.
12. Fawcett, S. E., & Magnan, G. N. (2001). *Achieving world-class supply chain alignment: Benefits, barriers, and bridges.* Phoenix, AZ: National Association of Purchasing Management.
13. Ibid. #9.
14. Cap Gemini, Ernst & Young. (2002) U.S. LLC, Georgia Southern and University of Tennessee. Operations excellence: The transition from tactical to strategic supply chains. 12th Annual Report on Trends and Issues in Logistics and Transportation.

15. Monczka, R., Trent, R., & Handfield, R. (2002). *Purchasing and supply chain management.* Cincinnati: South-Western College Publishing.
16. Reitman, V. (1997, February 3). Toyota halts Japan production after fire destroys factory. *The Wall Street Journal.*
17. Clark, D. (2005, January 12). Intel's next CEO charts new course. *The Wall Street Journal,* B1.
18. Nelson, D., Mayo, R., & Moody, P. E. (1998). *Powered by Honda.* New York: John Wiley & Sons, Inc.
19. Laseter, T. M. (1998). *Balanced sourcing.* San Francisco: Jossey-Bass Publishers.
20. Ibid.
21. Ibid.
22. *USA Today* (2005, January 31). Apple ranks as no. 1 brand; Al Jazeera makes top 5.
23. Ibid. #19.

Part II Epilogue

Designing the Global Supply Chain

Genius is 1 percent inspiration and 99 percent perspiration.

—Thomas Edison

Edison's prescribed combination of inspiration and perspiration is needed to design a business model that can beat global rivals by delivering outstanding value to customers. The task is made more difficult by rising customer expectations, rapidly emerging technologies, and evolving supplier capabilities. In such a world, the inspiration comes only after the perspiration inherent in vigilant scanning and rigorous analysis.

Scanning keeps managers in touch with the world in which their companies do business. Via scanning, managers are able to define the rules of competition and identify trends that foreshadow change in customer expectations and competitive strategies. By mastering the art and science of scanning, managers can avoid impending threats and take advantage of emerging opportunities before the competition realizes that the competitive landscape has changed.

Although the analysis begins with scanning, it certainly does not end there. Supply chain mapping coupled with strategic costing and core competency/outsourcing analysis helps managers structure SC resources for competitive advantage. Specifically, such analysis yields insight needed to answer two key questions. First, "What must be done to create customer value more efficiently than competing supply chains?" Second, "Who in our supply chain is best positioned to perform specific value-added activities?" Answering these questions enables managers to define the specific roles and responsibilities of

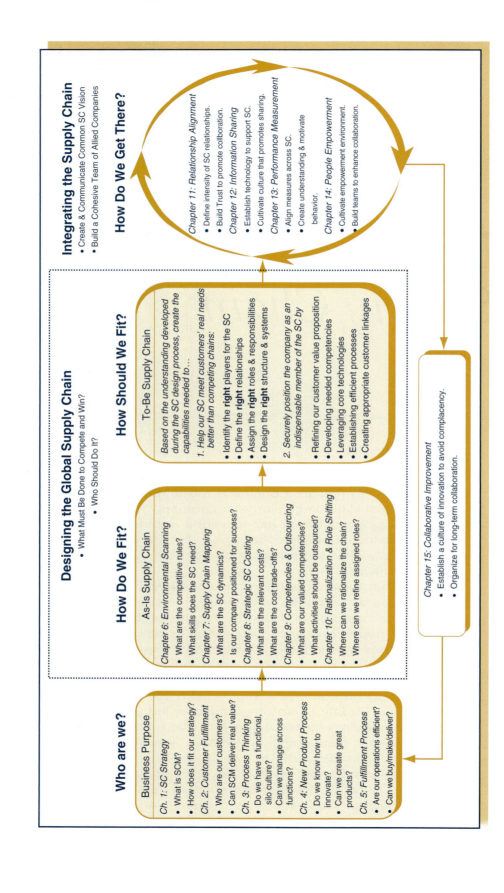

Designing the Global Supply Chain
- What Must Be Done to Compete and Win?
- Who Should Do It?

Who are we?

Business Purpose

Ch. 1: SC Strategy
- What is SCM?
- How does it fit our strategy?

Ch. 2: Customer Fulfillment
- Who are our customers?
- Can SCM deliver real value?

Ch. 3: Process Thinking
- Do we have a functional, silo culture?
- Can we manage across functions?

Ch. 4: New Product Process
- Do we know how to innovate?
- Can we create great products?

Ch. 5: Fulfillment Process
- Are our operations efficient?
- Can we buy/make/deliver?

How Do We Fit?

As-Is Supply Chain

Chapter 6: Environmental Scanning
- What are the competitive rules?
- What skills does the SC need?

Chapter 7: Supply Chain Mapping
- What are the SC dynamics?
- Is our company positioned for success?

Chapter 8: Strategic SC Costing
- What are the relevant costs?
- What are the cost trade-offs?

Chapter 9: Competencies & Outsourcing
- What are our valued competencies?
- What activities should be outsourced?

Chapter 10: Rationalization & Role Shifting
- Where can we rationalize the chain?
- Where can we refine assigned roles?

How Should We Fit?

To-Be Supply Chain

Based on the understanding developed during the SC design process, create the capabilities needed to...

1. Help our SC meet customers' real needs better than competing chains:
- Identify the **right** players for the SC
- Define the **right** relationships
- Assign the **right** roles & responsibilities
- Design the **right** structure & systems

2. Securely position the company as an indispensable member of the SC by
- Refining our customer value proposition
- Developing needed competencies
- Leveraging core technologies
- Establishing efficient processes
- Creating appropriate customer linkages

Integrating the Supply Chain
- Create & Communicate Common SC Vision
- Build a Cohesive Team of Allied Companies

How Do We Get There?

Chapter 11: Relationship Alignment
- Define intensity of SC relationships.
- Build Trust to promote collaboration.

Chapter 12: Information Sharing
- Establish technology to support SC.
- Cultivate culture that promotes sharing.

Chapter 13: Performance Measurement
- Align measures across SC.
- Create understanding & motivate behavior.

Chapter 14: People Empowerment
- Cultivate empowerment environment.
- Build teams to enhance collaboration.

Chapter 15: Collaborative Improvement
- Establish a culture of innovation to avoid complacency.
- Organize for long-term collaboration.

individual chain members. Managers are also able to identify their company's uniqueness and answer the critical question, "How should our company contribute to the entire chain's success?"

Finally, supply chain design is a dynamic process. Supply chains evolve over time. For example, new customers and suppliers join the SC team. New products are developed, and new facilities are constructed. As a result, most supply chains suffer from costly complexity creep. Simplification efforts must be used to keep supply chains manageable. Role shifting can then refine and coordinate the complementary capabilities of various chain members so that the chain can deliver unsurpassed value to the end customer.

To summarize, supply chain design is a company's "ultimate core capability" because it enables, or limits, the company's competitiveness. Supply chain design, however, requires both vision and analytical skills—it is a demanding and complex process. That reality is what makes SCM fun. And it is one reason why SC managers are in high demand.

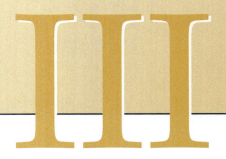
Collaborating Across the Supply Chain

PROLOGUE

> *It's not good enough to optimize the firm—we have to optimize the supply chain. But no one is king of the supply chain.*
>
> —JEFF TRIMMER, CHRYSLER

Although MIT's Charles Fine identified SC design as the "ultimate core capability," SC collaboration may be the more difficult capability to develop. Neither companies nor managers are accustomed to working synergistically across organizational boundaries. Just as many athletic teams with seemingly superior talent never become champions, many supply chains never learn to work together. Perhaps the distinguishing characteristic of championship-caliber athletic teams is that they have developed team chemistry. Great supply chains likewise cultivate "SC" chemistry—a common vision, an understanding of individual roles, an ability to work together, and a willingness to adjust and adapt in order to create superior value.

This third of the book's three modules discusses SC collaboration and explains why it is so important. Our discussion focuses on the practices and capabilities that foster collaboration to bind the members of the supply chain into a cohesive team. This module's five chapters are as follows:

- Chapter 11 presents the notion of relationship intensity and the relationship continuum. The emphasis is on cultivating appropriate relationships. After all, not all relationships should be treated equally. Trust and negotiation are discussed as key relationship-building elements.

The Supply Chain Road Map

Designing the Global Supply Chain
- What Must Be Done to Compete and Win?
- Who Should Do It?

Who Are We?

Business Purpose

Chapter 1: SC Strategy
- What is SCM?
- How does it fit our strategy?

Chapter 2: Customer Fulfillment
- Who are our customers?
- Can SCM deliver real value?

Chapter 3: Process Thinking
- Do we have a functional, silo culture?
- Can we manage across functions?

Chapter 4: New Product Process
- Do we know how to innovate?
- Can we create great products?

Chapter 5: Fulfillment Process
- Are our operations efficient?
- Can we buy/make/deliver?

How Do We Fit?

As-Is Supply Chain

Chapter 6: Environmental Scanning
- What are the competitive rules?
- What skills does the SC need?

Chapter 7: Supply Chain Mapping
- What are the SC dynamics?
- Is our company positioned for success?

Chapter 8: Strategic SC Costing
- What are the relevant costs?
- What are the cost trade-offs?

Chapter 9: Competencies and Outsourcing
- What are our valued competencies?
- What activities should be outsourced?

Chapter 10: Rationalization and Role Shifting
- Where can we rationalize the chain?
- Where can we refine assigned roles?

How Should We Fit?

To-Be Supply Chain

Based on the understanding developed during the SC design process, create the capabilities needed to…

1. *Help our SC meet customers' real needs better than competing chains:*
- Identify the **right** players for the SC
- Define the **right** relationships
- Assign the **right** roles and responsibilities
- Design the **right** structure and systems

2. *Securely position the company as an indispensable member of the SC by*
- Refining our customer value proposition
- Developing needed competencies
- Leveraging core technologies
- Establishing efficient processes
- Creating appropriate customer linkages

Integrating the Supply Chain
- Create and Communicate Common SC Vision
- Build a Cohesive Team of Allied Companies

How Do We Get There?

Chapter 11: Relationship Alignment
- Define intensity of SC relationships.
- Build trust to promote collaboration.

Chapter 12: Information Sharing
- Establish technology to support SC.
- Cultivate culture that promotes sharing.

Chapter 13: Performance Measurement
- Align measures across SC.
- Create understanding and motivate behavior.

Chapter 14: People Empowerment
- Cultivate empowerment environment.
- Build teams to enhance collaboration.

Chapter 15: Collaborative Improvement
- Establish a culture of innovation to avoid complacency.
- Organize for long-term collaboration.

340

- Chapter 12 shows how modern information technologies enable SCM. Popular technologies are discussed, but the focus is on technology's role in improving information sharing and SC collaboration.
- Chapter 13 details SC performance measurement. The vital role of measurement is discussed and specific SC measures and measurement practices are presented. Scorecards and benchmarking are evaluated.
- Chapter 14 highlights the role people play in driving SC initiatives. Collaboration depends on leveraging an empowered workforce's passion and creativity. The roles of training and teaming are emphasized.
- Chapter 15 discusses collaborative improvement. Long-term success requires constant improvement; therefore, two improvement philosophies are contrasted. Specific improvement programs are presented.

Chapter 11

Relationship Management

Do we understand relationship intensity? Can I help build SC relationships that deliver great customer value?

The Supply Chain Road Map

Integrating the Supply Chain
- Create & Communicate Common SC Vision
- Build a Cohesive Team of Allied Companies

How Do We Get There?

Chapter 11: Relationship Management
- Define intensity of SC relationships.
- Build trust to promote collaboration.

Chapter 12: Information Sharing
- Establish technology to support SC.
- Cultivate culture that promotes sharing.

Chapter 13: Performance Measurement
- Align measures across SC.
- Create understanding & motivate behavior.

Chapter 14: People Empowerment
- Cultivate empowerment environment.
- Build teams to enhance collaboration.

Chapter 15: Collaborative Improvement
- Establish a culture of innovation to avoid complacency.
- Organize for long-term collaboration.

After reading this chapter, you will be able to:

1. Identify the right type of relationship to build with SC members.
2. Discuss the benefits of improved relations from both buyer and supplier perspectives.
3. Describe the practices that promote successful alliance creation and management. Discuss the behaviors that impede collaboration among SC members.
4. Discuss the role of power and trust in establishing effective SC relationships.
5. Plan an effective negotiation—one that is capable of building strong SC relationships. Describe the elements of an effective negotiation strategy. Identify tactics that support win–win negotiations.

Opening Story: Relationship Management at Olympus

Another Friday morning task force meeting was only a few minutes away as Doug and Charlene stepped out of Doug's office and headed to the conference room. Doug was pleased with the progress the task force had made as it worked through the initial steps of the SC design process. Eyes had been opened to the opportunities available through SCM to improve customer service and reduce costs. Yet the experience of the past year led Doug to feel that the real work was only now beginning. After all, designing a supply chain was one thing; making it work was an altogether different beast.

PREVIOUSLY . . .

Already, Doug, and the entire team, had become aware of the fact that Olympus had not done a great job of managing its myriad SC relationships. An "ABC" analysis had revealed that managers at Olympus really did not understand the notion of relationship intensity. Joel Sutherland, the financial analyst on the team, was the first to note that, in many respects, Olympus had bought into the trade-press hype of tightly coupled, partnership relationships—even when they weren't appropriate. He had wondered aloud how much money had been wasted trying to build closer relationships when there was little or nothing to be gained.

Vijay Gilles, director of operations, had asked the opposing question, "How much money do you think we have left on the table by not initiating relationships with companies where collaboration would have yielded better solutions to customers' needs?" The task force agreed that relationship management was at the core of SCM and that Olympus had done a poor job of it, costing the company considerable competitive advantage.

Susan Mass, director of global supply, captured the team's overall feelings when she had sighed deeply and said, "You all know that we could and should do better, but the truth is, we really don't have a lot of experience building strong relationships. Alliances simply are not our forte. Besides, we've all read about so-called great relationships that over time proved to be less spectacular than advertised. Remember what happened to Chrysler, which supposedly had such great supply relationships only to find out that many of its suppliers were actually charging higher prices to Chrysler than to Chrysler's rivals. And then when DaimlerChrysler hit the financial skids, they put the screws to the supply base, demanding immediate and sustained price cuts. It seems that you just can't trust someone who works for another company to do the right thing for your own company."

David Amado had then dared to ask the daunting question, "We've picked apart other SC alliances. How do you think other members of our supply chain view us? Do you think they trust us to do the right thing for them or do you think that they believe we are out to take their lunch money?" Not surprisingly, nobody wanted to answer that question.

Everyone on the team knew of SC alliances that had failed to deliver the expected value that had prompted the closer relationship in the first place. Stories were shared about poorly aligned goals, promises made but not kept, relationships that lacked commitment, and lengthy, but rigid contracts that failed to govern interorganizational operations. As the team discussed the challenge of actually building the right relationships with the right SC members, it became evident that a little help would be needed, especially in the area of alliance management. Diane suggested that the team benchmark outstanding alliances to see what made them tick. Tameka felt that such an approach would take too much time and dilute their focus on other aspects of SC integration that needed to be addressed such as systems integration and performance measurement. He suggested that an outside consultant be brought in. Susan, however, argued against bringing in a consultant; she felt that the team had sufficient brainpower to develop a strategy for building winning SC relationships. The quandary Doug and the task force faced was how to proceed.

As Doug had pondered the dilemma of defining and establishing appropriate relationships with over 500 suppliers and 1000 customers, he had resorted to his common practice of taking his work home and talking it over with Charlene. Half joking, Doug had said, "Charlene, I wish you would come in next Friday and meet with the task force. We could sure benefit from your experience in building successful SC alliances, and no one outside the task force knows more about Olympus's SC initiatives than you."

Almost before he could finish the sentence, Charlene responded, "I'm in town next Friday; I'd be happy to join your task force for a day if . . . you'll join me in Rio for my presentation at the international logistics forum." That was an offer Doug couldn't refuse.

ENTERING THE CONFERENCE ROOM . . .

Doug greeted the assembled task force, saying, "Good morning. It's a beautiful day and we have a lot to accomplish. I believe you all know Charlene. She has agreed to spend the day with us to help us develop our relationship management infrastructure. I look forward to a productive meeting today."

1. If you were Charlene, where would you start?
2. What issues do you think will pose the greatest barriers to establishing "appropriate" relationships with Olympus's suppliers? What about customers?
3. What practices do you think Charlene will emphasize as the task force discusses building close SC alliances?

Open the window and look outside. It's a big world out there.

—Sakichi Toyoda

Supply Chain Relationships

Futurists describe a day when success will hinge on the agility and strength of the entire SC team rather than on the competitive power of any individual company. For instance, at Wal-Mart an emerging concern is whether some suppliers will have sufficient capacity to meet Wal-Mart's sourcing requirements as its global sales climb steadily to half a trillion dollars. Never before has a retailer attained such size. Nor has a retailer ever depended on its suppliers more than Wal-Mart to co-manage inventories and in-store displays.

Home Depot and Lowe's have a different concern. They work to differentiate themselves by carrying distinct brands and products in their stores. They don't want to look too much like each other. These two competitors already pressure many of their suppliers to pick sides. Both companies have been known to cut off suppliers that sold key product lines to the "enemy." Of course, this approach doesn't work with all supply relationships. Neither Home Depot nor Lowe's has the power to tell DeWALT or Makita, "If you sell to the competition, we won't carry your product." But, in the relationships where Home Depot or Lowe's is the 800-pound gorilla, they define the rules.

Toyota has taken still another approach to managing its SC relationships. Its goal has been to establish a strong and uniquely capable supply base. Toyota doesn't just work closely with valued suppliers; it has an ownership stake in them. When outside, global competitors began to look closely at working with Toyota suppliers, Toyota upped the ante by increasing its ownership stake in key suppliers. Toyota has invested in its suppliers' capabilities and wants to make sure that those capabilities don't end up making a competitor stronger.

For Wal-Mart, Home Depot, Lowe's, Toyota, and most other companies, the challenge and opportunity of SCM is to build an outstanding SC team by establishing the right relationships with the right SC players. Yet the most proactive SC companies find this to be difficult. No easy-to-follow road map exists. Besides, in a dynamic world filled with strong-willed managers, seemingly great relationships can deteriorate rapidly. Think Disney and Pixar. Despite the fantastic success achieved by this production–distribution duo, enough friction developed over shared risks and rewards that Pixar announced it would walk away from the alliance. Only after Michael Eisner, Disney's mercurial CEO, retired were the two companies able to reconcile key differences. Once again on speaking terms, Pixar agreed to be acquired by Disney.

Pixar's story points out another challenge in establishing the right relationships with the right players. Nobody knows for certain who will be tomorrow's right players. Before the 1997 release of *Toy Story*, Pixar's first digitally animated feature film, few people knew much about the company. No one anticipated that Pixar and digital animation would change the industry so rapidly. It only took Pixar's animation group 5 years to go from startup to star. Similar stories exist in most industries. In a world where tomorrow's new technologies and new business models are often hidden away in a garage or college dorm room, identifying and investing in the right SC relationships is a tough task. The task is made more daunting by the predisposition of most companies to use channel power to their advantage. Uneven power often leads to uneven relationships.

The futurists may be right—the day may come when key suppliers will have to choose which supply chain they are going to participate in. Such a world will require a different mind-set and a different set of skills than are commonly found in today's companies. Until then, SC managers must begin to realize that current and future success depends on their ability to identify outstanding partners and then develop appropriate relationships with them. Only then will their companies be able to build an SC team capable of winning over the long haul.

This defines today's management challenge: SC managers must learn to put together the best team of SC members possible regardless of geography or channel position. This means that SC managers must learn how to define and manage a diversity of relationships up and down the chain. Managers that can build the right relationships with the right SC players will enable their companies to participate as members of world-class SC teams. Relationship management is becoming a critical capability.

THE RELATIONSHIP CONTINUUM

A core principle of SCM is that not all relationships are created equal—nor should they be. Some relationships merit much more managerial attention and resource dedication than others. The typical company manages hundreds, if not thousands, of customer and supplier relationships—far too many to build close working relationships with each.

For example, Intel has hundreds of direct materials suppliers and thousands of indirect materials suppliers. Add in third-party and customer relationships and it is easy to see that even a company as successful as Intel cannot possibly invest in close working relationships with them all. As a result, Intel has made the strategic decision to manage a variety of relationships, ranging from simple, transactional relationships to intricate, resource-intensive strategic alliances (see Figure 11.1).

The transactional relationships do not receive much managerial time. Nor are they the target for much assistance or investment from Intel. They are managed for efficiency and are often transitory. As a rule, commodities are being purchased and the relationships themselves are often treated as if they too are commodities. The focus is on cost. Suppliers are under intense pressure to minimize both their product and relationship costs. Intel, like most other large companies, uses on-line bidding events (reverse auctions) to assure that it is getting the best price for these

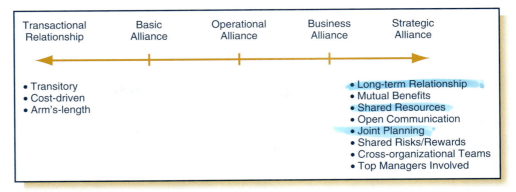

Figure 11.1 Relationship Intensity Continuum

components. Global sourcing is also used to keep costs down and the pressure on suppliers to perform up.

By contrast, the strategic relationships are closely scrutinized and carefully managed. Top management spends time and money to make sure these relationships are built on a solid foundation and for the long haul. Many of these relationships are managed looking out 2, 3, or even 5 years. These relationships are characterized by intensive and relatively open communication, supported by linked information systems. Information about production schedules and technology plans is shared. For this to work, Intel must protect sensitive customer and supplier information, making sure that it is kept strictly confidential. Mutual respect and benefits govern these relationships. Engineering resources and innovation ideas are often shared. Cross-organizational teams drive cooperative planning to solve problems and develop process and product technologies. Because of their resource-intensive nature, these strategic alliances represent only 5 to 10 percent of Intel's SC relationships. Intel's challenge is to determine which relationships merit this intensity of collaboration.

As the Intel experience illustrates, the question for SC managers is, "What type of relationship is appropriate?" The key word is "appropriate." Many companies, like Olympus in the opening story, have become caught in the mental-model trap that SCM means close working relationships. They have invested huge amounts of scarce resources to build the wrong relationships with the right customers and suppliers. Poor performance leads them to view the SC partner as the wrong partner. SC managers must learn to think in terms of relationship appropriateness and then build the skills to accurately define relationship intensity and then to build and sustain powerful alliances. After all, strategic alliances are much more resource intensive than simple transaction relationships. They also have a much greater potential to provide the company with a strategic advantage. But they only deliver on promise if a real opportunity exists in the first place and the right culture of cooperation is established.

To help it define relationship intensity, Intel uses ABC classification—a tool we have discussed several times in previous chapters (see Figure 11.2). Remember, ABC classification should be used as a starting point for evaluating the nature of specific relationships. A separate ABC classification should be performed for each type of SC relationship: customers, suppliers, and service providers. After performing an initial ABC classification based on the monetary value of individual relationships, managers should evaluate the qualitative factors that might lead a potential partner to have a

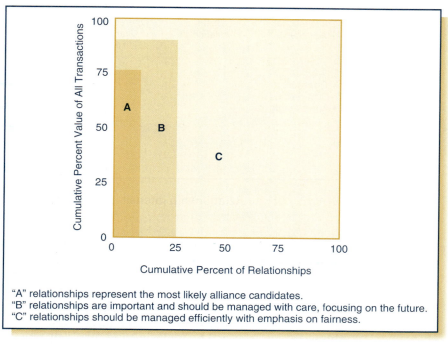

Figure 11.2 ABC Classification

- "A" relationships represent the most likely alliance candidates.
- "B" relationships are important and should be managed with care, focusing on the future.
- "C" relationships should be managed efficiently with emphasis on fairness.

dramatic impact on the organization's competitiveness. Some of the characteristics that suggest alliance formation are listed here:

- The relationship represents a large dollar volume, either in sales or in purchases.
- The SC member represents a large share of the company's business (again, either sales or purchases).
- The potential partner possesses skills, technology, or another unique aspect that cannot be found elsewhere.
- A strategic component, service, or upstream/downstream relationship is affected.
- Potential scarcity governs the marketplace.
- Intensive collaboration can create advantage: better quality, lower costs, shorter cycles, or unique service.

Of the preceding issues, the most critical may be whether closer coordination and collaboration can yield superior competitive advantage now and in the future. Unfortunately, many companies do not truly consider this issue in their relationship-definition process. Many others do a half-hearted job of evaluating it. Collaboration potential must become one of the criteria by which customers and suppliers are selected. It must also be incorporated into performance scorecards to evaluate the success of the relationship.

Even as SC managers pursue the quest to build strong partnerships with the most important "A" relationships, they must build an infrastructure that will enable them to maximize the value contribution of all SC relationships. Valuable "B"-level relationships that do not reach the importance required to justify building a strategic alliance must be managed with considerable care even though fewer resources are dedicated to collaborative ventures. Not only do non-strategic relationships represent a significant level of business activity but they also often evolve into more strategic relationships over time. Investing in good relations now can keep important doors open for the future. The reality that relationships evolve, key technologies change, and essential capabilities emerge (sometimes in the most unlikely places) suggests that even transaction-oriented, "C"-level relationships should be managed in a fair manner. Developing a reputation as an outstanding customer/supplier can help guarantee access to technologies and capabilities that have not yet been developed.

A warning: Many companies have promoted the idea that strategic collaborative relationships can be developed with one set of partners while other members of the chain can be "squeezed" for every last drop of value before being discarded. This is particularly true with respect to supplier relationships. Sophisticated matrixes are developed to classify suppliers into alliance and commodity relationships. The commodity relationships are then often "squeezed" via on-line bidding or the threat of global sourcing. Although squeezing saves money in the short run and is often easier than building efficient, fair relationships, it has its own risks. One of these is the risk of squeezing today a company that may develop tomorrow's key technology. Another pertains to the company's culture: Can companies really build a culture and the accompanying infrastructure to maximize relationship value across all relationships when it is treating 50 to 80 percent of its relationships as commodities? Most companies have found this balancing act to be very difficult to accomplish. They fail to build a culture of trust within their SC organization. The following sections discuss critical issues related to establishing productive relationships with companies at both ends of the relationship continuum.

MANAGING TRANSACTIONAL RELATIONSHIPS

Transactional relationships represent the majority of a company's SC relationships. Often 80 percent or more of all customer and supplier relationships fall into this category. A company's goal for these non-strategic relationships is twofold. First, the sheer number of non-strategic transactions dictates that companies strive for maximum efficiency in handling them. Again, both customers and suppliers appreciate efficiency—neither has the time or resources to waste with inefficient SC members. Efficiency affects relationship profitability. Second, it is vital to achieve good relations—a feeling held by other SC members that they are treated fairly. Fairness promotes return customer business and more responsive supplier support. Fair, efficient SC relations provide many returns, including:

- Lower administrative costs
- Lower product and/or service costs
- Better quality, innovation, and responsiveness
- Enhanced technical support
- The delivery of special services
- An opportunity to collect better competitive intelligence
- Fewer complaints and a better industry reputation
- More profitable relationships
- The opportunity to build closer, more collaborative relationships down the road

To summarize, customers are more patient, more likely to forgive the rare service failure, and more likely to provide a lifetime stream of profitable revenue. Suppliers are more willing to expedite an existing order, rush ship spare parts, or increase production to meet a sudden demand surge. In both upstream and downstream SC relationships, fair and friendly relations help keep negotiations simple, speed responses to inquiries, and facilitate the resolution of quality, service, or other problems. Good relations set the stage for more advanced future relationships—it is difficult to forecast which relationships will be important over a 5-year time period. By contrast, poor relations increase complaints; can take a solvable dispute to litigation, costing the company time and money; and can lead other SC members to engage in practices that drive up relationship costs. They can also lead potential suppliers or customers to dedicate constrained capacity or to share innovative ideas with competitors. For example, one apparel retailer makes extensive use of charge backs and other punitive measures when suppliers make mistakes; yet managers are surprised when they cannot get highly popular, fast-moving styles while competitors can.

Good SC relations begin with a company philosophy that says all SC members should be treated fairly and in a way that supports a mutually satisfying arrangement. Managers should be evaluated on their willingness and ability to foster proactive relations and should receive training in methods that promote them. The goal is to become a "preferred" customer or supplier. Some of the most important practices that lead to good SC relations are highlighted here. Each practice should be applied as appropriate, depending on the position, strength, duration, and importance of the relationship:

- *Personal contact:* Personal relationships generate goodwill and reduce miscommunication.
- *Clear specifications:* Product, process, and contract fulfillment specifications should be clearly stated to reduce confusion and ambiguity.
- *Timely payment:* Suppliers should be paid as quickly and easily as possible. At Payless ShoeSource, a 10-day, EFT payment cycle has been adopted to promote proactive relations.
- *Equitable treatment:* Policies should be applied equally. Preferred status should be based on real performance. Differences in service provided should be based on real profitability. Playing favorites creates suspicion and mistrust, damaging relations.
- *Training:* It often makes sense to provide marketing and category management support to customers and quality or other process training to suppliers. Training is an investment in skills and relationships.
- *Open communication:* Good electronic linkages and face-to-face communication skills are critical to good relations. SC managers need to learn to share all relevant information in a timely way.
- *Feedback:* Periodic surveys of suppliers and customers coupled with face-to-face feedback can build trust while helping improve the transaction process. Some possible questions to ask include "What can we do to make your job easier?" and "How could we work together to reduce your costs?"
- *Mutual consideration:* Managers should not unnecessarily burden other SC members. Delivery delays should be communicated quickly and changes in product and service specifications should be shared immediately. Differences in opinion should be discussed openly.
- *Give and take:* All suggestions received from other SC members should be evaluated quickly and feedback provided promptly.

- *Confidentiality:* Cost, technology, and performance information should remain strictly confidential.
- *Integrity:* SC managers should always exhibit a desire to fulfill all contract obligations without hassle or argument. They should model the integrity they expect to see.

SC managers must remember that we each view the world through a unique lens of personal experience. Every SC interaction has two sides. Building strong relations requires SC managers take a moment to consider the situation as it is felt on the other side of the relationship. One sales manager who used to be a purchaser commented on the different roles from her own experience: "When I was a purchaser, I really felt that I worked hard to be fair and make the relationship a positive one. Now that I am on the other side of the fence, I feel that purchasing managers are beating on me when they ask me to do the same things that I used to ask for." A little empathy can help build powerful SC relationships.

MANAGING STRATEGIC ALLIANCES FOR SUCCESS

Alliances are a core building block of winning SC teams. The fundamental principle driving SC integration is that closer, more collaborative alliances can yield mutually beneficial competitive advantage to the chain participants. When conceived and executed properly, SC alliances enable the partners to

- Focus on their individual strengths, potentially leveraging them into core competencies
- Manage the chain as a value system, optimizing resource usage across the chain
- Offer unique product/service packages and one-of-a-kind satisfaction opportunities
- Increase flexibility while spreading risk
- Learn from SC partners

SC managers should remember that a well-managed alliance provides specific, tangible benefits to both sides of the alliance. For example, founded on a collaborative philosophy, Honda's supplier training and development expertise has helped its suppliers improve their own internal processes on the way to creating a competitive SC model that has helped Honda become one of the world's premier auto manufacturers and the 26th most admired company in the world.[1] Both Honda and its suppliers are more profitable and growing their market share as a result of their collaboration.

As a rule, SC partnerships benefit the customer by lowering costs, improving product quality, enhancing responsiveness, decreasing order fulfillment times, speeding innovation, and yielding more productive use of resources. Suppliers benefit from longer-term, larger-volume contracts, which increase production stability, lower costs, and help justify investments in product and process technologies. Suppliers often gain access to the buyer's expertise in quality control and process engineering. In some cases, buying organizations even provide capital to upgrade the supplier's plant and equipment or finance the purchase of materials.

The mutual benefits available through alliances provide a strong incentive for proactive SC companies to seek closer, more collaborative partnerships. Because building winning alliances is hard, the following sections present a model for alliance development and discuss practices that promote and undermine alliance success.

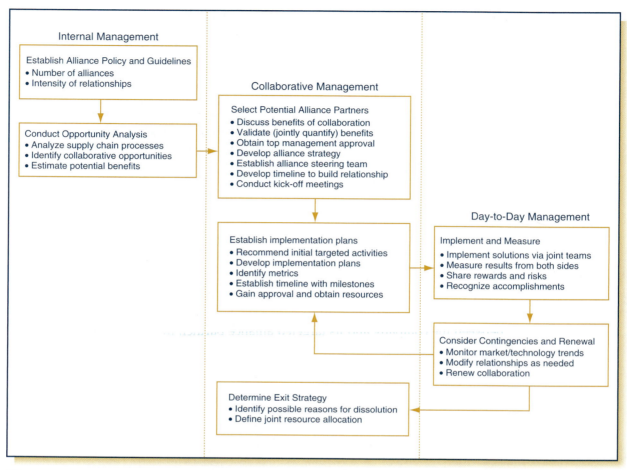

Figure 11.3 The Alliance Development Process

A Model for Alliance Management

Outstanding alliance performance requires careful planning and execution. Alliances tend to be long-term and resource intensive. They also evolve over time, with collaboration transcending traditional roles and responsibilities. The alliance development process occurs in three phases (see Figure 11.3).

Phase 1: Internal Planning for Alliance Success

Phase 1 emphasizes internal planning and takes place among a company's own management team. The question is, "What should our alliance strategy look like?" To answer this question, managers must assess the probability that the company can realistically improve competitiveness through closer relationships. Part of this assessment is aimed at ascertaining whether or not the company really has the mind-set, the skills, and the patience to build successful alliances. Great alliances do not just happen. Good communication, hard work, changed behaviors, realistic expectations, and a determination to work through difficulties and failures are all prerequisites to alliance building success.

If managers decide alliances can improve competitiveness and that the company is ready to proceed, an overall relationship management policy should be established.

The relationship continuum discussed earlier is a good starting point. A rigorous relationship screening and evaluation process should be established to help classify SC partners and define appropriate relationship intensity.

Managers should then conduct an opportunity analysis. Building on specific opportunities with well-defined and targeted outcomes improves the probability of alliance success. Specificity helps set expectations, promote open communication, and define roles and responsibilities. It also helps quantify the real, attainable benefits to be gained and shared. Although this analysis is often tedious and time-consuming, all of the scanning, mapping, costing, and competency analysis that has been performed in the SC design process provides a good starting point. Moreover, if the company has established fair and efficient relationships, it is likely that other members of the supply chain will offer alliances suggestions and be willing to participate in the opportunity analysis.

Phase 2: Collaborative Planning for Alliance Success

Phase 2 moves into collaborative planning. Once specific opportunities have been identified, defined, and prioritized, managers can begin to work with potential alliance partners. After initially approaching a potential partner with an idea for collaboration, the only way to truly know if it can deliver uniquely superior value is to explore the possibility together. This requires team-based collaborative planning between the company and its targeted alliance partner. Initially, the goal is to quantify the net impact of the potential alliance on both sides of the proposed partnership. This involves determining how the relationship will change, what new activities will be performed and who will do them, what investments will be needed, how much time and how many resources will be needed as well as who will provide them, and what benefits will be obtained and who will receive them. If the alliance is validated as viable and profitable for both sides, it will be possible to obtain the top management support that is critical to alliance success.

Once top managerial support is in place, an alliance steering team is put in place and an execution timeline is established. Many alliance initiatives launch with a kick-off meeting to formally acknowledge that the alliance is moving forward. Designed to generate excitement and momentum for the collaborative effort, these meetings are part planning, part promotion, and part celebration. The alliance steering team then goes to work to plan the nitty-gritty details that are part of changing the way two companies work with each other. Their job is to really get specific. At most companies, much of the previous discussion has been a little theoretical, oriented more toward "pie-in-the-sky" motivation than actual implementation. The focus is now on implementing specific relationship and operational improvement activities via goal identification, role specification, and the adoption of performance metrics and milestones. Both sides should be interested in clarifying minimum performance expectations, how changes in the technological and competitive marketplaces will be handled, and how shared resources and jointly developed technologies will be allocated. Contract templates and resource-sharing guidelines can be used to standardize the alliance creation process.

The final aspect of the up-front collaborative planning is to define the alliance exit strategy. Many companies unrealistically expect that the alliance will last forever. However, great alliances are entered into to build specific capabilities and achieve specific benefits. Over time, the competitive environment may change, new technologies may be developed, leadership at one or both partners may change, or the alliance may simply not deliver on its initial promise. Alliances, like technologies, may become obsolete or even dysfunctional. When this happens, it is necessary to exit the alliance. Companies should consider the contingencies and plan for this day right up front as part of the alliance definition process. A company's reputation as a good partner depends on its ability to end an alliance amicably.

Phase 3: Day-to-Day Management for Alliance Execution and Renewal

Phase 3 transitions to the day-to-day management of alliance activities by collaborative teams. These teams actually execute the plans and measure the results. This entails the hard work of managing change, people, and often technologies. Good process and project planning skills supported by frequent and open communication, strong leadership, and good team building help assure successful alliance execution. Patience is also needed. Alliances that truly change the nature of the relationship always run into problems. When these problems are anticipated, it is easier to be patient and work through them. Celebration is also an important aspect of alliance implementation. When great results are achieved, recognize and celebrate them. Celebrating affirms people's efforts and builds momentum. Indeed, SC leaders are paying greater attention to partner recognition programs. These programs generate goodwill and create visibility and thus momentum. Harley-Davidson brings its supply partners together for a supplier conference where it not only bestows its supplier-of-the-year awards but also shares design plans and lets suppliers ride its motorcycles. These conferences also create an opportunity to plan for future collaboration.

Because both the world and competitive imperatives change, SC managers must continually evaluate the alliance's performance and look for renewal opportunities. This involves active scanning of market conditions, customer needs, competitors' strategies, political shifts, and technology trends. The goal is to make sure that the alliance stays relevant and that it captures as much value as possible. Complacency or a sense of independence impedes the further development of many alliances. Many collaboration opportunities are missed. For example, despite its many collaborative ventures with Toyota, GM failed to get involved in Toyota's drive to hybrid engines. When gasoline prices rose dramatically in 2005, GM realized that it had missed an opportunity to improve its image and profitability. Joint planning and improvement teams can identify new opportunities and thus the need to modify the alliance or the incentive to grow it, possibly initiating a cycle of continuous collaborative improvement. One final comment: Each phase of the alliance process requires hard work and incurs certain risk. Building and sustaining collaborative alliances is tough.

Practices That Support Synergistic Alliances

Despite the allure of strategic alliances, great alliances are rare. For most companies, "synergistic alliance relationships" represent a very small fraction of all SC relationships—typically fewer than 3 to 5 percent of all relationships.[2] In part, the reason so few strategic alliances exist is by design; that is, the potential benefits available do not justify the investment in building the alliance. Another reason for the scarcity of synergistic SC alliances is that, as noted previously, they are hard to establish and maintain over time. Experience shows that alliance creation is a complex undertaking—there is no "silver bullet." Research suggests that a variety of practices are needed to transform a "preferred" relationship into synergistic collaboration. The following practices have been identified as vital to evaluating, establishing, and managing successful SC alliances. They are grouped according to the phase in the alliance development model to which they belong. Although most leading companies employ several of these alliance management practices, few have established a comprehensive alliance management process that incorporates them all.

Phase 1 Practices

- An alliance strategy is in place. A formal alliance policy is established complete with guidelines to govern alliances. Policies are needed to guide all aspects of an alliance from who key contacts will be to how resources will be shared and when investments will occur.
- A formal mechanism is used to identify and screen potential alliance partners.

Phase 2 Practices

- Clear and concise long-term contracts govern most successful alliances. They often run 1 to 5 years and are often considered to be "the key" to alliance success.
- Clear roles and responsibilities are defined and communicated. Explicitly stated roles and responsibilities reduce conflict and assure that key issues do not "fall between the cracks."
- Confidentiality agreements protect proprietary technologies and processes. Such agreements should specify how any jointly developed technology will be used in the future.
- Continuous improvement clauses are standard in most alliances. Improvement clauses target cost, quality, delivery, and innovation performance and specify both rewards and penalties.
- Exit criteria are spelled out at the very beginning of the relationship. Even productive relationships can become one-sided or cease to be mutually beneficial. The long term seldom means forever.

Phase 3 Practices

- Dedicated teams are used to foster "personal" relationships and establish continuity between alliance partners, facilitating collaboration, problem solving, and brainstorming activities.
- Technology linkages are established to make information exchange routine. Technologies that connect partners must be supported by a policy promoting frequent, honest, and open information sharing.
- A problem resolution methodology must be not just in place but also used to resolve the occasional misunderstandings or breakdowns that occur in even the best relationships.
- Risks and rewards are shared on a mutually acceptable basis. Synergy requires that both sides of an alliance benefit from the relationship—real alliances are not one-sided.
- Performance measures are aligned. When alliance partners use consistent measures to evaluate their own and each other's performance, problems are identified before they become crises.

Many less-tangible attributes and philosophies also need to be cultivated to support effective alliances. SC managers identify trust as the most critical facilitator of alliance success. Because of its key role in alliance collaboration, trust is discussed more fully later in the chapter. SC managers also frequently talk about the following intangibles as keys to successful alliances.

- Collaborative/joint efforts
- Collaborative continuous improvement
- Collaborative creativity and idea generation
- Cultural fit
- Mutual commitment to the relationship
- Mutual dependence
- Patience and perseverance
- Personal relationships
- Shared vision and objectives
- Trust
- Understanding of each other's businesses
- Willingness to be flexible and tailor services

Note the frequent occurrence of the words "shared," "collaborative," and "mutual." The shared nature of these attributes is difficult to cultivate and measure. Yet, it is critical. When one partner consistently puts forth 70 percent of the effort and resources while the other contributes only 30 percent, tension quickly develops. The underlying notion of each attribute is an emphasis on bringing the two parties together to help each achieve greater success than either could alone.

Attitudes and Behaviors That Impede Alliance Development

We have said it before, but the point is important enough to repeat: Great alliance relationships are hard to establish. They require both a change in philosophy and a change in practice. Unfortunately, many of the practices discussed earlier are under-utilized. Most managers report that their organizations lack clear alliance guidelines.[3] This reality represents a serious problem since guidelines are needed to determine (1) which relationships merit partnership status; (2) the intensity of specific relationships; (3) how key resources like intellectual property are to be developed, shared, and protected; and (4) when an alliance should be modified or even terminated. Proven guidelines would take a lot of the guesswork out of alliance management. More importantly, without up-front guidelines, few of the other practices are adequately established, and the alliance development process struggles to get out of Phase 1 successfully.

Beyond failing to implement the practices that promote alliance success, too many companies rely on size and power to motivate cooperation and, in the minds of less powerful SC members, to extract concessions. The power asymmetry that prevails in many SC relationships manifests itself in the way companies do (or do not) share risks and rewards. Even when an agreement has been made to share risks and rewards equally, identifying and quantifying them is extremely difficult. Further, today's emphasis on profit-and-loss statements and quarterly earnings reports leads managers to maximize their own companies' profits. Managers therefore find it difficult not to expropriate the economic benefits of alliance relationships at the expense of the alliance partner. This fact creates an adversarial feel in many alliances that is exacerbated by

- An unwillingness among managers to share sensitive, proprietary information
- The belief that an alliance partner is only as good as its last performance
- The failure to consider the realities of the partner's situation

Simply stated, few companies have made the organizational commitment to partnership relationships. The rest continue to hedge their bets, seeking the benefits of closer relationships without making enduring investments in those relationships.

The Role of Trust and Power in Supply Chain Relationships

Trust has been described as the foundation for effective SCM because it promotes collaboration, risk taking, and both shared information and shared resources.[4] At the same time, a lack of trust has been identified as the greatest obstacle to SC improvement.[5] The future of SCM depends on managers' willingness to commit to cultivating greater trust in alliance and other SC relationships.[6]

As a word, trust is heard whenever SC alliances are discussed; yet, as an actionable concept, trust is difficult to define. This fact has led some managers to be suspicious when they hear the word "trust"; this is true especially at smaller firms where managers feel whipsawed about by larger SC "partners." The title of a *BusinessWeek* article points to the challenge of building trust in a competitive world: "Supply Chain Squeeze: Big Clients Demand Cost Cuts—Now."[7]

Competitive pressures often lead to behavior that undermines trust. For example, a manager shared with pride the experience of being selected as the "Supplier of the Year" by a major Japanese company. He told about the wonderful evening at a downtown hotel where an extravagant banquet was held in honor of the supplier's outstanding performance. He then said, "That was a year ago. Just about a month ago we received a letter informing us that they were dropping us as a supplier because someone else beat our price by 2 cents a part."

Trust has numerous antecedents, including open information sharing, commitment, clear expectations, and follow through. The passage of time, high levels of performance, and the fulfillment of promises also promote trust. Finally, real trust exists only when both sides agree that it does. Relationships that one party describes as trust-based are often viewed as less mutually advantageous by the other side. To build trust, SC managers should keep in mind the following principles that define SC trust.

Trust Is Two Sided

Basic objectives often pull in different directions. The pivot point is channel power. Generally, buyers have it and suppliers do not. Managers at suppliers feel their customers use channel power to extract concessions. Buying organizations constantly seek to reduce costs while suppliers work to protect margins. But, as one manager has noted, suppliers feel that when "push comes to shove, it is almost always at our expense." Recent events seem to confirm this belief. *BusinessWeek* reported, "The ultimatum came in January: Cut your prices 30 percent, or the deal is off. But with margins already razor-thin, another cut was impossible."[8] *The Wall Street Journal* reported, "Chrysler yesterday demanded that its suppliers cough up 5 percent price cuts by January 1 and another 10 percent by 2003."[9] Table 11.1 highlights other issues that create divergent views and emotional distance between SC partners. The two-sided view of trust suggests that when the buyer says, "We need to squeeze costs out of the process," the supplier is likely to hear, "They plan to squeeze the margin out of us." Trust is hard to build when the power relationship is asymmetrical.

Trust Is Behavior

Trustworthy behavior tells supply chain partners they are valued. The easiest way to evaluate whether trust exists is to ask companies how their partners achieve their goals. If leverage is identified as the tool of choice, then trust is certain to be

Table 11.1 The Two-World View of Supply Chain Trust

	BUYER ORGANIZATION	SUPPLIER ORGANIZATION
Power	Have it!!!	Do not have it!!!
Corporate Objective	Reduce costs!!!	Protect margins!!!
Relationship Expectations	Have needs met—buying solutions	Be treated fairly
Communication Style	THE FACTS!	Seek to accommodate!
Problem Solving	Don't like to be corrected by suppliers!!!	View offers of help that occur only after problems arise as intrusive/controlling.
Definition of Win–Win	Suppliers should be happy if they are a little better off than before!	Expect to be compensated for value-added over the life of relationships!

missing in the relationship. Companies do not beat up SC partners that they value. Trust-based behavior is exemplified through on-time payment, the sharing of risks and rewards, and investing in each other's capabilities. The following scenarios show the variability found in relationship behavior.

- *Scenario 1:* A service provider was approached by a customer and told, "We've carefully examined the service you provide as well as what you charge for your service. We value what you do for us and think you need to charge us more. We want you to raise your rates because we want you to be successful over the long term. We can't rely on your service if you're not in business."
- *Scenario 2:* The cost savings promised by on-line bidding persuaded a consumer electronics company that had made the effort to build collaborative supply relationships to rationalize, "We will use reverse auctions to drive prices down by 30 percent and then resume our collaborative efforts."

Many companies try to get the best of both competitive and collaborative supply relationships. They define relationships as transaction-oriented or collaborative and then try to establish the mechanisms needed to manage different relationships effectively. This dichotomous approach can undercut a culture of trust. Wharton's Marshall Fisher pointed out that many companies, "decide to play the cooperative and competitive games at the same time. But that tactic doesn't work, because the two approaches require diametrically different behavior."[10]

Trust Requires Open Information Sharing

Managers must learn to share all information that affects a relationship's competitiveness. Leading companies share historical sales, production plans, and long-term forecasts as well as information on new product, market entry, and technology plans. Quarterly business reviews are also used to share feedback in both directions. Performance improvement is then expected. Open communication promotes strong and dynamic relationships that are capable of coming up with new ideas and unique products and services.

Trust Is Personal

Honda's Teruyuki Maruo recognized the role of personal relationships in building trust, saying, "Suppliers don't trust purchasing because purchasing means cost, but they must trust you. Suppliers must develop confidence in you. Suppliers may not trust purchasing, but you want them to trust you."[11] To help overcome its reputation for using its buying clout to squeeze suppliers, Wal-Mart instituted a program that called on each buyer's top 6 suppliers to evaluate the buyer's performance and behavior on an annual basis. The program's goal is to convince buyers to treat suppliers amicably. Wal-Mart still wants its buyers to be tough, but it expects them to be fair.

Trust Means Performance

Timothy Laseter noted, "The popular literature suggests that 'trust' is the key to effective customer–supplier relationships. But simply preaching trust as a new gospel is unworkable at best—and definitely naive."[12] Laseter alluded to the fact that there is no such thing as trust without consistent, outstanding performance. In fact, when asked to define trust, most SC managers emphasize the idea that both suppliers and customers perform to promise. Trust demands that companies do what they say they are going to do—the first time, all the time. As one manager explained, "I never lose sleep when I work with Jim because I know that he will deliver as promised even if he has to lose sleep."

Assessing Supply Chain Trust

The very nature of trust makes it hard for companies to objectively evaluate whether or not they have a trust-based culture. How many managers do you know who want to acknowledge that they work for a company that abuses its power and can't be trusted by other members of the supply chain? Because we all want to believe that we can be trusted and that we work for a trustworthy company, a realistic assessment of trust must incorporate perceptions of outside members of the supply chain.

Figure 11.4 shows a straightforward process for evaluating existing levels of trust and determining where improvement needs to be made. The process begins with a sincere desire to become a trusted SC partner. At many companies, this desire arises only after relationships become strained. Ford undertook a trustworthiness assessment after hearing repeatedly that its suppliers didn't trust Ford. Suppliers were much more eager and willing to work with Honda and Toyota. Interestingly, a 2005 survey of auto suppliers identified Toyota as the preferred OEM automaker to work with and Honda as the most trustworthy.[13] Why does it matter? Because over time, suppliers tend to shift engineering support and capital expenditure toward their preferred customers. Poor relations translate into diminished long-term support and competitiveness. Moreover, when Honda suffered a revenue shortfall in the early 2000s, it approached its suppliers for help. Because they wanted Honda as a long-term customer, they cut prices without a murmur. Seeking to capture the benefits of trust-based relationships, Ford undertook its trustworthiness assessment. It is, however, likely that companies that proactively assess trust—while relationships are working well—will be perceived as more credible in their trust-building initiatives.

Once a company decides to assess trust, managers must define the scope to the assessment. Will it be a functional assessment? Or will it look exclusively at supplier or customer relationships? Or will it evaluate the amount of trust throughout the chain? The selected scope will determine who should be involved. Once again, the very nature of trust argues for the use of an independent task force or outside assessor. It would be naïve to expect sales to objectively assess customer relationships.

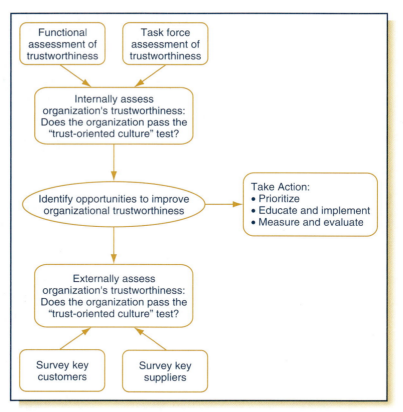

Figure 11.4 A Process for Assessing Trust in Supply Chain Relationships

Equally important, when it comes time to ask customers how they perceive the company's trustworthiness, they are far more likely to answer honestly if they feel that the assessor is unbiased and that their answers will be kept strictly confidential—reported only as part of the aggregate assessment. The actual assessment process should seek enough internal participation and external feedback to provide a valid and reliable understanding of the company's culture of trust. This will probably require at least 30 interviews with each participant group.

Two questions remain. First: "What should be assessed?" The 5 dimensions discussed earlier provide a good starting point. Second: "How should the assessment be utilized?" Overall levels of trust should be analyzed, as should each of the 5 dimensions of trust. The perceptions of each group surveyed should also be compared. Managers should be looking for gaps. Does one group feel that risks and rewards are shared equitably while the others do not? With data in hand, managers can set up internal and external brainstorming sessions, perhaps as part of a supplier conference or a customer advisory board meeting. The brainstorming should take a root-cause-analysis approach, seek to identify potential solutions, and establish a set of actionable priorities. If the company is committed to building trusting relationships, it will now have a road map to follow.

To summarize, many companies rely excessively on leverage to govern relationships. Both sides of alliances tend to be self-interested and pursue their own goals. Whenever those goals diverge, opportunistic behavior emerges. This opportunism destroys trust. Roger Blackwell summarized the cost incurred when trust is missing in SC relationships:

> If entrepreneurs and senior managers do not trust frontline employees, a firm cannot act with speed and efficiency. If a supplier does not trust a customer, then the supplier hesitates to suggest productivity changes. If customers don't trust suppliers, they cannot readily shift functions such as inventory replenishment to their supply chain partners. If employees do not trust management, they will not suggest changes that lead to better execution. Trust is the catalyst of progress in improved performance.[14]

MODERN NEGOTIATION AND RELATIONSHIP MANAGEMENT

One of the most important activities in relationship building is negotiation. Traditionally, negotiation was used to determine the specifics of an important contractual relationship. Price, quality, delivery, and compliance were the critical issues. Today, negotiation is a key tool in building competitive, world-class partnerships. Certainly, determining the nature of the contractual relationship is still important, but achieving high levels of trust and synergy are often the primary objectives of modern negotiation.

What Is Negotiation?

Negotiation is the formal communication process where two or more individuals meet face-to-face (or increasingly via electronic means) to discuss important issues and come to a mutually satisfactory agreement. Negotiations take place in many aspects of our daily lives. Families negotiate vital issues such as whether to eat out or cook at home, where to go on vacation, and how to allocate responsibility for household chores. Work colleagues negotiate such issues as team roles and responsibilities, day-to-day work assignments, or who will drive to lunch. Although these situations generally lack the preparation and organization found in negotiating SC relationships, they do involve the basics of the negotiation process. In each case, individuals involved in the negotiation have specific goals they are pursuing, communicate desires and listen to counterproposals, participate in a give-and-take concession process, and ideally arrive at a conclusion both sides find acceptable.

Though price, quality, and service are the topics most frequently discussed in negotiations, any issue that affects the performance of the relationship can be negotiated. Some additional topics, which demonstrate the range and diversity of issues that should be discussed, are listed here:

- Confidentiality, especially with respect to cost structure and proprietary technologies
- Continuous improvement expectations in quality, cost, and other relevant areas
- Contract duration and volumes
- Delivery schedules
- Joint research and development
- Nonperformance definitions and penalties/legal recourse for noncompliance
- Ownership and use of intellectual property that is jointly developed

- Provisions for terminating the relationship
- Shared resources including capital, personnel, and technology
- Technical assistance and support

Successful negotiations require the careful management of information, personal relationships, time, and power as the two sides of the negotiation work out a mutually beneficial arrangement. In most negotiations, neither side obtains all of its desired objectives. It is important to recognize that mutual benefit does not necessarily imply equality of benefits. Seldom do both sides of a negotiation come to the table with equal power and influence. The key for negotiation success is for both parties to improve their position, and their competitiveness, through the negotiation process. When this is not possible for whatever reason, then both sides are probably better off walking away from the process than accepting an agreement that is detrimental to either side's competitiveness. Though there are some managers who believe that failing to reach an agreement represents a negotiation failure, no agreement is better than a bad agreement.

When Is Negotiation Appropriate?

Negotiation is a time- and resource-intensive activity. The time and expense incurred in traveling to and from the negotiation site and in the negotiation itself can be substantial. However, this expense represents only a small fraction of the total negotiation cost. Pre-negotiation preparation can represent up to 90 percent of a successful negotiation.[15] Negotiation is most appropriately used when the costs of the negotiation can be viewed as an investment in future competitiveness. This occurs in high-dollar-value transactions, technologically complex or innovative situations, and highly uncertain/high-risk scenarios. Negotiation is valuable when it provides an opportunity to probe for unique value-added opportunities that might involve specialized capital investment, shared resources, the shifting of specific roles and responsibilities, or uniquely collaborative activities.

For example, Nestle, a large Swiss consumer packaged good company, provides capital to build dedicated warehouses that are then operated by third-party distributors. Negotiation is used to establish expectations, performance criteria, and measurement issues as well as other aspects of the long-term relationship including non-performance penalties. An element of brainstorming often accompanies these negotiations—mutual benefits often arise from shared learning that begins in the negotiation process. Negotiation also gives the two parties time to work out the details. Some questions to ask include "Is the buyer willing to share development costs?" "Are both sides willing to share the needed information and resources?" "Who assumes the risk if the effort does not work?" When appropriately pursued and executed, negotiation can lead to outstanding value creation.

Negotiation Philosophies

Most negotiations are driven by a conscious philosophy. For many years, the best negotiator was the one who could extract as many concessions as possible from her counterpart. This adversarial approach is known as the win–lose philosophy. Negotiators who pursue a win–lose negotiation feel that a fixed amount of value exists in the relationship, and the goal is to capture as much of the value as possible. Win–lose negotiating pits the customer and the supplier against each other—both sides pursue a hard line with fixed negotiating positions and a determined resistance to compromise. Leverage determines who wins and loses. The win–lose philosophy ultimately leaves the loser (usually the supplier) not only beaten but also lacking any real commitment to the buyer's success.

For example, in the early 1990s, Jose Ignacio Lopez, General Motor's purchasing czar, developed a reputation as a brutal negotiator. He broke the tradition of renewing 1-year contracts with established supply partners. Opening these contracts to competition, Lopez pitted suppliers against one another in an effort to obtain the lowest possible price. Although suppliers who had made extensive investments to develop new products for GM were irate, the strategy reduced GM's annual materials costs by $4 billion.[16] Over time, however, GM discovered that this approach reduced suppliers' commitment. For much of the following decade, many suppliers reserved their best ideas and highest level of support for more loyal customers. Others removed GM entirely from their preferred customer list. Over 10 years later, the same survey of auto suppliers mentioned earlier rated Toyota as the best customer with a total score of 415. GM scored 114—over 300 points lower. GM's experience suggests that over time there are no winners in win–lose negotiations.[17]

As a result, cooperative, win–win negotiating philosophies have become more popular. The fundamental tenet of win–win negotiating is that by working closely together, both the buyer and supplier can improve their competitiveness and profitability. Cooperation creates value while competition dissipates resources. Cooperation allows both sides to bring more energy and creativity to the table so that "hidden" options can be discovered. Steven Covey discusses the win–win philosophy: "It is a belief in the Third Alternative. It's not your way or my way; it's a better way, a higher way."[18] Several conditions must be present for win–win negotiation to be successful.

- Both sides must adopt a win–win mentality.
- Both sides must have a vested interest in a successful outcome.
- Both sides must view the negotiation as part of a larger or longer-term relationship.
- Both sides must recognize the other's needs and wants. The ultimate measure of success is the perception that the process has been fair and everyone's objectives have been met.
- Both sides must work jointly to create value. They share information and resources. When difficulties arise, cooperative efforts are undertaken to find an accommodating solution.
- Both sides must approach the negotiation with an attitude of trust.

Preparing for a Successful Negotiation

Negotiation experts concur that preparation is the most critical step in the negotiation process. Thus, the familiar saying, "Preparation Precedes Power" holds true for negotiating. Negotiators who do their homework by determining objectives, collecting information, analyzing strengths and weaknesses, or anticipating the other side's objections achieve superior outcomes. Having a well-thought-out plan allows them to argue positions persuasively, respond to the tough questions, recognize the tactics employed by the other side, and know when to conclude a good agreement or walk away from a bad one. Several "failings" common to negotiation preparation have been identified.[19]

- Negotiators fail to invest sufficient time in the planning process. It is impossible to effectively "cram" for an important negotiation—time must be committed before the negotiation.

- Negotiators fail to establish clear objectives. Without clear objectives, negotiators really do not know what their position on specific issues should be or when a good arrangement has been reached.
- Negotiators fail to consider their counterpart's needs. Only by knowing what the other side views as essential can a negotiator determine what concessions can be made on both sides.
- Negotiators fail to formulate convincing arguments for their positions. Without knowing both sides' strengths and weaknesses, negotiators cannot appreciate the source of their negotiating power and anticipate the ebb and flow of the actual negotiation.

Effective negotiators avoid these mistakes. They develop detailed plans, analyze the strengths and weaknesses of their position, and know where and when concessions are acceptable. They have done their homework to find out who their counterparts are and what their negotiation philosophy is likely to be as well as what tactics they are likely to employ. And they are lucky, but they define luck as the meeting point of preparation and opportunity. Great negotiators are not born; they are great because they prepare meticulously and they develop the skills needed to achieve superior outcomes. Successful negotiators use a systematic approach that consists of the following negotiation planning steps.

Develop Specific Objectives

The more specific the objectives, the more focused and better prepared the organization will be when the negotiation begins. One objective of any negotiation should be to reach a satisfactory agreement. Negotiations are too expensive to undertake without a firm commitment to find a common ground that meets both sides' basic wants and needs.

Establish an Effective Negotiating Team

Each department affected by the negotiation outcome should be represented on the team. Bringing the right technical expertise to the team is also vital. Finally, including experienced negotiators to either lead the negotiation or coach the lead negotiator is also a good idea. To assure proper team chemistry, the team members should be brought together early in the planning process to give them time to bond as well as to provide an opportunity to contribute throughout the planning process. Team members must also understand and agree to their specific roles and responsibilities both during the preparation and the actual negotiation.

Gather Relevant Information

Because information is power, successful negotiators take the research responsibility seriously. If a long relationship exists, the research burden is diminished because the negotiator is familiar with the other side's capabilities and negotiating style. Outside sources of information such as business publications, commercial databases, trade associations, financial statements, and Dunn and Bradstreet reports should also be evaluated. A tour of the other organization's operations is often a vital part of the pre-negotiation investigation.

Analyze Strengths and Weaknesses

Knowing the strengths and weaknesses of each side enables the negotiator to establish realistic expectations. This knowledge helps the negotiator develop an appropriate strategy and select winning tactics. Negotiators should understand (1) the motivations that underlie the potential relationship, (2) unique technologies or capabilities possessed by each side, (3) the availability of alternatives, (4) the time available for the negotiation, (5) trends in the competitive environment, (6) the skill and tendencies of the other side's negotiators, and (7) the financial position of each party.

Recognize the Other Side's Needs

A primary reason organizations negotiate is to determine where the give and take in the relationship will take place. As negotiators prepare, they must differentiate between the other side's absolute needs and the items on its wish list. By conceding a point that is important to the other party but not particularly vital to the negotiator, goodwill can be built at a low cost. This goodwill can then be expended on more critical issues.

Determine the Facts and the Issues

Facts are those items about which agreement is expected; they are the realities of the negotiation. By contrast, issues are those points about which disagreement is expected and which the negotiation is supposed to resolve. Once facts are agreed upon, time and effort can be dedicated to resolving the key issues such as what constitutes a fair and reasonable price or a late delivery. Although the majority of actual negotiating time should be spent narrowing the distance on key issues, the initial discussion of facts can help establish rapport and build the foundation for open and honest negotiations.

Establish a Position on Each Issue

Negotiators need to establish their own position on each issue and estimate the other side's positions as well. Most negotiators establish a realistic, achievable position. Based on this target, they work out pessimistic and optimistic scenarios. The pessimistic or worst acceptable position must be defined before the negotiation. When positions overlap, a little give and take by both parties can usually lead to a mutually acceptable arrangement. Failure to find a common ground on a critical point can undermine the entire negotiation. Neither side should expect to achieve optimal (or even target) results on every issue. Negotiators must be flexible and on occasion consider modifying their chosen position.

Plan the Negotiation Strategy

The strategy answers key overarching negotiation questions: Who will do the negotiating? Which issues should be discussed and in what sequence? Where is compromise acceptable? Where and when will the negotiation take place? How much of the organization's position should be revealed and when? How will the execution of the agreement be managed? The strategy provides guidance as the negotiation unfolds and provides the means by which progress is measured.

Select Appropriate Tactics

The tactical plan choreographs the actual negotiation process, arranging and directing the details required to get to a satisfactory agreement. It is the action plan. The tactics selected depend on the organization's negotiating philosophy, the negotiation objectives, and the strategy for the specific negotiation. A large variety of tactics are available—some are well suited to all negotiations while others are best used in collaborative negotiations and still others apply only to adversarial settings. Some tactics are unethical and should be avoided; however, the experienced negotiator should recognize when the other party is using them (see Table 11.2).

Table 11.2   Common Negotiation Tactics

Argue Based on Facts. Arguments that cannot be factually supported damage credibility.

Answer Questions Carefully. Experienced negotiators know that the proper answer to a question is truthful, advances the negotiator's tactical plan, and helps discern the supplier's objectives.

Be Considerate. Treating counterparts with respect and dignity almost never costs the well-prepared negotiator much in terms of position or outcome, but it does build goodwill.

Be Wary of Deadlines. An effective negotiator does not let deadlines force bad decisions. The use of arbitrary or meaningless deadlines diminishes credibility.

Best and Final Offer. The take-it-or-leave-it approach signals the need for a decision on a specific point. If the negotiator is not prepared to end the negotiation and the "bluff" is called, credibility is lost.

Do Not Be Afraid to Say No. It is better to say no than to agree to an unsatisfactory position. Being candid has merit.

Foot in the Door. Whenever an exceptional quote is received a negotiator should examine both motivation and capabilities to determine whether the offer represents a real long-term benefit.

High Ball. Win–lose negotiators sometimes begin a negotiation at an extreme position, expecting to make concessions.

Honesty and Openness. Win–win negotiations emphasize honest and open sharing of information.

Keep the Initiative. Some negotiators believe that the "best defense is a good offense." They establish initiative early and maintain it by probing the other side's position, asking for justifications and requiring supporting documentation.

Listen Effectively. Great listeners focus on not only the words but also the tone of voice and the pauses. Careful observation provides insight into the other side's position and real objectives.

The Missing Person. The deliberate absence of the person with the decision-making authority gives the negotiator extra time or an opportunity to escape negotiations that are not going well.

Never Give Anything Away. Win–lose negotiators often believe that the other side should make more and larger concessions. For every concession made, equal or greater concessions are expected from the other side.

Phantom Quote/Offer. Deliberately attempting to mislead the other side into believing that "a better quote (or offer) is waiting from another supplier (or buyer)" is unethical and risky.

Prioritize Issues. Two basic philosophies exist: (1) Discuss the most difficult issues first and (2) discuss the "easy" issues first to establish the trust that will help resolve more difficult issues.

Schedule Breaks. Scheduled breaks provide an opportunity to evaluate how things are going, discuss any surprises, gather additional information, and discuss strategies or tactics. The routine use of unscheduled breaks makes it difficult for the other party to draw meaning from a team's decision to call for an unscheduled break.

Security. Occasionally, unethical behavior ranging from the use of hidden microphones to the copying of work notes occurs. If in doubt, the negotiation should be conducted on-site at the negotiator's location.

Site Selection. Most negotiators prefer to host the negotiation to avoid travel and have access to needed information. The primary advantage of holding the negotiation at the other party's site is the option to "walk away" from negotiations that are not going well. Informal and comfortable settings are best for win–win negotiations.

Strong Initial Offer. Making a strong initial offer signals a desire to do business with the counterpart.

The Threat. A tactic often used in win–lose negotiations is the threat—"If you don't decide now, I can't promise that we will have the material when you need it." Frequent threats reduce credibility.

Use Diversions. Experienced negotiators divert attention away from the problematic issues by using a joke, an anecdote, or a well-timed break.

Use Positive Statements. Sometimes it is important to respond with a simple, "I see your point" or "Your point is well taken."

Use Questions Effectively. The right question can undermine an unacceptable position or deflect criticism.

Use Silence. Silence can be effectively used to avoid difficult questions, make the other side nervous, seek concessions without specifically asking for them, and redirect the discussion tactfully.

Practice the Negotiation

Because a company will have to live with the outcome (sometimes for years), strategically important negotiations should be thoroughly practiced before the real event. A mock negotiation can help simulate what might actually occur in the real negotiation. Both sides in a mock negotiation need to play their roles as realistically as possible to uncover flaws in the analysis, positions, or execution of the negotiating plan. Another technique is to present the negotiation plan (objectives, strategy, tactics, and agenda) to an internal panel of executives that aggressively dissects the plan, pointing out weaknesses and making suggestions for improvement. These internal panels have been called "Murder Boards" because their role is to pick apart the presentation.

Conducting Successful Negotiations

Negotiation is a dynamic process. Even the best preparation cannot guarantee success without careful execution. Great negotiators manage negotiation dynamics carefully. It has been estimated that approximately 60 to 70 percent of the benefits of the typical negotiated contract go to the side with the more skilled negotiator.[20] Most negotiations are conducted in 4 phases.

Phase 1: Fact Finding

An important role of the fact-finding session is to build rapport between the negotiators. In many countries, serious negotiations do not begin until the two sides have spent considerable time getting to know each other. Experience suggests successful negotiations are facilitated when the initial face-to-face meeting is limited to fact finding.

Phase 2: The Recess

The recess is used to reassess relative strengths and weaknesses, review and revise objectives, and reevaluate key issues. When the negotiation reconvenes, experienced negotiators prefer to address specific issues in order of perceived difficulty, starting with the least controversial issues. This approach builds on the rapport established in the fact-finding session.

Phase 3: Narrowing the Differences

Brainstorming, problem solving, and compromise are used to find a mutually agreeable position. When a specific issue deadlocks, the negotiation should move on to the next issue. Subsequent discussions can help break an earlier impasse. Effective negotiators often refer to common ground. They view issues independently and with an overall sense of give and take. They also separate people from positions, are careful never to attack the individual, and are quick to compliment their counterparts.

Thoughtful negotiators also keep an open mind, recognizing that good ideas often emerge during discussions. They are willing to work with potential partners to invent new options for mutual gain. In fact, skilled negotiators evaluate twice as many options per issue compared to average negotiators.[21] Finally, experienced negotiators recognize that fatigue slows thinking, clouds judgment, and can raise tensions. They arrange agendas to provide for sufficient rest before and during the negotiation.

Phase 4: Hard Bargaining

Hard bargaining should only be used when more cooperative efforts have failed. Because hard bargaining employs win–lose tactics and market power to get to a satisfactory deal, it should not be used when long-term partnership relationships are the goal.

Table 11.3 Characteristics of an Effective Negotiator

Ability to gain respect	Persistence
Ability to listen	Personal integrity
Analytical ability	Planning ability
Competitiveness	Problem-solving ability
Decisiveness	Quick, agile thinking ability
Desire to achieve	Self-control
Flexibility	Tact
Insight	Tolerance for ambiguity
Intelligence	Verbal clarity and language skill
Knowledge of human nature	Willingness to listen to others' ideas
Patience	Willingness to study and practice

Becoming a Skillful Negotiator

Experience suggests that although some individuals possess a quicker wit, more charisma, or stronger verbal aptitudes, almost anyone can improve their negotiating ability. Table 11.3 lists some of the characteristics and skills possessed by outstanding negotiators. It is interesting to note that all of these abilities can be developed or enhanced through training and practice. No one is born with negotiating knowledge and skills. Superior preparation that comes from hard work can help any manager become a more successful negotiator. Successful negotiators recognize that specialized training and practice are required, enter negotiations with high expectations (which they generally achieve), and are counted as among the most highly valued professionals in their organization.

CONCLUSION

Establishing good relationships with current and potential SC members is essential to the success of any company's competitive strategy. In today's cutthroat, yet resource-constrained world, the key is to establish an appropriate relationship with each member of the supply chain. Although the intensity of SC relationships will vary greatly, each relationship must be designed to achieve efficient, fair, and reasonable relations. Such a goal is critical to building a globally competitive "team" founded on the chemistry that comes from mutual respect, hard work, and a sincere desire for each team member to be more competitive. This chemistry facilitates proactive collaboration, role shifting, and truly synergistic performance, especially among the most important SC relationships.

Unfortunately, although there has been a lot of talk regarding cooperation among SC members, most companies are not as advanced in adopting the practices that make true teamwork a reality. Alliance building is a complex undertaking and no single practice, or group of practices, is capable of closing the cultural, emotional, physical, and strategic gaps that prevent synergistic collaboration. Thus, most companies have not put in place the skills and practices needed to build great SC alliances. As SC managers seek to obtain the market share and profitability benefits that can emerge over the lifetime of a collaborative relationship, they should keep the following points regarding alliance design and management in mind. They should

- View the alliance arrangement as the implementation of a strategic plan.
- Encourage the participants involved to consider their roles in terms of a value-added process.
- Make sure that the information needed to succeed is shared among participants.
- Set unambiguous goals, establish clear roles, and lay down firm rules.
- Measure performance rigorously.
- Consider the contingencies and develop an exit strategy—the long-term may not last forever.

SUMMARY OF KEY POINTS

1. Not all relationships are created equal—nor should they be. Some relationships merit much more managerial attention and resource dedication than others. Nonetheless, all relationships should be managed for efficiency and fairness.

2. Customer, supplier, and service provider relationships should be classified based on their strategic relevance and importance. Appropriate relationships should then be established. Relationship intensity and appropriateness is one of the most important concepts an SC manager needs to understand. The relationship continuum can help SC managers conceptualize and communicate relationship intensity.

3. Most SC relationships do not merit the time and attention invested in strategic alliances; but, all relationships should be managed proactively and as part of an overall SC strategy. Like all relationships, non-strategic relationships should be managed for efficiency and fairness.

4. Successful alliance strategies employ a 3-phase alliance development model. The first phase involves internal planning; the second focuses on a collaborative evaluation of specific opportunities; and the third focuses on execution of jointly developed plans.

5. Alliances are the building blocks of SC teams. When conceived and executed properly, SC alliances can help companies leverage their strengths, offer unique products/services, increase flexibility, and create learning opportunities.

6. Many tools and techniques have been identified as vital to evaluating, establishing, and managing successful strategic alliances. Some of the most important include the following:
   - An alliance policy is established and formal guidelines are used to manage alliances.
   - A formal mechanism is used to identify potential alliance partners.
   - Clear roles and responsibilities are defined and communicated.
   - Clear and concise long-term contracts govern successful alliances.
   - Confidentiality agreements protect proprietary technologies and processes.
   - Continuous improvement clauses are standard in most alliances.
   - Exit criteria should be spelled out at the very beginning of the relationship.
   - Risks and rewards are shared on a mutually acceptable basis.
   - A problem resolution methodology must be in place.
   - Technology is used to routinize information exchange.
   - Rigorous measurement alignment methodology keeps partners "on the same page."
   - Dedicated teams foster "personal" relationships and establish continuity.

7. Trust only exists when both sides agree that it does. Trust is manifest through behavior that tells SC partners they are valued. It requires open information sharing, is based on personal relationships, and is built on excellent performance.

8. Negotiation is the formal communication process where two or more individuals meet to discuss an issue or issues and come to a mutually satisfactory agreement.

9. Preparation is the most critical step in the negotiation process. Successful negotiators use the following planning steps:
   - Specific objectives are established.
   - An effective negotiation team is assembled.

- Relevant information is gathered.
- Strengths and weaknesses are analyzed.
- An effort is made to identify key needs for both sides.
- Facts and issues are defined.

- Positions are established on each important issue.
- A negotiation strategy is established.
- Appropriate tactics are identified.
- Important negotiations are practiced.

REVIEW EXERCISES

1. Describe the factors that should be considered in deciding what type of relationship to build with a specific customer or supplier.
2. Identify 10 practices that foster efficient, fair relationships with "C"-level customers and suppliers. Discuss two reasons managers should care about these relationships.
3. Describe the reasons companies should consider establishing closer relationships with important customers or suppliers. Identify the benefits buyers and suppliers should expect from an SC alliance.
4. Identify the most important tools and techniques that facilitate alliance development. What are some of the barriers to utilizing each of these techniques?
5. Discuss the counterproductive behaviors that impede alliance creation. Describe how you would mitigate the negative influence of these behaviors.
6. Define trust. Identify two current events—one that demonstrates a high level of trust and one that demonstrates the absence of trust. What are the performance implications discussed in each current event?
7. Discuss the issues involved in carrying out a successful negotiation. Do you have the skills to be a successful negotiator? Identify 3 areas in which you need training or practice.

Case   *How Close Is Too Close?*

Tim Tree, senior VP of supply chain management at Top Line Inc., sat silently in his office, pondering the ramifications of the formal letter of invitation that he held in his hand. The letter was from Top Line's most important customer, Dynamo Inc., and extended the unique opportunity to become one of only a few "Partner" suppliers to Dynamo. The letter pointed out that the "Partner designation represents the apex of Dynamo/ supplier relationships and is awarded exclusively to carefully selected suppliers with whom our Company shares common objectives and a commitment to a long-term, mutually beneficial interaction geared to meeting our customers' needs." Tim couldn't help but wonder whether Top Line was ready for the time and resource commitments required to participate in such a tightly coupled relationship.

As Tim considered what a "yes" or "no" decision might mean, he reflected on the changes that had taken place at Top Line over the past 24 months. Just a little over 2 years previously, Top Line had found itself perilously close to financial ruin. Quality levels were suspect, productivity was below industry standard, and it seemed that Top Line couldn't deliver product to key customers on time if its future depended on it (which it did).

The only thing standing between Top Line and bankruptcy was a set of 7 patents that protected Top Line's key process and product technologies. Unfortunately, the two most important patents were set to expire within 18 months. This fact spurred a new determination to improve Top Line's customer service capabilities. Tim and his team had approached Top Line's 10 most important customers in an attempt to find out just what constituted world-class service. After evaluating the customer feedback, Top Line embarked on a total quality campaign coupled with a lean logistics initiative. As a result, quality defects had dropped to an average of 250 parts per million, delivery performance had improved to almost 98 percent on time, and productivity had increased by over 15 percent. Sales had increased by almost 30 percent in the past year to $1.32 billion and Top Line had increased its market share to 8 percent of the global market.

Top Line's performance improvements had not gone unnoticed. In the past year, Top Line had received one

"Supplier-of-the-Year" award and had been granted "Key Supplier" status by Dynamo Inc. The entire senior management team at Top Line was certain the company was on the right track. Initially, the letter from Lisa Gecowets, VP of sourcing at Dynamo, seemed to confirm this feeling of renewed confidence, and everyone felt that the obvious answer was a resounding "yes!" Yet there were some questions about the amount of resource dedication needed to live up to Dynamo's expectations. Tim had been asked to investigate the matter further and provide a detailed recommendation regarding the nature of the relationship that Top Line should pursue with Dynamo. Tim's first step had been to scour the packet that had come with Lisa's letter to identify Dynamo's expectations of Top Line. Tim highlighted the key points as follows:

- Partner suppliers must work with Dynamo toward continuous improvement.
- Partner suppliers must share information regarding cost, technology, and resources.
- Partner suppliers must share real-time quality, inventory, and process change information.
- Partner suppliers must use cost-reduction programs to reduce costs 3 percent per year.
- Partner suppliers must participate in quarterly "Business Performance Reviews."
- Partner suppliers must attend Dynamo's annual supplier conference.
- Partner suppliers will be early participants in the new product design process.
- Partner suppliers commit, and receive, technical, production, and financial support to achieve shared goals.
- Planning and production schedules are integrated and order lead times reduced.

- Technology is shared, and protected, to create unique product/service offerings.
- Information is shared about business opportunities and opportunities to enhance profitability.
- Partner suppliers are sole sources for vital components.
- Partner suppliers are candidates for collaboration and resource sharing in the form of
  - Co-located engineering personnel
  - Vendor-managed relationships
  - Supplier-integrated manufacturing

Reviewing the list of expectations created a sense of concern deep in Tim's gut—he simply was not confident that Top Line could live up to the challenges. Communicating information real-time, sharing technology, integrating planning and production schedules, and dedicating resources to a customer's operations were not something Top Line was accustomed to doing.

Nevertheless, Tim saw tremendous opportunity to grow Top Line's capabilities and sales by working closely with Dynamo. His final recommendation had to be based on a realistic assessment of Top Line's ability to successfully collaborate with Dynamo despite its relatively constrained resources. Tim wondered whether the benefits of "Partner" status outweighed the costs. Was it possible that building a closer relationship with a key customer might not be the right thing to do?

CASE QUESTIONS

1. How would you suggest Tim analyze this opportunity?
2. What are the implications of saying "yes"? "No"? If the invitation is accepted, how can Tim assure a successful "partnership"?

ENDNOTES

1. Hjelt. P. (2003, May 12). Fortune global 500. *Fortune*, 97.
2. Fawcett, S. E., & Magnan, G. N. (2001). *Achieving world-class supply chain alignment: Benefits, barriers, and bridges*. Phoenix, AZ: National Association of Purchasing Management.
3. Bowersox, D. J., Closs, D. J., & Stank, T. P. (1999). *21st century logistics: Making supply chain integration a reality*. Oak Brook, IL: Council of Logistics Management. Ibid. #2.
4. Ibid, Bowersox. Hughes, J., Ralf, M., & Michels, B. (1998). *Transform your supply chain*. London: International Thomson Business Press. Kuglin, F. A.

(1998). *Customer-centered supply chain management*. New York: AMACOM. Nelson, D., Mayo, R., & Moody, P. E. (1998). *Powered by Honda*. New York: John Wiley & Sons, Inc.
5. Poirier, C. (1999). *Advanced supply chain management*. San Francisco: Berrett-Koehler Publishers, Inc.
6. Long, C., & Meyer, G. (1998). *Sacred cows make the best barbecue*. Seal Beach, CA: Vision+ Press.
7. Goldberg, S. B. (2001, April 23). Supply-chain squeeze: big clients demand cost cuts—now. *BusinessWeek*, 7–8.
8. Ibid.

9. Ball, J. (2000, December 8). Chrysler's checks to suppliers, shoppers to shrink. *The Wall Street Journal*, B4.

10. Fisher, M. L. (1997). What is the right supply chain for your product? *Harvard Business Review, 75*(2), 105–116.

11. Ibid #3, Nelson.

12. Laseter, T. M. (1998). *Balanced sourcing*. San Francisco: Jossey-Bass Publishers.

13. Tierney, C. (2005, August 9). Good relationships with automakers pay off for suppliers. *Detroit News*.

14. Blackwell, R. D. (1997). *From mind to market: Reinventing the retail supply chain*. New York: Harper Business.

15. Burt, D. N., Dobler, D. W., & Starling, S. L. (2003). *World class supply management*. Boston: McGraw-Hill Irwin.

16. Tully, S. (1995, February 20). Purchasing's new muscle. *Fortune*, 75–83.

17. Ibid #13.

18. Covey, S. R. (1989). *7 habits of highly effective people*. New York: Simon & Schuster.

19. Lewicki, R. J., & Litterer, J. A. (1993). *Negotiation: Readings, exercises and cases*. Homewood, IL: Irwin.

20. Ibid #15.

21. Monczka, R., Trent, R., & Handfield, R. (2001). *Purchasing and supply chain management*. Cincinnati: South-Western College Publishing.

Chapter 12

Information Sharing

What is an IS capability? Can I help leverage technology to support our SC strategy and deliver customer value?

The Supply Chain Road Map

Integrating the Supply Chain
- Create & Communicate Common SC Vision
- Build a Cohesive Team of Allied Companies

How Do We Get There?

Chapter 11: Relationship Alignment
- Define intensity of SC relationships.
- Build trust to promote collaboration.

Chapter 12: Information Sharing
- Establish technology to support SC.
- Cultivate culture that promotes sharing.

Chapter 13: Performance Measurement
- Align measures across SC.
- Create understanding & motivate behavior.

Chapter 14: People Empowerment
- Cultivate empowerment environment.
- Build teams to enhance collaboration.

Chapter 15: Collaborative Improvement
- Establish a culture of innovation to avoid complacency.
- Organize for long-term collaboration.

1. Discuss how technology enables an information-sharing capability to support SC collaboration.
2. Describe the various SC-related information technologies and information systems that have been developed over the past several decades.
3. Discuss the role of ERP systems as a collaboration enabler as well as the difficulties associated with their implementation.
4. Discuss the impact of the Internet and e-commerce on supply chain management.
5. Identify what information should be shared, who should be sharing this information along the supply chain, and the challenges involved in information sharing.

Opening Story: The Power of IT at Olympus

The weekend had finally arrived. After doing some long-neglected yard work, Doug sank down into his hammock to read the sports page and soak up some sun. As he quickly glanced through the rest of the paper, Doug came across an article in the business section on ERP systems. The title, "Managers Ask: Where Is ERP's Payoff?" Doug could relate. Olympus had begun investigating ERP almost 2 years ago. After some serious analysis, and over the objections of some managers who were certain ERP would turn out to be a money pit, the executive committee had decided to move forward. That was over a year ago. It had taken some time to select a software provider, but the system still wasn't up and running. And it was already well over budget.

Doug couldn't help himself. He started reading the article. Amazingly, the article seemed to be advocating ERP as an answer to better communication, coordination, and decision making. The article told some of the well-known ERP fiascos—the ones where ERP shut companies' order management systems down during peak season. Those incidents cost big names like Hershey and Whirlpool a fortune in money and more than a little bit of their pride. But the article went on to say, "Despite these well-publicized fiascos, the implementation hassles, and the high costs, leading companies are beginning to see the promised benefits. Although it is still too early to tell, ERP's beleaguered reputation may be in the midst of an extreme makeover."

Now that was a thought: the possibility of a real, tangible return on an IT investment. Doug wondered if and when that would be the case at Olympus. He hoped so. Olympus had long operated functional legacy systems that could barely talk to each other. Indeed, that was the motivation for going with the ERP system. That, and the fact that it seemed like everyone else was already headed down that path. Senior managers at Olympus did not want to be caught fighting tomorrow's competitive battles with yesterday's technology. Doug had participated in many of the ERP impact assessment meetings. Logistics had provided a wish list for the capabilities that it was looking for from an information system. The SC task force had even jumped into the fray since it seemed that the ERP decision would have a major influence on Olympus's emerging SCM strategy.

Hopes ran high that the ERP system would enable the type of collaboration that the task force was trying to make happen. Fears ran just as deep that the ERP implementation would distract Olympus at a critical juncture in the SCM implementation. That was a real concern for Doug. A concern that still loomed large—there were only so many resources to go around. But the biggest question for Doug, the one that never was fully answered, was, "What is technology's real role at Olympus?" The typical arguments had been made. ERP would solve Olympus's pressing data analysis and communication problems. IT was the long-awaited silver bullet. On the other side of the debate, some argued that IT was the source of all of their problems. Doug knew better—there were no silver bullets. And IT had a valuable contribution to make—Olympus, however, had never been able to articulate what exactly that contribution was or how it could be attained.

The heat of the noonday sun seemed to make the wheels in Doug's mind turn faster. Suddenly, he remembered Charlene pointing out months earlier that well-run supply chains are like well-choreographed ballets. He knew ballets, or any other performance that relied on cooperation, required great communication. People had to know what they were supposed to do every step of the way. If one person was out of place, even for a moment, the entire performance suffered. Intense and constant communication was a must!

Doug wondered how today's technologies could help ensure that everyone along the supply chain was moving in sync to the same tune. From the time he had first started looking into SCM, he had heard that information was the glue that holds supply chains together. He understood the theory, but he had never really seen it work that way. Past experience told him that he rarely had all of the information he needed to make timely, well-informed decisions. It seemed that something was always missing, lost, wrong, or kept behind locked doors.

The two nagging questions that had been bouncing around in the back of his mind seemed to crystallize. What was the real role of IT in SCM? The answer seemed clear: to enable choreography. What was the difference between information systems and real information sharing? This answer wasn't so clear. But Doug sensed that the answer built on technology's role as an enabler. If technology allowed for connections to be made so information could be shared, then there had to be a second piece to the puzzle. Something had to inspire people to want to connect. Something had to make it safe to share the information other managers needed to make good decisions. What was the missing piece? If he and the SC task force could define that piece, and bring it to life, IT could enable truly collaborative SC relationships. IT could enable better measurement up and down the supply chain. It could move Olympus, and the entire supply chain, toward the elusive goal of becoming a learning supply chain.

For the first time in his life, Doug was excited about IT. He could hardly believe it. Not wanting to lose these ideas, Doug jumped out of the hammock and ran to his office to jot down some notes. Startled to see Doug dashing through the house, Charlene yelled out, "What's the hurry?" Doug hollered back, "IT. I think I understand the potential of IT. I've just got to figure how to unleash its power!" Curious, Charlene followed Doug and with a quizzical look on her face asked, "Why are you so excited about IT all of a sudden? IT has never been high on your priority agenda."

"Give me a minute to make a few notes, then I'll tell you. In fact, all of this thinking has piqued my sweet tooth. Let's go down to the malt shop for a huge banana split. You can tell me what you think about IT and choreography."

Consider As You Read:

1. How is IT an enabler of SC collaboration? What keeps companies from using it successfully in this role?
2. What is the missing piece of the puzzle Doug has identified? Can you explain it? Why does a company need to make it safe to share information? Why does a company need to inspire people to want to connect?
3. How are IT and choreography related? What does the task force need to do to enable better SC choreography?

> *We believe those companies that position themselves to take advantage of the Internet to build information partnerships with their suppliers and customers have the potential to fundamentally change the face of global competition . . . and change our definition of the value we provide to our customers and constituents.*
>
> —MICHAEL DELL

THE IMPORTANCE OF INFORMATION

Technology drives global change.[1] As machine technology once transformed an agricultural economy into an industrial one, modern information technology (IT) is shifting our economy to not just a knowledge economy but also to a collaboration economy. Modern information technologies make SC integration possible.[2] Every critical SC process relies heavily on information flows across the product or service life cycle from concept to customer. Effective SC networks are held together and their value-added activities synchronized by the flow of information. Research, however, shows that information deficiencies rank second only to performance measurement as a serious hindrance to effective SC collaboration.[3] What does this mean? Managers have a lot of work to do to take full advantage of the magic of modern information technology.

Advances in information technology have facilitated the globalization of business and are enabling many of the changes taking place in SCM. Many managers credit the new information technologies that have emerged in the past 20 years for propelling SCM to the forefront of strategic discussions. By effectively harnessing and managing the information now available, organizations can design and operate their supply chains much more effectively and efficiently than ever before. As an example, consider that for hundreds of years businesses have relied on paper-based systems when exchanging goods and services. Today, leading companies no longer require paper purchase requisitions, purchase orders, invoices, receiving forms, or a manual accounts payable "matching process." All needed information can be transmitted electronically with minimal human intervention.

Changes in information technology provide new areas in which firms can differentiate themselves from competitors and cultivate genuine competitive advantages. Some have even stated that, given the current competitive climate, "little doubt remains about the importance of information and information technology to the ultimate success, and perhaps even the survival, of any supply chain management initiative."[4]

There are four reasons why timely and accurate information has become more critical for effective SC management than ever before.[5] First, to provide outstanding customer satisfaction, managers need information about order status, inventory availability, delivery schedules, shipment tracking, and invoices. And they need the information in real time. Second, information substitutes for inventory and other resources when dealing with uncertainty. Used effectively, information takes costs out of the supply chain. Third, information increases flexibility with regard to when, where, and how resources are utilized to gain a competitive advantage. Fourth, Web-based information sharing is changing relationships between buyers and sellers and redefining SC relationships.

Clearly, information technologies will play a critical role in determining the success of an organization's SC collaboration efforts. However, managers need to remember that technology is an enabler. It helps managers do things—some of which have never before been possible. Information technology must not be viewed as the goal or a "silver bullet" to solve all SC dilemmas or challenges. Automating bad processes simply helps you make mistakes faster and do the wrong things more efficiently. The wrong technology strategy adds neither real value nor customer satisfaction.

Companies that get their information technology strategies right recognize that two distinct, but related, components comprise an information capability. SC leaders invest in technology to connect people, both within their own company and across their supply chains. Technology makes it possible for various people, teams, functions, and organizations along the supply chain to work together. We call this first component **connectivity**. Having the technology to connect, however, is not enough. People have to want to use the technology to do something together. Otherwise, if there is no reason to collaborate, there is no reason to share information. This fact leads to a serious challenge. Information is power! Thus, every time valuable or sensitive information is shared, people make the conscious decision to give power away. Why is this important? It means that people have to both want to share and be willing to trust others to never abuse the shared power. Recognizing this, we call the second component of an information capability **willingness**. Only when companies can connect and they are willing to share needed information can technology help transform the individual members of a supply chain into a real team. Bringing connectivity and willingness together is hard work, but this is where modern technology delivers real competitive advantage.

ACHIEVING CONNECTIVITY THROUGH INFORMATION TECHNOLOGY

The ability to connect people and their ideas through hardware, software, and communication networks has revolutionized the way that businesses are managed. As one manager put it,

> Connectivity pays off in a way that mere information processing does not. Replacing carbon copy memos with publication quality, laser printer reports did not add much value, but using the Internet to route trucks to the right place does. My own experience is that personal computing had only a modest effect on my ability to generate and disseminate misinformation, but that e-mail and the Internet have made a big difference.[6]

Connecting computers at various levels of the supply chain has eliminated many steps that formerly required paperwork and human intervention. Orders can now be processed automatically. Production can be linked closely to consumer purchases at the point of sale. From the smallest microcomputer to the largest mainframe, computers are being interconnected or networked with each other across the globe.

Our goal throughout the following discussion is not to turn you into information systems experts. Rather, we want to help you gain a well-founded understanding of the functionality available in today's information systems. With this understanding, you will be able to work with the information systems experts to build the systems that make real sharing possible. You will then be able to improve the performance of the supply chain.

Brief History of Information System Connectivity

The connectivity ideal in SCM is to link the point of delivery of the final product to the end consumer all the way back to the initial point of production of any given component. The idea is to have an information trail that initiates and traces the product's physical trail.[7] To understand where we are on this connectivity journey, it is important to understand how technology has evolved. We will therefore take a brief look at the history of technology as a provider of connectivity.

Figure 12.1 shows the acronyms of the major business information systems on a timeline dating back to the 1960s. Several of these information systems are discussed in greater detail in this chapter. In their book, *The Extended Enterprise*, Davis and Spekman pointed out that "before integration of the supply chain is possible, the firm must mirror the same behaviors. Integration and cooperation must exist internally before you can do the same outside. This means that there can be no silos; information must flow openly, and functions/disciplines must cooperate and trust each other."[8] This suggests an inside to outside evolution pattern for systems development.

As Figure 12.1 illustrates, the development of SC information systems closely follows this inside-outside development approach. The development of these

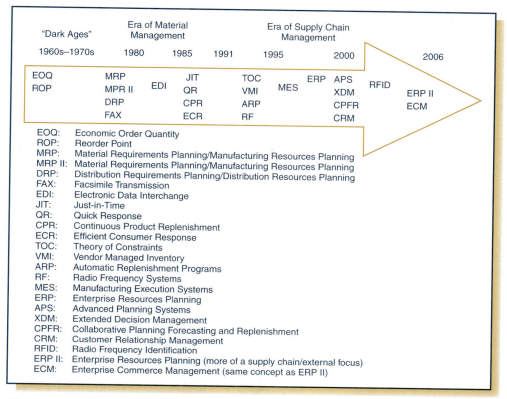

Figure 12.1 Development Timeline of Supply Chain–Related Information Systems

Source: Adapted from Davis and Spekman, *The Extended Enterprise.*

systems began with a very narrow focus on inventory and has gradually expanded to encompass other areas of the organization, progressively building on the structure of previous applications.[9] Many of these new developments have come from continuous improvement efforts facilitated by advances in technology. In addition, many of these new developments have been strategic in nature in an effort to respond to the rapidly changing competitive environment discussed in earlier chapters.

Economic order quantity (EOQ) and reorder point (ROP) systems were followed by material requirements planning (MRP) systems, which helped determine when orders should be placed for various components to avoid stockouts and excess inventory. Distribution requirements planning (DRP) systems, which extended MRP thinking to the distribution network, helped determine the correct amount of products to produce as well as the correct locations to which to ship finished goods. Figure 12.2 shows the relationship between these various systems.

These systems were followed by just-in-time (JIT), quick response (QR), continuous product replenishment (CPR), and efficient consumer response (ECR) systems that helped better match buyers' demands with the production and delivery of suppliers. These systems naturally grew into other systems such as vendor-managed inventory (VMI), where organizations are responsible for managing the inventory levels of their customers.

Customer relationship management (CRM) systems complemented these systems, helping companies track and analyze customer behavior. CRM systems also

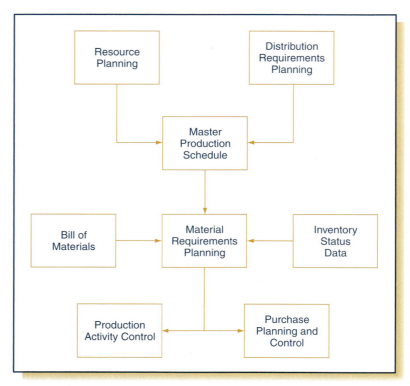

Figure 12.2   Interaction of Some Supply Chain–Related Information Systems

enabled managers to evaluate the effect of specific sales and marketing efforts. The term *customer relationship management (CRM)* encompasses all strategies, methodologies, tools, and other technology-based capabilities that help an enterprise organize and manage its customer relationships.[10] The focus of CRM is on providing optimal value to customers through pre-sale interactions, sales processes, and post-sale interactions. Much as EOQ, ROP, and MRP systems attempt to integrate and automate ordering and manufacturing processes within a company, CRM systems attempt to integrate and automate a company's various customer servicing processes. CRM systems allow companies to maintain all customer records in one centralized location that is accessible throughout the entire organization. Information for these records is collected, captured, and utilized during interactions between customers and the organization. This information gives managers an opportunity to customize solutions to individual customer needs. Managers can use the insight provided by CRM systems to improve customer service levels, enhance customer loyalty and retention, increase revenues from current customers, and acquire new customers.

ENTERPRISE RESOURCE PLANNING (ERP) SYSTEMS

During the late 1990s, companies noticed that many of their information systems operated independently of each other. These systems were often implemented on a functional or departmental basis. Each function (e.g., accounting, purchasing, engineering, human resources) had its own system, and seldom were these systems designed to work together. This lack of connectivity was often confounded by the use of different systems for different divisions or country operations. Companies maintained multiple databases (based on functional lines), entered similar data several times into these various databases, and had difficulty coordinating the information contained in these separate databases. For most companies, it was nearly impossible to carry out intricate, collaborative sales, marketing, purchasing, or logistics activities.

Managers knew that competitive realities required better connectivity. It was time to bring all of these disparate systems (often called "legacy systems") under one roof and allow them to communicate with each other. During the 1990s, over half of the *Fortune* 1000 began to replace their legacy systems with **enterprise resource planning (ERP)** systems designed to integrate transaction modules and provide a common and consistent database.[11] An ERP system is defined as "a single database surrounded by application programs that take data from the database and either conduct analysis or collect additional data for the firm."[12] ERP systems become a company's central nervous system. Information is entered only once and becomes available for anyone who needs it to make decisions. Information accuracy increased dramatically.

One way to understand the architecture of a typical ERP system is to view it in terms of the four primary business processes of the SCOR model (see Figure 12.3).

- Plan – which includes strategic and tactical planning as well as accountability/reporting (overall management, administration, finance, accounting, and human resource management).
- Source – which can be viewed from either side of the buyer–supplier relationship. From the supplier's point of view this process is the customer order management process. From the buyer's point of view this is the purchasing/sourcing process.

Figure 12.3 Typical ERP System Components

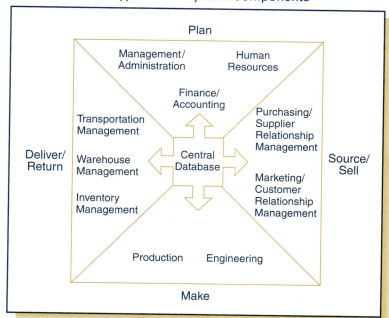

- Make – which involves the production, manufacturing, assembly, or service delivery processes.
- Deliver/return – both of which involve the organization's logistics, warehousing, and transportation processes.

ERP's real value is that it connects all information flows within the firm. Theoretically, specific transactions taking place in each business process are accessible and visible to everyone in the organization. For example, anyone wanting to find out how much inventory is in the warehouse, whether a particular order has been shipped, or when a supplier was paid can obtain this information by going through the system.

Enterprise resource planning (ERP) systems are viewed with both great optimism and serious skepticism. Some managers really believe they are the answer to the vast array of human, inventory, facility, and equipment management problems facing firms today. Others are confident that ERP systems will never deliver on promised benefits. Experience suggests that both arguments possess an element of truth. Some companies have been able to seamlessly integrate their ERP systems with suppliers and customers, demonstrating that such integration is possible. However, for many organizations, implementation problems lead managers to claim that ERP providers have "overpromised and underdelivered." ERP has become known for the challenges companies encounter during implementation.

ERP Implementation Issues

The concepts behind ERP systems make such good sense that it seems as though companies should have implemented them a long time ago. However, the process of implementing an ERP system in an environment where people are reluctant to change from their familiar legacy systems has proven to be a huge undertaking for most companies. Critical implementation issues include the following:

- *Never-ending implementation:* Many firms adopt ERP systems module by module, which makes the implementation seem like an endless nightmare.[13] Even simple implementations take a year or more. Complex implementations have taken close to a decade.
- *Importance of process mapping:* Each application captures data for and about a process. Planning for implementation requires that the process be well understood. Process mapping can help. As processes are mapped out in detail, managers gain a real understanding of how the processes work.
- *Process redesign:* During the mapping process, managers often discover that the process is very different from what they originally believed. They may find that the process should be redesigned or overhauled. Unfortunately, some managers choose to ignore process inefficiencies and proceed with the ERP implementation. Combining a new ERP system with a bad process usually leads to unsatisfactory results—the same old mistakes are made more rapidly. Thus, in many cases, the software system seems to be driving the implementation of new business practices and processes rather than supporting existing ones. Learning about the company's processes is often an unexpected benefit of ERP implementation.
- *Use of consultants:* Sometimes the experts setting up the new information systems are much better at computer programming than they are at business management.[14] SC managers need to know more about information systems and

technologies while information systems managers could benefit from a better understanding of SCM and business in general. There is a learning curve inherent in using any new technology. Knowledgeable consultants can help companies along this learning curve. However, relying solely on outside consultants is often a recipe for an expensive implementation that really doesn't meet the company's needs.

- *Excessive cost:* Developing and implementing SC information systems is costly and time-consuming. Without proper planning, costs and timelines can quickly escalate beyond budgeted amounts. A recent study revealed that the average total cost of ERP ownership ranged from $400,000 to $300 million with an average cost of $15 million.[15] Another study found that implementation time estimates and financial budgets are often exceeded by 50 to 100 percent or more.[16]

- *Resistance to change:* Internal employees and managers often prefer to use their existing legacy systems and are resistant to change, especially change that is hard to understand and is perceived as painful. ERP advocates need to do a better job of communicating the decision-making benefits of ERP systems.

- *Errors during implementation:* Sometimes companies learn about glitches or errors in their systems only after they have been implemented. The new system at Hershey Foods, for example, failed to capture 5 weeks of orders (including an order for 20,000 pounds of candy) just before Halloween. This resulted in a 19 percent drop in net income in the third quarter and a loss of a portion of the Christmas candy sales as well.[17] To avoid the problem, many organizations (1) gradually phase in new systems while phasing out old ones, (2) run both systems concurrently (in parallel) until the "bugs" have been worked out, or (3) utilize pilot projects at a limited number of divisions or locations as a sort of beta test of the new system.

- *Rapid technological change:* Rapid technological change has the potential to rapidly render new systems obsolete. This fact complicates cost–benefit analyses. Early adopters of a new technology have the benefit of being ahead of the competition, but also run the risk of acquiring an untested technology whose problems could disrupt the firm's entire operations.

The following 4-step ERP implementation process helps ensure that the business processes are effectively reengineered and improved:[18]

1. *Define the current process "as is."* An ERP implementation team of subject-matter experts document what the current process looks like.
2. *Define what the "best-in-class" business process should be.* At this point, the team must have a clear understanding of what the final objective of the process is. Further, they must understand what the ERP system will replace, and how the benefits are likely to occur.
3. *Develop the system.* This is an iterative process in which consultants work in conjunction with those managers who are most familiar with the business processes in question.
4. *Work through all final "bugs" and then "flip the switch."* A danger that often exists when flipping the switch—switching over from the old system to the new system—is that the company may not be ready for the change, nor is the system completely configured to handle the specific activities that keep the business running.

A valid concern voiced by managers is that expensive IT systems like ERP are hard to implement and are not the silver bullet to the company's information dilemma. Even so, many companies seem to be caught in a follow-the-competition mind-set. They just have to have the latest technology. This approach hampers the implementation of a capable information system.

The Future: ERP II?

According to Gartner vice president, Bruce Bond, traditional, inwardly connective enterprise resource planning (ERP) is dead, destroyed by the demand for greater collaboration among SC partners.[19] This reality is forcing companies to take the next step on the IT journey—the move to SC-wide information connectivity. Although some of the information generated by and contained in these previous systems was shared with other members of the supply chain, these systems were not designed to share the types and quantities of information that today's SC managers would like to share with other companies. ERP II and enterprise commerce management (ECM) systems have been proposed to overcome this limitation.

Brian Zrimsek, research director of the manufacturing applications strategies group at the Gartner Group, has identified some key differences between ERP and ERP II systems.[20] These systems differ in terms of their roles, domains, functions, processes, architectures, and data, among other items, as shown in Table 12.1.

The main difference between ERP and ERP II systems is collaboration, which appears to be a good idea. However, until managers can communicate seamlessly inside the firm, they cannot hope to do so with external parties like customers and suppliers. There is no point in providing inaccurate information to customers and suppliers. The ultimate goal is to create fully integrated SCM software packages. However, if businesses fail to address their current information system issues before migrating to ERP II systems, they run the risk of upgrading their problems, potentially making them bigger.

Table 12.1 Differences Between ERP and ERP II

Area of Difference	ERP	ERP II
Role	Concerned with optimizing an enterprise	Concerned with optimizing the supply chain through collaboration with trading partners
Domain	Manufacturing and distribution	All sectors/segments
Function	Manufacturing, sales and distribution, and finance processes	Cross-industry, industry sector, and specific industry processes
Process	Focused on the four walls of the enterprise	Connect with trading partners, wherever they might be, to take processes beyond the boundaries of the enterprise
Architecture	Monolithic and closed	Web-based, open to integrate and interoperate with other systems and build around modules or components that allow users to choose just the functionality they need
Data	Information generated and consumed within the enterprise	Information available across the supply chain to authorized participants

E-Commerce and the Internet

Once the companies in a supply chain have their information systems in place, these systems need to be able to communicate or speak with each other. Advances in communication mechanisms such as **electronic data interchange (EDI)** and the Internet have greatly facilitated this networked communication by eliminating some of the technology barriers and creating new opportunities for trading partners to share information along the supply chain. The cost of providing, collecting, and communicating information electronically has been dropping rapidly in recent years. These cost reductions and technological advances have led to the creation of a completely new and interconnected business environment. SC managers need to be aware of these changes and look for ways to incorporate them into their supply chains.

Electronic commerce has been defined as "the automation of commercial transactions using computers and networked communication technologies."[21] Electronic commerce therefore includes technologies such as EDI, the Internet, e-mail, electronic funds transfers, and electronic bulletin boards.

Some large firms have been using computer linkages to manage production and supply since the early 1980s. But these mainly specialized and proprietary systems have only been available to a limited number of participants. The Internet is leveling the playing field, giving other companies access to technologies that will accommodate similar linkages.

Companies use Internet standards internally as well as externally. The difference between intranets, Internets, and extranets is explained mostly by who is allowed access to the system. Intranets allow companies to implement applications on their own internal systems and avoid the difficulties associated with custom interfaces, incompatible types of hardware, and special connection procedures. Extranets typically allow limited access to certain applications and data to external companies such as suppliers and customers. Internet applications typically allow unlimited access.

The Internet is big business. U.S. online retail sales in 2005 were estimated at about $172 billion, representing about 6 percent of all retail sales.[22] Considerable growth is expected in the next several years. An Ohio State University survey predicts that the Internet will carry 20 percent of customer orders by the year 2010.[23] As exciting as this growth is, the fact remains that many businesses are not prepared to deal with the pressures such extraordinary demand will create. Even some of the biggest names in on-line retailing, such as Amazon.com and Sears.com, experienced significant glitches that blocked visitors from making purchases during recent holiday shopping seasons.[24]

Setting up a Web site and generating sales may be the easy part of an e-commerce supply chain. The difficulties come when companies have to source, make, and deliver on those sales. In December 2004, the two leading e-tailers, Amazon.com and Wal-Mart, had over 48 million and 32 million visitors, respectively.[25] To successfully complete the order fulfillment process for this level of traffic, companies need to have efficient, well-designed supply chains. Their purchasing, production, and logistics systems must be capable of handling the large sales volumes. Many companies have not realized the importance of these key processes and consequently have experienced order fulfillment difficulties.

As Figure 12.4 illustrates, the Internet can be used to both enhance value and reduce costs as it expands the efficient frontier of organizations.[26] Focusing first on costs, the Internet has helped companies achieve dramatically higher efficiency

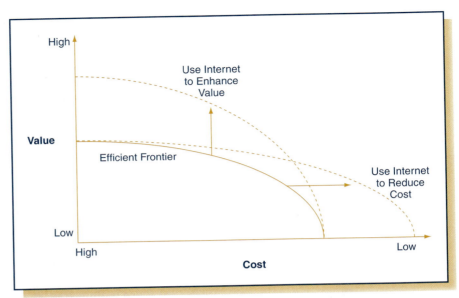

Figure 12.4   Effect of Internet on the Efficient Frontier

Source: Adapted from Chopra and Van Mieghem. Chopra, S. and J. Van Mieghem.[26]

levels. E-commerce allows for the centralization of inventory and shipping locations, which reduces overall safety stock requirements and inbound transportation costs. E-commerce also allows customers to perform the data entry tasks associated with placing an order, which reduces the redundancy of having to input this information multiple times during the order fulfillment process. E-commerce also reduces the costs of collecting and sharing demand and inventory information across the supply chain. Unfortunately, efficiency can cut two ways. In some instances, the efficiency effects of the Internet have driven prices of some products and services to a commodity status. Reverse auctions, where prices drop dramatically during the bidding process, exemplify this phenomenon.

Turning to revenues, the Internet enables real-time, global information sharing and interaction among supply chain members at all levels, from product development to the delivery to the end user.[27] This Web-based information sharing and interaction can improve revenues in several ways.

- E-commerce removes the time and location constraints associated with a physical retail location by providing customers throughout the world with 24/7 access to shopping and ordering.
- E-commerce allows direct sales to customers, thereby eliminating intermediaries and the profit margins that are associated with these intermediaries.
- E-commerce allows real-time access to information, which can be used to make better decisions about inventory levels, customer service levels, and trends in the marketplace.
- E-commerce allows the instantaneous and flexible introduction of products and product mixes made possible through e-commerce. Once a product becomes available, it can be added to the Web site immediately rather than having to wait for the next version of a catalog or the next shipment to a retail store.
- E-commerce allows customers to instantly pay for their orders, which reduces cash-to-cash cycles.

Although the impact of e-commerce has already been dramatic on the retail industry, its biggest impacts may yet be seen in its ability to encourage, enable, and facilitate SC integration. Companies have only begun to tap into the potential provided by these emerging technologies. The implementation of many of the concepts of SCM has been constrained due to the lack of the technological tools that they require. Tools like the Internet are beginning to eliminate these constraints, redefine functional roles within organizations, and change the relationships among SC members. The potential of these tools to help break down functional and organizational barriers by facilitating collaboration and information sharing holds great promise for future integration and collaboration efforts.

E-Marketplaces

One unique application of the Internet has been the creation of e-marketplaces. **B2B e-marketplaces** are defined as neutral Internet/Web-enabled entities through which companies may conduct buying and selling transactions for goods or services. Neutrality refers to the notion that an e-marketplace does not specifically represent a single buyer or a single supplier and that both buyers and suppliers are able to freely and independently participate in the e-marketplace.[28]

In terms of SCM, e-marketplaces can add value by helping companies identify new sources of supply or new customers. They can also help facilitate transactions between buyers and suppliers by being a mediator between the various parties. After interviewing executives at 50 e-marketplaces and surveying another 350 e-marketplaces, a research project[29] identified five types of e-marketplaces based on the functionality and the benefits they provide to buying organizations. These five types of e-marketplaces are identified in Table 12. 2.

These e-marketplaces were primarily being formed in highly fragmented industries with high dollar volumes such as agriculture, construction, transportation, printing, and business services. They make money by charging membership fees, transaction fees (flat or percentage), and through advertising. The study found that e-marketplaces (1) do not yield significant, repeatable price cuts, (2) are not the solution for all of a business's purchasing needs, and (3) are not a viable substitute for a company's supply management department.

For some, industry sponsored e-marketplaces (rather than neutral e-marketplaces), such as the automotive exchange, Covisint, are seen as a barometer of the future success of B2B e-commerce. However, their success, as with other information technology ventures, is ultimately linked more to collaborative processes than to e-commerce technology.[30]

E-marketplaces provide one way to link buyers and suppliers. The collaboration is the key element of the value they provide to buyers and suppliers. However, once the buyers and suppliers are brought together, the role of the e-marketplaces becomes less value-adding. E-marketplaces are not going to reduce the importance of good SC practices within organizations or completely take the place of other forms of supplier identification, supplier evaluation, or supplier selection in the future.

Radio Frequency Technology

Currently, there are two basic types of radio frequency technology being utilized in SC processes. The first type involves radio frequency transmissions between computer systems and mobile operators such as forklift drivers and order pickers within a relatively small area. These systems are used extensively in warehouse and DC

Table 12.2 Types of E-Marketplaces and Their Defining Characteristics

Type of E-Marketplace	Characteristics
Project/Specification Managers	• Primarily specialize in design and planning support. • Provide tools to plan and manage complex projects/processes for customers. Applications can range from designing a marketing brochure for a pharmaceutical company to optimizing a transportation network between a consumer products manufacturer and multiple retailers. • Provide collaboration tools to help customers increase speed to market and improve decision making on product development, ultimately improving potential revenues. • Help reduce the invoice price of purchased goods and services by helping buyers determine what to buy.
Supply Consolidators	• Identify the relevant supply base for a customer and conduct the purchasing transaction. • Help customers to design and plan the purchase and to establish the terms of purchase. • Bring together product offerings of many suppliers to increase the buyer's options. • Provide low cost and easy access to a fragmented base of suppliers that are either difficult to reach off-line or are so numerous that individual on-line tools are ineffective. • Effectively help customers reduce the transaction costs associated with searching through multiple paper-based catalogs, compare parameters across products, and manage accounts with numerous suppliers.
Liquidity Creators	• Establish the terms of purchase. • Create liquid, dynamic markets for commodity products traded between many buyers and sellers. • Provide liquidity for products that were previously too low-volume or nonstandard to warrant off-line exchanges. • Provide suppliers with a ready market for their product and buyers with a steadier source of supply. • Provide real-time price transparency across a wide base of suppliers, enabling customers to compare prices more effectively and more efficiently than previously possible.
Aggregators	• Primarily combine demand within and across buying enterprises and then use this combined market power to achieve lower prices from suppliers. • Primary role is to help customers reduce the price paid on a product or service by combining purchased volume across buyers and increasing competition among suppliers.
Transaction Facilitators	• Primarily transact and execute the purchase. Transaction facilitators generally focus on reducing complex, paper-based transactions between buyers and sellers.

operations. On-board computer systems give drivers instructions about where to pick up or place products. Specifically, in the order-picking scenario, the forklift driver uses a computer that is mounted on the forklift or contained in a portable tablet. The screen relays to the driver a picking list—all of the items she needs to pick (gather) for a specific order. The picking system determines the proper picking sequence based on product location, size, and weight. The driver simply looks at the screen and it tells her the location of the next item to be picked. It might even show her the best route to get there. When she finds the item, she scans a bar code on the box to confirm she has the right item. If it is the right item, she loads it and moves on to the next item on the list. The computer system automatically adjusts the inventory status for the product. When the order is complete, the screen indicates which dock to deliver it to. Once again, the driver scans a bar code located at the dock to confirm she is in the right place. These RF systems greatly improve picking efficiency and accuracy. They also improve inventory management and track individual worker productivity. In some of the more sophisticated systems, worker productivity is reported in real time—to the worker.

The second type of radio frequency technology involves the placement of **radio frequency identification (RFID) tags**—coded electronic chips—in the container or packaging of products. As these packages or boxes move throughout the chain, they can be scanned by a remote scanner for an identifying code or even for the list of contents. This type of technology has been utilized since the late 1990s in items such as ski-lift passes and key fobs that allow consumers to purchase gas at certain gas stations. One advantage that RFID tags have is that unlike bar codes, they do not need to be on the outside of the package or placed in a certain position for the scanner to be able to read the information. Further, they are less prone to damage. They can also hold much more information than bar codes and can be linked to Internet applications that can contain even more specific information about the product. Unlike bar codes, this information can be unique to every item, not just to a specific type of item or UPC code. What does it all mean? RFID tags make it easier to know where product is at all times as well as what condition it is in. The day may come when a customer can select items, put them in his shopping bag, and walk through a scanner. The RFID tags will all be scanned simultaneously and his credit card will be debited automatically. No more standing in lines. Greater retail productivity and better customer service are a driving force behind RFID adoption.

Overall, RFID tags have the potential to deliver a completely new level of transparency to supply chains and their customers. RFID tags will allow companies to generate real-time reports about exactly how much inventory is in a DC, how much inventory is on the truck that is scheduled to arrive that afternoon, as well as how much inventory a supplier has in stock and how much it expects to receive on its next shipment. Wal-Mart has seen the value of such transparency and as of January 2005 had 98 of its top 100 suppliers using RFID tags at the pallet level on at least some products they deliver to Wal-Mart. Wal-Mart's goal is to track goods with minimal human intervention. RFID has the potential to lead to labor savings, lower inventory costs, less theft, and an increased ability to ensure that items arrive where and when they are needed. However, even with Wal-Mart's assistance, many of its suppliers are finding RFID implementation difficult. Few can cost justify the RFID implementation. The technology is still immature and global standards are still being worked out.

Electronic On-Line Bidding Events: The Reverse Auction

Most people are familiar with the concept of an auction where buyers compete to purchase an item in a system that drives the price higher and higher to see who is willing to pay the most. Reverse auctions are when suppliers bid for a buyer's business (rather than buyers bidding for a seller's business). These auctions result in a downward pressure on the price of the product or service being sold. Electronic reverse auctions are simply auctions that take place over the Internet or some other electronic technology. Sun Microsystems spends about $1 billion per year in reverse auctions on items such as integrated circuits, disk drives, power supplies, and other production material.[31]

Most organizations verify supplier capabilities and prequalify suppliers as part of their reverse auction planning. Though electronic reverse auctions last only hours or minutes, the preparation for these auctions can take months. In addition to prequalifying suppliers, companies also need to carefully select the combination of goods or services that the suppliers will be bidding for. Then, to ensure that the resulting bids are comparable, the buying organization needs to make sure that all of the prequalified suppliers fully understand the requirements of the contract and the items up for bid.

Usually, the supplier that proposes the lowest bid is the one that receives the buyer's business. However, as with regular auctions where people may bid more than they can actually afford, many companies realize that it is easy for suppliers to get "caught up in the moment" and bid prices that are lower than they can actually produce the product or service for. Consequently, managers need to verify the capabilities of the lowest bidder after the auction. Only when suppliers are really capable of making high-quality product and delivering it on time should they be awarded the contract.

Although quality and delivery can be incorporated into the process, the reverse auction's real impact is on price. This focus on price and the competitive nature of reverse auctions can easily lead managers to make counterproductive decisions that are contrary to the SC principles of total cost of ownership and collaborative/cooperative relationships. Some suppliers refuse to participate in reverse auctions. Nonparticipation causes problems for companies like GM, Ford, and DaimlerChrysler, whose suppliers have been especially leery of reverse auctions given the automakers' historical focus on annual price reductions.[32]

Electronic reverse auctions represent one tool that SC managers can use to select suppliers and establish prices. However, before conducting a reverse auction, SC managers should carefully consider the process, the product or service, and the auction's potential ramifications on its long-term SC relationships.

Information Technology Summary

The software and technologies discussed here are representative of the SC-related information technologies in use today. Emerging technologies are changing the modern company's abilities to collaborate and become better integrated with its suppliers and customers. Since technological change continues to occur at an ever-quickening pace, new technological developments will continue to influence and shape the field of supply chain management in the future.

Adopting any new technology involves certain risks. However, early adopters can often obtain many benefits. If they approach their technology adoption and implementation decisions strategically, early adopters will likely be able to (1) exploit (either short-term or long-term) information advantages, (2) move quickly down the learning curve and position themselves to utilize transformational technologies in the future, and (3) help set the ground rules and the standards under which these technologies operate.

Neither cross-functional integration nor interorganizational SC collaboration could proceed very far without shared information. Most companies are therefore investing serious money and energy on their information technologies. Great information systems can collect, analyze, and disseminate accurate, real-time information regarding demand forecasts, inventory levels, delivery lead times, and quality levels. They can allow people to communicate and collaborate across a global SC network. They can even be used to drive learning. Yet many companies have often found that their efforts do not necessarily translate into real information sharing and collaboration. They are discovering that real information sharing requires investments in a culture of willingness to share decision-making information.

ACHIEVING INFORMATION SHARING THROUGH WILLINGNESS

For years, incompatible information systems have been blamed for poor SC coordination. The reality, for now at least, is that information systems often limit connectivity throughout the chain. Managers seldom have access to all the accurate information they need, when they need it, to make great decisions and coordinate activities. However, experience and research point to another, potentially bigger, problem than poor connectivity. That problem is a lack of willingness to share vital information. Systems and technology represent only half of the information dilemma—perhaps the easy half. The other half is a strident unwillingness of managers to share information with other members of their own firms or with supply chain partners.[33] Because willingness to share is critical to achieving high levels of SC collaboration, we will take a few minutes to look at four important questions:

- Why should information be shared?
- What information should be shared?
- When should information be shared?
- Who should be sharing the information?

Why Should Information Be Shared?

Information should be shared for many reasons. The most frequently discussed role of information in SCM is to substitute for inventory, reducing a company's costs. In a similar way, information substitutes for time, helping companies be more responsive to customer requests. Other potential, traditional benefits are listed in Table 12.3 by functional or departmental area. Simply stated, sharing information helps companies reduce costs, improve customer service levels, reduce lead times, improve profitability, increase quality levels, and enhance innovation.

Taking a different perspective, information can be used to change company and supply chain capabilities. For instance, information enables process redesign and reengineering. Information enables SC collaboration. Information can also be used to promote constant improvement and learning. These are powerful capabilities that can change the rules of the competitive game, enabling a company to win big!

What Information Should Be Shared?

Despite the increasing importance of SC strategies that are built on more open information sharing, most companies are stuck in a time warp—they typically don't share much more information today than they did 10 or 20 years ago. Most companies realize the importance of information and do share some information with their suppliers and customers, but the nature and scope of that information remains fairly limited. At a minimum, companies should be sharing the following types of information:[34]

Table 12.3 Potential Benefits of Increased Information

FUNCTION OR DEPARTMENT	POTENTIAL BENEFITS OF INCREASED INFORMATION SHARING
Sales	• Reduced costs by enabling higher sales productivity per salesperson • Increased sales through better information about customers • Higher customer service/satisfaction levels
Purchasing/ Operations/Logistics	• Better control over picking, shipping, and receiving • Reduction in transaction costs • Increased inventory accuracy • Reduced variability in the supply chain • Quicker reaction to supply chain problems • Lower inventory levels • Fewer missed production schedules • Increased visibility into processes • Reduction in the bullwhip effect • Better forecasts • Better coordination between manufacturing and distribution • More responsive suppliers • Better buyer/supplier relationships • Reduction in fleet costs through better planning of needs • Lead time reduction • More effective transportation
Finance	• Improved profitability • Increased invoice processing speed • Improved market share
Engineering/R&D	• Enhanced diffusion of technology and innovation

Sales Data and Sales Forecasts

In order to reduce the bullwhip effect, companies should share actual sales data with their suppliers along with their orders. Suppliers need to know why their customer ordered more this month than last month. Is it because the demand for their product increased, or is it because they are stocking up for an upcoming promotion, or is it simply because of a quantity discount that the supplier offered? Orders represent part of the picture. They need to be combined with actual sales information and promotion plans in order to make the best inventory management decisions. This is the goal of collaborative planning, forecasting, and replenishment (CPFR) programs.

Inventory Levels

One of the major concepts of SCM is the channel-wide management of inventory. Providing visibility into inventory levels can reduce the total level of inventory in the chain by reducing the amount of safety stock inventory that is required. Accurate inventory data for the entire chain would also improve production scheduling and help mitigate possible shortages due to supply disruptions upstream.

Order Status for Tracking/Tracing

Today's customers and companies want to know the real-time status of their order. They want to know that the order has been received. They want to know when the order will ship. If the order has shipped, they want to know when the order will arrive and whether or not the order is complete. Increasingly, they want to know where the order is in transit. Such information can be used to transship to other customers, DCs, or production facilities to help meet an unexpected need. Much of this information can be provided by allowing customers to directly link into a company's Web-based information system or the Web-based system of a supplier or transportation provider. This information can also be provided through a series of automated e-mails that update the customer about the progress of an order. Customers do not want to have to make several phone calls just to track down the status of an order.

Performance Metrics

Companies should be sharing performance metrics with suppliers and customers to let them know the status of their performance. These performance metrics can point out strengths as well as weaknesses of players on the SC team. This information can then be used to help improve the performance of individual players or provide the insight needed to shift tasks and processes to other members of the SC team.

Capacity and Capability Information

SCM requires joint planning between members of a supply chain. Capacity information is an important input to these joint planning sessions. SC partners need to know what current capacity levels are, if there are any potential capacity disruptions planned, and when new capacity is going to come on-line. For example, if a company is planning special maintenance or a production line change that will reduce its capacity, customers might want to move the timing of orders up to make sure they can obtain needed product. Similar information should also be shared for new capabilities that the company is bringing on-line. Knowing the plans of SC partners helps everyone prepare for possible shortages and better use their own and SC resources.

When Should Information Be Shared?

Most companies share a lot of information with suppliers and customers during the middle portion of a product's life cycle. Indeed, many of the information types we discussed in the preceding paragraphs focus on this part of the product life cycle. However, information sharing can have a greater impact at the beginning and end of the product life cycle.[35] More collaboration and information sharing at the design and introduction stage, for example, might change a company's decisions about how much of a new product to make, how it should be made, or how it should be priced. Better communication at the late maturity stage of the product life cycle might help companies avoid large quantities of obsolete inventory that needs to be heavily discounted in order to be sold. Better information sharing during the decline stage of the PLC can help better manage reverse logistics and recycling issues.

Who Should Be Sharing the Information?

Clearly, purchasing and marketing, functions that primarily deal with external organizations, should be sharing information with other members of the supply

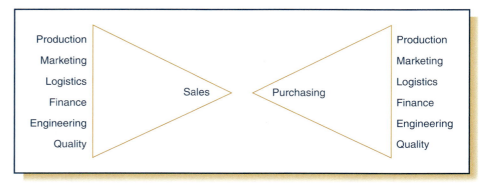

Figure 12.5   Bow-Tie Approach to Information Sharing
Source: Adapted from Cooper, M. C., L. M. Ellram, J. T. Gardner, and A.M. Hanks.[36]

chain. These information-sharing relationships are shown in Figure 12.5. This "bow-tie" approach has the majority of the two firms' functions far from each other in terms of communication, information sharing, and integration.[36]

An alternate approach, suggested by Sam Walton, proposes turning the various pieces of the bow-tie around into a diamond shape and allowing many functions within the organization to directly communicate with external organizations (see Figure 12.6). This approach is referred to as the *diamond approach*. This approach allows the engineering function of one organization to collaborate and work closely with the engineering function of the other organization. Similarly, this approach allows the outbound logistics function of the supplier to work in partnership directly with the inbound logistics function of the buying organization. In general, this approach creates many more points of contact and potential sources of integration and collaboration between the two organizations. Consequently, the diamond approach is much more in line with the core concepts of SCM, which encourage multiple levels of collaboration and integration between and among SC partners.

Challenges to Open Information Sharing

The notion that companies, and supply chains, could improve their performance by sharing the right information with the right partners at the right time is neither novel

Figure 12.6   Diamond Approach to Information Sharing

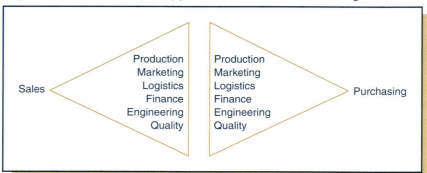

Source: Adapted from Cooper, Ellram, Gardner, and Hanks.

nor new. It is common sense. So, why don't companies share more information? Where does common sense break down, making frequent, honest, and open sharing a rare practice rather than common practice? Information sharing in a supply chain faces several hurdles.

Weak or Counterproductive Relationships

Proactive information sharing takes place only when good relationships are in place. Weak or adversarial relationships among organizations are a significant barrier to information sharing. Think about it: Would you share information with a company you do not trust? The odds are pretty good that any information you share under these circumstances will be used against you. On the other hand, strong, trusting relationships promote information sharing and cooperation among SC members.

This is a critical point: Technology can connect the firms in a supply chain but technology alone does not build close, trust-based relationships. However, when companies share common goals and want to build proactive, collaborative relationships, information sharing can improve relationship quality. Shared information is a key ingredient in the recipe for relationship success. In fact, one study found that information quality and information sharing (both depth and breadth) were two of seven attributes of supplier alliances that were found to really promote partnership success.[37]

As managers, you need to remember that not everyone is ready to share information equally. Some smaller members of an SC may lack the managerial or technological capabilities to share information. Others may not have yet decided that it is safe to share. Achieving needed levels of information sharing may itself require collaboration with and investment in SC partners. Likewise, the sooner an industry decides on information standards, the lower the cost for every member of the industry. For example, many smaller suppliers never adopted EDI systems simply because an industry standard was never established. Different customers used different standards and systems. Small suppliers simply could not afford to invest in all of the different standards being used.

People

People may not always be in a position to drive information sharing, but they are usually capable of wreaking havoc on such efforts. Reducing fear and getting buy-in is critical. This may require more open communication from top management regarding strategic and technology plans. It may require better employee training. Perhaps measurement and reward systems will have to be changed. Managers should ask, "Where are the barriers and how can we reduce them?" They should likewise ask, "What do we need to do differently to promote the new, desired behaviors?" Ultimately, willingness is a cultural phenomenon—a people issue. People, their concerns and their passions, should be explicitly considered as a company plans and implements its technology and sharing strategies. Chapter 14 focuses on building the culture and skills to support both information sharing and SC collaboration.

Power

You have heard it before—information is power. By nature, most people and organizations hold tenaciously onto the power that they possess. Once they have power, they are unwilling to share it or give it away. The same holds true for information.

Companies have traditionally guarded and filtered information in an effort to retain power and control.

Over the last two decades, there has been a general shift of power from manufacturers to retailers. Whereas Procter & Gamble once controlled its supply chain, Wal-Mart is the new channel captain. One of the trends that contributed to this power shift is the trend toward consolidation at the retail level within the supply chain. Large retail conglomerates have been created through mergers and acquisitions. Because of their size and market share, these organizations have more buying leverage and clout with suppliers. Further, and perhaps more importantly, retailers sit in a very important position in the supply chain: next to the end customer. They almost always have the best information about current demand patterns as well as trends in customer expectations and tastes. The way this information is shared not only influences SC efficiency but it also affects SC power. This fact leads many companies to hold onto information that could improve overall chain performance. SC leaders almost always bend, if not break, this rule of human nature. They know that sharing information helps the entire chain win in the marketplace. As the revenue and profit pie grows, there is more wealth to share among SC partners.

Trust

Of course, power and trust are related. If companies abuse power, they lose trust. Without trust, SC partners will not share information. Managers, by nature and experience, are skeptical about how information will be used. Trust reduces the fear that sensitive information will be used inappropriately. A lack of trust kills information-sharing initiatives. Even the most avid advocate of information sharing recognizes that there are rational limits to the amount and type of information that is shared. Trust is often the factor that determines where the boundary is drawn. The key point to remember is that sharing happens only when managers are comfortable with relationships and confident that any shared information will be used appropriately.

Security and Risk

One concern associated with information is the confidentiality and security of information shared. The information that an organization shares with its SC partners is among the most critical of its assets. Because of the inherent vulnerability of Web-based information-sharing methods, appropriate security measures need to be established for this asset on both the sending and receiving sides of the information exchange to protect against both external threats and internal abuses.[38]

Too Much Information

One problem companies face today is information overload. Technology allows the capture, analysis, and dissemination of mountains of information—far more than any manager could ever use. According to Tom Brunell, vice president of the Avnet Supply Network Solutions (SNS) organization, "Too much information, even flawless, is just as bad as too little. . . . Everybody doesn't need to know everything. We need to drill down more deeply into the implications of collaboration and define what type of intelligence is necessary for pivotal decisions."[39] Managers have to know what information is needed by individual managers to make great decisions. This information should then be provided in an easily accessible manner. Other information that is not needed for daily decision making may be made available through various search tools. For example, 3M has a knowledge management system in place that captures peoples' interests and expertise. When someone has an idea and is looking for some expert advice or a potential collaborator, she can access the knowledge system to find the right resource anywhere in the vast 3M network. The bottom line: Companies need to make sure that they are sharing the right amount of information with their key suppliers and key customers.

Lack of Standards

One major challenge to supply chain IT standardization is a lack of common terminology or communication standards. This challenge is being addressed by an IT industry consortium called RosettaNet, which is developing a common business language and universal standards for today's global supply chains. This challenge is also being addressed by the development of Extensible Markup Language (XML), a flexible computer language that facilitates information transfer between a wide range of applications.

Inaccurate Information

The quality of information available to SC managers is often inadequate. Inadequate information can lead to bad decisions; inaccurate information can lead to disasters. The difference is that managers take precautions when they know they are missing some key information. For example, they are likely to perform a contingency or sensitivity analysis. They may even run a series of brainstorming sessions to identify alternative scenarios or potential outcomes. By contrast, when managers think they have good information they do not take these extra, time-consuming steps. If the information turns out to be wrong, they are caught unprepared for the consequences.

Sometimes the inaccurate information comes from cost accounting and management control systems that were developed years ago in very different regulatory and competitive environments. New systems often need to be developed that provide the necessary useful information for SC decision making. Another source of inaccurate information may be an SC partner. Perhaps the partner is unaware that the information is bad. Other times, inaccurate or deceptive information may be passed along intentionally. Both behaviors adversely affect trust. Sharing deceptive information is unethical.

In summary, information sharing will continue to be an important component of SC collaboration activities for the foreseeable future. Advances in information technologies will accelerate such activities. But, the ultimate success of these activities depends on whether organizations can overcome the problems and challenges associated with building a culture of willingness to share information.

THE INFORMATION IRONY

Data, information, knowledge, and wisdom are all key components in what has been referred to as "the information irony."[40] The relationship between these various components is shown in Figure 12.7. Data is primarily produced by information technology (80 percent), rather than people (20 percent), and theoretically accounts for only about 10 percent of the potential for competitive advantage. In reality, however, great

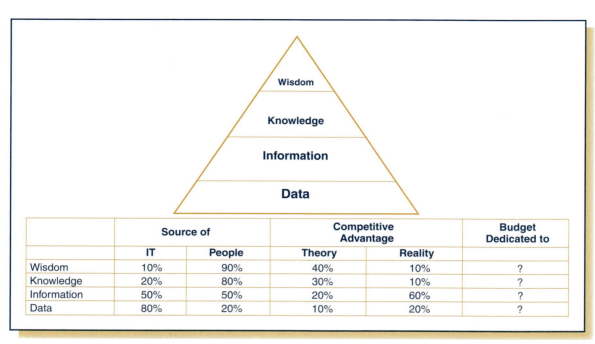

	Source of		Competitive Advantage		Budget Dedicated to
	IT	People	Theory	Reality	
Wisdom	10%	90%	40%	10%	?
Knowledge	20%	80%	30%	10%	?
Information	50%	50%	20%	60%	?
Data	80%	20%	10%	20%	?

Figure 12.7   The Information-Capability Hierarchy

data gathering and analysis capabilities probably yield 20 percent or more of a company's potential for competitive advantage. This reality results from the fact that many companies have not progressed very far up the information-capability hierarchy. Since relatively few companies are competing at the knowledge and wisdom levels, more advantage can be gained by being very good at the lower levels of the hierarchy. As companies learn how to build connectivity and willingness capabilities, this fact will change. Companies will either move higher up the hierarchy or suffer serious competitive losses.

Information emerges as data is collected, analyzed, and shared. Information is what managers use to make great decisions. The source of real information is less dependent on IT (50 percent) and more dependent on managers (50 percent) who design systems and use their outputs. In theory, information packs a greater competitive punch than mere data (about 20 percent). However, because so few companies compete on true knowledge and wisdom capabilities, information more than likely accounts for nearly 60 percent of a company's information-derived competitive advantage. The information level of the hierarchy is where most companies are today.

As we've noted, few companies have truly developed knowledge and wisdom capabilities. Knowledge is an organizational capability—the entire organization knows something that affects the culture and both the behavior and decisions that are made. Knowledge mobilizes proactive and productive behavior that builds both core competencies and world-class relationships. Great SC companies recognize the competitive potential of knowledge and are trying to build organizational cultures that can leverage a knowledge capability. Wisdom is the highest level of the hierarchy. It drives learning and collaboration. It allows a company to tell unique stories that build cohesiveness and momentum. In a sense, wisdom is the holy grail of business—it is the source of renewable advantage.

Why don't more companies pursue and develop knowledge and wisdom capabilities? The simple answer is, "They don't know how!" Both knowledge and wisdom are far more dependent on people and organizational culture than are data and information. That means that connectivity and technology sophistication can enable these higher-level capabilities, but that a culture of willingness is required to achieve them. So, what is the source of the irony? The irony is that companies invest much larger percentages of their time and financial budgets in information technology (i.e., hardware, software, infrastructure, etc.) that supports data and information capabilities rather than knowledge and wisdom capabilities. From a pure technology perspective, knowledge and wisdom are overlooked by most companies. Equally important, budgets also favor connectivity over willingness—technology over culture and people. The temptation to invest in the latest and greatest piece of information technology and a relentless focus on data and information leads many organizations to waste resources that might be better spent developing their human resources and training them on how to create, use, and disseminate knowledge and wisdom within the organization and along the supply chain. Managers need to take another look at their competitive focus and then carefully assess how their budgets are allocated.

WHAT DOES THE FUTURE HOLD?

In an effort to predict the future of many of the issues and technologies addressed in this chapter, an e-commerce-related Delphi study was conducted with 55 high-level SC executives.[41] As part of the study, the executives were asked to utilize a 7-point Likert scale (1 = highly unlikely to occur, 3 = somewhat unlikely to occur, 5 = somewhat likely to occur, 7 = highly likely to occur) to describe how likely each of various predictions were to occur within the next 5 to 10 years. The results of this study are shown in Table 12.4 and summarized in the following paragraphs.

- *Most likely to occur:* SC executives expect (1) an increased demand for on-line technical information, (2) an increased integration role for the purchasing functions of organizations, (3) the elimination of human intervention in the procurement-through-payables transaction process, (4) an improvement in efficiencies as a result of Web-based systems, and (5) the continued use of Internet/Web-based links with suppliers.
- *Least likely to occur:* Based on what SC executives believe is unlikely to happen, we can draw the following conclusions: (1) Web-based tools will not erode the leverage advantages of large buyers, (2) industry-sponsored e-markets will not become primary sourcing tools, (3) reverse auctions will not account for more than 20 percent of the spend, (4) neutral e-markets are less likely to be utilized than industry sponsored e-marketplaces, and (5) strategic alliances/relationships will not become less important as a result of e-commerce.

What do the SC executive responses really mean? We can expect an increased need for information and information sharing in and between organizations along the supply chain. The executives also recognize that there is no technology "silver bullet." Tools many managers thought would revolutionize SCM—such as reverse auctions and e-marketplaces—have a place, but they do not substitute for good thinking, sound decision making, and close collaboration.

Table 12.4 Future Trends in E-Commerce: A Supply Chain Management Perspective

PREDICTION	LIKELIHOOD
1 Buyers within your business unit will increasingly demand on-line access to technical information, such as product specification/configuration data.	6.2
2 As e-purchasing expands, your business unit's purchasing organization increasingly will play the role of supply chain integrator.	5.8
3 E-purchasing tools will enable your business unit's procurement-through-payables transaction process/cycle to be accomplished with minimal human intervention.	5.8
4 Web-based purchasing systems will drive purchasing/supply chain inefficiencies out of the system, allowing your business unit to reallocate resources to other, more critical areas.	5.7
5 The majority of your business unit's nonproduction/indirect material and services purchases will be done through direct Internet/Web-based links with your suppliers.	5.7
6 E-purchasing will facilitate the development of standard metrics, processes, and systems that will help integrate firms in your business unit's supply chain.	5.7
7 Easier access to firms via the Internet/WWW will help your business unit find and develop nontraditional, lower total-cost sources of supply around the world.	5.5
8 Consumption signals and orders from several levels down the supply chain will feed directly into the production planning systems of significant firms in your business unit's supply chain via Web-based systems.	5.3
9 Your business unit's buyers will increasingly rely on e-markets for information about potential suppliers.	5.3
10 Many e-markets that could potentially be used by your business unit will fail due to a lack of industry standards for commercial and technical information/data.	5.2
11 Your business unit will participate in Web-based electronic consortiums to leverage your purchases.	4.9
12 The majority of your business unit's production/direct material purchases will be done through direct Internet/Web-based links with your suppliers.	4.9
13 E-commerce will encourage and facilitate the removal of vertical/functional links from supply/value chains (e.g., distributors, retailers, etc.) within your business unit's supply chain.	4.7
14 E-purchasing will revolutionize your business unit's purchasing function to the point it no longer exists in the traditional sense.	4.7
15 The use of Internet/Web-based reverse auctions will increase the emphasis on price rather than focusing on the total cost of ownership within your business unit.	4.4
16 E-markets will drive industry standardization of goods and services in your industry.	4.3
17 Electronic reverse auctions, using third-party providers, will be the basis for supplier selection and price paid for at least 20% of your business unit's annual spend for nonproduction/indirect materials and services.	4.2
18 Electronic commerce will lead to increased outsourcing throughout your business unit.	4.0
19 Your business unit will mainly use e-markets for spot and low volume purchases.	3.9
20 Many of your business unit's suppliers will resist e-purchasing, and the associated technological integration, because of security/privacy concerns.	3.7
21 In the long run, Internet/Web-based reverse auctions will reduce the number of qualified suppliers in your business unit's supply chain.	3.6
22 Pricing/leveraging advantages of large buyers will be eroded due to the greater price discovery/knowledge that Web-based tools provide to smaller organizations within your industry.	3.5
23 Industry sponsored e-markets (e.g., Covisint, etc.) will be your business unit's primary sourcing and supply tool.	3.4
24 Electronic reverse auctions, using third-party providers, will be the basis for supplier selection and price paid for at least 20% of your business unit's annual spend for production/direct materials.	2.9
25 Neutral e-markets (e.g., E-Steel, Chemdex, FastParts, etc.) will be your business unit's primary sourcing and supply tool.	2.7
26 Strategic alliance/relationships will become less important to your business unit as e-commerce increases the number of suppliers and product/service offerings.	2.2

CONCLUSION

So, what is participation in a supply chain network worth? Metcalfe's Law states that the value of a network equals approximately the square of the number of users of the system (n^2). In other words, the more people there are on a network, the greater the value of the network to each user. This may apply directly to SC networks as well. If so, connectivity is an incredibly important concept and a goal that should be pursued by SC managers. However, experience shows that Metcalfe's Law needs to be tweaked a little bit to apply to SCM. A better law might be that the value of a network is influenced more by the willingness of the people or organizations on the network to share information than by the sheer number of people or organizations on the network. Only when the technology and human sides of information sharing come together can companies achieve the dramatic benefits that attract the managerial attention and financial investment in the first place. The critical need is to bring connectivity and willingness together and then to focus on moving up the information-capability hierarchy. Companies that play the knowledge and wisdom game will win every time when they compete against companies that are stuck on lower levels of the hierarchy. Managers need to step back and carefully consider their information capability development strategies.

SUMMARY OF KEY POINTS

1. There are two separate, but related, components of an information sharing capability: connectivity and willingness. Connectivity is the technological ability to share information. Willingness is the cultural phenomenon that promotes sharing and makes it safe to do so.

2. Advances in information technology are enabling many of the changes taking place in supply chain management. Among the most important changes in technology strategies has been the move to integrated enterprise resource planning (ERP) systems.

3. ERP systems are expensive and difficult to implement. However, their ability to give everyone access to the same data is a critical antecedent of real collaboration. Among the most important steps in improving the likelihood of ERP implementation success is the mapping and redesign of a company's process. It is likewise important to get the people affected by the implementation involved in the process. Finally, performance measures must be changed to support the implementation and use of ERP systems.

4. The Internet provides a whole new level of connectivity. As companies learn how to use the Internet more effectively, they will be able to drive efficiencies and revenues upward. Likewise, new opportunities for collaboration will emerge. Not surprisingly, the Internet will play an important role in winning SC strategies.

5. Managers need to dedicate some of their time to scanning initiatives to identify the new technologies that will enable connectivity and collaboration. They must then be willing to invest in what is often an arduous process of turning the new technology into a new capability. Radio frequency identification (RFID) tags provide an example of this technology development and adoption process. Within a few years, RFID will deliver a new level of transparency to supply chains and their customers.

6. For most companies, willingness is a harder capability than connectivity to build. Willingness requires a cultural transformation, but it unleashes the real competitive benefits of collaboration.

7. Basic types of information that companies must be willing to share include inventory levels, sales data, order status, sales forecasts, production schedules, and delivery schedules. However, managers must discover what information SC partners need to make good decisions. Sharing this information will improve SC performance.

8. Relationships, people, power, trust, security/risk, quantity of information, lack of standards, and inaccurate information all represent challenges that

must be overcome to improve information sharing within and between organizations.

9. Most companies find themselves at the lower levels on the information-capability hierarchy. Few companies have figured out how to build knowledge and wisdom capabilities, despite the competitive advantages available at these levels. Managers should reassess their information strategies and their budgets in an effort to better leverage the power of information in SCM.

REVIEW EXERCISES

1. Describe the relationship between information technology and information sharing.
2. Describe the possible benefits that companies can achieve by sharing information.
3. Describe how applying technology to bad processes can actually make things worse and what can be done to ensure that this doesn't happen.
4. Describe how ERP and ERP II systems were a logical extension of previous supply chain–related information systems.
5. If the Internet and other technologies reduce transaction costs (such as ordering costs) to zero, what effect might this have on the economic order quantity (EOQ) calculations discussed in Chapter 5?
6. Describe the steps that should be taken during ERP implementation to ensure that the information technology is closely aligned with the business processes.
7. Describe how the Internet and e-commerce can both increase revenues and lower costs.
8. Describe the different types of e-marketplaces.
9. Identify several types of information that should be shared between companies along a supply chain.
10. Describe two problems or challenges of information sharing and think of at least one way to help overcome each of these problems or challenges.

Case   *Supply-Base Reduction at Transport*

On May 18, 2004, Robert Ryan met with John Lucas, purchasing director of Transport Corporation at Transport's corporate headquarters in Phoenix, Arizona. "Your new assignment, as part of your recent transfer to the strategic sourcing manager position, is to make recommendations on how best to utilize information technology in our chassis and body parts supply-base reduction efforts. I expect your recommendations in 2 months," John said.

COMPANY BACKGROUND

Transport Corporation operates a fleet of nearly 30,000 trucks, one of the largest fleets in North America. The company provides transportation services to more than 25 million residential, municipal, and industrial customers across North America. With more than 1,200 operating and maintenance locations, Transport faces some unique challenges when it comes to replacement parts for its vehicles. In the past, these 1,200 locations have dealt with thousands of different parts suppliers across the country using separate legacy systems. Transport is currently in the process of moving toward centralized strategy development and price negotiation, but will still have decentralized order execution. On the corporate level, Transport now has 10 strategic sourcing teams working closely with employees throughout the company to define needs, find the best suppliers, and develop systems for streamlined purchasing.

One of the key points of Transport's overall business strategy involves implementing a procurement process that will leverage the company's size to realize savings and discounts through consolidation and reduction of the number of suppliers used. By reducing the number of suppliers it uses, Transport hopes to partner with select suppliers to ensure low prices, high quality, timely delivery, excellent customer service, and strong buyer–supplier relationships.

CHASSIS AND BODY PARTS PROJECT

One specific supply-base reduction project that Transport has recently undertaken involves chassis and body part purchases for their fleet of trucks. Chassis and body parts were selected for supply-base reduction efforts

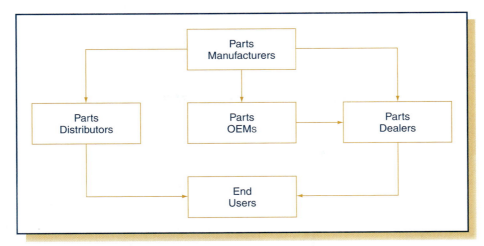

Figure 12.8 Key Players in Chassis and Body Parts Market

because the supply base was highly fragmented, the purchase volumes were not leveraged, there was no centralized purchasing process, this was a large area of spend that provided a good opportunity for savings, and because opportunities for product and information technology standardization existed. Currently, Transport purchases chassis and body parts from over 15,000 suppliers. Transport would like to create a preferred supplier list of 6 chassis parts suppliers and 6 body parts suppliers.

NATURE OF SUPPLY MARKET

The supply market for vehicle parts is comprised of many suppliers in a highly competitive struggle to earn customers. The products are readily available from many sources and supplier location has traditionally been an important selection criteria. Figure 12.8 lists the key players in the chassis and body parts market.

CASE QUESTIONS

1. What types of information technologies might be useful in Transport's supply-base reduction efforts?
2. What recommendations would you make to John?
3. How might reducing the number of suppliers facilitate the additional use of information technology and additional information sharing?
4. What benefits could be achieved in this situation through the proper use of information technology and information sharing?
5. What problems or challenges might Transport face as it implements these technologies?
6. Which would be more important for this project, information technology or information sharing? Why?

ENDNOTES

1. Chase, R. B., Aquilano, N. J., & Jacobs, F. R. (1998). *Production and operations management: Manufacturing and services, eighth edition.* New York: McGraw-Hill.
2. Lee, H. L., & Whang, S. (2001). E-business and supply chain integration, *Stanford Global Supply Chain Management Forum,* November 2001.
3. Fawcett, S. E., & Magnan, G. M. (2001). Achieving world class supply chain alignment: Benefits, barriers, and bridges, *Center for Advanced Purchasing Studies Focus Study Report.*
4. Handfield, R. B., & Nichols, E. L. Jr. (1999). *Introduction to supply chain management.* Upper Saddle River, NJ: Prentice Hall.
5. Bowersox, D. J., Closs, D. J., & Cooper, M. B. (2002). *Supply chain logistics management.* Boston: McGraw-Hill.
6. Krugman, P. (2000). Can America stay on top? *Journal of Economic Perspectives, 14*(1), 172.
7. Simchi-Levi, D., Kaminsky, P., & Simchi-Levi, E. (2000). *Designing and managing the supply chain.* Boston: McGraw-Hill.

8. Davis, E. W., & Spekman, R. E. (2004). *The extended enterprise: Gaining competitive advantage through collaborative supply chains.* Upper Saddle River, NJ: Prentice Hall.

9. Handfield, R. B., & Nichols, E. L. Jr. (2002). *Supply chain redesign.* Upper Saddle River, NJ: Prentice Hall.

10. Shah, J. R., & Murtaza, M. B. (2005). Effective customer relationship management through Web services, *The Journal of Computer Information Systems, 46*(1), 98–110.

11. Lawrence, F. B., Jennings, D. F., & Reynolds, B. E. (2005). *ERP in distribution.* Australia: South-Western.

12. Ibid.

13. Ibid. #3.

14. Adams, F. G. (2004). *The E-business revolution and the new economy.* Australia: South-Western.

15. Wisner, J. D., Leong, G. K., & Tan, K. (2005). *Principles of supply chain management: A balanced approach.* Australia: South-Western.

16. Ibid. #3.

17. Ibid. #9.

18. Monczka, R., Trent, R., & Handfield, R. (2002). *Purchasing and supply chain management, second edition.* Australia: South-Western.

19. Anonymous (2000). Are you ready for ERP II?, *TechRepublic,* September 13, 2000.

20. Anonymous (2001). Taking the pulse of ERP, *Modern Materials Handling, 56*(2), 44–49.

21. Ibid. #14.

22. Mangalindan, M. (2005). Online retail sales are expected to rise to $172 billion this year, *Wall Street Journal,* New York, May 24, D.5.

23. The Ohio State University (1998). *Careers Patterns Survey.*

24. Barbaro, M. (2004). The glitch that stole holiday buys; More holiday traffic means more jams for retailers' Web sites, *The Washington Post,* Washington, Dec 18, E.1.

25. McCourt, J. (2005). Online buying poised for growth, *Home Media Retailing, 27*(39).

26. Chopra, S., & Van Mieghem, J. (2000). Which E-business is right for your supply chain?, *Supply Chain Management Review,* July/August, 32–40.

27. Ibid. #8.

28. Kaplan, S., & Sawhney, M. (2000). E-hubs: The new B2B marketplaces, *Harvard Business Review,* May-June, 97–103.

29. *Center for Advanced Purchasing Studies Whitepaper (2000) entitled Coming into focus: Using the lens of economic value to clarify the impact of B2B E-marketplaces.*

30. Ibid. #8.

31. Carbone, J. (2005). Reverse auctions become more strategic for buyers, *Purchasing, 134*(20), 42.

32. Hannon, D. (2003). Suppliers: Friend or foe?, *Purchasing, 132*(2), 25.

33. Ibid. #3.

34. Lee, H. L., & Whang, S. (1998). Information sharing in a supply chain, *Research Paper No. 1549,* Stanford University Research Paper Series, July 1998.

35. Derrick, R. D. (2003). Challenging the bullwhip effect with advanced information sharing, *Outlook Point of View,* March 2003.

36. Cooper, M. C., Ellram, L. M., Gardner, J. T., & Hanks, A. M. (1997). Meshing multiple alliances, *Journal of Business Logistics, 18*(1), 67–89.

37. Monczka, R. M., Petersen, K. J., Handfield, R. B., & Ragatz, G. L. (1998). Success factors in strategic supplier alliances: The buying company perspective, *Decision Sciences, 29*(3), 553–576.

38. Kolluru, R., & Meredith, P. H. (2001). Security and trust management in supply chains, *Information and Computer Security, 9*(5), 233–236.

39. Brunell, T. (2002). Opinion: Too much information can clog the supply chain, *Electronics Supply and Manufacturing,* October 23, 2002.

40. Ibid. #3.

41. Center for Advanced Purchasing Studies (CAPS)—Research Project.

Chapter 3

Performance Measurement

Do we understand measurement? Can I use measurement to improve SC relationships and performance?

The Supply Chain Roadmap

Integrating the Supply Chain
- Create & Communicate Common SC Vision
- Build a Cohesive Team of Allied Companies

How Do We Get There?

Chapter 11: Relationship Alignment
- Define intensity of SC relationships.
- Build trust to promote collaboration.

Chapter 12: Information Sharing
- Establish technology to support SC.
- Cultivate culture that promotes sharing.

Chapter 13: Performance Measurement
- **Align measures across SC.**
- **Create understanding and motivate behavior.**

Chapter 14: People Empowerment
- Cultivate empowerment environment.
- Build teams to enhance collaboration.

Chapter 15: Collaborative Improvement
- Establish a culture of innovation to avoid complacency.
- Organize for long-term collaboration.

After reading this chapter, you will be able to:

1. Describe the role of measurement in shaping a company's culture and achieving results.
2. Discuss the strengths and weaknesses of traditional measurement practices.
3. Explain how world-class SC measurement improves alignment, emphasizes customer orientation, promotes process integration, and facilitates collaboration.
4. Identify and implement appropriate measures to manage and monitor important processes and relationships. Create unique, tailored measures.
5. Benchmark performance measures and leading-edge SC practices.

Opening Story: Measurement at Olympus

Doug sat comfortably at the back of the conference room, listening to members of the task force debate the efficacy of Olympus's measurement system. He had missed the previous week's task force meeting while he was in Rio de Janero with Charlene, but he was confident that Olympus was making good progress. During the past month all supply and customer relationships had been "ABC" classified and the task force was making progress developing a strategy and establishing the infrastructure to manage each type of relationship. The topic for the day's meeting had been to discuss performance standards for different levels of relationship intensity. However, the agenda had been sidetracked early when Diane Merideth, North American marketing manager, had railed, "No matter how well you think you're doing in manufacturing or logistics, we keep getting customer calls complaining about service failures. Customers really don't care about the whys or what-ifs; they simply want their product delivered on time and at the lowest possible cost."

This comment engaged every task force member, unleashing a firestorm of commentary. As the impassioned arguments ensued, Doug sat calmly, taking it all in. After all, Charlene had warned him this day would come, and it was good to get the "cards on the table." Nevertheless, it seemed that the time had come for Doug to join the fray and direct some of the energy toward finding a solution.

"If I understand correctly, the overriding theme this morning is that we need a comprehensive, but, flexible measurement system to drive operational excellence and promote collaboration up and down the supply chain. Is this correct?" Doug asked.

"That's right," Vijay affirmed, "but we feel handcuffed. It seems we are always trying to improve efficiencies to drive down costs and meet upper management targets for cost reductions. Yet that makes it tough to innovate since most of the new things we want to try require up-front investments, but do not guarantee immediate returns."

Susan agreed, adding, "Everything we do needs to tie directly into the P&L statement to get buy-in, but a lot of what we think might actually work is really tough to measure."

"Besides that," David interrupted, "half the time, what looks best for each of you according to the measures in place, really makes our life tough. Your cost-cutting translates into chaos and higher costs for us."

"I'm glad you understand the feeling," Vijay replied, "because that is exactly how we feel about some of the decisions made in logistics and sourcing. It seems that as we each strive for functional excellence, we create headaches for one another. Isn't that what we've been talking about all along?"

"That is a real concern," agreed Susan. "However, our greatest frustration is the constant emphasis on bottom-line results. We've been trying to change the nature of our supply relationships to capture greater creativity and collaboration, but the need to perform always brings us back to today's costs. Our suppliers sense this and feel that we are constantly trying to squeeze them. We are certain that more cooperative supplier relationships would yield real benefits down the road, but there is no reward to undertaking this journey. No offense, Joel, but you finance guys are killing us."

"No offense taken, Susan. You simply need to understand that in today's business world, finance is the language of business." Joel also noted, "And that means return on capital and quarterly profit reports. If we don't perform, our stock gets hammered. The market is not very forgiving."

Diane joined in again, reminding everyone, "Everything we've talked about represents someone's version of reality, but we seem to keep forgetting that we are in business to create and satisfy customers; yet the customer's perspective keeps getting lost in our debate."

"Perhaps that's because we really don't know what the customer wants. I've never seen a report indicating exactly how our important customers measure our performance. I know they use scorecards, but how do they actually put them together? What are their performance benchmarks for best in class?" David lamented. He added, "Tameka, is that information available?"

"No, it's not. But with a little commitment and effort, we could probably persuade some of our best customers to work with us to remedy that problem. That's really an issue that you and Diane need to drive. The systems group can help along the way."

Vijay chimed in, "We can all probably use some of that help, Tameka. I know that in operations we are not content with the information we are receiving, but its not just customer information that is missing. We really need to look at our current measures and get rid of some while adding others that would help us make better, more informed and holistic decisions."

"Before our plate gets too full, let's take a minute to see if we can pull a few golden nuggets from our discussion," Doug interjected. "Why don't we summarize the key points on the board? Let's start by acknowledging that much of what we do is tough to measure; at least, the current measures don't do a good job of tracking our efforts or capturing all of the pertinent results. David, would you do the honors and get us started by writing, 'A world-class SC measurement system needs to . . . what?' Based on what I've heard you say, I would begin the list with the following:

1. Connect our efforts to what customers really value and help us understand how they evaluate our performance.
2. Balance financial and cost measures with important, hard-to-quantify strategic measures that support longer-term initiatives.
3. Support functional excellence while promoting cross-functional communication and cooperation.
4. Help us understand our own processes across functional boundaries.
5. Communicate our expectations to suppliers, let them know where they stand, and direct their improvement efforts.

"What else needs to be on the list? And then how are we going to create this measurement system? Let's go to work and get this figured out!"

Consider As You Read:

1. What issues have led to Olympus's measurement problems? Are these unique to Olympus?
2. What else needs to be on the list? What are the important roles of a measurement system?
3. How would you suggest the task force create a world-class measurement system?

Not everything that counts can be counted, and not everything that can be counted counts.

—Albert Einstein

THE ROLE OF PERFORMANCE MEASUREMENT

Great SC companies like Dell, Lands' End, and Unilever are fanatical about measurement. Managers at these companies will tell you that SCM's most important goals—SC alignment, outstanding collaboration, and ultimately competitive advantage—all depend on great measurement. Even so, few companies have harnessed the power of measurement.[1] Thomas Monson described this power, noting, "When performance is measured, performance improves. When performance is measured and reported, the rate of improvement accelerates." Managers can capture this accelerated improvement by designing measurement systems to leverage the following roles of measurement.

- Measurement creates understanding!
- Measurement drives behavior!
- Measurement leads to results!

The time-honored saying "If you can't measure it, you can't manage it" is still commonly used today for the simple reason that it succinctly states an inescapable reality. Managers cannot effectively control processes that they do not understand, and they cannot fully understand a process without careful and accurate measurement. This adage thus highlights the most basic role of a performance measurement system: to provide insight into the nature and workings of value-added processes. This insight is central to SC strategy development and execution. A well-designed measurement system provides feedback regarding (1) customer requirements, (2) the company's and its suppliers' capabilities, and (3) the probable success of collaborative initiatives. Simply put, measurement creates understanding of SC processes and guides a company's progress toward real collaboration.

Measurement's second vital role is suggested by Tom Peters, who noted, "What gets measured, gets done." Measurement shapes behavior. Measurement is more critical than communication, training, or perhaps anything else when it comes to managing human behavior. This is true for both the managers responsible for developing competitive SC strategies as well as the workers who must execute them. Measurement's influence on behavior is pervasive because people pay very close attention to how they are measured. Think about it. What is one of first things that most students look at when they examine a course syllabus for the first time? The answer: They check to see how grades are determined. They want to know how they are being evaluated and they mold their expectations and behavior to the measures.

The same phenomenon holds true for people throughout the supply chain. Measurement practice speaks louder than words; therefore, it is critical to measure the right things. Many companies that jumped on the quality bandwagon experienced the frustration of persistent quality problems largely because they talked the quality talk while walking the cost-cutting walk. Because it is folly to hope for "A" if you are measuring "B," SC managers must adopt measures that truly promote collaborative behavior.

Finally, rigorous, thoughtful measurement always precedes high-level execution and the attainment of world-class results. The motto "Measure twice. Cut once" found on the occasional t-shirt emphasizes this third measurement reality: Results follow measurement. As important as it is to measure the right things, it is equally important to measure them correctly. When companies measure the right things using the right measures, good things happen. Harvard's Robert Kaplan has stressed the fact that good decision making requires correct measurement. He identified three characteristics that define "correct" measurement practice, noting that well-designed measurement systems must provide accurate and relevant information in a timely manner.[2] When managers have this type of information for every value-added process and each valued SC relationship, they can make effective decisions. When this type of information is appropriately shared up and down the supply chain, distinctive collaborative capabilities can be built. By contrast, incorrect measurement leads to non-aligned strategies, poor understanding, and inconsistent if not counterproductive behavior.

Unfortunately, experience shows that most companies' measurement systems fall short in one or more of these three basic roles of measurement.[3] As a result, they simply cannot pass the simple test presented by the following 3-item checklist.

☐   ☐   Our measurement system helps managers understand critical value-added processes.

☐   ☐   Our measurement system communicates expectations and promotes correct behavior.

☐   ☐   Our measurement system delivers high levels of targeted results.

The correct response to each statement should be, "Yes!"

TRADITIONAL MEASUREMENT

In the SC functions of purchasing, production, and logistics, five performance areas are regarded as essential to accomplishing customer service and profitability goals. These five areas are asset management, cost, customer service, productivity, and quality.[4] Most

Table 13.1   Frequently Used Performance Measures

	ASSET MANAGEMENT	COST	CUSTOMER SERVICE	PRODUCTIVITY	QUALITY
Sourcing	• Raw materials inventory levels • Raw materials inventory turns • Inventory obsolescence • Return on assets • Economic value-added	• Unit price • Acquisition cost • Total cost of ownership • Cost as a percent of sales • Administrative	• On-time delivery • Order to delivery cycle • Percent shipments expedited • Response time to inquiry	• Purchase orders per employee • Dollar spend per employee • Commodity teams per employee • Percent transactions automated	• Shipments rejected • Defect rate—parts per million • Percent suppliers certified • Percent orders from certified suppliers • Response to inquiry
Operations	• Work-in-process inventory • Inventory obsolescence • Return on assets • Return on investment • Economic value-added	• Direct labor costs • Manufacturing overhead • Costs per unit • Inventory carrying cost • Warranty costs	• Production to due date • Manufacturing cycle time • Back orders • New product lead time • Customer complaints	• Labor productivity • Equipment downtime • Changeover time • Engineering change orders • Total factor productivity	• Defect rate—parts per million • Percent rework or scrap • Statistical process control • Total hours quality training per year • Percent employees six sigma trained
Logistics	• Inventory turns • Inventory obsolescence • Return on assets • Inventory days supply • Economic value-added	• Inventory carrying cost • Total landed cost • Outbound freight • Warehousing labor costs • Administrative	• Fill rate • On-time delivery • Order cycle time • Complete orders • Customer complaints	• Units shipped per employee • Equipment downtime • Order productivity • Warehouse labor productivity • Transportation labor productivity	• Damage frequency • Order entry accuracy • Picking/shipping accuracy • Document/invoicing accuracy • Number of customer returns

companies put in place several measures from each area to monitor and manage a variety of value-added activities. Frequently used measures are shown in Table 13.1. Table 13.1 is far from exhaustive; in fact, the number of possible measures is almost limitless.

Asset Management

Successful companies invest in their future by investing in their capabilities; they also meticulously evaluate the return they obtain on those investments. Critical capital investments are made in facilities, equipment, technology, and inventory. Investments in facilities and equipment have been evaluated in terms of capacity utilization. A motorcycle facility that can produce 200,000 road bikes a year but is only making 150,000 is operating at 75 percent capacity—a utilization level that is probably too low to achieve efficiency and leverage scale economies. Most production facilities are designed to achieve maximum efficiency at about 90 percent of their capacity. Many services can operate at lower utilization levels and still be profitable. For example, in the airline industry, a load factor (a measure of the percent of seats occupied) above approximately 74 percent achieves profitability.

Historically, the goal has been to operate facilities and equipment as close to theoretical capacity as possible without jeopardizing routine maintenance, worker training, and other vital upkeep. However, in his book, *The Goal*, Eliyu Goldratt[5] pointed out that an excessive emphasis on capacity utilization generates excess inventory that can create chaos and confusion, greatly reducing a manager's ability to make good, competitive decisions. He emphasized the need to identify and carefully manage bottlenecks and constrained resources. According to his **theory of constraints**, the key to maximizing throughput is to alleviate the bottleneck, keeping it operating at maximum capacity all the time. All other operations should be scheduled at the capacity of the bottleneck. Managers should not be concerned by a little downtime at non-constrained resources.

Because working capital investments in inventory are often quite large, managers spend a lot of time managing inventories. The "lean" ideal is to have just enough inventory to keep operations running smoothly and meet customer needs. Too much inventory ties up capital and creates waste; not enough inventory creates costly disruptions and stockouts. Inventory levels are measured in terms of "days of supply" as well as turnover rates. Days of supply refers to the ratio of forecast production or sales to inventory available. For example, if expected daily sales are 410 motorcycles per day and 2,000 are in inventory, the manufacturer has just under 5 days of supply on hand. The "right" number of days supply varies by industry. In the automobile industry, dealers try to maintain about 60 days inventory on hand. Inventory turnover rates are typically calculated as follows:

$$\text{Inventory Turnover} = \frac{\text{Cost of goods sold during a time period}}{\text{Average inventory valued cost during the time period}}$$

It is important to note that the average inventory be determined using as many data points as possible, especially if inventory levels vary significantly. Imagine a situation where a manager counts inventory only at the beginning and ending points of a sales period. If beginning inventory is zero and ending inventory is zero, but large quantities of inventory were held throughout the sales period, the average inventory would be calculated to be zero. Inventory turns would be infinite—and infinitely misleading. Most companies are now targeting double-digit inventory turns. A few companies are achieving 20 to 40 turns per year.

Finally, perhaps the favored measure of asset utilization at the senior management level is return on assets, which is calculated as net profit divided by total assets. Individual projects are evaluated using a return on investment metric: net profit achieved divided by total project investments. One problem associated with the way rate-of-return metrics are occasionally used is that they place a heavy emphasis on short-run results. Vital investments that do not provide an immediate return may be forgone in favor of less strategically important initiatives that have an immediate bottom-line impact. Further, managers have a tendency to focus their efforts on areas over which they have the most direct control. In the case of ROA/ROI measures, managers have the greatest and most immediate control over the denominator. Managers can inflate the ratio by eliminating or postponing needed investments. Such decisions can prove debilitating over time. Although SC managers must carefully manage company assets, they must avoid placing too much emphasis on short-term ROA numbers.

Cost

Cost performance is viewed as critical and is tracked more carefully and comprehensively than any aspect of competitive performance. This is particularly true in the SC functions of purchasing, production, and logistics, which are often managed as cost centers. When competitive or economic challenges emerge, the instinct of most managers is to cut costs. For example, when the Japanese yen started to rise precipitously against the U.S. dollar, threatening the profitability of Japanese manufacturers, Toyota announced that it would cut costs like never before. Its resulting cost advantage yielded 2002 profits that were greater than the combined profits of DaimlerChrysler, Ford, and General Motors.

Managers must remember, however, that this instinct to cut costs can be dangerous if vital capabilities are undermined. Companies would frequently be better off working to build new competencies rather than simply cutting costs. Few companies have ever cut their way to greatness. Many managers fail to remember this. Why did cost-cutting work for Toyota? It was the external environment that had changed and required cost cuts—not Toyota's own poor or inefficient management. Toyota was a well-managed company that attacked cost-cutting as part of an overall strategy to build the best cars in the world. Cost-cutting was never viewed as the strategy. Companies that get this backwards often find themselves on a downward cost-cutting spiral that they cannot reverse.

Companies commonly monitor and report cost data at aggregate levels for each functional area as well as for specific activities such as warehousing, order processing, assembly, picking, and transportation. Costs are also evaluated as a percent of sales or of cost of goods sold. Comparison with historical or industry standards is common practice. By tracking changes, corrective action can be initiated or opportunities for improvement can be identified. Cost reductions in purchased inputs, made products, and delivered services translate directly into bottom-line profits. Southwest Airlines has leveraged its low operating costs into 30 consecutive years of profitability—an incredible achievement in the turbulent airline industry. Great companies like Southwest identify the activities that most impact total cost (e.g., airplane turnaround time at the gate and cross-trained employees), adopt appropriate metrics, and then manage consistently to these metrics.

Customer Service

Supply chain customer service consists of making the right products available for use or purchase when they are needed, where they are needed. Service measures usually focus on issues related to availability, time, and satisfaction. Key availability measures include fill rate, complete orders shipped, stockouts, and back orders. The most basic measure of fill rate is simply the number of items ordered by customers divided by the number of items delivered to customers. However, the complete order percentage (number of customer orders/number of orders delivered complete) is perhaps a better measure of service. After all, customers really do not like the hassle of tracking down items that are missing from an order. The stockout percentage measures the frequency that desired products are unavailable. When a stockout occurs, a customer can look to buy the item somewhere else, make a substitute purchase, or place a back order for the item. When combined with a stockout measure, the number of items back ordered is a good indication of a company's inability to meet its customers' availability requirements. Wal-Mart has built a dominant market position based on its ability to have products consistently available on the shelf where customers expect to find them.

Measures of time emphasize on-time delivery and cycle time. The percent of products delivered on time is an important measure in sourcing, operations, and logistics. A failure to deliver on time at any step in the value creation process threatens overall customer service and can increase costs. One company operating in the Caribbean struggled to meet manufacturing due dates. In order to deliver on time to customers, over 70 percent of its product had to be expedited via airfreight at a huge cost to the company. Many companies now include some form of on-time standard, complete with penalty clause, in their supply contracts.

Cycle times are an indicator of responsiveness and are measured in terms of elapsed time from order receipt to order delivery. Because short cycle times increase flexibility and a company's ability to meet the needs of varied but demanding customers, cycle-time reduction has become a major goal for processes ranging from new product development to manufacturing to customer order fulfillment. Steelcase's promise to deliver custom orders of office furniture in only 12 days is heavily dependent on achieving short cycles throughout the value-added process. Sony de Mexico survived because it created a short cycle-time advantage that could not be equaled by lower-labor cost Asian production sites.

A final measure of customer service that is widely employed is customer complaints. Waiting to hear from customers that they are not happy with a product or service is a poor substitute for measuring true customer satisfaction! Yet customer complaints are as close as many companies come to measuring satisfaction. Customer surveys represent a more proactive, but still relatively weak, approach to measuring service and satisfaction levels. More companies are employing focus groups, quarterly business reviews, customer advisory boards, and top management visits to gain a better understanding of customer perceptions of service levels.

Productivity

Productivity relates the outputs generated by an activity to the resources consumed by the activity and is usually expressed as a ratio; for example, units produced per labor hour. Although easy to define, productivity measurement is not always well understood. For example, how would you answer the question, "What does a reported productivity level of 15 'gizmos' per labor hour mean?" There are many possible answers to this question, but the most correct one is: "nothing." Without a basis for comparison, a report of 15 gizmos per hour provides no real understanding or foundation for decision making. To be useful, productivity measurement requires a comparison with past performance, competitor performance, or industry standards. Further, how would you respond to the statement, "Productivity growth is good"?

Most managers believe this statement is true and therefore set goals for productivity growth. Yet it is possible to increase order-picking productivity while accuracy decreases or damage levels increase. The real managerial issue is to determine why order-picking productivity increased. If the increase is due to better training, more clearly marked racks, or the use of radio frequency identification technology, then the productivity improvement is probably good. Steps should be taken to replicate the results elsewhere. Understood correctly, productivity measurement can help drive organizational learning.

Measuring productivity became popular during World War II—a time of scarcity and urgency. At the time, labor accounted for about 50 percent of the cost of goods sold. Labor productivity was thus a pretty good surrogate for overall productivity. Most companies still rely on labor productivity as their primary productivity measure despite the fact that labor often represents as little as 5 to 10 percent of the cost of a product. Wickham Skinner warned that the very way managers define productivity improvement and the tools they use to achieve it push their goal farther out of reach. He argued that roughly 40 percent of any manufacturing-based competitive advantage derives from long-term changes in manufacturing structure. Another 40 percent comes from major changes in equipment and process technology. The final 20 percent—no more—rests on conventional approaches to productivity improvement.[6] Similar relationships exist in the areas of sourcing and logistics. Although it is much harder to track, a measure of total factor productivity (where the denominator includes labor, materials, capital, and energy) would lead to better process understanding, more competitive decision-making, and a less-alienated workforce.

Quality

Customers place quality at the top of their priority list when purchasing a product or service. Basic measures of quality look at the functionality of a product or the reliability of a service. In sourcing and operations, the most common measure of quality is defect rate. Most companies today are targeting a parts-per-million defect rate. In fact, six-sigma quality suggests that only 3 out of 1 million items will be defective. To achieve this level of quality performance, products must be designed with greater thought toward quality and processes must be designed for both quality and stability. The emphasis on process quality has led to an almost universal use of statistical process control to assure that quality is built into every product, and frequently into every service. This emphasis on quality at the source has also led to the increased use of certified suppliers. Supply management professionals increasingly measure the percent of certified suppliers and the percent of orders (or dollars spent) from certified suppliers. Likewise, more companies are measuring the total hours of quality training provided to employees (and in some cases to suppliers' employees). The number of employees with six-sigma training is also being tracked.

In logistics, quality is reflected in service reliability. Are orders entered correctly? Are products picked accurately? Are documents filled out with precision? Do products arrive without loss or damage? In most cases, quality is tracked as a percentage of activities performed correctly to the total number of times the activity is carried out. For instance, if 99 out of 100 invoices were filled out without any error, the invoicing accuracy would be 99 percent. Damage frequency would be calculated as the number of damaged items divided by the total number of items shipped. In addition to tracking damage frequency, many companies track the total dollars represented by lost or damaged items as well as the number and dollar value of customer returns. A final quality issue involves the availability and accuracy of information. Is needed information available? And if it is, is it accurate? SC managers need to identify the types of needed information that are unavailable so that they can initiate systems changes that will make accurate information available for internal managers or external customers.

Caveats Regarding Traditional Measurement Practice

Although not inherently "wrong," traditional measurement practices have come under increasing criticism because they have not adequately met the decision-making needs of modern managers.[7] According to Robert Kaplan, traditional measures have been overly oriented toward short-term financial results and cost-cutting.[8] Further, they have not provided a holistic view of the company; nor have they promoted alignment or collaboration. Part of the problem with traditional measurement systems is that they have been designed to capture and communicate primarily functional information. The persistent emphasis on functional measures often leads to suboptimal decisions and counterproductive behavior. Measurement practice is often the major impediment to good SC thinking!

Moreover, recent competitive and environmental developments require more aggressive and innovative performance measurement to support better and more rapid decision making. Some of the key developments are highlighted here:

- Capable global rivals force companies to emphasize competitive dimensions beyond cost. Yet experience has shown that traditional measurement systems are best suited to providing cost information and do a relatively poor job of tracking other areas of performance.[9]
- Just-in-time or lean management substitutes information for inventory throughout the supply chain, requiring accurate information on a real-time basis.[10]
- Process management requires better measurement to simultaneously promote cross-functional agility and functional excellence.[11]
- Global networks depend on a broad range of measures to help make decisions concerning network configuration and coordination as well as day-to-day operational control.[12]
- Customer demands necessitate much better satisfaction information that comes straight from the customer.[13]

To manage the supply chain for competitive advantage, modern measurement systems must provide a broader array of real-time information that is better balanced between internally focused and externally oriented measures.

SUPPLY CHAIN MEASUREMENT

Nowhere have the inadequacies of traditional measurement been more evident than in supply chain management.[14] Across industries and channel positions, managers have discovered that delivering customer value profitably requires more than greater efficiency. It requires insight and alignment supported by collaboration and innovation. Measurement can promote these attributes. Indeed, improved measurement is essential to the development and execution of winning SC strategies. Superior SCM must emphasize goal alignment, customer satisfaction, process integration, total costs, and inter-organizational collaboration.

Alignment

Insight into one challenge confronting SC managers can be gained by exploring the question, "Does strategic intent translate into operational performance?" If the answer is "yes," then the strategic decision to adopt an strategy will lead to success. A "no" answer requires that managers find out why not. Research has answered the question, revealing that for many organizations there is no connection between strategic intent and operational performance.[15] Figure 13.1 illustrates this point by showing the relationships that exist among strategic intent, measurement, and performance. The diagram indicates that there is no correlation between strategic intent and performance or between strategic intent and measurement. But there is a strong correlation between measurement and performance. *What gets measured, gets done!* Why does the disconnect between intent and measurement exist? This question remains largely unanswered; however, it does present a warning to SC managers. They must make sure that the measures used throughout the organization are aligned with strategic objectives. Otherwise, strategic objectives will go unmet.

SC managers face two other alignment quandaries. First, inside their own companies, managers from a variety of functions are confronted by what they call "inconsistent," "counterproductive," "nonaligned," "nonsupportive," or "conflicting" performance measures. Second, these same adjectives describe discrepancies in measures among different members of the supply chain. At both levels, inconsistent or conflicting measures promote conflictive, and at times combative, behavior. For example, the marketing manager intent on meeting quarterly sales goals is not concerned with the situation on the production floor. The production manager who is focused on machine utilization and optimizing production schedules doesn't worry too much about the "rush" order placed by the marketing manager. In like manner, the marketing groups of many consumer products manufacturers offer special promotional discounts on products that they want to push into the market. Unwilling to pass up the great prices, retail buyers "forward buy" large quantities of the product, which then sit in the retailer's warehouse. The decisions made by managers on both sides of the transaction may appear to make sense based on the measures used, but they often increase total SC costs without improving service.

Nonaligned measures encourage turf protection, thwarting innovative practices. SC managers need to align key measures within their own organizations as well as up and down the supply chain.

Figure 13.1 Relationships Among Strategic Intent, Measurement, and Performance

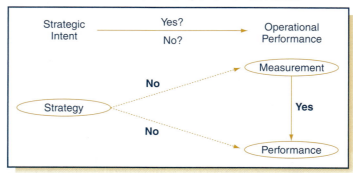

Customer Satisfaction

To meet customers' real needs, managers must understand what those needs are and have a clear view from the customer's vantage point of how well their company is performing. Traditional customer service measurement—which has relied on internally generated statistics regarding such things as fill rates, on-time delivery, and response time to inquiries—does not provide a clear understanding of customer expectations or satisfaction levels. At most companies, informal and infrequent approaches to assessing satisfaction are employed. Fewer than 50 percent of managers report the use of systematic programs to measure customer satisfaction.[16] A more concerted effort must be made to ask customers what services they truly value and then find out how they evaluate them. High service levels that are not highly valued by customers do not enhance competitive advantage but dissipate resources, often leading to diminished performance. Table 13.2 contrasts key characteristics of traditional and best-in-class customer service measurement practices.

Customer surveys are the method most used to obtain direct customer feedback. Surveys typically ask questions regarding overall feelings of satisfaction; the appropriateness and quality of the service or product; and customer experiences with specific aspects of the interaction such as timely delivery, rapid and accurate response to questions, and employee professionalism. Questions may also explore (1) opportunities for improving existing service, (2) suggestions for new services, and (3) customer perceptions of competitors' performance. Unfortunately, response rates are often very low because many customers do not take surveys seriously, making it difficult to gather pertinent and insightful information through surveys.

Some companies are therefore turning to personal interviews with important customers to find out what they are really thinking. Aspen Distribution, a regional third-party distribution company, sends senior managers on periodic "road tours" to visit customers and find out how Aspen can better meet their needs. The resulting personal relationships assure better access to more realistic information. Other approaches used to assess satisfaction and help develop customer-centric metrics include focus groups, expert panels, and customer advisory boards. Finally, some consumer goods companies have begun to "shadow" customers, following them around during a normal day or week to see how they actually use the company's product. Procter & Gamble has even placed cameras in customers' homes to get the real skinny on product use. Vendor-managed relationships that place employees on-site with the customer provide a comparable opportunity to get into the mind of the customer.

Table 13.2 Evolving Characteristics of Customer Satisfaction Metrics

TRADITIONAL PRACTICE EMPHASIZES...	BEST-IN-CLASS EMPHASIZES...
• Internal service measures over satisfaction measures	• External assessment that reveals what customers really think is important!
• Measures that are expressed as averages	• Absolute measures expressed in customer-centric terms!
• Measures that treat all customers the same	• Measures that recognize unique needs of individual customers!

The insight gained from customers should be used to align a company's valued-added processes and commensurate measurement practices to those of key customers. For example, Procter & Gamble has always used traditional fill rate measures. However, a better knowledge of customer needs led P&G to develop and emphasize a new measure, which showed the percentage of the time the product is actually on the shelf. The on-shelf-in-stock percentage emphasizes the fact that the consumer cannot buy the product if it is not on the shelf at the retail store level—regardless of the fill rate from the warehouse. P&G calls the in-store purchase decision "The First Moment of Truth." A high, on-shelf-in-stock percentage helps make sure that customers are not frustrated during this first moment of truth. On-shelf-in-stock measurement helps assess SC performance all the way to the customer. Of course, leveraging this measure requires high levels of communication among members of the supply chain.

At a large logistics services company, customer feedback identified the need to adopt measures of absolute service performance. Traditional measures that were expressed in terms of average performance levels (e.g., percent of shipments delivered damage free) were changed to absolute measures translated into customer-specific terms (i.e., damaged shipments delivered to a specific customer). A senior manager commented on this change, noting, "To say that we deliver 99.5 percent of our packages damage free might give us a false sense of well-being. To say that 5,000 customers received damaged packages from us on a particular day puts an entirely different perspective on our performance."

Direct customer feedback can be used to identify gaps in perception and practice, helping managers develop tailored services and custom measures. The closer relationship and better service delivered to important customers helps preempt competitors' efforts to capture market share.

Process Costing

Making good process decisions requires that costs be measured and compared across activities, departments, or even firms. Better process costing is the key. Two costing methods are particularly important: total costing and activity-based costing. First, total costing is a prerequisite to good process design and management. Total costs are simply the sum of all relevant costs for a given decision. For instance, the total cost of ownership is the cost most appropriately used in comparing substitute materials or alternative suppliers (TCO = Acquisition Cost + NPVΣ (Ownership Costs + Disposal/Scrap Costs)). Decisions made without good total cost information often produce a local optimum while creating greater overall costs for the organization.

SC managers are generally aware of the import of measuring total costs, but few actually use total costs as part of a comprehensive trade-off analysis. This reality reflects the fact that current total cost measures at many companies are incomplete and unreliable. Figure 13.2 illustrates the problem by showing the availability of logistics cost information. Ninety-four percent of logistics managers indicate that they have access to total cost information; however, these same managers acknowledge that they don't have access to one or more costs that should be included in a comprehensive total cost calculation. How can the impact of inventory or customer service decisions be accurately assessed when important cost data regarding the cost of back orders or service failures is missing? And this example only looks at logistics cost information; the problem of missing or unexamined data is more pronounced when the impact of a decision crosses functional boundaries.

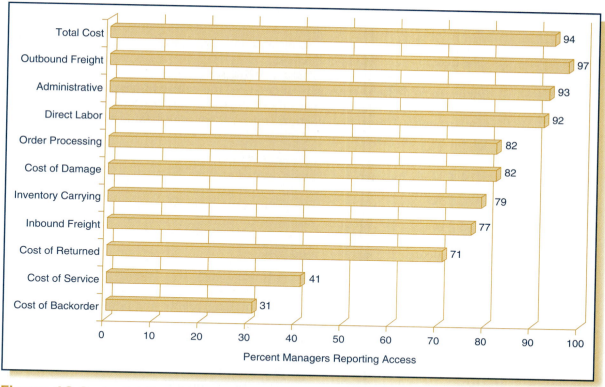

Figure 13.2 Availability of Total Logistics Cost Information

The challenge is exacerbated when total SC costs are being evaluated. Given the lack of accurate total cost data at the firm level, consider the challenge posed by evaluating costs across the supply chain (see Figure 13.3). Good SC design decisions including dis-intermediation and role shifting rely on accurate total costing. For example, when one supply chain entity incurs higher costs in order to reduce total SC costs, the SC members who benefit most must be willing to provide adequate

Figure 13.3 Total Supply Chain Cost

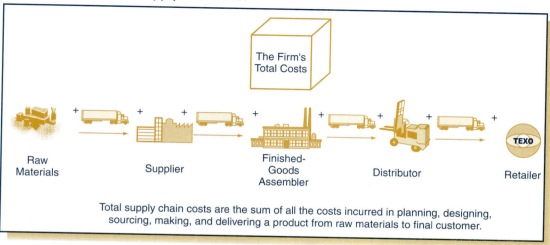

Total supply chain costs are the sum of all the costs incurred in planning, designing, sourcing, making, and delivering a product from raw materials to final customer.

compensation. Lacking accurate total cost information, it is impossible to quantify whose costs increase and whose decrease. As a result, managers make decisions that favor their own company's financial performance, even when the decisions reduce the overall chain's competitiveness.

Second, activity-based costing (ABC) links costs directly to the activities that drive them, helping managers understand the nature of important processes. ABC costing enables managers to evaluate the profitability of specific products, channels, or customers. Figure 13.4 illustrates the basic concepts behind activity-based costing. The following steps should be pursued:

- Identify the product or customer of interest.
- Identify the processes that are needed to make the product or serve the customer.
- Identify the activities that are performed in each process.
- Identify the specific resources that are consumed by each activity.
- Measure the cost of the resources consumed to make the product or serve the customer.
- Calculate the activity-based cost.

ABC costing requires process transparency and detailed information on products, customers, activities, and resource costs. It is tedious work. Nevertheless, ABC costing can greatly improve decision making, identifying opportunities to improve processes or providing the foundation to negotiate win–win relationships. When Inland Steel discovered that some of its "best" customers were actually unprofitable, managers used the ABC cost information to convince them that changes in the relationship were needed. At Torrington Supply Co., CEO Joel Becker took the same approach, telling a customer, "You're a great customer. You've been doing business with us for a long time, and we love you. But we need you to do something if we're going to continue to do business. We need you to help us reduce our transactions cost." And the customer did!

Supply Chain Measures

Superior measurement capability goes beyond functional excellence to facilitate collaboration throughout the entire supply chain. Yet the truth is that SC-wide metrics are almost never employed in actual day-to-day practice. One manager summed up the challenge, "Metrics are critical! We don't know what the new ones should be, but we need them."

Figure 13.4 Activity-Based Costing

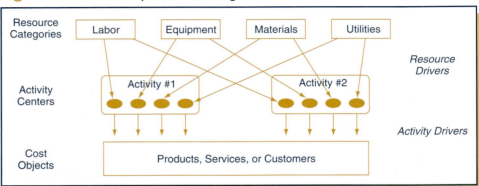

Table 13.3 Supply Chain Performance Measures

SC Inventory Days of Supply:	Total number of days of inventory required to support the supply chain—from raw materials to the final customer acquisition. Expressed as calendar days of supply based on recent actual daily cost of sales.
Cash-to-Cash Cycle Time:	The time required to convert a dollar spent to acquire raw materials into a dollar collected for finished product (total inventory days of supply + days sales outstanding – days payables outstanding).
Inventory Dwell Time:	The ratio of days inventory sits idle to days inventory is being productively used or positioned.
Customer Inquiry Response Time:	The average elapsed time between receipt of a customer call and connection with the appropriate company representative.
Customer Inquiry Resolution Time:	The average elapsed time required to completely resolve a customer inquiry.
Order Fulfillment Cycle Time:	The average actual lead times consistently achieved, in calendar days, from customer order to customer delivery. Includes order authorization to entry, entry to release, release to shippable, shippable to customer receipt, and receipt to customer acceptance.
On-Shelf-In-Stock Percentage:	The percentage of time that a product is available on the shelf, rack, or wherever the customer expects to find and buy it. Measures the supply chain's ultimate ability to satisfy the end customer.
Perfect Order Fulfillment:	A perfect order is an order that is delivered complete, on time, in perfect condition, and with accurate and complete documentation. Fulfillment is the percent of orders that are perfect (perfect orders/total orders).
Source/Make Cycle Time:	The cumulative time to build a shippable product from scratch—if you start with no inventory on hand or on order. Consists of total sourcing lead time, release-to-start build, total build cycle time, and complete build-to-ship time.
Supply Chain Response Time:	The theoretical number of days required to recognize a major shift in market demand and increase production by 20 percent.
Total Supply Chain Cost:	The sum of all the costs incurred in planning, designing, sourcing, making, and delivering a product broken down for each member of the supply chain.
Value-Added Productivity:	Total company revenues generated less the value of externally sourced materials expressed as a ratio of total company headcount.

Some of the metrics suggested for monitoring and managing SC activities are defined in Table 13.3. Most of these metrics like cash-to-cash cycle time and inventory dwell time still focus on a single firm's processes. Others like source/make cycle time and customer inquiry resolution time emphasize the dyadic buyer/supplier relationship. Three metrics—SC inventory days' supply, SC response time, and total SC costs—represent theoretical approximations. Occasionally these are estimated for a specific industry through special consortia efforts. For instance, the efficient consumer response (ECR) initiative in the food industry found that manufacturers, distributors, and retailers held over 120 days' supply of finished goods inventory. This finding revealed that while some firms had successfully reduced their own inventory levels, overall SC inventory had not been reduced. It had simply been shifted to other channel members. This understanding led to a dedicated effort to increase chain-wide collaboration in order to increase overall SC efficiencies and responsiveness.

Another measure that has captured the imagination of SC managers is the "perfect order." A perfect order is one that is received, processed, picked, packed, shipped, documented, and delivered on time without damage. An error of any kind creates an imperfect order. Leading companies that track perfect orders achieve perfect order percentages of only 80 to 90 percent. Remember, an order process consisting of 10 activities where the firm hits 97 percent for each activity would only

Table 13.4 Perfect Order Busters

• Order-entry error	• Missing information
• Ordered item is unavailable	• Late shipment
• Incomplete paperwork	• Inability to meet ship date
• Picking error	• Early arrival
• Customer deduction	• Inaccurate picking paperwork
• Damaged shipment	• Invoice error
• Overcharge error	• Credit hold
• Error in payment processing	

achieve a 73 percent perfect order accomplishment. Consultant William Copacino claims that nine out of 10 orders that fall short of perfection fail due to one of the perfect order busters listed in Table 13.4.[17] The value of the perfect order measure is twofold. First, it makes the need to improve obvious, helping the firm avoid complacency in the quest for perfection. Second, by tracking the root causes of perfect order failures, managers can dedicate resources to improve the order fulfillment process.

Of the measures discussed here, perhaps the one that has had the greatest impact on SC practice is cash-to-cash cycle time. Because of its widespread adoption, let's take a closer look at cash-to-cash cycle management and measurement. The prevalent use of cash-to-cash (C2C) cycle measures is a result of its direct impact on financial performance. Thus, the cash-to-cash cycle time is viewed as a critical means of communicating SC performance improvements to senior management. Remember, finance is the language of business. Cash-to-cash cycles show the direct financial benefit of SC initiatives. That is, SC practice can improve cash flows and reduce the cash-to-cash cycle, freeing up working capital to invest in new products, better processes, or more collaborative relationships. One CFO summarized this goal as follows:

> We have made working capital reduction a priority. . . . We are able to operate some of our businesses with negative working capital. Rather than putting money in inventory or receivables, we prefer to have our suppliers finance us by increasing our short-term liabilities, thus freeing up capital for other investments.

For many companies, the goal has become to attain negative C2C cycles. In other words, they are trying to achieve a negative working capital. Dell is often considered the role model for C2C cycle management. Dell's cash-to-cash cycle is negative. Let's take a look at recent cash-to-cash cycle times for Dell and H-P using the following equation. To calculate a company's cash-to-cash cycle, you need access to its financial statements, which can be found on-line in a company's annual report or at finance. yahoo.com or moneycentral.msn.com.

Cash-to-Cash Cycle = Total Inventory Days of Supply + Days Receivables – Days Payables

	Sales	Inventory	Receivables	Payables	Inventory Days	Days Receivables	Days Payables	C2C Cycle
Dell	$39,667	$ 358	$ 3,142	$10,201	3.29	28.91	93.87	–61 days
H-P	$73,061	$6,065	$19,030	$21,893	30.30	95.07	109.37	16 days

A brief glance at the numbers helps us understand why Dell is the leading computer company in the world. Dell's 70-plus day advantage over H-P allows it tremendous operating flexibility and financial freedom. If we look closer, we see that companies can improve their cash-to-cash cycles in two ways. First, they can establish highly efficient processes. Second, they can use leverage with other SC members, encouraging quick payment on sales or delaying payment to suppliers. Looking at Dell, we see,

- Dell's direct-to-customer business model is extremely efficient. Dell does not make and inventory computers at different points in the supply chain, hoping that someone will buy them. Dell makes computers to order. Most customers pay for the order immediately over the Internet when the computer is ordered. What does this mean? Dell can minimize inventories and receivables.
- Dell's channel power augments its efficient processes. That is, Dell's suppliers own the inventory used in Dell computers until the last possible moment—either co-locating facilities or providing inventory on consignment. This keeps inventory levels to an absolute minimum. The numbers also show that Dell does not pay its suppliers very quickly. However, Dell does pay 15 days more quickly than H-P. So, although Dell is tough on suppliers, on a relative basis, it pays to be a Dell supplier.

Of course, from a collaborative SC perspective, more efficient processes are the preferred approach to reducing cash-to-cash cycles. An SC mind-set can turn cash-to-cash management into a trust-building activity. One manager explained his company's approach to building strong relationships and a more competitive supply chain via cash-to-cash cycle management. He said, "Most large companies strive to reduce their cash-to-cash cycle, but not every company has the same cost of capital. Total supply chain costs can be reduced if the company with the lowest cost of capital accepts longer cash-to-cash cycles. We try to look at this as we manage relationships."

To summarize, SC measures provide a new perspective on operational performance and are changing attitudes as they provide added insight. However, obtaining relevant information across the supply chain remains a serious challenge. In many respects, while we know we need better SC-wide measures, we still don't know what the ideal set of SC measures looks like.

Scorecards

The balanced scorecard was introduced in the early 1990s in response to the shortcomings of traditional financial measures.[18] Scorecards create balance by featuring a set of qualitative measures in the formal measurement system. Over time, the balanced scorecard became a strategic management tool as objectives, measures, targets, and action plans were incorporated into the scorecard development process.[19] Today, the scorecard concept is widely used by leading SC companies to promote higher performance and more strategically focused relationships. Scorecards are used most frequently with suppliers, but a few companies have begun to use customer scorecards to help guide customers' efforts to become "customers of choice." The typical scorecard emphasizes total order performance by including measures of five critical dimensions—cost, quality, delivery, responsiveness, and innovation.

Scorecards' popularity stems from their intuitive appeal. For most of our lives, we have been receiving "report cards" that let us know just where we stand with respect to established standards. We also have developed a knack for using report cards to help us allocate our time and balance our efforts. Supplier scorecards thus provide a mechanism not just to evaluate supplier performance but also to communicate to suppliers exactly where they stand with regard to critical performance dimensions.

The proactive use of scorecards also focuses resource use to drive constant improvements in performance. Figure 13.5 shows an actual scorecard summary developed by a worldwide leader in the electronics industry. This scorecard communicates to suppliers that quality and delivery are the two most important evaluation criteria and lets suppliers know exactly what constitutes acceptable performance. The evaluation informs the supplier that it should work to improve its customer satisfaction score, which is explained in supporting documentation. The company that developed this scorecard summary uses quarterly business reviews with important suppliers to discuss current performance levels and share expectations. These reviews can last an entire day and can allow real feedback to be shared in both directions. They can also help refine existing measures and coordinate continuous improvement efforts. Some of the discussions are described as "blunt, even brutal" and real improvement is expected.

Increasingly, companies are posting scorecards to the Web. This provides a low-cost way to keep suppliers apprised of their performance because they can check their status as of their last shipment. Wal-Mart's "Retail Link" goes a step further, providing suppliers an opportunity to benchmark their performance to competing suppliers as well as to best-in-class suppliers across all product areas. Suppliers can also access training videos over the Web to help them close performance gaps that are identified. This proactive approach has taken some of the fear out of supplier evaluations because they are now viewed more as an opportunity to drive learning and improvement and less as a chance to punish poor performers.

In summary, scorecards (1) help companies select and monitor world-class suppliers, (2) support supplier recognition programs, (3) benchmark leading-edge practices, (4) disseminate best practice throughout the supply base, and (5) identify deficiencies that can be overcome through continuous improvement efforts.

Customized Measures

Many companies now develop customized measures to support their SC initiatives. They do so because a one-size-fits-all approach to measurement cannot effectively monitor and manage the diverse relationships found in modern supply chains. Uniquely supportive measures should be adopted to guide relationships that are

Figure 13.5 Supplier Scorecard Summary

Summary					Goals	
Suppllier Scorecard	Weight	Score	Weighted Score			
Quality	50%	5	2.5		Quality:	< 650 PPM
Delivery	30%	5	1.5		Delivery:	> 95%
Customer Satisfaction	10%	4	0.4		Customer Satisfaction	5
Impact Score	10%	5	0.5		Quality/Delivery Impact	5
Weighted Score =			4.9		Out of 5 Maximum	

Table 13.5 Characteristics of an Effective Measure

		This custom measure is...
YES	**NO**	
☐	☐	Aligned with organizational goals
☐	☐	Aligned with project goals
☐	☐	Customer oriented
☐	☐	Meaningful to workers, managers, and customers
☐	☐	Consistent across appropriate functions or departments
☐	☐	Promoting cooperative behavior both horizontally and vertically
☐	☐	Communicated to all relevant individuals
☐	☐	Simple, straightforward, and understandable
☐	☐	Easy to collect the needed data
☐	☐	Easy to calculate
☐	☐	Available on a timely basis—real time when possible
☐	☐	Strategic and tactical
☐	☐	Quantifiable
☐	☐	Designed to drive appropriate behavior
☐	☐	Designed to drive learning and continuous improvement
☐	☐	Designed to provide information that is actually used in decision making

established to achieve targeted objectives or to work on special projects. Adaptable measurement systems that can rapidly design and implement tailored measures foster the outstanding collaboration needed to succeed in today's dynamic global marketplace.

The power of tailored measures is that they communicate specific expectations, provide unique insight, and promote the behavior needed to leverage one-of-a-kind relationships. But measurement's power can work for or against strategic objectives, depending on how well the tailored measures are conceived and implemented. A checklist of the characteristics of an effective measure is provided in Table 13.5. Managers should evaluate every new measure against an appropriate checklist and seriously discuss each "no" that is checked. Too many "no" checkmarks suggests that the new measure may lead to poor understanding, counterproductive behavior, and unintended consequences. Managers should not implement any more measures than are absolutely necessary to achieve desired results.

BENCHMARKING

Benchmarking—the formal process of comparing the attributes of one organization to those of another—is a critical component of a company's performance assessment arsenal. Benchmarking helps a company assess and improve its own competitive abilities by helping managers stay abreast of state-of-the-art business thought and practice. The generic benchmarking process consists of 3 steps:

1. Define the "attribute" to be benchmarked and identify a best-in-class comparison company.

2. Document the comparison company's process at strategic and operational levels. Compare the best-in-class practices with the company's own methods, specifying any and all differences.
3. Develop a strategy, complete with specific methods, for adopting best practices and improving the organization's own process and performance.

Many companies actively benchmark performance metrics in order to establish and maintain a top-notch measurement system. SC executives openly acknowledge that it is necessary to find and use the best measures possible, even when the measures are developed elsewhere. The "perfect order" measure discussed earlier exemplifies a measure that once developed was rapidly adopted by SC leaders around the world. As well as looking at the metrics used by SC leaders, the search for great metrics might include secondary research that scours business books, trade magazines, and professional associations in search of appropriate metrics.

Just as finding, evaluating, and adopting good metrics is important, managers who believe in benchmarking actively seek to identify progressive SC processes and then learn as much as they can about them. The quest is to find better ways to perform key activities. Great benchmarkers live by the mantra, "Good practice is good practice, wherever it is found." As high-value-added processes are documented, firms identify opportunities to improve their own SC operations. Vigorous benchmarking not only guides specific process improvement efforts but also stimulates an attitude of continual learning. Unfortunately, far fewer firms benchmark processes than benchmark metrics.

One of the greatest challenges encountered in benchmarking is to identify the right company to use as the benchmark. Over the years, several types of benchmarking have been adopted in an effort to drive the learning process. Competitive benchmarking, evaluating the best practice of a leading competitor, is often viewed as the most relevant approach to benchmarking. However, few competitors that do something incredibly well are willing to allow the competition to come in and get an intimate look at how they do business. Even so, in a global economy, it is often possible to find a competitor that is willing to open its doors for some form of benchmarking exercise. General Motors and Ford learned a great deal about lean operations from their fiercest Japanese rivals, including Toyota.

Non-competitive (or non-restricted) benchmarking entails looking to companies in other industries for examples of best practice. The classic example of non-competitive benchmarking involved Xerox's quest to improve its distribution system. Xerox's choice of a benchmark company was the catalog retailer L.L. Bean. Other companies, including some in the food and personal care industries, have since benchmarked L.L. Bean's order fulfillment process. Internal benchmarking is a final type of benchmarking that is of interest to large, global companies. For example, Johnson & Johnson has over 150 different business units, giving it numerous opportunities to find and disseminate best practice.[20]

Managers interested in benchmarking should be aware of at least three caveats. First, effective benchmarking depends on the competitive attitude of a company's management team. An example involving two Japanese companies competing in the same industry illustrates this point. The managers at the industry's largest and most established company did not see any value in comparing themselves to anyone. After all, they were the best. At the second firm, a relative newcomer to the industry, managers stressed the need to constantly look to other companies—in and outside their industry—to find better ways to manage key processes. The established competitor encountered stagnant sales and a growing expenses-to-sales ratio while the "inquisitive" firm enjoyed double-digit sales growth and improved profit margins. The companies' attitude toward benchmarking is not the sole cause of the distinctly different performance results; however, managers at the "hungry" firm believe that what they have learned through benchmarking has helped them improve customer service and SC productivity.

Second, aggressive benchmarking affects managers' perceptions of their own firm's performance. In a study of logistical competencies, managers were asked to evaluate their relative performance vis-à-vis leading industry competitors along 32 different capabilities.[21] These evaluations were then compared to each company's level of benchmarking aggressiveness. Firms classified as non-benchmarkers identified themselves as the outstanding performers for 15 of the 32 capabilities. Limited benchmarkers considered themselves to be the highest performers for another 15 of the 32 capabilities. Extensive benchmarkers claimed to be the best performers for only two capabilities. Rather than providing evidence that benchmarking leads to decreased performance, it seems that managers who are actively involved in benchmarking initiatives have a more realistic view of their own company's capabilities. For non-benchmarkers, "ignorance is bliss" and can lead to complacency.

Finally, research has shown that high-performing SC companies are likely to be active benchmarkers.[22] Benchmarking, however, by itself does not enable a company to become the world's best at any activity. That is, the essence of benchmarking is copying best practice, not creating best practice. Although benchmarking deserves a place in the competitive arsenal, SC managers must not become overly dependent on it.

CONCLUSION

In a world where the performance bar is constantly rising, measurement practice must improve at an equal pace. High-performance organizations like Kraft Foods, Schneider National Logistics, and Wal-Mart have learned this vital lesson. They realize that measurement practice is more a matter of attitude than anything else. An organization's attitude toward measurement establishes the focus and boundaries of the measurement system and determines the effectiveness of its efforts to use measurement to achieve competitive advantage.

One executive expressed his company's attitude toward measurement as follows:

> If it moves we measure it. We measure for how much it costs to move, what resources were used, did we move it to the right place without damaging it and how long it took. If it doesn't move, we measure how long it stays there and what resources are consumed while it sits. This framework is applied to the measurement of products, people, and equipment. Finally, we try to measure whether we did it as well as or better than anyone else could do it.[23]

This description clearly highlights a desire to use measurement to gain insight and understanding regarding every organizational process and resource. It highlights the fact that great companies are compulsive about measurement, viewing measurement as the platform on which competitive position, distinctive capabilities, and SC collaboration are built. Because leading companies view enhanced measurement as a prerequisite to outstanding performance, they invest in comprehensive measurement programs. These programs

- Make accurate, detailed, relevant, and timely information accessible to managers for strategic planning and daily decision making.
- Track a broad range of measures from all 5 supply chain areas—asset management, cost, productivity, service, and quality.
- Employ metrics that are easily understood by everyone.
- Make trade-offs visible and processes transparent.
- Incorporate customer-centric and process-oriented measures.
- Create alignment with both corporate strategy and customer expectations.
- Document the progress that is being made and that drives learning.
- Facilitate the benchmarking and adoption of best practices—wherever they are found.
- Create competitive power because they lead to better decisions and more appropriate behavior.

Performance measurement practice stands at a crossroads—many managers know that to achieve best-in-class status they need to improve their companies' measurement systems. But they are not sure exactly how to make the needed changes happen. Initial efforts should focus on clearly defining strategic intent and evaluating the fit and suitability of existing measures. Greater effort is needed to define desired outcomes and then to adopt relevant measures to facilitate and promote enhanced performance in those areas. Increasing communication and paying attention to potential disconnects between strategy and measurement can jump start the improvement process. Managers can also look to consortiums, industry initiatives, and professional associations like the Supply Chain Council and the Institute for Supply Management for insight into both tried and true measures as well as the development of new metrics. Additional, creative efforts to design new measures may be needed to support distinctive capabilities, meet customers' needs, and facilitate collaboration. Some of these efforts can and should take place within individual firms as managers and workers are brought together to discuss key activities and measurement opportunities. Similarly, to expand perspectives and better understand the needs of other SC members, managers from customers and suppliers can be included in the efforts to build a powerful measurement system. A nominal group technique might provide a useful forum for brainstorming unique and customized measures.

Finally, managers should remember that modern information technology makes it possible to collect, manipulate, and disseminate information that was unavailable just a few years ago. Technology allows many aspects of SC performance that were previously difficult to assess to be measured in an accurate and timely manner. For example, in the past, companies measured delivery performance from the perspective of on-time shipment—because they could not tell exactly when shipments actually arrived. Using satellite communication and on-board tracking systems, on-time delivery to customers can now be tracked in real time. When this data-capturing capability is coupled with better database technology, managers can utilize information for better decision making in such important but diverse areas as supplier selection and evaluation, facility design and location, and order cycle reduction. The accessibility and reliability of the data collected, stored, and communicated via today's technologies provide a strong incentive to take measurement issues into account in the design of technology systems.

SUMMARY OF KEY POINTS

1. A company's ability to monitor and manage its value-added processes as well as those of its SC partners depends on its measurement capability.

2. Measurement performs three vital roles: It creates understanding, shapes behavior, and leads to operational performance and results.

3. Traditional measurement practice has emphasized five critical areas: asset management, cost, customer service, productivity, and quality. Most companies implement multiple measures in each of these areas to monitor and improve their value-added capabilities.

4. Measurement can be used to create alignment. Three areas should be considered: alignment between strategy and measurement, alignment among measures used across functional areas, and alignment of measures employed up and down the supply chain.

5. Customer-focused measures are needed. A special effort must be made to find out what customers value and how they evaluate performance. Customer-centric measures should be tailored to important customers.

6. Process costing is a critical step in managing world-class processes. Accurate total costing and activity-based costing create process transparency and make trade-offs visible.

7. Tremendous effort has been dedicated to develop SC measures. Three popular measures are SC inventory days of supply, cash-to-cash cycle time, and perfect order fulfillment. Most SC measures do not capture what is going on across the entire supply chain.

8. Scorecards incorporate financial and key qualitative measures to communicate expectations, evaluate performance, and motivate improvement.

9. Most companies should adopt tailored measures to help them manage particularly important processes and relationships. Managers need to know what constitutes an effective metric.

10. Benchmarking can help companies identify and emulate best practice. Good benchmarking practice looks at best-in-class metrics and practice wherever it is found.

REVIEW EXERCISES

1. Identify and discuss three roles of performance measurement. From your own experience, identify good and bad examples of measurement practice that illustrate each role.

2. Identify and discuss three measures used in the following areas: asset management, cost, customer service, productivity, and quality.

3. Explain why strategic intent does not translate into operational performance. Discuss the reasons for the lack of alignment within the company and across the supply chain.

4. Discuss the characteristics of a customer-centric measurement system. Develop a flowchart to highlight the critical steps in establishing a customer-centric measurement system.

5. Explain why SC total cost analysis is not performed more often. Discuss the implications of this measurement failure.

6. Describe several challenges to the development of effective SC-wide measures Which SC measure do you think is most effective?

7. Go on-line to find the financial statements for Wal-Mart and Kroger. Compare their cash-to cash cycles. Describe what you see. Infer how each company manages its cash-to-cash cycle.

8. Explain the benefits of the balanced scorecard methodology. Explain why scorecards are used in buyer/supplier relationships. Discuss the benefits of posting scorecards to the Web.

9. Identify the characteristics of an effective measure. Describe how modern information technology supports the adoption of tailored metrics.

10. List the steps involved in the benchmarking process. Explain why benchmarking is important and when it is appropriate. Who should a company benchmark?

11. What is meant by the statement, "Great companies are compulsive about measurement"? Describe the core traits of a world-class measurement system.

Case   *The Gorilla's Dilemma*

Mark Meiers, director of global procurement at PharmaCorp, stared deeply into the mirror, ruefully pondering the marvel of reflection. Mark considered carefully the fact that people see the world not as it is but as they are, looking through the lenses of personal experience. He realized that the same principle held true for the way that people view themselves—they tend to look only from a selective perspective. With this thought in mind, Mark mulled over some of the comments he had heard over the past 4 days at the World Pharmaceutical Exposition in Basel, Switzerland. He had been taken aback when he talked to Thomas Rue, a professor at St. Gallen University, about some research that Thomas had just completed on the theme of buyer/supplier trust. Thomas noted that he had heard more than once during his supplier interviews that PharmaCorp was an "absolutely brutal" customer. Mark's response had come quickly: "We are tough, but I've never considered us to be 'brutal.' What do we do that makes them say that?" Thomas outlined a series of behaviors, most of which involved Pharma's use of its industry-dominating size to "squeeze" suppliers.

Further investigation during the expo revealed that many suppliers hated doing business with Pharma. Mark couldn't believe that suppliers viewed Pharma as "ruthless" and "greedy." Because Mark and his sourcing colleagues considered themselves to be tough, but fair,

he had been surprised at the rancorous tone and tenor of the comments he had heard. Suddenly, Mark didn't like the reflection that he was seeing—it presented some real vulnerabilities. Was it possible that suppliers were inclined to share their best ideas with, and allocate scarce capacity to, rivals? This possibility worried Mark. As Mark considered the long-term implications of this negative supplier sentiment, he wondered what could be done to improve PharmaCorp's reputation among industry suppliers.

BACKGROUND AND COMPETITIVE SCENARIO

As the millennium began, the sourcing group at PharmaCorp recognized that the pharmaceutical industry was undergoing a challenging transition. Two issues were driving dramatic change: the expiration of vital patents and an increase in the cost of R&D. The end of patent protection for many top-selling drugs meant that margins would come under severe pressure. At the same time, the search for new, blockbuster drugs was becoming more and more expensive. The combination of smaller margins and higher R&D costs threatened industry profitability. To cope with this dual challenge, key industry players were striving to increase market power and R&D budgets through mergers and acquisitions. Several giants had been created in recent years (see Table 13.6).

Table 13.6   Major Global Pharmaceutical Companies

COMPANY	MERGER AND ACQUISITION PARTICIPANTS	YEAR	2002 SALES
Merck	No major acquisitions		$51.8 billion
Johnson & Johnson	Acquired Depay	1998	$36.2 billion
	Acquired Cordis	1997	
	Acquired Biopsys Medical	1996	
GlaxoSmithKline	Glaxo Wellcome & Smith Kline Beecham	2000	$33.9 billion
Pfizer	Acquired Pharmacia	2003	$32.4 billion
	Acquired Warner Lambert	2000	
Bayer Group	Acquired Aventis Crop Science	2001	$31.7 billion
	Acquired Lyondell Chemical	1999	
Novartis	Ciba & Sandoz	1996	$20.9 billion
Bristol-Myers Squibb	Acquired Dupont Pharmaceutical	2001	$18.1 billion
Abbott	Acquired BASF Pharmaceuticals	2001	$17.6 billion
Euro exchange rate = $1.07; British pound exchange rate = $1.60			

PharmaCorp had been an active player in the recent merger and acquisition frenzy. In fact, with almost $50 billion in annual, worldwide sales, Pharma had become the 800-pound gorilla of the industry. With Pharma's newfound behemoth status, Mark, and his sourcing team, saw an opportunity in the challenging environment not just to survive but to thrive. By driving costs out of purchased materials and increasing sourcing's efficiency, Pharma's profitability and cash flow could be improved (and sourcing's image within PharmaCorp could be greatly enhanced). To take full advantage of the new opportunity, the global procurement team had adopted a variety of assertive sourcing practices:

- Supply-base reduction had been used to concentrate Pharma's purchases.
- Purchasing requirements were aggregated globally to increase buying power.
- Aggressive target costing was used to establish prices to be paid for key supplies.
- Global suppliers were constantly sought after to create the threat of alternative supply sources.
- Reverse auctions had been employed to enhance competition among suppliers.
- Pharma had established a cost analysis team to "estimate" bottom-line supplier costs.
- Every buyer had received extensive training in negotiations.

The use of these practices combined with the global procurement team's aggressive goal of driving acquisition cost to the lowest level in the industry had yielded a decrease in materials cost of almost 20 percent in the past 18 months.

IMPROVING SUPPLIER RELATIONS

Mark was pleased with the tremendous gains that the global procurement team had made in helping PharmaCorp establish itself as the industry's profit leader. He knew that those profits were being invested heavily into R&D in the hunt for new blockbuster drugs as well as for cures to serious diseases. In fact, at 20 percent of revenues, Pharma's R&D budget was the largest in the industry. Despite these successes, Mark knew that something needed to be done to improve Pharma's image among its supply base. Because poor supplier relations posed a significant threat to Pharma's long-term success, Mark was preparing to establish a task force to study the problem and make a recommendation within the next 6 weeks. Mark wondered what guidelines he should give the task force. He felt confident that Pharma needed to maintain its sourcing advantage and was reluctant to give up the practices that had led to such outstanding results. But, he also realized that perhaps a cultural shift was needed to take some of the "toughness" out of the buyer/supplier interactions. Simply stated, he wanted to really achieve the elusive goal of tough, but fair.

CASE QUESTIONS

1. In what ways do you think that performance measurement may have contributed to the poor supplier relationships?
2. How could measurement be used to establish parameters for tough but fair supplier relationships?
3. How could measurement be used to change the culture at Pharma so that it is more conducive to the development of tough but fair supplier relationships?

ENDNOTES

1. Fawcett, S. E., & Swenson, M. J. (1998). Customer satisfaction from a supply chain perspective: An evolutionary process in enhancing channel relationships. *Journal of Consumer Satisfaction, Dissatisfaction and Complaining Behavior, 11*, 198–204.
2. Kaplan, R. S. (1991). New systems for measurement and control. *The Engineering Economist, 36*(3), 201–218.
3. Ibid. #1.
4. Bowersox, D., Daugherty, P., Droge, C., Rogers, D., & Wradlow, D. (1989). *Leading edge logistics: Competitive positioning for the 1990s.* Oak Brook, IL: Council of Logistics Management. Bowersox, D. J., Calantone, R. J., Clinton, S. R., Closs, D. J., Cooper,

M. B., Droge, C. L., Fawcett, S. E., Frankel, R., Frayer, D. J., Morash, E. A., Rinehart, L. M., & Schmitz, J. M. (1995). *World class logistics: The challenge of managing continuous change.* Oak Brook, IL: Council of Logistics Management. Bowersox, D., Closs, D. J., & Stank, T. P. (1999). *21st century logistics: Making supply chain integration a reality.* Oak Brook, IL: Council of Logistics Management.
5. Goldratt, E. (1992). *The goal.* New York: North River Press.
6. Skinner, W. (1986). The productivity paradox, *Harvard Business Review, 65*(4), 55–59.
7. Kaplan, R. (1984). Yesterday's accounting undermines production. *Harvard Business Review,*

95–101. Eccles, R. (1991). The performance measurement manifesto. *Harvard Business Review, 69*(1), 131–137.

8. Ibid. #2.
9. Fawcett, S. E., & Clinton, S. R. (1996). Enhancing logistic performance to improve the competitiveness of manufacturing organizations. *Production and Inventory Management Journal, 37*(1), 40–46.
10. Schonberger, R. J. (1986). *World class manufacturing.* New York: The Free Press. Bagchi, P. K., Raghunathan, T. S., & Bardi, E. J. (1988). The implications of just-in-time inventory policies on carrier selection. *Logistics and Transportation Review, 23*(4), 373–384. Lieb, R. C., & Miller, R. A. (1988). JIT and corporate transportation requirements. *Transportation Journal, 27*(3), 5–10.
11. Wells, M. (1996). *VP logistics, Hershey Inc.* Speech at Michigan State University.
12. Porter, M. (1986, Winter). Changing patterns of international competition. *California Management Review,* 9–40. Fawcett, S. E. (1992). The status and impact of logistics issues in the success of co-production via maquiladoras. *International Journal of Logistics Management, 2*(2), 30–41.
13. Stock, J., & Lambert, D. (1992). Becoming a "world class" company with logistics service quality. *International Journal of Logistics Management, 3*(1), 73–80. Ibid. #4, Bowersox (1995). Ibid. #1.
14. Ibid. #4.
15. Ibid. #2
16. Ibid.
17. Copacino, W. C. (1993). Creating the perfect order. *Traffic World, 32*(2), 26.
18. Ibid. #2.
19. Kaplan, R. S. (1996). The balanced scorecard is more than just a new measurement system. *Harvard Business Review, 74*(3), S3–S4. Kaplan, R. S. (2000). Having trouble with your strategy? Then map it. *Harvard Business Review, 78*(5), 167.
20. Bowersox, D. J., Closs, D. J., & Cooper, M. B. (2002). *Supply chain logistics management.* Boston: McGraw Hill.
21. Ibid. #4, Bowersox (1995).
22. Ibid. #4, Bowersox (1999).
23. Ibid. #4, Bowersox (1995).

14

People Management: Bridge or Barrier to SCM

Are our people a bridge or barrier to SCM? How can I cultivate a culture of collaboration?

The Supply Chain Road Map

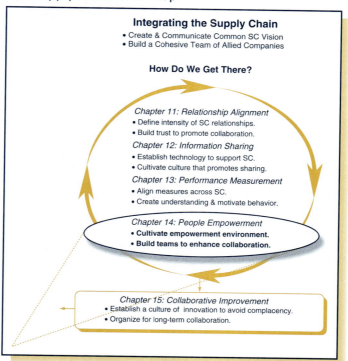

Integrating the Supply Chain
- Create & Communicate Common SC Vision
- Build a Cohesive Team of Allied Companies

How Do We Get There?

Chapter 11: Relationship Alignment
- Define intensity of SC relationships.
- Build trust to promote collaboration.

Chapter 12: Information Sharing
- Establish technology to support SC.
- Cultivate culture that promotes sharing.

Chapter 13: Performance Measurement
- Align measures across SC.
- Create understanding & motivate behavior.

Chapter 14: People Empowerment
- **Cultivate empowerment environment.**
- **Build teams to enhance collaboration.**

Chapter 15: Collaborative Improvement
- Establish a culture of innovation to avoid complacency.
- Organize for long-term collaboration.

433

After reading this chapter, you will be able to:

1. Describe the characteristics of an SC manager.
2. Describe the vital role people play as a bridge or barrier to SC collaboration.
3. Explain how to cultivate a culture of empowerment. Discuss the ABCs of empowerment.
4. Explain the importance of investing in employee capabilities through training, especially in the areas of cross-training and teaming.
5. Discuss why developing and integrating human and technological resources is critical to developing world-class processes.

Opening Story: People As the Bridge to SCM Success at Olympus

"Charlene, it's going to be a beautiful day. I just hope I live to enjoy it. Remind me, why do we get up at 5:20 A.M., lace up the tennis shoes, and run 5 miles every morning?"

"That's easy, Doug, it's because we love to see the sun rise."

"But we could do that sitting on the back patio, Charlene."

"That may be so, but we wouldn't live as long, especially with all that junk you eat when you travel. You don't really want to weigh 300 pounds do you, Doug? Besides, I thought you liked this quiet time to talk about the most pressing events in your SC transformation."

"That's true but, Charlene, do we really have to be cruising along at a 6-minute mile pace?"

"I hope you don't exaggerate so much at work; we're barely running 7-minute miles. Before you get too winded, tell me about that HR dilemma you mentioned yesterday."

"That's a great idea! I'll do that. As you know, we've made a world of progress over the past year and a half. We documented the potential benefits of SCM and persuaded Joe Andrus to let us move forward. We've mapped the supply chain and picked a couple of pilot projects to show that SCM really can help us compete. We've defined our core competencies and developed an outsourcing strategy. We're in the process of putting in place a segmented customer success program. We're pretty close to defining relationship intensities up and down the chain. And our new measurement system is coming along nicely. But we have a long way to go with the information systems, not to mention the strategic costing initiative and the SC rationalization effort. Everyone on the task force is excited about the progress we've made, but we're running out of steam. Tuesday afternoon, Susan, Vijay, and David stopped by my office to discuss the agenda for tomorrow's task force meeting. Apparently, there was some sort of glitch in the e-mail. They weren't there to complain, but talk about being winded—I could tell that they are exhausted. The majority of the task force workload

---

has fallen squarely on their shoulders and it shows. I don't think any of us thought that this initiative would require so much of our heart and soul over such a long time. I'm worn out myself—and SCM is my passion."

"Doug, it seems to me that the answer is obvious. Your task force has carried Olympus up the SC mountain into rarified air. It's only natural that you're all winded. You've all been working two full-time jobs—your own plus the task force's. I know that SCM has become your 'baby,' but it's time to share the passion and the workload with others throughout the company."

"You're probably right, Charlene, but that's a whole new game. So far, we've controlled or at least touched almost every detail. It'll be tough to let go. We haven't even considered how to make the hand-off, but you're right, real success means that SCM has to become part of the culture and structure at Olympus. It'll have to become part of everyone's job, not just the task force's project. But while the task force understands the power of systems thinking and collaboration, systems thinking hasn't taken hold across the company. Although we have some really bright, talented functional managers, we don't have a lot of middle management with an SC mind-set or collaboration skills. How can we let go, if there isn't a strong team to pass the baton to? I suppose we really should have thought of this before, but. . . . You've worked through this process with other companies. Where do you think we should begin?"

"That's a good question, Doug. You've been fortunate to have Joe's support and your task force is made up of wonderful people who possess a lot of clout with their individual functions, but you still need to consider how you are going to get everyone to buy in. You'll need broad-based understanding and support and that means training. Based on the nature of SCM, you'll need a pretty extensive program that runs from the CEO to the production floor. That'll be a tough sell, both in terms of money and time."

"That's wonderful, Charlene, just one more thing to benchmark! How come every time we have one of these chats, it costs me time and money?"

"Don't worry, Doug, the advice is free. While you're at it, you will want to build a culture of empowerment, which as I recall is not exactly Olympus's forte. And speaking of time and money, empowerment doesn't come cheaply. But down the road, you will find it to be a necessary investment. Olympus's people might not have the mind-set and skills to take the SCM baton and run with it, but they can easily drop it if they want to. Besides, people are the only asset you have that adapts and learns. They are your only true source of creativity and competitiveness. Despite everything else you've accomplished, if you cannot figure out how to capture the energy and passion of your people, Olympus will never be world class, at least not for long."

"You're right, Charlene, and just in time. I've only got enough kick left for the sprint to the corner. I'll race you!"

"You're on; I just hope you have enough kick left to carry SCM across the finish line!"

Consider As You Read:

1. How did Doug and his team get so caught up in SCM that they forgot to get everyone involved? What are the dangers of having the task force do it all? Can SCM thrive if it doesn't become part of the culture?
2. What should an SC training program look like? Who should be involved? How much training is needed and for how long?
3. What is a culture of empowerment? What does it look like? How should Doug go about cultivating it?

> *We know how to invest in technology and machinery, but we're at a loss when it comes to investing in people.*
>
> —PETER SENGE

THE SUPPLY CHAIN MANAGER

What is "the" SC manager? The truth is that many managers from engineering to marketing touch critical SC processes from new product development to order fulfillment. Many other managers have line responsibility for the core SC functions of planning, sourcing, making, and delivering. But not all of these managers are true SC managers. True SC managers are not defined by functional position or job description. They are defined by mind-set and skill set. SC leaders feel strongly that the true SC manager possesses strong functional skills, sees the big picture, analyzes trade-offs rigorously, builds collaborative relationships, executes with discipline, exemplifies leadership, and embraces change.[1] Few managers possess this combination of attitudes and skills. This reality threatens the implementation of winning SC strategies. In their book *The Extended Enterprise*, Edward Davis and Robert Spekman call our attention to this educational deficiency, saying, "It is essential that we recognize that most managers do not currently possess the skills or mind-set needed to operate in an extended enterprise environment."[2]

Why the concern? The simple answer: Without the right people, SC strategies will not be envisioned, nor will they be executed! SCM requires change. Companies must change the way they organize resources—the way they do business. The transformation to a winning SC strategy is every bit as difficult as the one Jim Collins describes in his best-selling business book *Good to Great: Why Some Companies Make the Leap . . . and Others Don't*. Interestingly, Jim Collins identifies two people issues as prerequisites to making the leap from good to great. First, a Level-5 leader must be in place. Level-5 leaders possess vision, humility, and determination. They embrace change because they know change is necessary. Second, the company must have the right people on the bus and then make sure each person is in the right seat.[3] Experience suggests that the same two characteristics are needed to go from company-versus-company competition to a supply chain-versus-supply chain world.

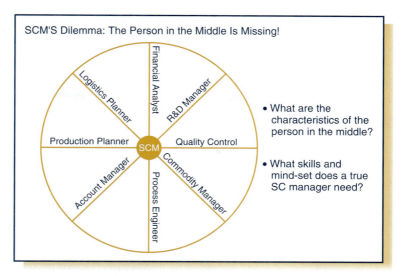

Figure 14.1 Today's Supply Chain Manager

Unfortunately, finding the right people to invite onto the SC transformation bus is a real challenge. A VP of technology and supply management at Intel described this as Intel's greatest SC challenge. He explained, "We can find great entry-level people—the ones with strong functional skills. But, finding people who can bring everyone together to work as a cohesive team is a real challenge. They're just not out there." He then depicted companies as wheels with a variety of functional spokes (see Figure 14.1). Each spoke is a needed functional expert. Take any spoke away and the wheel moves forward more slowly. However, for the wheel to be a wheel, the spokes must be held together with a powerful hub—the true SC manager. The VP then described the person at the hub as "the holistic thinker with collaboration skills." He then lamented, "This person in the middle is missing!" Absent the hub, the wheel can bear neither the weight of competition nor the burden of collaboration. The company cannot win the competitive race.

Managers at leading SC companies everywhere recognize Intel's dilemma as their own.[4] They know that to win the competitive race—the SC marathon—they must become much more effective at developing the SC manager at the hub of the wheel. They realize that although this is not their strength, developing the true SC manager is not something that can simply be outsourced to human resources. They recognize that Peter Senge's quote is dead-on accurate: Putting the "wheel" together will require a dramatically new approach to investing in people. It will also require real empowerment so that the hub and the spokes can work together to create customer value. The following discussion describes how a company can invest in and develop a strong team of SC managers.

THE MOST VALUABLE ASSET?

Every company must someday ask, "What is the true source of our company's competitive advantage?" Few managers seem to grasp the importance or implications of this question and their response to it. Getting the answer right will determine their company's future!

A brief history: For the past 20 years, managers have invested in technology as if they viewed technology to be the source of competitiveness. Most have discovered that whether it's hardware or software, anyone can buy and implement the "hottest" technology. The fact is that competitors replicate most technological advances within a year. This is true of both product and process advantages. As a result, the race for technological superiority usually ends in parity.

Even as the technology race continues at most companies, a few companies have focused on their companies' people as the most important competitive resource. They treat the people who work for the organization as the foundation of their companies' competitive capabilities. Take, for instance, David Neeleman, CEO at JetBlue Airways. He argues that JetBlue's destiny depends on its people's passion:

> Great companies and great dynasties and great empires, most of those were not defeated externally. They were defeated from within. Our greatest challenge going forward is how can we continue to inspire our crew members on a daily basis? How can we keep them motivated and let them know the impact they have on our customers? That's our greatest challenge, and that's what keeps me up at night.

JetBlue's rapid growth in a struggling airline industry suggests that Neeleman may be onto something. Perhaps it is not coincidence that JetBlue's effort to tap the creativity and contribution of the human resource to satisfy customer needs mirrors Southwest Airlines' drive to leverage its people as a source of advantage. Remember, Southwest has racked up a remarkable 30 consecutive years of profitable operations.

Of course, managing the human resource for competitive advantage is not a new concept. For many years, and across most industries, managers have identified their employees as their companies' most valuable asset. In the early 1980s, one manager at Ford Motor Company noted, "Human resources—that is what gives you the competitive edge. Everybody's buying the high-tech equipment. . . . The only competitive edge we'll have over anyone else is our human assets."

The problem is that although managers often talk about the importance of people, relatively few live up to their own rhetoric. Robert Levering emphasized this point with the subtitle of his book *A Great Place to Work: What Makes Some Employers So Good (and Most So Bad)*. Scott Adams, creator of the Dilbert comic strip, has taken up this theme, identifying the great management lies (see Table 14.1). Number one on his list of lies is, "Employees are our most valuable asset."[5] Adams's "Great Management Lies," which focus on the way companies manage the human resource, expresses the cynicism that is felt by many workers and managers alike across the supply chain. Such cynicism threatens the collaboration that is needed to identify and implement winning SC strategies. Cynics and skeptics do not create value; they undermine collaboration. Breaking the cycle of cynicism is crucial to SC success. Rick Blasgen, an outspoken advocate for SCM, emphasized this point, saying, "People are either the bridge or the barrier to supply chain management."

As an SC leader, Procter & Gamble invests in its people as a bridge, placing them at the heart of P&G's collaboration strategies. P&G's emphasis on people is not new. In fact, managers at P&G still talk about the following 1947 quote from then CEO Richard R. Deupree: "If you leave us our money, our buildings, and our brands, but take away our people, the Company will fail. But if you take away our money, our buildings, and our brands, but leave us our people, we can rebuild the whole thing in

Table 14.1   The Great Management Lies, by Scott Adams

1. Employees are our most valuable asset.
2. I have an open-door policy.
3. You could earn more money under the new plan.
4. We're reorganizing to better serve our customers.
5. The future is bright.
6. We reward risk takers.
7. Performance will be rewarded.
8. We don't shoot the messenger.
9. Training is a high priority.
10. I haven't heard any rumors.
11. We'll review your performance in 6 months.
12. Our people are the best.
13. Your input is important to us.

a decade." These managers claim that the essence of the quote still holds true today—people are still P&G's most valuable asset.

P&G's emphasis on people emerges from its belief that winning the hearts of customers (both retailers and consumers) requires not just the quest for high productivity but also the unleashing of people's passion to collaborate. Richard Antoine, P&G's global human resource officer, notes that collaboration is critical to success. "The days of the lone-ranger manager who thinks, 'Everyone else is my rival,' are over. Individual performance still matters, but you won't perform well in this complex world if you aren't collaborating with and getting help from lots of people."[6]

P&G's emphasis on teamwork starts with the CEO, A. G. Lafley. He encourages teamwork by example. P&G's Antoine says, "He always asks managers to give him two different approaches and present the pros and cons of each. And at meetings, A. G. says, 'Before you jump in and inject your own point of view, make sure you listen and truly understand the other's point of view.'" A. G. Lafley insists that teamwork take place everywhere at P&G. As a result, managers are now working across divisions to cross-promote products like Gillette's Venus razors and P&G's Always feminine-care products. Just a few years ago such collaboration would not have happened. Managers from different divisions were too busy competing to see who could outsell one another. Lafley also stresses collaboration with customers, asking employees to watch how customers use products and to find out what their real needs are. P&G also works with retailers, helping them devise new and better performance measures. P&G even helped one retailer improve its distribution operations, going so far as to pay half of the costs of upgrading the dock where P&G products were delivered.

To really inspire collaboration, however, requires more than just encouragement. Collaboration must become part of the fabric of the company's culture. P&G has therefore made finding people who know how to collaborate a part of its hiring process. Potential employees are screened for nine important skills, one of which is the ability to collaborate (see Figure 14.2). These same skills are emphasized in corporate communications, training programs, and perhaps most importantly, in annual performance reviews. P&G isn't interested in creating just great products; P&G expects its people to foster creativity and collaboration. P&G believes that for

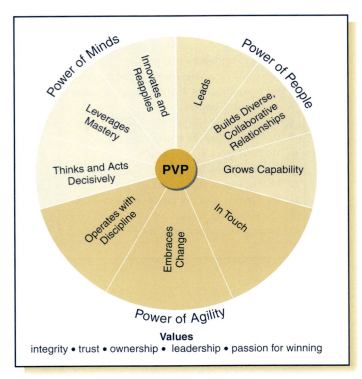

Figure 14.2   Procter & Gamble's Leadership Development Attributes

people to be the bridge to successful SC collaboration, they must be viewed as more than a commodity—they must be hired and trained not simply for the work their hands can do but also for their ability to collaboratively make P&G and its SC partners more competitive.

To summarize, proactively managing people does not always lead to outstanding SC collaboration. The other practices on the SC road map must also be implemented. However, a disgruntled workforce is almost always in a position to undercut any SC initiative. Similarly, managers who feel threatened because they know they don't have the needed collaboration skills stand in the way of greater SC collaboration. High levels of buy-in and commitment are needed throughout the organization and across the supply chain to attain the levels of collaboration needed to achieve process and product breakthroughs. Commitment to collaboration begins with how a company invests in its people's collaboration capabilities.

INVESTING IN EMPLOYEE CAPABILITIES

When designing a training program, managers must decide how much investment is enough. SC guru Bud Lalonde provided insight into this question. After years of studying SC career success, Lalonde proclaimed that to avoid obsolescence within 5 years, a person needed to consistently invest 10 percent of her time in acquiring new skills. That translates into 200 hours of skill enhancement per year. The clear implication is that much of the burden for skill acquisition falls on the shoulders of the individual. The bad news is that Lalonde made this announcement in the mid-1990s. By the early 2000s, Lalonde said the world had changed, exclaiming that an amazing 20 percent of an individual's time must be allocated to continuous learning to avoid obsolescence in a scant 3 years. The obsolescence curve has compressed—and it looks like today's dynamic environment is making learning a lifelong quest. This idea has been succinctly stated as follows: "Education . . . must reach everyone and it will have to go all through life. If you stop, you become obsolete, you cease to be competitive." Visionary SC companies like P&G are catching this vision and dedicating the resources needed to build world-class SC managers.

John Deere has been a leader in SC education. Deere put in place a comprehensive training program that helps new managers build skills, current managers upgrade skills, and suppliers expand skills. Deere believes so strongly that education builds competitiveness that it offers over 50 courses not only to Deere employees but also to the personnel of first-tier and selected second-tier suppliers. An important point here is that Deere realizes that it must help its SC partners build skills. By inviting partners to join in the training, the entire SC team becomes more competitive. Table 14.2 lists many of the courses offered by Deere. Note the breadth and variety of opportunities employees have to expand their capabilities. The odds are pretty good that you will need many of these same tools in your managerial toolkit. Deere is committed to helping its people become more effective SC managers. Of note, beyond helping employees gain specific job-related skills, many courses are offered to help managers broaden their personal horizons.

In addition to upgrading skill sets, these professional development classes bring managers together in a learning environment where they can build relationships. As managers get to know each other, they develop confidence in each other's competencies. The investment in training becomes an investment in SC team building, reducing the time required to make teams effective. Reticence toward team assignments decreases and managers become dedicated to team success as they go through training together. More will be said about the need for cross-training in the next several pages.

The Cross-Trained Worker

The cross-functional worker came into the spotlight with the emergence of lean manufacturing.[7] In fact, the lean philosophy is built around a cross-trained, empowered, and responsible workforce.[8] At Toyota, the inventor of lean production and arguably the world's best auto manufacturer, world-class process capabilities depend on the development and integration of people and technology systems. A tour of a Toyota's assembly line in Toyota City, Japan, reveals that workers are never idle—they are constantly moving with purpose, and seemingly without wasted effort. Moreover, the workers move in synch with the machines on the assembly line in a carefully choreographed display of precision and efficiency. The human and technology systems have been integrated. The payoff is clear—Toyota achieves (1) outstanding productivity, (2) high quality ratings, (3) remarkable concept-to-market-development times, (4) consistently satisfied customers, and (5) unbeatable levels of profitability year after year.

Several facets of Toyota's approach to people management merit discussion. First, in Toyota's JIT system where small-lot-size inventories are the norm, the role of the worker is critical because a problem anywhere in the process threatens to bring production to a halt. Toyota therefore invests heavily in the problem-solving skills of

Table 14.2 Training Courses Offered at Deere & Company

- Advanced EDI
- Advanced Product Quality Planning
- Apples and Oranges
- Application of ABC Data
- Benchmarking
- Business Report Writing
- Cash Flow Analysis
- Cell Manufacturing
- Compensation Strategies and Incentives for CI
- Conflict Resolution: Team Operating Skills
- Continuous Process Improvement
- Continuous Process Improvement (Advanced)
- Continuous Quality Improvement
- Cost/Price Analysis
- Creative Focus
- Customer Service—A Strategy for the Future
- Customer Service II
- Cycle-Time Reduction
- Decision Focus
- Design of Experiments
- Developing Communication for Increased Collaboration
- Developing Employees
- Developing High Performance Teams
- Effective Facilitation
- Effective Job Skills
- Facilitator Skills
- Failure Mode & Effects Analysis
- Finance for the Non-Financial Manager
- Group Problem Solving
- Interviewing Techniques
- Introduction to ISO/QS-9000
- Inventory Management
- ISO/QS-9000 Internal Auditor/ Team Training
- ISO/QS-9000 Quality System Documentation
- Job Instruction Workshop
- Leadership Skills
- Mistake Proofing
- Presentation Skills
- Preventive Maintenance for Cycle-Time Reduction
- Preventing Discrimination and Sexual Harassment
- Process Mapping
- Project Management
- Root Cause Analysis
- Setup Reduction
- Teaching Techniques
- Team Effectiveness
- Team Effectiveness II
- Team Focus
- Team Problem Solving
- Time Management
- Win–Win Negotiations
- Working in a Changing Environment
- World-Class Manufacturing
- Writing Skills

its workforce, focusing the training on the problems each individual is in the best position to solve. Individual workers are given full responsibility for their own work and then held accountable for their own performance. But a worker's responsibility does not stop at this; instead, workers are expected to maintain their own equipment, to keep their workstations along with the surrounding area clean, to help each other when difficulties arise, and to contribute to the continual improvement of the production process.

Second, job descriptions at Toyota are quite broad. When Toyota took over management of General Motor's Freemont, California, assembly facility as part of the NUMMI joint venture, it reduced the number of job descriptions from over 200 to 3. By giving workers more responsibility and then providing them with a challenging work environment, Toyota avoids the monotony of uninteresting, narrowly focused tasks. Workers are motivated to be both productive and creative. Perhaps the most vital aspect of the worker's job description is the emphasis placed on every individual's participation in continually improving both product quality and the manufacturing system.

Third, the notion of **"jidoka"** or line stop plays a key role in the Toyota production system. The jidoka philosophy gives individual workers the authority to shut down the entire production line when quality or other problems arise. Responsibility for action is given to those individuals who have the best information and are most familiar with the situation regardless of official title. Of note, the word "jidoka," translated from the Japanese kanji, literally means "man and machine system." Giving individual workers the authority to shut down an entire production line requires that workers possess not just good production skills but also a high level of familiarity with the entire production process and sound judgment. Worker participation in every facet of the value-added process is the social norm—a social norm that fosters systems thinking and collaboration. This practice differs sharply with many companies where a worker's participation is frequently limited to suggestion boxes. Of course, to make this all possible, Toyota had to make a series of clear choices to (1) view its workers as an integral part of the value-added system, (2) invest time and money in worker training, and (3) delegate to workers diverse responsibilities and real authority. These are the keys to building a truly cross-trained workforce—and a workforce that is a viable competitive weapon.

One final point deserves mention. The ability to integrate workers more fully into the value-added process depends on the relationship between management and the workforce. If an adversarial relationship exists, attempts to increase worker participation are met with skeptical resentment. In a setting where the workers take responsibility for their own work and actively participate in problem solving, the role of the manager becomes one of facilitating a team approach.[9] This role is very similar to that of the coach in the athletic world. Yet, few managers possess the teaching and communication skills of an effective coach. Too often, managers also lack the mind-set of a coach, a mind-set that leads them to constantly ask how they can share the company's success with their workers.[10] Cross-training only works when workers are empowered to participate and given the chance to make real decisions that make an impact. They must then be rewarded for the value they create. When this occurs, the "we-against-them" attitude evaporates, replaced by a spirit of cooperation directed toward meeting customers' needs and whipping the competition.

The Cross-Experienced Manager

Effective collaboration requires a dedicated emphasis on building a "cross-experienced" management team. The goal is to provide managers with an understanding of the roles and challenges inherent in managing diverse value-added activities throughout the company. To develop cross-experienced managers, companies like DaimlerChrysler and Motorola have instituted extensive management trainee programs for new-hire SC managers. A typical training program provides a new manager with some degree of experience—3 to 6 months in each position—in a variety of functional areas. At Motorola, all new materials managers go through a 6-month rotation program that enables them to see how different, related functions actually work. The trainee also has an opportunity to build relationships that will reduce barriers to cross-functional cooperation. Another leading organization believes so strongly in creating cross-experienced managers that it is experimenting with a 2-year rotation program that gives management trainees an opportunity to experience firsthand 4 to 6 different assignments in the following areas: the assembly line, production control, purchasing, logistics, marketing, accounting, and finance. A well-designed rotation program helps managers

- Develop an appreciation for the needs and wants of customers
- Become intimately familiar with the product and the value-added process
- Gain a better perspective of what goes on in the different functional areas and how the functional areas work (or don't work) together to meet organizational goals
- Learn the "language" spoken in each area (in preparation for future intra-organizational communication)
- Establish relationships with other managers that will be useful in future decision-making responsibilities and collaborative initiatives
- Develop an appreciation for the workers that make the product or, in the case of service industries, interface with customers
- Gain an understanding of the role that outside suppliers (both product and service) play in product development, production, and distribution

Of course, cross-functional experience should continue throughout a talented manager's professional life. This basic pattern of job rotation can be used for managers in mid-career. That is, managers can be periodically transferred among functions for short periods of time. This practice is quite expensive, but it communicates that the company is serious about systems thinking and teamwork. Occasional assignments to cross-functional task forces and project teams help managers apply and retain their cross-functional perspective. Working on cross-functional teams and special assignments in other functional areas helps keep managers in touch with the needs, responsibilities, and constraints of different organizational units. Such assignments should extend to teams that involve both suppliers and customers. Honeywell uses interorganizational teams as a standard part of its new product development efforts.

When a rotation program is coupled with classroom training and professional development workshops, managers better understand the nature of the organiza-tion, its culture, and strategy. As noted, critical training focus should be on the value, role, and cultivation of a system's perspective. Understanding the need for better collaboration and its influence on the firm's culture and strategy positions managers to make integrative decisions. Additional points of interest for training include the following:

- an overview of the organization focusing on its history, culture, and objectives
- a review of customers, their needs, wants, and success factors
- an analysis of key suppliers, including their competencies and capacities
- exercises in communication, teamwork, and paradigm shifts
- specific instruction regarding the firm's performance measures and reward system

Linking training modules to a rotation program inculcates a sense of teamwork and cooperation among the company's management team.

As managers gain relevant experience across areas, they gain the perspective and insight needed to manage effectively in an SC world. Unfortunately, the cost of these management development programs makes them difficult to justify. After all, new managers must spend from 6 months to 2 years in rotation before they fill the positions for which they were hired. This represents a serious investment by a company. Given today's highly mobile managers often change employment after only 3 to 5 years, companies hesitate to establish the extensive programs needed to cultivate cross-experienced managers. In one instance, a company with a reputation for developing outstanding cross-experienced managers scaled back its training program after competitors made a practice of hiring away its newly trained managers. Competitors had found that it was easier and less expensive to "headhunt" bright and capable managers than to establish their own training programs.

Cross-Functional Teams

Michael Hammer has suggested that teams will provide the foundation of organizational design.[11] Already, teams are found throughout the supply chain, impacting most critical processes (see Table 14.3). You may have noticed that we have talked

Table 14.3 Types of Teams That Impact Supply Chain Performance

Type of Team	Team Objectives
Advisory Councils	A variety of teams help design and manage the supply chain including internal, senior-level steering committees, customer advisory boards, and supplier councils. These boards provide feedback, expedite communication, and garner commitment for key initiatives.
Capital Equipment	Capital equipment teams design and acquire needed equipment. Several tasks must be performed to meet key objectives: (1) Determine the necessary specifications, (2) select an adequate supplier, (3) conduct negotiations, and (4) install and maintain equipment.
Commodity	Commodity teams develop the expertise and relationships needed to establish a strategy for managing the acquisition of important commodities over time. They also investigate and select one or more sources for a given material or service.
Cost Reduction	Cost-reduction teams take many forms and consist of many different players. The fact that sourced inputs represent 50 to 80 percent of the cost of good sold suggests that considerable effort be targeted at improving both supplier relations and supplier processes.
Customer Relationship	Dedicated customer teams work to build relationships and understand specific customer needs as well as to respond to customer inquiries and resolve customer problems. These teams increasingly work to design tailored services for the most important customers.
Cycle-Time Reduction	Cycle-time reduction teams are responsible for taking time out of key processes such as order fulfillment. The increased use of collaborative planning, forecasting, and replenishment and vendor-managed replenishment has made inclusion of outside representatives valuable.
Information Systems	Information systems teams determine the information needs of the firm and then design the information systems to provide this information. Information systems specialists run the team but they need the input from the areas where information is either collected or used.
Inventory Control	Inventory teams seek to reduce inventory levels while providing an uninterrupted flow of materials. Sourcing, operations, and marketing work to develop dock-to-stock, lean-materials, and coordinated promotions/replenishment systems
Problem Solving	Numerous ad hoc teams or task forces are put together to solve specific problems, drive the adoption of new technologies, or implement a strategic initiative. These teams are almost always dissolved upon completion of the specific task.
Product Development	Product development teams reduce the time needed to bring a product from concept to market. These teams consist of representatives from marketing, production, purchasing, engineering, and quality assurance, as well as representatives form both customers and suppliers.
Quality Improvement	Quality teams work to improve the quality of products and processes. Members come from production, purchasing, quality assurance, and engineering. More companies are including supplier and customer representatives to assure that they define quality appropriately.
Supplier Development	Supplier development teams help suppliers upgrade process engineering, manufacturing, and quality capabilities. These teams consist of representatives from selected suppliers as well as from production, sourcing, quality assurance, and engineering.
Value Analysis	Value analysis teams study a product or process and all of its components to determine how to produce the product at a lower cost or with improved quality. These teams often include representatives from engineering, marketing, operations, and purchasing.

about specific teams and their important roles in almost every chapter of the book. Cross-functional and interorganizational teaming can help bridge the "chasms" that prevent collaboration. In some organizations, the belief in the team experience is so firmly ingrained that a manager's progress up the leadership ladder is based in part on her capacity to contribute to team success.

Properly designed and managed teams can go a long way toward reducing communication barriers. Better communication leads to greater collaboration, reduced turf protection, and better overall decisions. Decision making no longer focuses on local optimums; rather, it emphasizes total organizational performance. Despite these benefits of cross-functional teams, teams are not a universal answer. Further, because teams are composed of people, they are not always easy to manage, even when they are the best approach to problem solving. Training plays a vital role in helping managers learn how to design and manage effective teams. At Deere, many courses are dedicated to the team process. Among these courses are the following.

- Conflict Resolution: Team Operating Skills
- Developing Communication for Increased Collaboration
- Developing High Performance Teams
- Effective Facilitation
- Facilitator Skills
- Leadership Skills
- Team Effectiveness
- Team Effectiveness II
- Team Focus
- Team Problem Solving

Team Appropriateness

SC managers must learn how to evaluate the dynamics that impact team success (see Table 14.4). They must also learn how to identify and weigh the pros and cons of teaming before putting a team together to deal with an important managerial issue (see Table 14.5). The greatest advantage of cross-functional teams is the opportunity to bring a diverse set of talents and expertise together to make decisions or solve problems. Good team communication leads to more rapid and more

Table 14.4 Factors That Impact Team Dynamics and Success

• Availability of resources	• Measures used for team and team members
• Clarity of team objectives	• Supplier involvement
• Commitment of members to the team	• Team autonomy/mandate
• Complexity of team assignment/task	• Team cohesiveness
• Executive management support	• Team leadership
• Functional/technical skills of team members	• Team longevity
• Open and honest team communication	• Team member personalities
• Organizational experience with teams	• Team process skills of team members
• Overall organizational support for team success	• Team reward structure
• Performance feedback and information support	• Team size

Table 14.5 Advantages and Disadvantages of Teams

ADVANTAGES OF TEAMS	DISADVANTAGES OF TEAMS
• **Decision Ownership**. Cross-functional teaming builds ownership in the solution of choice. Even when additional time is needed to arrive at a consensus, the overall implementation is faster because of the ownership that has been created.	• **The Never-Ending Debate**. When a team is composed of talented, but unyielding people, consensus is hard to reach. A dominant team member can forestall meaningful progress. Since no one is individually responsible, tough decisions are never made.
• **Leveraged Diversity**. By bringing diverse opinions and expertise together more creative decisions are brought to light. As team members challenge current practice or a proposed idea without attacking each other, the entire team can dig a little deeper in the quest to find a better way.	• **Groupthink**. A strong desire to "go along to get along" can prevent teams from challenging weak ideas or analysis, even when the needed information is readily available. The result is mediocre decision making. It is important to stress not only the quality of the team process but also the quality of the team outcome.
• **Faster Task Completion**. Teaming reduces the temporal and physical distance that information needs to travel, leading to shorter task completion times. Trust creates a willingness to compromise, which helps the team make integrative decisions and implement the chosen plan of attack.	• **Social Loafing**. On occasion, team members settle back and let the rest of the team carry the load. This is called "team process loss" or "social loafing" and occurs when individual accountability is not tracked. The ability to "hide" allows people to avoid committing to the team process. Such individuals may be committed to the success of the organization, but simply focus their efforts on other responsibilities.
• **Better Organizational Understanding**. As team members interact, they get to know the constraints encountered by other team members. They take this understanding back to their own areas. Slowly but surely, a better understanding of the entire organization is shared throughout the company.	• **Peer Pressure**. The team process can exert great pressure on team members to alter their decision-making behavior in order to belong to the group. If they lower their standards or accept a group decision that they do not agree with, the team influence is negative. Going against deeply held ethical beliefs to support the team can create a sense of uneasiness that reduces a member's commitment to the organization.

thorough decision execution. Indeed, putting all of the right people in the same room and getting them to focus on a common goal changes the dynamics of decision making.

Well-run teams can bridge functional boundaries, unlock creative power, and drive the development of distinctive competencies; however, they are tough to manage because each team member not only possesses a functional bias but also comes to the team with a personal style and certain idiosyncrasies. Individualists find it particularly difficult to work on synergistic teams. Further, team members have many other responsibilities that require their time and commitment. Most companies do not know how to measure team performance and compensate team members for their individual contributions. As a result, almost everyone has participated on a dysfunctional team at least once.

Team Composition

Teams are not without cost. For example, team members almost always continue to fulfill normal responsibilities in their own functional or divisional areas. Participating on a team can distract from these everyday responsibilities. Too much team participation can lead to burnout. Serious thought must therefore be given to who should participate on a team. The careful selection of team members can help overcome socialization difficulties before they arise, contributing to team success.

Further, effective teams have a strong leader who has good people skills, strong credibility with other team members, and significant team experience. Addressing the following questions can streamline the team design process:

- Is there a well-defined goal that can be clearly articulated and communicated?
- Is a variety of expertise and experience really needed?
- What time commitment is really required?
- Who are the best people—those with the right knowledge and experience—to serve on the team?
- What assignments do these individuals currently work on? Can they really add more value by working on the team? Can their other responsibilities be effectively performed by other individuals?
- Who will lead the team? Does this individual have the skills and clout necessary to guide the team?
- Does the team composition take into account different personalities and working styles?

One caveat must be highlighted. The selection of team members usually focuses on functional expertise. Member credibility and influence are also taken into account in the design of many teams. But, the role of personalities and working styles is often overlooked. Kathy Kolbe, a consultant in the area of team composition, has found that teams formed without looking at inherent working styles are often dysfunctional. Kolbe argues that everyone approaches work in an instinctive way and that team performance is enhanced when the right set of working styles are all found on the team.[12] She has identified four primary working styles:

- *The Quick Starter*—Highly energetic, sees an opportunity and quickly mobilizes energy
- *The Fact Finder*—Very meticulous and oriented toward detail and analysis
- *The Follow Through*—Determined and focused on carrying out a task to its completion
- *The Implementer*—Very task oriented, with a particular penchant for hands-on work

Highly productive teams include individuals who are oriented toward each working style. Several other instruments including the Meyers-Briggs personality profile and the Learning-Style Inventory developed by David Kolb have been used to help design more effective teams.

The Team Process

A well-thought-out task that is supported throughout the organization is a prerequisite to success. If the team goal cannot be articulated or the organization is unwilling to put the needed resources behind the team effort, the team is destined to struggle. One apparel manufacturer set the ideal example when the CEO brought the team together and announced unequivocally that the team's task of designing an integrative supply chain was "the most important challenge that the firm had faced in the past 20 years." He then made certain that resources were available to support the team's efforts. Despite this company's success, experience has shown that even when the team consists of the right people, a clear objective is articulated, and senior management support is in place, most organizational cultures are not designed to promote and support team decision making. The following points are requirements for transforming the group into a team:

- *Common goal*—Successful teams possess a common goal that motivates all team members.
- *Leadership*—Teams are led by well-respected managers who understand team dynamics.
- *Communication*—Open, constructive communication is fundamental to team success.
- *Cooperation*—Effective teams cooperate even when this means that someone must compromise.
- *Specific roles*—Team members understand their specific roles and responsibilities.
- *Measurement*—Clear and precise performance measurement facilitates team success.
- *Individual responsibility*—Each member is held accountable for individual and team performance.
- *Resources*—Adequate resources, including information, are made available to the team.
- *Time*—True "chemistry" emerges as team members spend quality time working together.

Because some teams greatly outperform their counterparts, great effort has been dedicated to understanding exactly what makes a team tick. As early as 1965, the team development process was described as a 4-stage process, which became widely known as forming, storming, norming, and performing.[13] A fifth stage of adjourning has since been added.[14] By working through each stage of the team development process, team effectiveness can be enhanced.

- **Forming** is the process of deciding who should belong to the team.
- **Storming** is the process of establishing common ground and identifying individual roles and responsibilities. Storming establishes direction, purpose, roles, responsibilities, and rewards for both the overall team and each team member.
- **Norming** is the process of establishing team rules and procedures. Norming helps the team find its own uniquely collaborative rhythm. At this stage, individual players begin to work as a synchronized team.
- **Performing** is the process of identifying problems and opportunities, establishing a plan of attack, and then implementing the plan. A well-designed, well-trained team often finds that performing is the easiest part of the team process.
- **Adjourning** involves the up-front definition of key milestones and a specific ending point in terms of outputs and a target completion date. Once a team completes its designated task, it should disband, freeing up resources for continuous improvement elsewhere.

Team Measurement

Many companies recognize the need for team members to bond, and provide team members an opportunity to participate in mountaineering, rope courses, or other socialization activities that require real teamwork not just for success but also for survival. The goal of these activities is to break down the traditional barriers that exist back at the office, helping improve communication, establish trust, and build important relationships. However, team members return to work to measures that promote individual, and/or functional, excellence. The power of measurement overpowers the relationships that began to take shape during the team-building exercise. Team-building activities that are not supported by collaborative measures become fun but expensive get-to-know-you sessions.

Companies like Honeywell that use teams extensively realize that performance measures must be modified to support the team process. Perhaps the biggest challenge is to find the right balance between team-based measures and individual measures. Too much emphasis on team outcomes can lead to social loafing and a loss of individual motivation. Not enough emphasis on team-oriented measures and the team process can be undermined as individuals optimize their own personal performance. General Electric adopted a measure of what it calls "boundarylessness" in order to identify and weed out individuals who are not well suited for teamwork. Such individuals obstruct the free flow of ideas and disrupt team cohesiveness and effectiveness.[15] In today's multicultural world, socialization efforts and performance measurement must be brought together to help build effective teams.

The team dynamic is just that—dynamic. Companies that know how to use teams know that (1) some projects are better suited for teams than others, (2) some people work better on teams than others, and (3) time and resources must be dedicated to the team development process. Trying to use teams without investing in their development often costs much more in wasted motion and lost opportunity than taking the time up front to form, storm, and norm.

ESTABLISHING AN EMPOWERMENT CULTURE

Investing in the systems thinking and collaboration skills of workers provides the greatest returns when the company makes commensurate investments to establish an **empowerment culture**. An empowerment culture makes it possible for managers and teams to learn, to innovate, and to create unprecedented customer value. An empowerment culture precedes the creation of the knowledge worker and the learning organization. Take note: The SC manager described at the beginning of this chapter is "the" knowledge worker.

Why is this important? Because the knowledge worker is a worker who can recognize opportunities, analyze problems, and proactively move to find creative solutions. The knowledge worker is able to work effectively as a member of a task force or cross-functional team as well as being able to share key insight across organization boundaries.[16] The impact of the knowledge worker on the development of new products and outstanding processes is tremendous. In fact, many companies like 3M have invested in the "knowledge" systems to catalog expertise so that it can be shared throughout the entire organization. One of 3M's nontraditional products, fly-fishing line, came into existence when an avid fly fisherman from 3M noted that his fishing line did not have the sinking characteristics that he desired. He knew that, somewhere within 3M, the materials knowledge existed to develop a better fly line. Searching the 3M knowledge database, he was able to find the right person to help solve his fishing problem and create a new product for 3M. Creativity, enthusiasm, and access to the right people with the right expertise is critical to 3M's goal of achieving 25 percent of its sales from products introduced within the last 4 years.

Empowerment at Newmont Gold

Intense competition, evolving technologies, and a constant emphasis on increased profitability placed tremendous pressure on the materials management group at Newmont Gold to perform at ever higher levels. However, the department's culture was reactive and the managers were less than fully committed to innovation and teamwork. Changing the culture to promote creativity, passion, and collaboration promised to be a slow and tedious process. Yet this is exactly what the new materials director needed to do. From the outset, the director's focus was on getting everyone to take personal responsibility for getting the materials group to be best in class. A new mind-set coupled with a renewed commitment to learning and performance was needed to involve every individual and unleash the wealth of creativity and experience found within the materials group. To bridge this cultural chasm, three foundation pillars had to be put in place before the pathway to world-class performance could be built (see Figure 14.3).

Leadership Style

An empowerment culture requires managers who are leaders and coaches. Although this role transformation from boss to coach has been preached from the pulpit of change for over 20 years, most managers do not understand what it really means to be a coach. A critical role of coaching is recruiting. With this in mind the materials director at Newmont adopted the philosophy that his most important job was to "get the right people in the right place and then get out of their way" so that they are free to perform. Of course, this style requires a shared vision, clearly communicated expectations, skill enhancement through targeted training, consistent and fair performance measurement, and aligned incentives. This might be summarized as the "7 rights" of people management:

1. Get the *right* people.
2. Communicate the *right* expectations.
3. Provide the *right* training.
4. Measure the *right* things.
5. Reward the *right* behavior.
6. Support with the *right* resources.
7. Give them the *right* opportunity (i.e., get out of the way).

Figure 14.3 The Pathway to People Empowerment

Leadership   Goal Setting   Communication/Teamwork

Workers and managers who possess a desire and an ability to learn thrive within this environment and contribute both the ideas and the energy needed for constant innovation. However, the personal responsibility required in this setting will lead some individuals to self-select out and seek a less demanding work environment.

Goal Setting

Great coaches rely on aggressive and systematic goal setting. Vital to effective goal setting is the need for perspective. The Newmont materials director emphasized a need to constantly look backward—"backward from the future." The operative question here is, where do we want and need to be in the future to be successful? Looking backward from this vantage point yields two additional questions: Where are we now? and How are we going to "evolve" to get to where we want to go? When everyone is focused on identifying critical success factors and setting goals that will help the organization evolve and develop key capabilities, innovation and change happen without coercion. Change is no longer viewed as a threat, but as an opportunity to excel. One manager noted, "We don't accept mediocrity; we set goals!" Aggressive goal setting drives out complacency, helping to sustain the momentum of an empowered workforce.

Two tools that were used to assure that goal setting and goal attainment permeated the mind-set of the materials group were a best practices program and a performance measurement tracker. The best practices program identified vital activities, set performance goals for each activity, and aggressively benchmarked performance. Some of the areas targeted for best practice included supply base optimization, supplier review and analysis, and alliance implementation. The performance measurement tracker drove goal setting down to the individual level, requiring that workers meet with their immediate supervisors in a mentoring or coaching setting. Together, each worker/supervisor team identified and assessed the competencies that the worker needed to excel. This process helped identify what the worker does well and where opportunities for improvement exist. Annual goals are set with specific timelines for important milestones. Quarterly reviews are held to discuss progress and assure that the resources are available to facilitate goal achievement.

For the personal goal setting to work, the materials director had to make sure that (1) failure was not punished and (2) group leaders genuinely sought to help their workers succeed. First, while failure was not encouraged, managers recognized that when people try new things and establish stretch goals, desired outcomes are not always achieved. The key is to "learn and go on." An oft-repeated question at Newmont was, "Did you learn something?" Second, managers worked closely with those who were struggling to achieve, meeting with them on a weekly basis if necessary. Managers had to adopt the philosophy that "We don't give up on people unless they give up on themselves." Experience showed that most people get on track and establish patterns of achievement and success. On rare occasions, workers decided that expectations were just too high and opted for other employment.

Communication and Teamwork

Enhanced communication and teamwork is the final piece of infrastructure needed to support empowerment. Great coaches know how to communicate expectation, correction, and praise. They use communication to teach and build the team while motivating the individual. While expectations are high at Newmont, they are clearly communicated so that everyone knows where the materials group is headed and what role each individual is expected to play to move the group forward. An exhaustive monthly report, which started as a performance scorecard, helps track progress in key areas while providing an opportunity for more precise communication. Each supervisor within the materials group turns in a monthly report, which is then carefully evaluated by the materials director. He highlights important areas and asks for clarification where needed before returning the report to the supervisors, who are then expected to respond to issues of concern. The monthly report facilitates goal attainment while helping to keep communication clear and constant. As a result, each individual feels and takes greater responsibility for the success of the materials group.

The other side of the communication/teamwork pillar at Newmont is that workers are constantly recognized for their contributions to the group's success. The materials group put in place a system where individuals nominate their peers for their accomplishments and contributions. Monthly gatherings are held as part of the recognition process. Thus, not only are specific achievements recognized but a sense of camaraderie is also built. By design, the program recognizes the contributions of not just individuals within the materials group but also those that come from individuals from other departments as well as from outside suppliers.

Empowerment unleashed tremendous creative power and increased the motivation and commitment of the entire materials department. Empowerment began the drive down the road of constant innovation toward the destination of best in class.

The "ABCs" of an Empowerment Culture

Unleashing the creativity and contribution of an empowered workforce presents one of the most puzzling challenges managers face in today's business world. However, experience and research have provided some summary clues for managers determined to piece the puzzle together.[17] Three distinct puzzle pieces, referred to as the "ABCs," are particularly important to building a culture of impassioned empowerment.

Affirmation

"A" stands for the need to affirm the workforce, providing positive reinforcement and communicating to the workforce that they truly are valued. To assess the level of affirmation in the culture, managers should ask, and meticulously answer, two questions,

- What do we do to make our employees feel incompetent and unappreciated?
- What do we do to make our employees feel competent and valued?

Issues like training, measurement, and pay need to be assessed. But to really get a feel for the way employees see the culture, managers must look at simple daily behaviors. For example, the query, "Didn't you read your e-mail?" is often interpreted as an incriminating statement by the employee who is late for a meeting. Most managers who undertake an evaluation of their own style are surprised to find that they do many things that undermine their attempts to make employees feel valued. Similarly, they are disappointed to find that the list of specific behaviors that communicate competence and value is much shorter than the list that expresses a lack of appreciation. It has been suggested that for every criticism, nine points of reinforcement are needed to create balance. Few managers understand the importance of affirmation; even fewer live the behaviors needed to establish an affirming culture. Great coaches know how to correct mistakes while recognizing successes in a way that their players come to view their criticisms as an attempt to help the player succeed. This is a mark of an affirming culture.

Belonging

"B" represents the innate need that people have to feel that they belong. When people feel that they are just drops of water in the vast organizational ocean, they seldom bring their best ideas or their highest level of effort to work with them. After all, they feel that even their best efforts will be lost in the labyrinth and go unrecognized and unrewarded.

The need to create a sense of belonging is important in most settings; however, it is absolutely essential in some cultures. For example, collectivist cultures such as those found in Latin America and Asia place particular importance on belonging to a team. Individual performance almost always improves when workers feel a sense of responsibility for the success of the team. One major electronics manufacturer set up a maquiladora operation in Mexico and was shocked to suffer 18 percent employee turnover per month. Huge training costs, lost productivity, and poor quality offset the benefits of Mexico's low labor costs and threatened the operation's viability. As managers investigated the cause of the high turnover, they found that workers felt no connection with the company. Workers would therefore leave for other work at the slightest provocation. By adopting a few simple practices, the company dropped the turnover rate to about 3 percent a month. Managers began to hold monthly parties to celebrate workers' birthdays. A volleyball net was set up behind the facility for workers to play games during their lunch breaks. And the company sponsored a soccer team in the city soccer league. The increased sense of community radically altered the workers' attitudes toward the company and their role and responsibility for its success.

Table 14.6 presents typical statements from employees regarding the characteristics of an employee-oriented organization. Most of these statements focus on the value employees place on feeling like they belong; that is, that they are part of the fabric of the organization. This desire to belong has been reiterated year in, year out by *Fortune* magazine's list of the "100 Best Companies to Work For." *Fortune's* list is compiled from feedback obtained directly from employees. Figure 14.4 summarizes

Table 14.6 Employee Statements on the Characteristics of an Employee-Oriented Organization

- *Services for employees—e.g., a gym and health-related programs*
- *Benefits and salaries suggest company cares about employees*
- *Company asks for employees' opinions and input for decisions*
- *Treat each person as an individual*
- Employees understand their position and are knowledgeable
- Company continuously trains and updates skills of employees
- *Employees are happy doing their job*
- *Allowing employees to advance and grow in the organization*
- *Open communications between employees and immediate boss*
- *Meetings are more like town hall discussions*
- *Management is openly willing to receive feedback*
- Trains employees beyond job requirements
- *Company is generous with benefits*
- *Fair level of pay—competitive level*
- *Provides services to employees that are not job related*
- *Work space is clean, user friendly*
- *Employees use updated equipment*
- *Well run human resource department—easy access to services*

Bolded, italicized statements all relate a company's efforts to invest in a sense of belonging.

Figure 14.4 Factors That Make a Company a Great Place to Work

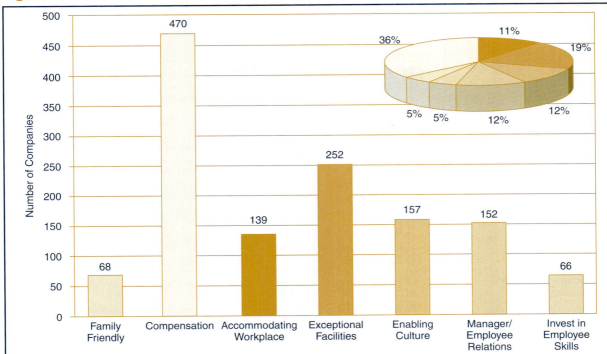

Factors That Contribute to Employees Perceptions

Characteristic	Employee Perceptions of Characteristic
Compensation	Employees view compensation as the hallmark of a great company to work for. It is not that workers aspire to riches, but they do want to be treated fairly, and they regard a company's financial package as the acid test of fairness. They simply want their companies to "put their money where their mouth is"! Great companies have learned to combine salary, bonuses, stock options, insurance programs, and the company retirement plan into a comprehensive package that communicates a concern for their employees' well-being. They have learned that the company's success must be shared with all of the people who contribute to that success.
Family Friendly	Employees feel a need to make work fit within a more holistic lifestyle. The goal is to balance work with personal and family needs. As companies respond to this expectation, they are offering an assortment of services and benefits including family counseling, savings bonds for children, college tuition grants, parental leaves, time off to attend parent–teacher conferences, and lactation rooms for new mothers. Despite an expressed desire among employees for a more family-oriented work environment, most companies struggle to balance the demands of a fiercely competitive global economy with the needs of their workforce.
Facilities	Employees welcome a well-designed workplace that is located in a safe and aesthetically pleasing setting. They like the convenience of on-site child care, on-site medical care, or on-site concierge services. Some companies even offer massages, dry cleaning, travel services, and pet care. Another feature employees find very attractive is access to exercise programs and fitness facilities. Companies like Detroit Diesel and Lands' End have built beautiful and complete athletic facilities at their corporate headquarters. Access to these facilities year round is a perk that keeps many part-time seasonal workers coming back year after year to help Lands' End fulfill customer orders during the Christmas rush.

Figure 14.4 Continued

Accommodating Workplace	Employees view flexibility as an important perk. Today's workers enjoy the convenience that comes with the opportunity to schedule their own hours. Shorter workweeks, telecommuting, and flextime programs all allow workers to balance work and family obligations. Paid vacations and opportunities to take time off without pay also provide for personal renewal. The sabbatical, which allows a worker to take 6 months to a year off to develop new skills and broaden personal horizons, has become popular in recent years. Great companies recognize the need to avoid burnout and provide workers opportunities for revitalization.
Enabling Culture	Employees express a desire to work for an ethical company. Many feel it is important to work for a company that promotes diversity, is environmentally sensitive, and is involved in the community. Paid time for charity or volunteer work is particularly attractive. People like to work where they can be themselves, possess high levels of autonomy, and make a contribution that goes beyond building a better product or delivering higher levels of service. Great companies create a culture that makes it possible for their people to make a difference in colleagues' and customers' lives while improving the community in which they live.
Manager/Employee Relations	Personable managers who take the time to know their employees and acknowledge their accomplishments and concerns are a key source of corporate enthusiasm. Former GE chief Jack Welch's practice of writing personal notes to colleagues generated great respect and admiration throughout the organization. Such behaviors promote open communication and facilitate a sense of collegiality. Further, employees are eager to know that their ideas are valued and they seek to be empowered. They want to be trusted. Employee councils, established to tap ideas and resolve problems, are popular. Employees also want to be involved in the interviewing, hiring, and other activities that impact their working environment.
Invest in Employee Skills	More than ever, employees recognize the need to stay current with the latest developments in their fields of expertise. Obsolescence comes rapidly in the global economy. Employees see company-sponsored education programs as extremely beneficial. In addition to specific skills-based training and tuition reimbursement programs, popular education initiatives focus on ethics, personal improvement, and life skills. Unfortunately, high training costs have led many companies to make a conscious decision to place the onus for lifelong education on the shoulders of their employees.

the characteristics of these outstanding companies. As you look over these characteristics, consider how each creates a sense of belonging. Ultimately, the question for every manager is, "Does my company look and act like a great place to work?"

Competence

"C" emphasizes the need to invest in employee capabilities throughout the organization. Investing in the human resource is one of the great challenges managers face today. So many other needs exist that it can be difficult to stretch the budget far enough to cover all of the investment needs. Competitors are often bringing new products to market on shorter cycles and it seems as if everyone is investing in new technologies. Not wanting to be left behind, managers dedicate scarce capital to these areas, leaving the training budget of many companies tight if not inadequate. Of course, the fact that employee loyalty is at all-time lows makes it difficult to justify investing in people who may be working for the competition tomorrow. Despite these realities, a failure to invest in the knowledge and skills of the workforce can stifle the company's long-term capabilities and competitiveness. Equally important, a failure to invest in worker competence manifests an attitude that workers really are not valued. Managers should consider the following questions to assess whether or not a culture of empowerment through competence enhancement is being built.

- What is expected from our employees? Are they meeting these expectations fully?
- How do we train our employees? Are there incentives to pursue personal skill development?
- How much do we invest in our employees' skills compared to other investments?
- What specific new job-related skills have you helped employees build?
- What specific non-job-related life skills have you helped employees build?

If employees are not performing at or above industry standard, no formal training program is actively promoted, investments in people are low in comparison with other investments and below best-in-class standards, and managers cannot identify specific skills they have helped employees develop, it is time to rethink the company's competency-building strategy. Affirmation and belonging are important, but without competence, an empowerment culture will not emerge.

Managers that know and manage the "ABCs" can expect to develop a passionate and creative workforce that embraces both change and collaboration. As a result, they will see higher levels of productivity, quality, innovation, customer service, and employee morale.

INTEGRATING PEOPLE AND TECHNOLOGY SYSTEMS

Perhaps the two greatest potential strengths of any company are its human and technological resources. Few companies do a good job of developing these two resources. Even fewer effectively integrate them to achieve a competitive advantage. The propensity of many organizations is to buy the latest and most popular technology available and then hope that it can be implemented successfully. Recent efforts to implement enterprise resource planning (ERP) systems illustrate the challenge that accompanies this strategy—many organizations have taken twice as long and spent twice as much as initially budgeted. The ERP challenge was foreshadowed by similar difficulties in implementing electronic data interchange (EDI), robotics, flexible manufacturing systems, and other technological advances.

Although many organizations embrace technology, efforts to develop human resources are often meager by comparison and poorly structured. Few training budgets equal those designated for technology despite estimates that systematic and structured investments in training can provide up to twice the return as investments in technology.[18] Further, the answer to the question, "what makes factories flexible?" has been found to be a cross-trained workforce, not technological investment.[19] Jack Welch, the iconic former CEO at General Electric, consistently noted that one of the most vital jobs of senior management is to develop the people within the organization.

Transforming technological and human resources into a formidable competitive weapon requires a change in attitude regarding their development and use followed by their strategic integration. The following points must be kept in mind as managers invest in and develop these vital resources.

- The organization's needs must be matched with the technology's capabilities. As a general rule, the simplest technology that will meet product and process needs should be given priority. Such technologies generally cost less and are easier to implement.
- The organization's technology strategy should support the firm's long-term approach to building world-class value-added processes. This rule requires early thinking about how technology and human systems will interact to create value.
- The following technology pitfalls should be avoided: the "follow-the-leader" mentality, the "shiny-hardware" syndrome, and the "island of automation." Every technology investment should be carefully justified and closely tied to a real capability that is needed and that can realistically be achieved.
- The firm must view its workforce as a critical resource and commit the necessary capital to training programs. A critical point here is that once management starts investing in workers, it must also give the workers the responsibility and opportunity to use their increasing skills.
- Managers must develop a greater familiarity with the organization's value-added processes and key technologies. Appreciating and understanding the abilities of line workers and managers in other disciplines is needed to coordinate and integrate competitive efforts.
- Adequate organizational support must be in place to implement and support new technologies. Appropriate performance measures that do not penalize workers and that promote "revolutionary" process enhancement should be adopted.

The final step in leveraging human and technological resources is to integrate them. If adequate workforce training is coupled with the adoption of the appropriate process technologies, all that remains is for the company to make the integration of the two a priority.

CONCLUSION

In his book *Clockspeed*, Charles Fine argued that the notion of sustainable advantage had become outdated, a victim of compressed technology cycles and a dynamic world. Yet some companies like Southwest Airlines and Wal-Mart demonstrate a remarkable ability to achieve profitable growth year after year. What is it that has sustained these companies' success? Arguably, their perennial success derives from their ability to harness the learning and passion of the workforce. They train their workers, empower them to serve customers, and expect them to come up with ideas to improve both day-to-day operations and the organization's business model. They have become learning organizations. For example, when a Wal-Mart associate in Arizona notices that Hispanic customers are looking for a kind of cookware known as a caldero, she mentions this and calderos are soon on the shelf.[20] More formal experimentation is also encouraged and has led Wal-Mart to become the world's largest grocer less than a decade after entering the market. Wal-Mart is experimenting with vacations, flower delivery, used-car sales, and online DVD rentals. Wal-Mart listens to and learns from customer complaints. One customer tells the following story about Wal-Mart:

> I telephoned the Bentonville, Arkansas, headquarters of Wal-Mart to complain about its store in La Plata, Argentina. The switchboard immediately rang the vice president of international operations, who picked up his own phone. He thanked me for calling, asked detailed questions about my dissatisfaction, and inquired whether I was willing to repeat my story for his Latin American VP. He transferred me straight away, and an even more detailed conversation followed. Then I was asked if I would be willing to talk with the Argentinian store manager if he called me. Ten minutes later my phone in Connecticut rang.
>
> On my next trip to Argentina, a year later, the store had been transformed. No wonder Wal-Mart is the world's largest retailer.[21]

The question is, "Can Wal-Mart and other learning companies perpetuate the cultures that made them great despite their own success and their increased size?" After all, most successful companies sooner or later succumb to complacency, and large companies fall victim to bureaucratic inertia. Perhaps this is why it has been said, "Those whom the Gods wish to destroy they bless with 40 years of success." Recognizing that workers are a company's most valuable asset, investing in their collaboration skills, and establishing a culture of empowerment may be the best way to avoid a destiny of demise—it is the only way to create a team of true SC managers.

Summary of Key Points

1. True SC managers are not defined by functional position or job description. They are defined by mindset and skill set. Great SC managers possess strong functional skills, see the big picture, analyze trade-offs rigorously, build collaborative relationships, execute with discipline, embrace change, and exemplify leadership.

2. Successful companies like JetBlue and P&G recognize that people are a company's most important asset—the only asset capable of creating and collaborating. They design key HR processes such as hiring, training, and promoting around the need to identify, build, and keep collaborative people.

3. Training must reach everyone and continue all through life; otherwise, the obsolescence curve will overtake a company's workforce. This reality is particularly true in SCM where the competitive rules are constantly changing and the necessary skill sets are relentlessly changing.

4. Cross-functional workers are critical to the implementation of collaborative SC strategies. The keys to building a cross-functional workforce are (1) view workers as an integral part of the value-added system, (2) invest time and money in worker training, (3) delegate to workers diverse responsibilities and real authority, and (4) change the nature of the manager/worker relationship to give workers the opportunities to use their cross-functional experience and skills.

5. Cross-experienced managers are just as important as cross-functional workers, but perhaps harder to find. The cost of rotation programs combined with the lack of loyalty in the workplace make it very difficult to justify the efforts needed to help managers become holistic, systems thinkers.

6. Cross-functional teams are the lifeblood of many SC initiatives. Training can lead to better team design and management. It is also needed to help individuals feel more comfortable as a team member and contribute to a team's success.

7. Creating an empowerment culture requires managers who are leaders and coaches. Managers who coach their employees understand the "seven rights" of people management: right people, right expectations,

right training, right measurement, right rewards, right resources, and right opportunity.

8. The "ABCs" of an empowerment culture are affirmation, belonging, and competence.

9. For people to truly be a bridge to effective SCM, management must make a conscious decision to simultaneously develop and integrate the organization's human and technology systems.

REVIEW EXERCISES

1. Explain why people are a company's most important resource. Discuss why many managers talk about the importance of their people and then fail to invest in them.
2. Think back to the best work experiences of your life. What made these experiences so good? Likewise, what factors contributed to negative work experiences?
3. Describe your impressions of Deere's training philosophy and course offerings. Explain why more companies do not provide this type of training.
4. Explain the reasons cross-training is an investment and not just a cost.
5. Discuss the benefits of a cross-experienced management team.
6. Based on your own experience, describe the challenges and benefits of working on a team. Discuss the challenges of designing and managing a successful team.
7. Describe the aspects of Newmont Gold's empowerment program that you like. What would you change to make it even better?
8. Identify an example of each of the "ABCs" of an empowerment culture as they are practiced at your workplace. Do you use the "ABCs" in your relationships?
9. Describe the characteristics of a great place to work. Identify the pros and cons of establishing each characteristic.
10. Explain why Toyota does such a good job of making their workers an integral part of the value-creation process while others do not.

Case   *Collaboration's Missing Link*

Doris Mauer, Migdi's normally energetic and enthusiastic VP of SCM, was ticked and tired. She sat exhausted in her window seat on Flight 217 from Cincinnati to Zurich. Just a few hours earlier, she had received an unexpected text message. It was bad news! The collaborative planning project with Nestle was underperforming and Nestle had decided to opt out after the pilot concluded. Doris knew the project wasn't going well, but she had hoped that Migdi could smooth ruffled feathers and use the experience as a stepping-stone. Now, it looked more like a stumbling block. Migdi's executive council wasn't very patient with programs and projects that didn't provide instant, tangible returns. Doris wondered what the fallout would be.

As competitive pressure from Aldi and Tesco ratcheted up, Doris knew that Migdi had to get its act together. Collaboration with key consumer product companies was the only way Migdi could hope to hold off the hard-charging competition. Migdi needed to get its SC costs down to offer prices closer to those that made the discounters so popular. And Migdi really needed to leverage its assortment, displays, and special offerings to create a unique shopping experience for its customers. To do either, Migdi needed more than passive support or mere cooperation from its SC partners. Migdi needed their passionate collaboration.

Doris hated to admit it, but Migdi was really struggling with collaboration—at every level. Migdi had always had good people, if a bit insular. But Migdi's success had led to a little complacency. Success had also kept feelings of jealousy hidden behind all-knowing smiles. Turf protection had always been an issue. After all, Migdi was a marketing company at its core. Everyone knew that. Marketers made the decisions, and marketers received the recognition. People in other functional areas did their best to support Migdi's marketing mission. That was before the onslaught of fierce competition. Now, with the discounters changing the rules of the competitive game, resentment was bubbling to the surface.

Doris was confident many of her colleagues hadn't even noticed the tension. Some acted as if they hadn't noticed Aldi either. If she weren't battling to stem the competitive tide and trying to drive collaborative initiatives, she might not have seen the threats either. But she saw the symptoms every day: foot dragging, information hoarding, competition for recognition, and other subtle clues that Migdi's culture was dysfunctional. As a result, Migdi had lost touch with the marketplace. If it hadn't, Migdi might have responded to the discounters before they grew into a major threat. Migdi also lacked the discipline to execute and take costs out of its processes while keeping product on its shelves. Worse, the culture had kept Migdi from developing a core of managers who knew how to leverage capabilities and build collaborative relationships internally and with SC partners.

Doris's greatest fear was that the culture at Migdi had settled into an uncomfortable "comfort zone" that would make embracing the changes needed to win customers' hearts almost impossible. That's why she was in Cincinnati in the first place. She was attending a P&G-sponsored retail development workshop. One of the topics on the agenda—"Embracing Change"—had caught her attention. As she checked into it, she became more intrigued. The focus would be on assessing a company's culture to determine whether it was capable of generating the passion needed to respond to competitive threats and innovate its way to success.

Gary Rhoads, the workshop leader, had taken an interesting approach. Before he said anything else, he asked, "Does your company have a culture of despair or delight? Do you know the difference?" His point: If you live at a company with a despair culture, the odds of your being able to collaborate or innovate are zilch! Gary didn't mince words, and he shared both anecdotes and hard numbers from years of research to back up his story. Winning companies don't just focus on delighting customers; they build a culture of delight internally as well. It was that culture that captured the hearts and minds of employees, enabling them to bring passion to work every day. It made it safe for them to take risks, unleashing their creativity. Delight precipitated collaboration.

Doris looked down at her notes. She had a big red checkmark next to another question Gary had asked: "How would your employees describe their working environment?" At that point, Gary had asked everyone to fill out a short 11-question diagnostic (see Table 14.7). The questions were simple and all each manager had to do was put a checkmark in one of two boxes. For example, one question asked, "How would our employees describe their working environment?" If employees feel they are stuck in "dead-end" jobs, a checkmark went in the left-hand column. If they view the workplace as family friendly, the

checkmark went in the right-column. After evaluating each of the 11 statements, a total score was calculated. Gary had said that a score under 6 signaled a need for immediate intervention. Likewise, a score of 9 or greater indicated the company was well on its way to establishing a culture that promotes creativity and collaboration. Doris was shocked; by her own estimation, Migdi fell below the "immediate intervention line." She wondered how Midgi's employees would respond to the 11 questions if given the chance. She wasn't sure she wanted to find out.

Her notes continued: "It's vital to remember that no easy-to-follow formula exists to transform a company's people into a bridge to SC success. Creativity and passion emerge from philosophy and culture. The first is easy to articulate; the second is difficult to cultivate." She could relate—it was easy to talk about collaboration but very hard to really make it happen. Her notes included a series of bullet points as a final checklist for her to consider as she evaluated whether or not Migdi treated its workforce as a strategic, value-added resource.

- Do we view workers as a vital competitive asset?
- Do we invest in workers through training?
- Have we expanded workers' roles so they can actively contribute?
- Have we shifted authority to workers whenever possible?
- Have we devised and implemented appropriate performance measures?
- Do we compensate and recognize employees in a way that tells them they are valued?
- Do we consistently strive to build mutual respect between workers and managers?

She couldn't help but feel that Migdi was in real trouble. Doris wondered if the simple exercise included with the 11-question diagnostic would really work. Could it be that simple? She knew better, but it might be the first steps she and Migdi needed to take. Now that the angst had dissipated, she saw a glimmer of hope. Doris decided it was time for a good night's sleep. Work was waiting back in Switzerland.

CASE QUESTIONS

1. How does a company's culture influence its collaborative capabilities? Why is this so important?
2. What makes a culture of despair so debilitating? What makes a culture of delight so empowering?
3. How should Doris proceed over the long haul to help Migdi develop managers capable of winning in a collaborative SC world? Develop a road map that identifies key steps and needed resources.

Table 14.7 Does Your Organizational Culture Support Creativity and Collaboration?

PREDICTORS OF DESPAIR	SCORE 0	SCORE 1	PREDICTORS OF DELIGHT
• Dead-end job	☐	☐	• Opportunities to learn
• Little control over tasks and job	☐	☐	• Possess autonomy
• Top management is unfair	☐	☐	• Managers seek suggestions
• Ethics—going against my judgment	☐	☐	• Values-based environment
• Must deal with rejection	☐	☐	• Positive impact on others' lives
• Must deal with uncertainty	☐	☐	• Understand role and receive feedback
• Narrow job tasks and responsibilities	☐	☐	• Complete whole jobs
• Compensation among industry's worst	☐	☐	• Compensation shows I'm valued
• Rigid and demanding workplace	☐	☐	• Flexible and accommodating workplace
• Workplace displaces family	☐	☐	• Workplace family friendly
• Physical facilities are poorly maintained	☐	☐	• Exceptional facilities—work and play

Total Score: _____

Scores under 6 indicate a need for immediate intervention.

Scores over 9 suggest a culture that promotes creativity, learning, and collaboration.

**The first steps to cultural overhaul**:

If action is needed to bring creativity and collaboration into the workplace, try the following exercise.

- Break your team into groups of 3 to 6 people.
- Have _each_ group member brainstorm 5 to 10 ideas to create a great place to work.
- Bring the group back together to discuss the individually generated ideas.
- As a group, select the 3 to 5 ideas that can be most impactfully implemented.
  - Make these best practice ideas the target for pet projects.
  - Establish priorities for the remaining ideas.
- Bring all of the groups together and share both sets of ideas. Refine and establish priorities.
- Allocate resources.
- Document implementation and results.

ENDNOTES

1. Fawcett, S. E., & Magnan, G. N. (2001). _Achieving world-class supply chain alignment: Benefits, barriers, and bridges._ Phoenix, AZ: National Association of Purchasing Management.
2. Davis, E. W., & Spekman, R. E. (2004). _The extended enterprise: Gaining competitive advantage through collaborative supply chains._ Upper Saddle River, NJ: Prentice Hall.
3. Collins, J. (2002). _Good to great._ New York: HarperCollins.
4. Fawcett, S. E., Magan, G., Ogden, J., Cooper, B. In press.
5. Adams, S. (1997). _The Dilbert Principle._ New York: Harper Business.
6. Hymowitz, C. (2006, February 13). Rewarding competitors over collaborators no longer makes sense. _The Wall Street Journal,_ p. B1.
7. Sugimori, Y., Kuunokim, K., Cho, F., & Uchikawa, S. (1977). Toyota production system and kanban system materialization of just-in-time and respect-for-human system. _International Journal of Production Research, 15_(6), 533–564. Schonberger, R. J. (1982). _Japanese manufacturing techniques: Nine hidden lessons in simplicity._ New York: The Free Press. Schonberger, R. J. (1986). _World class manufacturing._ New York: The Free Press.
8. Abernathy, W. J., Clark, K. B., & Kantrow, A. M. (1983). _Industrial renaissance._ New York: Basic Books, Inc.

9. Wheelwright, S. C. (1985, Spring). Restoring the competitive edge in U.S. manufacturing. *California Management Review*, 27–42.

10. Hayes, R., & Wheelwright, S. (1984). *Restoring our competitive edge: Competing through manufacturing.* New York: John Wiley & Sons, Inc.

11. Stewart, T. (1996, August 19). It's a flat world after all. *Fortune*, 197–199.

12. Kolbe, K. (1989). *Conative connection—acting on instincts.* Reading, MA: Addison Wesley Publishing. Kolbe, K. (1993). *Pure instinct: business' untapped resource.* New York: Random House.

13. Tuckman, B. (1965). Developmental sequences in small groups. *Psychological Bulletin*, 63, 384–399.

14. Tuckman, B., & Jensen, M. (1977). Stages of small group development revisited. *Group and Organizational Studies, 2*, 419–427. Lawson, J., & Bourner, T. (1997). Developing communication within new workgroups. *Journal of Applied Management Studies*, 6(2), 149–167.

15. Sherman, S., & Hadjian, A. (1995, November 17). How tomorrow's leaders are learning their stuff. *Fortune*, 90–100. Hymowitz, C., & Murray, M. (1999, June 21). Raises and praise or out the door. *The Wall Street Journal*, pp. B1, B4.

16. Fawcett, S., Rhoads, G., & Burnah, P. (2004). People as the bridge to competitiveness: Benchmarking the "ABCs" of an empowered workforce. *Benchmarking: An International Journal, 11*(4), 346–360.

17. Ibid.

18. Jacob, R., Rao, R. M., & Musi, V. J. (1995, April 3). The struggle to create an organization. *Fortune*, pp. 90–97.

19. Upton, D. M. (1995). What really makes factories flexible. *Harvard Business Review, 73*(4), 74–84.

20. Useem, J. (2003, March 3). One nation under Wal-mart. *Fortune*, 64–80.

21. Chichester, G. (2003, March 17). No. 1 Wal-mart: letter to editor, *Fortune*, 30.

Chapter 15

Collaborative Innovation

Is the curse of complacency a threat? Can I use collaborative innovation to build a sustainable advantage?

The Supply Chain Road Map

Integrating the Supply Chain
- Create & Communicate Common SC Vision
- Build a Cohesive Team of Allied Companies

How Do We Get There?

Chapter 11: Relationship Alignment
- Define intensity of SC relationships.
- Build trust to promote collaboration.

Chapter 12: Information Sharing
- Establish technology to support SC.
- Cultivate culture that promotes sharing.

Chapter 13: Performance Measurement
- Align measures across SC.
- Create understanding & motivate behavior.

Chapter 14: People Empowerment
- Cultivate empowerment environment.
- Build teams to enhance collaboration.

Chapter 15: Collaborative Improvement
- Establish a culture of innovation to avoid complacency.
- Organize for long-term collaboration.

1. Explain why innovation is needed. Discuss the perils of complacency and the characteristics of learning.
2. Describe two generic continuous innovation strategies, give an example of each strategy, and discuss their advantages and disadvantages.
3. Identify the characteristics of an effective continuous improvement program. Describe the features of a culture of innovation.
4. Define collaborative, SC innovation. Identify and discuss the role, pros, and cons of diverse collaborative innovation initiatives. Explain when and why a company would employ each initiative.
5. Discuss the importance of establishing the infrastructure to support long-term collaborative innovation. Explain the role of both executive governance and SC advisory councils.

Opening Story: Avoiding Complacency at Olympus

6:15 A.M.

"Whew, Doug, that was a killer run! Where'd you get all the energy? You really pushed the pace today—I clocked us at just over 6-minute miles."

"Well, Charlene, today is celebration day. I wanted to set the right tone. Besides, I'm excited for our task force. After 2 years of hard work, the team gets to show off a little this afternoon. I'm confident that we'll have some great results to report in the management review with Joe Andrus and the executive council. It feels good to be crossing the SCM finish line!"

"You're right, Doug," Charlene sighed, out of breath. "It has been a long haul and you deserve to celebrate, but you're not done yet."

Puzzled, Doug queried, "What do you mean, we're not done?"

"You'll see," Charlene whispered sheepishly. "We can talk more tonight at the restaurant. You can let me know what happened and I can share a little news with you. Right now, I've got to shower and get to work."

10:00 A.M. TASK FORCE MEETING

"Good morning. Today's the big day. Let's take a few minutes to go over the final numbers you'll be reporting this afternoon. Susan, we'll start with you and work our way around the table."

"Thanks, Doug. Our total spend is down 3 percent despite Olympus's sales growth. Over 90 percent of our purchases are with certified suppliers and we've almost eliminated charge backs for OS&D shipments. Defective materials have been reduced by 50 percent over the past year. And we have reduced the supply base by almost 30 percent. We feel pretty good about what's happening."

"Thanks, Susan. Vijay, what's going on in operations?"

"Good morning, everybody. Susan really has done a great job with our suppliers, as has Diane with our top customers. The timely delivery of higher-quality materials combined with better demand forecasting has improved our production scheduling, helping us reduce downtime by 40 percent. Better management of our product reformulations has reduced our maintenance costs by 12 percent. We've practically eliminated overtime. Our defect rate has been cut in half and we are making schedule 97 percent of the time. We estimate that these improvements have saved over $4 million this past year."

"That's great, Vijay. Diane, tell us about marketing."

"What more can I say than to report that Goliath just named us 'Supplier of the Year.'"

"That's fantastic," David interjected. "Just 2 years ago we were in Goliath's doghouse."

"That's right, David," Diane continued. "Better information sharing and more responsive logistics have really improved our service levels. We haven't missed a delivery window at any of our top 10 customers for the past 3 quarters. As a result, sales are up 15 percent and we forecast even better growth next year. We've been invited to work on a couple of exciting new initiatives with key customers. Life is good!"

"Well done, Diane. David, what's the skinny in logistics?"

"As Diane already noted, our on-time delivery is up. More importantly, we have developed a tailored logistics capability that helps us better meet the service requirements of our most important customers. Logistical efficiency has also improved. Specifically, we have shuttered two DCs and reduced the number of carriers we use by 20 percent. We now ship 10 percent of our product on customers' trucks. While our fill rate is up, our days of inventory have dropped from 35.4 to 20.9 and our turns have increased from 10.4 to 19.9. As a percent of sales, logistics costs have fallen by almost 2 percent."

"Not bad, David, not bad at all. So Joel, how do the operating improvements translate to the bottom line?"

"From a financial perspective, SCM is providing a solid return. Olympus's profit margin is 13.5 percent, up from 8 percent a year ago. And our ROA has climbed to 27 percent, up from 16 percent. And as you all know, our stock price is up 18 percent this year. We are clearly headed in the right direction."

"Great, Joel—even Tim Rock should like those numbers. I think we have a compelling story to tell. I look forward to sitting back and watching you make our presentation this afternoon—you've done a great job. Let's break early for lunch. I'll see you all in the conference room at 2:45 P.M."

4:47 P.M. IN THE CONFERENCE ROOM AFTER THE MANAGEMENT REVIEW

"Doug, that was quite a presentation your team made. I think even Tim was impressed," Joe Andrus smiled as he congratulated Doug. "SCM has delivered some outstanding results. Olympus's future looks bright, but for how long? You know how quickly things can go south. Just look at

Carrefour. They're our largest customer outside the United States. Five years ago, they looked invincible. Today, the rumor mill says Carrefour is vulnerable to a hostile takeover."

"Joe," Doug interrupted, "I'm not sure I want to hear what you're going to say next. The last 2 years have been a rough ride."

"I'm sure they have. Nevertheless, we both realize that Olympus's recent competitive woes resulted from complacency. We didn't adapt; we weren't meeting customers' needs. We can't let that happen again. Your team has helped set a new course for the company. Now, we'd like you to take on a new role at Olympus—chief supply chain officer. As a member of the executive council, we want you to make SC processes and thinking part of Olympus's culture. We need to be lean and *innovative*! Anyway, congratulations, we'll talk again early next week. For now, take your team out to dinner and celebrate. Tomorrow, start thinking about where you want to take SCM next. We trust you, Doug, and want to see what you can do for an encore!"

Consider As You Read:

1. Explain how the results achieved by the SC task force could actually lead to complacency.
2. If you were Doug, where would you focus your efforts to (a) keep complacency at bay, (b) drive constant innovation, and (c) make SC thinking part of Olympus's culture?
3. What cultural and structural barriers is Doug likely to encounter as he continues the SC journey?

> *Sooner or later, something fundamental in your business world will change.*
>
> —ANDREW GROVE, INTEL[1]

> *I absolutely, all the time, remember that complacency is the enemy of innovation.*
>
> —HOWARD STRINGER, SONY[2]

THE DYNAMICS OF SUCCESS

The one constant in today's business climate is change. For years, the sages of management foresaw this day. Joseph Schumpeter, the Austrian economist, coined the term "creative destruction" in 1942 to describe the endless cycle of entrepreneurial innovation that makes existing companies obsolete.[3] Peter Drucker defined the "age of discontinuity"—a time when emerging technology and a world economy would disrupt the status quo, creating a dynamic, tumultuous marketplace.[4] Andrew Grove proclaimed that, "only the paranoid survive" in a market where the rules of competition can be rewritten seemingly overnight.[5]

Today, as never before, the forces of entrepreneurial spirit, economic globalization, and technological innovation converge to drive unyielding and unpredictable change. To survive, companies must innovate at the pace and scale of the marketplace. To do so, they must constantly scan the environment, looking for trends and identifying disruptive technologies before these technologies change the competitive rules. They must monitor not just core markets but also the periphery because new competitors can come from almost anywhere. They must benchmark customers' needs, competitors' capabilities, and best-in-class processes. Simply stated, today's companies must learn to adapt, to create new markets, and to develop new customers. To keep their new customers, they must establish cultures of continuous improvement.

The Perils of Complacency

Unfortunately, few companies possess the DNA to pursue relentless innovation and constant improvement. Recent history suggests that sustaining outstanding performance beyond 15 to 20 years is rare even for the best companies.[6] Companies appear to go through a life cycle of innovation, growth, maturity, and decline (see Figure 15.1). The question is, "How long will each stage last?" Success, it seems, breeds bureaucracy and complacency. As they grow, companies become more complex. They are weighed down by policies and procedures that discourage innovation. Managers hold to the mental models that led the company to its original success. Cultural and structural inertia prevent managers from adapting to the evolving rules of a changing competitive game.

Worse, successful companies are tempted to use their scale and resources to postpone real change. For example, in the early 2000s, facing fierce competition from

Figure 15.1   The Company Life Cycle

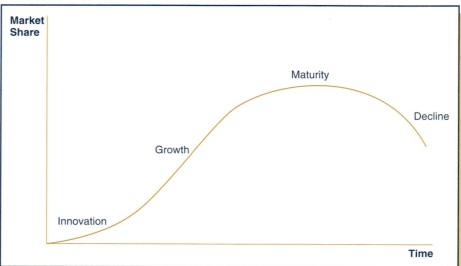

Toyota and Honda, General Motors resorted to massive discounting to sell cars. Although discounting slowed GM's market share slide, it did very little to solve GM's real problem—the need to design and build vehicles customers wanted to buy. Such tactics as discounting are unsustainable. They destroy profitability, reducing the company's long-term ability to invest in innovation. Moreover, they can preserve just enough momentum to keep the company from facing the brutal facts and making needed changes. Complacency leads to decline.

Unable to reinvent themselves on a continuing basis, corporate titans like A&P, GM, IBM, PanAm, and Sony all became vulnerable to more entrepreneurial companies. Once household names, A&P and PanAm have disappeared from the market. A&P's demise is illustrative of the perils of complacency. Founded in 1859, A&P was its era's Wal-Mart. By 1929, A&P operated 15,000 stores—more than any retailer before or since—and emphasized a familiar slogan, "Everyday low price." When threatened by a new retail format known as the supermarket, A&P closed 9,500 old-fashioned groceries, adopted a new distribution model, and opened a flood of supermarkets. The result: By 1950 A&P was second in sales only to General Motors. A&P owed its success to an undeviating focus on a core idea—to sell as much merchandise as possible at the lowest possible prices. A&P's dominance ended with the death of owner John Hartford. New leaders forgot the core idea, defined A&P as a set of existing stores, and allowed complacency to take over. Relative newcomers led by Kroger soon displaced A&P. A German conglomerate now owns the remnants of A&P.[7]

Once a company becomes complacent and vulnerable to competitive threats, it is difficult to turn things around. Of the companies mentioned earlier, only IBM has successfully reinvented itself to emerge from a competitive malaise. Once the world's leader in computing technology, IBM found itself unable to compete against the Compaqs, Dells, and H-Ps of the world. The solution was to reposition itself in the market as a technology service provider. IBM's transformation from a hardware company to a services provider was completed in 2005 with the sale of its storied PC business to Lenovo, a Chinese conglomerate. Companies like GM and Sony have struggled for years to rekindle the competitive fire and regain their market dominance. They have found that changing a company's DNA is a daunting task!

The Learning Organization

The best bet to avoid complacency and decline is to create a culture of organizational learning. Market leaders like Dell, Toyota, and Wal-Mart have leveraged learning into sustained sales growth and industry-leading profitability. Each has also been driven by a core ideal that has motivated the search for excellence. For example, Sam Walton believed passionately that Wal-Mart's mission is to "Lower the cost of living for the people of the world." Managers at Wal-Mart have never lost sight of this goal as they have worked to create customer value. Wal-Mart's ability to develop new customers by entering new market segments and geographic regions throughout the 1990s and early 2000s led to year-to-year sales growth of almost 15 percent. If it can continue to learn and thus find or develop new markets at the same pace, Wal-Mart will hit a mind-boggling half-trillion dollars in sales by 2010.

By the same year (2010), Toyota has set the goal to become the world's largest automaker. The quest is fueled by a relentless pursuit of excellence focused on making customers' lives better. Jim Press, Toyota's North American marketing leader, explains, "The Toyota culture is inside all of us. Toyota is a customer's company. Mrs. Jones is our customer; she is my boss. Everything is done to make Mrs. Jones's life better. We all work for Mrs. Jones."[8] Underlying Toyota's success is the Toyota Production System (TPS), often called JIT or lean production. The TPS creates an unmatched value combination of flexibility, quality, and cost. Nonetheless, constant efforts are made to improve it. The Toyota culture requires that Toyota people always step out of the "comfort zone." As each target is achieved, a new, more demanding goal is set.

At Dell, the company culture is permeated with the belief that the status quo (no matter how good) is never good enough. Michael Dell's focus is always on what could be done better—and at a lower cost. His mantra is "Celebrate for a nanosecond, then move on." Dell folklore includes a story about the opening of Dell's first factory in Malaysia. To acknowledge the event, Michael Dell sent the manager in charge one of his old running shoes. The message was clear: Job well done, but remember this is just the first step in a marathon. This unyielding focus on improvement has helped Dell earn more than 550 business-process patents. One patent covers a way to configure manufacturing stations that improves productivity fourfold over a standard assembly line. As Massachusetts Institute of Technology's Erik Brynjolfsson has noted, "They're inventing business processes. It's an asset that Dell has that its competitors don't."[9]

The lesson to be learned from these three leaders is simple: Continued success requires constant learning. Companies that cultivate a culture capable of embracing constant change and mastering continuous improvement can avoid the perils of complacency and achieve strong, sustained performance. Whether a company slides into complacency or becomes a learning organization begins with its attitude toward innovation.

INNOVATION STRATEGIES

While many companies fall into the complacency trap, others recognize that to compete they must innovate. The question is, how? Over the years, companies have pursued two paths to innovation. Figure 15.2 shows these paths.

Transformational Innovation

The first path emphasizes **transformational innovation** and relies on strategic breakthroughs in process or product technology. Amazon.com's on-line bookstore represents transformational process technology. Intel's ever-faster microprocessors exemplify transformational product technology. Transformational innovation is attractive because it changes the competitive rules, giving the transformation leader a dramatic competitive advantage.

On the downside, companies that pursue transformational innovation often become dependent on potential strategic breakthroughs. What happens if such breakthroughs do not occur? Or, what happens if a competitor achieves a breakthrough that cannot be easily copied? Relying exclusively on transformational innovation is a high-risk, high-potential-gain innovation strategy. The following example illustrates how transformational innovation can change an entire industry, bringing new players to the forefront of the competitive stage while relegating traditional powers to the background.

By the late 1990s, Apple Computer looked like a company on the verge of extinction. Its share of the personal-computing market had shrunk to a tiny 2 percent. But behind the scenes a turnaround was being orchestrated. The transformation would be

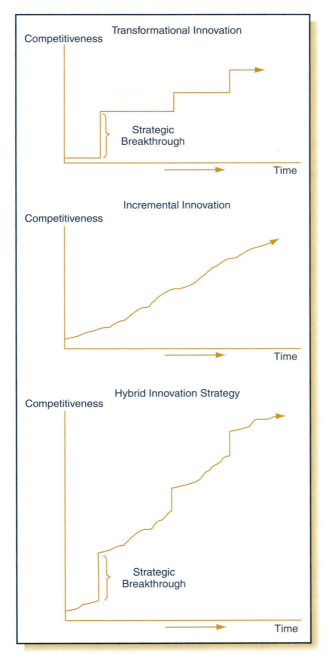

Figure 15.2 Innovation Philosophies

built on a new Unix-based operating system called OS X. Steve Jobs had told the OS X development team to treat the project as a "moon shot"—that is, as an all-or-nothing bet on the company's future. After 3 years of intensive development, OS X was introduced in 2001. The new operating system brought a level of stability and security to the market that other operating systems lacked. It also made plug-and-play of camcorders and other consumer gadgets possible.

However, third-party software developers were unwilling to develop new, sexy software applications for the Mac. Jobs determined that "If nobody wants to help us, we're just going to have to do this ourselves." Apple soon launched a series of user-friendly applications designed to help consumers manage their digital lives. A bundle of five applications called iLife (iMovie, iPhoto, iDVD, GarageBand, and iTunes) enabled users to edit movies, create digital slide shows, record their own music, and manage digital music, photo, and video libraries. Apple had differentiated the Macintosh from Windows-based PCs and positioned it at the center of consumers' emerging digital universe.

More importantly, the foundation was in place for more dramatic innovation. iTunes made it possible to manage a digital music library, but users couldn't access their music away from the computer. A portable, digital music player was needed. Nine months later, the iPod was launched. The iPod incorporated a sleek, attractive appearance, a modified version of the iTunes jukebox software for a user-friendly interface, and a hard disk for storing vast music libraries. The next step was to create an on-line store for buying downloadable songs. Apple's iTunes Music Store opened in 2003 and sold 1 million songs in the first 6 days. Over the next 18 months, Apple turned its software competence and "user experience" into one of the world's most popular brands, selling 250 million downloadable songs and almost 10 million iPods. That gave Apple a 62 percent share of the on-line music market and a 70 percent share of the portable hard-disk digital music player market. For an entire generation of young consumers, Apple had become a core brand representing the digital lifestyle. Along the way, Apple had rewritten the competitive rules for the computer, consumer electronics, and music industries.[10]

Incremental Innovation

The second path to innovation involves continuous, incremental improvements. Toyota has set the standard for continuous improvement. **Incremental innovation** strategies rely on creating a systemic capability. That is, improvements must take place everywhere and all the time. Continuous improvement companies therefore solicit innovation ideas through a variety of methods from suggestion boxes to business plan contests to on-line brainstorming sessions. They know that everyone regardless of position or tenure must be involved in innovation. Gary Hamel, innovation guru and author of *Leading the Revolution*, argues, "The real returns come from harnessing the imagination of every single employee every single day."[11] After all, good ideas are good ideas whatever the source—and this includes SC partners.

For example, at W. R. Grace's chemical-manufacturing division, 34 on-line brainstorming sessions generated 2,685 ideas, 76 new products, and 67 distinct process improvements.[12] At W. L. Gore, the creator of Gore-Tex fabric, if an employee can convince a group of colleagues to invest some of their own time on an idea, the idea becomes an official project. At Google, the goal is to make Google obsolete before someone else does. Google encourages employees to devote up to 20 percent of their time to pet ideas, called "Googlettes," in the pursuit of the "next" Google.[13] The goal at each company is to build momentum through incremental improvements to constantly raise the competitive bar and make the company a moving target.

Despite its competitive potential, continuous improvement strategies are not widely employed. Many companies prefer transformational innovation to continuous improvement. They would rather rewrite the competitive rules with big, bold ideas than build an environment of persistent experimentation. Yet, in today's intensely competitive environment, success depends as much, if not more, on continual productivity gains and consistent innovation than on occasional, dramatic breakthroughs in process technology or product design.

Constantly improving already good products and processes is needed because all advantages are difficult to protect. Most new products can be imitated, and often improved on, by competitors within a year and 60 to 90 percent of all learning available through process development diffuses to competitors.[14] Continuous improvement is therefore needed to stay ahead of the competition. Moreover, pursuing innovation through a series of small, incremental steps does not preclude the development or adoption of strategic breakthroughs. In fact, the attitudes, skills, and technical competence needed to pursue continuous improvement prepare a company to quickly assimilate breakthroughs whenever and wherever they occur (see Hybrid Innovation Strategy in Figure 15.2).

Regardless of a company's choice of innovation strategy, creating a learning organization is a real challenge. Gary Hamel warns, "To truly enhance the innovation capacity of an organization is going to take 3 to 5 years. It's tough."[15] It's tough because it requires a clear sense of what innovation is. Hamel argues that many companies mistakenly define innovation as invention; they view it in terms of products only. Samuel Palmisano, CEO of IBM, helps define the type of innovation needed in today's marketplace, saying, "Let's be clear on the meaning of innovation. It's a lot more than invention. Innovation is the intersection of invention and insight. It is the fusion of new developments and new approaches. . . . Innovation is focused less on things and more on ideas, collaboration, and expertise."[16]

It's also tough because true innovation capacity requires a sense of urgency and a risk-taking perspective that few large companies possess. Art Collins, CEO of Medtronic, notes, "The tough part is that many times you've got to change before the real requirement to change is necessarily seen. That means people will make mistakes. You've got to give people the opportunity to make mistakes, to fail, and not to crucify them for doing that. . . . That's easy to say, but hard to do."[17] Technologist Bill Joy echoes, "If you want a culture of innovation, you can't punish people for attempting great things and sometimes failing."[18]

Finally, enhancing an organization's innovation capacity is tough because it requires sustained investments to build a culture of innovation. Such a culture begins with trust and promotes the sharing of ideas. Individual expertise is nurtured and valued. Specific skills including communication, coaching, and project management are cultivated across the workforce. Money is set aside to explore ideas, some of which are a little off the wall and some of which come from outside the company's own walls. Bill Joy favors "small, quirky, controversial projects." He argues that, "If everyone thinks an idea is okay, how can it be innovative?"[19] A. G. Lafley, the architect of P&G's turnaround, looks for ideas everywhere: "The P&G of 5 or 6 years ago depended on 8,000 scientists and engineers for the vast majority of innovation. The P&G we're trying to unleash today asks all 100,000-plus of us to be innovators." He adds, "I'm a big believer that we sometimes need help in solving problems. So I have set a goal to get half of our innovation from outside. We're in the 20 percent range now, up from 10 percent 3 or 4 years ago. We have even worked with competitors."[20]

The fact that innovation can be nurtured, even strategically planned and pursued, is emphasized by the following three case studies. While each company pursues a different path to innovation, they all establish a culture and specific programs to unleash people's curiosity and reward them for acting on their innovation impulses.

Pet Projects at Newmont Gold

At Newmont Gold, a need to reduce materials costs and achieve more consistent innovation led to the implementation of the Pet Project Program. The idea was to

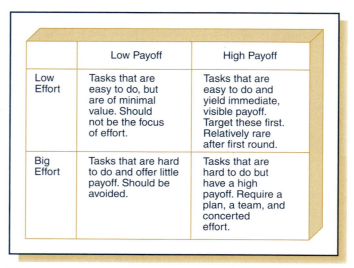

	Low Payoff	High Payoff
Low Effort	Tasks that are easy to do, but are of minimal value. Should not be the focus of effort.	Tasks that are easy to do and yield immediate, visible payoff. Target these first. Relatively rare after first round.
Big Effort	Tasks that are hard to do and offer little payoff. Should be avoided.	Tasks that are hard to do but have a high payoff. Require a plan, a team, and concerted effort.

Figure 15.3 The Pet Project Assessment Matrix

engage the creativity and experience of each member of the materials group to identify improvement opportunities. To get the program going, the following question was asked: "What are the problems that need improving that we haven't gotten around to yet?" With this question in mind, every member of the team was asked to submit one or more pet project ideas. The simple matrix shown in Figure 15.3 was used to prioritize potential projects.

The process to approve pet projects was designed to weed out low payoff projects while encouraging individual initiative. The approval process consisted of the following 7 steps:

1. Every member of the group is responsible for submitting at least one "pet" idea.
2. The compiled list is refined and reduced to a Top 20 list using the assessment matrix.
3. Each individual selects a pet project to lead based on interest and expertise.
4. Each individual enrolls team members who share an interest and passion for the project.
5. The team submits a proposal with milestones, responsibilities, and a completion date.
6. Proposals are reviewed by group leaders who then submit a prioritized list.
7. The final list is reviewed by the materials director to provide coordination and assure resource availability.

The key to a successful Pet Project Program is 100 percent employee participation. Every employee is expected to be a project leader and to take ownership for improving performance within the materials department. Each project leader must enroll team members. No one is forced to work on any given project. Everyone knows that they are free to decline participation. Enrolling team members means finding people who share excitement and passion for making the project successful. That is, people are encouraged to participate only if they are truly interested and can contribute in a meaningful way.

Figure 15.4 shows the pet project proposal form. To be complete, each proposal must include (1) the project's primary goal, (2) a plan of action that specifies the activities to be performed, (3) important milestones, and (4) a targeted completion date.

Pet Project Name ________________

Goal Completion Date

Project Leader ________ Team Members ________

Milestones Completion Date

1.
2.
3.

Promised Actions	Who's Responsible	Promised Date	Completion Date
1.			
2.			
3.			

Figure 15.4 Pet Project Proposal

Each activity is tied to a team member who is identified as the activity owner. Finally, as part of the pet project process, everyone is expected to look for and eliminate "zero-based" activities. These are activities that are currently performed for no other reason than "it's always been done this way." Such jobs are identified, evaluated, and eliminated. Eliminating zero-based activities frees up time for pet projects while improving both efficiency and effectiveness. The zero-based job duties that are eliminated each month are highlighted in a monthly report turned in to the director of the materials group.

The Pet Project Program achieved outstanding buy-in among employees—over 136 pet projects were identified. More importantly, many high-value projects were completed. In the procurement group alone, which consists of 17 employees, 16 of 18 approved pet projects were successfully completed. The 50 employees in the materials group successfully completed 80 of 84 approved pet projects. Some of the projects that made the Top 20 list follow:

- Inventory reduction through consignment
- Supplier reduction
- Alliance formation program
- Procurement card
- Supplier "report card" program
- Zero-based work duties
- Backup transportation for bulk commodities

The first-year impact was remarkable. The formal strategic alliance project produced consignment and stockless inventory arrangements that streamlined operating processes, shortened replenishment lead times, and reduced total inventory costs by 18 percent. The Pet Project Program unleashed tremendous creative power and increased the motivation and commitment of the entire materials department.

FrameworkS at Johnson & Johnson

As the twentieth century came to a close, senior management at Johnson & Johnson (J&J) felt a clear need to challenge existing assumptions regarding the company's growth prospects. Amassing sales of over $23 billion, the company had become a worldwide market leader in the health care products industry. Johnson & Johnson owed its success to a culture of entrepreneurial vigor and a decentralized management structure. The J&J brand was well known, but the company consisted of 170 distinct and *independently minded* operating companies. The independent structure that had propelled the company's growth posed a threat to its future.

The problem was twofold. First, senior management worried that Johnson & Johnson might become a victim of its own success by embracing the false assumption that the traditional ways of doing things would continue to power growth.[21] Complacency threatened innovation and renewal. Second, to succeed in a market changing at a dizzying pace, the company needed to remain nimble and flexible while capturing critical mass on a global scale. Ralph Larsen, then CEO at Johnson & Johnson, described the challenge:

> It was apparent that we needed to do something that would further align idea creation and decision making at the senior levels of our company with the realities of our extraordinarily dynamic marketplace. . . .
>
> We realized we needed to create a powerful agent of change within Johnson & Johnson. This was not a simple proposition. Inherent in our decentralized approach is discomfort with well-intentioned, corporate-wide programs that can end up placing a layer of distracting top-down governance and bureaucracy on line operations. How, then, were we to go about informing our operating management worldwide about the increasingly serious, company-wide challenges we faced? How could we inspire our leaders to embrace a more unified perspective? How could we share the very best thinking and ideas as well as the vast experience and resources in our company? How could we establish an environment in which we could break down organizational, functional and geographic barriers and act in concert on challenges best met through a cooperative approach? And, how could we accomplish all of this while preserving, better yet, strengthening our decentralized management?[22]

Johnson & Johnson's answer was a process called FrameworkS. The goal of FrameworkS was to help leadership throughout the company (1) more effectively understand the marketplace, (2) better define customer expectations, and (3) identify new opportunities for growth. The capital "S" reminded everyone that multiple "frames" of reference needed to be used to understand the company's diverse businesses.

FrameworkS required the executive committee to identify and explore the most pressing issues that the company would face in coming years. Such topics have included e-commerce and leadership development. Once a company-wide issue is identified, a FrameworkS team is put together by the executive committee. The clearest thinkers, sharpest business managers, and most knowledgeable market and technology experts are sought for each team. Team members are drawn from the executive committee, senior corporate staff, and the management boards of the distinct operating companies. The team conducts detailed research on the topic of interest. Appropriate Johnson & Johnson operations are visited, other companies' practices benchmarked, and academic experts consulted. The research process can take up to 6 months.

Findings are thoroughly discussed and evaluated in a multi-day meeting attended by the executive committee and all of the members of the FrameworkS team. FrameworkS meetings provide an open and lively forum where facts are presented, ideas exchanged, and mind-sets challenged. The fact that members of the FrameworkS team often come from diverse operating businesses and have had very little previous interaction with each other creates a unique dynamic. Fresh perspectives are shared. Invigorating discussion results. The best options and opportunities for Johnson & Johnson are identified.

After the meeting, management teams craft and implement action plans to take advantage of the identified opportunities. For example, one FrameworkS team determined that a new type of leader with a different set of competencies was needed to drive future growth. To communicate this need, the team established the company's Standards of Leadership, which defines five clusters of competencies Johnson & Johnson managers are expected to develop and demonstrate (see Figure 15.5). Specific activities including training, performance measurement, and succession planning are designed to build these competencies among the company's global management team.

The FrameworkS process energized Johnson & Johnson's global management team. The executive committee gained a better appreciation for how others see the company. Leaders among the operating businesses learned from one another and more aggressively pursued emerging market opportunities. An eagerness to embrace the ambiguity and change of a global marketplace emerged. The result: Johnson & Johnson started new businesses, entered new markets, and established new programs to build the skills needed to innovate and grow in the twenty-first century.

Figure 15.5 Johnson & Johnson's Standards of Leadership

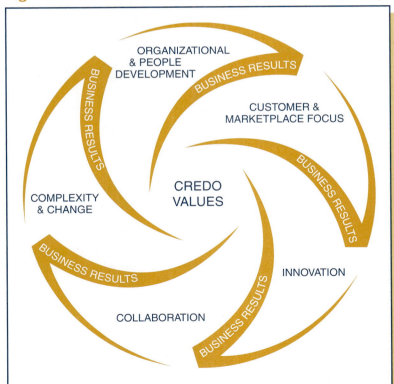

Employee Initiative and Innovation at 3M

From its inception, 3M has been an innovator. 3M's culture of innovation was firmly entrenched by William L. McKnight. McKnight joined the company in 1907 as an assistant bookkeeper and became its president in 1929. His style was to empower people. He emphasized that investing in people was the most important pathway to growth, stating his basic management philosophy in 1948:

> As our business grows, it becomes increasingly necessary to delegate responsibility and to encourage men and women to exercise their initiative. This requires considerable tolerance. Those men and women, to whom we delegate authority and responsibility, if they are good people, are going to want to do their jobs in their own way.
>
> Mistakes will be made. But if a person is essentially right, the mistakes he or she makes are not as serious in the long run as the mistakes management will make if it undertakes to tell those in authority exactly how they must do their jobs.
>
> Management that is destructively critical when mistakes are made kills initiative. And it's essential that we have many people with initiative if we are to continue to grow.

McKnight's objective, of course, was to capture the innovative ideas of all 3M employees, known as 3Mers. Joseph Wiese, the visionary behind the first-ever color copier, explains, "At 3M, innovation is everyone's job. Those who show talent, initiative and creativity will be given a chance to pursue their research dreams—regardless of their formal training and background." The link between an individual's ideas and innovation is almost sacred at 3M. In fact, 3Mers often cite the 11th Commandment: "Thou shalt not kill an idea." They also talk about 3M's storied innovation history not just with pride but also with a hope that they can be a part of 3M's future success stories. Innovation stories are part of 3M's culture and are chronicled on the company's Web site. The hope is that sharing success stories will challenge and encourage 3Mers everywhere to find innovative solutions to customer problems. The constant stream of innovation at 3M has helped 3M develop a line of 55,000 products across more than 30 core technologies.

Everywhere you look within 3M efforts are made to make personal initiative part of the culture. Desi DeSimone, former CEO at 3M, described 3M's 10 Commandments for building a culture of innovation:

1. Give people time to follow their dreams. 3M gives its people 15 percent of their time to devote to their research ideas. The Web site notes, "3M innovation is practical observation, coupled with imaginative research. At 3M, innovation is given time to grow."
2. Make it a part of the expert's job to share their knowledge. 3M expects its best engineers and scientists to openly share their knowledge to help colleagues with their own projects. Art Fry, co-inventor of Post-it Notes, points out, "The 3M dedication to innovation is always a team effort."
3. Results must be measured. While personal initiative is encouraged and supported, goals must be defined and progress tracked. 3M's most famous measure is for 30 percent of all sales to come from products introduced in the past 4 years.
4. Anticipate customer needs. According to Desi DeSimone, "The most interesting products are the ones that people need but can't articulate that they need."

5. Recognition is necessary. Not only are success stories part of 3M folklore but 3M sponsors its own "Oscar" night with eminent innovators being inducted into the Carlton Society—3M's Hall of Fame.
6. Be honest and know when to say no. Managers listen to every idea. As a result, 3M tries a lot of little ideas, keeps the ones that work, and discards the ones that don't.
7. Promote a career, not a job. 3M rarely resorts to layoffs to cut costs because a creative culture only persists if creative people feel secure with their future.
8. Internationalize your management team. International experience broadens perspectives, helping managers understand worldwide customer needs. Up to 75 percent of 3M's top managers have at least 3 years of international experience.
9. Keep spending on research and development. 3M has made it a habit to raise its R&D budget each year—even in slow economic conditions. 3M's R&D budget has exceeded $1 billion in recent years.
10. Wall Street isn't always right. Wall Street emphasizes quarterly earnings; 3M focuses on basic, long-term decisions. A culture of innovation is built over the long haul.[23]

3M recognizes that perpetuating a culture of innovation in a market where cost pressures are intense is a serious threat to its future. To adapt, 3M has made operational excellence a quest equal to its drive for organic growth. 3M Acceleration—an initiative to increase the efficiency and impact of new product development—has been adopted. The goal is to double the number of quality ideas and to improve the speed, efficiency, and success with which products are launched, tripling the value of successful new product launches. Six-sigma tools, new metrics, and stretch goals have been implemented to (1) ensure that the voice of the customer is at the heart of the innovation process and (2) bring discipline to the actual new product introduction process. To assure that the company will continue to invest in its future, the budgeting process directly links resource commitments to new product commitments. At 3M a "renaissance in innovation" is being pursued to connect the company to its customers so that 3M can take full advantage of higher-impact, customer-inspired product innovations.

To summarize, Newmont Gold, Johnson & Johnson, and 3M demonstrate that it is possible to plan for continuous innovation. Specific programs like Pet Projects, FrameworkS, or 3M Acceleration can be put in place to identify improvement opportunities. A company's culture can be built to promote innovation. Bringing passionate people together to share their ideas and then cooperatively pursue them is the key to continuous innovation. Unfortunately, few companies make capturing the best thinking and innovative imagination of their workforce a priority. Those that do turn innovation into a source of competitive renewal.[24]

COLLABORATIVE INNOVATION INITIATIVES

The need for constant innovation goes beyond the four walls of the company. The entire supply chain must be involved. The old saying "A chain is only as strong as its weakest link" is particularly true when it comes to innovation. As the competitive battleground shifts from company versus company to supply chain versus supply chain, avoiding obsolescence means promoting learning everywhere across the chain. Modern companies must therefore play a more active role in the learning that takes place up and down the chain.

Collaborative innovation across the chain provides two advantages. First, creative, talented people can be found in companies all along the chain. Harnessing their experience and best thinking makes sense. A study by PricewaterhouseCoopers revealed that over 50 percent of money-making ideas come from customers, suppliers, or competitors.[25] Second, many innovative SC practices are too costly for a single member of the chain to undertake. For example, fast-cycle product development relies on collaboration. At one manufacturer, 8 of 10 engineers in its corporate R&D facility are supplier personnel. The result: Better coordination has led to shorter development cycles and higher-quality, lower-cost products. The manufacturer and its suppliers have shared in the market share gains. By working together, sharing resources, companies can improve their own as well as the entire chain's competitiveness.

Opportunities to collaborate are almost boundless, limited only by SC partners' willingness to try something new. For example, to compete against lower-cost Asian rivals, Hayward Pool Products adopted lean manufacturing. Hayward's ability to cut waste, streamline assembly lines, and capture market share caught the attention of other small manufacturers. Managers at Hayward decided to share what they had learned. In a weeklong crash course, executives from 40 other firms came to learn about lean manufacturing. After a day in the classroom learning basic lean manufacturing principles, the executives were given an opportunity to put their new knowledge to work. Divided into teams, they visited Hayward's factory floor. Their task—observe various aspects of Hayward's manufacturing process and come up with ideas to improve it. Eager to test what they have learned, and bringing fresh perspective to the task, the "guest consultants" almost always generate good, usable ideas. Hayward benefits from more efficient processes and the visiting executives return home ready to make their own companies more lean and competitive.

Figure 15.6 identifies five fairly common collaborative initiatives. The nature and effectiveness of these initiatives vary greatly. Suggestion programs tend to be simple, low-cost programs that are easy to set up and require minimal collaboration and resource sharing. The potential payback is also usually limited. At the other end of the spectrum are resource-intensive supplier or customer process improvement programs. DaimlerChrysler has loaned key suppliers one or more process engineers for a year or longer. The engineers help the suppliers reengineer their own processes to improve efficiency and quality. Supplier personnel learn process improvement skills that they can then share across the company as well as with their own suppliers.[26] Each of these collaborative initiatives is discussed in greater detail next.

Collaborative Improvement Suggestion Programs

Sometimes all that is needed to get customers or suppliers to share great ideas is to ask them. Suggestion programs do this. John Deere has had great success with its Cost Reduction Opportunities Process (JDCROP). Like most suggestion programs, JDCROP encourages suppliers to submit cost-reduction suggestions to Deere for evaluation by Deere engineers. Somewhat unique is Deere's promise to evaluate and respond to the supplier within 20 working days. Viable suggestions are approved. A joint supplier–Deere team then works to make the suggestion a reality. The first year's savings are shared 50/50, giving both partners in the improvement effort a tangible reason to be creative and to strive for excellence. Suggestion programs often go beyond cost and quality to target cycle-time reduction, tailored services, and new product development.

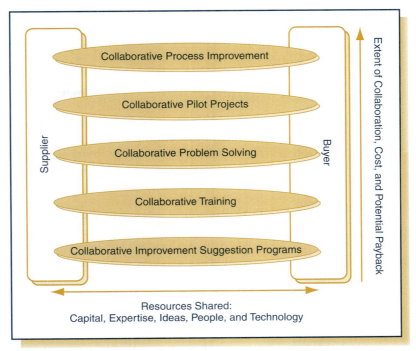

Figure 15.6 Collaborative Innovation Initiatives

Collaborative Training

To deliver outstanding value to the end customer, every member of the chain must operate efficient processes capable of producing high-quality outputs. Unfortunately, many companies lack such processes. They also lack the managerial talent and capital to build them. The only viable way to improve their processes is to get help from SC members who possess needed expertise and experience. SC leaders therefore make it a practice to provide training to valued channel partners.

John Deere, for example, invites supplier personnel to participate in every class or seminar that is offered to Deere's own employees. Certified suppliers are even encouraged to invite their own suppliers to participate in Deere-sponsored education programs. Deere knows that it must do everything it can to help build the skills of the entire SC team.

Beginning in 2003, 3M adopted a very different approach to helping SC partners build needed skills. Through a program called "Six Sigma with Our Customers," 3M employees began sharing their six-sigma expertise with customers. The goal is to help customers learn to use six sigma to improve their operations and solve their most pressing problems. James McNerney, former CEO at 3M, explained the motivation behind the program:

> "Six Sigma with Our Customers" is all about working to solve our customers' most important issues and realize their largest opportunities, as they define them. We are investing in their success and our success simultaneously. Our employees work on customer projects in customer factories, warehouses and offices—wherever the work needs to be done.
>
> The result is not only new and stronger relationships with key customers, but also new insights into the real-world problems our customers face.

We have more than 130 customer projects today, and we expect that number to triple over the next few years. I am confident that "Six Sigma with Our Customers" will make a significant impact on our growth all around the world.[27]

Collaborative Problem Solving

Problems, large and small, arise in the normal course of managing SC relationships. Companies with an innovation mind-set view problems as an opportunity to learn. When a problem is discovered, a problem-solving team comprised of buyer and supplier personnel is formed. The team searches out the root cause, brainstorms a solution, and takes action. Joint problem solving is used to improve products, processes, and relationships.

Collaborative problem solving can also mitigate the impact of an unexpected disaster. For example, Aisin, a key Toyota supplier, suffered a catastrophic fire that burned a key facility to the ground. The factory had been Toyota's primary (99 percent) source of a crucial brake valve. A survey of the damage revealed that most of Aisin's 506 highly specialized machines were useless. Because Toyota only kept 4 hours of inventory on hand, within hours of the fire, Toyota had to shut down its 20 Japanese assembly plants. Drastic action was needed. A "war room" was set up and a collaborative problem-solving team mobilized. The objective: to get the needed P-valve back in production.

Aisin provided blueprints for the 200 P-valve variations. Toyota asked other suppliers for help. New jigs were designed, tooling improvised, and machine tools adapted to make the P-valve. By Wednesday evening, 5 days after the fire, the first usable P-valves arrived at Toyota's production plants. The quick action was possible because of the type of relationships Toyota had built with its suppliers. Suppliers never asked how they would be compensated for coming to Toyota's rescue. They trusted Toyota. After all, they had participated with Toyota on many previous problem-solving efforts.[28]

Collaborative Pilot Projects

Supply chain innovation, by nature, involves a tremendous amount of experimentation. For every lucrative initiative implemented, many fruitless concepts are considered and discarded. Great SC companies improve their odds of pioneering innovative practices by establishing an efficient approach to help them validate groundbreaking ideas and test new programs. Collaborative pilot projects are often used.

Many collaborative pilot projects do not yield desired results. A prerequisite to using them successfully is to find a partner that possesses the patience of Thomas Edison as well as his penchant for testing idea after idea until he found one that worked. On one occasion, a reporter visited Edison to ask about a new substitute for lead in the manufacture of storage batteries. Edison commented that he had made 20,000 experiments, but none had worked. The reporter asked, "Aren't you discouraged by all this waste of effort?" Edison replied, "Waste! There's nothing wasted. I have discovered 20,000 things that won't work."

Nabisco's adoption of collaborative planning, forecasting, and replenishment (CPFR) shows the value of working with a proven and willing partner. CPFR helps trading partners work together to reduce forecasting errors and increase product availability through synchronized replenishment. The goal is to more fully satisfy the demands of end customers at lower costs. Successful implementation requires a commitment to cooperative planning, open information sharing, and coordinated fulfillment. In other words, CPFR requires that companies change the way they work with each other.

When CPFR was first introduced in 1998, few retailers were willing to give it a chance. Nabisco turned to Wegmans, a grocery retailer that had proven to be a close ally in previous innovative ventures. The two worked closely to design a pilot test to validate CPFR's promised benefits. The trusting relationship they had developed on other pilot projects mitigated many implementation challenges. The pilot yielded outstanding results. CPFR increased the sales of Nabisco's product line by over 50 percent while reducing inventory by a third. Nabisco used these results to promote CPFR to other retailers. Over 300 companies have participated in CPFR projects since its introduction, achieving inventory reduction of 10 to 40 percent while improving in-stock product availability by 2 to 8 percent.

Collaborative Process Improvement

Process improvement initiatives are often the most resource-intensive form of collaborative innovation. They incorporate and extend the other four collaborative ventures to help SC partners dramatically improve their own capabilities. Companies like DaimlerChrylser and Rockwell Collins have dedicated a large portion of their process engineering staffs to assist key suppliers in process redesign efforts. Similarly, leaders like GE with its "At the Customer; For the Customer" (ACFC) initiative have made helping customers improve their operations a key part of their customer fulfillment strategies. Honda, however, pioneered and popularized the sharing of engineering talent as part of its supplier development program, dubbed *BP*. BP stands for,

- *Best Position*—Achieve global competitiveness.
- *Best Productivity*—Improve the process.
- *Best Product*—Improve quality and deliver.
- *Best Price*—Decrease cost.
- *Best Partners*—Build a synergistic long-term relationship.[29]

Honda's BP approach involves lending a process development team to a supplier for a period of 3 months to teach the supplier's management and workers the BP process. The goal: to help suppliers learn the skills needed to become more competitive and more self-reliant. BP's 3-month time horizon provides ample time to complete a meaningful project. Besides, as Teruyuki Maruo, the father of the BP process, acknowledges, "If you have seen no changes after 3 months, it is not going to work."[30]

The BP process follows Deming's 4-stage Plan Do Check Act (PDCA) model shown in Figure 15.7. The "plan" stage begins by identifying a good supplier development opportunity. Honda uses a supplier selection matrix to quantify opportunities. Selection criteria include total spend, quality level, delivery performance, and cost competitiveness. Issues such as long-term commodity strategy, projected program life of supplied parts, and past working relationship are also considered. Honda personnel then meet with leading candidates to (1) provide an overview of the BP process and (2) discuss the amount and type of supplier commitment required for success. This meeting provides a final opportunity to assess the supplier's cultural readiness to proceed in the BP process. If the decision is made to go forward, the supplier must identify a full-time project manager, provide a dedicated war room to manage the

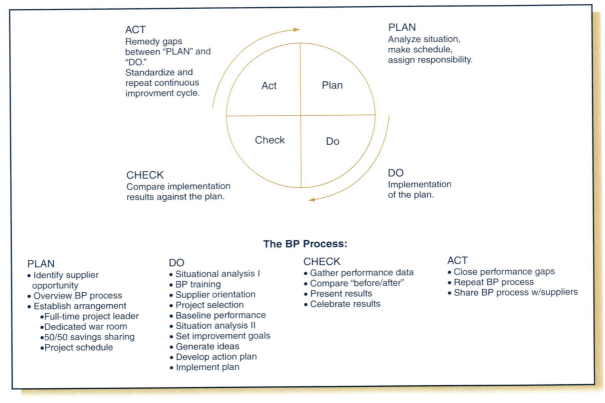

Figure 15.7 Honda's BP Process

Source: Adapted from Nelson, D., Mago, R., & Moody P. E.[29]

project, agree to a 50/50 savings sharing arrangement, and establish a project start date and schedule.

The "do" stage starts the 13-week clock and begins with a detailed situation analysis at Honda's assembly facility. Honda engineers spend 2 to 3 days learning everything they can about the supplier's parts and how they are used. They also examine the parts' cost, quality, and delivery history. With this background, Honda conducts a daylong training seminar to familiarize the supplier's team members with the BP philosophy as well as the tools and techniques that will be used. The next step is to hold a supplier orientation meeting to communicate the goals of the BP process with the supplier's workforce.

Now that introductions have been made, the team is ready to identify a targeted project—a production line, a specific process, or an entire department. Each potential "model line" is carefully analyzed to identify the best opportunity. The joint supplier–Honda team then meets with the people who work on the model line in an hour-long meeting. Questions are answered, concerns are listened to, and the workers are asked for their suggestions. During this meeting, the team starts to build trust with the "experts" who know most about the process. It is now time to document the model line's baseline or "before" performance.

The real work is just beginning. A thorough analysis of the model line is performed using the 3As—go to the Actual place, study the Actual parts, and understand the Actual situation. Process maps and Pareto charts help make sense of the data. Specific goals can now be set and ideas for making improvements generated. Although the BP team will have many ideas, the team must actively engage the line workers to identify improvement opportunities. As workers share ideas, the ideas are posted on a wall so that everyone can see them. They are then prioritized. Workers' names are written next to their ideas, making it possible for them to track the implementation and the impact of their ideas. Action plans are jointly brainstormed and implemented by the workers, the supplier's engineering and maintenance staff, and the BP team.

When the redesigned line is up and running, the "check" stage begins. Performance data is collected and the "after" metrics calculated in the exact same way as the "before" measures. This makes a direct comparison possible so that improvements can be quantified. If specific goals are not obtained, plans can be made to reach them. The BP process concludes with a management review. The line workers present the results to an audience comprised of managers from both the supplier and Honda. Finally, it is time to celebrate the results.

What results should a supplier expect? Honda has conducted hundreds of BP projects with its suppliers. On average, quality goes up by 30 percent and labor productivity increases almost 50 percent. More importantly, the supplier's employees understand the BP process and are ready and excited to test it out on other processes. The supplier's culture has been changed—a mind-set of continuous improvement established.

ORGANIZING FOR LONG-TERM COLLABORATION

Building the learning supply chain requires a governance infrastructure that makes ongoing collaboration among SC partners easy. Figure 15.8 models the practices used by SC leaders to do this. Certain aspects of the model are not new. For example, innovation is built on the foundation of functional expertise. The challenge is to become more collaborative while enhancing functional expertise. For most companies teaming is the vehicle for driving collaboration. Increasingly, personnel from SC partners are included as team members. And the use of "guest" engineers/managers who work as team members on-site at a partner's facility is common at leading companies. However, fewer companies effectively employ executive governance and SC advisory councils as core components of their governance structures.

Executive Governance Councils

The supply chain governance council can help mitigate internal resistance to SC initiatives. At Hewlett-Packard, the role of the governance council is twofold: first, to "maintain ongoing executive-level awareness of business initiatives to avoid reinventing the wheel" and second, to "coordinate supply chain activity throughout the company." Senior executive participation is mandated and membership is limited to divisional executives with authority to allocate resources. The goal is to focus on company-wide initiatives to capture cost savings, drive productivity enhancements, and offer innovative solutions to customers. The council has helped unify divisional managers and led to harmonized policies and procedures.

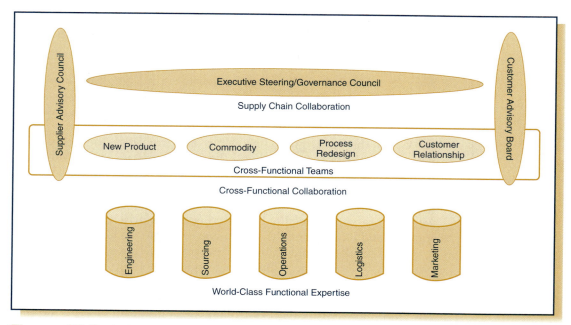

Figure 15.8 Using Supply Chain Governance to Promote Long-Term Collaboration

Collaborative initiatives that have been coordinated through the governance council include global lean operations, postponement manufacturing, and Internet-based virtual sourcing.

At Rockwell Collins, a senior-level SC steering committee was established to increase cross-functional interaction and establish buy-in for specific initiatives. Turf issues are to be fought and resolved by the steering committee, allowing lower-level managers to focus on implementing the initiative rather than seeking approval and obtaining resources. The steering committee meets weekly to fulfill the following roles:

- Serve as champion and mentor
- Establish rules of engagement
- Acquire resources
- Provide encouragement and motivation
- Perpetuate rewards and recognition
- Facilitate communication
- Facilitate goal alignment
- Inculcate a customer satisfaction mind-set

Although the specific roles and responsibilities of a governance council vary, the members of the council typically meet in integration sessions to consider and evaluate proposals. Pros and cons are openly discussed, as are potential impacts and possible problems. Once a proposal is completely understood and refined, its viability is assessed. Attractive projects are adopted and promoted. Political battles and resource issues are addressed and dealt with by the governance council. When the council does its job well, implementation cycles for key SC initiatives are greatly reduced.

Supply Chain Advisory Councils

Supply Chain advisory councils bridge strategic distances between a company and its SC partners. These councils are used as sounding boards for new ideas as well as for the dissemination of best practice. Rockwell Collins has established both a supplier advisory council and a customer advisory board to help it work more closely with key partners. The supplier council is composed of a dozen senior-level company managers and 16 senior executives from highly valued suppliers. The advisory council meets quarterly and acts as a board of directors for the supply-base management process. The council engages the supply base to actively critique and continuously improve the supply acquisition process. The council evaluates new ideas and practices to assure that they make sense from the suppliers' perspective. Council feedback acts as an early warning system, helping the company avoid alienating key suppliers. The objective is to help the company become a favored customer with the supply base. The council also speeds the sharing of technology and best practices among the supply team. Finally, the council helps plan and participates in the annual supplier conference. Feedback from the supplier advisory council has led to the following:

- Earlier supplier involvement in product and process design, especially among the engineering teams
- Better corporate-to-corporate communication
- A policy of using preferred suppliers first
- Enhanced relationships via ERP/EDI/Internet
- Better forecast sharing

The customer advisory board works in a similar fashion. Representatives from key customers are asked to participate as members of a board that meets at least annually to provide insight into how Rockwell Collins can better meet customer needs. Key topics discussed include product development, service support, and resource-sharing opportunities.

CONCLUSION

To survive in today's fast-paced, ever-changing market, companies must perform at ever-higher levels. Operational excellence is critical. However, continued success mandates constant, unrelenting innovation. Innovation must take place everywhere and can be pursued through incremental or transformational strategies. Each strategy has its place. Indeed, to remain relevant, companies are increasingly finding that they must pursue both at the same time. To do this, they must build a culture that unleashes the passion and creativity of the workforce. Then they must implement specific programs like Newmont Gold's Pet Projects or Johnson & Johnson's FrameworkS to harness the power of new ideas.

Even greater opportunities to create distinctive, hard-to-imitate advantage are available through SC collaboration. Collaborating across company borders can increase process efficiency, deliver superior products, and promote a sense of urgency that can keep complacency at bay. The advantage of collaborative innovation is that it provides a company access to a richer resource base—ideas, experience, know-how, and capital. The disadvantage comes in the form of justifying the investment and coordinating the initiative. SC leaders like Honda are finding that the advantages outweigh the disadvantages. They are showing that the learning supply chain may be the best source of sustainable competitiveness.

Regrettably, achieving advantage through collaborative innovation requires higher levels of managerial commitment than are often in place among today's companies. Opportunistic behavior makes it difficult to pursue more resource-intensive collaborative innovation initiatives. Stock price valuations seldom recognize the potential long-term return that comes from up-front investments in a supplier's or customer's capabilities. A *BusinessWeek* article that looked at GE's customer development initiative concludes, "For GE, of course, the larger question is whether pouring a lot more resources into customers will pay off for GE's bottom line."[31] Skeptics abound.

Honda, however, is convinced. Honda estimates that every dollar invested in supplier development yields an 800 percent return.[32] The fact is that more companies are experimenting with collaborative innovation, enticed by the desire to achieve similar returns or driven by the fear of being left behind. Each new success story builds momentum for SC collaboration.

SUMMARY OF KEY POINTS

1. The forces of entrepreneurial spirit, economic globalization, and technological innovation are changing the nature of competition. Companies must constantly innovate to avoid becoming irrelevant. Unfortunately, success itself creates cultural and structural impediments that hinder innovation.

2. Dell, Toyota, and Wal-Mart have shown that it is possible to avoid the perils of complacency. These companies epitomize the learning organization. For every goal that is achieved, a more demanding goal is set. Continuous improvement has become part of the culture.

3. Over the years, companies have pursued two paths to innovation. Transformational innovation relies on strategic breakthroughs in process or product technology. Incremental innovation focuses on harvesting the benefits of a continuous flow of small improvement ideas.

4. To enhance a company's innovation capacity takes 3 to 5 years. Managers must correctly define innovation in terms of "ideas, collaboration, and expertise." They must create a sense of urgency and make taking risks safe. They must nurture a culture of innovation through sustained investments. Finally, they must involve everyone all the time.

5. Innovation doesn't just happen. Newmont Gold, Johnson & Johnson, and 3M demonstrate that innovation can be nurtured and planned. Specific programs like pet projects and FrameworkS can be implemented to identify great ideas. A company's culture can be designed to promote innovation.

6. The need for constant innovation extends beyond the four walls of the company. The entire supply chain must be involved. Modern companies must take an active interest in the innovation and improvement capabilities of their SC partners.

7. Opportunities for collaborative innovation are almost limitless. Five types of programs have been widely implemented among SC leaders: collaborative suggestion programs, collaborative training, collaborative problem solving, collaborative pilot projects, and collaborative process development.

8. Honda popularized collaborative process improvement through its supplier development program dubbed *BP*. The essence of these programs is the sharing of engineering talent with partners who need help improving their internal processes. Honda estimates that for every dollar invested, it achieves an 800 percent return.

9. Building the learning supply chain requires more than ad hoc programs. Frequent, ongoing collaboration is needed. Executive governance and supply chain advisory councils are being used to reduce the turf protection often encountered in SC innovation. These councils act as sounding boards for new ideas as well as a means for identifying and disseminating best practices.

1. Identify the primary forces that threaten to make companies irrelevant. How does each force change the competitive rules, making it necessary for companies to innovate? How can a company anticipate and prepare for each type of market disruption?

2. Why does Sony's new CEO, Howard Stringer, call complacency "the enemy of innovation"? How do once great companies like Sony and General Motors become complacent? Explain how a company can avoid the perils of complacency.

3. Identify and discuss the characteristics of the learning organization. Identify a company in the industry you would like to work in that has mastered the art of continuous innovation. What specifically has it done to develop its culture of innovation?

4. Identify, compare, and contrast the two primary paths to innovation. What skills are needed for each? When is each appropriate? Why do many companies fail to pursue either approach?

5. Briefly discuss Newmont Gold's, Johnson & Johnson's, and 3M's approaches to instilling innovation into their cultures. How are their approaches similar? In what ways are they different? Why does each work?

6. Explain why it is imperative to drive innovation up and down the supply chain. Identify and discuss several practices that are commonly used to promote SC innovation and improvement.

7. Describe Honda's BP supplier development program in detail. Create a flowchart that shows the primary steps in the program. What are the goals associated with each step? If Honda has been so successful with BP, why don't more companies use this type of program?

8. Explain the need for governance mechanisms that promote ongoing communication and collaboration up and down the supply chain. Discuss the specific roles of both executive governance councils and supply chain advisory councils. What are the primary benefits of each? What are the challenges a company is likely to encounter as it attempts to implement these governance mechanisms?

Case   *The Case for Supply Chain Advisory Boards*

"Thanks for the match, Bob. There's nothing like a little tennis to work off the frustration of a tough week. Have a great weekend and I'll see you bright and early Monday morning."

Tim Thomas was glad that he had worked off a little aggression on the court—it beat taking it home with him. Tim's frustration was an artifact of the torturously slow pace of change at his company, C^2, a leader in the biotech arena. For the past year, Tim had been trying to revamp C^2's supply chain strategy. Competitive pressure and customer demands dictated a need for greater collaboration up and down the supply chain to reduce costs and shorten concept-to-market cycles. However, managers across C^2 viewed greater integration as a threat to their autonomy and C^2's future. They argued that in the fast-paced biotech industry it would be too easy to "tie our wagon to a plow horse when a thoroughbred is needed, and vice versa." They were reluctant to commit their time, effort, and budgets to modifying C^2's corporate culture and structure to support the needed integration. Tim decided that people are definitely the barrier to

change. Lacking full-fledged support from his functional colleagues and having obtained only perfunctory support from his tennis partner and C^2's CEO, Bob Haskins, Tim was uncertain how to proceed.

As C^2's director of global sourcing, Tim had only a day earlier returned from a visit to Cedar City, Iowa, where he had spent a few hours with Lindy Robison, Rockwell Collins's director of sourcing. Tim had met Lindy at a workshop in Dallas, Texas, and had been intrigued by Lindy's presentation on building support for SCM. Lindy had emphasized that four types of commitment are needed to enhance competitiveness via SCM: top management support, broad-based functional support, channel support from customers and suppliers, and structural support. None of the four were present at C^2. But Tim was too stubborn to abandon his quest for a more interactive supply chain.

In the hope of identifying something he might do to turn things around at C^2, Tim had arranged to fly out to Iowa to pick Lindy's brain. Shortly after lunch, Lindy had mentioned that some of the best ideas had come from customers and suppliers through an advisory board system adopted by Rockwell Collins. Tim had thought, "Advisory boards might be the answer; after all, Bob is into teams, and advisory boards look like a low-cost opportunity." Tim and Lindy had spent the rest of the day discussing the nature and role of advisory boards. During the flight home, Tim transcribed his notes, as follows:

- Advisory councils can mitigate resistance and facilitate collaboration! Rockwell Collins uses three types of advisory boards.
- A senior-level SC steering committee increases interaction and helps create buy-in for specific initiatives. The steering committee meets weekly to (1) serve as an SCM champion and mentor, (2) establish rules of engagement, (3) acquire resources, (4) provide encouragement and motivation, (5) perpetuate rewards and recognition, (6) facilitate communication, (7) facilitate goal alignment, and (8) inculcate a customer satisfaction mind-set.

  My thoughts: Are items 6, 7, and 8 enough of a selling point to at least get Bob's attention and get the ball rolling? Could a streamlined steering committee generate enough success to justify a more robust committee in the future?

- A supplier alliance advisory council composed of Rockwell managers and senior executives from valued suppliers meets quarterly and acts as a board of directors for the supply process. The council engages the supply base to critique and improve the supply acquisition process. One objective is to help Rockwell become a "favored customer with the supply base." The council facilitates the sharing of technology and best practices. Feedback from the council has led to tangible outcomes:
  - Earlier supplier involvement in product/process design, especially among the engineering teams

- A policy of using preferred suppliers first
- Better corporate-to-corporate communication and enhanced connectedness via ERP/EDI/Internet
- Better sharing of forecasts

  My thoughts: I can do this! Can we generate enough good ideas/improvements/successes to create momentum for other collaborative initiatives? Who should participate: in-house? suppliers?

- A customer advisory board brings representatives from key customers together on an annual basis to provide insight into how customer needs can be met. Products, services, and resource-sharing opportunities are discussed. Customers can be difficult to enlist for participation.

  My thoughts: I can't make this happen; I can only suggest; maybe implore. If we can do something with the supplier board, this might happen down the road. What can I do to push this along?

As Tim tucked his racket and gear into the trunk, he wondered whether or not he could leverage advisory boards to change minds at C². Could he get Bob to back the creation of a steering committee? Would suppliers bring their best efforts and ideas to an advisory council? Would his own supply team embrace a supplier advisory board? What else could he/should he do to get people excited about SC collaboration? These and other questions filled his mind, but he had been away from home most of the week. It was Friday evening and time to shift gears and mind-sets so that he could have fun with his family. Tim's motto was "first things first" and he believed quantity time was a prerequisite to quality time in team building—especially at home.

CASE QUESTIONS

1. How would you address Tim's thoughts? Has he missed anything?
2. What team formation and team management advice would you give Tim?

ENDNOTES

1. Grove, A. (1996). *Only the paranoid survive.* New York: Currency.
2. Kelly, K., & Dvorak, P. (2005, March 16). Resuscitating Sony. *The Wall Street Journal*, p. B1.
3. Schumpeter, J. A. (1942). *Capitalism, socialism and democracy.* New York: Harper & Row.
4. Drucker, P. (1969). *The age of discontinuity: Guidelines to our changing society.* New York: Harper & Row.
5. Ibid. #1.
6. Foster, R., & Kaplan, S. (2001). *Creative destruction: Why companies that are built to last underperform the*

market—And how to successfully transform them. New York: Currency.

7. Collins, J. (2002). *Good to great*. New York: HarperCollins; Useem, J. (2003, April 14). *Fortune 500*. *Fortune*, 87–90.

8. _____ (2005, January 27). Toyota: The car company in front. *The Economist*.

9. Park, A., & Burrows, P. (2003, November 3). What you don't know about Dell. *BusinessWeek*, 74–84.

10. Schendler, B. (2005, February 10). How big can Apple get? *Fortune*.

11. Kirkpatrick, D. (2004, September 6). Innovation do's and don'ts. *Fortune*, 239–240.

12. Fisher, A. (2004, November 29). Get employees to brainstorm online. *Fortune*, 72.

13. Ibid. #11.

14. Ghemawat, P. (1986, September–October). Sustainable advantage. *Harvard Business Review*, 53–58; Ohmae, K. (1987, Spring). The triad world view. *Journal of Business Strategy*, 8–19.

15. Ibid. #11.

16. Palmisano, S. J. (2003, November 17). How the U.S. can keep its innovation edge. *BusinessWeek*, 34.

17. Florian, E. (2004, March 8). Special: CEOs on innovation. *Fortune*.

18. Joy, B. (2004, November 15). Large problem. *Fortune*, 214.

19. Ibid. #18.

20. Ibid. #17.

21. Larsen, R. S. (1998). *The CEO series*. FrameworkS CEO Series (21).

22. Ibid.

23. Loeb, M. (1995, January 16). Ten commandments for managing creative people. *Fortune*.

24. _____. (2002). *3M annual report: Proud past, bright future.*_____. (2003). *3M annual report: Global + speed + innovation.*

25. Ibid. #12.

26. Nelson, D., Moody, P. E., & Stegner, J. (2001). *The purchasing machine*. New York: The Free Press.

27. Ibid. #24.

28. Reitman, V. (1997, February 3). Toyota halts Japan production after fire destroys factory. *The Wall Street Journal*.

29. Nelson, D., Mayo, R., & Moody, P. E. (1998). *Powered by Honda*. New York: John Wiley & Sons, Inc.

30. Ibid.

31. Brady, D. (2003, October 13). Will Jeff Immelt's new push pay off for GE? *BusinessWeek*, 94–98.

32. Ibif. #29.

Part III Epilogue

Collaborating Across the Supply Chain

We shape our homes; thereafter, they shape us.

—WINSTON CHURCHILL

What is supply chain management?

Supply chain management is the design and management of seamless, value-added processes across organizational boundaries to meet the real needs of the end customer.

Supply chain management is a philosophy supported by managerial practices that promote the building of a world-class *SC TEAM* via the selection of the *right* players and the establishment of the *right* relationships. The goal of the *TEAM* is to meet the real needs of the end customers, profitably. We have talked about two key issues: SC design and SC collaboration. SC design identifies and brings together a group of companies with complementary competencies. SC collaboration turns these companies into a cohesive, championship-caliber *TEAM*.

Creating the *TEAM* is the tougher task. After all, a company's stock price depends on its, not the *TEAM's*, performance. Many companies never learn to collaborate—they simply pursue arms-length, adversarial relationships as they fight for a bigger piece of their chain's revenue pie. Thus, the first step to building a *TEAM* is to learn how to define and develop appropriate relationships. Not all relationships are created equal, nor should they be. Each relationship's potential to create unique value should be evaluated to determine where it belongs on the relationship continuum. Every relationship should strive for efficiency, fairness, and trust.

The Supply Chain Road Map

Designing the Global Supply Chain

- What Must be Done to Compete and Win?
  - Who Should Do It?

Who are we?

Business Purpose

Ch 1: SC Strategy
- What is SCM?
- How does it fit our strategy?

Ch 2: Customer Fulfillment
- Who are our customers?
- Can SCM deliver real value?

Ch 3: Process Thinking
- Do we have a functional, silo culture?
- Can we manage across functions?

Ch 4: New Product Process
- Do we know how to innovate?
- Can we create great products?

Ch 5: Fulfillment Process
- Are our operations efficient?
- Can we buy/make/deliver?

How Do We Fit?

As-Is Supply Chain

Chapter 6: Environmental Scanning
- What are the competitive rules?
- What skills does the SC need?

Chapter 7: Supply-Chain Mapping
- What are the SC dynamics?
- Is our company positioned for success?

Chapter 8: Strategic SC Costing
- What are the relevant costs?
- What are the cost trade-offs?

Chapter 9: Competencies & Outsourcing
- What are our valued competencies?
- What activities should be outsourced?

Chapter 10: Rationalization and Role Shifting
- Where can we rationalize the chain?
- Where can we refine assigned roles?

How Should We Fit?

To-Be Supply Chain

Based on the understanding developed during the SC design process, create the capabilities needed to...

1. Help our SC meet customers' real needs better than competing chains:
- Identify the **right** players for the SC
- Define the **right** relationships
- Assign the **right** roles & responsibilities
- Design the **right** structure & systems

2. Securely position the company as an indispensable member of the SC by
- Refining our customer value proposition
- Developing needed competencies
- Leveraging core technologies
- Establishing efficient processes
- Creating appropriate customer linkages

Integrating the Supply Chain

- Create & Communicate Common SC Vision
- Build a Cohesive Team of Allied Companies

How Do We Get There?

Chapter 11: Relationship Alignment
- Define intensity of SC relationships.
- Build trust to promote collaboration.

Chapter 12: Information Sharing
- Establish technology to support SC.
- Cultivate culture that promotes sharing.

Chapter 13: Performance Measurement
- Align measures across SC.
- Create understanding & motivate behavior.

Chapter 14: People Empowerment
- Cultivate empowerment environment.
- Build teams to enhance collaboration.

Chapter 15: Collaborative Improvement
- Establish a culture of innovation to avoid complacency.
- Organize for long-term collaboration.

494

Building collaborative *TEAMS* means investing in information sharing, measurement systems, and people. An information capability starts with technology—the ability to collect and disseminate the information needed to make great decisions. Because information is power, the ability to leverage information for competitive advantage requires a culture of trust, a willingness to share. Combining technology and willingness can create institutional knowledge and promote learning. Measurement creates understanding and motivates collaborative behavior. It provides alignment, getting everyone on the *TEAM* to work together. People, of course, drive learning and are either a bridge or a barrier to collaboration. Getting people to bring their best ideas to work is critical. So is empowering them with the skills to analyze and coordinate across functions as well as to work in teams. Add in a culture of innovation and the right programs to promote collaborative improvement, and the *SC TEAM* is positioned to win both now and in the future.

The best of the best companies around the world are shaping not just collaborative but also winning *SC TEAMS*. Their success stories are shaping an exciting and challenging environment for tomorrow's SC managers.

APPENDIXES

Appendix A

TCO Analysis-Printer purchase	BASE CASE TCO Analysis	
	Option 1: All laser printers	Option 2: Mix of laser and deskjet
ASSUMPTIONS AND BASE DATA		
Number of laser printers	400	50
Price per printer	$1,000.00	$1,000.00
Number of deskjet printers		2,100
Price per printer		$150.00
Price per toner	$120.00	$120.00
Pages per toner	5,000	5,000
Pages per year	7,500,000*	3,750,000**

*Assume average usage of 75 printed-page sides per day across all users.

**Assume average usage of 300 printed-page sides per day for administrators only; the rest is other users.

Price per cartridge		$35.00
Pages per cartridge		500
Pages per year		3,750,000
Laser average repairs per year	.0417	.0417
Cost	$175.00	$175.00
Annual repair cost	$2,916.67	$364.58
Deskjet average repairs per year		.0057
Cost		$100.00
Annual repair cost		$1,200.00
Disposal Value		
Laser	$100.00	$100.00
Deskjet		($15.00)
Useful life	4 years	4 years
CALCULATION OF TCO		
Cost of printers		
Laser (Number of printers × price)	$400,000.00	$50,000.00
Deskjet (Number of printers × price)		$315,000.00
Monthly		
(Pages/pages per toner) × cost of toner	$15,000.00	$7,500.00
Monthly cost of cartridges		$21,875.00
DISCOUNTED TCO		
Price of printers		
Laser	($400,000.00)	($50,000.00)
Deskjet		($315,000.00)

(continued)

	BASE CASE TCO Analysis	
TCO Analysis-Printer purchase	Option 1: All laser printers	Option 2: Mix of laser and deskjet
Toner, PV, 4 years	($638,704.77)	($319,352.38)
Cartridges, PV, 4 years		($931,444.45)
Repairs		
Toner, PV, 4 years	($124,192.59)	($15,524.07)
Cartridges, PV, 4 years		($51,096.38)
Disposal		
Laser, PV, received in 4 years	$32,258.06	$4,032.26
Deskjet, PV, received in 4 years		($25,403.23)
TCO		
Discounted for Present Value	($1,130,639.30)	($1,703,788.26)

TCO Analysis-Printer purchase
Sensitivity Analysis: Reduced Toner Page Yield

	Option 1: All laser printers	Option 2: Mix of laser and deskjet
ASSUMPTIONS AND BASE DATA		
Number of laser printers	400	50
Price per printer	$1,000.00	$1,000.00
Number of deskjet printers		2100
Price per printer		$150.00
Price per toner	$120.00	$120.00
Pages per toner	4,000	4,000
Pages per year	7,500,000*	3,750,000**

*Assume average usage of 75 printed page sides per day across all users.

**Assume average usage of 300 printed page sides per day for administrators only; the rest is other users.

Price per cartridge		$35.00
Pages per cartridge		500
Pages per year		3,750,000
Laser average repairs per year	.0417	.0417
Cost	$175.00	$175.00
Annual repair cost	$2,916.67	$364.58
Deskjet average repairs per year		0.1
Cost		$100.00
Annual repair cost		$1,200.00
Disposal Value		
Laser	$100.00	$100.00
Deskjet		($15.00)
Useful life	4 years	4 years
CALCULATION OF TCO		
Cost of printers		
Laser (Number of printers × price)	$400,000.00	$50,000.00
Deskjet (Number of printers × price)		$315,000.00

(*continued*)

	Option 1: All laser printers	Option 2: Mix of laser and deskjet
Monthly (Pages/pages per toner) × cost of toner	$18,750.00	$9,375.00
Monthly cost of cartridges		$21,875.00
DISCOUNTED TCO price of printers		
Laser	($400,000.00)	($50,000.00)
Deskjet		($315,000.00)
Toner, PV, 4 years	($798,380.96)	($399,190.48)
Cartridges, PV 4 years		($931,444.45)
Repairs		
Laser, PV, 4 years	($124,192.59)	($15,524.07)
Deskjet, PV 4 years		($51,096.38)
Disposal,		
Laser, PV received in 4 years	$32,258.06	$4,032.26
Deskjet, PV received in 4 years		($25,403.23)
TCO Discounted for Present Value	($1,290,315.49)	($1,783,626.35)

TCO Analysis-Printer purchase
Sensitivity Analysis: Reduced Cartridge Price

	Option 1: All laser printers	Option 2: Mix of laser and deskjet
ASSUMPTIONS AND BASE DATA		
Number of laser printers	400	50
Price per printer	$1000.00	$1000.00
Number of deskjet printers		2100
Price per printer		$150.00
Price per toner	$120.00	$120.00
Pages per toner	5000	5000
Pages per year	7,500,000*	3,750,000**

*Assume average usage of 75 printed page sides per day across all users.

**Assume average usage of 300 printed page sides per day for administrators only; the rest is other users.

	Option 1: All laser printers	Option 2: Mix of laser and deskjet
Price per cartridge		$10
Pages per cartridge		500
Pages per year		3,750,000
Laser average repairs per year	.0417	.0417
Cost	$175.00	$175.00
Annual repair cost	$2,916.67	$364.58
Deskjet average repairs per year		0.1
Cost		$100.00
Annual repair cost		$1,200.00

(*continued*)

	Option 1: All laser printers	Option 2: Mix of laser and deskjet
Disposal Value		
Laser	$100.00	$100.00
Deskjet		($15.00)
Useful life	4 years	4 years
CALCULATION OF TCO		
Cost of printers		
Laser (Number of printers × price)	$400,000.00	$50,000.00
Deskjet (Number of printers × price)		$315,000.00
Monthly		
(Pages/pages per toner) ×		
cost of toner	$15,000.00	$7,500.00
Monthly cost of cartridges		$6,250.00
DISCOUNTED TCO		
price of printers		
Laser	($400,000.00)	($50,000.00)
Deskjet		($315,000.00)
Toner, PV, 4 years	($638,704.77)	($319,352.38)
Cartridges, PV 4 years		($266,126.99)
Repairs		
Laser, PV, 4 years	($124,192.59)	($15,524.07)
Deskjet, PV 4 years		($51,096.38)
Disposal,		
Laser, PV received in 4 years	$32,258.06	$4,032.26
Deskjet, PV received in 4 years		($25,403.23)
TCO,		
Discounted for Present Value	($1,130,639.30)	($1,038,470.79)

CASES

Case 1   *Creating a Cycle of Satisfaction*[1]

Linda Fernandez smiled as she reviewed the latest market study on Whirlpool's newest product introduction—the Ideale. Whirlpool claimed that the Ideale was the world's lowest-cost automatic washing machine.

The Ideale concept had emerged 18 months earlier as part of Whirlpool's global market expansion strategy and had cost the company $30 million. The good news was that the Ideale looked like it might be the "hit" product Whirlpool needed to shore up its position as one of the world's premiere white goods companies. At least the customer comments Linda was looking at indicated that the Ideale had "home-run" potential. For example, Silvia Oliveira, Brazilian housewife, had said,

> She's my second mother. Before she came along I spent hours bent over the washing tub. Now, I can put Ideale to work and do other things, like tend my children, cook dinner, and even visit my mother.

THE IDEALE STORY

Years earlier, Whirlpool had identified the need to bring an inexpensive washing machine to market in developing countries around the world. The low-income consumer market worldwide was absolutely huge. Equally important, Whirlpool was convinced that if it could successfully sell to the younger generation—which was often 50 percent of the population in developing countries—it would have built-in consumers for its more expensive, higher-end appliances over time as its customers aged and increased their earning power. Unfortunately, Whirlpool's initial attempts had failed to take off. These early efforts had focused on stripping down existing products to reduce their cost. But at a price point of $300 dollars, these low-cost washers were still too expensive for consumers in key markets like Brazil, China, and India.

Despite this failure, designers at Whirlpool persevered. After all, the 30 million low-income households in Brazil, one of Whirlpool's best international markets, appeared eager to buy a washer if only someone would make a high-quality, low-cost machine. Independent surveys showed that automatic washers were popular—the second most coveted item among low-income consumers. Only cell phones were more coveted. Besides, just 25 percent of households in Brazil, 8 percent in China, and 4.5 percent in India had automatic washing machines. There was plenty of room for growth. In fact, Whirlpool executives were confident that a low-cost machine like the Ideale would boost washing machine market penetration by 20 percent in 2 years.

Therefore, a concerted effort was undertaken to design a low-cost washer from scratch. To do this, Whirlpool researchers began to explore the washing habits and mind-set of poor Brazilian homemakers. Focus groups and home visits were initiated. Dozens of representative families were "adopted" by Whirlpool researchers to provide feedback throughout the development process. Designers quickly discovered several salient facts:

- Washing clothes by hand required homemakers to spend hours bent over the washing tub—a chore they disliked immensely.
- Low-income Brazilian homemakers do laundry more frequently than their upscale counterparts.
- Homemakers were willing to live with a slower spin cycle as long as the clothes still had the appearance of being "wrung automatically."
- Brazilian housewives liked seeing the machine operate. They also had a habit of washing floors underneath furniture and appliances.
- Low-income consumers viewed washers as a status symbol and were insulted that less-expensive appliances were often unattractive.
- Brazilians prefer cheery and rounded styling—control panels that included yellow buttons and blue lettering were perceived as stylish.
- White was a favored color because homemakers associated it with cleanliness.

Contemporary research in China and India yielded similar results. However, some differences were identified. For instance, Chinese homemakers disdained white because it dirties easily. Indian consumers felt similarly.

---

[1]Jordan, Miriam and Karp, Jonathan, (2003, December 9). "Machines for the masses." *Wall Street Journal.*

Space constraints in Chinese homes meant that washers are often kept in the living room, often situated under shelves. Finally, consumers in each country preferred wash cycles to have names that were culturally unique.

The research strongly suggested that a lucrative market awaited the introduction of a well-designed automatic washer. Because the typical Brazilian worker earned only about $220 per month, it was determined that the retail price point had to be between $150 and $200—less than half the average price of $462 in the United States.

To meet this overriding imperative, it was decided that the washing machine would have to be designed and manufactured in a low-labor-cost country. Fortunately, Whirlpool's Brazilian factories were among its most advanced. Its rapidly growing Brazilian design staff consisted of highly skilled, technically competent low-cost engineers and industrial designers. This design team could "Latinize" U.S. designs as well as conceptualize and develop entirely new products for worldwide consumers.

The breakthrough that made the Ideale possible occurred when the Brazilian design team decided that a single-drive system that washed and spun without switching gears would meet the needs of low-income consumers. By eliminating the multiple-drive system, costs could be reduced dramatically. The single-drive technology was also unique enough for Whirlpool to apply for patents in key markets worldwide. The other major design change was to build a smaller machine with only a 9-pound capacity. The focus groups confirmed that these changes were good enough for the targeted consumers.

The market research also suggested some finer design points. For instance, the Brazilian machine was designed to stand high on four legs. It also came with rounded styling and a transparent, acrylic lid. Although the Brazilian version was available only in white, the Chinese version was marketed in light blue and gray, and the Indian machine in green, blue, and white. Further, in China, where millions of low-income consumers rely on bikes for transportation, the company chose a name for the heavy-duty cleaning cycle that translated as "grease removal." In India, the setting for delicate fabric was named "sari."

LINDA'S CHALLENGE

As Linda perused the market report, she was pleased to see that in the first 15 days, Whirlpool shipped twice the number of machines that it expected to sell in the first month. Early sales in China were equally promising. Her task was to take the early market results and quantify the 5-year expected return. If the numbers looked as positive as she hoped, she would then prepare an after-action report that identified the "good, the bad, and the ugly" of the Ideale development process. The goal was to create a cycle of satisfaction that could be used to guide future winning product development efforts.

QUESTIONS

1. Assume the following:
   - The sales price to consumers is $150.
   - The retailers' markup is 50 percent.
   - Whirlpool's after-tax profit margin is 4 percent.
   - The hurdle rate is 20 percent.
   - Populations are as follows: Brazil, 182 million; China, 1.286 billion; and India, 1.049 billion.
   - Family size are as follows: Brazil, 4.01; China, 3.70; and India, 4.91.
   - Market penetration for each of the first 2 years is equal and sales increase by 10 percent per year for years 3, 4, and 5.

   What is the expected 5-year net present value?
2. Benchmark Ideale's development process to help Whirlpool establish a winning approach to future global development efforts.

Case 2   *Getting the Data Right*[1]

Nicole Holdaway sat perplexed. As director of supply chain operations at Best Inc., she was responsible for making sure the right product was on the shelf for customers to buy. She was to do so at the lowest possible inventory costs. Until recently, she had felt pretty good about Best's ability to manage the inventory–service trade-off. After all, the company had invested millions in information technology to help managers track inventory from point of sale back to key suppliers' distribution centers. But after a 3-month study of inventory data accuracy, Nicole knew Best's inventory data wasn't accurate. Dramatic improvements were needed. The question was, "If technology investments hadn't improved inventory accuracy, what would?"

THE HISTORY OF BAR-CODE TECHNOLOGY[2]

Nicole couldn't help but think back to her high school days in the late 1970s when she worked as a grocery cashier. Back then cash registers were a place to store money. The idea of bar codes and databases had been completely foreign to her. Ringing up a customer's sale was a laborious task that depended on prices being clearly stamped on each item. Smeared prices required a price check that could cause long lines of customers to back up. Such lines led to palpable customer frustration.

Bar codes and scanners changed everything. Nicole thought it interesting to recall that the first retail bar-code transaction actually took place before she started working as a cashier. On June 26, 1974, a checkout clerk at a Marsh supermarket in Troy, Ohio, made history as she slid a pack of Juicy Fruit gum over a bar-code scanner. Despite expectations, the use of bar codes didn't take off. Instead, bar-code adoption was so anemic that in 1976 *BusinessWeek* published an article titled, "The Supermarket Scanner That Failed." However, by the early 1980s mass merchandisers led by Kmart were adopting the technology. Retail practice was forever changed. Nicole smiled as she wondered if history would repeat itself with the RFID technology the industry was just beginning to adopt.

By the 1990s, bar codes and databases had changed distribution management farther up the supply chain. Procter & Gamble had achieved double-digit productivity gains and inventory reductions. Kimberly-Clark had reduced shipping errors by over 50 percent. Warehouses up and down the supply chain put bar codes on cases, pallets, racks, and dock doors. Mobile scanners made it possible to track inventory from picking to shipping.

Nonetheless, Nicole knew that the most dramatic gains had taken place at the retail level. Wal-Mart was probably the leader in bar-code innovation, using bar codes to make cross-docking possible. Wal-Mart even put a bar code on every price label on every shelf. Associates, armed with wireless scanners, are able to scan the tags and then make price changes, place an order, or look up sales histories. Wal-Mart was even able to track sell-through rates, enabling it to position product where it would sell faster. Managers across the industry widely believed that Wal-Mart not only knew what was selling better than its suppliers but also understood purchasing habits better than consumers themselves.

Knowing what she knew about the revolutionary success of bar-code technology, Nicole couldn't help but rely on the inventory data provided by Best's information system. Bar codes had transformed industry practice, seemingly allowing stores to track the flow of goods and automatically place precise replenishment orders. Further, suppliers could now use point-of-sales information to synchronize production schedules to real-time customer purchases. In theory, inventory could be reduced without reducing service levels. But at Best Inc. the theory had broken down, and Nicole needed to find out why.

INVENTORY ACCURACY AT BEST INC.

Questions regarding Best's inventory accuracy arose when a disgruntled customer had written a letter to Best's VP of marketing, Kristine Thomson. The letter's tone riveted Kristine's attention.

[1]Raman, Ananth, DeHoratius, Nicole, and Ton, Zeynep. (2001, May). The Achilles' Heel of Supply Chain Management. *Harvard Business Review.*
[2]Varchaver, Nicolas. (2004, May 31). Scanning the globe. *Fortune.*

Dear Ms. Thomson:

I've been a loyal customer for over a decade, but I am so frustrated that I doubt I'll ever shop at Best again. Responding to an ad in your weekly circular, I visited your local store to buy an electronic keyboard. After 10 minutes of searching, I asked a clerk for help. Since the product wasn't on the shelf, he checked the computer, which said the item was in stock. After another 30 minutes spent in fruitless search, the clerk promised to track the product down, get it on the shelf, and give me a call. He never called!

I stopped by the store on two other occasions during the week. The product was not on the shelf and your clerks could not find it anywhere in the store. Why do you make promises you can't fulfill? For the last several years, I have spent over $4,000 a year at Best. But no more! I'll take my business and your profits to your competition from now on.

Regards,
Tamara Masters

Kristine had promptly called Nicole, asking her to look into the situation and report back within the week.

Nicole had quickly looked up the inventory status of the missing keyboard and found that 42 units were recorded as in stock. She then called the store manager, asking him to do a thorough physical count of the item. None were found. This finding led Nicole to bring in an outside consultant to help perform a physical count at all of Best's retail stores. Amazingly, the physical audit showed that the actual inventory matched the computer records only 35 percent of the time. Worse, many of the disparities were huge.

Before the physical audit, managers at Best had thought their systems were achieving 99 percent inventory accuracy. Analysis of the disparities suggested that the profit implications were dramatic. Excess inventory and lost sales probably reduced Best's profits by between 10 and 20 percent.

The disappointing findings regarding inventory accuracy together with the profit-impact estimates led Nicole to look deeper into the inventory accuracy problem. Her continued analysis identified a secondary problem—the phantom stockout. Many items reported as out of stock at the service desk were found someplace in the store, either in the wrong place on the sales floor or lost in the back room. Nobody knew for sure how many customers had left the store empty-handed and perhaps mad because they couldn't find what they were looking for.

Finally, adding insult to injury, before a new retail location was opened for business, a physical audit was performed. Even before the doors were opened to customers for the first time, the computerized inventory system had the wrong quantities for one in three SKUs. The average discrepancy was an unbelievable 25 percent.

Now that Nicole understood the magnitude of the problem, she wondered what her next steps should be.

QUESTIONS

1. What are the sources of the data inaccuracies at Best Inc.?
2. What changes does Nicole Holdaway need to implement to eliminate the data inaccuracies? Where should she start?
3. Is RFID the answer?

Case 3   *Supplier Quality at Triton Diamond*

The meeting on supplier quality ended at 3:10 P.M. without having accomplished one of Tim Rock's major goals. Tim Rock, senior purchasing manager at Triton Diamond, was disappointed—he had hoped that his proposal to offer advantageous payment terms to preferred suppliers would be approved; unfortunately, the plan had been rejected by the chief financial officer. Thinking about the CFO's final comments, "We just can't do that. We can't offer some suppliers special payment terms," Tim wondered how he could entice Triton's suppliers to cooperate more fully in Triton's new supplier quality improvement program.

THE TRITON DIAMOND COMPANY

By the fall of 2007, Triton Diamond, a leading manufacturer of polycrystalline diamond (PDC) inserts, had been in its new manufacturing facility in Denver, Colorado, for almost a year. Triton had moved to the larger facility to accommodate a rapid expansion in demand for Triton's PDC inserts. The dynamic growth of the previous 3 years—sales had increased by about 20 percent in each of those years (see Figure 1)—had meant that Triton needed more space for both manufacturing and research and development activities. Even with the move to the new facility, Triton's continued explosive growth over the past year already necessitated a major expansion. Sales for 2007 were expected to break the $350 million mark.

Triton's rapid growth came largely from providing low-cost, high-quality products delivered on time. More specifically, the growth in sales resulted from Triton's

unique technological position as well as its willingness to tailor product offerings to meet customers' specific needs. As the holder of over 20 product and process patents (with several more under review), Triton had established itself as a technological leader and thus a preferred supplier of PDC inserts for use in oil and gas drilling operations.

Triton also dedicated tremendous resources to joint research and development projects. Triton was committed to building close working relationships with key customers. The objective was to provide customers with the highest quality of standard, customized, or proprietary products possible. In many instances, achievement of this goal required joint research in product development. This emphasis on joint research and product customization had led to a dramatic expansion in product offerings—from 11 distinct inserts in 2003 to over 160 different finished products in 2007. Combining close working relationships, advanced technology, and a solid reputation for quality had positioned Triton as a leader in the polycrystalline diamond industry.

TRITON'S QUALITY TRACK RECORD

Technological uniqueness had paved the way for Triton's entry into the market; however, a reputation for delivering high-quality inserts was vital for Triton to sustain growth into the future. In the tight-knit oil and gas drilling industry, customer experiences were widely shared. Any quality problem quickly became known throughout the industry. Word-of-mouth endorsement was therefore critical to building and maintaining recognition as a preferred supplier of PDC inserts.

Because a reputation for poor quality meant a quick exit from the market, managers at Triton had always viewed quality as important (see Table 1). However, the quest for quality became formalized in 2001 when Superbdrill, one of Triton's largest customers, obtained ISO 9000 certification. Superbdrill strongly urged its major suppliers, including Triton, to likewise become ISO certified. As a result, Triton sought and obtained the ISO 9002 certification from the same certifying agency that had certified Superbdrill. In 2004, Triton renewed its certification; however, the ISO 9001 certification was obtained. ISO 9001 certification extended the quality certification to Triton's research and development activities. This was an important milestone given Triton's desire to use joint research and development to facilitate close working relationships and create switching cost.

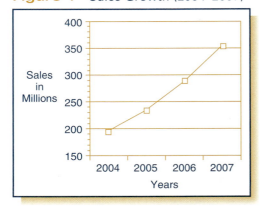

Figure 1   Sales Growth (2004–2007)

Table 1 Triton's Quality Policy

Customer Satisfaction is a relentless focus of all company objectives.

We are committed to delivering defect-free products.

We are committed to delivering products on time.

We are committed to responding to customer problems with all of our resources.

We are committed to providing the most current and advanced level of technology.

We are committed to meeting and exceeding the needs and expectations of our customers.

By 2005, Triton had achieved a standard of excellence with respect to quality, on-time delivery, and pricing. In fact, DrillMaster, a major Triton customer, named Triton as its "Number 1" vendor for 2005. During the year, Triton had delivered over 60,000 parts to DrillMaster. Incoming inspection found only 13 discrepancies for a 99.99 percent vendor efficiency rating. This performance constituted "Best-In-Class" status and led to a special commendation from DrillMaster, which stated:

Triton consistently supplied PDC cutters that met our requirements, were delivered on time and were competitively priced. Your company responded to our needs in a consistent and professional manner. The DrillMaster Management Team extends our thanks and congratulations for your "Team Effort" and a job well done.

More important than the official commendation was the fact that Triton had achieved "Level 1" vendor status, which meant DrillMaster would no longer conduct receiving inspection on incoming parts. Managers at Triton were excited to have met the standards necessary to be named a "dock-to-stock" supplier. This accomplishment not only validated Triton's official Quality Policy, which was posted in highly visible locations throughout Triton's manufacturing facility, but also prompted Tim to think about the viability of extending "dock-to-stock" certification backward to Triton's suppliers.

MOTIVATING SUPPLIER QUALITY

Tim Rock had joined Triton in 2002—shortly after the initial ISO certification. He quickly realized that much of Triton's success rested on its reputation for producing extremely high-quality PDC inserts. Tim had also recognized that purchasing had a significant opportunity to impact Triton's competitiveness through the acquisition of low-cost, high-quality materials.

Triton purchased from approximately 400 suppliers, which were classified into three levels. Level 1 suppliers provided materials that were used directly as components of PDC inserts. Each PDC insert consisted of two principal components: a tungsten carbide base and a polycrystalline diamond cutting surface. Because of the composition of the inserts, Tim referred to them as "bread and butter products." In effect, the tungsten base was the bread and the PDC the butter. Given the simple nature of a PDC insert, only 12 suppliers were classified as Level 1 suppliers. However, these 12 suppliers represented over 50 percent of all purchase dollars. Level 2 suppliers provided inputs used in the production process. Triton actively sourced from 100 Level 2 suppliers, spending about 30 percent of the purchasing budget with these suppliers. The remaining 300 suppliers were all Level 3 suppliers and provided inputs that supported both operations and administration.

Tim dedicated much of his time and effort to building and improving relationships with the Level 1 suppliers. In fact, to support Triton's quality emphasis, Tim completed the training needed to be certified as an ISO auditor in 2004. Tim used this training to help suppliers improve their quality processes. For example, in a visit to Tungsten Specialist Incorporated (TSI), Triton's leading supplier of tungsten carbide substrates, Tim noted that TSI was not matching the specification sheet it received from Triton with the final materials certification. Although this finding helped explain why Triton occasionally received lots that did not meet the required specifications, it raised serious questions about the quality practices at TSI.

The fact that the quality of the tungsten carbide substrate was critical to the performance of the finished PDC insert led Tim to initiate a study of tungsten carbide suppliers. Triton had been purchasing tungsten carbide substrates from three suppliers; however, 99 percent of its tungsten carbide substrates were sourced from TSI. After surveying both existing suppliers as well as other buyers of substrates, Tim decided that TSI was the best source of substrates and that it would be more appropriate to "tighten up" the relationship rather than start over with a new supplier.

The decision to "tighten" the relationship with TSI provided an excellent opportunity to begin to extend supplier certification backward to Triton's Level 1 suppliers. Tim led a purchasing team effort in the design of a 3-stage supplier certification program. Via this program, suppliers would be designated as approved, preferred, or certified. To move from approved to preferred, a supplier had to (1) deliver five lots of product that passed inspection without any defects (these lots also had to make it through production without any issue or failure), (2) complete a quality agreement, and (3) demonstrate the use of a self-auditing process control program. To obtain certified, "dock-to-stock" status, a preferred supplier had to maintain delivery of another five lots without issue or defect.

Tim was certain that extending certification backward to Triton's suppliers was vital to future success. He was worried, however, that simply recognizing suppliers as certified would not provide enough motivation to get suppliers to want to become a "Triton Certified Supplier." Tim felt that providing suppliers with a nice plaque to hang in the reception room was a nice start but that the truly exceptional quality performance that he desired to see from Triton's suppliers would need some kind of "bottom line" motivational mechanism.

Tim recognized some basic challenges to providing such a "bottom line" motivation. First, Triton's relatively small size had historically prevented it from being a dominant customer for most of its suppliers. Second, in the case of TSI, Triton already purchased 99 percent of its substrates from TSI. As a result, it would be difficult to promise increased volumes unless Triton continued its rapid growth. Finally, as with the idea of offering special payment terms to certified suppliers, any "bottom line" initiative needed to be approved by senior management.

Tim wondered what he and Triton could offer to Level 1 suppliers to get their attention and motivate them to improve their quality practices.

QUESTIONS

1. How quickly should he move to get suppliers on board?
2. What might he do to get the CFO and other top management to support some form of financial reward for certified suppliers?
3. Compare Tim's idea for motivating supplier quality improvement to supplier development efforts used by companies like Honda and Deere. Are there any similarities?

An earlier version of this case was written at a case-writing workshop sponsored by the Institute for Supply Management.

Case 4

Quality Upstream at HI-TECH Semiconductor

The quality review meeting had just ended. Ty Rock, purchasing director at HI-TECH Advanced Materials, left the room more than a little frustrated. Despite Ty's best efforts to improve supplier quality, incoming materials continued to fall below the established standards. Worse yet, Ty knew that quality requirements were only going to increase over the next year. After all, HI-TECH's customers seemed to be insatiable in their demand for higher levels of quality. Indeed, it was the insistent urging of HI-TECH's most important customers that had led HI-TECH to undertake an arduous quality improvement effort known as the Standardized Supplier Quality Assessment (SSQA). Given the continued customer-driven quality pressure HI-TECH was under, Ty's mandate was clear—he had to figure out how to get HI-TECH's key suppliers to ramp up their quality.

THE QUALITY CHALLENGE

As a supplier of semiconductor manufacturing equipment to customers such as Intel, Motorola, and National Semiconductor, HI-TECH's quality dilemma had its roots in events that had transpired over a dozen years earlier. Rapidly losing market share to fierce Asian semiconductor manufacturers, members of the Semiconductor Industry Association had received government approval to establish a cooperative research and development organization called SEMATECH. SEMATECH began operations in 1987 with 13 charter members with the primary objective of developing advanced semiconductor manufacturing technologies. By cooperating with Sandia National Laboratories, Oak Ridge National Laboratory, and the Electrical Power Research Institute, SEMATECH rapidly became a major force in helping the major semiconductor manufacturers stem the competitive tide. By 1992, U.S. semiconductor manufacturers had captured 44 percent of the worldwide semiconductor sales to lead the world in chip sales for the first time since 1984.

One aspect of SEMATECH's commitment to global leadership was the development of the Standardized Supplier Quality Assessment. SSQA was designed as a tool to assist suppliers in developing a comprehensive quality-driven operating system. The goal was to achieve the highest quality products delivered on time and at a reasonable cost. SSQA involved 114 distinct elements organized into 3 major modules:

1. Module 1 was based on the International Standards Organization quality standard—ISO 9000.
2. Module 2 was based on Malcolm Baldrige National Quality Award criteria.
3. Module 3 was based on Motorola Quality Software requirements.

With a unified voice, the SEMATECH members "invited and encouraged" their first-tier suppliers, Including HI-TECH, to implement SSQA if they wanted to retain preferred supplier status. The first-tier suppliers were provided some initial training in SSQA implementation and then given 6 months to document their practices using the 114 SSQA elements as guidelines. At the end of the 6 months, a team of managers from SEMATECH companies visited HI-TECH to go over the process and help identify the key areas for improvement. With opportunities to improve identified and targeted, HI-TECH was able to dramatically enhance its quality performance.

SEMATECH initially worked with HI-TECH and the other first-tier suppliers to extend the implementation of SSQA upstream. However, the leverage dynamics were quite different and almost no progress was made. Whereas SEMATECH companies spoke with a common voice and represented the vast majority of its first-tier suppliers' sales, second-tier suppliers sold to a variety of customers outside the semiconductor industry. Further, most of the second-tier suppliers were very small and resource constrained. For example, NPF, one of HI-TECH's key sheet metal suppliers, had a total of 147 employees working in 2 shops. NPF sold to all of the major semiconductor first-tier suppliers as well as to companies in the commercial and defense aerospace industries. Companies like NPF balked at the idea of implementing SSQA, arguing that it simply did not fit their situation. SEMATECH quickly turned the responsibility for upstream quality improvement over to the primary first-tier players like HI-TECH.

A STREAMLINED APPROACH

To alleviate the resource concerns of the upstream supply base, several representatives from the first-tier suppliers modified the basic SSQA program, selecting the elements most applicable to small businesses. The result was the Small Business Operating System (SBOS), which consisted of only 44 critical elements. SBOS was initially launched in 1995. Unfortunately, SBOS was not received any better than its predecessor. The semiconductor industry was thriving and there was no imminent and pressing need for change. To complicate matters, the primary first-tier suppliers were communicating different expectations to the upstream supply base. Without a common voice, it was easy for the second-tier suppliers to just say no to SBOS.

THE CURRENT DILEMMA

By 1998, the success of the mid-1990s had disappeared. Huge amounts of excess capacity plagued the industry, and semiconductor prices had plummeted. Further, new manufacturing capabilities were coming on line, creating considerable uncertainty regarding the new technological standards for the industry. The combined impact of these two events was that the major semiconductor manufacturers dramatically scaled back their purchases of manufacturing equipment. Capital expenditures dropped by as much as 70 percent. This precipitous decline was quite painful for HI-TECH and the other first-tier suppliers. This downturn forced the entire semiconductor industry to reevaluate its competitive position.

HI-TECH, together with the other first-tier suppliers, refocused on the quality issue and brought SBOS back to the forefront of its strategic initiatives. In fact, for the first time, all of the key first-tier suppliers agreed that improving quality was mandatory and that SBOS represented a viable and practical approach. Unfortunately, getting the second-tier suppliers to seriously look at SBOS continued to be a serious challenge. NPF's management team was representative of the lower-tier suppliers as it voiced the opinion that SBOS was still too resource intensive. Besides, NPF's managers argued that simply focusing on ISO 9000 might be more beneficial because ISO certification might be more readily accepted by its non-semiconductor customers.

As Ty thought about the past 5 years and the previous efforts to implement SBOS, he wondered what it would take to get suppliers like NPF to adopt SBOS. One thing was clear: Supplier quality performance was inadequate and it was his job to help suppliers get quality right, right now.

QUESTIONS

1. What are the comparative strengths of a customized quality certification program like SBOS and a general quality certification program like ISO 9000?
2. What do you see as the most important barriers to achieving widespread acceptance of SBOS? Can Ty realistically expect to overcome these barriers? How would you suggest he proceed?

An earlier version of this case was written at a case-writing workshop sponsored by the Institute for Supply Management.

Case 5   *Quality Issue/Consequential Damages*

Blackstone Healthcare purchases dextrose (a sugar product) that goes into many intravenous (IV) finished good product codes. On a recent shipment, the required quality control inspection was performed and the batch of dextrose product was released to production. During production, an inspector noticed that there appeared to be foreign contamination in the finished product. At this point, all production was stopped, and the raw materials quarantined.

Upon further testing of the final product, it was confirmed that there was contamination and that it came from the dextrose used. Blackstone Healthcare had significant investment in the now unusable product in-process and finished goods made from this contaminated lot of material. The dextrose alone was worth $125,000. Blackstone Healthcare's in-process investment was determined to be $1.5 million. Blackstone Healthcare's agreement with the supplier states that the supplier will not be liable for any consequential damage, but only the value of the raw materials that it supplies.

Blackstone buys about $12 million in dextrose each year, and is one of the top three customers to this organization. The supplier has about $500 million in total sales from all products, about $75 million to Blackstone. Blackstone has another qualified supplier, but this supplier could not meet 100 percent of Blackstone's immediate needs. It would take about 3 months for that supplier to gear up and about 9 months for Blackstone to develop a new second source. Help Blackstone prepare for its meeting with the dextrose supplier by addressing the following questions.

QUESTIONS

1. What are the facts and advantages that the buyer can leverage during the negotiation process?
2. What outcome do you think that Blackstone would like?
3. What outcome do you think that the dextrose supplier would like?
4. What are the facts and the advantages that the supplier may try to leverage?
5. What counterlevers can be designed to diffuse the supplier's position?
6. What should be done to prevent this from happening in the future?

Case 6   *Chatham, Ltd., Market Analysis*

The Stretchum Company was Chatham, Ltd.'s, sole approved source for elastomeric products for 10 years. Elastomeric products are used in the production of many bandages and other sterile medical supplies. Most of these products were latex-based. In 2005, Stretchum announced an unjustified price increase of 10 percent on all the items Chatham, Ltd., purchased from them. This represented approximately a $1.5 million annual increase for Chatham, Ltd.'s, rubber products. These products are critical to Chatham, Ltd., and are used in products that account for over 30 percent of Chatham, Ltd.'s, sales of products and support services.

Chatham, Ltd., was one of Stretchum's top 20 customers. Chatham, Ltd., could not determine whether Stretchum had passed a similar increase on to its other customers, but suspected that it had passed on price increases of various percentages. Chatham, Ltd., performed a quick analysis of the cost drivers underlying Stretchum's operations and determined that there had been no major cost increases. Stretchum is a big supplier of elastomeric products to the health care sector.

The rubber used in Chatham, Ltd.'s, products requires FDA approval at a cost of approximately $500,000, and takes 9 to 15 months. There are several other suppliers in the market who would like to be qualified to do business with Chatham, Ltd., that appear on the surface to be viable options. In addition, Chatham, Ltd., was in the process of qualifying a new latex-free rubber material from different sources, although that approval was about 6 to 12 months down the road.

Stretchum knew that Chatham, Ltd., had no immediate alternatives and refused to negotiate. When asked to justify the increase, Stretchum responded, "We need to protect ourselves from the potential liability we may face in the legal system by doing business with health care companies." At least for the short term, Chatham, Ltd., had to absorb the increases during that year.

QUESTIONS

1. Perform a competitive analysis of Chatham, Ltd.'s, situation, and be prepared to discuss.
   a. What are Chatham, Ltd.'s, strengths?
   b. What are Chatham, Ltd.'s, weaknesses?
2. How should Chatham, Ltd. work to overcome its weaknesses and build on its strengths in the longer term?
3. From Chatham, Ltd.'s, standpoint, what are its immediate alternatives in terms of its current best alternative to a negotiated agreement (BATNA)? In other words, what, if anything, can Chatham, Ltd. do today?

Case 7   *Evaluating a Leader's Strategy for Managing Procurement Leverage*

Stacey Daniels, procurement strategy manager at Nexis Computing, a contract manufacturer (CM) of laptop computers, PDAs, and other high-tech electronics, was checking her e-mail early one morning when a headline caught her eye: "Dell aims to establish a new model for notebook procurement." Stacey clicked on the link and scanned the article. It appeared that perhaps a new purchasing strategy was taking hold in the electronics industry. Stacey was very aware that her organization counted on getting price leverage with its suppliers of parts. It either marked these parts up in order to get a higher, but "invisible" profit from its customers, or, in very competitive situations, used that savings to reduce the price to its customer and win the business. Either way, Stacey knew the important role that the procurement organization played in working with suppliers to reduce the price of parts. She wondered how Dell's new model would affect relationships with suppliers. She also wondered if there were any holes in Dell's new model that would allow Nexis to somehow continue to enjoy the benefits of supplier price leverage.

Here is what Stacey read:

- Dell met with its key global component suppliers and global notebook contract manufacturers to change Dell's notebook production and procurement model. The goal of the meeting was to reduce the current price-cutting competition among CMs, especially that which is aimed at direct negotiations with component suppliers.

- The practice of direct CM negotiations with component suppliers destroys component price visibility, which makes it difficult for Dell to determine the fair price to pay for the finished product. Direct CM negotiation also strains component suppliers.

- Dell will begin to utilize an on-line bidding system for procurement of key components and oversee delivery of components used in its notebooks to contract manufacturers. The contracted price for the components will be visible to all CMs. Dell will give CMs a handling charge on top of the contracted price.

Stacey knew that this would be of great interest to Nexis's top management, as Nexis was always trying to win some business from Dell. It would also be of interest if Nexis's current customers started to use this approach in dealing with Nexis. Stacy quickly drew a diagram of what she believed the system would look like, based on the description in the brief article (see Figure 1).

Figure 1   Possible Sourcing Relationship

As Stacey looked at this diagram, she wondered about the controls and the relationship issues. With that in mind, please answer the following questions.

QUESTIONS

1. How might this new model have an effect on CMs' relationships with their suppliers?
2. Based on Figure 1, how and/or where could contract manufacturers still potentially take advantage of component suppliers' pricing?
3. What controls could Dell put in place to preempt the problems you identified in question 2?
4. Modify Figure 1, if necessary, to incorporate your controls.

5. If you were a component supplier to Dell, how would you feel about this arrangement?
   a. Do you have any suggestions you would like to give Dell to improve upon this process?
   b. If you don't like this process, why did you think component suppliers would agree to follow it?
   c. Would you be willing to help Dell in terms of monitoring the CMs' compliance with the T&Cs of the contract? Why or why not?

Facts in this case were taken from Shen, Steven. (2003, December 1). Dell aims to establish a new model for notebook procurement. *DigiTimes Systems Daily News.* www.digitimes.com. Nexis is a fictitious company, and all of the information about Nexis is for classroom purposes only.

Case 8

A Mandate for Costs Reduction Due to the Competitive Environment

In 2007, global economies are creating new competitive challenges for every organization and OnTarget is no different.

THE ORGANIZATION

During the past several years OnTarget has moved from a dominant competitor in its industry environment to one of intense competition. Top management saw this competitive environment emerging and understood that it would be necessary to reduce costs in order to remain competitive. Global Procurement, along with every other group within OnTarget, was charged with developing strategies for corporate-wide cost reductions.

The Global Procurement group has identified two general areas that it would like to attack. First, inventories are too high throughout the company. These inventories include both maintenance parts and indirect materials. Second, some materials costs have been increasing at the rate of 4 to 5 percent per year. This is higher than the Producer Price Index. These price increases cannot be tolerated because competition is forcing OnTarget to have flat or even declining prices to customers. Thus, these price increases cut directly into OnTarget profits, hampering its competitiveness. The company believes that the expenses can be reduced because a benchmarking project revealed that these increases were above the industrial average.

The company is a large organization with three different operating units. Accordingly, each unit is responsible for millions of dollars worth of expenditures. Each unit is rather large and sells somewhat different products. Hence, the units do not "talk" among themselves as much as desirable. This is partially due to geographic differences but also because the operations have a tradition of independence.

A centralized Global Procurement Department provides services to each unit. Some individuals within the centralized department are assigned to separate operational functional units with the company. For instance, one unit has a large expenditure of a major packaging material. A global procurement professional is responsible for managing this major expenditure even though the individual does not directly report to that unit.

COST REDUCTION: A FIRST STEP

The Global Procurement group's first step was to conduct an organization-wide spend analysis. Through this analysis, the amount spent with every supplier was identified. One important observation was that one large supplier, Extel, provided product and services to each of the company's three main units. Furthermore, in terms of spend, Extel was one of the top five suppliers for the entire corporation. Some of the goods were purchased from a number of long-term agreements, whereas certain capital goods and services were purchased as a result of competitive bidding. Within the long-term agreements, clauses were included allowing the supplier to increase prices. In hindsight, this is most unfortunate for OnTarget.

The supplier had a good reputation in the industry and does business with virtually all firms in OnTarget's industry. OnTarget is dependent on some of Extel's proprietary technology and specialized products. Other items purchased from Extel are available from other sources. Extel's service and quality were generally considered good to excellent by OnTarget, and excellent by Extel itself. Extel has expressed an interest in increasing its business with OnTarget and offering more services and different arrangements.

COST REDUCTION: A SECOND STEP

Because Extel represents such a large corporate spend, the Global Procurement group decided to further investigate the buyer–supplier arrangement. Several interesting patterns emerged. First, different units were buying the same products from Extel without any coordination among themselves. Furthermore, different sales representatives were selling the same item to different units at different prices. It was not uncommon for two or three sales representatives to be working on agreements with two or three company buyers at any one time. Second, in one unit, the company was making an extremely large purchase from this supplier. Unfortunately, the buyer–supplier relationship was bumpy in this unit as many accusations of price increases, poor deliveries, and changing demands were frequently traded between the buyer and supplier.

A third finding was that in two units major services were being purchased from this supplier. Although the services were slightly different, the purchase of these services was not being coordinated.

COST REDUCTION: A THIRD STEP

The company has a target to reduce expenses. Because of the competitive environment, the company must reduce costs in order to remain competitive. The items purchased from this particular supplier have been identified as a potential area for cost reduction.

Please address the following issues.

QUESTIONS

1. How can Global Procurement reduce costs by working with this supplier? The strategy should contain at least three methods or ideas for cost reduction.
2. What barriers do you see to implementing your recommendations? How might these barriers be overcome?
3. What sort of relationship should OnTarget seek with Extel? Why?
4. What issues and inefficiencies might OnTarget need to address within its own operations?
5. How can OnTarget really determine if Extel is as good as OnTarget thinks it is?

GLOSSARY

activity-based cost management (ABCM) A managerial accounting approach that attempts to match the indirect costs with the activities and products or services that actually generate those costs, the same way traditional accounting systems handle direct costs.

activity-based costing The direct tie between specific costs and customers that create them.

adjourning The final stage of the team development process that includes the up-front definition of key milestones and a specific ending point in terms of outputs and a target completion date.

B2B e-marketplaces Neutral Internet/Web-enabled entities through which companies may conduct buying and selling transactions for goods or services.

benchmarking A method for comparing and quantifying operational performance to establish internal targets based on "best-in-class" results.

best-in-class When a company achieves a reputation in the marketplace for performing a value-added activity as well as or better than anyone else.

best practice analysis Identifying and describing production and managerial practices that result in outstanding levels of performance.

bill-of-materials (BOM) A list of all the subassemblies, intermediate parts, and raw materials that go into a product. The BOM shows the quantity and precedence relationship of each part required to make an assembly.

blanket order Specifies the overall terms of agreement for a given time period, often one year or more.

breadth complexity The range and variety of products made available by one business.

bullwhip effect Exaggerations of fluctuating demand through the supply chain as suppliers overcompensate to avoid stock outages and then underanticipate future demand. Supply chain coordination can reduce the effect and the associated cost of inventory.

business model A company's business model defines how resources will be used to create value for the customer. In an SC environment, special attention must be given to how the resources from different members of the chain will be combined to deliver unparalleled value.

business process outsourcing (BPO) A process that includes everything from logistics to human resource management, payroll processing, purchasing, marketing, sales, accounting, administration, and information technology.

cash flow The timing of cash payments and receipts that can make a difference in a company's liquidity, not just the amount of these flows.

center-of-gravity approach A facility location approach that minimizes the distance traveled or the costs involved in shipping to and from the various locations along the supply chain.

collaborative innovation A path to innovation that seeks to avoid obsolescence by promoting learning everywhere across the chain.

collaborative planning, forecasting, and repleishment (CPFR) CPFR is the sharing of forecasts, promotion plans, and other related information among members of the supply chain in an effort to reduce inventories, improve availability, and enable automatic replenishment. In its simplest form, CPFR involves collaboration to jointly forecast and plan requirements.

commodity A group of like items that the organization purchases. Examples of commodities include paper, molded plastic parts, and travel services.

compatibility The need to align network-design decisions to the company's overall strategy.

competencies The skills and processes that are developed to create promised value.

concurrent NPD The use of a cross-functional team to develop a new product with a targeted unit cost; the approach advocated by most SC leaders.

configuration The decision of where to locate value-added activities.

connectivity Various people, teams, functions, and organizations along the supply chain working together.

contingency theory The theory that business decision making depends on and affects the competitive environment and the organization's performance. Contingency theory is the foundation of industrial organizational theory and resource-based theory.

contract manufacturing Manufacturing by a third party that makes an end product under another company's brand.

control Refers to the day-to-day decisions involved in managing operations.

coordination Refers to the challenge of integrating geographically dispersed activities.

core competence The set of skills and processes that produce a competitive advantage.

core competency Something that a company does so well that it provides the company a competitive advantage.

corporate social responsibility (CSR) A critical issue that requires companies to be aware of what is often called the *triple bottom line*: economic, environmental, and social performance.

cost driver analysis Relates to what processes, activities, and decisions actually create costs in the supply chain.

cost leadership One company in every industry achieves the lowest cost position among its rivals—this is the cost leader. All other companies must differentiate themselves along another competitive dimension.

cost performance The measure of a business's efficiency to create a product of acceptable value with minimal cost to the consumer.

critical path method (CPM) A project management tool that helps project managers schedule and monitor the various activities associated with a project in a way that helps complete the project on time. CPM assumes that managers know how long individual activities that comprise the project will take to complete.

customer relationship management (CRM) A systematic effort to better manage specific customer relationships to increase revenue generation and profitability. CRM often involves the adoption of CRM software, which is software developed to increase the sophistication of customer segmentation.

customer segmentation The identification of unique groups of customers who possess similar needs.

customer success factors The capabilities that direct customers need to satisfy their downstream customers.

data-mining Simply stated, data mining is the process of analyzing data to identify patterns or relationships. Modern data mining is enabled by sophisticated software and involves the systematic process of searching through large volumes of data to uncover relationships hidden in transaction data history. Data mining is sometimes referred to as Knowledge-Discovery in Databases.

decision trees A decision-making tool that graphically displays the underlying decision process. Decision trees make conditional decisions with "branches" that represent different potential payoffs.

delivery Fast, consistent order cycle time with limited variability.

demand chain The supply chain as seen by customer-focused marketers.

depth complexity The number of available options a customer can choose from within a product category.

design for initiative (DFX) A product development team mandate to improve a specified supply chain factor, X, through careful design. For example, products may be "designed for" optimizing manufacturing, supply, and/or usability.

differentiation A strategy that requires a company to develop a product that reduces price, thus causing shifts in the market and competition.

dis-intermediated When a company is shifted out of the supply chain.

distribution center (DC) Distribution centers are warehouses where goods are stared and sorted to provide more rapid and cost-effective replenishment. Product is placed closer to potential customers and can be mixed and matched to improve the utilization of truckload space.

dwell time ratio The number of days in the logistics process that inventory sits idle compared to the number of days the inventory is moving.

early supplier involvement (ESI) The practice of including suppliers in the new product development process in order to tap their expertise in designing the product, process, and supply chain.

economic value-added (EVA) The surplus value generated by an investment, calculated by subtracting taxes and the cost of capital from operating profit.

electronic commerce (e-commerce) An automated, computerized environment for commercial transactions.

electronic data interchange (EDI) The inter-organizational, computer-to-computer communication of business transactions such as orders, confirmations, invoices, and shipping notices.

empowerment culture An environment by managers where employees can learn, innovate, and create unprecedented customer value.

end customer The primary monetary contributor to the supply chain. This is where a business firm should direct its marketing and service initiatives.

enterprise resource planning (ERP) Systems designed to integrate transaction modules and provide a common and consistent database.

environmental scanning The acquisition and use of information about events, trends, and relationships in an organization's internal and external environments.

expected value analysis For decisions involving uncertainty, expected value analysis provides a rational approach for selecting the best course of action. The expected value is calculated by multiplying the probability of each outcome by its forecast payoff.

facility layout   A type of design decision that determines the positioning of equipment, the flow of materials, and the number of times each item must be handled.

facility location   One type of design decision that determines the most effective place to locate a factory; manufacturers focus primarily on labor costs or resource proximity.

fill rate   The percent of products ordered that are actually delivered.

flexibility   The ability of a firm to adjust to fluctuating economic environments, changing schedules, and unexpected events.

forecasting   A control decision that provides an estimate of what products need to be produced and when they need to be produced.

forming   The process of deciding who should belong to a team.

functional organization   The grouping of resources into specialty departments, such as accounting, finance, logistics, marketing, operations, and purchasing.

functional shiftability   A process that shifts roles to the SC member best positioned to perform them.

Gantt chart   Graphical portrayal of a project's activities over time. Gantt charts make due dates and other time-critical issues visible so that managers can better manage individual as well as groups of projects.

incremental innovation   The second path to innovation, which involves continuous, incremental improvements.

industrial organization (IO) theory   The theory that business decision making should be driven by the analysis of market forces including suppliers, buyers, existing rivals, potential rivals, and providers of substitute products.

information sharing   The promotion of process management by communicating strategic objectives and organizational roles.

infrastructure   The physical, bricks-and-mortar assets a company uses in the value creation process.

insourcing   The internal production of a product.

integrated product development (IPD)   IPD refers to the team-based approach to product development. By working in a cross-functional team, product and process design decisions can be made concurrently or simultaneously, greatly reducing the time required to take an idea from concept to market. Better communication during the development process also leads to superior ideas and a better end product.

integrated supply   Having one or more distributors handle all of the items, rather than ordering from a large number of manufacturers or small distributors.

inventory control   A control decision that determines how much and when to make specific products.

jidoka system   Toyota system which allows workers to "stop the line" when they discover production problems. The Japanese symbol for jidoka literally translates into "man and machine system."

key performance indicators (KPI)   Also known as key success indicators (KSI), KPIs are quantifiable measurements that reflect a company's critical success factors. They define and measure the company's progress toward organizational goals.

logistics   The process of transporting and storing goods, assuring that inbound materials are available for operations and that outbound finished products are available when and where the customer wants to buy them; as defined by the Council of Logistics Management (CLM), the process of planning, implementing, and controlling the efficient, cost-effective flow and storage of raw materials, in-process inventory, finished goods and related information from point of origin to point of consumption for the purpose of conforming to customer requirements.

make-or-buy   The decision to insource or outsource.

materials management   Inbound logistics.

MRO   Abbreviation for "maintenance, repair, and operation." MRO items are the support materials that must be purchased to support business operations. These items are not direct materials or services used in the production and delivery of a product or service.

negotiation   The formal communication process where parties discuss issues and come to a mutually satisfactory agreement.

norming   The stage of the team development process of establishing team rules and procedures; helps the team find its own uniquely collaborative rhythm.

offshoring   Another name for outsourcing to a different country.

operating profit   Profit from the sales of goods and services, before interest expenses, investment results, and taxes.

operations   The process of converting sourced inputs into a product or service that customers value.

outsourcing   The process of moving an aspect of production, service, or business function from within an organization to an outside supplier.

Pareto principle   A rule that suggests that 80 percent of an outcome are generated by 20 percent of an activity. For example, 80 percent of a companies sales are often generated by 20 percent of its customers.

penalty clause   An agreement specifying a penalty for late payments or deliveries.

performing   The stage of the team development process of identifying problems and opportunities, establishing a plan of attack, and then implementing the plan.

physical distribution   Outbound logistics.

postponement strategy   When a company postpones final manufacturing, assembly, packaging, labeling or other value-added activities until a final customer order is received.

privatization   Outsourcing by a government or a public agency.

process design   A design decision that involves technology selection and work design.

process reengineering   The discipline and practice of capturing the current "as-is" state of a process and defining the desired future "to-be" process configuration; the radical redesign of business processes made possible by improved information technology.

product design   One type of design decision that represents the company's ability to profitably capture future market share.

product life cycle (PLC)   A marketing concept that states that products and services evolve through a life cycle, and that the specific management concerns vary with each stage of the life cycle.

product positioning   The understanding of your customers and positioning the total package to meet their needs, which is critical to customer loyalty.

production   Conversion of sourced inputs into a product or service that customers value.

profit   A measure of how much a company makes after paying all its expenses; also called *net profit*.

profit before tax   Operating profits less interest expenses, plus or minus results from investments and other activities.

program evaluation review technique (PERT)   A project management technique that helps project managers schedule and monitor the various activities associated with a project in a way that helps complete the project on time. PERT assumes uncertainty regarding individual activity times, combining estimates for best-case, most-likely, and worst-case scenarios to plan project durations.

purchase order (PO)   A document that specifies the terms and conditions of the purchase agreement and initiates supplier action.

purchase requisition   A document used to clearly describe and communicate needs to sourcing.

purchasing   Acquisition of the inputs used to support production and day-to-day business activities.

quality   A measure of whether or not a product lives up to customer expectations.

quality control   A control decision that focuses on designing, building, and inspecting quality into both the process and the product.

radio frequency identification (RFID) tags   Coded electronic chips usually found in the container or packaging of products. RFID tags are used to provide better inventory tracking and management.

resource-based theory   The theory that business decision making should center on the management of internal resources to establish hard-to-replicate competitive advantages and core competencies.

resources   All assets, including people, technology, infrastructure, materials, and money.

reverse auctions   When suppliers bid for a buyer's business (rather than buyers bidding for a seller's business). Usually refers to a real-time on-line bidding scenario.

reverse marketing   Reverse marketing is the process of recruiting a supplier to provide an item or a service. It involves the buyer taking the initiative to create a supply market for a product or service that is not otherwise available. The buyer is asking the supplier to do something that it is not currently able to do. Reverse marketing often relies on good relationship marketing skills.

scheduling   A control decision in which aggregate planning determines what needs to be produced and provides a rough idea of the timing for the desired production.

scorecards   A system of creating balance by featuring a set of qualitative measures in the formal measurement system.

service gap   Insufficient service or an inability to meet customers' needs due to a lower-level of standards than customer expectations.

sequential NPD   A traditional approach to NPD based on strict functional boundaries where each area does its part on the product and passes it along to the next function.

sourcing   The process of acquiring the inputs used to support production and day-to-day business activities.

storming   The stage of the team development process of establishing common ground and identifying individual roles and responsibilities. Storming establishes direction, purpose, roles, responsibilities, and rewards for both the overall team and each team member.

strategic cost management   Using cost management techniques to reduce the organization's costs and improve profit while supporting its value proposition.

supplier certification   The formal process of working with selected suppliers to evaluate and improve supplier quality.

supply chain advisory councils   Organizations that bridge strategic distances between a company and its supply chain partners.

supply chain analysis   The examination of the management of the flow of information, inventory, processes, and cash from the earliest supplier to the ultimate consumer, including the final disposal process.

supply chain management (SCM)   The design and management of seamless, value-added processes across organizational boundaries through the integration of people and technological resources to meet the real needs of the end customer.

supply chain rationalization   The process of systematically evaluating the company's operating network, suppliers, customers, and product offerings to find and eliminate inefficiencies and redundancies.

SWOT analysis   Analysis of a company's strengths, weaknesses, opportunities, and threats.

synergies   Cooperative interactions that result in higher efficiency and a better net product.

system boundaries   The members of a system.

systems thinking   The holistic process of considering both the immediate local outcomes and the longer-term system-wide ramifications of decisions.

target price   What the customer is willing to pay for the product.

theory of constraints   The theory that the key to maximizing throughput is to alleviate the bottleneck, keeping it operating at maximum capacity all the time.

third-party logistics (3PL)   Using a supplier to provide some combinations of logistics activities.

tiering   A type of aggregation opportunity that involves the move from buying individual parts to the purchase of complete modules.

total cost of ownership   A philosophy for understanding all relevant SC-related costs of doing business with a particular supplier for a particular good/service, or the cost of a process, or particular SC design.

trade-off   The compromising of one production process for another (for example, compromising quality for cost).

transformational innovation   The first path to innovation; relies on strategic breakthroughs in process or product technology.

triadic presence   The ability of a company to operate in three major world markets—the United States, the European Union, and Asia.

value chain   A set of interconnected, internal business functions that is responsible for the decision-making processes to determine supply chain values. These functions can include executive management, research and development (R&D), supply management, operations, logistics, marketing, human resources, accounting, finance, and information technology.

value proposition   The value a company promises to deliver to customers.

value proposition analysis   How an organization competes; an essential element of corporate strategy.

value stream mapping   A specific application of process mapping, based on lean manufacturing principles.

vendor managed inventory (VMI)   In its broadest application, VMI involves the supplier generating orders for the customer. VMI programs vary tremendously and can involve generating orders based on demand information communicated by computer or by an on-site visit. Resource intensive VMI programs involve the placement of supplier personnel at the customer's location where they not only manage inventory levels but also participate in other decisions regarding the suppliers' product, including new product development, line extensions, transportation management etc.

willingness   The desire to share and the ability to trust in an information sharing situation.

INDEX

NUMBERS

3M, 35, 450, 481
3PL (third-party logistics) operations, 160, 283
5S principles (Toyota), 147
6σ (six sigma) program, 32
   3M sharing of, 481–482
   quality measure, 414
"7 rights" of people management, 451
80/20 rule, 44, 64

A

A&P, 469
ABC classification, 44–45, 317, *323*, 323, 347–348, *348*
ABCM. *See* activity-based cost management (ABCM)
accountability, for product cost targets, 117
activity-based cost management (ABCM), 46, 259–263, 420, *420*
   decision making with, 262
   implementation problems, 262–263
   and total cost of ownership, 418
ad hoc teams, 445
Adams, Scott, "10 Great Management Lies," 438, 439
adjourning, in team development process, 449
Advanced Consumer Products, Inc. (ACP), 260
Advanced Micro Devices (AMD), 286
advisory councils, 445, 487
aesthetics, and quality, 33
affirmation, in empowerment culture, 453
"age of discontinuity," 468
aggregation opportunity, 324
aggregators, 388
agricultural productivity, 85
Airbus, 82
airfreight, 156, 157–158
airlines, cost forecasting, 165
Aisin plant fire, and Toyota, 136, 320, 482
alignment, supply chain measure for, 416
alliances. *See also* strategic alliances
   in globalization, 202
Amazon.com, 48, 121
   breadth and depth, 314
   flexibility, 34
   inventory, 252
   outsourcing decisions, 293
   value proposition, 251
   Web site visitors, 385
American Airlines, 150

American Customer Satisfaction Index, 37
American Express, 92
Apple Computer, 38, 82, 108, 250, 470–471
approval, of suppliers, 139
arm's-length relationship, for outsourcing, 295
"as-is" supply chain map, 19, *20*
ASIC (application specific integrated circuit), 103
Aspen Distribution, 417
assembly productivity, 33
asset management, frequently used performance measures, 410, 411–412
Atari, 103
attribute control charts (*p*-charts), 56
automotive industry. *See also specific companies*
   modular products, 227
Avandamet, 56
   averages
   managing to, 30
   simple moving, 165–166
   weighted moving, 167

B

B2B e-marketplaces, 387
backward pass, 238
backward process integration, 11
BancOne, 110–111
bar-code technology, 498
beachheads for expansion, 202
Bean (L.L.), customer service policy, 48
Becker, Joel, 420
Beer Game, 25–27
belonging, in empowerment culture, 453–454, 456
benchmarking, 425–427
best-in-class cost, 115
best practices, dissemination, 152
Bezos, Jeff, 314
Blackwell, Roger, 21, 361
blanket order, 140
Blasgen, Rick, 439
BMW, 204
BMW 7 Series, 312
Boeing, 165
Bombardier Aerospace, 208
Bond, Bruce, 384
BoschSeimans, sourcing and logistics, 134–135
boundarylessness measure, 450
bow-tie approach to information sharing, *394*
Bowersox, Donald, 153

BPO (business process outsourcing), 283, 292–294
brainstorming, in TCO analysis, 266–267
breadth complexity, 314
Briggs, Robert, 314
Brunell, Tom, 396
Brynjolfsson, Erik, 470
Bucklin, Duane, 202
Buell Motorcycle, 110
bullwhip effect, 10, *10*
Bureau of Economic Analysis, 198
business models, 1
   strategy's role in defining, 16–17
business process outsourcing (BPO), 283, 292–294
Business Week, 48, 357
buyer-directed sourcing, 225
buyers, skill level required for outsourcing, 299–300

C

C2C (cash-to-cash) cycle time measure, 421, 422
Canon, 35
Cap Gemini study, 319
capacity, sharing information about, 393
capital
   outsourcing to conserve, 284
   total cost of ownership analysis of purchase, 265
capital equipment teams, 445
Carese, 330
Carrefour, 17, 134
   and Wal-Mart, 203
carrying costs, 173
cash flow, 121–123, *122*
cash-to-cash cycle time measure, 421, 422
Caterpillar, 84, 313
cause and effect diagram (fishbone; Ishikawa diagram), *63*, 63–64
celebration of alliance implementation, 354
center-of-gravity approach to facility location, 208–209
centralized organizational structure, pros and cons of, 310
change
   attitudes about, 452
   as constant, 467
   resistance to, and ERP, 383
chemistry, in championship teams, 6
Chrysler, 357
complexity supply chain, *308*

Wells, Mike, 92
Wheelwright, Steven, 188
Whirlpool, case study, 496–497
White, David, 217
Wiese, Joseph, 478
Wilde, Oscar, 248
willingness in information capability,
    377–378
win-lose philosophy of negotiation, 362
win-win philosophy of negotiation, 363
wisdom, 398–399
W.L. Gore, 472
workforce. *See* employees

World Trade Organization (WTO), 197
W.R. Grace, 472

X

X-bar charts (variable control charts),
    57–58
X-Box video-game system, 284–285
Xerox, 35
    benchmarking by, 426
    supply relationships, 316
XML (Extensible Markup Language), 397

Y

Yamaha, 35
    yield
    management, 150
    in semiconductor business, 56

Z

Zaki, Wahib, 204
zero-based activities, eliminating, 475
Zrimsek, Brian, 384